S0-BYD-338

Popular Musicians

Popular Musicians

Volume 2

The Doobie Brothers - Paul McCartney

Editor

Steve Hochman

Project Editor

McCrea Adams

SALEM PRESS
Pasadena, California   Hackensack, New Jersey

Managing Editor: Christina J. Moose
Project Editor: McCrea Adams
Acquisitions Editor: Mark Rehn
Research Supervisor: Jeffry Jensen
Production Editor: Yasmine A. Cordoba
Photograph Editor: Karrie Hyatt
Copy Editors: Lauren M. D'Andrea; Douglas Long
Research Assistant: Jun Ohnuki
Design and Layout: James Hutson

∞ The paper used in these volumes conforms to the American National Standard for Permanence of Paper for Printed Library Materials, Z39.48-1992(R1997)

Library of Congress Cataloging-in-Publication Data

Popular Musicians / consulting editor, Steve Hochman ; project editor, McCrea Adams.
p. cm.
Includes discographical references and index.
ISBN 0-89356-986-0 (set : alk. paper). — ISBN 0-89356-987-9 (vol. 1 : alk. paper). — ISBN 0-89356-988-7 (vol. 2 : alk. paper). — ISBN 0-89356-989-5 (vol. 3 : alk. paper). — ISBN 0-89356-990-9 (vol. 4 : alk. paper).
1. Musicians — Biography — Dictionaries. 2. Musical groups — Dictionaries.
I. Hochman, Steve, 1956-

ML105.P66 1999
781.64'092'2—dc21 99-11658
[B] CIP

Second Printing

PRINTED IN THE UNITED STATES OF AMERICA

Contents

Popular Musicians

Popular Musicians

The Doobie Brothers / Michael McDonald

The Doobie Brothers

ORIGINAL MEMBERS: Tom Johnston (b. 1948), John Hartman (b. 1950), Patrick Simmons (b. 1950), David Shogren

OTHER MEMBERS: Michael McDonald, Mike Hossack (b. 1950), Jeff "Skunk" Baxter (b. 1948), Tiran Porter, Keith Knudsen (b. 1952), John McFee (b. 1953), Cornelius Bumpus (b. 1952), Chet McCracken (b. 1952), Bobby LaKind (1945-1992)

FIRST ALBUM RELEASE: *The Doobie Brothers*, 1971

Michael McDonald

BORN: St. Louis, Missouri; February 12, 1952

FIRST ALBUM RELEASE: *If That's What It Takes*, 1982

MUSICAL STYLES: Rock and roll, country rock, rhythm and blues, pop

One of the most popular bands in the United States in the 1970's, the Doobie Brothers, along with such groups as the Allman Brothers Band and Lynyrd Skynyrd, took rock concerts to an unprecedented level. Previously, most concerts had been small, cozy events, but these 1970's bands played to sold-out crowds in the country's largest stadiums and helped pioneer the trend of concert-related merchandising. The Doobie Brothers were also quite prolific, releasing an average of one album per year for a decade.

The Doobie Brothers' initial twelve-year career, which began in 1970, took a winding path, with the band changing personnel and musical styles several times. After their breakup in 1982, many members went on to solo careers, although only Michael McDonald achieved notable success.

Origins. The Doobie Brothers formed in 1970 when John Hartman, Tom Johnston, and David Shogren, members of a little-known group named Pud, added a fourth member named Patrick Simmons and adopted the name Doobie Brothers from the California slang term for a marijuana cigarette. The band played small engagements in the San Francisco Bay area before recording a self-titled album for Warner Bros. in 1971. The album was largely ignored, and the band subsequently made the first of several personnel changes by replacing Shogren with Tiran Porter and adding another drummer, Michael Hossack.

Guided by Johnston's songwriting, the Doobie Brothers then recorded *Toulouse Street* in 1972, an album characterized by a strong guitar rhythm, a double-drum format, and tight harmonies. Unlike the group's debut album, *Toulouse Street* achieved quick success and eventually sold more than one million copies. It yielded several hits, including "Listen to the Music," "Rockin' Down the Highway," and "Jesus Is Just Alright." The 1973 album *The Captain and Me* followed the same pattern, with hits "Long Train Runnin'" and "China Grove."

The next album, *What Were Once Vices Are Now Habits* (1974), incorporated some changes, although the basic sound of the music stayed the same. Jeff "Skunk" Baxter, formerly the lead guitarist for Steely Dan, appeared on this album, although he did not actually join the group until the following year, giving the band an unusual three-guitar format. Hossack left the group during the recording of this album and was replaced by Keith Knudsen. This album sported the memorable single "Black Water," which became the group's first number 1 hit in the United States.

The McDonald Era. In 1975, founding band member Johnston was forced to leave the group due to health problems. Left without their lead vocalist and primary songwriter, the Doobie Brothers invited keyboardist Michael McDonald, also a Steely Dan alumnus, to join the group. McDonald and Baxter were mostly responsible for the material on the band's next two albums, which gradually shifted the group's focus from guitar country rock to a keyboard-based pop and rhythm-and-blues combination. McDonald's distinctive tenor and ballad songwriting proved popular with U.S. audiences, and the 1978 *Minute by Minute* album earned four Grammy Awards, including three for the single "What a Fool Believes," which had been coauthored by McDonald and non-band member Kenny Loggins.

This success, however, ultimately led to further personnel changes. Citing the pressures of fame and the music industry, Baxter and Hartman both left the band in 1979. New members John McFee, Chet McCracken, and Cornelius Bumpus were recruited for the 1980 album *One Step Closer*, which was fairly well received even though the band had already passed the crest of its popularity. The band spent the next two years trying to regroup, but did not record any new studio albums during this time. In September of 1982, the Doobie Brothers announced that they would dissolve after a farewell concert in Los Angeles' Griffith Park, from which a live double album was recorded.

Separate Ways. After the Doobie Brothers' breakup, most of the band members remained in the music industry. Simmons and Johnston released solo albums that were not notably successful, while Baxter turned to the production aspect of the business. McFee and Knudsen formed a country-rock band called Southern Pacific, which recorded several country hits in the 1980's before disbanding in 1991.

McDonald was the most successful of the former Doobies, producing several solo albums. Other projects included cowriting Carly Simon's hit single "You Belong to Me" and lending distinctive backup vocals to Christopher Cross's "Ride Like the Wind." McDonald also duetted on several notable singles, including "Ever Changing Times" with Aretha Franklin and "On My Own" with Patti LaBelle, which became a number 1 hit.

The Doobies Revisited. Due partly to popular demand and partly to the sluggishness of some of the members' individual careers, the Doobie Brothers reunited in 1987 and 1988 for a well-received tour by almost all of the band's former members, including Johnston and McDonald. Audiences' enthusiasm sent several of the members, though not McDonald, back to the recording studio, where they were joined by percussionist Bobby LaKind. This session resulted in a 1989 album titled *Cycles*, which was moderately well received. The 1991 *Brotherhood* was not as successful, however. Perhaps realizing that audiences preferred their 1970's music, the Doobie Brothers toured off and on throughout the 1990's, occasionally with McDonald joining them. Recognized as a significant influence on classic 1970's rock, the Doobie Brothers' music remained popular enough that a total of four different greatest-hits albums were eventually released, attaining respectable sales. —*Amy Sisson*

For the Record

John Hartman has recalled that when fellow members of his group dubbed themselves the "Doobies," he did not know what the name meant. One day Dyno Rosen read Hartman a passage from *Rolling Stone* containing the line, "they were smoking a doobie." When Hartman asked Rosen what it meant, Rosen replied, "You idiot! It's a joint."

SELECT DISCOGRAPHY

Doobie Brothers

■ ALBUMS

The Doobie Brothers, 1971
Toulouse Street, 1972
The Captain and Me, 1973
What Were Once Vices Are Now Habits, 1974
Stampede, 1975
Takin' It to the Streets, 1976
The Best of the Doobie Brothers, 1976 (compilation)
Minute by Minute, 1978
One Step Closer, 1980
Best of the Doobies Volume II, 1981 (compilation)
Cycles, 1989
Brotherhood, 1991
Listen to the Music: The Very Best of the Doobie Brothers, 1993 (compilation)

Michael McDonald

■ ALBUMS

If That's What It Takes, 1982
That Was Then: The Early Recordings of Michael McDonald, 1982 (compilation)
No Lookin' Back, 1985
Take It to Heart, 1990
Blink of an Eye, 1993

SELECT AWARDS

Grammy Awards for Record of the Year, Song of the Year (Kenny Loggins and Michael

McDonald), and Best Arrangement Accompanying Vocalist(s) (Michael McDonald) for "What a Fool Believes"; for Best Pop Vocal Performance by a Duo, Group, or Chorus for *Minute by Minute*, all 1979

SEE ALSO: Allman Brothers Band, The; Eagles, The; Little Feat; Loggins and Messina / Kenny Loggins; Miller, Steve; Steely Dan.

The Doors

ORIGINAL MEMBERS: Jim Morrison (1943-1971), Ray Manzarek (b. 1935), Robby Krieger (b. 1946), John Densmore (b. 1944)
FIRST ALBUM RELEASE: *The Doors*, 1967
MUSICAL STYLE: Rock and roll, blues

The Doors' first album appeared in 1967, a time when the counterculture, the hippie movement, Vietnam War protests, and psychedelic drug use were sweeping across the United States. The Doors were unusual in a number of ways. Primarily, at a time when many other new bands, particularly the San Francisco bands such as Jefferson Airplane, sang of community, peace, and love, the Doors jolted listeners with a much darker view of life. The lyrics of Jim Morrison probed the subconscious, uncovering violence, paranoia, and unfettered sexual desires. This vision struck a chord with millions of listeners in the late 1960's as events in the United States—assassinations, riots, protests, the escalating Vietnam War—turned increasingly grim.

Aided by several hit singles and Morrison's brooding good looks, the Doors enjoyed a few years of considerable popularity. After the death of Morrison in 1971 they faded from view, only to find renewed interest beginning in the late 1970's, when their music influenced a new generation of musicians and radio listeners. *Rolling Stone* magazine responded to this reawakened interest with a 1981 cover photograph of Morrison with the caption "He's hot, he's sexy, and he's dead."

Forming the Band. Ray Manzarek and Jim Morrison met while both were taking film classes at UCLA. In 1965 they met again on the beach at Venice, California, a beach community adjacent to Los Angeles. According to keyboardist Manzarek, Jim Morrison recited some lines from "Moonlight Drive" ("Let's swim to the moon/ Let's climb through the tide/ Penetrate the evening/ That the city sleeps to hide"). Manzarek remembers suggesting that they start a band and "make a million dollars." They recruited guitarist Robby Krieger and drummer John Densmore, and the group began rehearsing in Manzarek's beachfront apartment in Venice. They were unable to find a bass player they liked, so Manzarek played the bass parts on a keyboard with his left hand. Morrison suggested a name for the group taken from poet William Blake, who had written: "When the doors of perception are cleansed, man will see things as they truly are, infinite." (Author Aldous Huxley had also used the phrase "doors of perception" as the title for a book relating his experiences with psychedelic drugs.)

The Doors soon became part of the highly creative music scene in Los Angeles in the mid-1960's. The Doors were not an instant hit in Los Angeles clubs, but they eventually built a following. They were signed to a recording contract by Elektra Records, a relatively small folk-oriented label.

Breaking on Through. The first album, titled simply *The Doors*, was a stunning debut. Produced by Paul Rothchild and released in January of 1967, it became part of the sound track for a generation during 1967's "summer of love." The album contained the timeless hit "Light My Fire," which held the number 1 spot for three weeks in the summer of 1967. Other songs on the album included the hard-driving "Break on Through" and the beautiful, eerie "Crystal Ship." However, it was Morrison's variation of the Oedipal theme in "The End" that most clearly defined what would become the key elements in his work: violence ("father . . . I want to kill you"), sin with no hope of redemption (Oedipal sexual desire for the mother), and, above all, death ("this is the end/ beautiful friend"). Shortly before they signed their recording contract, the group had performed a particularly graphic live version of "The

The Doors, late 1966: John Densmore, Robby Krieger, Ray Manzarek, Jim Morrison (AP/Wide World Photos)

End" that caused them to be fired from their job as house band at the Whisky-A-Go-Go when the club's manager was repulsed by the song.

Other Albums. The bands's next two albums, *Strange Days* (1967) and *Waiting for the Sun* (1968), were released fairly quickly and were again produced by Rothchild. *Strange Days* included the haunting "People Are Strange" and "Moonlight Drive." *Waiting for the Sun* went to number 1 on the album charts in 1968 and contained "Five to One," "The Unknown Soldier," and the group's second and last number 1 single, "Hello I Love You." *Waiting for the Sun* also included "Not to Touch the Earth," a section of a longer piece entitled "Celebration of the Lizard." "Not to Touch the Earth" is notable for concluding with the quietly spoken lines "I am the lizard king/ I can do anything," which resulted in Morrison being nicknamed the Lizard King.

After the third album the band's output was less consistent in quality, and the group's problems involved in working with the unpredictable, and frequently drunk, Morrison increased. The critics' response to the band was generally less kind that it had been originally. *The Soft Parade* (1969) contained some oddly middle-of-the-road string and horn arrangements ("Touch Me" was a number 3 single), and *Morrison Hotel/Hard Rock Cafe* (1970) contained no hits, although years later its "Roadhouse Blues" became a classic-rock radio staple. With the release of *L.A. Woman* in 1971, the band's fortunes took an upturn, as it contained two singles that entered the Top 20, "Love Her Madly" and "Riders on the Storm." This was their first album not produced by Rothchild; it was produced by the band with longtime engineer Bruce Botnick.

"No One Here Gets out Alive." In the spring of 1971, after finishing *L.A. Woman,* Morrison decided to go to Paris with his wife, Pamela Courson, to escape Los Angeles and, he hoped, to do some writing. Courson found him dead in the bathtub of their hotel room on July 3, 1971. He was twenty-seven years old. Morrison is buried in the famous Pere-Lachaise cemetery in Paris. (Other notables interred there include composer Frederick Chopin, and writer Victor Hugo.) Morrison's headstone is covered with scrawled tributes from fans and quotes from his lyrics.

Jim Morrison's behavior drew headlines during the band's career, and his legend still threatens to overshadow his and the Doors' considerable musical and poetic achievements. His unquenchable thirst for alcohol and drugs and his erratic behavior was well-documented and confirmed by friends. (Many have also noted, however, that Morrison could—especially when sober—be a gentle and kind person.) In interviews he delighted in manipulating the media, giving journalists a "performance" and making controversial and sometimes false and contradictory statements. He stated that his parents and family were all dead, for example, when in fact both parents and a brother were very much alive (his father was an admiral in the Navy).

Morrison's brushes with the law were well-publicized. He was arrested for inciting a riot at a 1968 concert in New Haven, Connecticut, by telling the crowd that he and his girlfriend had been attacked and sprayed with mace by the police backstage. He was also arrested after being drunk and disorderly on an airplane. The most infamous incident occurred in Miami in March, 1969, when the drunken singer unzipped his pants onstage. It was said that he exposed himself, but this point has been debated, and there has never been a definitive answer to the "did-he-or-didn't he?" issue. Nonetheless, Morrison stood trial for indecent exposure and public drunkenness. He was convicted, sentenced to six months' hard labor, and fined $500. The case was still on appeal at the time of Morrison's death.

The Doors' Sound. Each member of the Doors contributed important elements to the sound. Guitarist Krieger was a folk and flamenco enthusiast, as evidenced by his playing on "Spanish Caravan." He also mastered the bottleneck slide guitar and was a superbly sensuous, melodic guitarist. Krieger's songwriting skills surfaced when he brought one of his first efforts to an early group rehearsal. The song was "Light My Fire." He also wrote a number of other important Doors songs, including "Love Me Two Times" and "Touch Me."

Manzarek was the chief arranger, and it was his job to give musical shape to Morrison's poetic landscapes. His catchy keyboard parts were an essential element of the Doors' success. Playing Vox and Guild organs and other assorted keyboards—as well as creating the distinctive bass lines on the early albums—he provided a foundation of sound on which the others could build. Manzarek was classically trained but retained a garage-band enthusiasm in his playing.

Drummer Densmore had a jazz background and was a solid time keeper. His jazz influences are apparent in the cymbal and snare-drum work in "Break on Through." He anchors the long keyboard and guitar solos on "Light My Fire" perfectly, and he plays precise and dramatic accents in long pieces such as "The End" and "When the Music's Over."

Morrison's mysterious, dark lyrics echo the works of nineteenth century French poets Arthur Rimbaud and Charles Baudelaire. His rich, soulful baritone is among the most distinctive voices in rock. Moreover, with his movie-star looks, hedonistic lifestyle, and early death, Morrison has taken his place alongside such figures as James Dean and Marilyn Monroe as a pop-culture icon.

For the Record

According to *Disk* magazine, Jim Morrison always said that his main guide to poetry was Friedrich Nietzsche's *The Birth of Tragedy from the Spirit of Music*: Morrison "combined Nietzsche with a little freshman psychology and a lot of very broad images (the sea, the sun, the earth, death) and came up with Morrison therapy. . . . Cut your ties to the establishment past, swim in your emotions, suffer symbolic death and rebirth."

Legacy. After the breakup of the Doors, Krieger and Densmore briefly played together in the Butts Band; Krieger later recorded and played on his own, and Densmore pursued acting. Manzarek released two solo albums and later collaborated with Philip Glass. Manzarek also produced the early albums by Los Angeles punk band X, which recorded an uptempo version of the Doors' "Soul Kitchen." The Doors were influential on many punk and new wave bands.

Interest in Jim Morrison and the Doors' music remained strong through the 1990's, with fans buying over a million Doors CDs and tapes per year. Many books have been written about the band and Morrison, including memoirs by band members Densmore and Manzarek. Morrison's book of poetry *The Lords and the New Creatures* (1970) is still available, as are some posthumous collections. Good concert footage of the band has been released on video. Manzarek has noted that the Doors were a hit-and-miss live band: When they were "on," the performance was great, but when they were not it could be terrible. (The performance level of the band was largely dependent on the condition of the lead singer on any given night.)

Directors Francis Ford Coppola and Oliver Stone have both made contributions to the cinematic legacy of the Doors. The soundtrack for Coppola's 1977 Vietnam War film *Apocalypse Now* effectively used "The End." It provided an ominous and powerful underscore to montages of napalm bombing runs. Oliver Stone's controversial 1991 film *The Doors* featured Val Kilmer as Morrison. As biography, the film must be taken with a grain of salt, as Stone took a number of liberties with the facts. Band members loudly protested the portrayal of Morrison as a drunken louse and the fact that the film focused extensively on the destructive relationship he had with longtime girlfriend Courson. —*John W. Clark*

SELECT DISCOGRAPHY

■ SINGLES

"Light My Fire," 1967
"People Are Strange," 1967
"Hello I Love You," 1968
"Touch Me," 1969
"Love Her Madly," 1971
"Riders on the Storm," 1971

■ ALBUMS

The Doors, 1967
Strange Days, 1967
Waiting for the Sun, 1968
The Soft Parade, 1969
Morrison Hotel/Hard Rock Cafe, 1970
Absolutely Live, 1970
L.A. Woman, 1971
Best of the Doors, 1985 (compilation)
The Doors, 1997 (4-CD boxed set)

SELECT AWARDS

Rock and Roll Hall of Fame, inducted 1993

SEE ALSO: Buffalo Springfield; Byrds, The; Jefferson Airplane; Velvet Underground.

The Dream Syndicate

ORIGINAL MEMBERS: Steve Wynn (b. 1960), Karl Precoda (b. c. 1961), Kendra Smith (b. 1960), Dennis Duck (b. 1953)

OTHER MEMBERS: Paul Cutler (b. 1954), Dave Provost, Mark Walton (b. 1959)

FIRST RELEASE: *The Dream Syndicate*, 1982 (extended-play single)

MUSICAL STYLES: Rock and roll, alternative, country rock

With a droning sound reminiscent of the Velvet Underground, the Dream Syndicate emerged from the Los Angeles club scene in the early 1980's as part of the "paisley underground."

The Beginnings. Vocalist and guitarist Steve Wynn and bassist Kendra Smith joined musical forces while at the University of California at Davis in 1981. Moving to Los Angeles, they connected with guitarist Karl Precoda and drummer Dennis Duck. Their self-titled debut extended-play single in 1982 attracted some critical notice, while their first full-length album, *The Days of Wine and Roses*, recorded and released the same year, established them as a significant band in the alternative music scene of the early 1980's. "Tell Me When It's Over"

Dream Syndicate (Paul Natkin)

was that album's and the band's quintessential track. Wynn's feedback guitar and tortured vocals, reminiscent of the Velvet Underground's "Waiting for the Man" and "Heroin," result in a memorable and original song, one that helped solidify the band's identity. That song and album, however, represented the band's peak in popularity and commercial appeal.

Paisley Underground. "Paisley underground" was a term made up to identify a loosely knit group of Los Angeles bands in the early 1980's who shared a strong interest in original songwriting and openly acknowledged the influences of 1960's rock groups. The name derived from their 1960's influence and their tendency to wear paisley shirts. Other groups associated with the paisley underground were Rain Parade, 3 O'Clock, and Green on Red. A 1983 tribute album to paisley underground inspirations was recorded by Smith, Precoda, and Duck, along with members of the Bangles, Rain Parade, and 3 O'Clock. Entitled *Rainy Day*, it featured covers of tunes by bands and performers from the 1960's who influenced the paisley underground scene, including the Beach Boys, the Byrds, Jimi Hendrix, and the Who.

By 1983 the band had begun to splinter with the departure of Smith and, in 1984, Precoda. *Medicine Show* (1984) alienated some fans who considered it too commercial for their liking, although the album was well received by the media. *Out of the Grey* (1986) showed Wynn's growing interest in a country-rock, Neil Young-influenced sound. That album's undistinguished country-rock sound, however, further alienated the band's old fans, failing to point in any clear direction for Wynn's songwriting and performing.

The End. Moving further in the direction of country rock, Wynn enlisted former Neil Young producer Eliot Mazer to contribute to the Dream Syndicate's 1988 release, *Ghost Stories*, a follow-up to *Out of the Grey*. Their popularity continued to decline, and 1989's *Live at Raji's*, recorded early that year at a popular punk-rock club in Los Angeles, represented the end of the Dream Syndicate. A compilation entitled *Tell Me When It's Over: The Best of Dream Syndicate (1982-1988)* was released in 1992. It provides an excellent survey of The Dream Syndicate's recording career.

Legacy. After the Dream Syndicate dissolved, Steve Wynn soldiered on as a solo artist. In 1993 he formed a group called Gutterball and released an album. In addition, he has recorded a number of solo efforts, the most highly regarded being *Kerosene Man* (1990) and its follow-up, *Dazzling Display* (1992).

After leaving the Dream Syndicate in 1983, Kendra Smith formed a band called Opal. She experimented with different kinds of sounds later on her solo releases. On *Five Ways of Disappearing* (1995), she plays a pump organ, which, coupled with her clear, lovely voice, results in a unique sound. Critics have found her work reminisicent of avant-garde musician Brian Eno.

—*Benjamin Pensiero*

SELECT DISCOGRAPHY

■ ALBUMS

The Days of Wine and Roses, 1982
Medicine Show, 1984
Out of the Grey, 1986
Ghost Stories, 1988
Live at Raji's, 1989
Tell Me When It's Over: The Best of Dream Syndicate (1982-1988), 1992 (compilation)

SEE ALSO: Creedence Clearwater Revival / John Fogerty; Eno, Brian; Velvet Underground; Young, Neil.

The Drifters

ORIGINAL MEMBERS: Clyde McPhatter (1932-1972), Bill Pinckney (b. 1925), Andrew "Bubba" Thrasher, Gerhart "Gay" Thrasher, Willie Ferbee

OTHER MEMBERS: Johnny Moore (1934-1998), Bobby Hendricks (b. 1937), Ben E. King (b. Benjamin Earl Nelson, 1938), Rudy Lewis (1936-1964), Gene Pearson, Johnny Terry

FIRST SINGLE RELEASE: "Money Honey," 1953

MUSICAL STYLES: Rhythm and blues, doo-wop, gospel

The Drifters can be thought of as one of the most important groups in 1950's music. Organized in 1953 to showcase the vocal talents of Clyde McPhatter, the group all but disbanded when McPhatter was drafted in 1954; it was reformed in 1959 to record the unusual and successful "There Goes My Baby." The group flourished in the early 1960's with a number of lead singers performing a wide range of songs. Johnnie Moore continued to lead a version of the Drifters in public appearances into the 1990's.

The Beginnings: Clyde McPhatter. In the early 1950's, Billy Ward and the Dominoes featured the clear, gospel-inflected tenor of Clyde McPhatter. After McPhatter left the group in 1953, Atlantic Records president Ahmet Ertegun signed him to a contract and, after a false start with another backup group, hired Bill Pinckney, Willie Ferbee, and Andrew and Gerhart Thrasher to back him up. They started to record in mid-1953, and "Money Honey," the group's first release, was a hit.

At this time, the type of music the Drifters played was generally known as "race music." (Jerry Wexler's term, "rhythm and blues," was just beginning to be used.) It was considered too rough and suggestive for the "sensitive" ears of the white audience, which was protected from the alleged suggestiveness of such Drifters songs as "Honey Love," with lines such as "I need it in the middle of the night." As a result, these songs, highly successful on the rhythm-and-blues charts, did not appear on the white best-seller lists.

In 1954, however, the Drifters found a way to reach white listeners with their version of an American holiday classic. On their "White Christmas," the words are first chanted by bass Bill Pinckney, then swung up-tempo by McPhatter. One music reviewer called it a "vulgar barnyard travesty of a beloved American classic," but the Drifters' version crossed over to the white charts. By this time, however, fate had split up the Drifters in the form of a draft notice for McPhatter.

Life After McPhatter. McPhatter's departure seemed to leave the group without a reason for being, but they continued to perform. Johnny Moore sang lead on such successes as "Soldier of Fortune," "Fools Fall in Love," and "Ruby Baby." Bobby Hendricks briefly joined the group to sing "Drip Drop."

Through the efforts of disc jockey and rock promoter Alan Freed and others, the predominantly white pop music scene had become far more welcoming to rhythm-and-blues talents than when the Drifters had formed. At this point, the Drifters were little more than a name, owned by manager George Treadwell, and when Treadwell heard a group called the Crowns (at times known as the Five Crowns), he offered them the chance to replace the original Drifters.

The new Drifters were destined to have not just different personnel, but a different sound. The legendary songwriting team of Mike Leiber and Jerry Stoller, authors of several songs the Drifters had recorded, produced their records. At the first session, Leiber and Stoller took a blues song written by lead singer Ben Nelson (who would soon change his name to Ben E. King) and added a South American rhythm background and a string section (unheard of for rhythm-and-blues music at the time), creating the classic "There Goes My Baby" (1959). From then on they no longer sounded like a traditional rhythm-and-blues vocal group; the close harmonies of the five singers had been supplanted by a lead singer backed by many instruments and a girls' choir. Nevertheless, this introduced a recording phase that includes most of the beloved songs people now associate with the Drifters.

"There Goes My Baby" was the crossover song that put the Drifters back in the public eye. They

The 1964 Drifters lineup: Billy Davis, Gene Pearson, Charlie Thomas, Johnny Moore, Johnny Terry (Archive Photos/Frank Driggs Collection)

began recording the music of the most popular songwriters of the time, such as Doc Pomus and Mort Shuman and Gerry Goffin and Carole King. With Ben E. King singing lead vocals, they went on to record such successes as "Dance with Me" and "This Magic Moment." In 1960, before leaving for a solo career, King had one last session with the group, in which they recorded what may be the best-known Drifters song (it is also the title of a book about them): "Save the Last Dance for Me." By then the Drifters were used to changing lead singers. Rudy Lewis took the lead on songs such as "Please Stay" (1961),"Up on the Roof" (1962), and "On Broadway" (1963).

On May 20, 1964, the Drifters had a recording session scheduled, but they learned that Rudy Lewis had died suddenly the night before. (Rumors of a drug overdose were never proved.) Johnnie Moore, who had been with the group in its Crowns incarnation, had returned a year earlier, and he stepped up to sing lead on "Under the Boardwalk," which was destined to be the group's last major hit. Like many other popular rhythm-and-blues acts, the Drifters began covering white middle-of-the-road music, and like most of those, they lost their old audience without attracting a new one.

Continuation and Influence. The group continued touring with Johnnie Moore singing lead, despite competition from other alleged "Drifters" groups (including one led by Bill Pinckney). Their songs have been rerecorded by others, going back to Dion's solo versions of "Ruby Baby" and "Drip" in the early 1960's. Jay and the Americans covered "This Magic Moment" in 1969. In 1978 George Benson revived "On Broadway," and in 1979 James Taylor had a hit with "Up on the Roof."

The Graduates. Clyde McPhatter would go on to a solo career, with songs strongly reminiscent of his Drifters work, now welcomed on the pop stations, including such hit singles as "Treasure of Love," "Without Love," and "Long, Lonely Nights," but he left Atlantic Records in 1959 and had little success with other labels. He developed problems with alcohol and other drugs, which made him an unreliable performer and contributed to his early death in 1972. Bobby Hendricks, who sang lead on "Drip Drop," went on to a solo career, in which his best-known song was "Itchy Twitchy Feeling." Ben E. King was quite successful in his own right, notably with his first single, "Spanish Harlem," and with "Stand by Me," which was a hit in 1961, and then again in 1986, when it was revived for the film of the same name.

—Arthur D. Hlavaty

SELECT DISCOGRAPHY

■ SINGLES

"Money Honey," 1953
"Honey Love," 1954
"White Christmas," 1954
"Soldier of Fortune," 1956
"Fools Fall in Love," 1957
"Drip Drop," 1958
"There Goes My Baby," 1959
"This Magic Moment," 1960
"Save the Last Dance for Me," 1960
"I Count the Tears," 1960
"Loneliness or Happiness," 1961
"Please Stay," 1961
"When My Little Girl Is Smiling," 1962
"Up on the Roof," 1962
"On Broadway," 1963
"Under the Boardwalk," 1964

■ ALBUMS

The Drifters' Golden Hits, 1968
Their Greatest Recordings: The Early Years, 1971
Rockin' & Driftin': The Drifters Box, 1996 (three-CD boxed set, compilation)

SELECT AWARDS

Rock and Roll Hall of Fame, inducted 1988

SEE ALSO: Coasters, The.

For the Record

In 1993, Clyde McPhatter became one of the first rock-and-roll singers to appear on a United States postage stamp, along with Elvis Presley and five others.

Duran Duran

ORIGINAL MEMBERS: Simon LeBon (b. 1958), John Taylor (b. 1960), Nick Rhodes (b. Nicholas Bates, 1962), Andy Taylor (b. 1961), Roger Taylor (b. 1960)
OTHER MEMBERS: Warren Cuccurullo (b. 1956)
FIRST ALBUM RELEASE: *Duran Duran*, 1981
MUSICAL STYLES: Pop, rock and roll

Duran Duran was one of the first true music-video bands. Using colorful, stylish images and the proliferation of music videos to promote their teen-friendly pop songs, they captured a youthful generation's eye and ear. A springboard for many of its members' side projects and solo outings, which were usually more mature in nature, Duran Duran remained the most visible and popular vehicle for its main core of Simon LeBon, Nick Rhodes, and John Taylor.

New Romantics. In 1978, art students Nick Rhodes and John Taylor took the name for their just-forming band from the 1968 film *Barbarella*, which featured an evil character named Dr. Duran Duran. With Rhodes playing keyboards and John Taylor handling bass, the two went through a number of other bandmates in their search for a full-time lineup. One of these erstwhile members was vocalist Stephen Duffy, who soon decided that Duran Duran was too synthesizer-heavy. (Ironically, Duffy's first album, which was released during the 1980's, was almost entirely dependent on synthesizers.) Meanwhile, guitarist Andy Taylor and drummer Roger Taylor (none of the Taylors are related), signed up for the band. In 1980, drama student dropout Simon LeBon joined the group as vocalist. With that, the band's lineup was complete.

To appeal to teenage audiences, the members took on an extremely glamorous image common to a new musical movement, the new romantics, which placed superficial image ahead of substance. With their good looks, gaudy 1980's outfits, and much makeup and hair dye, they fit the style perfectly. Appropriately, Duran Duran's songs, with catchy melodies and vapid lyrics, were overlooked due to their flashy image. Rum Runner, a popular club for the new romantics, became a frequent venue for Duran Duran's live appearances.

This Is "Planet Earth." Duran Duran's first single release, "Planet Earth," was in 1981. By then, the public had noticed their immaculate dance-pop music and haircuts. "Planet Earth" went to number 12 on the U.K. charts, readying new fans for an entire album, *Duran Duran*, which reached number 3. Two other singles, "Girls on Film" and "Careless Memories," followed. This success proved them a major musical sensation. One year later, they followed up with *Rio*.

MTV was established during the early 1980's, making music videos popular. Music videos allowed bands to visualize their songs and put them to pictures. If the images were popular, the song would become popular and sell millions of copies. Duran Duran quickly became part of this trend. Their single "Rio" was a prime example of Duran Duran's talents. Lyrically silly, it featured passages such as "Wow!/ Moving on the floor now babe, you're a bird of paradise/ Cherry ice cream smile, I suppose it's very nice." In the video, the band sailed crystal-blue waters and dressed stylishly, with beautiful models everywhere. *Rio* also launched the singles "Hungry Like the Wolf," an equally danceable pop tune, and the ballad "Save a Prayer." Although the music press chose to disregard this light music, teen-oriented publications capitalized on it, endlessly featuring articles and foldouts of Duran Duran, who were a big teen sensation.

"The Reflex." By 1983's *Seven and the Ragged Tiger*, their image and music had become increasingly sophisticated, suggesting a need for more adult acceptance. The album debuted at number 1, and with some dazzling videos, Duran Duran were ubiquitous on MTV and the radio. "The Reflex" was one of the hit singles, with a still quirky yet catchy set of lyrics: "The reflex is an only child he's waiting in the park/ The reflex is in charge of finding treasure in the dark/ And watching over lucky clover isn't that bizarre/ Every little thing the reflex does leaves you answered with a question mark." They immediately followed this accomplishment with a dark and futuristic full-

Duran Duran (Archive Photos/Express Newspapers)

length video, *Arena*, which featured the song "The Wild Boys." This was Duran Duran's peak.

The Split. In 1984, the group broke into two decidedly different spin-offs, both of which abandoned Duran Duran's teen appeal. John Taylor and Andy Taylor joined with singer Robert Palmer to become Power Station, a rock-oriented group. Nick Rhodes, Roger Taylor, and Simon LeBon, meanwhile, took the synthesizer-driven new romanticism to a much more serious and dark level with Arcadia. Both groups' efforts were considered proficient and listenable but without heart.

In 1985, Duran Duran reconvened to record the title track for the film *A View to a Kill.* John Taylor went on his own for a sound-track song, "I Do What I Do," for the film *9½ Weeks.* That year, starvation in Africa caught the world's attention, and musician Bob Geldof took the initiative to organize Band Aid, recording a song to raise relief money. "Feed the World" featured many popular musicians of the day, including Duran Duran. In their final live appearance with all five original members, Duran Duran played at Band Aid's live benefit concert, Live Aid.

In 1986, artistic differences put aside, John Taylor, Rhodes, and LeBon reformed as Duran Duran. Their 1986 release, *Notorious,* did not receive the response previous albums had, although the music press took them more seriously and the title track went to number 2. *Big Thing* (1988) experienced similar problems, with its biggest single, "I Don't Want Your Love," reaching number 4. *Decade,* a compilation album, was released in 1989, and another musician joined the group, Brooklyn-born guitarist Warren Cuccurullo. *Liberty,* their 1990 album, went largely unnoticed.

The Rebirth. After three years, Duran Duran made the comeback they had desired. *Duran Duran (The Wedding Album),* from 1993, contained one of their strongest compositions, "Ordinary World." It peaked at number 3 and again put Duran Duran in the public eye. Their look and sound were refined, even with Rhodes's constantly changing hairdo. *Thank You,* in 1995, was a tribute album in which they covered classic rock songs, including Lou Reed's "Perfect Day."

John Taylor grew more and more independent of the band, recording a sound-track for the 1994 film *Mi Vida Loca* and more Power Station tracks. In 1997, after recording some tracks for Duran

For the Record

Nick Rhodes, in 1983, produced an album for the pop group Kajagoogoo. Kajagoogoo's biggest hit was "Too Shy."

Duran's next album, *Medazzaland*, he departed to pursue a solo career.

Legacy. Arguably the most prolific group of new romantics, not to mention the most enduring, Duran Duran truly paved the way for MTV musicians, helping to establish music videos as an integral part of the music world. They would invariably be remembered for their 1980's videos, music, and style. —*Lawrence Ferber*

SELECT DISCOGRAPHY

■ ALBUMS

Duran Duran, 1981
Rio, 1982
Seven and the Ragged Tiger, 1983
Arena, 1984
Notorious, 1986
Big Thing, 1988
Decade, 1989 (compilation)
Liberty, 1990
Duran Duran (The Wedding Album), 1993
Thank You, 1995
Medazzaland, 1997

SELECT AWARDS

Grammy Awards for Best Video Album for *Duran Duran* and Best Video, Short Form, for "Girls on Film"/"Hungry Like the Wolf," 1983

SEE ALSO: Culture Club / Boy George; Michael, George / Wham!; Palmer, Robert.

Bob Dylan

(Robert Allen Zimmerman)

BORN: Duluth, Minnesota; May 24, 1941
FIRST ALBUM RELEASE: *Bob Dylan*, 1962
MUSICAL STYLES: Blues, country, country rock, folk, folk rock, rock and roll, rockabilly

While Bob Dylan's secretiveness and moodiness have created many myths and legends about his private life, much of his biography is well known. He grew up in Hibbing, Minnesota; his father, Abraham, moved the family when the young Robert Zimmerman was six. Dylan began playing the guitar at the age of twelve, becoming deeply influenced by the "hillbilly" and folk music of singers Woody Guthrie, Pete Seeger, and Leadbelly, as well as the urban blues of John Lee Hooker, Muddy Waters, and Willie Dixon. With the advent of rock and roll, Dylan listened to Elvis Presley, Buddy Holly, and Little Richard and began forming small local bands. Dylan performed in Minnesota coffeehouses. He also read the poetry of Beat writers such as Allen Ginsberg, Gregory Corso, and Jack Kerouac, who helped shape his image and lyrical style.

In 1959 he briefly attended the University of Minnesota, where he adopted the surname Dylan after Welsh poet Dylan Thomas. Moving to New York City in 1961, Dylan made a pilgrimage to the deathbed of his idol, Woody Guthrie, and quickly became a fixture in Greenwich Village coffeehouses. By spring of that year, Dylan held second billing to John Lee Hooker at Gerde's Folk City and worked with other folksingers such as Ramblin' Jack Elliott, Dave van Ronk, and Tom Paxton. After playing harmonica on a few other peoples' albums, Dylan was noticed by legendary producer and talent scout John Hammond, who signed him to Columbia Records. Columbia employees who did not like Dylan's music quickly predicted that he would have no success and were heard to refer to him as "Hammond's folly." With one short defection, Columbia would be Dylan's recording label for the next forty years.

After Dylan signed with manager Albert Grossman, *Bob Dylan* was released in 1962. Largely a collection of traditional American folk songs, it caused a minor sensation in the folk-music world. Nonetheless, Hammond was replaced by producer Tom Wilson for the next four albums.

The Freewheelin' Bob Dylan (1963) established Dylan's reputation as an acoustic folksinger and original songwriter who emphasized protest material such as "A Hard Rain's a-Gonna Fall," "Blowin' in the Wind," and "Masters of War." Dylan's unique, harsh, nasal voice, his wheezing harmonica—which he wore on a neck holder so he could play guitar and harmonica at the same time—and his talking-blues delivery were also hallmarks of his third album, *The Times They Are a-Changing* (1964). The title track became an anthem for the growing protest movement, as did "Blowin' in the Wind," a song covered by the folk trio Peter, Paul and Mary; in 1963 their version went to number 2 on the charts, the first hit version of a Dylan song.

By 1964 Dylan was the undisputed king of the folk world. He had already become something more than a songwriter and performer—he was a hero and an icon to folk-music lovers, Civil Rights workers and protesters, and even members of the political faction known as the New Left. He and folksinger Joan Baez, with whom he was romantically involved for a time, had made triumphant appearances at the annual Newport Folk Festival, the most prestigious folk venue in the country.

Changes. In 1965 Dylan made major changes in his musical direction that launched him to the top of the new "counterculture" vanguard. In the mid to late 1960's it was a place he shared only with the Beatles and perhaps the Rolling Stones in terms of influence, leadership, and widespread interest. In his 1965 concerts and albums Dylan broke open the possibilities for popular music, not only by creating new musical fusions but also by emphasizing the intellectual, enigmatic dimensions possible in poetic wordplay. Further, much to his discomfort, Dylan was the model for rock musicians being elevated from simple performers to spokespeople for a generation—it was a mantle that Dylan himself did not want.

Change had already been evident in his 1964 album *Another Side of Bob Dylan,* which demonstrated his move from protest to more personal, confessional lyrics. No one, however, was prepared for the cultural revolution sparked by Dylan's Newport Folk Festival appearance on July 25, 1965, when he came on stage with an electric guitar and sang surrealistic lyrics backed by the loud Paul Butterfield Blues Band. Horrified folk purists denounced the performance as well as Dylan's next album, *Bringing It All Back Home* (1965), which included songs such as "Subterranean Homesick Blues." The music revealed Dylan to be an innovator who was quickly becoming far removed from his folk roots.

It would be hard to overestimate the influence of Dylan on the pop music of the late 1960's. Dylan had already written far more songs than he wanted to record himself, and innumerable other artists recorded his songs, both the well-known and obscure ones. In 1965 alone, the Byrds version of Dylan's "Mr. Tambourine Man," Cher's rendition of "All I Really Wanna Do," and the Turtles' version of "It Ain't Me, Babe" all hit the Top 20. In addition, hundreds of solo artists and groups jumped on the folk-rock bandwagon with their own Dylan-influenced material. Barry McGuire's "Eve of Destruction" and Simon and Garfunkel's "Sounds of Silence" were both number 1 hits in 1965. In 1966 came the Mamas and the Papas' "California Dreamin'." Donovan (already nicknamed the "British Dylan") added electric rock instruments to his act. The Beatles and Dylan influenced each other. John Lennon, in particular, possessed a strong sense of the absurd and a delight in wordplay, and Dylan's work inspired him to free his songwriting; the more abstract lyrics of *Sgt. Pepper's Lonely Heart's Club Band* and *Magical Mystery Tour* (both 1967) are the most obvious examples. Other British bands from the Kinks to the Rolling Stones also wrote songs showing the Dylan influence.

Dylan's innovations continued with *Highway 61 Revisited* (1965), with much critical attention focused on Dylan's cryptic, streetwise imagery. The album's extraordinary opening track, "Like a Rolling Stone," is probably one of the most influential songs in rock history. That song (clocking in at over six minutes in length), as well as the album's "Desolation Row," an eleven-minute surreal opus, helped set the stage for the album-oriented material that would soon lead to FM radio's rise to prominence and lessen the importance of the three-minute singles preferred by the AM Top-40 stations.

On tour, Dylan found himself the center of an increasingly unmanageable circle of musicians, writers, fans, and hangers-on that gave him little privacy. His breakup with singer Joan Baez, for example, became public property when Baez stormed out during filming of the 1965 documentary *Don't Look Back* by filmmaker D. A. Pennebaker. This offbeat movie, filmed during a Dylan tour of Great Britain, remains an important examination of Dylan during this period. Touring

Bob Dylan in 1963: folk sensation (AP/Wide World Photos)

sometimes cynical, even nasty. His lyrics were witty and playful, by turns sensible and willfully inscrutable. (People undoubtedly read more into his lyrics than Dylan had ever intended.) These factors together inspired scholarly analysis as well as idolization and interest that occasionally turned into obsession. A man named A. J. Weberman proclaimed himself a "Dylanologist" and dug through Dylan's trash for clues.

Dylan was clearly in need of rest. He had moved upstate from New York City to Woodstock, New York, and he had an accident on his motorcycle near there on July 29, 1966. It was reported that he suffered a broken neck and had to spend many months recuperating in seclusion. (It has since been speculated that his injuries were not that serious and that he simply wanted to withdraw, but this is not known.) Recuperating near Woodstock, Dylan spent the year working with the Band on songs later released as *The Basement Tapes* (1975; the material had been released previously on a number of bootleg recordings).

later in 1965 and 1966 with an electric backup band, called simply the Band (who went on to their own distinguished career), Dylan and the band were often heartily booed.

Dylan's creativity continued to flow in 1966 with the release of *Blonde on Blonde,* a two-record set containing "Rainy Day Women #12 & 35," a song widely banned for its drug references (Dylan repeatedly sings, "Everybody must get stoned"). "Sad-Eyed Lady of the Lowlands" was another lengthy song. Dylan later declared that it was about his wife, Sara Lowndes, whom he married on November 22, 1965.

Dylan's personality had become removed and mysterious—sometimes humorously whimsical,

In 1968 the album *John Wesley Harding* signaled yet another change in direction. Dylan's voice had mellowed, and the new songs were more traditional in scope if not in imagery. The music was far from the psychedelic sounds of the period. Yet Jimi Hendrix, who had been performing Dylan songs for some time, recorded "All Along the Watchtower" for his 1969 album, *Electric Ladyland.* While many bands were covering Dylan tunes, most notably the Byrds, whose canon was heavily reliant on Dylan songs, Hendrix's release became the most popular Dylan cover of the era.

Dylan ended the 1960's with *Nashville Skyline*

(1969), the last album of his major influential period. *Nashville Skyline* was dominated by country-music influences and even included a duet with country singer Johnny Cash. The album yielded Dylan's most successful single to date, "Lay, Lady, Lay" and is credited with paving the way for the country-rock fusion of groups such as the refurbished Byrds, Poco, and later the Eagles.

The Early 1970's. Dylan puzzled and disappointed most critics and fans by opening the new decade with two unenergetic albums, *New Morning* and *Self-Portrait,* both 1970 releases extolling family life with songs Dylan may have hoped would downplay his reputation into a more realistic context. *New Morning* was dismissed as undistinguished, as was *Self-Portrait,* an ironically titled collection of country tunes written by other artists that was widely ignored. In the same year, MacMillan published *Tarantula,* a book containing many sketches reminiscent of Dylan's *Blonde on Blonde* era, to disappointing responses from critics and the public. Still, the second collection of Dylan's most successful material, *Bob Dylan's Greatest Hits, vol. 2* (1971) contained five new, vibrant songs. *New Morning* included "If Not for You," a collaboration with former Beatle George Harrison, whose own version of the song appeared on his 1970 *All Things Must Pass* set. Twenty-three years would pass before a third collection of greatest hits would appear, an indication of Dylan's declining popular success in the decades after *Nashville Skyline.*

In 1972 Dylan made a guest appearance at George Harrison's Concert for Bangladesh benefit, but he seemed dry of new ideas. The following year he wrote and performed the score for Sam Peckinpah's Western film *Pat Garrett and Billy the Kid.* Most of the music was instrumental, featuring acoustic guitar work, but one vocal track, "Knockin' on Heaven's Door," became another success as a single and has remained one of Dylan's most enduring compositions. Dylan also had a part in the film, playing a character named Alias.

In 1974 Dylan made a surprising move by briefly leaving Columbia Records to join David Geffen's new Asylum Records, giving the label his latest release, *Planet Waves.* This set, although it sold well, was an artistic disappointment (although the song "Forever Young" was later a modest hit for Rod Stewart); even a tour with the Band did not calm speculation that Dylan might be past his prime.

Renewal. In 1975, ten years after he "went electric," Dylan seemed reinvigorated. He returned to Columbia Records and released three high-quality albums in one year: the long-awaited *Basement Tapes* with the Band (although this was old material), *Blood on the Tracks,* and *Desire. Blood on the Tracks,* containing "Tangled Up in Blue" and "Lily, Rosemary, and the Jack of Hearts," was widely hailed as his best work in years, and some critics called it his best album. Dylan was not to release another record to such a positive response until 1997's *Time out of Mind. Desire,* while not the equal of its predecessor, had its share of highlights, notably "Hurricane," a return to Dylan's socially conscious lyrics. The song comes to the defense of Rubin "Hurricane" Carter, a boxer whom Dylan and others believed had been falsely imprisoned for murder. (Eventually the law agreed. In 1976 the New Jersey Supreme Court threw out Carter's conviction. He was then retried and reconvicted. In 1985 the second conviction was also overturned.) The album also featured "Sara," a lover's lament from Dylan to his wife during their divorce. *Desire* also helped launch the career of singer Emmylou Harris, who sang second vocals on the album.

During 1975 Dylan's live performances also

For the Record

During the late 1980's Bob Dylan explained why he was glad to have started his musical career during the turbulent 1960's: "Everything happened so quick in the '60's. There was just an electricity in the air. It's hard to explain—I mean, you didn't ever want to go to sleep because you didn't want to miss anything. It wasn't there in the '70's and it ain't there now."

showed his renewed energy. Friends Joan Baez and Byrds' guitarist Roger McGuinn joined Dylan's "Rolling Thunder Revue," a touring company designed to play small venues rather than large stadiums. Dylan's entourage, which included poets Allen Ginsberg and Anne Waldman, was recorded and filmed for the planned production of a film about the tour. The tour was as much a literary as musical experience, with Dylan accompanying Ginsberg on a pilgrimage to Beat writer Jack Kerouac's grave in Lowell, Massachusetts. Dylan included a reading of Ginsberg's verse in the final cut of his film project, ultimately named *Renaldo and Clara*. The four-hour movie, released three years later, seemed to encapsulate yet another lull in Dylan's creative powers. The self-absorbed film raised no public or critical interest, nor did the 1978 album *Street Legal*, which seemed a miscalculated attempt to capture the flavor of old. The one high point of the year was his appearance in *The Last Waltz*, an all-star concert filmed by Martin Scorsese honoring the retirement of the Band from the stage.

More New Directions. In 1979, Dylan startled the music world by declaring himself a convert to fundamentalist Christianity. His next three albums, *Slow Train Coming*, *Saved* (1980), and *Shot of Love* (1981), were lyrically and musically gospel-driven, with choirs sometimes joining Dylan in the studio. The one single to enjoy success from this trilogy, "Gotta Serve Somebody" from *Slow Train Coming*, won Dylan his first Grammy Award, and he performed the song in one of his rare televised appearances on *Saturday Night Live*.

Dylan then produced a series of uneven albums beginning with *Infidels*, a collection produced by Dire Straits leader Mark Knopfler. Its successor, *Empire Burlesque* (1985), did nothing to help Dylan's eroding reputation. Other low points included his 1985 appearance at Live Aid with Rolling Stones members Keith Richards and Ron Wood and his starring role in the ill-fated 1987 film *Hearts of Fire*. Still, comments he made onstage at the Live Aid show inspired singer Willie Nelson to inaugurate the Farm Aid concert series designed to assist American farmers.

Dylan gained a reputation beginning in the late 1970's and continuing into the 1990's for performing notoriously uneven concerts; some were undoubtedly almost unlistenable. With a band blasting behind him, he would sometimes race through songs at breakneck speed, mumbling or shouting the lyrics so unintelligibly that audiences could not even determine what song he was playing. One critic said that it sounded as though Dylan were trying to explode his old songs from the inside. By the mid-1990's, however, Dylan had calmed down and generally returned to a less assaultive live style.

By 1986 Dylan himself was beginning to say that it might be time to retire. Instead, he began a series of collaborations. First he toured with the Grateful Dead in early 1987. Dylan quickly began a second tour, this time with Tom Petty and the Heartbreakers. His most successful collaboration, however, occurred the following year with Jeff Lynne, Tom Petty, George Harrison, and Roy Orbison, who recorded as the Traveling Wilburys. They produced two albums (in 1988 and 1990, the second without Orbison after the singer's death). The decade ended with the critical success of 1989's *Oh Mercy*. Produced by Daniel Lanois, *Oh Mercy* foreshadowed the sparse style of albums to come. It included the song "Man in a Long Dark Coat," which newcomer Joan Osborne covered on her 1995 debut album, *Relish*.

Recognition and New Work in the 1990's. The 1990's were a decade of both honors and new successes for Dylan, although the decade began on a low note. *Red Sky at Morning* (1990) was a surprisingly thin album despite guitar work from Texas blues guitarist Stevie Ray Vaughan. Soon Dylan's reputation was renewed again, this time by major retrospectives. With *Biograph* (1985), Columbia Records collected some of the alternate tracks, rehearsal outtakes, and other unreleased material long pirated by "bootleg" companies. This set was soon superseded by 1991's *The Bootleg Series*, a boxed set impressively overviewing Dylan's recording career.

In 1991 Dylan performed for the Grammy Awards ceremony, at which he was honored with a National Association of Recording Arts and Sciences Lifetime Achievement Award. Another tribute was 1992's all-star thirtieth anniversary celebration at Madison Square Garden. Dylan himself played, as did an amazing range of other performers, including Neil Young, who cheerfully christened the event the "Bobfest." Dylan's own major live performances included an appearance at Woodstock '94 and his ebullient 1994 set for the *MTV Unplugged* series. In May, 1997, Dylan became seriously ill with a viral infection in the sac around his heart. By August he was back on tour, appearing before Pope John Paul II at a eucharistic conference in Bologna. In December of that year, he received a Kennedy Center Honors award, with President Bill Clinton in attendance.

Dylan's recordings, too, found renewed critical interest. *Good As I've Been to You* (1992) and the Grammy-winning *World Gone Wrong* (1993) were solo acoustic versions of blues and folk songs which highlighted Dylan's guitar playing rather than compositional skills. Then, returning to the dark, sparse style of *Oh Mercy*, Dylan hired that album's producer, Daniel Lanois, to give him the sound that resulted in *Time out of Mind* in the fall of 1997. Including many bluesy numbers, the gritty recording was quickly and widely hailed as Dylan's best since *Blood on the Tracks*, earning the Grammy Award for Album of the Year in 1997.

Legacy. From his folk beginnings, largely emulating Woody Guthrie, Dylan went on to adopt the personae of a major voice of the Civil Rights movement, a folk-rocker, the rock-and-roll poet laureate, a major innovator, a country boy, a mystic visionary, and a world-weary traveler of many roads. No other songwriter has been as influential or as copied as Dylan has since the 1960's, and it is unlikely that any other musician has been the subject of as many articles, books, films, scholarly studies, anthologies, and printed collections of lyrics. His importance is immeasurable. His influence has been direct and acknowledged by such artists as the Beatles, Lou Reed, Roger McGuinn, Bruce Springsteen, Elvis Costello, David Bowie, Patti Smith, Sinead O'Connor, and Frank Zappa. Younger artists of the 1990's—including Lucinda Williams, Beck, Jewel, Pavement, and hip-hop protesters the Fugees—also have paid homage to Dylan. Dylan's legacy was also manifested by the success of the band the Wallflowers, a group headed by his son Jakob. —*Wesley Britton*

SELECT DISCOGRAPHY

■ ALBUMS

Bob Dylan, 1962
The Freewheelin' Bob Dylan, 1963
The Times They Are a-Changin', 1964
Another Side of Bob Dylan, 1964
Bringing It All Back Home, 1965
Highway 61 Revisited, 1965
Blonde on Blonde, 1966
John Wesley Harding, 1967
Nashville Skyline, 1969
Planet Waves, 1974
Blood on the Tracks, 1975
The Basement Tapes, 1975
Desire, 1975
Slow Train Coming, 1979
Saved, 1980
Infidels, 1983
Biograph, 1985 (compilation)
Oh Mercy, 1989
The Bootleg Series, vol. 1-3 (Rare and Unreleased) 1961-1991, 1991 (compilation)
MTV Unplugged, 1995
Time out of Mind, 1997

SELECT AWARDS

Grammy Award for Best Rock Vocal Performance, Male, for "Gotta Serve Somebody," 1979
Rock and Roll Hall of Fame, inducted 1989
Grammy Award for Best Rock Performance by a Duo or Group with Vocal for *Traveling Wilburies Volume One*, 1989 (with others)
Grammy Lifetime Achievement Award, 1991
Grammy Award for Best Traditional Folk Album for *World Gone Wrong*, 1994
Kennedy Center Honors Award, 1997
Grammy Award for Album of the Year for *Time out of Mind*, 1997

SEE ALSO: Baez, Joan; Band, The; Byrds, The; Cash, Johnny; Guthrie, Woody; Hendrix, Jimi; Orbison, Roy; Petty, Tom, and the Heartbreakers; Springsteen, Bruce; Wallflowers, The.

E

Sheila E.

(Sheila Escovedo)

BORN: Oakland, California; December 12, 1957
FIRST ALBUM RELEASE: *The Glamorous Life*, 1984
MUSICAL STYLES: Pop, rock and roll, funk, Latin

One of the few women to find success in the male-dominated pop percussion field, Sheila E. did not originally intend to become a solo artist. Her early success playing with Diana Ross, Marvin Gaye, and her father, Pete Escovedo of Santana, along with her high-profile friendship with Prince, led her to score several hits of her own in the mid-1980's. Her first album, *The Glamorous Life*, typified her high-energy, Latin-influenced funk-rock sound.

The Beginnings. The daughter of Santana drummer Pete Escovedo, Sheila E. grew up surrounded by musicians but otherwise had no formal musical training. By the age of seven, she had learned to play the drums, and when she was a teenager, she began to tour with her father's Latin band, Azteca. Sheila E. quit high school to go on the road and recorded several albums with Azteca. By the late 1970's, she had become an in-demand studio musician, playing with Diana Ross, Marvin Gaye, and Herbie Hancock. However, this seemingly overnight success did not come without obstacles. "Once I started coming out to Los Angeles to do session work when I was 17 or 18, I noticed, recording with top session players, a lot of the male drummers really resented me for being in the room with them," she has said. "I couldn't understand it. I was doing what I love to do. . . . It was very hard. I felt like I had to prove myself as a player, and I still do. I still have to prove I can play."

A Pivotal Meeting. In 1978, Sheila E., who was still using her full last name, met the artist then known as Prince, leading to a friendship that would prove pivotal to her career. They first worked together when Sheila E. recorded "Erotic City," a duet with Prince on the B side of his number 1 1984 hit, "Let's Go Crazy." Sheila E. has said, "I love recording with Prince. The sky's the limit with him. There are no rules in the studio. Nothing matters as long as the energy is there."

Under Prince's tutelage, Escovedo became Sheila E. the solo act with a retooled, sexy image. She toured with him as his opening act during his 1984-1985 Purple Rain tour, which coincided with the release of her debut album, *The Glamorous Life*. The title track went to number 7 on the pop charts, her biggest hit to date, while "Belle of St. Mark" reached number 34. The album earned multiple nominations for Grammy and American

Sheila E. (Lissa Wales)

Music Awards. Her subsequent albums were less successful: *Sheila E. in Romance 1600* only hit number 50 in 1985 but included "A Love Bizarre," a duet with Prince that went to number 11.

Touring the Globe. As the 1980's wound down, Sheila E. temporarily put aside her solo career to join Prince for the *Sign '☮' the Times* album, world tour, and film. Her eponymous third album, released in 1987, peaked at number 56 with the number 68 "Hold Me" its most successful single. In 1991, Sheila E. released *Sex Cymbal,* her least successful album, reaching only number 146 on the charts. She spent much of the 1990's playing session work and touring as the leader of four different bands that spanned styles from Latin, jazz, and funk to gospel, rhythm and blues, fusion, and Brazilian blues.

A Television First. In 1998, Sheila E. had another career milestone when she was tapped to become the music director for *The Magic Hour,* a short-lived syndicated late-night talk/variety show hosted by basketball great Earvin "Magic" Johnson. The first woman to hold a music director position for a late-night show, Sheila E. also cowrote the hour-long program's theme music with her brother, Peter Michael Escovedo.

—*Robert DiGiacomo*

SELECT DISCOGRAPHY

■ ALBUMS

The Glamorous Life, 1984
Sheila E. in Romance 1600, 1985
Sheila E., 1987
Sex Cymbal, 1991

SEE ALSO: Prince; Santana, Carlos.

For the Record

"I'd rather be in the back playing in a band. I don't always have to be in the limelight. . . . Really, I never even thought I'd ever be a solo artist. Who would ever think a percussion player would be a solo artist?" —*Sheila E.*

The Eagles

ORIGINAL MEMBERS: Glenn Frey (b. 1948), Don Henley (b.1947), Bernie Leadon (b. 1947), Randy Meisner (b. 1948)

OTHER MEMBERS: Don Felder (b. 1947), Joe Walsh (b. 1947), Timothy B. Schmit (b. 1947)

FIRST ALBUM RELEASE: *The Eagles,* 1972

MUSICAL STYLES: Country rock, folk rock, rock and roll

In 1971 a group of musicians who were originally assembled to be Linda Ronstadt's backup band formed one of the most successful rock bands of the 1970's, the Eagles. They combined traditional folk and country harmonies with rock guitars, and their lyrics portrayed outlaws and hustlers of the old and new West. Strong playing and writing abilities, perfectionism in the studio, and shrewd management led to a gold debut album, three consecutive number 1 albums, five number 1 singles, three Grammy awards, and induction into the Rock and Roll Hall of Fame in 1997.

The Beginnings. The Eagles were a product of the folk-rock and country-rock movements of the late 1960's and early 1970's. Although none of the four founding members was originally from Los Angeles, they formed Ronstadt's backup band there and are often considered a Los Angeles band. Glenn Frey was the first to accept a position as guitarist with Linda Ronstadt's band. In need of a drummer, he called upon Don Henley, whom he had met at the Troubadour club in Los Angeles.

Originally from Gilmore, Texas, Henley had found his way to the Troubadour with a band called Shiloh. As drummer and lead singer of the band, Henley became acquainted with the duo Longbranch Pennywhistle (J. D. Souther and Glenn Frey), who also frequented the Troubadour. Henley accepted Frey's offer to audition for the Ronstadt band. Henley and Frey formed a successful partnership from the beginning. Ronstadt's producer, John Boylan, recruited the former bass guitarist of Rick Nelson's group, Randy Meisner, and lead guitarist Bernie Leadon, formerly of the Dillard and Clark Expedition and the Flying Burrito Brothers.

The Eagles Hotel California *lineup: Glenn Frey, Don Henley, Timothy B. Schmit, Don Felder, Joe Walsh* (AP/Wide World Photos)

The Eagles Take Flight. With future mogul David Geffen as their manager, this quartet amiably left Ronstadt to pursue a career on their own. After spending some time in Colorado to write songs, rehearse, and polish their performances in local clubs, the Eagles recorded their debut album in London under the direction of veteran producer Glyn Johns. Both the first single, "Take It Easy" (cowritten by Frey and Jackson Browne), and the album, *The Eagles* (released in July, 1972), went gold. It was a solid debut that embodied a down-to-earth approach with its strong vocal harmonies and easygoing rhythms. Two other singles, "Peaceful Easy Feeling" and "Witchy Woman," also made appearances on the *Billboard* charts.

Their second recording effort, released in the spring of 1973, was the concept album *Desperado,* in which the songs were loosely tied to the tale of the outlaw Doolin-Dalton gang. Their fascination with the Wild West firmly established the Eagles as part of the California culture. Both the title song and the single "Tequila Sunrise" were modest hits. ("Desperado" was later a bigger hit for Linda Ronstadt.) In 1974 the Eagles prepared to work on their third album, *On the Border.* The band asked Bill Szymczyk to take over for Glyn Johns as record producer and changed management from Geffen to Irving Azoff. Szymczyk took the Eagles in a slightly different direction with his strong rhythm-and-blues orientation. When the album was released in March, 1974, the Eagles announced that they had added a fifth member, guitarist Don Felder, recognized as one of the best slide guitarists in the industry. *On the Border* easily surpassed gold-record levels and contained the band's first number 1 single, the ballad "Best of My Love."

In June, 1975, the Eagles released their fourth album, *One of These Nights,* which easily sold more than a million copies and yielded three hit singles: "Lyin' Eyes," "Hollywood Waltz," and "Take It To the Limit." Amidst this tremendous success grew rumors of internal problems among the band members. By the end of 1975 Leadon had left the group to form the Leadon-Georgiades Band and was replaced by Joe Walsh, former lead guitarist with the James Gang and a successful solo artist in

For the Record

Eagles manager Irving Azoff commented on the band to Irwin Stambler as the Eagles were working on the *Hotel California* album, "Even more than before, they all want to take their time. To us melodies, lyrics, and vocals all are really—and equally—important. And that's why we say the Eagles are the Beach Boys of the '70's."

his own right. Walsh had toured with the Eagles in 1973 and was also managed by Irving Azoff's Front Line Management. This change in personnel did not prove to be detrimental: Their first album with Walsh was number 1 on the *Billboard* charts for eight weeks and was the biggest-selling album of their career. *Hotel California* (1976) sold nine million copies worldwide in its first year of release alone and contained two number 1 singles, the title track and "New Kid in Town." Henley later described the title song as "a reggae song, with Spanish influences, about the state of America." The lyrics of "Hotel California" describe the tantalizing California dream of a sunny paradise that can become a prison. Much of their later work expressed a similar dark and introspective view of life. This album's "Life in the Fast Lane" became a staple of FM rock playlists.

Another shift in personnel took place in 1979 when Randy Meisner left the band to pursue a solo career. He was replaced by former Poco bass guitarist Timothy Schmit. In October of 1979 this latest lineup released the album *The Long Run*. Not as critically acclaimed as their previous efforts, and three years in the making, the album did achieve platinum status and yielded three Top-10 singles: "Heartache Tonight," "The Long Run," and "I Can't Tell You Why."

The End of an Era. In the early 1980's both Henley and Frey turned their attention to solo work. As internal dissension grew, Irving Azoff, the Eagles' manager, made the formal announcement in May of 1982 that the Eagles had disbanded. Soon after, Don Felder began work on a solo career with the release of his album *Airborne* in 1983 before leaving the music business to pursue a career in real estate. After working with the Eagles on their last studio album, Schmit toured with Jimmy Buffett and released three solo albums. Walsh played on albums for Stevie Winwood and Richard Marx, recorded several solo albums, and in 1980, as part of a campaign to register voters, ran for president of the United States as an independent candidate. Glenn Frey attained a moderate degree of success as a solo artist with such Top-40 hit songs as "The Heat Is On," "Sexy Girl," and "Smuggler's Blues" in the 1980's, but he failed to attain the same level of success as longtime friend and songwriting partner Henley. Henley's first solo album, *I Can't Stand Still* (1982), marked the beginning of his solo career.

A Reunion. As unlikely as it may have seemed in the early 1980's, the 1990's saw a reunion of the Eagles in a live collection aptly titled *Hell Freezes Over.* (In years past, when asked about the possibility of an Eagles reunion, Henley had said that it would occur "when hell freezes over." For one thing, Henley had tired of Walsh's antics on the road; Walsh would do things such as attacking hotel-room walls with a chain saw.) The unexpected reunion was occasioned by the release of an album entitled *Common Thread.* It contains many of country music's prominent artists (Travis Tritt, Clint Black, and Trisha Yearwood, among others) performing their renditions of Eagles songs. The public response was so overwhelming that the album reached double-platinum status. When Tritt was asked to make a music video to accompany his version of "Take It Easy," he declined, stating that "the only way I'd do a video is if we got the Eagles back together." Tritt was just as shocked as everyone else when the Eagles agreed to perform in the video. From that experience they decided to do a reunion tour. As a testament to the quality of their music and to their large following, their 1994-1995 "Hell Freezes Over" tour of the United States became one of the highest-grossing concert tours on record.

—Kimberly Morgan

SELECT DISCOGRAPHY

■ ALBUMS

The Eagles, 1972
Desperado, 1973
On the Border, 1974
One of These Nights, 1975
Hotel California, 1976
Their Greatest Hits 1971-1975, 1976 (compilation)
The Long Run, 1979
Eagles Live, 1980
Greatest Hits Volume 2, 1982 (compilation)
Best of the Eagles, 1985 (compilation)
Hell Freezes Over, 1994

SELECT AWARDS

Grammy Award for Best Pop Vocal Performance by a Duo, Group, or Chorus for "Lyin' Eyes," 1975
Grammy Award for Record of the Year for "Hotel California," 1977
Grammy Award for Best Rock Vocal Performance by a Duo or Group for "Heartache Tonight," 1979

SEE ALSO: Buffalo Springfield; Byrds, The; Henley, Don; Ronstadt, Linda.

Steve Earle

BORN: Fort Monroe, Virginia; January 17, 1955
FIRST ALBUM RELEASE: *Guitar Town*, 1986
MUSICAL STYLES: Country, country rock, rock and roll

After spending most of his life establishing himself as one of the most respected and original songwriters in Nashville, Steve Earle squandered his talent in a haze of drug and alcohol abuse that almost killed him. Always a rebel, as a teenager he had protested the Vietnam War; as a country recording star, he continued his activism by playing at Farm Aid concerts and later becoming involved in such organizations as Not In Our Name, a group led by actors Tim Robbins and Susan Sarandon protesting capital punishment. It is his dark, brooding songwriting skills and his alternative-country style, however, that are most likely to make him a legend.

The Texan Moves to Nashville. Raised near San Antonio, Texas, Earle received his first guitar at age eleven and mastered it by age thirteen. He left home at sixteen and married his first of six wives when he was nineteen. Moving to Nashville, he played in local bands, recording with country legend Guy Clark in 1975. Clark, along with Nashville hero Townes Van Zandt, influenced the young Earle not only in their blues-based country songwriting style, but also in their hard-drinking ways. That year he also met Emmylou Harris, who would be one of his many supporters, singing his songs and having him record on her albums. In 1975 he also appeared briefly in Robert Altman's film *Nashville*.

He struggled for years in Nashville, writing songs for seventy-five dollars per week, working odd jobs and playing in various bands. Finally, in 1986, his *Guitar Town* was released to immediate critical success. At the time, Nashville was turning out shallow, sentimental ballads, and Earle's songwriting was original and true, and he was declared an heir to the spirit of Hank Williams. A rockabilly Duane Eddy-influenced album, *Guitar Town* featured unusually political lyrics for a country singer and gained him immediate respect as a great songwriter. His next album, *Exit O* (1987), received even more critical acclaim, and the song "I Ain't Ever Satisfied" gained some airplay on rock radio stations. Nashville was, so far, avoiding his music.

Copperhead Road (1988), his most commercially successful album, was even more rock-oriented, and the title track received extensive airplay in the United States and the United Kingdom. His rec-

For the Record

In 1975 Steve Earle almost received his big break when Elvis Presley was set to record his song "Mustang Wine." Presley never showed up for the session, however, and died soon after.

ord label, MCA, quickly switched him from their country label to their pop label, another division where he did not exactly fit. *The Hard Way* (1990), was followed by his *Shut Up and Die Like an Aviator* in 1991. Commercially, both fared poorly, causing MCA to let his contract expire. Earle's longtime drug habit had started at the age of thirteen with heroin, and by the early 1990's it had grown so far out of control as to make him a liability.

Jail Time. With no record label, Earle's crack cocaine problem escalated to the point where the prolific songwriter would not write a single word or note of music for four years. Constantly selling his guitar for the drugs, he was eventually arrested for drug possession and sent to jail in 1994. What he called his "vacation in the ghetto" may have ultimately saved his life. In jail, he completed a drug rehabilitation program successfully and was released early.

Despite being clean and sober, no major record label would sign him, so he wrote songs for others. Finally, a Nashville independent label released his acoustic *Train a Comin'* in 1995. He also appeared on the sound track of Tim Robbins's 1995 film *Dead Man Walking*. After that, he started his own label, E-Squared, and released two excellent albums, *I Feel Alright* in 1996 and *El Corazón* in 1997. In addition to being a vehicle for his own music, the E-Squared label is also dedicated to championing the alternative-country sounds of up-and-coming groups such as the V-Roys. Earle, with Ray Kennedy, known as the Twangtrust, produce all of the E-Squared albums in addition to many other recording artists' albums in Nashville.

Far-Reaching Influence. Like Lyle Lovett and Dwight Yoakam (who are also difficult to categorize and outside the country mainstream), Earle is a respected talent who is more comfortable with the alternative-rock crowd than with the traditional Nashville country crowd. Probably more influential than he will ever be popular, his songwriting, singing, producing skills, and great guitar playing can be heard through work with Harris, Lucinda Williams, Nanci Griffith, Jerry Douglas, Kris Kristofferson, and Brian Setzer, to name just a few.

—Kevin M. Mitchell

SELECT DISCOGRAPHY

■ ALBUMS

Guitar Town, 1986
Exit O, 1987
Copperhead Road, 1988
The Hard Way, 1990
Shut Up and Die Like an Aviator, 1991
Train a Comin', 1995
I Feel Alright, 1996
El Corazón, 1997

SEE ALSO: Eddy, Duane; Lovett, Lyle; Williams, Hank; Yoakam, Dwight.

Steve Earle (Paul Natkin)

Earth, Wind, and Fire

ORIGINAL MEMBERS: Maurice White (b. 1941), Wade Flemons (1940-1993), Don Whitehead, Verdine White (b. 1951), Sherry Scott, Phillard Williams, Michael Beale, Chester Washington, Leslie Drayton, Alex Thomas

OTHER MEMBERS: Philip Bailey (b. 1951), Larry Dunn (b. 1953), Al McKay (b. 1948), Ralph Johnson (b. 1951), Andrew Woolfolk (b. 1950), Fred White (b. 1955), Roland Laws, Roland Bautista, Jessica Cleaves (b. 1948), Johnny Graham, Don Myrick (d. 1993), Louis Satterfield (b. 1957), Michael Harris (b. 1953), Sheldon Reynolds

FIRST ALBUM RELEASE: *Earth, Wind, and Fire*, 1972

MUSICAL STYLES: Soul, funk, rhythm and blues

Drummer Maurice White organized Earth, Wind, and Fire in Chicago in 1971. His vision was to build a band with a philosophical foundation espousing universal happiness and spiritual brotherhood. The group's reputation was built on its exuberant stage act with shifting rhythms, sudden dynamic changes, and visual showmanship.

The Beginning. White was raised in Memphis, Tennessee, and by age six was a featured soloist at his church. As the youngest member of a local quartet, the Rosehill Jubilettes, White learned about life on the road while traveling to southern churches. Influenced by the rhythm and blues of Sam Cooke and Lou Rawls, White began his career as drummer after witnessing marching bands. He began working with high school friend Booker T. Jones, who would later form the Memphis instrumental group Booker T and the MG's.

With Jones, White played with the club band the Mad Lads. Moving to Chicago, he played his first session on Betty Everett's "You're No Good." He did various session work for Vee Jay Records and became Chess Records' full-time drummer from 1962 to 1967, playing for Billy Stewart, Little Milton, Etta James, Howlin' Wolf, Sonny Boy Williamson, and Willie Dixon.

His first professional tour was with jazz virtuoso Ramsey Lewis, who trained White in management. White started his own company, Hummit Productions, with Wade Flemons and Don Whitehead, both singers and keyboardists. In 1969, the three called themselves the Salty Peppers and recorded "La La Time," releasing it on their own Hummit label. A Capitol Records representative heard the song, and the label decided to distribute it nationally.

Earth, Wind, and Fire. White decided to expand the group's scope and purpose, choosing the name Earth, Wind, and Fire from his astrological chart, which did not contain the fourth element, water. With singer Sherry Scott and younger brother Verdine White, he recruited the other members of the original ten-piece lineup.

After two lackluster albums for Warner Bros., the group disbanded. With brother Verdine, White hired new members Philip Bailey, Larry Dunn, Roland Laws, Roland Bautista, Ralph Johnson, and Jessica Cleaves. Performing as the warmup band for singer John Sebastian at New York's Rockefeller Center, the group attracted Columbia Records president Clive Davis, who bought the group's contract. In spring of 1972, the new lineup recorded *Last Days and Time.* With primarily original music and two cover songs, the album received considerable airplay on college radio stations, who opened new markets for the band. In the winter of the following year, they released *Head to the Sky* with three new members, earning their first two legitimate hit singles, "Evil" and the title track.

Going Platinum. The follow-up, *Open Our Eyes* (1975), was the group's first platinum album without Cleaves, who had left the band to marry. Becoming an eight-piece group, the band released its first Top-30 hit, "Mighty Mighty." Another *Open Our Eyes* track, "Devotion," also rose on the charts, and its spiritual, metaphysical lyrics indicated the band's future direction.

In 1974, the group was the only black band at the major "California Jam" rock concert before opening for Sly and the Family Stone at New York's Madison Square Garden. Their next album, *That's the Way of the World* (1975), went double platinum, and included their first number 1 single, "Shining Star." Another White brother, Fred, joined the ensemble as they moved into larger stadiums. Their next double-platinum seller, the live two-album *Gratitude* (1975), was an unprecedented seller for a black group in that era.

Earth, Wind, and Fire's next platinum album, *All 'n All* (1977), was inspired by Brazilian music and further explored metaphysical themes. The group's onstage act had expanded to include imaginative magical trappings from magician Doug Henning, including the band vanishing from the stage. In 1978, they received three Grammy Awards, notably for their version of the Beatles' "Got to Get You into My Life" from the film *Sgt. Pepper's Lonely Hearts Club Band,* in which the group appeared.

After a brief 1979 flirtation with disco, the group earned another Grammy for "After the Love Has Gone" from their next double-platinum seller, *I Am. I Am* was quickly compared with the Beatles' 1969 *Abbey Road* and was considered their most influential album. In December, 1979, they appeared at the United Nations for a United Nations International Children's Emergency Fund (UNICEF) benefit concert, but the band felt they were becoming too commercial. While dissension over White's beliefs began to split the group, they released *Faces* (1980), the album that broke the platinum-selling streak. After taking time off, the band returned to the charts with 1981's *Raise.*

Disintegration and Reformation. While the group continued to sell respectably in the 1980's, pressures to outdo their previous work and remain innovative sent band members into solo careers. From late 1983 through early 1987, the group was dormant.

In 1987, Earth, Wind, and Fire returned with "System of Survival," followed by a nine-month tour. Three years later, the reenergized band issued their last Columbia release, *Heritage.* Returning to Warner Bros. in 1991, the group began a new series of albums. On September 15, 1995, they were honored with a star on the Hollywood Walk of Fame, and they were nominated for the Rock and Roll Hall of Fame in 1997. —*Wesley Britton*

For the Record

Maurice White got the name of Earth, Wind, and Fire from ideas he picked up in his astrological chart. After learning that his sign, Sagittarius, contained only earth, air, and fire, he changed "air" to "wind" and used the resulting combination as the name for his new group. He then proceeded to find members who matched his spiritual ideals.

SELECT DISCOGRAPHY

■ ALBUMS

Earth, Wind, and Fire, 1971
Last Days and Time, 1972
That's the Way of the World, 1975
I Am, 1979
Electric Universe, 1983
Beat It to Life, 1986
In the Name of Love, 1997

SELECT AWARDS

Grammy Award for Best Vocal Performance by a Group for "Shining Star," 1975

Grammy Awards for Best R&B Instrumental Performance for "Runnin'" and Best R&B Vocal Performance by a Duo, Group, or Chorus for *All 'n All,* 1978

Grammy Awards for Best R&B Instrumental Performance for "Boogie Wonderland" and Best R&B Vocal Performance by a Duo, Group, or Chorus for "After the Love Has Gone," 1979

Grammy Award for Best R&B Performance by a Duo or Group with Vocal for "Wanna Be with You," 1982

SEE ALSO: Beatles, The; Booker T. and the MG's; Cooke, Sam; Dixon, Willie; Rawls, Lou.

Sheena Easton

(Sheena Shirley Orr)

BORN: Bellshill, Scotland; April 27, 1959
FIRST ALBUM RELEASE: *Take My Time,* 1981
MUSICAL STYLES: Pop, rock and roll

Despite her enormous talent, Sheena Easton's career has been the subject of much criticism and controversy. Born Sheena Shirley Orr, Easton grew up in Scotland and studied performance at the Royal Scottish Academy of Music and Drama in Glasgow. After an eight-month marriage ending in divorce, Easton's career was launched by a British documentary about her transformation from an amateur into a polished professional performer. Critics accused Easton of passively allowing the media to mold her into a commercial package, and some even felt that her singing was too imitative of Barbra Streisand.

For the Record

Sheena Easton's early career is an example of a self-fulfilling prophecy. In 1979 a British television program, *The Big Three*, decided to follow her path to stardom for a year. When its documentary aired in mid-1980, Easton's first single, "Modern Girl," had not been successful. However, the show itself made her a star overnight: Her second single, "9 to 5" ("Morning Train" in the U.S.), shot to number 3 on the British pop chart. When her first single was re-released, it went to number 6, making Easton the first female British singer in a quarter of a century to have two songs in the Top 20 at the same time.

Forging Ahead. This criticism did not stop Easton's career, however. Her first single, "Modern Girl," was well received in England, and her next single, "Nine to Five" (retitled "Morning Train" in the United States), was an export hit, soaring to the top of the U.S. pop charts in a short time. Due to her sudden popularity, she was chosen to sing "For Your Eyes Only," the title track of the 1981 James Bond film. Unusually, the film's opening credits featured Easton herself, in a format similar to the MTV music videos that became popular in the 1980's. To round out her successful year, Easton was awarded the 1981 Grammy Award for Best New Artist.

Over the next few years, Easton became the first music artist to have recorded Top-5 hits in five different categories on the *Billboard* charts: pop, black, country, dance, and adult contemporary. She sparked even more controversy by winning a Grammy Award in the Mexican-American category, which some found inappropriate in light of Easton's Scottish descent.

Finding a Direction. For several years after arriving in the United States, Easton continued to sing wholesome pop songs, such as the hits "When He Shines" and "He Could Have Been with Me." In 1983, she recorded the popular duet "We've Got Tonight" with Kenny Rogers. Easton also married her former manager, Rob Light, and this period of her life was marked by moderate, although not spectacular, success.

However, Easton was frustrated in both her personal and professional lives. She wanted a tougher sound but had a hard time finding material until she was offered "Strut," a fast-paced dance-rock tune that was later nominated for a Grammy Award. Soon after, she asked singer Prince to write a song for her; the result was 1985's "Sugar Walls," a song with such suggestive lyrics that it was banned from several radio stations and denounced by conservative groups as pornographic. Easton continued her association with Prince by singing backup vocals on his "U Got the Look" in 1987.

Other Projects. At the end of 1986, Easton divorced her second husband after two years of marriage. At the same time, she began pursuing her long-held dream of acting. In 1987, the producers of the popular television show *Miami Vice* announced that the main character, played by Don Johnson, would get married on the show. Easton initially had difficulty getting an audition, and the part ultimately went to actress Lorraine Bracco. However, when Bracco became ill a few days into filming, Easton was called at the last minute to replace her and filmed four episodes of the show. Other acting projects eventually included William Shatner's science-fiction television series *Tek War* and a stint on Broadway as Aldonza in Mitch Leigh, Dale Wasserman, and Joe

Darion's *Man of La Mancha.* Most of these projects were not well received by critics, nor was her 1995 album, *My Cherie.* Easton adopted a baby boy that year, stating that her lack of a permanent relationship did not make motherhood inappropriate.

While Easton's career has spanned an impressive range of projects, some critics feel that her transience marks a lack of artistic maturity. While few would dispute the fact that Easton has a strong, beautiful voice, it could be argued that she never has really found her niche in the music world. —*Amy Sisson*

SELECT DISCOGRAPHY

■ SINGLES

"For Your Eyes Only," 1981

"We've Got Tonight," 1983 (with Kenny Rogers)

■ ALBUMS

Take My Time, 1981

You Could Have Been with Me, 1982

Madness, Money and Music, 1982

Do You, 1985

The Lover in Me, 1988

The World of Sheena Easton: The Singles, 1993 (compilation)

My Cherie, 1995

SELECT AWARDS

Grammy Award for Best New Artist, 1981

Grammy Award for Best Mexican/American Performance for "Me Gustas Tal Como Eres," 1984 (with Luis Miguel)

SEE ALSO: Miguel, Luis; Prince; Streisand, Barbra.

Echo and the Bunnymen

ORIGINAL MEMBERS: Ian McCulloch (b. 1959), Will Sergeant (b. 1958), Les Pattinson (b. 1958)

OTHER MEMBERS: Pete De Freitas (b. 1961)

FIRST ALBUM RELEASE: *Crocodiles,* 1980

MUSICAL STYLES: Pop, rock and roll

A product of the post-punk Liverpool, England, club scene, Echo and the Bunnymen are perhaps best known for their moody remake of the Doors' "People Are Strange" (with former Doors member Ray Manzarek both producing and playing on the track), which was used as a theme for the 1987 vampire film *The Lost Boys.* Despite a strong cult following in Great Britain, Echo and the Bunnymen never achieved commercial success in the U.S. market.

Crucial Three. Echo and the Bunnymen can trace their roots to the breakup of the Crucial Three in 1977. This dissolution freed vocalist Ian McCulloch to put together his own band. By the end of 1978, McCulloch had gathered guitarist Will Sergeant and bassist Les Pattinson. Along with a drum machine that the band had christened Echo, the Bunnymen made their first public appearance at a Liverpool club called Eric's. In March, 1979, Echo and the Bunnymen released their first single, "Pictures on My Wall," on the independent Zoo label. Later that year, Echo was replaced by a human drummer, Peter de Freitas. The release of two other singles, "Monkeys" and "Rescue," combined with a fervent touring schedule, led to a recording contract with Korova and the group's first album, *Crocodiles,* which was released in 1980. *Crocodiles* was a critical success and reached number 17 on the British album charts.

Echo and the Bunnymen followed up the release of *Crocodiles* with an extensive tour of the United Kingdom. The "Crocodiles" tour established the apocalyptic stage show that was to become the group's visual trademark. Sporting camouflage, Echo and the Bunnymen would perform in a thick dry-ice fog in an attempt to evoke the visual imagery of the 1979 film *Apocalypse Now.*

Success. In 1981, Echo and the Bunnymen followed up their early success with a U.S. tour, a live extended-play single, *Shine So Hard,* and a new studio album, *Heaven up Here,* which reached number 10 on the British album charts. A string of successful singles was followed in 1983 by *Porcupine,* Echo and the Bunnymen's third studio album, which reached number 2 on the British charts. Their fourth album, *Ocean Rain* (1984), described by the self-produced publicity packages that accompanied the album as "the greatest album ever made," climbed to number 4 on the British charts for 1984 and cracked the Top 100

Echo and the Bunnymen (Paul Natkin)

in the United States. In 1986, a greatest hits collection, *Songs to Learn and Sing*, hit number 6 on the British charts.

After a long musical silence, the band resurfaced in 1987 with *Echo & the Bunnymen*, which featured former Doors member Ray Manzarek as a musical guest. Reaching number 4 on the British charts, *Echo & the Bunnymen* also made it to number 51 on the the U.S. charts, making it their most successful U.S. release. This collaboration with Manzarek would prove very fruitful for the band, as the Manzarek-produced cover of the Doors' "People Are Strange" became a hit after it was used as the theme for the film *The Lost Boys* in 1987.

Troubles. The U.S. tour supporting *Echo & the Bunnymen* was derailed when McCulloch was thrown by a fan twelve feet from the stage into an orchestra pit. McCulloch left the Bunnymen in 1988 for a solo career. His solo debut album, *Candleland* (1989), was a critical and commercial success in the United Kingdom.

Tragedy struck the band in 1989 when De Freitas was killed in a traffic accident. The remaining Bunnymen signed Damon Reece to replace De Freitas and Noel Burke (formerly of St. Vitus' Dance) to replace McCulloch, and they fulfilled their contractual obligations to Korova with the 1990 release of *Reverberation*, which failed to chart. Meanwhile, McCulloch's solo career spanned many groups and numerous albums, culminating with a 1995 band called Electrafixion, which brought McCulloch and Sergeant back together for a Bunnymen-influenced album entitled *Burned*.

Nothing Lasts Forever. In 1997, the surviving members of Echo and the Bunnymen returned to the studio to record the first new Bunnymen album (with McCulloch) in ten years. *Evergreen* was released on July 1, 1997, and was supported by a rigorous tour schedule and an official Website. Despite the multimedia marketing, *Evergreen* posted only moderate sales. —*B. Keith Murphy*

SELECT DISCOGRAPHY

■ ALBUMS

Crocodiles, 1980
Heaven up Here, 1981
Porcupine, 1983
Ocean Rain, 1984
Echo & the Bunnymen, 1987
Reverberation, 1990
Evergreen, 1997

SEE ALSO: Doors, The.

Duane Eddy

BORN: Corning, New York; April 26, 1938

FIRST ALBUM RELEASE: *Have "Twangy" Guitar—Will Travel*, 1958

MUSICAL STYLES: Rock and roll, rockabilly, country, pop

Duane Eddy is one of the few successful instrumentalists in the history of rock and roll; he is to rock music what Chet Atkins is to country music. Although he does not play with the quickness of Atkins, he set a style at the outset of rock and roll that was to influence many guitarists to follow. His distinctive twangy-guitar sound, with its use of reverb and tremolo and its minimalist technique, effectively made this instrument the most important in rock and roll, and his string of hits in the late 1950's spawned a whole generation of guitarists who emphasized the bass strings to effect a driving and haunting sound. In 1960, the *New Musical Express* poll in the United Kingdom voted Eddy the World's Top Music Personality. He appeared in three films and released some twenty-seven albums.

No Formal Training. Eddy received his first guitar when he was five, and his father taught him a few basic chords. He listened to popular music on the radio and was fascinated by the singing cowboys Roy Rogers and Gene Autry. At the age of ten, he performed "Missouri Waltz" on a lap steel guitar for a local radio station; the guitar was a present from an aunt. Five years later he acquired his first electric guitar, a Gibson Les Paul. By this time, he and his family had moved to Arizona, and many of his early hit records were recorded in Phoenix. In his teen years, Eddy formed a country band that played music indebted to such musicians as Chet Atkins, Merle Travis, Les Paul, and Jerry Byrd. He has also cited such jazz artists as Django Reinhardt, Barney Kessel, and Louis Armstrong as favorite musicians.

In his mid-teens, Eddy recorded one of Chet Atkins's tunes at his local radio station in Coolidge, Arizona. Jimmy Delbridge, a local piano player, heard it and contacted Eddy; the two began to perform together, and thus began the group that would later become famous as Duane Eddy and the Rebels (Jimmy Delbridge would become known as Jimmy Dell). The group developed a style that clearly derived from the cocky, brooding rebelliousness of such 1950's icons as

Duane Eddy in 1975 (Archive Photos)

Marlon Brando, James Dean, and Elvis Presley. Eddy's clothing, hairstyle, and serious demeanor reflected the image of young people in such films of the time as *The Wild One* (1954), *Rebel Without a Cause* (1955), and *Blackboard Jungle* (1955). "Lonely" and "rebel" are notable words in his hits "Rebel Rouser" and "The Lonely One."

When Eddy was eighteen, he traded his Gibson for a Gretsch 6120 and used this guitar for nearly all of his early hits. On two hits, "Because They're Young" and "Kommotion," Eddy played a six-string bass. By 1956, he had also made the acquaintance of disc jockey Lee Hazlewood, who became his producer and cowriter. In 1958, several of his tunes appeared on the charts: "Movin' 'n' Groovin'," "Rebel Rouser," "Detour," and "Cannonball." The Duane Eddy "twang" had arrived. Most songs featured the solo riffs of Eddy using the lower strings (the bass sound), bridged with saxophone solos and backed by a rhythm section that often included shouts, howls, and whoops provided by a group called the Sharps. Eddy returned the favor by playing on their record "Have Love, Will Travel" in 1958. Quite a number of hits followed until 1963, when he released his last big hit, "Boss Guitar." Eddy would not be prominent on the pop charts until twenty-three years later, when in 1986 he recorded with the Art of Noise and won a Grammy Award for the single "Peter Gunn," a tune he had first recorded in 1958.

That Twangy Guitar. A glance at the names of his many albums will clearly indicate the association of the word "twangy" with Duane Eddy: for example, *Have "Twangy" Guitar—Will Travel, The "Twangs" the "Thang," "Twangin'" Up a Storm,* and *The Biggest "Twang" of Them All.* Eddy admits the label was a gimmick, and he says, "I really don't know what 'twangy' means." A dictionary will indicate that "twang" has several meanings, but most relevant is that which refers to a harsh, quick ringing sound produced by plucking a string. The word refers to the distinctive sound Eddy delivers mostly from the lower four strings of his guitar. This sound is also the result of creative use of technology in the studio. A DeArmond outboard tremolo box creates a pulsing sound, and an empty water tank with a speaker at one end and a microphone at the other provides an echo.

Innovations. The introduction of the "twang" was itself an innovation, but to get that sound Eddy and collaborators had to take advantage of the technology available. They not only employed devices such as the tremolo box and echo chamber but also used overdubs. At first this overdubbing was a necessity because the saxophone player, Plas Johnson, was not in Phoenix where the main recording took place. The saxophone parts were recorded in Los Angeles and then integrated with the rest of the music. On the first album, *Have "Twangy" Guitar—Will Travel* (1958), Eddy included a version of B. B. King's "Three-30-Blues." This willingness by a white musician to enter the world of the blues is indicative of the beginnings of change in modern popular music and of its effect on race relations. Eddy's stance on this challenging of the race barrier is also evident in his appearance in December, 1958, at the Apollo Theatre in Harlem, New York. For a while he was the only white performer in the theater, and his appearance there marked only the second one by a white artist (the first had been Buddy Holly). By the time of the album *The "Twangs" the "Thang"* (1960), Eddy and Hazlewood began to conceive of the album as more than just a disparate group of tunes highlighted by a hit single or two. The album became a project in itself, and several theme albums followed: *Girls! Girls! Girls!* (1961), *Twistin' 'n' Twangin'* (1962), *Surfin' with Duane Eddy* (1963), and *Duane Eddy Does Bob Dylan* (1965) are examples.

For the Record

"It's certainly my opinion that he stood at the crossroads of rock and roll and transformed things by putting the musicians up front. Duane came along and was a real musician out front. It really all started for me in rock and roll with Duane Eddy."

—*John Fogerty, 1991*

In 1987, Capitol Records released the album *Duane Eddy*, and on this record Eddy plays with such well-known artists as Paul McCartney, George Harrison, Ry Cooder, and John Fogerty, who later inducted Eddy into the Rock and Roll Hall of Fame. Eddy has also appeared several times on Country Music Television. —*Roderick McGillis*

SELECT DISCOGRAPHY

■ SINGLES

"Rebel-'Rouser," 1958
"Forty Miles of Bad Road," 1959
"Because They're Young," 1960
"(Dance with the) Guitar Man," 1962

■ ALBUMS

Have "Twangy" Guitar—Will Travel, 1958
The "Twangs" the "Thang," 1960
Girls! Girls! Girls!, 1961
Twistin' 'n' Twangin', 1962
Surfin' with Duane Eddy,, 1963
Duane Eddy Does Bob Dylan, 1965
The Best of Duane Eddy, 1965 (compilation)
Twangy Guitar, 1970
Duane Eddy, 1987
Twang Thang: The Duane Eddy Anthology, 1993 (compilation)

SELECT AWARDS

Grammy Award for Best Rock Instrumental Performance (Orchestra, Group, or Soloist) for "Peter Gunn," 1986 (with the Art of Noise)
Rock and Roll Hall of Fame, inducted 1992

SEE ALSO: Atkins, Chet; Beach Boys, The; Cash, Johnny; Dale, Dick; Orbison, Roy.

Electric Light Orchestra

ORIGINAL MEMBERS: Jeff Lynne (b. 1947), Roy Wood (b. 1946), Bev Bevan (b. 1944), Rick Price

BEST-KNOWN LINE-UP: Jeff Lynne, Bev Bevan, Richard Tandy (b. 1948), Kelly Groucutt (b. 1945), Mik Kaminski (b. 1951), Melvyn Gale (b. 1952), Hugh McDowell (b. 1953)

OTHER MEMBERS: Mike Edwards, Michael D'Albuquerque, others

FIRST ALBUM RELEASE: *No Answer*, 1972

MUSICAL STYLES: Pop, rock and roll, disco

Formed in Birmingham, England, in 1971, the Electric Light Orchestra (ELO) grew out of the successful British rock band the Move. Led by Roy Wood and Jeff Lynne, ELO attempted to blend pop songcraft with classical grandeur, eventually discovering a formula that transformed the group into one of the most successful "hit machines" of the 1970's. Although attrition among the group's members and changes in musical fashion caused ELO to disband in 1986, Jeff Lynne continued to find outlets for his unique sound, both as a producer and as a member of the rock and roll super group, the Traveling Wilburys.

"Move"-ing On. From its beginnings in 1966, the Move contained the nucleus of what would later become the Electric Light Orchestra. Multiple instrumentalist Roy Wood and drummer Bev Bevan were both part of the original ELO lineup. Jeff Lynne, who would later emerge as ELO's leader, joined the Move in 1969, shortly after the release of its *Shazam* album. As if to foreshadow ELO's classical leanings, the Move based "Night of Fear," its first single, on Russian composer Peter Ilich Tchaikovsky's *1812 Overture.*

The conflict among the members of the Move over the group's direction resulted in frequent lineup changes and wide-ranging musical experimentation. Indeed, the group's very eclecticism may have accounted more than anything else for their failure to establish a large following in the United States. When Wood and Lynne announced in 1971 that the Move would become the Electric Light Orchestra and that more lineup changes would follow, few who had followed the group were particularly surprised.

Misses, Hits, and More Misses. At first, the Electric Light Orchestra appeared as likely to fail in the United States as the Move had. ELO's debut album, 1972's *No Answer*, yielded only one minor hit (the five-minute "10538 Overture") and was distinguished mostly by the failure of its rock and classical elements to cohere. The group's 1973 album, *Electric Light Orchestra II*, with the eleven-minute "Kuiama" and the eight-minute "Roll Over

For the Record

During the first part of their 1978 world tour in support of the *Out of the Blue* album, ELO performed inside a 250,000-pound, laser-equipped "spaceship" that remains one of the most spectacular stage sets in the history of live rock. Ironically, elements of the performance were not "live" at all; nearly ten years before Milli Vanilli was shamed from the music business for lip-synching, ELO was known to enhance its "spaceship" performances with prerecorded strings and vocals.

Beethoven," did little to change the general perception of Lynne as a talented but self-indulgent band leader. (Wood left shortly after the release of *No Answer.*)

With *On the Third Day* (1973), however, the group's vision began coming into focus, and both *Eldorado* (1974) and *Face the Music* (1975) contained Top-10 hits. The 1975 album *Ole ELO* collected the best-known songs from ELO's first five albums and went gold. The lineup had solidified as well. Joining Lynne, Bevan, and keyboardist Richard Tandy were bassist Kelly Groucutt, violinist Mik Kaminski, and cellists Hugh McDowell and Melvyn Gale. Although Kaminski, McDowell, and Gale participated mainly in the group's live performances (the albums' orchestral sections were often performed by full orchestras), they were included in all ELO photos and personnel listings until the 1979 *Discovery* album.

It was this seven-man lineup that toured in 1976 in support of *A New World Record*, the group's first platinum album. The album yielded three hit singles, the second of which, "Do Ya," had been a minor hit for the Move in 1972, and the third of which, "Telephone Line," became their third Top-10 and first gold single.

Out of the Blue, into the Black. Further evidence of the group's popularity was the success of its 1977 *Out of the Blue* album. Despite the popularity in the 1970's of two-record live albums, two-record studio albums were seldom attempted. (Fleetwood Mac's *Tusk* would not appear until 1979). Nonetheless, *Out of the Blue* became the group's second platinum album, and the singles "Turn to Stone," "Sweet Talkin' Woman," and "Mr. Blue Sky" helped the group maintain a presence on Top-40 airwaves into the fall of 1978.

By this time, the ELO sound had become extremely ornate. Lynne and Groucutt frequently overdubbed their Beatlesesque vocal harmonies into simulated choirs when they were not using actual choirs, and orchestras augmented by Tandy's futuristic synthesizer sounds turned up on almost every track. Although the results, like many of Lynne's lyrics, were often clever, the cumulative effect was becoming heavy handed. Perhaps it was a sense of having reached a saturation point that led the group to lighten both its membership and its sound for *Discovery.* Only Lynne, Bevan, Tandy, and Groucutt were pictured on the album's inner sleeve.

Whatever its reasons, the newly streamlined ELO placed four of *Discovery*'s tracks in the Top 40 in an era when two singles per album was the norm and three a happy exception. By the end of 1980, the group's 1979 *Greatest Hits* album and subsequent soundtrack to the film *Xanadu* (1980) had sold another three million copies.

The Descent. Over the next six years, ELO released three albums, only one of which—the 1981 album *Time*—went gold. All three yielded Top-20 hits, with "Hold On Tight" becoming the group's fifth Top-10 single, but the appearance of the 1986 *Balance of Power* album on the relatively minor CBS Associated label and the reduction of the "orchestra" to three members suggested that the group had worn out its welcome. By 1987, Bevan was filling the drum seat for Black Sabbath.

Lynne immediately became a highly sought-after producer, developing connections that culminated in his joining Bob Dylan, Tom Petty, Roy Orbison, and George Harrison in the rock and roll super group the Traveling Wilburys. With each superstar's identity disguised by a Wilbury family nickname, Lynne was "Otis Wilbury" on the group's 1988 debut and "Clayton Wilbury" on its

1990 sequel. (His 1990 solo album, *Armchair Theatre*, caused little excitement.) Because the sound that Lynne had crafted for ELO owed a great deal to the Beatles, many considered his joining the Traveling Wilburys, which contained former Beatle Harrison, particularly fitting.

—*Arsenio Orteza*

SELECT DISCOGRAPHY

■ SINGLES

"Can't Get It Out of My Head," 1975
"Evil Woman," 1975
"Telephone Line," 1977
"Don't Bring Me Down," 1979
"I'm Alive," 1980
"Hold On Tight," 1981

■ ALBUMS

No Answer, 1972
Electric Light Orchestra II, 1973
On the Third Day, 1973
Out of the Blue, 1977
Secret Messages, 1983
Balance of Power, 1986
Traveling Wilburys, Volume One, 1988 (Jeff Lynne, Bob Dylan, George Harrison, Tom Petty, Roy Orbison)
Afterglow, 1990 (boxed set)

SELECT AWARDS

Grammy for Best Rock Performance by a Duo or Group with Vocal, for *Traveling Wilburys, Volume One*, 1989 (Jeff Lynne, with the Traveling Wilburys)

SEE ALSO: Black Sabbath; Dylan, Bob; Orbison, Roy; Petty, Tom, and the Heartbreakers.

Emerson, Lake, and Palmer

ORIGINAL MEMBERS: Keith Emerson (b. 1944), Greg Lake (b.1948), Carl Palmer (b. 1947)

FIRST ALBUM RELEASE: *Emerson, Lake, and Palmer*, 1970

MUSICAL STYLE: Progressive rock

Founded in 1970 and heralded as one of rock's first "supergroups", Emerson, Lake, and Palmer (ELP) played their first major performance at the Isle of Wight Festival. The week-long event, a British version of Woodstock, was an opportunity for ELP to play for a large, enthusiastic crowd at a trans-Atlantic forum featuring a "who's who" of rock contemporaries that included Jimi Hendrix, the Doors, the Moody Blues, and Jethro Tull.

Keith Emerson, Greg Lake, and Carl Palmer were not novices to British progressive rock. Once nicknamed "the Jimi Hendrix of the Hammond organ," Emerson was keyboardist with the Nice. Lake played bass and sang with King Crimson. Emerson and Lake were acquainted, as King Crimson and the Nice had been booked together on concert dates. They shared similar musical interests and ambitions, and at a coincidental meeting at San Francisco's Fillmore West they discussed the possibility of forming a group.

After a series of auditions, Palmer, a talented young drummer who had worked with Atomic Rooster and the Crazy World of Arthur Brown, was invited to join. ELP's early repertoire was a varied mix of tunes from King Crimson and the Nice, original rock material written by Lake, and Emerson instrumental pieces derived from jazz and classical sources.

A New Sound. At the time of ELP's formation, there was skepticism about the viability of a guitarless rock band, regardless of the established capabilities of the membership. However, the keyboard-trio format ultimately worked to the group's advantage. Palmer's role was expanded to include the use of a battery of symphonic and ethnic percussion instruments. Lake developed a more linear, melodic approach to playing bass guitar that went well beyond the traditional role of outlining the chord changes. Lake also served as producer and wrote much of the group's material.

Two other factors came into play. First, Lake occasionally played guitar on recordings and on stage, particularly on his showcase numbers. Second, Emerson was the first keyboard player to make the Moog synthesizer an essential part of his sound, using it as a solo instrument and to provide psychedelic effects. Developed in 1964 by American physicist Robert Moog, the synthesizer could electronically produce and alter the basic properties of sound (dynamic level, pitch, tone quality) in an infinite array of possibilities. This early synthesizer could play only one note at a time, however, so overdubbing was necessary in the studio to produce chord textures with it. In live performance, more than one unit had to be used to play two notes or sounds at a time. Early synthesizers were also not programmable, so the player had to adjust an array of knobs to change sounds.

Emerson took to the Moog immediately and instinctively, both in the studio and in live performance. On stage, he stood between two Hammond organs, one with a large modular Moog synthesizer on top. While playing outlandishly fast and complicated keyboard parts on synthesizer and the two organs, he managed to turn knobs to adjust the synthesizer without losing a note. (Emerson enjoyed stage theatrics in general, standing on top of the organ and rocking it back and forth, sticking long knives into it, playing it backwards, and balancing the organ on its corner and then slamming it to the floor.)

Albums and Tours. The band's first album, *Emerson, Lake, and Palmer*, was released in 1970. It contained "Take a Pebble," a showcase for Emerson's versatility on the piano, and "Lucky Man," the group's first single. The album *Tarkus* (1971) followed, one side of which is a largely instrumental suite that features Emerson on the organ. This album in more aggressive than the first. A live album, *Pictures at an Exhibition*, their reworking of the piece by Modest Mussorgsky, was also released in 1971. *Trilogy* appeared in 1972, and here the band's elements come together well, with Lake's vocals and Emerson's keyboard work on various instruments complementing one another. *Trilogy* contained the notably laid-back single "From the Beginning" and the band's version of American composer Aaron Copland's "Hoedown." On *Brain Salad Surgery* (1973) the band went largely in the direction of apocalyptic science fiction. The distinctive cover art was by Swiss artist— Geiger, who later designed sets for the film *Alien*. The lyrics (often an ELP weak point) were supplemented by

Keith Emerson (Michael Ochs Archive)

King Crimson lyricist Peter Sinfield. (They were also supplemented by Romantic poet William Blake, as the album opens with "Jerusalem," a musical setting of Blake's poem.) *Brain Salad Surgery* was loud and bombastic, with the Moog synthesizer more prominent than ever.

Throughout these years ELP maintained a heavy touring schedule, and the theatrical elements of their show included a large rotating drum platform and, eventually, a dummy piano that spun around in the air with Emerson "playing" while belted to the bench. In many ways *Brain Salad Surgery* was the epitome of the ELP sound, and the band seemed not to know where to go from there.

Citing the stresses brought on by success, ELP neither toured nor recorded during a two-year period in 1975 and 1976. Increasingly, each member of the trio had become involved in musical projects outside the group (film, composition, solo work, collaboration with others). Their major solo projects were eventually were combined on the double album *Works Volume I* (1977). Three sides were solo efforts, and side 4 was an ELP side, including their version of Copland's "Fanfare for the Common Man."

In 1977 Emerson Lake and Palmer launched their most ambitious tour to date. Staffed with a seventy-five-member symphony orchestra and chorus, three 18-wheelers, a large behind-the-scenes crew, and a payroll obligation of $20,000 per day, ELP embarked on a seventh U.S. tour. Although the venture met with financial difficulty (the orchestra had to be jettisoned after three weeks to cut costs), the tour seemed to signify ELP's return. Yet the *Works* album had not been particularly successful, and the band soon apparently lost interest in continuing.

The Breakup. In 1978 the group gave a final live performance and, after one last half-hearted album (the dreadful *Love Beach*) in 1979, Emerson, Lake, and Palmer disbanded. After the breakup, each member pursued individual musical endeavors. Palmer had a commercially successful run in the 1980's with the progressive pop-rock group Asia. Lake released solo work. Emerson scored some films, including the 1981 Sylvester Stallone film *Nighthawks*. There were also variants of the original ELP lineup. In the mid 1980's Emerson and Lake joined with drummer Cozy Powell to form a trio. Emerson and Palmer teamed with bassist/vocalist Robert Barry to form the band 3.

Finally, the original members reunited in 1991 to record a film score, and the reunion led to a new ELP album, *Black Moon* (1992). The group also resumed touring—on a much smaller scale than in their 1970's heyday—and planned to do additional recording. *Black Moon* did not sell well, but the band discovered that it still had a fan base that would attend live shows. In 1994 Emerson developed a medical problem in his arms that affected his playing, and the band's plans were put on hold. A disheartened Emerson feared that he might never tour again. He recovered, however, and the band toured in 1996 with fellow British band Jethro Tull, and again in 1998.

Pop Music and the Classics. Emerson's adaptations of classical works, and his use of classical elements in his own writing, can be viewed in a larger historical context. A "give and take" relationship has long existed between popular and classical music, and Emerson's effort to connect the classics with the idiom of rock was a continuation of a practice in place for many years. Tin Pan

For the Record

When ELP formed in 1970, there was talk about including an established lead guitarist to complete the roster, and Jimi Hendrix was contacted about joining the band. Had he accepted the offer, ELP would have become HELP.

§

Composer Aaron Copland, when asked in the 1970's if he had heard ELP's version of his "Hoedown," replied lightheartedly that he had, and although it was not quite what he had written, he enjoyed it. He added that he also enjoyed the royalty checks he had received for it.

Alley songwriter George Gershwin tried to break into the "legitimate" music field with his *Rhapsody in Blue.* Master symphonist Igor Stravinsky wrote a jazz-inspired clarinet concerto for swing band leader Woody Herman, and Copland wrote for Benny Goodman. The multifaceted Leonard Bernstein had a dual career as composer of *West Side Story,* playing on Broadway, while he served as conductor of the New York Philharmonic.

Adapting and expanding classical works by casting them in a new context for an unlikely audience proved to be a successful venture for Emerson, Lake, and Palmer. Examples include "Pictures at an Exhibition," a multiple-movement piano suite by the nineteenth century Russian composer Modest Mussorgsky, "Fanfare for the Common Man" and "Hoedown" by Copland, and excerpts from the first piano concerto of Argentinean composer Alberto Ginestera, which appeared on *Brain Salad Surgery.* The ELP versions were not intended to be literal transcriptions. Copland's brief, stately fanfare became a ten-minute excursion with jazz and blues undertones. Tempo and timbre were drastically altered, yet the arrangements were logical extensions of the original versions. "Toccata," the ELP adaptation of the Ginestera concerto, captured and reinforced the fierce rhythmic power of the original, which was influenced by South American Indian ritual dance music. In a meeting between Emerson and Ginestera, the elder musician assured Emerson, after hearing the supercharged ELP version, "That is the way my music should be played."

—William M. Camphouse

SELECT DISCOGRAPHY

■ ALBUMS

Emerson, Lake, and Palmer, 1970
Tarkus, 1971
Pictures at an Exhibition, 1971
Trilogy, 1972
Brain Salad Surgery, 1973
Works Volume I, 1977
The Atlantic Years, 1992 (compilation)
The Return of the Manticore, 1993 (boxed set)

SEE ALSO: Asia; Genesis; Hendrix, Jimi; King Crimson; Yes.

En Vogue

ORIGINAL MEMBERS: Cindy Herron-Braggs (b. 1965), Maxine Jones (b. 1966), Terry Ellis (b. 1966), Dawn Robinson (b. 1968)

FIRST ALBUM RELEASE: *Born to Sing,* 1990

MUSICAL STYLES: Rhythm and blues, pop, hip-hop

San Francisco Bay-area producers Denzil Foster and Thomas McElroy struck gold when they auditioned vocalists for a rhythm-and-blues girl group who could incorporate hip-hop rhythms into their tight four-part harmonies. Cindy Herron-Braggs, Maxine Jones, Terry Ellis, and Dawn Robinson barely knew one another when they auditioned, but Foster and McElroy knew right away that the blend of voices was right. Within a year they had become a hit female vocal group, with "Born to Sing" (number 21) and "Hold On" (number 2) making the charts in 1990.

Creation. Foster and McElroy, former members of Club Nouveau, had had a number 1 hip-hop hit with Bill Withers's classic, "Lean on Me." After leaving the group, they envisioned the creation of a girl group that would combine the best of the 1960's doo-wop tradition with 1970's soul and 1990's hip-hop grooves. Emphasizing sultriness and intelligence, as well as vocal proficiency and glamour, they presented En Vogue to Atlantic Records, who signed them to a record deal in 1990.

Success. En Vogue's first album, *Born to Sing* (1990), saw both the title track and "Hold On" hit the Top 40 and push the album to number 21 on the pop charts. Their follow-up did even better. *Funky Divas* (1992), was a production masterpiece, mixing pop, rock, rap, reggae, and soul for a mainstream sound that went triple platinum and peaked at number 8. "My Lovin' (You're Never Gonna Get It)" (number 2) and "Free Your Mind" (number 8) both earned plenty of video time for displaying the quartet's glamorous clothes and confident personalities.

After their early success, the band was in high demand for magazine covers, personal appearances, and even a Diet Coke commercial for director Spike Lee. Herron, a former Miss Black California, had a role in the 1992 film *Juice.* The group

En Vogue (Paul Natkin)

hit the charts again in 1993 performing "Whatta Man" (number 3) with Salt-n-Pepa and releasing the Top-10 extended-play single *Runaway Love.* They also opened for Luther Vandross's 1993 sold-out tour.

The group took three years off to start families and pursue solo projects, returning in 1996 with "Don't Let Go (Love)" (number 2) from the *Set It Off* sound track. While recording their third album, *EV3* (1997), Robinson left the group to pursue a solo career. The album's first single, "Whatever," was penned and produced by Babyface.

For the Record

Early in their career, En Vogue performed elaborately arranged renditions of the national anthem at Los Angeles Lakers and Golden State Warriors professional basketball games.

Legacy. Though the group frequently has been compared to 1960's groups such as the Supremes, they have considered their musical inspirations to be more funky groups such as the Emotions and Sister Sledge. Unlike most of the 1960's girl groups, En Vogue rotated lead vocals among all of the group members. Their success paved the way for similar girl groups such as SWV, Jade, and TLC. —*John Powell*

SELECT DISCOGRAPHY

■ ALBUMS

Born to Sing, 1990

Remix to Sing, 1991

Funky Divas, 1992

EV3, 1997

SELECT AWARDS

Soul Train Music Awards for Entertainers of the Year and Best Soul/R&B Album for *Funky Divas*, 1992

MTV Video Music Awards for Best R&B Video, Best Dance Video, and Best Choreography for "Free Your Mind," 1993

Soul Train Lady of Soul Award for Best R&B Group Single for "Don't Let Go (Love)," 1997

SEE ALSO: Babyface; Salt-n-Pepa; Supremes, The; TLC.

The English Beat

ORIGINAL MEMBERS: Dave Wakeling (b. 1956), Andy Cox (b. 1956), David Steele (b. 1960), Everett Morton (b. 1951)

OTHER MEMBERS: Ranking Roger (b. Roger Charlery, 1961), Saxa (b. c. 1930), Wesley Magoogan, David "Blockhead" Wright

FIRST ALBUM RELEASE: *I Just Can't Stop It*, 1980

MUSICAL STYLES: Ska, pop

Formed in Birmingham, England, in 1978 in the aftermath of the punk and new-wave movement, the English Beat were leaders in England's ska revival. While other revivalist groups foundered when the craze peaked, the English Beat were able to stay afloat for several years with their bright melodies and politically astute lyrics.

The Beginnings. The punk movement that had taken England by storm in 1977 had many positive attributes, but one thing it was sadly lacking was a sense of humor. The English Beat was not only out to capture that genre's brooding audience, but also to offer them an element of fun. Started by hometown pals Dave Wakeling (vocals, guitar), guitarist Andy Cox, bassist David Steele, and drummer Everett Morton, the original foursome built a loyal fan base through steady pub performances. The addition of black rapper Ranking Roger and an older Jamaican saxophone player who went by the name of Saxa really gave the English Beat its soul. (Saxa was said to have played with the Beatles in their Liverpool days and earlier with ska stars such as Prince Buster and Desmond Dekker).

In 1979, the group's hard work on stage caught the attention of Jerry Dammers of the Specials, who signed them to his 2-Tone record label. Attracted not only by the group's catchy, sometimes frenzied sound, but also its strident antiracism lyrics, Dammers invited the band into England's ska inner circle, where they befriended other bands such as Madness. The English Beat's first single, a catchy cover of the Miracles' "The Tears of a Clown," quickly entered the U.K. Top 10 and almost immediately turned the band into the darlings of *Top of the Pops*, England's television music series, with Wakeling's cool mannerisms in sharp contrast to the frenetic pace of Ranking Roger.

In time, the band parted company with 2-Tone and made an arrangement with Arista to form its own subsidiary label, Go Feet, which provided the band with some commercial muscle while allowing them to retain an independent-label feel. Three singles released on the label in 1980 reached England's Top 10: "Hands Off . . . She's Mine," "Mirror in the Bathroom," and "Too Nice to Talk To."

Politically Aware. Known for their leftist leanings, the band used their lyrics to foster political awareness, reaching a head with the song "Stand down Margaret," which offered some biting musical advice to then-Prime Minister Margaret Thatcher ("I see no joy/ I see no sorrow/ I see no chance of your bright tomorrow.") The English Beat's debut album, *I Just Can't Stop It* (1980), contained many hit singles and reached the number 3 spot on the British album charts.

Beginning of the End. By the end of 1980, the ska boom was losing its edge as the bands most associated with the genre started trying new things: Madness became more pop-oriented, the

For the Record

The English Beat was known as the Beat in every country but the United States. They added "English" to avoid confusion and legal problems with a Los Angeles power-pop band also called the Beat. The Los Angeles Beat never broke through on the charts, although they did write and record the original "Hangin' on the Telephone," later covered by Blondie.

Specials' music became a bit gloomier. The English Beat, meanwhile, headed into a more reggae-oriented sound with mixed results. The band's second album, *Wha'ppen* (1981), was a critical disappointment, although it did yield the hit "Drowning/All out to Get You." As the hits stopped coming, the English Beat turned its attention to the United States (though known as simply the Beat elsewhere, in the United States they called themselves the English Beat to avoid confusion with a Los Angeles band). The band's third and final album, *Special Beat Service* (1982), did include two minor U.S. hits, "I Confess" and "Save It for Later."

The Last Year. In an ironic twist, 1983, while being the year the band truly fell apart, also brought them their biggest chart hit, a remix of "Can't Get Used to Losing You" from their first album. Wakeling and Ranking Roger decided to stay together and formed General Public, which had a hit in 1994 with their remake of the Staple Singers' "I'll Take You There"; Cox and Steele, meanwhile, regrouped as Fine Young Cannibals.

—*Nicole Pensiero*

SELECT DISCOGRAPHY

■ ALBUMS

I Just Can't Stop It, 1980
Wha'ppen, 1981
Special Beat Service, 1982

SEE ALSO: Special, The.

Brian Eno

BORN: Woodbridge, Suffolk, England; May 15, 1948
FIRST SOLO ALBUM: *Here Come the Warm Jets,* 1973
MUSICAL STYLES: Ambient, progressive rock

Brian Eno's public creative career began in 1972 as a member of the rock group Roxy Music. Through the influence of minimalism, experimental and avant-garde music, electronics, and non-Western music, Eno's later works would be characterized as ambient music. Aside from his own compositions, Eno is recognized as being a superior record producer. Although Eno may not be considered a mainstream artist, he does have a loyal following.

Influences. From 1964 to 1966 Eno attended the Ipswich Art School, and in 1969 he received a Diploma in fine art from Winchester Art School. Eno never received any formal training in music. He was, however, raised near a United States military base where he was able to hear and be influenced by much of the contemporary American music styles of the 1960's as well as big-band jazz. Eno's musical influences from the 1960's are primarily the Velvet Underground and the Who. Later influences include composers John Cage and Erik Satie and minimalist composers La Monte Young, Terry Riley, and Steve Reich.

Brian Eno in 1981 (Deborah Feingold/Archive Photos)

Roxy Music. Although Eno's first band, the Maxwell Demon, was formed in the 1960's, his true career began in 1971 with the organization of the British rock group Roxy Music. Founding members include Eno (synthesizer, tape player, and composition), Bryan Ferry, Andy Mackay, Phil Manzanera, and later, Paul Thompson. In 1972 Roxy Music signed with E.G. Management and released several albums. Eno's work on the synthesizer set a new trend, but he left Roxy Music in 1973 over disagreements with Ferry. Without Eno, Roxy Music continued as a group until officially disbanding in 1982.

The Progressive Rock Period. In 1973 Eno released his first solo album, *Here Come the Warm Jets,* which anticipated the developments of the new-wave rock of the 1970's. Other albums of this genre include *Taking Tiger Mountain (By Strategy)* (1974) and *Another Green World* (1975). *Another Green World* marked a turning point in Eno's composition with fewer lyrics and a definite influence of minimalism and electronics. It was the first album where he is listed as the composer of all the pieces, and most of the instruments were played by Eno himself. *Before and After Science* (1977) is Eno's last solo progressive rock album. Two years in the making, *Before and After Science* was a calmer, more contemplative music which received critical acclaim. Eno, realizing that he preferred recording to performing, independently created his own record label, Obscure Records, which released eight albums during the 1970's. Dedicated to experimental music, Obscure Records included pieces by contemporary composers Gavin Bryars, Christopher Hobbs, John Adams, Max Eastley, John Cage, Jan Steele, Michael Nyman, the Penguin Cafe Orchestra, Tom Phillips, Fred Orton, and Harold Budd.

Ambient Music. In 1975, while walking home from a session, Eno was hit by a taxi and nearly died. While in the hospital he gained a new revelation toward sound and his music. In May of 1975 Eno released *Discreet Music* in this new style which he called ambient music. Between 1978 and 1982 Eno produced four albums which he called the ambient series. It was a quiet, gentle music with an emphasis on timbre and an obscured basic pulse. These were generally longer works which received mixed reviews from the critics. The ambient series includes *Ambient 1: Music for Airports* (1979), composed mostly by Eno; *Ambient 2: The Plateaux of Mirror* (1980), a collaboration between Eno and composer Harold Budd; *Ambient 3: Day of Radiance* (1981), with compositions by hammer-dulcimer player Laraaji; and *Ambient 4: On Land* (1982), composed mostly by Eno. Eno also released his *Music for Films* in 1976. This limited edition of five hundred copies was reissued in 1978 as a single album, and then again in the ten-album retrospective boxed set *Working Backwards, 1983-1973.* Although largely ignored by the press, *Music for Films* would earn Eno the reputation as a sound-track producer. *Music for Films, Volume II* followed in 1983 as part of *Working Backwards, 1983-1973.* Eno's ambient compositions are considered to be an influence in the development of the new-age movement.

Sound Tracks. During the 1980's Eno gained importance as a sound-track composer. This includes producing the "Prophecy Theme" for David Lynch's film *Dune* (1984), music for the public television series *Creation of the Universe,* and background music for the acclaimed Nova film *The Miracle of Life. Apollo: Atmospheres & Soundtracks* (1983, cowritten with Daniel Lanois and Roger Eno, Brian's younger brother) was commissioned for Al Reinhert's documentary on the Apollo missions to the moon. In 1984 Sony Japan commissioned Eno to compose a multimedia work that would be available only on a newly developed recording format—the compact disc. The result was *Thursday Afternoon,* released in 1985. By the mid-1990's Eno had released four new albums: *Wrong Way Up* (1990) with John Cale,

For the Record

Brian Eno composed the three-second segment of music audible upon startup of Microsoft's Windows95 for the personal computer.

The Shutov Assembly (1992), which consists of varied ambient pieces, *Nerve Net* (1992), and *Neroli* (1993), which is minimalist.

Collaborator and Producer. Eno has appeared as an instrumentalist on at least twenty-three albums. He has appeared on albums with the conceptual rock group 801, on two albums with King Crimson guitarist Robert Fripp, and on three albums with David Bowie. Eno collaborated in 1981 with David Byrne of Talking Heads on the album *My Life in the Bush of Ghosts* and on the music for Twyla Tharp's Broadway production of *The Catherine Wheel.* Eno's expertise in the recording studio would be sought out after 1975, and he has produced at least twenty-three albums on which he is not listed as a composer. The rock acts whose work Eno has produced include John Cale, Robert Calvert, Talking Heads (*Remain in Light*), Ultravox, Devo, and U2 (including their successful 1991 release *Achtung Baby*).

Trained as a visual artist, Eno is also successful in the area of audiovisual installations. Since 1979 he has had numerous shows in galleries and other public places where he combines music with video and sculpture. In 1990 Eno began a series of meetings with musician-composers Laurie Anderson and Peter Gabriel to plan a theme park called Real World in Barcelona, Spain, which would celebrate technological achievements.

—Brent Register

SELECT DISCOGRAPHY

■ ALBUMS

Roxy Music, 1972 (with Roxy Music)
For Your Pleasure, 1973 (with Roxy Music)
Here Come the Warm Jets, 1973
Taking Tiger Mountain (by Strategy), 1974
Another Green World, 1975
Discreet Music, 1975
Before and After Science, 1977
Music for Films, 1978
Ambient 1: Music for Airports, 1979
My Life in the Bush of Ghosts, 1981 (with David Byrne)
Ambient 4: On Land, 1982
Apollo: Atmospheres & Soundtracks, 1983
Music for Films, Volume II, 1983
Thursday Afternoon, 1985
Nerve Net, 1992
The Shutov Assembly, 1992
Neroli, 1993

SELECT AWARDS

Grammy Award for Album of the Year for *The Joshua Tree,* 1987 (producer; with U2 and Daniel Lanois)
Grammy Award for Producer of the Year, 1992 (with Daniel Lanois)

SEE ALSO: Anderson, Laurie; Bowie, David; Devo; Gabriel, Peter; Roxy Music / Brian Ferry; Talking Heads / David Byrne; U2.

Enya

BORN: Gweedore, Ireland; May 17, 1961
FIRST ALBUM RELEASE: *Enya,* 1986
MUSICAL STYLES: New age, Celtic

Enya has enjoyed much success as a recording artist by combining the sensibilities of new-age music with the more traditional sounds of her native Ireland. She first came to worldwide attention with "Orinoco Flow," the hit single from her 1988 album *Watermark.* Enya released several more albums during the 1990's, including *Shepherd Moons* (1991), for which she won a Grammy Award. Throughout her career, she has remained a rather enigmatic figure, seldom performing and giving few interviews.

Musical Background. Born Eithne Ní Bhraonáin, Enya grew up the fifth of nine children born to musical parents in the small town of Gweedore, County Dore, Ireland (Enya is an anglicized form of her first name). Her father led a popular show group, and her mother taught music in the local school. Building upon this musical heritage, two of Enya's elder brothers and two uncles formed An Clann As Dobhair (the Family from Dore) in 1968. The band also accepted Enya's sister Marie and shortened its name to Clannad a few years later, going on to achieve international acclaim with its blend of traditional and contemporary sounds.

The Enya Trinity. Enya joined the family ensemble in 1980 but left two years later when Clannad and its longtime manager and producer, Nicky Ryan, parted ways. Believing strongly in Enya's potential, Ryan took her under his professional wing. He even invited her to stay in his and his wife Roma's Dublin home. The three soon developed a musical partnership—Enya providing melodies, Ryan producing and arranging, and Roma penning lyrics—that would yield platinum success. Indeed, the trio has worked so closely together that it has sometimes been said that Enya is actually three people rather than one.

Enya's first major achievement came in 1985 with her score for the David Puttnam feature *The Frog Prince*. However, this merely served as prelude to her breakthrough project, a 1987 British documentary entitled *The Celts*. Enya contributed a number of songs to the series, which were then released as an album known as both *The Celts* and *Enya*. On it, one can already hear the the exotic blend of Irish and new-age influences that would bring fame to Enya.

Watermark. The album drew the attention of Rob Dickins, who signed Enya to the WEA Music label, making possible Enya's next venture, 1988's *Watermark*. From the opening notes of the first selection, the album bathes the listener in voluptuous sonorities. Enya's tender vocals soar above lush strings, thick synthesizer pads, a celestial chorus, and an occasional woodwind solo. Roma Ryan provided poetic, evocative lyrics for all of the songs, some in English, others in Gaelic or Latin.

Not every song on *Watermark* is a soothing ballad. In particular, the hit single, "Orinoco Flow," is quite upbeat. Buoyed by the song's unanticipated popularity, the album quickly went platinum, selling in excess of four million copies. Many in the press hailed the album as a masterpiece of new-age music, tasteful and artfully executed, which lent substance to a genre that is often little more than treacle. Reviewers also applauded Enya for bringing attention to Irish music. Her approach may not have been traditional, but it did seem to capture the essence of her homeland.

Enya released several albums during the next decade. The follow-up to *Watermark*, *Shepherd Moons*, hit the stores in 1991. It sold even better than its predecessors, with sales of ten million copies worldwide, and won a Grammy Award for Best New Age Album. *The Memory of Trees*, Enya's next release, did not appear until the very end of 1995 and sold less well than *Watermark* or *Shepherd Moons*. Enya then released a greatest-hits album in 1997, *Paint the Sky with Stars: The Best of Enya*.

A handful of songs from Enya's various albums have been distributed as singles and extended-play singles by both WEA and her U.S. label, Reprise. None has sold as well as "Orinoco Flow." A number have also found their way into various films, including *Green Card* (1990), *Far and Away* (1992), *Toys* (1992), and *The Age of Innocence* (1993). In addition, Enya's music has been used

Enya (Reprise/Simon Fowler)

in television commercials to help sell everything from diet drink mixes to ocean cruises.

Perfectionism. In general, Enya's career has been shaped by two important factors. The first has been her perfectionism. She has, for instance, been known to record more than five hundred vocal takes for just one song. Enya's perfectionism results in immaculate albums but does hinder her ability to release enough of them to satisfy her fans.

The other career-shaping element has been the complexity of Enya's recordings combined with her penchant for performing many of the songs' parts herself. Since she sings her own background vocals, she has difficulty performing her music live. Enya has not performed in concert to any significant extent—a few television performances, one for the King of Sweden and another for Pope John Paul II, notwithstanding. Added to her reluctance to perform is a distaste for the limelight; she has granted few interviews and has not spent time in the public eye.

Eschewing the public spotlight has lent mystique to Enya's enigmatic persona (living in an Irish castle has only heightened this aura of mystery). Also, her remoteness from fans has forced music, rather than personality, to be the center of her career, something in which Enya takes obvious pride: "People don't know what I look like or anything about me, but they know the music. I enjoy that, because that's what's really important."

While Enya has enjoyed a good deal of critical acclaim, many in the press have been less than charitable. Her music has been called exaggerated and anonymous by her detractors. However, her defenders enjoy the contemplative soulfulness and pretty harmonies she offers. Whatever else critics have said of Enya, they have agreed that she has lent a distinctive voice to popular music. It is true, though, that Enya appears to have become tied in to her particular style. Artistically, she has not ranged far from the music first heard on *The Celts.* However, record sales have proven that there is a large market for Enya's unique sound.

—David Lee Fish

For the Record

Concerning her private lifestyle, Enya has said, "Just because you're a pop star, it doesn't mean that you have to be seen in nightclubs. And I find it really strange. A person has to have a choice, and my choice is to be somewhere else."

SELECT DISCOGRAPHY

■ ALBUMS

Enya, 1986
Watermark, 1988
Shepherd Moons, 1991
The Memory of Trees, 1995
Paint the Sky with Stars: The Best of Enya, 1997

SELECT AWARDS

Grammy Award for Best New Age Album for *Shepherd Moons,* 1992

SEE ALSO: McKennitt, Loreena.

Gloria Estefan

BORN: Havana, Cuba; September 1, 1957
FIRST ALBUM RELEASE: *Live Again/Renacer,* 1977 (with Miami Sound Machine)
FIRST SOLO ALBUM RELEASE: *Cuts Both Ways,* 1989
MUSICAL STYLES: Latin, pop

Popular music in the United States derives from many sources. Although music from Latin America has frequently enjoyed wide acceptance in the United States—for example, the tango in the early twentieth century and the rumba during the big-band era of the 1930's and 1940's—lasting success for musical performers from Latin America has usually been difficult to achieve. Perhaps the most difficult challenge for a Latino performer is to gain acceptance as a crossover artist, or someone who builds and holds audiences for his or her work in both Latin and U.S. popular music. Gloria Estefan is one of the few vocalists and songwriters to accomplish this feat.

Early Years. Gloria Estefan's family background and early years gave little indication that she would become a major popular music star in the United States. Her father, José Manuel Fajardo, was a respected athlete who became a member of the security guard for Cuban President Fulgencio Batista Zaldívar. Her mother, Gloria García de Fajardo, was a schoolteacher. Fidel Castro overthrew the Batista government in 1959, making José Fajardo and other security personnel enemies of the new revolutionary state. The Fajardos fled Castro's Cuba and faced the difficult adjustments to life in the United States as refugees from a revolution. Gloria's father was one of more than one thousand Cubans who participated in the Bay of Pigs invasion in 1961. This military operation, supported by the United States, failed to overthrow Castro. Gloria's father was captured and held prisoner for more than one year. Soon after his release, José Fajardo joined the United States military and fought in the Vietnam War. He returned to the Fajardo home in Miami in 1968. It soon became apparent that he was suffering from a serious disease.

As Gloria entered her teenage years, she took on the emotionally distressing task of nursing her father, once a strong athlete and soldier, as his body gradually degenerated from the fatal affliction (which may have been multiple sclerosis or a reaction to exposure to the herbicide Agent Orange in Vietnam). An intelligent and sensitive person, Gloria carried her burdens quietly at home. She had little contact with her peers. Instead she turned to her schoolwork and to music. She was an excellent student and also revealed a talent for playing the guitar and singing. She enjoyed listening to popular music, especially the Carpenters, Johnny Mathis, Barbra Streisand, Diana Ross, and legendary Cuban vocalist Celia Cruz. Although these influences would be apparent in later years, Gloria did not sing in public. She played the guitar and sang only within the family circle.

Breakthrough. After graduation from high school in 1975, Gloria overcame her shyness and began to sing at parties in the Miami area, where her warm but strong voice impressed her listeners.

Gloria Estefan (Paul Natkin)

Invited to sing at a wedding, she made an especially favorable impression on band organizer and musician Emilio Estefan. He convinced her to join his band, which eventually became known as the Miami Sound Machine. Music was only a part-time occupation for Gloria; she continued her education at the University of Miami, from which she graduated with a degree in psychology in 1978. She and Emilio were married a few weeks later. Their long-term collaboration proved to be fruitful in both marriage and music. The Miami Sound Machine reached beyond Miami to audiences in the Caribbean and Latin America. By 1984, the band had a large following in the His-

For the Record

Gloria Estefan revived the conga, a type of Cuban dance music first made popular in the United States by a youthful Desi Arnaz in the late 1930's. To participate, dancers form a line and place their hands on the hips of the person in front of them. The entire line moves forward to the rhythm of the conga music, usually performing three steps and a kick. More than eleven thousand concertgoers formed a conga line at a Miami Sound Machine performance in Burlington, Vermont, in June of 1986. Two years later in Miami, 119,984 celebrants joined Estefan and the band to dance in the longest conga line in history.

panic market, but Gloria and Emilio were determined to break into the largest popular music empire of all: the English-language audience in the United States.

Their breakthrough into the U.S. pop music market came with the release of the album *Primitive Love* in 1985. The album featured the soft, melodic ballads "Words Get in the Way" and "You Made a Fool of Me," but the spark that caught the public's attention was the rapid-fire number "Conga." Gloria had experimented with this traditional form of Cuban dance music, but Emilio was skeptical about its reception by audiences in the United States and Europe. The enthusiastic response, however, to the conga numbers during the band's tour of Holland, England, and the United States convinced Gloria and Emilio to include an updated version on their 1985 album. Kiki García, a talented percussionist and composer, jotted down the words and music as the group traveled from Amsterdam to London. The results were evident in the fast-paced mix of lyrics and rhythm that exploded as effectively on the album as it did for live audiences. Soon conga lines snaked across the fields and floors of Miami Sound Machine concerts. The "Conga" single simultaneously reached the upper levels of the pop, African American, and Latin charts in the United States. Gloria and the Miami Sound Machine had made their breakthrough.

International Stardom. In a business in which many performers fade away after one year or less in the limelight, Gloria and Emilio faced the challenge of finding the right material to follow *Primitive Love.* The next two albums, *Let It Loose* (1987) and *Cuts Both Ways* (1989), not only established Gloria's enduring popularity but also marked her maturity as a composer and vocalist. The original members of the Miami Sound Machine began to drift apart, however. Some sought new opportunities, and others seemed to resent the growing influence of Gloria and Emilio. One of Gloria's most successful singles, "Rhythm Is Gonna Get You," from the album *Let It Loose,* was written in collaboration with Kiki García, who departed soon after its release. Supported by new musicians, Gloria gained confidence as a composer. These two albums contained several of her original compositions, including "Can't Stay Away from You," "Here We Are," and "Don't Wanna Lose You," but her most personal lyrical statement came in "Oye Mi Canto" ("Hear My Voice"). Gloria wrote the words and shared credit for the music with Jorge Casas and Clay Ostwald. The lyrics convey several messages. The combination of English and Spanish words sung to a throbbing Afro-Cuban beat constitutes a declaration of the legitimacy of crossover music as a popular art form. The lyrics also express Estefan's concerns for tolerance and reconciliation that transcend political, cultural, and ethnic boundaries.

At a peak of international stardom that extended from Japan to Europe, Gloria was the victim of a serious highway accident that nearly crippled her and threatened her career. On March 20, 1990, in the midst of the successful *Cuts Both Ways* tour, Gloria's bus was hit from the rear by a heavy truck. The impact threw Gloria from the bunk where she was resting, resulting in a cracked spinal column that required extensive surgery including the implantation of two eight-inch metal rods to protect the injured spine. Several months of arduous physical therapy restored most of her agility, and she eventually resumed her busy schedule.

In the 1990's, Gloria's attention turned to her cultural roots in Cuba and her family roots in Miami. She released two albums, *Mi Tierra* (1993) and *Abriendo Puertas* (1995), that drew from the folk and popular musical traditions of her island homeland. Like Linda Ronstadt's 1987 *Canciones de Mi Padre* (based on Ronstadt's Mexican background), Gloria's albums not only were directed toward a Latin American audience but also were intended to lead fans in the large U.S. market to an appreciation of a Latin genre. Meanwhile, Gloria and Emilio had established a home in the Cuban community of Miami. The Estefan family (including two children, Nayib and Emily) had achieved material success and Gloria was a symbol of the melding of Cuban and Latin American traditions with the expansive popular culture of the United States. —*John A. Britton*

SELECT DISCOGRAPHY

with Miami Sound Machine

■ ALBUMS

Live Again/Renacer, 1977
Eyes of Innocence, 1984
Primitive Love, 1985
Let It Loose, 1987

Gloria Estefan solo

■ ALBUMS

Cuts Both Ways, 1989
Into the Light, 1991
Mi Tierra, 1993
Abriendo Puertas, 1995
Destiny, 1996

SELECT AWARDS

Tokyo Music Festival First Prize for "Conga," 1986
Billboard Pop Artist of the Year, 1988
Broadcast Music Incorporated Songwriter of the Year Award, 1989
Grammy Award for Best Tropical Latin Album for *Mi Tierra*, 1993
Grammy Award for Best Tropical Latin Album for *Abriendo Puertas*, 1995

SEE ALSO: Carpenters, The; Mathis, Johnny; Ronstadt, Linda; Ross, Diana; Streisand, Barbra.

Melissa Etheridge

BORN: Leavenworth, Kansas; May 29, 1961
FIRST ALBUM RELEASE: *Melissa Etheridge*, 1988
MUSICAL STYLE: Rock and roll

Melissa Etheridge's unique contribution to rock and roll is a product of her strong musical background, including youthful exposure to a variety of instruments as well as some professional training at the Berklee College of Music. While she is well known for her social activism and has become an alternative lifestyle icon, it is her music that first made her a public figure and that continues to be her best gift to the world.

It Was Always "When." As a child, Melissa Etheridge's idol was Reggie, of the television cartoon band the Archies. Etheridge got her first guitar when she was eight years old, and when she was ten she composed her first song, "Don't Let It Fly Away (It's Love)." At the age of eleven she entered her first talent contest, at a local mall, singing a song she wrote herself, about an orphaned Vietnamese child. She did not win, but the audience response was overwhelming, and she was hooked. From then on she played churches, teachers' conventions, retirement homes—any gig she could get. She believed from the start that she was going to be a star. "Melissa always had an amazing amount of self-confidence," her mother told Rolling Stone magazine. "She never, ever said, '*If* I am able to do something in music.' It was always *when*."

By the time she was in high school, Etheridge knew she was gay. Her father accepted the revelation calmly, but she was twenty-three before she was able to talk openly with her mother. Her contemporaries were fairly accepting. "High school was fine," she said. "I don't have any sad stories to tell about it. I had a talent, and people knew about it, so I had friends." Her songs appealed equally to gays and straights, with references to universal feelings and a non-gender-specific beloved.

While still in high school Etheridge learned to play piano, drums, saxophone, and clarinet, and listened to all the music she could find. One summer, she listened to the Beatles' *Sgt. Pepper's Lonely Hearts Club Band* every day. Looking back, she realized, "It totally changed my life. I started realizing, words are important. Melodies are nice but words can make you think. You can get to people's bodies with music and if you can make somebody think, then you've got their whole attention."

She attended more carefully to the finer points of music and lyric-writing, and on graduating she decided to study her craft at the Berklee College of Music in Boston. Studying music, however, was no substitute for playing music, and she dropped out before the year was through to play wherever she could find work. "Part of me wishes I had stayed longer so that I would be a more accomplished musician," she later said. "I would certainly play guitar better. But I didn't have the patience."

Finding a Niche. Etheridge moved to Los Angeles just as the band Guns n' Roses was becoming popular. "There were no coffeehouses or places to play acoustic music," she said. "I actually followed my lifestyle and, for social reasons, went to the gay and lesbian bars. And I'd notice a little piano tucked away in the corner, so I asked if I could play, and I guess I developed a niche from there."

Eventually, Chris Blackwell of Island Records heard her play in one of these bars and signed her to his label. In 1988 she released her self-titled debut album, which went platinum. *Brave and Crazy* and *Never Enough* followed suit, and the latter's track "Ain't It Heavy" brought Etheridge her first Grammy Award.

The Triangle Ball. Although never really in the closet, Etheridge came out to the world at the Triangle Ball, a gay and lesbian fete for President Bill Clinton's 1993 inauguration, surprising herself as much as anyone. "I knew that I wanted to come out. I was tired of the hiding and not being able to be upfront. But it was spontaneous to do it there."

Melissa Etheridge (Lissa Wales)

Far from inciting a backlash, Etheridge's coming out brought positive recognition and publicity galore. *The Advocate* dubbed her "Rock's Great Dyke Hope." "I don't really understand what it means," she laughed. "Am I saving rock and roll or am I saving dykes?" She had no regrets. "Best thing I did in my life, no doubt about it. A weight off my shoulder, knowing you have nothing to hide. There's nothing more powerful."

A Dream Come True. The high point of her life, by her own estimation, was her appearance on "MTV Unplugged" with Bruce Springsteen. "That would be what you call a dream come true," she said. Springsteen was something of an idol for Etheridge, who has often been referred to as the "female Bruce Springsteen." "I used to sing Springsteen songs at the top of

For the Record

As respected as Melissa Etheridge may be musically, there are those who do not agree with her fashion sense: She made *People* magazine's "Worst Dressed" list in 1995.

my lungs when I was a kid, because he was singing about a girl and I could relate," she told *Entertainment Weekly.* "But I think not having female singers like him leaves out women who are strong and straight and feel those things, too."

Another idol of Etheridge's was Janis Joplin, whom she was planning to play in the film biography *Piece of My Heart* from a script by her partner, Julie Cypher. To prepare for the part, she performed with Joplin's band, Big Brother and the Holding Company. She also paid tribute to Joplin at Woodstock '94, attracting many favorable comparisons and a storm of attention from the music press.

Continued Controversy. Although her music clearly cuts across all lines, Etheridge's sexuality has gained a great deal of attention as well, and she has not exactly run from it. She and longtime lover Cypher posed together naked for an ad for People for the Ethical Treatment of Animals (PETA). The caption read, "I'd rather go naked than wear fur." Predictably, the ad caused quite a stir. Not so predictable, at least to Etheridge, was the most vocal source of objections—AIDS activists (whose cause she long supported) objected to PETA's stand on the use of animals in research and chastised her vigorously for "switching camps." Etheridge decided not to do any more "visible work" for PETA.

Cypher and Etheridge's relationship made headlines again in January of 1997, when Julie gave birth to a daughter, Bailey Jean, whom the couple were raising together. Etheridge said she and Cypher would like to have three children.

The title of Etheridge's 1995 hit album, *Your Little Secret,* refers not to her sexuality, as many people understandably believed, but was a nod to her fans on the Internet. "I was lurking on my Website where my fans talk to each other and I guess you can't say you overheard because I oversaw one fan talking to the other about, 'Well, Melissa's made it now, she's real big, I guess she's not our little secret anymore.' As a nod, as a little wink, as an irony at this point, I call it *Your Little Secret* because no, I'm not." *—Jean McKnight*

SELECT DISCOGRAPHY

■ ALBUMS

Melissa Etheridge, 1988
Brave and Crazy, 1989
Never Enough, 1992
Yes I Am, 1993
Your Little Secret, 1995

SELECT AWARDS

Grammy Award for Best Rock Vocal Performance, Female, for "Ain't It Heavy," 1992
Grammy Award for Best Rock Vocal Performance, Female, for "Come to My Window," 1994

SEE ALSO: Joplin, Janis; Springsteen, Bruce.

The Eurythmics / Annie Lennox

The Eurythmics

ORIGINAL MEMBERS: Annie Lennox (1954), David Stewart (b. 1952)
FIRST ALBUM RELEASE: *In the Garden,* 1981

Annie Lennox

BORN: Aberdeen, Scotland; December 25, 1954
FIRST ALBUM RELEASE: *Diva,* 1992
MUSICAL STYLES: Rock and roll, rhythm and blues

Gaining admittance to a respectable middle-class school, Annie Lennox had formal instruction in piano, voice, and flute. Her flute studies led to her 1971 acceptance at the Royal Academy of Music in London. There, her musical education exposed her to traditional Scottish folk music, Broadway musicals, classical music, and Motown pop. This eclectic mix of influences would immeasurably contribute to Lennox's vocal stylings as well as to her easy familiarity with stagecraft and the video camera.

Roots. Working as a waitress while attending the academy, Lennox met guitarist, writer, and producer Dave Stewart with whom Lennox began a romantic liaison. After Stewart left the folk-rock group Longdancer, the two organized the short-lived band the Tourists, a combination of new-wave sounds with Beatles- and Talking Heads-influenced pop.

Dissatisfied with the Tourists' direction, the duo formed the Eurythmics in 1980, beginning their collaboration of self-produced records and videos built on Lennox's voice and striking, androgynous appearance and Stewart's behind-the-scenes electronics capabilities. In order to shed her blond-bombshell image in the Tourists, Lennox began wearing men's suits and dressing like Elvis Presley before creating more unusual fashion statements on stage. Their first project, *In the Garden*, was a commercial failure, deemed a heavy-handed mix of cold electronic sounds and musical dramatics. Four singles from the album, "Never Gonna Cry Again," "Belinda," "This Is the House," and "The Walk" also failed to arouse interest. The couple then ended their romantic relationship but chose to continue the professional partnership. In 1982, they released "Love Is the Stranger," which gave them renewed confidence despite its initial lackluster commercial response.

Trendsetting Hitmakers. In January of 1983, the Eurythmics' second album, *Sweet Dreams (Are Made of This)*, became one of the most successful small business ventures of the 1980's. The title track, produced on an eight-track recorder in a loft above a picture framer's shop, was an immediate best-seller, reaching number 1 in the United States. "Love Is the Stranger" was reissued, this time a marked success, as were the next singles culled from the album, "Who's That Girl" and "Right by Your Side." During the filming of the video for "Who's That Girl," Stewart met Bananarama singer Siobhan Fahey, whom he subsequently wed.

Touch (1983), the duo's sound track for the 1984 film, was a disappointment, and their sound track for the film *1984* was even disliked by the film's director. *Be Yourself Tonight* (1985) showed a new direction for the band, with less synthesizers and more guitar-driven melodies. A major success was "Sisters Are Doing It for Themselves," on which Lennox duetted with American soul singer Aretha Franklin. Other hits from the album included "Here Comes the Rain Again" and "Sexcrime."

In 1985, Lennox developed throat problems and canceled the group's scheduled appearance at the Live Aid benefit concert, but the new single, "There Must Be an Angel" topped British charts. Later that year, Lennox made her film debut in *Revolution*, sharing the screen with actors Donald Sutherland and Al Pacino. "Julia" was a relative failure on the charts, but April's release of "Would I Lie to You" became a signature song for the duo.

Stewart also began his own solo projects, producing records for Bob Dylan, Tom Petty, Bob Geldof, Mick Jagger, Feargal Sharkey, and Daryl Hall of Hall and Oates. The Eurythmics returned in 1986 with *Revenge*, another single-producing collection including "Thorn in My Side," "Miracle of Love," and "When Tomorrow Comes." "Missionary Man," while a less powerful album track, was remixed for single release and proved to be one of the group's most innovative hard-rock songs. In England, the group received special attention for their *Rough and Tough at the Roxy* extended-play single of four live songs.

The 1987 followup, *Savage*, was less successful, with "I Need a Man" being the collection's one highlight. The Eurythmics' acoustic performance

For the Record

After starting out as "Catch and the Tourists," Annie Lennox and David Stewart renamed themselves the Tourists, then the Eurythmics. They took the word from Emil Jacques-Dalcrose, who had coined it for a miming-dancing system he developed to teach music to children.

of "You Have Placed a Chill" at the 1988 South African political leader Nelson Mandela birthday concert received critical praise, and later that year, Lennox duetted with Al Green on "Put a Little Love in Your Heart." In 1989, the Eurythmics released their most successful album since *Sweet Dreams (Are Made of This)*, *We Too Are One*, which stayed number 1 until 1990. In that year, the group's last singles, "(My My) Baby's Gonna Cry" and "The King and Queen of America" ended the nearly decade-long streak of hits.

Solo in the 1990's. In 1991, the Eurythmics' career was summarized with the issue of their *Greatest Hits* collection, and in 1993, selections from their live 1983-1989 appearances were released. Lennox's first solo album, 1992's *Diva*, was also issued as her first full-length video. Critics found the effort a logical extension of the later Eurythmics' sound, with two tracks, "Legend in My Living Room" and "Walking on Broken Glass," the standouts. Her second solo project, *Medusa*, yielded her distinctive art-vocal hit, "No More I Love You's." Much of this album centered on Lennox's return to interpretations of older rock standards, including Procol Harum's "A Whiter Shade of Pale," the Clash's "Train in Vain," and the Pretenders' "There's a Thin Line Between Love and Hate." In 1996, Lennox issued her second full-length solo video, *Live in Central Park*.

Dave Stewart also released solo albums, but with less success. *Dave Stewart and the Spiritual Cowboys* (1990) and *Honest* (1991) were taken out of production by 1998, leaving only *Greetings from the Gutter*, a 1995 release, available at music stores. His standout rendition of "Instant Karma," performed at a 1991 tribute to John Lennon, was aired on U.S. cable television alongside performances by the surviving former Beatles, Michael Jackson, Prince, Cyndi Lauper, and many other rock luminaries. —*Wesley Britton*

SELECT DISCOGRAPHY

■ ALBUMS

The Eurythmics

In the Garden, 1981
Sweet Dreams (Are Made of This), 1983
Touch, 1983
1984: For the Love of Big Brother, 1984 (sound track)
Touch Dance, 1984
Be Yourself Tonight, 1985
Revenge, 1986
Savage, 1987
We Too Are One, 1989
Greatest Hits, 1991 (compilation)
Live 1983-1989, 1993

Annie Lennox

Diva, 1992
Medusa, 1995

SELECT AWARDS

Grammy Award for Best Rock Performance by a Duo or Group with Vocal for "Missionary Man," 1986

SEE ALSO: Franklin, Aretha; Green, Al; Petty, Tom, and the Heartbreakers.

The Everly Brothers

MEMBERS: Isaac Donald Everly (b. 1937), Philip Everly (b. 1939)

FIRST SINGLE RELEASE: "The Sun Keeps Shining"/"Keep a-Lovin' Me," 1955

MUSICAL STYLES: Rock and roll, country rock, pop rock

The Everly Brothers were not only among the most important rock-and-roll stars, but also among the most influential musicians of any era. They set unmatched standards for close, two-part harmonies and contributed some of the best elements of country and pop music to early rock and roll. Their legacy is felt enormously in all rock acts that feature harmonies, from the Beatles to later roots rockers such as Dave Edmunds and Nick Lowe.

The Beginnings. Isaac Donald Everly was born on February 1, 1937, in the small town of Brownie in Kentucky. (The town no longer exists, except for some old smokestacks.) Philip Everly was born in Cook County hospital in Chicago on January 19, 1939. Their parents, Ike Everly and Margaret Embry, had moved from Waterloo, Iowa, to Chicago to continue their career in music. Ike, an excellent guitar player, and Margaret, who played the bass fiddle, traveled around the Midwest playing mostly in fairs and clubs. Ike was one of the few authentic guitarists in American music. The influence of his thumb-picking style can be heard in the music of such players as Merle Travis, Chet Atkins, and Mark Knopfler.

In 1945 the Everly family settled in Shenandoah, Iowa, where they had found a job on radio station KMA. The money was reasonable, and they agreed that Shenandoah provided the right atmosphere for their boys to grow up in. Don and Phil started singing when they could barely speak, and their father taught them to harmonize and to play the guitar. By the ages of six and eight, they had joined their parents each morning on a radio show.

The Everly Family Show. Soon the Everlys moved to a larger house, and they lived a good life in Shenandoah for almost nine years. In 1947 the owner of KMA radio died and his son took over the station. Live entertainment shows on radio were becoming old-fashioned; in 1951 the Everly family was fired. A smaller station, KFNF, offered them a job, but it was necessary for both parents to work extra jobs in order to support the family. Therefore, they decided to find better circumstances.

In 1953 the family moved to Knoxville, Tennessee, where they worked on WROL radio, performing two shows per day and getting paid ninety dollars per week. When the money ran out, Ike got in touch with Chet Atkins in Nashville. It was not long before Atkins had one of Don's songs, "Thou Shalt Not Steal," recorded by Kitty Wells. It

The Everly Brothers (Warner Bros./Archive Photos)

was a hit and the decision was made to split up the family act and send the brothers to Nashville. The first two years were difficult; Ike worked as a barber, and Margaret was a beautician to help support the boys while they solicited record companies. They auditioned for almost every record company in Nashville, but failed to get a contract. Just when they were about to give up, they were finally signed to Columbia Records. In 1955, the first Everly Brothers single, "The Sun Keeps Shining"/"Keep a-Lovin' Me," was released.

From Disaster to Success. Don and Phil suffered repeated rejections by record executives who did not know what to do with them. Finally, in February, 1957, the Everly Brothers signed with Cadence Records, released "Bye Bye Love," sold more than two million records, and began a career that established them as one of the most influential duos in the history of recorded music. Years later Bob Dylan paid tribute to Don and Phil, saying, "We owe these guys everything. They started it all." The Everly Brothers' major hits included "Wake Up Little Susie" in 1957, "All I Have to Do Is Dream" and "Bird Dog" in 1958, and "Cathy's Clown" in 1960. Among their other significant singles were "Gone, Gone, Gone," "The Price of Love," "Love Is Strange," and "Bowling Green."

Through the 1960's, Don and Phil continued to write, perform, and record. In 1970 they had their own highly rated television special, "Johnny Cash Presents the Everly Brothers."

Breakup and Reunion. Since 1957 the Everly Brothers have performed in more than seven hundred cities in the United States and Canada. From 1959 to 1973 they toured the world, and maintained regular tours in Great Britain. Their careers continued to do well in the early 1970's, but the ravages of life in the spotlight began to wear the brothers down. On July 14, 1973, the Everlys decided to go their separate ways: Don moved back to Nashville, and Phil stayed in Los Angeles. They did not see much of each other for ten years, and both worked on solo careers.

In 1983, Don and Phil decided to work together again. On September 22 and 23, at the Royal Albert Hall in London, the Everly Brothers performed two historic concerts before thunderstruck capacity crowds. The reunion concert was released as a double album and aired around the world as a cable television special. The album went gold and brought them a new contract.

The Everly Brothers made three albums for Mercury/Polygram. Their first, *EB 84*, was released in September, 1984. In 1986 *Born Yesterday* was released, and in 1989 their last album for Mercury, *Some Hearts*, was released. *EB 84* went gold in various countries around the world. The Everly Brothers ended their contract with Mercury/Polygram in 1990.

Still in demand worldwide, the Everlys would continue to tour six to eight months per year, performing for audiences in Europe, Australia, and North America. Each summer they would return to their ancestral homeland to give a benefit concert for the economically depressed coal-mining community in Muhlenberg County, Kentucky. The proceeds from this yearly "Everly Brothers' Homecoming Music Festival" go to the Everly Brothers' Foundation, a charity which provides aid for scholarships and community projects.

—*'Inoke F. Funaki*

For the Record

In January, 1986, Don and Phil Everly were two of the original inductees into the Rock and Roll Hall of Fame. Having sold more than forty million records and created a sound that is beyond the fads and whims of the music industry, they were honored as two artists who laid the foundation for an art form that created a cultural revolution.

SELECT DISCOGRAPHY

■ SINGLES

"Bye Bye Love," 1957
"Wake Up Little Susie," 1957
"All I Have to Do Is Dream," 1958
"Bird Dog," 1958

"('Till) I Kissed You," 1959
"Let It Be Me," 1960
"Cathy's Clown," 1960
"Crying in the Rain," 1962

■ ALBUMS

Everly Brothers, 1958
Songs Our Daddy Taught Us, 1959
The Fabulous Style of the Everly Brothers, 1960
A Date with the Everly Brothers, 1961
Christmas with the Everly Brothers, 1962
Rock n' Soul, 1965
Two Yanks in England, 1966
Hit Sound of the Everly Brothers, 1967
Roots, 1968
The Everly Brothers' Show, 1970
Nashville Tennessee Nov 1955, 1981
EB 84, 1984
All They Had to Do Was Dream, 1985
Born Yesterday, 1986
Mercury Years, 1993
Heartaches 'n' Harmonies, 1994
Original British Singles, 1995

SELECT AWARDS

Rock and Roll Hall of Fame, inducted 1986
Hollywood Walk of Fame, star awarded 1986

SEE ALSO: Atkins, Chet; Beatles, The; Berry, Chuck; Charles, Ray; Diddley, Bo; Hollies, The; Lewis, Jerry Lee; Perkins, Carl; Presley, Elvis; Simon and Garfunkel; Wells, Kitty; Who, The.

F

Fairport Convention. *See* Richard Thompson

See Richard Thompson

José Feliciano

BORN: Lares, Puerto Rico; September 10, 1945
FIRST ALBUM RELEASE: *The Voice and Guitar of José Feliciano,* 1964
MUSICAL STYLES: Latin, pop, soft rock, folk rock

The second of twelve children born to a laborer in Lares, Puerto Rico, José Feliciano was stricken by congenital glaucoma and left permanently blind at birth. He expressed a fascination for music at a very early age, beginning to learn guitar, accordion, and other instruments at the age of three. Feliciano was largely self-taught, but he practiced diligently and listened to a wide range of music. He was particularly fond of classical guitarist Andrés Segovia, jazz gutarist Wes Montgomery, and vocalist Ray Charles. In 1950, his family moved to New York City's Spanish Harlem area. When he was nine years old, he made his concert debut at New York's El Teatro Puerto Rico in the Bronx.

Rapid Rise to Fame. During his high school years, Feliciano began playing at the coffeehouses in Greenwich Village, New York. In 1962, he dropped out of high school in order to become a full-time musician, his meager earnings helping to support his large family. His coffeehouse jobs led to important developments: He met his manager and first wife, Hilda Perez, at the Cafe Id, and he was offered a contract with RCA after performing at New York's Gerde's Folk City.

In 1964, his first recordings were released. His first single was "Everybody Do the Click," and his first album was *The Voice and Guitar of José Feliciano,* which included flamenco stylings. He also appeared at the Newport Jazz Festival during this year. In 1965, his second album, The *Fantastic Feliciano,* was released. After releasing *A Bag Full of Soul* in 1966, Feliciano began to record successful Spanish-language albums for RCA International, including *Sombras . . . Una Voz, Una Guitarra, Mas Exitos de José Feliciano* and *El Sentimiento, La Voz y La Guitarra de José Feliciano.* He played for an audience of 100,000 in Buenos Aires, Argentina, and two of his singles, "La Copa Rota" and "Amor Gitana," were hits on the Latin charts.

The year 1968 was very important for Feliciano. On his new album, *Feliciano!* he included a cover of a recent song by the Doors, the U.S. rock group popular with the rapidly peaking youth counterculture. "Light My Fire" was the hit single from their own debut album, released just the year before, and its style was rather heavy and aggressive. Feliciano's version was lighter and more romantic and, of course, had a touch of bluesy salsa. Defying the conventional marketing wisdom of not promoting a cover until well after the release of the initial version, "Light My Fire" was promoted for airplay and was a smash hit, entering the U.S. Top 5 and eventually becoming a gold record. In the same year, he recorded a cover of "Hi Heel Sneakers" by Tommy Tucker, which was also successful. A follow-up album, *Feliciano! #2,* was quickly released by the energetic young musician in the same year and also became a gold record.

Also in 1968, Feliciano generated a good deal of controversy when he was invited to sing the U.S. national anthem during the fifth game of the World Series in Detroit. This was at the height of the Vietnam War, and many Americans were very sensitive about anything related to issues of patriotism and loyalty. Like the U.S. flag, "The Star-Spangled Banner" was an especially emotional symbol at this time, and Feliciano's Latin- and jazz-inflected version, sung before an audience of thirty thousand, disturbed some listeners, just as it delighted others. The performance had been recorded and was released as a single, becoming yet another hit in that eventful year.

Continuing his almost frenzied pace of recording, Feliciano released three albums in 1969: *Souled*, *Alive Alive-O!*, and *Feliciano/10 to 23*. Also in this year, he won a Grammy Award for Best New Artist. Although single releases from his newer recordings were not smash hits, one of the albums (*Souled*) earned platinum status. He had established a solid base of fans all over the world and would continue touring and recording. His Christmas song "Feliz Navidad"(1970) has entered the standard holiday repertoire.

Television in the 1970's. During the 1970's, Feliciano was especially active in the medium of television. His theme song for the popular sitcom *Chico and the Man* entered the Top 100 singles chart in 1974. He also appeared on other shows such as *KungFu* and *McMillan and Wife*. Along with his English-language recordings, such as his 1973 album, *Compartments* (produced by blues guitarist Steve Cropper), and his work with singer Joni Mitchell on "Free Man in Paris," he also released several Spanish-language recordings.

Awards. In 1980, Feliciano started working with the newly formed Latin branch of Motown Records, which released *José Feliciano*, an English-language album. He won Best Latin Pop Performance Grammy Award that year as well. In 1982, he married his second wife, Susan Omillion, whom he had met in 1971. The following year, Feliciano released *Escenas de Amor*, a Spanish-language album that was popular with the Hispanic audience, but *Romance in the Night*, his second English-language album with Motown, was less successful. After switching to the EMI label, Feliciano earned three Best Latin Pop Performance Grammies for various albums, in 1984, 1987, and 1990. He continued to play and record in a wide range of settings, recording with the Vienna Symphony Orchestra in 1987.

Adding the roles of father, educator, and entrepreneur to that of singer and guitarist, Feliciano's life in the 1990's was even more diverse than before. Along with spending time with his children, he became involved in an instructional video project, plans for a restaurant in Las Vegas, Nevada, and other ventures. At the same time, he continued to record and concertize. *Americano* was released internationally by Polygram in 1996, and smaller labels continued to issue albums with new versions of his most famous songs mixed with new covers.

José Feliciano's music and career bridged Hispanic American, Anglo American, and African American cultures. He inspired millions of physically challenged with his positive attitude, perseverance, and brilliance as an artist. —*Alice Myers*

SELECT DISCOGRAPHY

■ ALBUMS

Feliciano! 1968
Feliciano/10 to 23, 1969
Alive Alive-O! 1969
Feliz Navidad, 1970
Me Enamore, 1983
I'm Never Gonna Change, 1988
Steppin' Out, 1990
Americano, 1996
On Second Thought, 1997
And the Sun Will Shine, 1998

SELECT AWARDS

Grammy Awards for Best New Artist and Best Contemporary Pop Vocal Performance, Male, for "Light My Fire," 1968
Grammy Award for Best Latin Pop Performance for "Me Enamore," 1983
Grammy Award for Best Latin Pop Performance for "Lelolai," 1986
Grammy Award for Best Latin Pop Peformance for "Cielito Lindo," 1989
Grammy Award for Best Latin Pop Peformance for "Por Que te Tengo Que Olvidar?" 1990

Bryan Ferry. *See* Roxy Music / Bryan Ferry

The Fifth Dimension

ORIGINAL MEMBERS: Billy Davis (b. 1940), LaMonte McLemore (b. 1940), Ron Townson

(b. 1941), Marilyn McCoo (b. 1943), Florence LaRue Gordon (b. 1944)

OTHER MEMBERS: Michael Bell, Trish Turner, Marjorie Barnes, Danny Beard

FIRST SINGLE RELEASE: "I'll Be Loving You Forever," 1966

FIRST ALBUM RELEASE: *Up, Up, and Away*, 1967

MUSICAL STYLES: Pop, rhythm and blues, soul, jazz

Like the Mamas and the Papas and the Friends of Distinction, the Fifth Dimension represented a whole new generation of pop vocal groups who arrived on the music scene in the mid-and late 1960's with soaring songs of love, peace, and happiness. Mixing semipsychedelic clothing, flamboyant choreography, and sunny optimism, they signaled a decisive break from the drab dress and post-World War II suburban sentimentality of their immediate predecessors and mainstream competition, the Lettermen, the Vogues, the Johnny Mann Singers, and others.

What Is Hip? As late as the mid-1960's, counterculture music—rock and rhythm and blues—was in stiff competition with the pop music of Bobby Darin and the sophisticated sounds of Frank Sinatra. For some fans and performers, the lines were clearly drawn. There was either rock and rhythm and blues, or there was pop music (even Motown's black pop), which was the music of the establishment.

There were a few musicians and singers, however, who tried to bridge the gap between the styles. As Motown artists did, they wanted to combine the energy and excitement of rock and rhythm and blues with the urbane sophistication of Tin Pan Alley pop music. In 1967, a group of idealists calling themselves the Fifth Dimension broke out of the pack and made the charts with

The Fifth Dimension performing in Baltimore in 1968 (Archive Photos)

"Go Where You Wanna Go" and "Up, Up, and Away." The slick arrangements, boy-girl harmonies, and idealistic lyrics ("We can sail among the stars together/ you and I/ for we can fly") condemned the group to irrelevance as far as the members of the rock revolution were concerned. At the same time, the content of the Fifth Dimension's lyrics (as in "Age of Aquarius" and "Up, Up, and Away") were suspected by some critics of promoting or sanctioning drug use. Like other pop groups, the Fifth Dimension was tagged with the dismissive label "middle of the road," a term which does define, in a positive way, exactly the path the group was trying to pave.

From Blues to Balloons. The Fifth Dimension was formed out of the remains of the Hi-Fi's, a vocal group which specialized in singing pop-tinged gospel and blues. LaMonte McLemore, a photographer for the Miss Bronze America beauty contest of 1963, convinced Miss Bronze, Marilyn McCoo, to form the group with his friends Harry Elston and Floyd Butler. The Los Angeles residents eventually toured with Ray Charles but musical conflicts broke up the quartet. Elston and Butler left to form their own group, the Friends of Distinction.

Meanwhile McLemore's cousin, Billy Davis, came up from St. Louis where he had been in a number of groups, including the Emeralds, which had some regional success. McLemore sought out two more friends to complete the group. Ron Townson had been classically trained as a vocalist and directed his own gospel group, the Celestial Choir. Florence LaRue had just started teaching after completing her reign as Miss Bronze America, 1962; she'd become friends with McCoo when McCoo had passed on the Miss Bronze America crown to her in 1963.

The group, now called the Versatiles, began rehearsals in 1966 and auditioned for manager Marc Gordon, who then introduced them to producer-performer Johnny Rivers. Rivers liked the group but not the name. Ron Townson is credited with coming up with the group's new name, the Fifth Dimension. Rivers signed the group to his new label, Soul City Records, and put them with Motown songwriter Willie Hutch who wrote their first single, "I'll Be Loving You Forever." A typical Motown rhythm and blues/pop song, "I'll Be Loving You Forever" did not make the charts. The second single, a John Phillips song, "Go Where You Wanna Go," found the group imitating Phillips's group, the Mamas and the Papas. The song was a hit, making the Top 20 in early 1967. A third song, "Another Day, Another Heartache," though again done in the style of the Mamas and the Papas, revealed a personality distinctive to the group.

By spring of 1967, Rivers was working on the group's first album but halted production midway through to attend a songwriting festival. There he met a young songwriter, Jimmy Webb, who had been inspired by a hot-air balloon flight to write a song called "Up, Up, and Away." Rivers brought the song to the Fifth Dimension who loved it on first hearing, recorded it almost immediately, and released it before the album was finished. "Up, Up, and Away" was a runaway hit, making instant stars of both the group and the young songwriter.

Recording Classics. The Fifth Dimension had a string of hits between 1967 and 1972, and while "Up, Up, and Away" is justly considered its signature song, it was not as big or daring as the 1969 double-sided single, "Aquarius/Let the Sunshine In." Culled from the hit Broadway musical *Hair*, "Aquarius/Let the Sunshine In" was the group's biggest hit, selling more than two million copies. The band's trio of Laura Nyro songs—"Stoned Soul Picnic," "Sweet Blindness," and

For the Record

In 1968 Billy Davis lost his wallet in a cab in New York. Fortunately, the finder returned it to him. To show his gratitude, Davis invited the man to a Fifth Dimension performance. The man turned out to be one of the producers of the Broadway musical *Hair*. He invited the group to a performance, where they first heard "Aquarius."

"Wedding Bell Blues" were also top sellers.

Like most pop stars' albums of the 1960's, the Fifth Dimension's albums are mostly compilations of hit or potential hit singles. Yet they have at least one classic album in their repertoire, *The Magic Garden* (1968) written, arranged, and produced by Jimmy Webb. A follow-up to their first album, *Up, Up, and Away* (1967), *The Magic Garden* featured complex arrangements, alternating rhythms within songs, odd, psychedelic lyrics and instrumentation (the sitar was a favorite of Webb in these early recordings), and a variety of musical styles, from classical interludes and wry satires ("Paper Cup") to Burt Bacharach/Hal David imitations ("The Girls' Song") and John Lennon/Paul McCartney tributes ("Ticket to Ride").

Legacy. Marilyn McCoo and Billy Davis left the group in 1975 and went on to have a fairly successful career as a duo, hitting the charts with songs such as "You Don't Have to Be a Star" and "I Hope We Get to Love in Time." The Fifth Dimension's last chart record was "Love Hangover" (1976), which lost the chart battle to Diana Ross's version of the same song. The group continued on into the 1980's and 1990's, with LaMonte McLemore and Florence LaRue the only original members remaining.

In attempting to bridge pop, soul, gospel, and rock, the Fifth Dimension embodied the high idealism of the 1960's. As artists such as Janis Joplin and Jimi Hendrix did for rock and roll, the Fifth Dimension tried to expand the possibilities of pop music. —*Tyrone Williams*

SELECT DISCOGRAPHY

■ ALBUMS

Up, Up, and Away, 1967
Stoned Soul Picnic, 1968
Greatest Hits on Earth, 1975
Anthology, 1986

SELECT AWARDS

Grammy Awards for Record of the Year (wr. with Marc Gordon and Johnny Rivers), Best Contemporary Single, Best Contemporary Group Performance (Vocal or Instrumental), and Best Performance by a Vocal Group for "Up, Up and Away," 1967

Grammy Awards for Record of the Year (with Bones Howe) and Best Contemporary Vocal Performance by a Group for "Aquarius/Let the Sunshine In," 1969

SEE ALSO: Campbell, Glen; Mamas and the Papas, The.

Ella Fitzgerald

BORN: Newport News, Virginia; April 25, 1917
DIED: Beverly Hills, California; June 15, 1996
FIRST SINGLE RELEASE: "Love and Kisses," 1935
MUSICAL STYLES: Jazz, pop

Ella Fitzgerald is regarded by many as the greatest singer in the history of jazz. Fitzgerald was among other notable black artists, such as jazz singer Billie Holiday, bandleader, composer, and jazz pianist Duke Ellington, and poet Langston Hughes, who, in the 1920's, fueled the artistic and cultural explosion known as the Harlem Renaissance.

The Beginnings. Growing up outside New York City, Ella Fitzgerald earned her earliest success at the age of sixteen by winning an amateur contest held at the historic Harlem Opera House. Winning the twenty-five dollar prize with her performance of "Judy" and "The Object of My Affection" (two songs made popular by her early influences, the Boswell Sisters), Fitzgerald would later refer to this experience as "the turning point of my life."

Fitzgerald's first professional performing experience was in 1935 when she appeared for a week-long engagement with Tiny Bradshaw's Band at the Harlem Opera House. It was here that she would make an important contact with Bardou Ali, who worked for drummer and bandleader Chick Webb. Ali first introduced Fitzgerald and Webb, thus starting a relationship that would prove both professionally and personally significant in both their lives.

At age seventeen, Fitzgerald joined Webb's band as part of a vocal duo with Charlie Linton. Webb's band was one of the leading bands in New York City and performed at some of the most prestigious clubs, exposing Fitzgerald to large audiences. Her first appearance with Webb's band was at Yale University, and within one week she performed at the Savoy, one of the most popular clubs in Harlem, New York. During this time she was named Best Female Vocalist in the 1937 *Down Beat* Readers Poll, which was the first of her many national and international awards. Fitzgerald's career took off with hits such as "A-tisket, A-tasket" (1938), which topped the song charts for seventeen weeks. Fitzgerald's swinging style, combined with Webb's high energy drumming, helped define the rhythmic phenomenon that gave this music its name: swing.

Ella Fitzgerald (Paul Natkin)

While enjoying real success in her professional life, Fitzgerald's personal life was suffering. Her mother passed away one year prior to Fitzgerald joining Webb's band, leaving her without parents and without a clear direction in life. Webb not only provided her with a career path but also developed a father-figure relationship with her. Fitzgerald's time with this band proved to be some of the happiest and most important years of her life.

In June of 1939, only four years after Fitzgerald joined his band, Webb died of pneumonia. As its most likely heir, Fitzgerald took over the band under the name Ella Fitzgerald and Her Orchestra, leading the band, if in name only, for three years.

The Bebop Era. As jazz evolved in the 1940's, so did Fitzgerald's career. Big bands began to die out in favor of smaller jazz groups, elaborate orchestrations gave way to the more individually oriented art form of improvisation, and the increasing complexity of jazz appealed more to sophisticated listeners than to dance music fans. During this time, Fitzgerald developed her own improvisatory solo vehicle—scat singing.

Scat singing is a means of improvisation that makes use of nonsense syllables and mimicry, especially of jazz instruments. Fitzgerald was a master at this technique. Coupling her scat singing with the playfulness of her voice, Fitzgerald would frequently imitate the legendary jazz trumpeter and vocalist Louis Armstrong.

Throughout the 1940's, Fitzgerald became enthralled with this music. In 1947 she briefly toured, and later that year she performed at New York City's Carnegie Hall with one of the most important figures in jazz, Dizzy Gillespie. Gillespie and contemporary Charlie Parker have been credited with the advent of what many would agree to be the most important period of jazz, the bebop era.

Jazz at the Philharmonic. In 1948, shortly after marrying her second husband, jazz bassist Ray Brown, Fitzgerald was introduced to promoter Norman Granz. Granz, founder of Verve Records, established a concert series that aimed to promote racial integration and civil rights. Known as "Jazz at the Philharmonic," Granz's endeavor strived to elevate the perception and treatment of jazz and jazz musicians through profitable performing and recording contracts. In 1954, Granz became Fitzgerald's manager, and in 1955 he signed her to his record label after skillfully negotiating her former contract with Decca Records. This relationship launched Fitzgerald's career to greater popularity and fame than she could have imagined.

The advent of long-playing records allowed for more substantial recording endeavors than were possible with earlier records. Granz had Fitzgerald record the *Songbook* recordings, each of which featured Fitzgerald singing a single composer's contributions to the popular American song repertoire. The first of these, entitled *Ella Fitzgerald Sings the Cole Porter Songbook* (1956), included the vastly successful "Night and Day" and "I've Got You Under My Skin." Subsequent *Songbook* projects featured the music of Rodgers and Hart (1956), Duke Ellington (Volume I, 1956 and Volume II, 1957), George and Ira Gershwin (1958-1959), Harold Arlen (1960), Jerome Kern (1964), and Johnny Mercer (1964). Her album *Ella Fitzgerald Sings the Irving Berlin Songbook* (1958) won her the first of what would be many Grammy Awards. It is quite possible that Ira Gershwin said it best: "I never knew how good our songs were until I heard Ella Fitzgerald sing them."

These recordings suited Fitzgerald's voice famously. With her light, pure tone and impeccable diction, she voiced a depth and range of expression that captivated the listener. Compositions such as "Honeysuckle Rose" and "Lady Be Good" demonstrated her uncompromising sense of swing and imaginative harmonic vocabulary, bringing subtlety and life to these standard works. Alternatively, songs such as "Miss Otis Regrets" featured her quiet humor and insightful approach to phrasing which remain unequaled.

With these recordings, Fitzgerald gained an internationally acclaimed reputation. Under the management of Granz she would go on to record many other significant albums, including projects with such jazz greats as Louis Armstrong (*Ella and Louis,* 1956; *Porgy and Bess,* 1957), Count Basie (*Ella and Basie: On the Sunny Side of the Street,* 1963), and Duke Ellington (*Ella and Duke at the Cote d'Azur,* 1967).

Life Achievements. Fitzgerald's place in history is supported by the distinction of collecting more Grammy Awards than any other jazz singer, being named Best Female Vocalist in *Down Beat* Readers Polls eighteen years in a row, and receiving a Kennedy Center Award and the National Medal of the Arts, presented to her by the President of the United States. In addition, she has been dignified with honorary doctorates from some of the most prestigious academic institutions in the United States, including Yale and Dartmouth Universities.

In 1996, Ella Fitzgerald died after suffering deteriorating health. She left behind a legacy of greatness. While in her personal life her happiness was always in question—she was orphaned at a young age, married and divorced twice, and continually battled weight problems—for Ella Fitzgerald, what always mattered most was the chance to sing for her fans, a task she did prolifically and beautifully. *—Mark Sheridan-Rabideau*

SELECT DISCOGRAPHY

■ ALBUMS

Ella Fitzgerald Sings the Cole Porter Songbook, 1956
Ella and Louis, 1956 (with Louis Armstrong)
Ella Fitzgerald: Jazz at the Philharmonic, 1957
Ella and Basie: On the Sunny Side of the Street, 1963

SELECT AWARDS

Grammy Awards for Best Vocal Performance, Female, for *Ella Fitzgerald Sings the Irving Berlin Songbook* and Best Jazz Performance, Individual, for *Ella Fitzgerald Sings the Duke Ellington Songbook,* 1958

Grammy Awards for Best Vocal Performance, Female, for "But Not for Me" and Best Jazz Performance, Soloist, for *Ella Swings Lightly,* 1959

Grammy Awards for Best Vocal Performance Single Record or Track, Female, for "Mack the Knife" and Best Vocal Performance, Album, Female, for *Mack the Knife—Ella in Berlin,* 1960

Grammy Award for Best Solo Vocal Performance, Female, for *Ella Swings Brightly with Nelson Riddle,* 1962

Grammy Award for Lifetime Achievement, 1967
Grammy Award for Best Jazz Vocal Performance for *Fine and Mellow,* 1979
Kennedy Center Award for Contributions to American Music, 1979
National Medal of Arts Award, 1987
Grammy Award for Best Jazz Vocal Performance, Female, for *All That Jazz,* 1990
Grammy Awards for Best Historical Album and Best Recording Package—Boxed for *The Complete Ella Fitzgerald Songbooks,* 1994

SEE ALSO: Bennett, Tony; Charles, Ray; Cole, Nat "King"; Coltrane, John; Davis, Miles; Sinatra, Frank.

Fleetwood Mac

ORIGINAL MEMBERS: Mick Fleetwood (b. 1947), Peter Green (b. 1946), John McVie (b.1945), Jeremy Spencer (b. 1948)
BEST-KNOWN LINEUP: Lindsey Buckingham (b. 1947), Mick Fleetwood, Christine McVie (b. 1943), John McVie, Stevie Nicks (b. 1948)
OTHER MEMBERS: Bekka Bramlett (b. 1968), Bob Brunning, Billy Burnette (b. 1953), Danny Kirwan (b. 1950), Dave Mason (b. 1946), Rick Vito (b. 1949), Dave Walker, Bob Welch (b. 1946), Bob Weston
FIRST ALBUM RELEASE: *Peter Green's Fleetwood Mac,* 1968
MUSICAL STYLES: Blues, pop, rock and roll

Will the Real Fleetwood Mac Please Stand Up was the title of a 1973 live bootleg album. The title jokingly refers to the band's many changes, both in personnel and in style. From late 1960's British blues band to mid-1970's pop powerhouse, Fleetwood Mac's mercurial, decades-spanning career has touched on two continents and a half-dozen musical styles.

The Beginnings. The original Fleetwood Mac was founded in 1967 by guitarists Peter Green of the British blues band John Mayall's Bluesbreakers and Jeremy Spencer. Green recruited Bluesbreakers drummer Mick Fleetwood and bass player John McVie, and a blend of their surnames gave the new band its name—Fleetwood Mac. The combined guitar power of Green (who had replaced Eric Clapton in the Bluesbreakers) and Spencer, considered one of England's best bottleneck-style guitarists, won praise from reviewers and carried their first album, *Peter Green's Fleetwood Mac* (1968), onto the British charts. A second album, *Mr. Wonderful* (1968), was released only in Britain.

In 1969, the band added yet another guitarist, Danny Kirwan, and recorded their third album, *English Rose.* One of Green's compositions, "Black Magic Woman," was later covered by Santana and became their signature song. Two more albums followed in 1969, *The Pious Bird of Good Omen* and *Then Play On,* and from them, Fleetwood Mac had three of Britain's top-selling singles, "Albatross," "Man of the World," and "Oh Well."

The First Big Breakup. The year 1970 should have been a great one for Fleetwood Mac. Instead, they lost Green due to personal problems during a tour of Germany. In what was to become standard operating procedure, the band played on, adding McVie's wife, keyboard player Christine Perfect, to the mix. Perfect (later McVie) had been a member of the British band Chicken Shack and had sung with Spencer Davis. Soon after, Jeremy Spencer vanished during a 1971 California tour. It was later learned that he had joined a religious cult, the Children of God, and abruptly cut his ties to the outside world.

Bob Welch became Fleetwood Mac's first American member in 1971, replacing Spencer. Welch was a veteran of a Las Vegas show band and had backed artists James Brown, Aretha Franklin, and Fontella Bass. Kirwan was fired and replaced by Bob Weston and Dave Walker, both of whom only stayed with the band a short time. To add to the confusion, manager Clifford Davis set Weston and Walker up with a band, called them Fleetwood Mac, and booked a U.S. tour. The real Fleetwood Mac spent most of 1974 in court putting a stop to it. Throughout their troubles, the varying combinations managed to record a string of albums on the Reprise label: *Future Games* (1971), *Bare Trees* (1972), *Mystery to Me* (1973), and *Heroes Are Hard to Find* (1974).

The 1997 Fleetwood Mac reunion: Mick Fleetwood, Lindsey Buckingham, Stevie Nicks, Christine McVie, John McVie (Reprise/David LaChapelle)

The Supergroup. Fleetwood Mac moved to California in 1974, but by then, Bob Welch had already had enough. Undaunted, Fleetwood and the McVies started looking for a place to record their next album. To show off the acoustics of his Sound City studio, prospective producer Keith Olsen played an album recorded there—the self-titled debut by California duo Buckingham/Nicks. Fleetwood liked what he heard, both from the studio and from self-taught guitar virtuoso Lindsey Buckingham. Initially, Buckingham balked at the offer to join the band, stating that he and partner/girlfriend Stevie Nicks were a package deal. The offer was then extended to both of them.

The new Fleetwood Mac immediately went to the studio. Christine McVie's voice blended smoothly with the new duo's two-part harmonies, and Buckingham's studio wizardry brought a new dimension to the band. Their 1975 *Fleetwood Mac* album sold five million copies and featured the hit singles "Over My Head," "Say You Love Me," and "Rhiannon," a signature Nicks tune that introduced audiences to her captivating trademark gypsy-witch persona.

Despite the success of *Fleetwood Mac,* no one was quite prepared for 1977. The McVies' marriage ended, Fleetwood's marriage ended, and the long-term relationship between Buckingham and Nicks ended. The band also recorded *Rumours* at the Record Plant in Sausalito, California. Singles such as "Go Your Own Way," "Don't Stop," and "You Make Lovin' Fun" saturated the airwaves, and "Dreams," (a song written by Nicks about the end of her relationship with Buckingham) became Fleetwood Mac's first number 1 single. Romantic turmoil made for great music, and *Rumours* went on to become the best-selling album

For the Record

Fleetwood Mac's eleventh album, *Rumours* (released in February, 1977), set a number of impressive records. In October, 1987, it hit its 397th week on the British pop charts, breaking a record held by Meat Loaf's *Bat out of Hell.* By the end of 1991 it had raised this record to 443 total weeks. Meanwhile, the album set an American record for nonsound-track albums by topping the chart for 31 weeks (a record later broken by Michael Jackson's *Thriller*) and sold more than 14 million copies.

of all time, a record which stood until Michael Jackson's *Thriller* ousted it in 1982.

After a tour and a brief hiatus, Fleetwood Mac returned to the studio in 1979 with the daunting task of recording the follow-up to *Rumours.* Determined not to merely copy the successful formula of the last album, Buckingham forced the band in a different direction, recording many of the tracks in his home studio. The result, *Tusk* (1979), was an experimental mix of music, vocals, and studio alchemy. *Tusk* did not reach the stellar level of *Rumours,* but it did go platinum and produce two Top-10 singles, including the title song, which featured the University of Southern California marching band. The *Tusk* tour also spawned a live album in 1981.

Following solo albums by Buckingham, Fleetwood, and Nicks, the band reunited to record *Mirage* in 1982. Critics considered *Mirage* a safe album, a retreat to the *Rumours* format without the *Rumours* chemistry. More solo albums followed, this time with Christine McVie trying her hand. It seemed as if the band were finished.

The Second Big Breakup. Internal difficulties forced the dissolution of the popular 1970's lineup in 1987. Buckingham was the first to leave. "The creative atmosphere was next to nil. . . . It was pretty nuts. It had gotten to the point where it was hard to work." He had stopped work on his in-progress third solo album in favor of the band's 1987 release, *Tango in the Night,* and did not want to tour in support of the album. Skilled in the art of carrying on, Fleetwood Mac added two guitarists, Billy Burnette and Rick Vito, and went on the road.

It was the beginning of the end, however. The new lineup released one album in 1990, *Behind the Mask,* which failed to produce a hit and was the first Fleetwood Mac album since 1975 that did not go platinum. A dispute over song rights between Nicks and Fleetwood led to her departure in 1993. Christine McVie's status was less clear. She appeared on 1995's *Time* along with new members Dave Mason and Bekka Bramlett, but did not tour. Following the dismal performance of *Time* and a tour as part of a nostalgia package with Pat Benatar and REO Speedwagon, Fleetwood and John McVie reluctantly put the band to rest.

However, the seeds of reunion were planted during the 1992 presidential inauguration. President Bill Clinton had used Fleetwood Mac's feel-good anthem "Don't Stop" as his campaign theme song, and it seemed only fitting that the *Rumours*-era lineup close the celebration with a "one time only" performance.

While the performance did not put the band back together, it did put the members back in touch. When Buckingham needed a drummer and sounding board for his fourth solo album, he turned to Fleetwood. John McVie came in to play a little bass, Christine McVie added some harmonies, and tentatively, Fleetwood Mac came together to celebrate the twentieth anniversary of *Rumours.* Recorded live in 1997 during a series of "invitation-only" MTV concerts, *The Dance* debuted at number 1 on the *Billboard* album chart, and Fleetwood Mac began touring once more.

—*P. S. Ramsey*

SELECT DISCOGRAPHY

■ ALBUMS

Peter Green's Fleetwood Mac, 1968
English Rose, 1969
Then Play On, 1969
Kiln House, 1970
Future Games, 1971

Bare Trees, 1972
Heroes Are Hard to Find, 1974
Fleetwood Mac, 1975
Rumours, 1977
Tusk, 1979
Tango in the Night, 1987
The Dance, 1997

SELECT AWARDS
Grammy Award for Album of the Year for *Rumours*, 1977
Rock and Roll Hall of Fame, inducted 1998

SEE ALSO: Clapton, Eric; Cocker, Joe; Eagles, The; Jethro Tull; Santana, Carlos.

The Flying Burrito Brothers. *See* Gram Parsons

John Fogerty. *See* Creedence Clearwater Revival / John Fogerty

The Foo Fighters

ORIGINAL MEMBERS: Dave Grohl (b. 1969), Pat Smear (b. 1960), William Goldsmith, Nate Mendel
OTHER MEMBERS: Taylor Hawkins, Franz Stahl
FIRST ALBUM RELEASE: *Foo Fighters*, 1995
MUSICAL STYLES: Alternative, grunge, hard rock

Upon the suicide of Nirvana front man Kurt Cobain in 1994, many critics assumed that the careers of the surviving members of the band had ended. However, drummer Dave Grohl surprised many by fashioning a post-Nirvana career as the leader of the band Foo Fighters. The band triumphed both critically and commercially and became perennial fixtures on MTV and the pages of *Rolling Stone* and *Spin* magazines.

Solo Project. The band's debut, *Foo Fighters* (1995), was written and performed solely by Grohl (except for one appearance on guitar by Greg Dulli of the Afghan Whigs). Like Nirvana's music, the Foo Fighters' borrowed both from punk and hard rock, emphasizing both catchy melodies and an energetic, distorted, guitar-based sound. Also like Nirvana's, the lyrics on the album were often hard to understand due to Grohl's tendency to sing (or scream) incoherently. However, where Cobain's lyrics outlined his intense self-doubt and depression, Grohl's were often nonsensical. The first single, "This Is a Call," opened with the lyrics, "Ritalin is easy/ Ritalin is good."

There were exceptions to the nonsense, most notably the single "I'll Stick Around." Initially, the track, with its angry refrain, "I don't owe you anything," was rumored to be about Cobain. However, lines such as "How could it be I'm the only

The Foo Fighters' Dave Grohl (Ken Settle)

one who sees your rehearsed insanity," led many to conclude the song's subject was Cobain's widow, Courtney Love of the band Hole, known for her wild, attention-grabbing antics. In interviews, Grohl remained evasive as to the subject of the song, though he allowed that it was not about Cobain.

Becoming a Full Band. After the album was completed, but before it was released, Grohl put together a full lineup of Foo Fighters, in April of 1995, for their slot as the opening act for punk rocker Mike Watt's U.S. tour. With Grohl on guitar and vocals, the band was rounded out by second guitarist Pat Smear of the legendary early 1980's Los Angeles punk band the Germs (as well as the final Nirvana tour lineup), bassist Nate Mendel, and drummer William Goldsmith, who had previously served as the rhythm section for the Seattle band Sunny Day Real Estate.

The album was well received by critics, who were surprised to discover that there was another talented songwriter from Nirvana. At a time when the music world was dominated by bands such as Bush and Candlebox, who were accused of stealing Nirvana's ideas and legacy, Foo Fighters were seen by many as a more genuine article, if only because of the band's obvious connection to the already legendary Nirvana. Additionally, the band featured the supremely charismatic Smear, whose energetic and camp demeanor (he displayed a fancy for cross-dressing) naturally put him in the spotlight. He became a frequent presence on MTV, serving as a correspondent on the station's fashion show, *House of Style*.

New Album and Lineup Changes. The Foo Fighters' second album, *The Colour and the Shape* (1997), unlike the first, featured the full band lineup. Immediately after the recording of the album, however, Goldsmith left the band and was replaced by Taylor Hawkins, former drummer for Alanis Morissette.

Whereas the first album had a fairly raw production sound, on *The Colour and the Shape*, the band took a slightly more glossy, radio-friendly approach to guitar rock. The album also marked a new sense of vocal and lyrical confidence on Grohl's part. He not only enunciated more clearly on this album, but made his lyrics more personal, addressing matters such as his recent divorce. Although the album performed well on the charts and spawned the hit singles "Monkey Wrench," "Everlong," and "My Hero" (the latter of which was also rumored to be about Cobain), the media attention that had greeted the first album had lessened. On September 4, 1997, at a preshow performance at the MTV Video Music Awards, Smear announced his departure from the band and was promptly replaced on stage by Franz Stahl.

—*Michael Pelusi*

For the Record

The name Foo Fighters refers to World War II slang for unidentified flying objects (UFOs). The band's label (owned by Capitol) is named Roswell, for the town in New Mexico where UFOs allegedly landed in the 1940's. The band also showed their mystical allegiance by appearing on two albums related to the alien conspiracy television drama *The X-Files*: the 1996 *Songs in the Key of X* album and the 1998 sound track to *The X-Files* film.

SELECT DISCOGRAPHY

■ ALBUMS

Foo Fighters, 1995

The Colour and the Shape, 1997

SELECT AWARDS

MTV Video Music Award for Best Group Video for "Big Me," 1996

SEE ALSO: Hole; Nirvana.

Foreigner

ORIGINAL MEMBERS: Mick Jones (b. 1944), Ian McDonald (b. 1946), Lou Gramm (b. 1950), Dennis Elliott (b. 1950), Al Greenwood (b. 1951), Edward Gagliardi (b. 1952)

OTHER MEMBERS: Rick Wills (b. 1947), Johnny Edwards, Bruce Turgon, Jeff Jacobs (b. 1962), Mark Schulman
FIRST ALBUM RELEASE: *Foreigner*, 1977
MUSICAL STYLES: Rock and roll, pop

Foreigner's combination of slow ballads and moderately hard rock dominated by guitars and keyboards pioneered the musical style known as adult-oriented rock (AOR). Their success paved the way for other AOR groups such as Journey, Styx, and REO Speedwagon.

The Beginnings. Guitarist and vocalist Mick Jones, the founder of Foreigner, began his musical career in the early 1960's as a member of Nero and the Gladiators. He later worked with artists such as Johnny Halliday, Wonderwheel, Spooky Tooth, Leslie West, and Ian Lloyd. In early 1976 he met Ian McDonald, who had played multiple instruments for King Crimson. Jones and McDonald joined with vocalist Lou Gramm, drummer Dennis Elliott, keyboardist Al Greenwood, and bassist Edward Gagliardi in New York to form Foreigner. The band took its name from the fact that Jones, McDonald, and Elliott were British (Gramm, Greenwood, and Gagliardi were American).

The band's self-titled first album, released in March of 1977, was an immediate success. It stayed in the Top 20 in the United States for one year, sold more than three million copies, and produced three major singles. "Feels Like the First Time" reached number 4, "Cold as Ice" reached number 6, and "Long, Long Way from Home" reached number 20. Foreigner toured the United States in 1977 and 1978, then released another hit album, *Double Vision* (1978). This album was even more successful, with the singles "Hot Blooded" reaching number 3 and "Double Vision" reaching number 2.

Changes. The first of several changes in the membership of Foreigner occurred in April of 1979, when Gagliardi was replaced by bassist Rick Wills. The band then released another successful album, *Head Games*, with the singles "Dirty White Boy" reaching number 12 and "Head Games" reaching number 14. In 1980 McDonald and Greenwood left the band and were not replaced. Despite this loss, the remaining members of Foreigner released an even more successful album, *4*, which reached number 1 in the United States in 1981. The album included the hit singles "Urgent," "Juke Box Hero," "Break It Up," and the group's first hit ballad, "Waiting for a Girl Like You."

After taking a three-year break from touring and recording, Foreigner released *Agent Provocateur*, which included the hit singles "That Was Yesterday" and "I Want to Know What Love Is." The latter song, another slow ballad, was the group's greatest hit, reaching number 1 in the United States and in the United Kingdom.

Solo Careers and More Changes. In 1987 Foreigner released *Inside Information*, which included the hit singles "Say You Will" and "I Don't Want to Live Without You." Gramm released the solo album *Ready or Not*, which included the hit single "Midnight Blue," in 1987, and *Long Hard Look*, featuring the hit single "Just Between You and Me," in 1989. Jones also released a self-titled solo album in 1989. Foreigner faced its greatest crisis when Gramm left the band to form a new band, Shadow King, which released a self-titled album in 1991. Jones replaced Gramm with vocalist Johnny Edwards, who appeared on the 1991 album *Unusual Heat*.

In 1994 Gramm returned to Foreigner, but Will and Elliott left the band that year. The band added bassist Bruce Turgon, keyboardist Jeff Jacobs, and drummer Mark Schulman. The new Foreigner

For the Record

Foreigner holds an unusual distinction in *Billboard* chart history. In late 1981, its "Waiting for a Girl Like You" held the number 2 position on the charts for ten weeks—longer than any other single had held that position. It was kept out of the number 1 position throughout the ten weeks by the same song—Olivia Newton-John's "Physical."

released *Mr. Moonlight* in 1994 and began touring in 1995. Although the albums of the 1990's produced no major new hits, Foreigner continued to draw large crowds to its concerts, while its hits of the 1970's and 1980's continued to appear frequently on the radio. —*Rose Secrest*

SELECT DISCOGRAPHY

■ ALBUMS

Foreigner, 1977
Double Vision, 1978
Head Games, 1979
4, 1981
Records, 1982 (compilation)
Agent Provocateur, 1984
Inside Information, 1987
Unusual Heat, 1991
The Very Best . . . and Beyond, 1992 (compilation)
Mr. Moonlight, 1994

SEE ALSO: Boston; Journey; King Crimson; REO Speedwagon; Styx.

The Four Seasons / Frankie Valli

The Four Seasons

ORIGINAL MEMBERS: Frankie Valli, Tommy DeVito (b. 1936), Nick DeVito, Hank Majewski (d. 1969)

OTHER MEMBERS: Bob Gaudio (b. 1942), Nick Massi (b. 1935), Joe Long, Gerry Polci (b. 1954), Don Ciccone (b. 1946), Jerry Corbetta (b. 1947), Larry Lingle (b. 1949)

FIRST ALBUM RELEASE: *Sherry and 11 Others*, 1962

Frankie Valli
(Francis Castelucio)

BORN: Newark, New Jersey; May 3, 1937

FIRST ALBUM RELEASE: *Inside You*, 1975

MUSICAL STYLES: Rock and roll, pop

One of the most venerable groups in rock history, the Four Seasons have several distinctions, not the least of which is having risen to fame at the very moment the "British invasion," led by the Beatles, was sending most U.S. rock bands to premature oblivion. Between 1962 and 1967, Four Seasons recordings remained on the charts almost continuously, thanks to twenty-nine hit songs, and the group sold about fifty million records.

Equally impressive, for different reasons, has been the group's longevity. It originally formed in 1956 and—through many changes in personnel—was still active four decades later. Through all the changes it experienced, however, one thing remained constant: Its lead singer, Frankie Valli, provided the group's solid core and gave it a distinct identity. A natural tenor with a three-octave range, he could effortlessly sustain a distinctive falsetto voice that became the group's inimitable trademark. In an era in which few female voices were heard in rock music, the Four Seasons offered a unique androgynous sound that rock fans tended either to love or to hate.

Origins. Born Francis Castelucio, Frankie Valli took his stage name from Texas Jean Valley, a country singer he had admired as a child. He grew up in Newark, New Jersey, where he began recording professionally as a soloist and in groups while still a teenager in the early 1950's. One of his teen groups, the Variatones, became the forerunner of the Four Seasons. Its membership included Hank Majewski, Tommy DeVito, and the latter's brother, Nick DeVito. After the Variatones were renamed the Four Lovers, they scored a hit with "You're the Apple of My Eye," a big enough hit for them to be invited to appear on *The Ed Sullivan Show* in 1956.

The Four Lovers' early success proved to be a fluke. Over the next few years they achieved little, until a record producer named Bob Crewe took an interest in them. At his suggestion they brought in a new member, Bob Gaudio, a veteran of the Royal Teens (remembered for the 1958 novelty hit "Short Shorts"). A keyboardsman and songwriter, Gaudio's challenge was to create a new sound and image for the group, which at Crewe's suggestion, was renamed the Four Seasons, after a local cocktail lounge.

In 1962 the Four Seasons' recording of Gaudio's "Sherry" was featured on Dick Clark's *American Bandstand* television program. In September the song reached number 1 on the charts. This success opened the gates to a flood of hits that flowed without interruption for more than five years. These included Gaudio and Crewe's "Big Girls Don't Cry" (1962) and "Walk Like a Man" (1963), both of which followed "Sherry" in going gold.

In 1964, after the Four Seasons switched from Vee Jay to the Phillips label, they quickly scored their fourth number 1 song with "Rag Doll" and narrowly missed gold with "Dawn (Go Away)" a year later. Their other Top-10 singles during this period included "Let's Hang On" (1965), "Working My Way Back to You" (1966), "I've Got You Under My Skin" (1966), "Tell It to the Rain" (1966), and "C'mon Marianne" (1967). Their albums also were among Phillips' best-selling albums.

In the late 1960's the Four Seasons' popularity ebbed as rock styles changed. Their attempt to catch onto the psychedelic fad with the painstakingly produced *Genuine Imitation Life Gazette* in 1965 was a disappointing failure. *Half and Half*, released in May, 1970, made the lower end of the charts then faded. By then it was evident that their popularity as recording artists had crested.

Soon all the members from a decade earlier but Valli and Gaudio were gone. Crewe returned as a producer in 1972, but nothing they recorded worked. Nevertheless, they remained a major draw in nightclubs and on the college circuit as they continued touring.

Valli's Solo Career. Although Valli stayed with the Four Seasons, he had solo aspirations that began in his teenage years. As early as 1953 he recorded his first single, "My Mother's Eyes." Through his long performing career he often juggled solo and group performing. In 1967, while the Four Seasons were still going strong, he scored his first solo hit, "I Can't Take My Eyes Off You." With the decline in the group's popularity in the 1970's, he put more energy into his solo act and had a hearing problem that had threatened permanently to deafen him surgically corrected.

In 1974 Valli signed with Private Stock and had several solo hits, beginning with "My Eyes Adored You" (written by Crewe and Kenny Nolan), which reached number 1 in 1975. He had less success, however, with a series of albums on several labels, including *Frankie Valli Is the Word* (1978), *The Very Best of Frankie Valli* (1979), and *Heaven Above Me* (1981).

By this time the Four Seasons were nearly defunct; however, they soon made an impressive comeback. "Who Loves You" reached number 3 in 1975, and "December 1963 (Oh, What a Night)" hit number 1 a year later. Despite these successes, Valli announced in early 1977 that he was through performing with the Four Seasons. The following year he enjoyed his biggest solo hit ever with the theme from the popular film *Grease*, which sold more than seven million records.

In 1980 Valli and Gaudio—who together owned the group and the rights to its name—reassembled the Four Seasons with guitarists Larry Lingle and Don Ciccone, keyboardist Jerry Corbetta, and drummer Gerry Polci. Afterward, the group underwent further changes but usually worked with at least six members.

—R. Kent Rasmussen

For the Record

The use of "December 1963 (Oh, What a Night)" on the sound track of the hit film *Forrest Gump* in 1994 put the Four Seasons song back on the charts, where it had reached number 1 nearly two decades earlier. Thanks to its reincarnation, it set an all-time record for a single, with a total of fifty weeks on the charts.

SELECT DISCOGRAPHY

The Four Seasons

■ SINGLES

"Sherry," 1962
"Big Girls Don't Cry," 1965
"Walk Like a Man," 1963
"Dawn (Go Away)," 1964
"Rag Doll," 1964
"Let's Hang On!" 1965
"Working My Way Back to You," 1966
"I've Got You Under My Skin," 1966

■ ALBUMS

Four Seasons Entertain You, 1965
Working My Way Back to You, 1965
Genuine Imitation Life Gazette, 1965
Gold Vault of Hits, 1967
Half and Half, 1970
Chameleon, 1972
Story, 1975
Who Loves You, 1975
Helicon, 1977
Frankie Valli and the Four Seasons: 25th Anniversary Collection, 1987 (4-CD set with both group and solo material)

Frankie Valli

■ ALBUMS

Frankie Valli Is the Word, 1978
The Very Best of Frankie Valli, 1979 (compilation)
Heaven Above Me, 1981

SELECT AWARDS

Rock and Roll Hall of Fame, inducted 1990 (early 1960's members of the Four Seasons)

SEE ALSO: Beach Boys, The; Beatles, The.

The Four Tops

ORIGINAL MEMBERS: Levi Stubbs (b. Levi Stubbles, 1938), Renaldo "Obie" Benson (b. 1947), Abdul "Duke" Fakir (b. 1935), Lawrence Payton (1938-1997)

FIRST ALBUM RELEASE: *Four Tops*, 1965

MUSICAL STYLES: Rhythm and blues, soul, pop

In the 1960's, Berry Gordy's Motown Records dominated the rhythm and blues and pop charts. Among the most popular groups in America were four Motown groups: Diana Ross and the Supremes, the Temptations, Smokey Robinson and the Miracles, and the Four Tops. All four groups were known for their exceptional talent, but over the decades the Four Tops outlasted their Motown peers as well as other rhythm and blues, pop, and soul groups. While other groups experienced personnel changes, the Four Tops did not. Indeed, the group remained intact for forty-three years until death claimed one of its members.

The Early Years. Four teenage natives of Detroit, Michigan—Levi Stubbs (lead singer), Duke Fakir (first tenor), Lawrence Payton (second tenor), and Obie Benson (baritone)—began singing together in 1954 at local social functions and in amateur contests. The young men were known as the Four Aims, and a major musical influence was the popular rhythm and blues group the Ink Spots. The Four Aims sang backup or appeared as an opening act for such established performers as Count Basie, Brook Benton, Billy Eckstine, and Della Reese and evolved into a popular nightclub act. During this period, another group called the Ames Brothers also became increasingly popular. As a result, the Four Aims decided to change the group's name to avoid being mistaken for the Ames Brothers. Stubbs, Fakir, Payton, and Benson selected the name the Four Tops and recorded songs for Chess Records, Red Top Records, and Columbia Records but produced no hit singles.

The Motown Sound. After performing for nearly a decade, the Four Tops signed with Berry Gordy's Motown Records in 1963. This was the same year that Gordy assigned the highly talented songwriting-producing team of Brian Holland, Lamont Dozier, and Eddie Holland to write for the Supremes, who were known as the no-hit Supremes. Once the Supremes began recording Holland, Dozier, and Holland songs, they became musical superstars. The three producers worked their same magic on the Four Tops and created songs that showcased Stubbs's powerful voice as well as the group's exquisite four-part harmony. From 1964 to 1967, the Four Tops recorded their biggest hits, each written by Holland, Dozier, and Holland, including "Baby I Need Your Loving" (the Four Tops' first gold record), "I Can't Help Myself (Sugar Pie, Honey Bunch)," "It's the Same Old Song," "Something About You," "Shake Me, Wake Me (When It's Over)," "Reach out I'll Be There," "Standing in the Shadows of Love," "Bernadette," and "You Keep Running Away."

The Four Tops' hit records proved that they, along with Motown's other superstars, were instrumental in creating the legendary Motown Sound, which Gordy labeled the "Voice of Young America." Gordy envisioned the Motown Sound

The Four Tops in 1966 (Express Newspapers/Archive Photos)

as good music that people of all races would enjoy and as a way to abolish racial barriers in popular music. The Four Tops helped Gordy achieve his goals. The Four Tops began to be in demand everywhere and appeared at a variety of venues, including the Apollo, the Copacabana, the Hollywood Bowl, Coconut Grove, and Carnegie Hall. They also toured abroad. In England, they sold out the famed Royal Albert Hall twice in one evening.

During the 1970's, the Four Tops recorded three successful albums with the Supremes: *The Magnificent Seven* (1970), *The Return of the Magnificent Seven* (1971), and *Dynamite* (1971). In 1983 the Four Tops sang with another legendary Motown group, the Temptations, during the Emmy-winning television special *Twenty-Five Years of Motown.* On the television program, the two groups participated in a "battle of the bands," during which the Four Tops sang classic Temptations' hits while the Temptations sang classic Four Tops' hits. Although both groups gave stellar performances, there was one major difference: The Four Tops had no replacement personnel, while only Melvin Franklin and Otis Williams remained as original members of the Temptations.

Legacy. The Four Tops continued singing without a change in personnel until 1997, when Lawrence Payton died. Until his death, the four men sang together without a personnel change for forty-three years, a feat that no other rhythm-and-blues or pop recording group has matched. The remaining Four Tops, Levi Stubbs, Obie Benson, and Duke Fakir, agreed that Payton could not be replaced and therefore continued on as a trio.

The Four Tops recorded more than thirty-six albums, and the group sold more than 50 million records worldwide. For more than four decades, the group set recording and performing standards for other groups to emulate. Of even greater significance is the fact that the Four Tops recorded some of the most popular songs of the twentieth century. —*Linda M. Carter*

SELECT DISCOGRAPHY

■ SINGLES

"Baby I Need Your Loving," 1964

"Without the One You Love (Life's Not Worthwhile)," 1964

"Ask the Lonely," 1965

"I Can't Help Myself (Sugar Pie," 1965

"It's the Same Old Song," 1965

For the Record

The Four Tops' amazing career would have ended in 1988 had they not been delayed by the taping of a television program in England that caused them to miss Pan Am flight 103. The plane crashed in Lockerbie, Scotland, and there were no survivors.

"Something About You," 1965
"Shake Me, Wake Me (When It's Over)," 1966
"Reach out I'll Be There," 1966
"Standing in the Shadows of Love," 1966
"Seven Rooms of Gloom," 1967
"I'll Turn to Stone," 1967
"Bernadette," 1967
"You Keep Running Away," 1967
"Walk Away Renee," 1968
"If I Were a Carpenter," 1968
"Still Water (Love)," 1970
"MacArthur Park," 1971
"(It's the Way) Nature Planned It," 1972
"Ain't No Woman (Like the One I Got)," 1973
"When She Was My Girl," 1981

SELECT AWARDS
Rock and Roll Hall of Fame, inducted 1990
Hollywood Walk of Fame, received star 1997

SEE ALSO: Supremes, The; Temptations, The.

Peter Frampton

BORN: Beckenham, Kent, England; April 22, 1950
FIRST ALBUM RELEASE: *Wind of Change*, 1972
MUSICAL STYLES: Pop, rock and roll

An established session guitarist, Peter Frampton worked with a number of British bands before going solo in 1971. Frampton produced one of the top-selling albums of the 1970's with the 1976 release of *Frampton Comes Alive!*, a double album recorded in San Francisco. *Frampton Comes Alive!* featured his trademark "talkbox," a guitar effects device that allows words to be formed by routing the sound through a mouthpiece.

Frampton's Camel. Frampton first played guitar in public at a Boy Scout talent show when he was only eight years old. He performed Cliff Richard's "A Girl Like You." Eight years later, in 1966, he joined the British band the Herd. In 1969, along with Steve Marriott (formerly of the Herd and Small Faces), he formed Humble Pie. Frampton and Marriott claimed to have created Humble Pie in an attempt to gain credibility as musicians instead of being "mere pop idols." After three albums with Humble Pie, including the relatively successful *As Safe As Yesterday Is* (1969), Frampton decided to go solo. The impetus for this decision came when George Harrison invited Frampton to play on Harrison's epic *All Things Must Pass* album in 1972. Humble Pie continued on through many incarnations until the death of Marriott in 1991.

Signed to a solo contract with A&M Records, Frampton collaborated with, among others, Ringo Starr and Billy Preston for his debut album *Winds of Change* (1972). *Winds of Change* failed to reach the Top 100 in the U.S. album charts and

Peter Frampton (Fotos International/Archive Photos)

was followed one year later by *Frampton's Camel*, which also failed to crack the Top 100. However, through steady touring and annual album releases, Frampton began to make his mark. 1974's *Something's Happening* peaked at number 25. The next year, *Frampton* topped out at number 32. At this point, Frampton and his band were performing as many as two hundred concerts per year. The blue-collar approach paid off when the breakthrough to superstardom came in 1976.

"Do You Feel Like We Do." In April of 1976, Frampton released the double album *Frampton Comes Alive!* Recorded live at the Winterland Ballroom in San Francisco, the album contained the Frampton trademark songs "Show Me the Way," "Baby I Love Your Way," and the voicebox classic "Do You Feel Like We Do." All three singles reached at least number 12 on the U.S. charts. The parent album topped the album charts for a total of ten weeks in 1976, including five weeks in a row at number 1. *Frampton Comes Alive!* stayed on the Billboard album charts for nearly two years and eventually sold in excess of fifteen million copies.

In 1977, Frampton released *I'm in You*, which topped out at number 2 on the U.S. album charts en route to double-platinum sales. *I'm in You* also produced two moderately successful singles, "I'm in You," which peaked at number 2 in the United States, and a remake of Stevie Wonder's "Signed, Sealed, Delivered (I'm Yours)," which, with Wonder playing harmonica, reached number 18.

Sgt. Pepper's Lonely Hearts Club Band. In July of 1978, Robert Stigwood's torpid film version of the Beatles' famous album *Sgt. Pepper's Lonely Hearts Club Band*, featuring Frampton as Billy Shears, reached U.S. theaters. The film was blasted by critics, but the sound track, which featured Frampton, the Bee Gees, Aerosmith, Steve Martin, Billy Preston, and Earth, Wind, and Fire, was a success, peaking at number 5 on the U.S. album charts.

After recovering from a near-fatal car crash in the Bahamas in 1978, Frampton's 1979 album *Where I Should Be* proved to be a moderate success, topping out at number 19 on the U.S. charts. Two years passed before *Breaking All the Rules* was released in 1981, followed one year later by *The Art of Control*. Poor album sales led to Frampton and A&M Records parting company by the end of the year.

Signed by Virgin/Atlantic Records, Frampton released the synthesizer-driven *Premonition* in 1986 to a lukewarm critical response and lackluster sales. After a brief period of silence, Frampton released the weak-selling *When All the Pieces Fit* in 1989. Returning to session work, Frampton worked with such acts as Lynyrd Skynyrd before returning to touring as a part of "classic rock" package events. —*B. Keith Murphy*

SELECT DISCOGRAPHY

■ ALBUMS

Wind of Change, 1972
Frampton's Camel, 1973
Something's Happening, 1974
Frampton, 1975
Frampton Comes Alive!, 1976 (live)
Where I Should Be, 1979
Breaking All the Rules, 1981
When All the Pieces Fit, 1989
Peter Frampton, 1994
Frampton Comes Alive II, 1995 (live)

SEE ALSO: Bee Gees, The; Fleetwood Mac; Harrison, George; Wonder, Stevie.

Aretha Franklin

BORN: Memphis, Tennessee; March 25, 1942

FIRST SINGLE RELEASE: "Today I Sing the Blues," 1960

MUSICAL STYLES: Soul, blues, gospel, rhythm and blues, pop, rock and roll

The reigning "Queen of Soul" for more than four decades, Aretha Franklin is one of the most prominent female vocalists in the history of popular music. The quintessential crossover artist, Franklin has played the Apollo Theatre as well as the Lincoln Center. She received an award from Martin Luther King, Jr., and entertained at a Presidential Inauguration. She has performed duets with everyone from Smokey Robinson to Frank

Aretha Franklin (Paul Natkin)

Sinatra. These days, when she sings her most famous anthem, "Respect," it is no longer an angry demand; it is more a confident statement of fact for an extraordinary woman's extraordinary career.

The Gospel Legacy. Franklin was raised with the gospel music of the black church and grew up with urban rhythm and blues. Her father, Reverend C. L. Franklin, one of the most famous black preachers in the North and an accomplished gospel performer, presided over a large congregation at Detroit's New Bethel Baptist Church. Franklin was six years old when her mother walked out on the family. Barbara Franklin, who also had a great gospel voice, died four years later. The three Franklin sisters routinely sang at their father's church and accompanied him on the evangelical circuit. Franklin met legendary gospel singers Mahalia Jackson, Clara Ward, James Cleveland, and Sam Cooke on these tours, and their musical influence stayed with her throughout her career.

The Long Apprenticeship. While still in her teens touring on the gospel circuit with her father, Franklin flirted with the idea of trying the big pop and rhythm-and-blues markets. Gospel performer Sam Cooke, who had just made the switch to pop, encouraged the young girl to sign with his label, RCA. Instead, Franklin was enticed to go to New York City and Columbia Records by John Hammond. Hammond's resume was impressive; he had promoted the careers of Billie Holiday and Bessie Smith and would soon sign the 1960's folk icon, Bob Dylan. Despite Hammond's knack as a talent scout and producer, Franklin was mishandled at Columbia. Her first efforts with the label, "Today I Sing the Blues" (1960), "Won't Be Long" (1961), and "Operation Heartbreak" (1961) received limited distribution in an exclusively black market. After recording ten albums with the label, Franklin earned only one minor pop hit, a cover of the old Al Jolson show tune "Rock-a-Bye Your Baby with a Dixie Melody" (1961). Hammond intended to turn Franklin into a female Nat "King" Cole, a suave black song stylist acceptable to a broader white audience. In reality, the label's strategy only pulled Franklin further away from her gospel roots and rhythm-and-blues repertory. After six years, Franklin ended up owing Columbia money while other former gospel singers such as Cooke, Wilson Pickett, and Sam and Dave, who had signed with other labels, enjoyed success in the crossover market. As soon as her contract with Columbia ended, Franklin jumped ship to Atlantic Records where she began a long and productive association with Jerry Wexler.

The Atlantic Records Years. The years at Columbia served as an important apprenticeship, developing Franklin's versatile range and teaching her the subtleties of instrumentation and arrangement. By the time she teamed up with producer Wexler and arranger Arif Mardin, she knew how she wanted to sound. From their first sessions together in Muscle Shoals, Alabama, Wexler allowed Franklin an unusual degree of artistic freedom. Wexler and his team, fifteen years before, had employed the same approach to develop a distinctive niche for Ray Charles. The combination of mellow, fluid Southern soul that marked the Atlantic recordings and the more hard-hitting Detroit rhythm and blues and gospel foundations that Franklin brought with her yielded a phenomenal run of hits. The string of Atlantic successes included "I Never Loved a Man (the Way I Love You)" (1967), "Respect" (1967), "Chain of Fools" (1968), "Think" (1968), "Share Your Love with Me" (1969), "Call Me" (1970), and "Spirit in the Dark" (1970). With her incredibly wide range, Franklin seemed unafraid of tackling works composed by others, from blues to mainstream pop. Few singers, before or since, could handle both Otis Redding's rhythm-and-blues tune "Respect" and John Lennon and Paul McCartney's pop classic "Eleanor Rigby." She could sound earthily sensual in Carole King and Gerry Goffin's "(You Make Me Feel Like) A Natural Woman" (1967), or sophisticatedly upbeat in Burt Bacharach and Hal David's "I Say a Little Prayer" (1968). Franklin was the first rhythm-and-blues and soul artist to successfully record albums in addition to singles. These Atlantic-produced albums encompass everything from uptempo dance hits and down-and-dirty blues to the Franklin speciality—evocative and dreamy ballads.

Public Prominence, Private Turmoil. Franklin's musical style achieved national stardom among a broad multicultural and multigenerational audience. Her legions of fans made her the female recording artist with the most million–sellers in the history of the industry. A symbol of black as well as feminist pride, Franklin represented the rare black female who had achieved both creative control and financial inde-

For the Record

Aretha Franklin deserves her crown as the Queen of Soul. Her four-decade career has been punctuated by remarkable achievements. The first female inductee in the Rock and Roll Hall of Fame and the youngest Kennedy Center Honoree, she has won more Grammy Awards than any other female entertainer in history. She has graced the cover of *Time*, and she sang at the inauguration of President Bill Clinton and the funerals of Mahalia Jackson and Martin Luther King, Jr.

pendence. Her personal life, however, had been in disarray for several years. Before her marriage to Ted White in 1961, Franklin in her teenage years had given birth to two sons. Always reticent in interviews and protective of her own and her family's privacy, Franklin never publicly revealed the identities of her first two children's fathers. Her third son, Teddy Jr., born during her marriage to White, was also a musician and has worked as a guitarist with his mother's band. Franklin's deteriorating marriage to White was widely covered by the media. On at least one occasion, White hit Franklin in public and, on another, he shot her production manager. The couple divorced in 1969. During the same year, Franklin's father, active in civil rights issues in Detroit and nationally, organized a conference for black separatists that erupted in a violent confrontation with Detroit police. Franklin was reported to have begun drinking heavily during these troubled times and she had a few skirmishes with the law for reckless driving and disorderly conduct.

The 1970's brought more public success and personal changes. A relationship with her road manager Ken Cunningham produced a fourth son. A second marriage to actor Glynn Turman in 1978 lasted six years. Her concerts had evolved into Las Vegas-style megaproductions, and Franklin acquired a reputation for outrageously revealing and less-than-flattering costume excesses. While musical tastes changed, Franklin's career careened on. Still the unchallenged pop diva, she left Atlantic Records in 1980 for a deal with Arista, designed to position her for another commercial blitz. She collaborated with George Benson on the 1981 release *Love All the Hurt Away* and worked with Luther Vandross that same year to produce *Jump to It.* Cast in the 1980 blockbuster film *The Blues Brothers,* Franklin parodied her usual extravagantly glamorous image by singing "Think" in a dowdy apron and fuzzy slippers. This cameo appearance introduced her music to a whole new generation.

Once again, however, her personal life was marked by tragedy. Franklin moved to Detroit to nurse her father, who had lapsed into a coma after being shot in a 1979 burglary at his home. By the end of the decade, Franklin had suffered the deaths of her father, her sister and collaborator Carolyn, and her brother and manager Cecil. Remarkably, she kept recording for an ever-expanding audience. Responding to changes in the music industry in the 1980's, she produced music videos that received extensive coverage on MTV. Her eclectic range and crossover appeal had never been greater. The 1985 album *Who's Zoomin' Who* delivered several hit singles, a Top-20 duet with the British group the Eurythmics, and guest performances by Dizzy Gillespie, Carlos Santana, and Tom Petty's Heartbreakers. Her next album in 1986, *Aretha,* featured a version of the Rolling Stones signature piece "Jumpin' Jack Flash," arranged and accompanied by Stones guitarist Keith Richards. That album also produced a Grammy Award-winning duet with pop crooner George Michael, "I Knew You Were Waiting (for Me)."

An Enduring Legacy. Aretha Franklin's achievements are legendary: She was the first woman inducted into the Rock and Roll Hall of Fame in 1987, the youngest recipient of a Kennedy Center Honors award, and the winner of more Grammy Awards than any other female performer. Leaving a trail of recordings in every genre behind her, from pure gospel and funky soul to blissful ballads, Franklin did not slow down in the 1990's. She would continue to tour, write, arrange, and record her own material. She would also sample the creative efforts of younger talent, working with artists such as Sean "Puffy" Combs. An international superstar, Franklin has earned the title "Queen of Soul." She is a larger-than-life icon of twentieth century popular culture. Her work changed the complexion of American music, bringing the races and the generations together and fusing gospel, rhythm and blues, soul, and pop to create a distinctive and enduring sound.

—Janice Monti-Belkaoui

SELECT DISCOGRAPHY

■ ALBUMS

The Tender, the Moving, the Swinging Aretha Franklin, 1962

I Never Loved a Man the Way I Loved You, 1967

Aretha: Lady Soul, 1968

Aretha Now, 1968
Aretha Franklin: Soul '69, 1969
Aretha's Greatest Hits, 1971
Young, Gifted, and Black, 1972
Amazing Grace, 1972 (with James Cleveland)
The Best of Aretha Franklin, 1973
Love All the Hurt Away, 1981
Jump to It, 1982
Who's Zoomin' Who, 1985
Aretha, 1986
The Queen of Soul, 1992
Aretha's Greatest Hits (1980-1994), 1994

SELECT AWARDS
Grammy Awards for Best R&B Recording (with Jerry Wexler) and Best R&B Solo Vocal Performance, Female, for "Respect," 1967
Grammy Award for Best Soul Gospel Performance for *Amazing Grace*, 1972
Grammy Awards for Best R&B Vocal Performance, Female, for *Aretha* and Best R&B Performance by a Duo or Group with Vocal for "I Knew You Were Waiting (for Me)" (with George Michael), 1987
Rock and Roll Hall of Fame, inducted 1987
Grammy Legend Award, 1991
Grammy Award for Lifetime Achievement, 1994
Kennedy Center Honors, 1994

SEE ALSO: Benson, George; Charles, Ray; Cole, Nat "King"; Cooke, Sam; Dylan, Bob; Jackson, Mahalia; James, Etta; Lennon, John; McCartney, Paul; Michael, George / Wham!; Pickett, Wilson; Robinson, Smokey; Sam and Dave.

Lefty Frizzell

BORN: Corsicana, Texas; March 31, 1928
DIED: Nashville, Tennessee; July 19, 1975
FIRST SINGLE RELEASE: "If You've Got the Money, I've Got the Time" / "I Love You a Thousand Ways," 1950
MUSICAL STYLE: Country

Born to an oil-field worker and his wife, William Orville (Lefty) Frizzell and his six bothers and sisters moved frequently from town to town in eastern Texas and western Arkansas. Living in poverty, Lefty had to quit school before he finished the sixth grade. When he was twelve years old his mother bought a guitar for him from a tenant farmer, who taught him to play a few chords. His main inspiration was Jimmie Rodgers, to whom he listened every night on records. His real hero, however, was Ernest Tubb. Frizzell memorized all his songs and played them on guitar. It is said that Frizzell got his nickname after winning a schoolyard fight with a boy much bigger than he was, though the accuracy of this story is subject to some dispute.

Early Days. Frizzell began singing at Saturday night dances in 1943 to help his family get enough to eat. (His father disappeared into the Army after volunteering at age forty-three.) His mother got him his first radio job at a small station in Paris, Texas, in 1944, a fifteen-minute early-morning program of solo playing and singing. The next year he married Alice Lee Harper, a Texas girl. They moved to Dallas and then New Mexico, where their first child, Lois Aleta, was born. For several months Frizzell worked as a bus driver for a group of missionaries traveling from town to town throughout the Southwest. While on these trips he began writing songs and sending them to his wife.

In 1947 Frizzell had another radio show, a daily fifteen-minute program that paid $3.75 a week. The show originated in Roswell, New Mexico, where the young father also performed every Saturday night at a bar called the Cactus Garden. Here he began "fooling around," as he put it, with the "wild gals" who chased cowboys and cowboy singers. One summer night a fourteen-year old girl was "slam-banged" in the parking lot, as she reported to the sheriff, by three musicians, one of whom was Lefty Frizzell. He pleaded guilty to statutory rape and spent the next six months in the county jail. While in prison he wrote more songs to his wife, creating a series of songs begging for forgiveness. One of these was entitled "A Thousand Ways."

After he was released from jail, Frizzell and his wife and child moved frequently. He worked on oil wells as a roustabout, and he sang in honky-tonk saloons in western Texas and eastern New Mexico. In July, 1950, he had his first recording session in Dallas with a group called the Tune Toppers. Two of the songs became extremely popular and were headed to the top of the country music charts by early 1951: "I Love You a Thousand Ways" and "If You've Got the Money, I've Got the Time." This success led to Frizzell's first appearance on the Grand Ole Opry on December 30, 1950. It also led to money, women, and great quantities of liquor. A party had begun, and Frizzell never wanted it to end.

Rise and Fall. The year 1951 saw great success for Frizzell. He toured with Hank Williams and had three songs in *Billboard's* Country Top 10: "I Want to Be with You Always," "Look What Thoughts Will Do," and "I Love You a Thousand Ways." Each song stressed themes of joy, casual romance, and a forgiving or nonexistent wife. He made his first national television appearance and joined the Grand Ole Opry as a regular. Frizzell now drove a Cadillac, had his own tour bus (driven by his father), and had a major problem with alcohol. He drank almost constantly, leading to numerous accidents. He gained a reputation as a singer with endless numbers of girlfriends who was never prepared or on time for a performance. His shows continued to break attendance records, however, and he had enough money to buy a new house in Beaumont, Texas, for his wife, who was pregnant again, as well an airplane. The new child, Rickey Rodger, was born in December of 1951.

In the next year he had seven best-selling songs, but these would be his last for more than ten years. He quit the Opry in 1952 and signed with a new manager, but he was unable to overcome his reputation as a unreliable, heavy-drinking, troublemaker. By the end of 1953 he was twenty-five years old, was almost broke, and seemed to be near the end of his career. He sold his house and his airplane and moved to Bakersfield, California, where another son was born. In 1958 he cut a Marty Robbins tune, "Cigarettes and Coffee Blues," that was his first hit in six years. Then he recorded "The Long Black Veil," a great song that became a classic but never made it to the Top 10. (It was later recorded in 1968 by the Band for their first album.) Frizzell's career hit bottom in 1961, when he was playing for thirty-five dollars a night in Bakersfield bars. In an attempt to rebuild his life he moved his family to Nashville, Tennessee, where he checked into a clinic for his drinking problem.

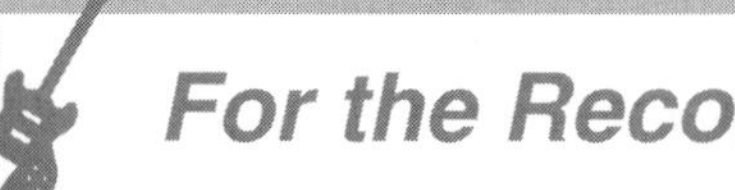

For the Record

Frizzell had a remarkable singing style—he would take short, simple words and hold them out, adding extra notes and syllables. He once said, "To me, every word has a feeling about it. . . . I want to hold one word through a whole line of melody, to linger with it all the way down. I didn't want to let go of that no more than I wanted to let go of the woman I loved. I didn't want to lose it."

The Last Years. His efforts to beat his alcoholism unfortunately had little success. He tried to start his own music company, Golden Eye Music, and had two songs on the charts in 1964-1965, "Saginaw, Michigan"—a song about a poor boy meeting a rich girl and her mean-spirited father, which went to number 1—and the very sad tune "She's Gone, Gone, Gone." Nothing else made it. Frizzell's wife became a "born-again" Christian and threw him out of their house many times for drinking. All he wanted to do was write, sing, and fish, but he mostly drank. He tried singing at rodeos. He signed a contract with ABC records in 1972, but he was worn out, overweight, and constantly drunk. His election that year to the Songwriters Hall of Fame did not improve his career. A few songs from the period, written with Whitey Shafer, captured his mood: "That's the Way Love Goes," "I Never Go Around Mirrors" (possibly one of the saddest, most heartbreaking songs ever recorded), and "I Can't Get over You to Save My Life." The lyrics reveal his loneliness, desperation, and fear of dying. His greatest fear, he said, was to die by himself.

He continued making appearances, and in August, 1974, he recorded "Life's Like Poetry" by Merle Haggard. This would be his last recording. His wife finally filed for divorce in April, 1975, and he gave his last concert in Indianapolis, Indiana, in July. A few days later, on July 18, he suffered a massive stroke, alone in his Nashville house, and died of cardiac arrest on his way to the hospital at the age of forty-seven. Frizzell's songs and music influenced many country singers, including Johnny Cash, Stoney Edwards, and Willie Nelson. His influence was most strongly seen in the career of Merle Haggard, who learned much from Frizzell—and tried to copy his singing style—when they were both living in Bakersfield.

—Leslie V. Tischauser

SELECT DISCOGRAPHY

■ SINGLES

"If You've Got the Money, I've Got the Time" / "I Love You a Thousand Ways," 1950
"Always Late (with Your Kisses)" / "Mom and Dad's Waltz," 1951
"The Darkest Moment (Is Just Before the Light of Day)," 1953
"You're Humbuggin' Me" / "Cigarettes and Coffee Blues," 1958
"Knock Again, True Love" / "The Long Black Veil," 1959
"When It Rains the Blues" / "Saginaw, Michigan," 1963
"She's Gone, Gone, Gone" / "Confused," 1965
"That's the Way Love Goes" / "I Never Go Around Mirrors," 1973

■ ALBUMS

The Legendary Lefty Frizzell, 1973
The Best of Lefty Frizzell, 1991
Lefty Frizzell: Life's Like Poetry, 1992 (12-CD set)

SELECT AWARDS

Nashville Songwriter's Hall of Fame, inducted 1972
Country Music Hall of Fame, inducted 1982

SEE ALSO: Cash, Johnny; Haggard, Merle; Nelson, Willie; Rodgers, Jimmie; Tubb, Ernest.

The Fugees

ORIGINAL MEMBERS: Wyclef "Clef" Jean (b. 1971), Lauryn "L" Hill (b. 1976), Prakazrel "Pras" Michel (b. 1973)
FIRST ALBUM RELEASE: *Blunted on Reality*, 1994
MUSICAL STYLES: Hip-hop, funk, rhythm and blues, folk

In 1991, two high school students, Lauryn Hill and Prakazrel Michel, began rapping together in South Orange, New Jersey. Their group, originally called the Tranzlator Crew, soon evolved from a duo to a trio with the addition of Wyclef Jean, Michel's cousin who had recently moved from Brooklyn to New Jersey. What emerged was a three-headed hip-hop monster, prepared to define their place in the world of rap music.

Tranzlator Crew. Blessed with Michel's keen business sense and production expertise, Hill's buttery vocals, and Jean's eclectic musical sensibilities, the Tranzlator Crew began making plans for their first album. Unfortunately, in the early 1990's, many record companies resisted signing any acts other than gangsta rappers. The style had a choke hold on the rap industry, and many record company executives were more interested in exploiting the popularity of gangsta rap than promoting and encouraging the overall growth of hip-hop.

After a series of unsuccessful auditions, the trio's luck finally changed. Two talent scouts from Philadelphia, Pennsylvania, Chris Schwartz and Joe Nicolo from RuffHouse Records, watched as the Tranzlator Crew rapped and sang John Lennon's "Imagine," culminating with Hill's earthy alto floating over Jean's acoustic guitar. When the audition was over, the Tranzlator Crew had found a label.

The group's first album, *Blunted on Reality* (1994), was greeted with a lukewarm reception by the rap world. While some critics praised its innovative sound, others felt the album was a complete failure. Furthermore, the album's overall thematic approach as an alternative form of hip-hop distanced the group from their rap peers. Critics suggested that Hill leave the group and embark on a solo project, an endeavor which would make proper use of her talent. Despite such skepticism, two singles from the album gave a glimpse at the group's potential: "Vocab" and "Nappy Heads." Even though they were remixes of the original songs, these tracks demonstrated the vitality of the group's music as well as their dedication to the fundamental musical creativity and lyrical expertise that constitute rap music.

Despite their rocky start, the Tranzlator Crew remained determined to succeed. The group changed their name to the Fugees, renegotiated their contract with RuffHouse, and embarked on a new project. According to the group, the first album's failure was primarily due to their willingness to sacrifice their collective vision for the album in order to obtain a record deal. The group returned to South Orange and the Booga Basement, the production studio spearheaded by Jean and sponsored in large part by Hill with the money she made as a soap opera actress as a teen. It was here that the true artistic vision of the group became a reality.

Refugees. The failure of the group's first album forced them to think seriously about their place in the hip-hop world. The name Fugees (short for refugees) was originally chosen as a nod to Michel and Jean's Haitian roots. Michel explained, "We decided to call ourselves the Fugees because when we were growing up, people used to call us refugees—as if we were the only people seeking refuge from our land. What we're saying is that everyone is a refugee, whether mentally or physically, from your country, from your life. And it's in that sense that our music is refugee music."

Jean, a preacher's son, emigrated with his family to Brooklyn from Haiti when he was nine. Michel, the son of Haitian parents (his father was a church deacon) attended Rutgers University in New Jersey as a philosophy major. Hill, who studied at Columbia University, considered pursuing a degree in history. For some listeners, the group's diverse interests, cultural roots, and intellectual pursuits place them outside of the stereotypical roughneck hip-hop image. In essence, they have at times found themselves to be refugees from the industry and their peers. For critics who questioned their skills on the first album, it was time to settle the score.

The Score. When the Fugees released their second album, *The Score,* in 1996, they did so with the intent of revealing their unique approach to rap. With gangsta rap fading from the music scene, the industry was becoming much more open to an expansion of hip-hop beyond the self-effacing lyrics of the gangsta-rap genre. The Fugees wanted to voice the fundamental lyrical and musical founda-

The Fugees: Wyclef Jean, Lauryn Hill, Prakazrel Michel (Ruff House/ Columbia/Marc Baptiste)

For the Record

"I was fifteen years old, makin' my little money off the soaps. Wyclef was so determined. . . . I used to hit him off with whatever I could every now and then and he would buy another piece of equipment. Over time, he accumulated a complete studio." —*Lauryn "L" Hill*

tions of hip-hop. In doing so, they pushed the form to new levels, similar to groups such as Arrested Development and the Roots, where live music, jazz sensibilities, and a keen social awareness often placed them at odds with more mainstream, popular rap music.

The Score has a film motif, with each song representing a different scene which adds to the flavor and texture of the entire album. With "Ready or Not," Hill's layered harmonies fell thick over listeners' ears, demanding that they prepare for the second coming of the Fugees. This song displays the group's ability to combine humor, talent, and knowledge in a package that can reach, and even affect the lives of, black children. The remainder of the album presents a musical montage—a collection of images that build upon and transcend earlier themes. In "Zealots," Jean responds to critics who said that Hill should venture out on her own. "The Beast" takes a look at police violence against African Americans, while "Fu-gee-la" plays with Teena Marie's sensual crooning classic "Ooo La La La."

Where "Family Business" expands the limit of family to those who share common oppressions, "Killing Me Softly with His Song," a cover of Roberta Flack's 1974 triple Grammy Award-winning original, establishes the themes of family and musical ancestry as vital parts of the Fugees' makeup. From "Cowboys," a song which questions the motivations of gun-toting lyricists, to "No Woman, No Cry," a cover of Bob Marley's reggae classic, the Fugees establish world music as the palette from which they paint their musical portrait.

Legacy. The Fugees' music marked the beginning of a new age of hip-hop. It was an age where healing, musicality, and experimentation would come to the fore and allow the world of hip-hop culture to define and re-define itself from within.

—*Shanna D. Greene*

SELECT DISCOGRAPHY

■ ALBUMS

Blunted on Reality, 1994

The Score, 1996

Bootleg Versions, 1996

SELECT AWARDS

Grammy Awards for Best Rap Album for *The Score* and Best R&B Performance by a Duo or Group with Vocal for "Killing Me Softly with His Song," 1996

SEE ALSO: De La Soul; Grandmaster Flash; Hendrix, Jimi; Queen Latifah.

Funkadelic. *See* George Clinton / Parliament / Funkadelic

G

Kenny G

(Kenneth Gorelick)

BORN: Seattle, Washington; June 5, 1956
FIRST SOLO ALBUM RELEASE: *Kenny G*, 1982
MUSICAL STYLES: Jazz, pop, rhythm and blues, soft rock

Kenny G is one of the few instrumental performers to have achieved the same levels of popularity and attention enjoyed by vocalists. Starting out as a backup musician, he recorded his first solo album in 1982 and continued going strong as a solo performer with subsequent releases.

Inspiration. Kenneth Gorelick grew up in Seattle, Washington. He became interested in the saxophone when he was ten years old after seeing a saxophonist performing on *The Ed Sullivan Show.* His mother encouraged him and rented a saxophone. He played the instrument in school bands and gained a reputation for diligent and consistent practice. While his experiences at Franklin High School helped him learn to read music notation and work with other musicians, he also developed a keen musical ear by playing along with records at home. Grover Washington, Jr., was one of his early influences. The subtle blues inflections of these artists required great control over tuning, and, by trying to imitate them, Kenny G independently developed a musical vocabulary that would form the basis of his own unique style.

When Kenny G was seventeen years old, an unusual opportunity to apply these skills arose when famous rhythm-and-blues singer Barry White, giving a concert in Seattle, needed a saxophonist to play in his Love Unlimited Orchestra. In Kenny G's own words, "They needed a sax player who could read and solo in a soulful style, and I really was the only person in Seattle that could do both." Kenny G's high school band director recommended him for the job, and, bypassing the usual route of wedding receptions and nightclubs, the young student, playing his first paid performance, found himself onstage with a major recording artist. He rose to the occasion and got a standing ovation for his solo.

Kenny G (Paul Natkin)

Practice Makes Perfect. Kenny G continued to work hard at both music and academics. He also played with pianist Liberace and again with Barry White during the singer's subsequent visits to Seattle. After graduating from Franklin High School, Kenny G went to the University of Washington (1974-1978), where he studied music under Roy Cummings, the university's jazz band director. Cummings broadened Kenny G's horizons by exposing him to the music of great jazz saxophonists such as John Coltrane (who had reintroduced the soprano saxophone in the mid-1960's), Charlie Parker, and Sonny Rollins. Although he loved music and practiced several hours per day, Kenny G majored in accounting so that he could keep his career options open. He also took private lessons from Seattle musician Johnnie Jessen and, during his college years, maintained some of his contacts in the popular music field. He also played with Cold, Bold, and Together, a local rhythm-and-blues group.

After graduating magna cum laude from the university, Kenny G auditioned for Jeff Lorber, a musician based in Portland, Oregon. Kenny G passed the audition and joined Lorber's band, the Jeff Lorber Fusion. This was another important point in Kenny G's career, since this group, although based in the Northwest, was a nationally known act. Kenny G played with the band from 1979 to 1982. With Lorber, he toured the United States for the first time and gained valuable experience. Lorber's band recorded with Arista Records, and Kenny G attracted the attention of Arista's president, Clive Davis, who decided to record a Kenny G solo album.

Solo Stardom. Kenny G's first solo album, *Kenny G*, was recorded in 1982. It was produced by Lorber and was heavily influenced by Lorber's ideas. Kenny G's second album, *G Force* (1984), was produced by Kashif, a vocal-oriented rhythm-and-blues producer whose tastes were more in line with Kenny G's. This album sold almost 200,000 copies and helped establish Kenny G as a solo artist. Kenny G's third album, *Gravity* (1985), also produced by Kashif, was not as successful. Although Kenny G played several instruments on the album, including synthesizers, flute, and alto sax as well as his trademark soprano saxophone, the instrumentals were blended with vocal pieces. For his next album, Kenny G wanted to emphasize instrumentals and a more consistent mood, and Arista Records agreed.

The result was the hit album *Duotones*, released in 1986. In the course of working on the album, Kenny G felt that he had found his stylistic voice. *Duotones* included the single "Songbird," which rose to number 4 on *Billboard*'s pop chart. "Songbird," which eventually became a platinum single, was written for Lyndie Benson, who became his wife. Kenny G performed the song on *The Tonight Show* on network television.

The next two albums, *Silhouette* (1988), which was self-produced, and *Breathless* (1992), were internationally successful and set new sales records for instrumental music. Kenny G began to go on world tours and recorded with famous vocalists Whitney Houston, Aretha Franklin, George Benson, Michael Bolton, and Natalie Cole. His sixth album, *Live* (1989), was a double album of concert performances and was released with a companion video, which was also very popular. *Breathless* (1992), his seventh album, set a record by staying at first position on the Contemporary Jazz chart for over one hundred weeks. "Forever in Love," a single from this album, earned a Grammy Award. Kenny G's eighth album, *Miracles: The Holiday Album* (1994), set new records for sales in the holiday category and included a cover of "White Christmas." His ninth album, *The Moment* (1996), included a duet with vocalist Toni Braxton titled "That Somebody Was You."

Style. Kenny G's music is very accessible to listeners, and this has always been an important value for him. He tends to favor romantic moods with slower tempos (ballads), and his treatment of melodies is very similar to that of popular vocalists. Being an instrumentalist, however, he has often been placed in a jazz category by music industry executives. This status has been questioned by many jazz critics, who prefer more profuse improvisation and more melodic and rhythmic tension. Kenny G, however, has always presented himself as a popular musician. Since his technical abilities match those of his compatriots

For the Record

Using a technique known as "circular breathing," Kenny G set a world record for the longest note held on a wind instrument on December 1, 1997. The total time was 45 minutes and 47 seconds.

in the jazz world, his emphasis on a simpler style is more a matter of choice than necessity.

—*Alice Myers*

SELECT DISCOGRAPHY

■ ALBUMS

Kenny G, 1982
G Force, 1984
Gravity, 1985
Duotones, 1986
Silhouette, 1988
Live, 1989
Breathless, 1992
Miracles: The Holiday Album, 1994
The Moment, 1997
Six of Hearts, 1997
Havana, 1997

SELECT AWARDS

Grammy Award for Best Instrumental Composition for "Forever in Love," 1993
Hollywood Walk of Fame, received star 1997

SEE ALSO: Mangione, Chuck; White, Barry.

Ana Gabriel

BORN: Sinaloa, Mexico
FIRST ALBUM RELEASE: *Tierra de Nadie*, 1988
MUSICAL STYLES: Latin, pop

From the mid-1980's through the 1990's, Ana Gabriel, one of Mexico's premier singer-songwriters, was at or near the top of the Latin charts in the United States and many South American countries. With an explosive and gritty voice perfectly fitted to the emotional roller coaster of love, passion, and pride inherent in ranchera music, she managed to bridge the gap between traditional ranchera stars of the past and modern Latin pop stars. In "Voy a Ser" ("I'm Going to Be," 1991), for instance, she sang: "I'm going to make you love me even more than yesterday/ And after I've got you in my hands/ I'll make sure you pay dearly for your deceit," appealing to the modern woman's demand for respect. Delivered with what one critic called "the most powerful voice in Spanish-language music," Gabriel convinced her fans that she was both contemporary and true to her Mexican roots.

Though she was musically inclined from a young age, Gabriel received her musical break when she won second prize in the "Valores Juveniles" competition with her song "No Me Lastimes Mas." Soon after, she was signed by Sony Records. "Pecado Original" marked a turning point in her career and became her best-known record.

Gabriel's "Luna" (1993) was her seventh number 1 Latin hit, setting a record for a female artist and clarifying why she has been one of the biggest selling female artists of all time. After experimenting with pop rhythms on *Vivencias* (1996), she returned to her mariachi ranchera roots on *Con un Mismo Corazon* (1997), which hit the Latin Top 10, as did its first single, "A Pesar de Todos." An unusual feature of the album was the dual offering of the title track, one a solo by Gabriel, and one a duet with Mexican star Vicente Fernandez. Gabriel, who has won Latin Music awards in both the regional Mexican and pop categories, joins Selena and Proyecto Uno as the only artists to win in two different genres. —*John Powell*

SELECT DISCOGRAPHY

■ ALBUMS

Tierra de Nadie, 1988
Quien Como Tu, 1990
Un Estilo, 1990
Mi Mexico, 1991
The Best, 1992
Luna, 1993
Ayer Y Hoy, 1994
Joyas de Dos Siglos, 1995
Vivencias, 1996
Con un Mismo Corazon, 1997
The Best: The Latin Stars Series, 1998

SELECT AWARDS

Billboard Latin Music Pop Female Artist of the Year Award, 1993
Billboard Latin Music Mexican Album of the Year Award, Female, for *Con un Mismo Corazon*, 1997

SEE ALSO: Ronstadt, Linda; Selena, Jon Secada.

Peter Gabriel

BORN: Woking, Surrey, England; February 13, 1950
FIRST ALBUM RELEASE: *Peter Gabriel*, 1977 (first solo release)
MUSICAL STYLES: Rock and roll, art rock, alternative rock

From his time as lead singer for Genesis in the 1960's and early 1970's to his own successful solo career, Peter Gabriel has displayed a gift for communicating emotional experiences through his lyrics and music. Nearly all of his music has dealt with themes and stories that go well beyond the typical pop song, and Gabriel's constant striving to provide a moving experience on his albums and in live performances has made him stand out as one of the most original musicians to achieve popular success.

Beginnings. Gabriel's experiences in music began when he was a youth at Charterhouse, an elite British boarding school, where his shy and introverted nature was at great odds with the discipline of a traditional prep school education. Music became his escape from this environment, and as Gabriel trained his voice and learned to play flute, drums, and piano he also formed bonds with friends who would one day form the band Genesis.

As lead vocalist for Genesis from 1967 to 1975, Gabriel's unusual and powerful voice gave a focus to the band's often lengthy art-rock pieces. As the band matured, he brought his interest in the theater into his performances and started wearing masks and costumes to help express the mythic themes of the group's music. A shy, soft-spoken person offstage, he used the costumes and masks to free his onstage persona. Perhaps for this reason, some form of mask, costume, or makeup remained part of his live performances until the 1996 tour to support the album *So.*

As Genesis progressed, Gabriel added to the theatrical aspects of their presentation. As much as his unique voice, Gabriel's quirky sense of humor and theatrical antics made Genesis stand out among other progressive-rock bands. His last tour with the group, performing the double album *The Lamb Lies Down on Broadway* (1974), was the height of a trend of increasingly wild costumes and set designs. Gabriel had written nearly all the lyrics for the album and provided its story line (unusual for Genesis, usually a very collaborative band). The album therefore gave him a glimpse of what it might be like to work beyond the confines of the group. (The 1998 release *Genesis Archive 1967-1975* contains a powerful full performance of *The Lamb Lies Down on Broadway* from the 1975 tour.)

Peter Gabriel (Geffen/Alan Beukers)

Beyond Genesis. Feeling caught in the machine of the band's album-tour-album-tour cycle, Gabriel left Genesis in 1975 to spend time with his family and take control of his artistic future. His first solo album was produced by American producer Bob Ezrin and released in 1977. (It was titled *Peter Gabriel*, as, confusingly, were his next three albums as well.) It yielded the infectious single about his decision to leave Genesis,

"Solsbury Hill." It was an important album for Gabriel, allowing him the chance to prove his artistic validity outside Genesis. Though a few of the orchestrated tracks on the album are reminiscent of the grand musical themes that Gabriel and Genesis had composed together, in general Gabriel steered clear of mythic stories and purposefully arranged his songs to give an impression quite different from his work with Genesis.

For his second album Gabriel hired avant-garde guitarist (and leader of King Crimson) Robert Fripp as producer. Fripp wanted the album to capture the sense of a live band performance—a definite change from the sound of Gabriel's first album. In retrospect, the resulting stripped-down feel of the album does not seem to mesh well with Gabriel's musical inclinations. Nonetheless, the album has a number of excellent tunes, such as "On the Air" and the single "D.I.Y." Yet compared with the rest of Gabriel's work, the songs seem stark and lacking in color. What comes through quite well, however, is his ability to communicate deep emotional feelings that range from the melancholic despair of "Home Sweet Home" to the rebellious antics of a character called Mozo in "On the Air."

Breakthrough. Gabriel's third album, released in 1980, was his breakthrough in terms of establishing his own sound. His interests in African music and high technology meshed into an original style that was both striking and unique.

Working with producer Steve Lilly White, whose atmospheric approach to music had broken new musical ground in his work with the Irish band U2, Gabriel explored unique arrangements. He added kalimba runs, haunting saxophone solos, and rich synthesizer pads to emphasize a song's subject matter. Gabriel also insisted that the drumming on the album use no cymbals. The album saw Gabriel extending his ability to express a wide range of emotions through music with his unique and original arrangements, a trait that is well shown on "Family Snapshot," "Biko," and the album's mildly successful single, the antiwar anthem "Games Without Frontiers." The sessions also gave rise to the 1980's "Phil Collins" drum sound, created when Collins (in the role of a session drummer) began playing a tom-tom rhythm against the delay of a gated reverb set up by engineer Hugh Padgham. The huge sound that resulted laid the foundation for songs such as "Intruder." Gabriel experimented with building songs from the rhythms up, rather than the traditional method of writing songs first, then finding backing drums to fit them.

Gabriel's forth album, subtitled *Security* in its American release, saw him explore even more diverse themes and extend the style established on his previous album. *Security* was his first gold album. Many of the songs (among them "The Rhythm of the Heat," "San Jacinto," and "The Family and the Fishing Net") were inspired by cultural rituals and reflected Gabriel's interest in ethnic music and traditions. Others ("I Have the Touch," "Wallflower," and his first Top-40 single, "Shock the Monkey") expressed emotional responses to the modern world. No matter what the subject, Gabriel managed to use cutting-edge technology but to humanize it by his ability to express human experiences.

In 1984 Gabriel released his first live solo album, *Peter Gabriel Plays Live,* a double album that showcased the best of his solo material and demonstrated his and his band's ability to blend cutting-edge technology with a passionate live performance. That same year Gabriel's interests in world music and culture prompted him to establish the World of Music, Arts, and Dance (WOMAD) Festival, a traveling event that brought Middle Eastern and African music, dance, and art to the West. During this time he also used his

For the Record

Though subsequent tours of WOMAD proved successful ventures, the first was a financial disaster that nearly bankrupted Peter Gabriel. His mates from Genesis decided to help him out: They did a one-time reunion concert with Gabriel, and the proceeds cleared his debts.

talent for expressive atmospheric sound to create the music for Alan Parker's film *Birdy.* The resulting sound track won him the Grand Jury Prize at Cannes.

Pop Stardom. In 1986 Gabriel's fifth studio album, *So,* saw him mature as an artist on a number of levels. The album was coproduced by Daniel Lanois. Gabriel's use of technology was tempered by a more delicate response to the emotional underpinnings of the songs, as seen in "Don't Give Up," "Mercy Street," and "In Your Eyes." At the same time, the lighter tunes presented him as less "arty" and eccentric. With songs such as the funky "Sledgehammer," a number 1 hit, and "Big Time" (number 8), Gabriel let a more immediate connection to life shine through his songs. The whimsical stop-animation videos accompanying these two songs were immensely popular on MTV. The album went to number 2 and propelled Gabriel into the ranks of pop stardom.

Gabriel's next project saw him utilize the connections he had established with artists during his involvement with WOMAD; it also let him draw upon his own knowledge of world music.

He created a dense and sophisticated sound track for the film *The Last Temptation of Christ.* The album, a powerful work entitled *Passion,* gave him the chance to work closely with world-class Muslim percussionists, instrumentalists, and vocalists.

Many of the musicians and sounds he discovered on *Passion* strongly influenced Gabriel's next album, *Us* (1992). Most of the songs reflect Gabriel's painful soul-searching after his divorce from his wife of many years. The resulting album is a layered, even denser work than *Passion.* Though *Us*'s many levels of overdubbed sound are rich, the overall heavy tone loses some of the immediate connection with life that had surfaced on *So*'s lighter tracks. Nevertheless, backed by Gabriel's status as well as the airplay of the singles "Steam" (number 32) and "Digging in the Dirt" (number 52), *Us* climbed to number 2 on the charts. The subsequent tour spawned another live double album, *Secret World Live* (1994).

Gabriel's tapestries of sound and his interest in world music have influenced a number of artists' approaches to popular music. His pioneering use of synthesizers, processed drums, ethnic percussion, music videos, and music technology in general has never strayed far from his desire to connect emotionally to the themes of his songs.

—*Todd A. Elhart*

SELECT DISCOGRAPHY

■ ALBUMS

Peter Gabriel, 1977
Peter Gabriel, 1978
Peter Gabriel, 1980
Peter Gabriel: Security, 1982
Peter Gabriel Plays Live, 1983
Birdy, 1985 (sound track)
So, 1986
Passion, 1989 (sound track)
Us, 1992
Secret World Live, 1994

SEE ALSO: Collins, Phil; Genesis.

Marvin Gaye

BORN: Washington, D.C.; April 2, 1939
DIED: Los Angeles, California; April 1, 1984
FIRST ALBUM RELEASE: *The Soulful Moods of Marvin Gaye,* 1961
MUSICAL STYLES: Pop, soul

The career of Marvin Gaye mirrored his personal life: It was a mixture of fabulous success and long periods of despair and isolation. One of the brightest stars in the galaxy of artists included in the Berry Gordy family at Motown Records, Gaye constantly searched for a way to balance the struggle between his head and his heart, to come to terms with his personal relationship with God, and to try to mend the damage caused by his relationship with his father, Marvin Gay, Sr. (Marvin Gay, Jr. added the *e* to his name when he began his musical career.) Gaye fought with his father his entire life, which ended on April 1, 1984, one day before his forty-fifth birthday. He was killed by his father during an argument in the Gay home in Los Angeles.

Dreams of Destiny. Marvin Pentz Gaye was born in Washington, D.C., on April 2, 1939, the oldest son of a charismatic preacher. Raised in a housing project in the slums of Washington, D.C., Gaye experienced a strict religious upbringing. The church was eccentric—it was a small Pentecostal subculture that celebrated the Jewish High Holy Days and observed the Sabbath on Saturday. The only joyful part of the church experience for Marvin was the music, and he learned to play the piano by ear as a child, possessing a natural ability to sing. He began singing in church around the age of three, and by the age of five he sometimes traveled with his father on the evangelist circuit.

Gaye's mother worked as a domestic and was the main source of the family's financial support. The Reverend Gay was a part-time postal worker, but he was often not working at all. He was a violent man, beating his children severely for minor mistakes or the slightest misbehavior. Gaye sought refuge and found his only comfort in music.

While attending high school, Gaye studied drums, piano, and guitar. Along with friends, Marvin also formed his first singing group, the D.C. Tones. More interested in skipping school than attending, and unable to concentrate on formal studies, he quit high school before graduation to join the Air Force, but was discharged a short time later in 1957. The discharge, while classed as "honorable," said that he could not adjust to regimentation and authority.

On the Road to Motown. Returning to Washington, D.C., Marvin joined a professional group called the Marquees with a few of his former high-school friends from the D.C. Tones. They patterned themselves after a group called the Moonglows, who had a hit in 1955, "Sincerely," that became a doo-wop classic. (Doo-wop was a group vocal style that developed during the 1950's; it used dazzling, dense harmonies and had sparse instrumentation, often a simple guitar and string bass.) When they met blues and pop artist Bo Diddley, things began to happen. Diddley became a great influence on Gaye's musical style, strengthening his ties to the blues tradition and the country church. Diddley also produced the Marquees' first single record, "Wyatt Earp" backed with "Hey, Little School Girl." Marvin believed he was destined for a career as a solo artist, and the opportunity came when he met Harvey Fuqua. Fuqua was involved in blending new combinations of styles and sounds in American popular music; he also led the Moonglows. Fuqua had a talent for anticipating trends as teenage music started growing in the late 1950's and early 1960's. He became Gaye's mentor and played a part in his career until the end, producing Gaye's final album, *Midnight Love,* in 1982, which featured Gaye's comeback hit "Sexual Healing."

In 1959 Fuqua invited Gaye to join a new version of the Moonglows, and they left for Chicago to record in the Chess studios. Although Marvin was working as a background vocalist, Fuqua recognized the special quality in his voice and was the first to recognize dance music as Gaye's strength.

Marvin Gaye in 1983 (Paul Natkin)

By the end of the 1950's, different sounds from Ray Charles to Jackie Wilson were attracting a new generation of teenagers. The Moonglows' records were not selling well, and Fuqua thought that he could promote Marvin Gaye as a solo artist. Fuqua and Gaye settled in Detroit when their tour ended, and they recognized a new sound developing. That new sound would soon find a home in what became the largest black-owned business in the country: Berry Gordy's Motown Records. It was not long before the paths of Fuqua, Gaye, and Gordy intersected.

Berry Gordy, Jr.'s entrepreneurial family had settled in Detroit in the 1920's. While Gordy's love was music, and he tried to make a living in it, his record store went bankrupt trying to sell jazz records. In order to support his family, one of the jobs he took was working on an automotive assembly line. Determined to pursue his love of music, however, Gordy quit the automotive business after two years, using the skills learned on the assembly line to begin producing other artists along with his sister Gwen, who had a natural talent for business and had already starting making records. By 1960 Harvey Fuqua had also started a small record label, eventually working with the label owned by Gwen Gordy. Berry Gordy's business was growing and, eventually, when Fuqua needed cash, Gordy bought Gaye's contract. While Marvin had looked upon Fuqua as a father figure, he strongly desired success and was anxious to become a part of Motown. He eventually married Gordy's older sister Gwen, seventeen years his senior.

Success. Marvin worked as a backup singer and drummer for Smokey Robinson before recording his first album as a solo artist, *The Soulful Moods of Marvin Gaye,* in 1961. With his sights still set on becoming a ballad singer much like Frank Sinatra, this album was jazz oriented. Motown still thought they would have more success with Gaye as a dance-music artist for the teenage market, however, and he next recorded the song "Stubborn Kinda Fellow," which entered the Top 10 of the rhythm-and-blues charts. This success was followed by a long succession of Motown hits such as "Hitch Hike," "Pride and Joy," "Can I Get a Witness," and "Wonderful One."

For the Record

"My dream was to become Frank Sinatra. . . . Now this is going to surprise you, but I also dug Dean Martin and especially Perry Como. They weren't monster singers, but I liked their relaxed presentation. . . . When I finally got some money together over at Motown in the sixties, I used to sport Perry Como's sweaters. I always felt like my personality and Perry's had a lot in common. —*Marvin Gaye*

(from David Ritz's *Divided Soul: The Life of Marvin Gaye,* 1985)

Gaye also recorded a number of vocal duet records with singer Mary Wells on the 1964 album *Together* and the 1967 hit "It Takes Two" with Kim Weston. His most successful partnership at Motown was with Tammi Terrell. For two years they recorded a string of hits, written and produced by Nickolas Ashford and Valerie Simpson, such as "Ain't No Mountain High Enough" and "Ain't Nothing Like the Real Thing."

Perhaps Gaye's most lasting solo hit was "Heard It Through the Grapevine," recorded in 1968. As his success grew, he demanded more independence at Motown, and he followed that hit with the 1971 album *What's Going On,* one of the first sophisticated concept albums. The songs on this album were written and produced by Gaye and reflected his growing concern for the political and social situation in the United States, influenced by the demand for civil rights by African Americans and the protests and demonstrations surrounding the Vietnam War. Widely regarded as a classic, the album was an important and lasting contribution to the music of that generation.

Troubled Man. While continuing to experience success in his career, Marvin's personal life was in ruins. He went through periods of constant touring followed by periods of almost total isolation, cutting himself off from friends and family. He even moved to Europe for a few years, in part to escape his personal problems but mainly to escape his tax problems with the Internal Revenue Service.

Gaye eventually returned to the United States and signed with CBS Records in 1981, recording what was to be his last album, *Midnight Lover*, in 1982, featuring the Grammy Award-winning "Sexual Healing." Suffering from debilitating paranoia brought on by a dependency on drugs, he moved into his parents' home in Los Angeles. In close quarters, Marvin's feelings toward his father became ever more resentful, and the two fought violently. Finally, during a heated argument on Sunday morning, April 1, 1984, his father shot him to death. Since Gaye's death, his popularity and interest in his music has increased. Gaye has become as icon of American popular culture, and the power of his music and its message survive.

—*Jo Ann Collins*

SELECT DISCOGRAPHY

■ SINGLES

"Pride and Joy," 1963
"How Sweet It Is to Be Loved By You," 1964
"I'll Be Doggone," 1965
"Ain't That Peculiar," 1965
"It Takes Two," 1967 (with Kim Weston)
"Your Precious Love," 1967 (with Tammi Terrell)
"Ain't Nothing Like the Real Thing," 1968 (with Tammi Terrell)
"I Heard It Through the Grapevine," 1968
"Let's Get It On," 1973
"Got to Give It Up," 1977
"Sexual Healing," 1982

■ ALBUMS

The Soulful Moods of Marvin Gaye, 1961
That Stubborn Kinda Fellow, 1963
Live on Stage, 1963
Together, 1964 (with Mary Wells)
How Sweet It Is to Be Loved by You, 1965
In the Groove, 1968
You're All I Need, 1968 (with Tammi Terrell)
What's Going On, 1971
Trouble Man, 1972 (motion-picture sound track)
Let's Get It On, 1973
Midnight Love, 1982
The Master (1961-1984), 1995 (4-CD boxed set)

SELECT AWARDS

Grammy Awards for Best Rhythm and Blues Instrumental Performance and Best Rhythm and Blues Vocal Performance, Male, for "Sexual Healing," 1982
Rock and Roll Hall of Fame, inducted 1987

SEE ALSO: Charles, Ray; Diddley, Bo; Robinson, Smokey; Sinatra, Frank; Wilson, Jackie.

Crystal Gayle

(Brenda Gayle Webb)

BORN: Paintsville, Kentucky; January 9, 1951
FIRST SINGLE RELEASE: "I've Cried (the Blue Right out of My Eyes)," 1970
MUSICAL STYLES: Country, pop

Born Brenda Gayle Webb in Paintsville, Kentucky, in 1951, Gayle was the youngest of Ted and Clara Webb's eight children and the only one to be born in a hospital. At the time of her birth, her father was a miner working in the Van Lear mines, which closed in 1955. Upon the mines' closing, the Webb family moved from its Butcher Hollow, Kentucky, home, later made famous by the film *Coal Miner's Daughter*, to Wabash, Indiana, where Gayle grew up. By the time of the family's 1955 move, Gayle's older sister, who was to become the country music legend Loretta Lynn, had married, moved out of the family home, had children, and was in the Northwest, performing on radio shows and competing in talent contests.

Style. Both Gayle and Lynn have said that they grew up in different families. The differences in their early lives have contributed to the differences in their musical styles and sounds. Lynn's style is pure country, both in subject matter and in voice quality. Gayle has pursued themes associated with country music, particularly the heartbreak of male-female relationships, but her rendition of those themes is generally more sophisticated and more controlled than Lynn's. Gayle's smoother, more controlled voice and her mid-America sound have made her audience appeal much wider than Lynn's. However, Lynn's true country sound and her deep emotional appeal guaranteed her a more loyal following than Gayle has ever had.

Beginnings. Gayle recorded her first single, "I've Cried (the Blue Right out of My Eyes)," on the Decca (later MCA) label in 1970. By the time nineteen-year-old Gayle had made her first recording, Lynn had become the acknowledged "Queen of Country Music." Without a doubt, Lynn's prominence contributed to Gayle's ability to procure a recording contract. Certainly Gayle did not have to work as hard as Lynn to win media attention or to get her records played. Nevertheless, Gayle was definitely a unique talent, and her success was hers alone. In 1974 she signed with United Artists, and, for the next decade, she was a force within the realm of country music.

Crystal Gayle (Archive Photos/Laurence Agron)

Career Success. Gayle has received many awards for her recordings and performances. In 1978 she was the first female country artist to have an album go platinum, *We Believe in Magic.* This success was followed by another platinum album, *When I Dream,* in 1978. In 1979 Gayle was the first country star to tour China. In 1979 she also had two gold albums, *Miss the Mississippi* and *Classic Crystal.* From 1976 to 1987 Gayle had seventeen number 1 hits on the *Billboard* charts, the last of which, "Straight to the Heart" (1987), stayed in the Top 100 for twenty-two weeks.

Legacy. Crystal Gayle has made two significant contributions to country music. First, she was one of the first country entertainers to have her music accepted by an audience of not exclusively country music fans. In 1977, "Don't It Make My Brown Eyes Blue" crossed over from the country charts to the pop charts.

Second, Gayle's style encouraged a wider range of performers to sing country music. While the topics and themes of Gayle's music were the topics and themes of traditional country music, her voice was different from the female voices which had sung traditional country. Her voice sounded more like mainstream America than the voices of her predecessors, thus, she appealed to a much wider audience than most country singers of the late 1970's and early 1980's. Her widespread appeal caused a greater variety of performers to become interested in singing country music. Hearing Gayle perform caused other performers to think that they could also sing country music even without a high-pitched voice or a nasal resonance.

—*Annita Marie Ward*

For the Record

In 1996, upon returning to Paintsville, Kentucky, to dedicate the Country Music Highway, Crystal Gayle said, "Even though I did not grow up here, this is my heritage. This is my roots, and this is definitely my home."

SELECT DISCOGRAPHY

■ ALBUMS

When I Dream, 1978
Miss the Mississippi, 1979
A Crystal Christmas, 1986
50 Original Tracks, 1993 (compilation)

SELECT AWARDS

Academy of Country Music Female Vocalist of the Year Award, 1976, 1977, 1979

Grammy Award for Best Country Vocal Performance, Female, for "Don't It Make My Brown Eyes Blue," 1977

Country Music Association Female Vocalist of the Year Award, 1977, 1978

Grammy Award for Best Recording for Children for *Sesame Country*, 1981 (with the Muppets, Glen Campbell, Loretta Lynn, and Tanya Tucker)

SEE ALSO: Lynn, Loretta.

J. Geils Band

ORIGINAL MEMBERS: J. Geils (b. Jerome Geils, 1946), Danny Klein (b. 1946), Magic Dick (b. Richard Salwitz, 1945), Peter Wolf (b. Peter Blankfield, 1946), Stephen Jo Bladd (b. 1942), Seth Justman (b. 1951)

FIRST ALBUM RELEASE: *The J. Geils Band*, 1970

MUSICAL STYLES: Rock, rhythm and blues

Often called the "American Rolling Stones," the J. Geils Band was a good-time, partying group based in the Boston area during the 1970's and 1980's. Drawing their inspiration from the great artists of rhythm and blues, they made music devoid of pretense, an invigorating blend of classic soul and bar-band rock. Despite their name, they were fronted not by guitarist J. Geils, but by vocalist Peter Wolf, a transplanted New Yorker who was one of rock's most captivating showmen, a former fast-talking disc jockey who understood the meaning of entertaining an audience.

Having Fun. Like the Rolling Stones' Mick Jagger, Wolf embodied ceaseless energy onstage. In an era when many bands indulged in long, screaming guitar solos, pretentious, complex song structures, and a serious attitude toward their music, the J. Geils Band kept things down to basics with catchy, soulful tunes and much unapologetic fun. Without being a throwback, they instinctively understood what made rock and roll great when it first came into existence.

The band's six members were all virtuosos. Keyboardist Seth Justman wrote most of the group's original material (they also performed many covers of classic and obscure rhythm-and-blues songs) and supplied much of the melody, particularly in the band's more commercial, pop-oriented, later period. Geils himself was a fiery and crisp, if understated, guitar player who always provided the perfect tasteful lick for a given song. Magic Dick was one of the greatest harmonica players in the blues and rock world, and the rhythm section of bassist Danny Klein and drummer Stephen Jo Bladd was always in perfect synchronization, supplying a solid foundation to the music. Even when the band graduated to playing arenas in the 1980's, they still managed to make audiences feel as if they were in a crowded club somewhere on Chicago's South Side.

The Beginnings. The J. Geils Band formed in Boston in 1967. Before the six-man lineup came together, guitarist Geils fronted the J. Geils Blues Band, an acoustic trio. Geils, Klein, and Magic Dick all shared a huge admiration for the soul, blues, and jazz greats of the day, from James Brown to Little Walter and Ray Charles to John Coltrane. The band was popular on the booming

For the Record

"I think to see it was to believe it. The J. Geils Band was a real American band—six guys with a love of music, really feeling blessed that we were able to prevail and keep going. We were no frills, no tricks, just hard, sweaty rock and roll. And when we hit the stage, it was showtime!"

—*Peter Wolf, 1993*

folk music scene in Cambridge, Massachusetts.

Peter Wolf had moved to Boston from the Bronx, New York, and had spent much of his adolescence attending rhythm-and-blues concerts at Harlem's famed Apollo Theatre. Wolf was a huge jazz fan, and he was equally enamored of the motor-mouthed disc jockeys of rock and roll's golden age, Alan Freed, Jocko Henderson, and Symphony Sid among them.

Wolf attended the Boston Museum of Fine Arts School, but he was more interested in his job as a disc jockey on Boston station WBCN. He formed a band in which he could indulge his love of soul music, the Hallucinations, which also included drummer Stephen Jo Bladd. The Hallucinations played the same club circuit as the J. Geils Blues Band (who soon eliminated the word Blues from their name), and in 1967 Wolf and Bladd joined the Geils team to create a new, more electric rock and soul band. Some of their first shows were backing up blues giants such as Muddy Waters and John Lee Hooker. The final addition came in 1969 when Seth Justman, a versatile keyboardist and songwriter, joined the lineup, which then remained solid until 1983.

One Big Party. It did not take long for the J. Geils Band to be signed to a record deal. They had quickly become a fixture at Boston's most important club, the Tea Party, when they were discovered by a talent scout from Atlantic Records, one of the most important rhythm-and-blues and rock record companies. Their first album, simply titled *The J. Geils Band,* was released in late 1970 and consisted of some original material and covers of some of their favorite soul and blues songs, as did their second album, 1971's *The Morning After.*

While many other bands of the day were content to stand still onstage and play indulgent solos, the Geils sextet was constantly animated, in the tradition of their soul heroes. Wolf, in particular, traversed the stage as quickly as he spoke, leaving both himself and audiences breathless. Some were skeptical as to whether the band could transfer that power to recordings, but the resulting *Live: Full House,* recorded in Detroit, Michigan, in 1972, proved they could, and it would remain one of the classic live albums of the era. *Live: Blow Your Face Out,* from 1976, is another.

Peter Wolf of the J. Geils Band (Ken Settle)

Throughout the 1970's and early 1980's, the J. Geils Band continued to dazzle audiences throughout the United States with their classy showmanship and stripped-down approach to soul rock. Primarily regarded as a live act, the band had no major sellers, and only one album, 1973's *Bloodshot,* made the Top 10. However, they were one of the most respected bands performing, a guaranteed good time for anyone who saw their show or bought an album.

By 1977, with the release of their album *Monkey Island,* the band had started to shift gears musically, heading to more of a mainstream pop-rock sound. By 1981, with the release of *Freeze-Frame,* they had found the right combination of roots music and pop to be able to reach the mass audiences. *Freeze-Frame* was a number 1 album, and it yielded two smash singles, the number 1 "Centerfold" and the number 4 title track.

The Show Comes to an End. Things were still going well for the J. Geils Band, at least on the surface, when, in 1983, Wolf left the band (or was fired, depending on the version of the story). Although the band continued without him, their only album without Wolf, 1984's *You're Gettin' Even While I'm Gettin' Odd*, was neither a critical nor a commercial success, and they soon broke up. Wolf, meanwhile, fared better on his own, recording intermittently. His first solo album, *Lights Out*, was a moderate success in 1984, as was the same-titled single. He rarely performed live after the breakup of the band, however, leaving younger fans with only the legacy of the dynamic performer he once was.

In the mid-1990's Geils (then calling himself Jay) and Magic Dick teamed for a new round of shows and recordings, but they could never recapture the magic of the 1970's and 1980's. Justman, Bladd, and Klein, meanwhile, seemingly disappeared from the rock scene. —*Jeff Tamarkin*

SELECT DISCOGRAPHY

■ ALBUMS

The J. Geils Band, 1970
Live: Full House, 1972
Bloodshot, 1973
Live: Blow Your Face Out, 1976
Monkey Island, 1977
Sanctuary, 1978
Love Stinks, 1980
Freeze-Frame, 1981
Anthology—House Party, 1993

SEE ALSO: Brown, James; Charles, Ray; Hooker, John Lee; Rolling Stones, The; Waters, Muddy.

Genesis

ORIGINAL MEMBERS: Peter Gabriel (b. 1950), Tony Banks (b. 1951), Mike Rutherford (b. 1950), Anthony Philips (b. 1951), Chris Stewart

OTHER MEMBERS: Phil Collins (b. 1951), Steve Hackett (b. 1950), Ray Wilson (b. 1968)

FIRST ALBUM RELEASE: *From Genesis to Revelation*, 1969

MUSICAL STYLES: Progressive rock, pop

Formed in 1966, the British rock band Genesis survived through the 1990's despite the departure of its lead vocalist Peter Gabriel in 1975, the distraction of a solo career for his successor Phil Collins, the dwindling of its numbers to three, and then Collins's departure in 1996. In the early 1970's Genesis represented the trend of progressive rock at its grandest level. By 1980 it had redefined itself with a more commercially successful sound and won over a mainstream audience in America and the United Kingdom.

The Early Days. The origins of Genesis trace back to an elite British public school (roughly equivalent to a prep school in America) called Charterhouse and to the merger of two student bands, the Garden Wall and the Anon. Vocalist Peter Gabriel, keyboardist Tony Banks, and drummer Chris Stewart made up the former, while guitarist Anthony Philips and bass guitarist Mike Rutherford were members of the latter. Gabriel and Banks would later name Otis Redding and the Beatles as important early influences.

In addition to singing, Gabriel played the flute, an unusual but not unprecedented element in rock music. The new band was named by their first producer, Jonathan King of Decca Records, a Charterhouse alumnus. Their first single, "The Silent Sun," was released in 1968, followed by the little-heard album *From Genesis to Revelation* in the next year. The group's fortunes began to change for the better with the signing on of their fourth drummer, Phil Collins, who had already gained professional experience in the group Flaming Youth before joining Genesis in August, 1970. With the arrival of creative guitarist Steve Hackett soon after, Genesis became a well-balanced ensemble of considerable musical talent.

While none of their early albums scored much commercial success, Genesis built a loyal concert audience drawn to the group's long song suites and elaborate stagecraft and lighting—all destined to be hallmarks of a Genesis concert. Gabriel's typically ornate lyrics, with their kaleidoscopic imagery, benefited from the versatility and expressive force of his high tenor voice. Gabriel donned strange costumes and masks, including batwings, a fox head, and giant flower petals. All the members of Genesis except Gabriel sat down when they performed in the early years, so it was entirely up to Gabriel to entertain the audience visually.

Like other groups in the progressive rock movement of the early 1970's, Genesis showed little interest in producing either traditional love songs or dance music. Their musical style, too, was alternative, having little in common with the rhythm-and-blues roots of much other 1960's rock. The songs of Genesis tended to be thematic—focusing on some aspect of the modern world or on history or myth.

Selling England by the Pound of 1973, the first Genesis release to gain measurable attention in the United States, can be considered a concept album, a cycle of songs depicting the state of affairs in modern England. From it came the successful single "I Know What I Like (in Your Wardrobe)." The long track "The Battle of Epping Forest," about a gang fight, contained elaborate punning by Gabriel and impressive tempo, mood, and rhythm shifts from the band.

The Lamb Lies Down on Broadway. The group's longest and most complex project was the double album entitled *The Lamb Lies Down on Broadway* (1974), developed from a story by Gabriel recounting the surrealistic journey of a New York City street kid named Rael. Rael's life changes with the appearance of two strange signs: a dark mass descending on Manhattan and a lamb lying down on Broadway. He must then suffer various ordeals, meet supernatural creatures (including Death, in the form of the "Supernatural Anesthetist"), and chase after his elusive brother John, finally to be delivered back home with new spiritual insights.

Each of the album's four sides amounted to a suite of continuous music in which individual numbers were connected by instrumental transitions that prepared changes of mood and key. A number of the instrumental sections were lengthened into longer mood pieces that advanced the story without words and showcased the band's players. In particular, Tony Banks's solos on the introduction to the title track and elsewere are typical of the playing expected of the keyboard

Genesis in 1977: Steve Hackett, Tony Banks, touring drummer Chester Thompson, Mike Rutherford, Phil Collins (Archive Photos)

player in an early 1970's progressive rock band and stand comparison to the work of his contemporaries Rick Wakeman of Yes and Keith Emerson of Emerson, Lake, and Palmer.

A tour of 102 concerts brought the work to audiences throughout Europe and the United States. On the album much of the story line must be deduced from the liner notes; in concert Gabriel narrated pieces of the story during the breaks. In addition to singing all the songs, Gabriel indulged himself with bizarre costumes and an animated stage presentation, gesticulating and dancing around the stage to take full advantage of the lighting and smoke effects.

The Collins Era. After the completion of the *Lamb Lies Down on Broadway* tour, Genesis faced a major crisis when Gabriel announced that he was leaving the band to pursue a solo career. A huge number of vocalists auditioned before the remaining members decided to designate their drummer, Phil Collins, lead singer. The decision was in fact a logical one, since Collins regularly provided backing vocals and had sung lead on single tracks from the albums *Nursery Cryme* and *Selling England by the Pound.* Moreover, Collins could produce a delicate high tenor that bore a resemblance to Gabriel's voice. Inevitably, Collins found himself leaving his drum set and advancing front and center for his singing duties. He quickly developed his own brand of stage theatrics. First Bill Bruford (formerly of Yes) and then Chester Thompson were hired as replacement drummers for the band's live shows. Collins continued to drum on their studio work.

Genesis released two albums as a quartet, then the departure of Steve Hackett reduced the group to a trio. The change did not reduce record sales: The aptly named 1978 album *. . . And Then There Were Three* went gold. From then on, Genesis moved closer to commercial pop, incorporating drum machines, more synthesizers, slick arranging, and the talents of professional studio musicians, including horn players from the funk band *Earth, Wind, and Fire.* The title of the group's platinum album *ABACAB* (1981) reveals a bit of self-mockery: ABACAB is shorthand for a standard arrangement pattern for pop songs. The new gambit proved highly successful. The single "In Too Deep" (theme song for the film *Mona Lisa*) made the U.S. Top-10, as did the album *Invisible Touch* and its number 1 selling title song (1986). Genesis continued to tour, releasing *We Can't Dance* in 1991 and some live albums.

When Collins departed in 1996, he was replaced by Ray Wilson, and the new lineup released *Calling All Stations* in 1997. —*David Haas*

For the Record

During the 1980's, Princess Diana let it be known that Genesis's 1976 album *A Trick of the Tail* was her favorite rock album.

§

Before becoming a professional musician, Phil Collins had a career as a child actor. He appeared as an extra in the film *A Hard Day's Night.*

SELECT DISCOGRAPHY

■ ALBUMS

Trespass, 1970
Nursery Cryme, 1971
Foxtrot, 1972
Selling England by the Pound, 1973
Genesis Live, 1973
The Lamb Lies Down on Broadway, 1974
A Trick of the Tail, 1976
. . . And Then There Were Three, 1978
Duke, 1980
Three Sides Live, 1982
ABACAB, 1981
Invisible Touch, 1986
We Can't Dance, 1991
The Way We Walk, Volume 1: The Shorts, 1992
The Way We Walk, Volume 2: The Longs, 1993
Calling All Stations, 1997
Genesis Archive, Vol. 1: 1967-75—The Gabriel Years, 1998 (4-CD boxed set)

SEE ALSO: Collins, Phil; Emerson, Lake, and Palmer; Gabriel, Peter; King Crimson; Yes.

Vince Gill

BORN: Norman, Oklahoma; April 12, 1957
FIRST ALBUM RELEASE: *Can't Hold Back*, 1979 (with Pure Prairie League)
FIRST SOLO ALBUM RELEASE: *Turn Me Loose*, 1983
MUSICAL STYLES: Progressive bluegrass, country

As the son of a banjo-playing federal judge, Vince Gill was attracted to bluegrass music at an early age. It should come as no surprise that Gill became proficient on the banjo, but by his high school years he had also mastered the guitar. While in high school he organized a bluegrass band, Mountain Smoke, that gained sufficient notoriety to be invited to open a concert for the pop group Pure Prairie League. Upon graduation, Gill, an accomplished athlete, entertained ideas of a professional career as a golfer, but it was music that ultimately lured him away from his Norman, Oklahoma, home. When the Kentucky-based bluegrass band Bluegrass Alliance extended to him the opportunity to play with the extremely talented musicians Sam Bush and Dan Crary, Gill accepted.

Early Musical Experience. After a twelve-month stint with the Alliance, Gill moved to Los Angeles for a two-year tenure with Sundance, a band led by bluegrass fiddler Byron Berline. A major turning point in his career came in 1979, when he accompanied a friend who was auditioning for a position with the Pure Prairie League. Gill's intent was to determine if the League's members remembered him from the concert in which his band, Mountain Smoke, opened for the group. Not only did they remember him, but to Gill's delight, they offered him a position as lead singer.

Gill performed with Pure Prairie League for three years, during which time he participated in recording three albums: *Can't Hold Back* (1979), *Firin' Up* (1980), and *Something in the Night* (1981). The magnitude of his talent as a multi-instrumentalist and vocalist became evident in 1980 when his song "I'm Almost Ready" resulted in a Top-40 pop hit for Pure Prairie League. Concurrent with the band's success, Gill participated in several recording sessions which also helped to advance his career. From 1979 to 1981, he busied himself in the studio with Byron Berline (*Outrageous*, 1980), Rosanne Cash (*Seven Year Ache*, 1981), and Rodney Crowell (*Rodney Crowell*, 1981).

While his music career was still in its infancy, Gill demonstrated musical skills that forecast his future stardom. He was an excellent vocalist and songwriter, and his proficiency on seven instruments (banjo, Dobro, guitar, fiddle, mandolin, electric guitar, and drums) placed him in high demand for recording sessions with established artists. In addition to his own solo projects, from 1979 to 1997 Gill appeared on more than one hundred recordings involving the elite of country and bluegrass music.

Ladder of Success. A number of factors contributed to Vince Gill's successful climb up country music's ladder of stardom, but his association with Rodney Crowell's band the Cherry Bombs played a major role. In 1981, following his success on the Top-40 pop charts, Gill left the Pure Prairie League and moved to the West Coast, where he obtained a position as guitarist with Crowell. A major career break came for Gill in 1983, when Tony Brown, a former keyboardist for Crowell, signed Gill to a recording contract with RCA Records. Unfortunately, Brown, who was eventually to play a major role in Gill's success, accepted a position with MCA Records before Gill could record his first solo project. However, another former Cherry Bomber, bassist Emory Gordy, Jr., produced Gill's RCA debut album, *Turn Me Loose* (1983).

Gill and his family moved to Nashville, Tennessee, in 1984, about the same time "Victim of Life's Circumstance," his second single off *Turn Me Loose*, cracked country music's Top-40 chart. This began a run of successful singles that lasted into the 1990's. Gill's next two albums on RCA produced several Top-10 hits, including "If It Weren't for Him" (featuring harmony vocals from Rosanne Cash), "Oklahoma Borderline," and "Cinderella." The positive public reaction to his music was encouraging, but Gill's career, musically speaking, was yet to really take off. It was his continued involvement as a multifaceted musician that aided his career advancement. Gill performed on the recordings of such artists as Conway Twitty, Bonnie Raitt, Emmylou Harris, Lyle Lovett, Patty Loveless, Suzy Bogguss, George Jones, and Reba McEntire. He also cowrote songs with Rosanne Cash and toured with Harris's band in the late 1980's.

Based upon his diverse involvement and success in country music, in 1989 Gill signed a recording contract with MCA, which reunited him with Tony Brown, the man who had initially signed him with RCA. Brown was instrumental in launching a very promising musical career for Gill. Every one of Gill's six MCA albums sold more than one million copies. His first MCA release, *When I Call Your Name* (1989), was an eclectic work that included everything from honky-tonk to contemporary pop, but was the perfect vehicle for showcasing Gill's diverse talents as a singer-songwriter. The title cut, which featured vocal assistance from Patty Loveless, won a Grammy Award and two Country Music Association (CMA) Awards. When the album went platinum, Gill was firmly established as a country music superstar.

When Gill left RCA for MCA, his music took on a more traditional sound, which accounts in part for his rise to stardom. Ricky Skaggs had popularized a back-to-basics style in the early 1980's that called for a "rootsier," or more traditional, sound, and Gill seemed to be emulating the neotraditionalist approach. This is especially evident in his *Pocket Full of Gold* (1991), a hit album with high bluegrass vocals, traditional country arrangements, and contemporary production.

Accomplishments. If sales figures are significant in measuring an artist's success, then it should be noted that Gill's next five MCA projects sold in excess of ten million copies. His recordings *Pocket Full of Gold* and *I Still Believe in You* (1992) sold two million and three million copies, respectively, and *Let There Be Peace on Earth*, his 1993 Christmas album, went platinum. *When Love Finds You*, released in 1994, went triple-platinum, and *Souvenirs*, a 1995 collection of favorites, sold more than one million copies. (This latter project provides an excellent introduction to Gill's work.)

In addition to his impressive sales figures, Gill's charting success is note worthy. He began a string of Top-10 hits in 1990 that ran for five consecutive years and included the number 1 hits "Take Your Memory with You," "I Still Believe in You," "Don't Let Our Love Start Slippin' Away," "One More Chance," and "Tryin' to Get Over You." The success of his 1994 triple-platinum release, *When Love Finds You*, was based in large measure on the hit songs "What the Cowgirls Do" and "Whenever You Come Around." This album not only made the Top 3 on the country music chart but also crossed over and made the Top 10 on the pop album chart.

Gill's *High Lonesome Sound* (1996), produced by Tony Brown, in many ways mirrors his first MCA recording, as Gill attempted to expand his sphere of artistry and venture into diverse fields of music. Half the songs on the album were written by Gill and the other half he cowrote. *High Lonesome Sound* features a great deal of Gill's award-winning guitar playing (which had been reserved previously for his live performances), and it includes such variant styles as roadhouse blues with a screaming blues guitar and bluegrass with Alison Krauss and her band Union Station. The title cut, "High Lonesome Sound," was voted to be the 1997 Bluegrass Song of the Year by the International Bluegrass Music Association (IBMA).

In addition to his IBMA Award, Gill's numerous honors include eight Grammy Awards, fifteen Awards from the Country Music Association, and his 1992 induction into the Grand Ole Opry.

—*Wayne M. Bledsoe*

SELECT DISCOGRAPHY

■ ALBUMS

Turn Me Loose, 1983
Things That Matter, 1984
Way Back Home, 1987
When I Call Your Name, 1989
Best of Vince Gill, 1989 (compilation, boxed set)
Pocket Full of Gold, 1991
I Never Knew Lonely, 1992
I Still Believe in You, 1992
Let There Be Peace on Earth, 1993
When Love Finds You, 1994
Vince Gill and Friends, 1994
Songs from the Heart, 1994 (Australian import)

Souvenirs, 1995 (compilation)
Essential Vince Gill, 1995 (compilation)
Super Hits, 1996 (compilation)
High Lonesome Sound, 1996
The Key, 1998

SELECT AWARDS

Grammy Award for Best Country Vocal Collaboration for "Restless," 1991 (with Ricky Skaggs and Steve Wariner)

Country Music Association Male Vocalist of the Year Award and Song of the Year (Songwriter's Award) for "When I Call Your Name," 1991 (wr. with Tim Dubois)

Country Music Association Male Vocalist of the Year Award and Song of the Year (Songwriter's Award) for "Look at Us," 1992 (wr. with Max D. Barnes)

Country Music Association Entertainer of the Year and Male Vocalist of the Year Awards, Album of the Year Award for *I Still Believe in You,* Vocal Event of the Year Award for "I Don't Need Your Rocking Chair" (with others), Song of the Year (Songwriter's Award) for "When I Call Your Name" (wr. with Tim Dubois), all 1993

Country Music Association Entertainer of the Year, Male Vocalist of the Year, and Album of the Year Awards for *Common Thread: The Songs of the Eagles,* 1994 (with others)

Grammy Award for Best Country Vocal Performance, Male, for "When Love Finds You," 1995

SEE ALSO: Cash, Rosanne; Harris, Emmylou; Jones, George; Judds, The / Wynonna Judd; Lovett, Lyle; McEntire, Reba; Mattea, Kathy; Parton, Dolly; Raitt, Bonnie; Twitty, Conway.

For the Record

Vince Gill declined his first invitation to perform at the Grand Ole Opry—a major honor among country musicians—so that he could attend a recital being given by his daughter.

The Gin Blossoms

ORIGINAL LINEUP: Doug Hopkins (1961-1993), Scott Johnson (b.1952), Bill Leen, Phillip Rhodes, Jesse Valenzuela, Robin Wilson

FIRST ALBUM RELEASE: *Dusted*, 1989

MUSICAL STYLES: Rock and roll, country rock, alternative

The Gin Blossoms seemingly came out of nowhere with a pair of rock-and-roll hits from their double-platinum major-label debut album in 1992, and returned to obscurity almost as quickly, breaking up in 1997 after only their second major album. Yet the band's Southwest-flavored, guitar-based pop music with its self-deprecating lyrics remained popular, and several songs continued to receive airplay even after their creators' second release faded from the charts in mid-1996.

A Slow Start. The Gin Blossoms had their roots in Tempe, Arizona, with bass player Bill Leen and guitarist Doug Hopkins forming the band in the mid-1980's. Guitarist and singer Jesse Valenzuela joined Leen and Hopkins in 1987, and acoustic guitarist Robin Wilson signed on in 1988, eventually replacing Valenzuela as the lead vocalist. Drummer Phillip Rhodes rounded out the quintet.

The Gin Blossoms first claimed national attention in 1989 with *Dusted*, released on the independent San Jacinto label. After signing with A&M Records, the band released a five-song extended-play single, *Up and Crumbling*, in 1991. That was followed on August 4, 1992, by *New Miserable Experience*, which features twelve songs, including six written or cowritten by Hopkins, who had been fired from the band (and replaced by guitarist Scott Johnson) in early 1992 after failing to overcome problems with alcohol and depression. The extended-play single did not garner much attention despite the Gin Blossoms' touring, and neither did the full-length album, at least initially.

Success and Tragedy. The Gin Blossoms began picking up steam in the summer of 1993 behind "Hey Jealousy," which entered *Billboard* magazine's Hot 100 singles chart on July 24, and

The Gin Blossoms (Paul Natkin)

alternative music to which the band was supposed to be a counter. Hopkins, who was heavily influenced by alcohol, lived long enough to earn a gold record for *New Miserable Experience*, on which he received credit despite being ousted before its completion. He left a Phoenix detoxification center in the first week of December, 1993, and shot himself to death in his Tempe home.

When one listens to the songs Hopkins wrote for *New Miserable Experience*, which include "Lost Horizons," "Pieces of the Night," "Hold Me Down" with Wilson, and "Cheatin' " with Valenzuela, it is apparent alcohol was often on his mind. "Lost Horizons" ("Drink enough of anything to make this world look new again/ Drunk, drunk, drunk in the gardens and the graves") and "Hold Me Down" ("When those doors swing open and all the drinks are passed around/ Anytime the pickins look too easy . . . hold me down") are classic drinking songs. Even the lighthearted country tune "Cheatin'" opens in a bar: "It was early and I'd had my share . . . " Though Hopkins's songs were sung in a bouncy, upbeat style by Wilson, and his music has a catchy pop quality, a closer listen suggests there is more to the story than what is in the words.

"Found Out About You," which entered the chart on November 20. Both eventually became Top-25 hits. In fact, *New Miserable Experience* was faring so well during a musical period dominated by dark-themed grunge and alternative music, it was rereleased by A&M with a completely different booklet and artwork. Other tracks off *New Miserable Experience* also began getting airplay, with the cheerful "Allison Road," written by Wilson, and the mellow "Until I Fall Away," written by Wilson and Valenzuela, receiving plenty of notice. Listeners and critics compared the band's music to that of the Byrds, R.E.M., and Tom Petty for its use of vocal harmonies, rhythm, and guitars. The band toured extensively in support of *New Miserable Experience* from the time it was released, and as the songs' airplay increased, so did the crowds. The Gin Blossoms quickly earned a reputation as a top live act.

The irony of the Gin Blossoms' musical style—up-tempo pop conjuring images of the open deserts of the Southwest, fast cars, and dark bars—is that the lyrics are every bit as tortured as the

For the Record

The name Gin Blossoms comes from an expression for burst blood vessels in the nose stemming from heavy alcohol use. The band name was inspired by a picture of comedian W. C. Fields and his chronically red nose.

Big hits "Hey Jealousy" and "Found Out About You" are fun songs, but careful listening reveals the sorrow and bitterness underneath.

It took the Gin Blossoms almost four years after *New Miserable Experience* to release another album, with *Congratulations I'm Sorry*—the title referring to the mix of success and tragedy during the years between albums—reaching stores February 13, 1996.

Meanwhile, "Til I Hear It from You," from the sound track of the unmemorable 1995 film *Empire Records*, proved a huge success. The song, written by Valenzuela, Wilson, and Marshall Crenshaw, became one of the band's biggest hits and was the most-added-track in a variety of radio formats in its first week of release. That success led observers to believe the band would thrive even without Hopkins's writing talents.

Not to Be. Fans and critics were eager to hear *Congratulations I'm Sorry*, which debuted at number 10 on the *Billboard* 200 album list, higher than *New Miserable Experience* had ever reached. The first single, "Follow You Down," likewise proved successful, topping "Til I Hear It from You" in airplay and suggesting the Gin Blossoms were going to be chart toppers for years to come. All five band members took writing credit for "Follow You Down" and took turns penning the songs on the album. The "Follow You Down" single, with "Til I Hear It from You" on the B-side, reached *Billboard*'s Top 10 and spent almost one year on the chart.

However, *Congratulations I'm Sorry* evidently was not worth the wait. Critics felt that, while it was a decent album with music that could be considered typical Gin Blossoms fare, it lacked magic, and many forgettable tracks could not match the infectious nature of earlier hits. The album simply did not equal *New Miserable Experience*. The second single, "As Long as It Matters," faded quickly. Despite more fervent touring by the band, *Congratulations I'm Sorry* vanished from the Top 200 in four months, and the album was completely forgotten by the end of the year. Despite earning another gold record for its outstanding early performance, it did not approach the sales success of *New Miserable Experience*.

Aftermath. After the success of "Til I Hear It from You" and the early sales of *Congratulations I'm Sorry*, many were confident the Gin Blossoms could thrive without Hopkins, and band members denied they had anything to live up to as far as songwriting was concerned. Those predicting lasting success may have spoken too soon. *Congratulations I'm Sorry*'s fast fade in 1996 suggests the star-crossed guitarist Hopkins had a knack for writing music, the loss of which the band's skill, energy, and popularity could not overcome. The Gin Blossoms' members dissolved back into the Arizona music scene after a three-year run as surprise stars of the rock charts, leaving a small but popular musical legacy. —*Eric Strauss*

SELECT DISCOGRAPHY

■ ALBUMS

Up and Crumbling, 1991 (EP)
Dusted, 1989
New Miserable Experience, 1992
Congratulations I'm Sorry, 1996

Gipsy Kings

ORIGINAL MEMBERS: Nicolas Reyes, Andre Reyes, Jacques Baliardo, Maurice Baliardo, Tonino Baliardo
FIRST ALBUM RELEASE: *Allegria*, 1983
MUSICAL STYLE: Latin

Few other ethnic music ensembles have achieved the popular success of the Gipsy Kings. They have done so with an exotic blend of flamenco and other musics dubbed rumba flamenca. The core of the group consists of brothers from the Reyes and Baliardo families, offspring of well-known gypsy musicians. In the 1980's, the Gipsy Kings had an international dance hit with "Bamboleo."

Beginnings. What was to become the Gipsy Kings began in the late 1970's when the sons of two famous gypsy flamenco musicians, José Reyes and Manitas de Plata, formed their own ensemble. Singer Reyes and guitarist de Plata enjoyed much success as performers during the 1960's, selling millions of records and bringing traditional flamenco music to a wide audience. Their sons began with less ambitious goals. They first played at weddings and festivals in the gypsy communities of southern France from which they hailed. They also performed as street musicians and billed themselves as Los Reyes.

The husky, impassioned singing of Nicolas Reyes and the fiery guitar playing of Tonino Baliardo formed the heart of the ensemble. They excelled at multiguitar versions of a Spanish music known as Sevillana. The members of Los Reyes eventually landed in St. Tropez, France, where they performed at posh parties. Changing their name to the Gipsy Kings, they released a few albums that attracted little attention. Only a small core of devoted fans followed the group.

A New Sound. This changed when the Gipsy Kings met up with producer Claude Martinez. He thought the group had great potential but needed a musical makeover. Under his direction, the ensemble shed some of its traditional sound for a more contemporary one that combined the sensibilities of the Sevillana with other Mediterranean musics and a hint of pop-dance. It was a new musical hybrid that deserved its own name, rumba flamenca.

Rumba flamenca made the music of the Gipsy Kings more accessible to the general listener and paved the way for the sensation generated by their 1987 singles "Bamboleo" and "Djobi Djoba." No one could have anticipated their huge impact. It began in France, where the popularity of the songs in dance clubs earned the Gipsy Kings a recording contract with Sony. Rereleased on their platinum album *Gipsy Kings* (1987), the songs made the group a European phenomenon. "Bamboleo" enjoyed the most popularity. The toe-tapping, head-nodding epidemic quickly spread across the globe.

Fame. By the time the commotion had subsided, the Gipsy Kings had emerged as the best-known gypsy band on the planet. They quickly capitalized on their fame with extensive touring and were soon one of the most popular acts on the road. The group even sold out London's Royal Albert Hall and were invited to perform at the inaugural ball for President George Bush, quite an accomplishment for a group singing in their gipsy dialect of Gitane.

The personnel for the Gipsy Kings would vary somewhat in the years since "Bamboleo," but their musical style has remained largely unchanged. Slow or fast, it is always passionate. This is the mark of flamenco, which is clearly heard in Nicolas Reyes's soulful singing. Although it can be relaxed in ballads, his raspy, tense voice strains for high notes as he shouts out fervent lyrics in faster paced numbers. Reyes is also adept at covering nonflamenco styles, with his version of "My Way" from the 1987 album bringing wonderful new life to a tired old classic.

Throughout the 1990's, the Gipsy Kings worked hard to sustain their popularity through frequent touring and a number of albums released on various labels. While none of their songs would match the success of "Bamboleo," the group has sold over thirteen million albums worldwide and would continue to dominate world music charts. Director Peter Weir selected their song "Sin Ella" for the sound track to his 1993 film *Fearless*. The Gipsy Kings have also been the subject of two television documentaries. —*David Lee Fish*

SELECT DISCOGRAPHY

■ ALBUMS

Gipsy Kings, 1987
Mosaique, 1989
Este Mundo, 1991
Gipsy Kings Live, 1992
Love & Liberté, 1993
The Best of the Gipsy Kings, 1995 (compilation)
Tierra Gitana, 1996
Compas, 1997

The Go-Go's

ORIGINAL MEMBERS: Belinda Carlisle (b. 1958), Jane Wiedlin (b. 1958), Charlotte Caffey (b. 1953), Margot Olaverra, Elissa Bello

BEST-KNOWN LINEUP: Belinda Carlisle (b. 1958), Jane Wiedlin (b. 1958), Charlotte Caffey (b. 1953), Gina Schock (b. 1957), Kathy Valentine (b. 1959)

FIRST ALBUM RELEASE: *Beauty and the Beat*, 1981
MUSICAL STYLES: Pop, rock and roll

The Go-Go's (Paul Natkin)

Formed in Hollywood in 1978 as a punk girl group originally calling themselves the Misfits, the Go-Go's gradually shed their punk baggage, emerging as reliable purveyors of snappy, hard-edged pop. Their success inspired record companies to discover and market all-female rock groups in record numbers. With the exception of the Bangles, however, none of those groups came near the Go-Go's in terms of either popularity or musical quality. The Go-Go's broke up in 1984, and despite the temporary nature of the occasional reunions, they would remain one of the most popular all-female rock groups of all time.

Getting Serious. Although more rock girl groups formed during the punk years of the mid- to late 1970's than had formed during any other period in rock history, few, if any of them, sought commercial acclaim. Groups such as the Slits and the Raincoats, for instance, were content to stay within punk's experimental parameters. It was in such an environment that Belinda Carlisle, Charlotte Caffey, and Jane Wiedlin came together as the Go-Go's.

At first neither they nor the Hollywood punk crowds for whom they played seemed to expect much from them in terms of musicianship or songcraft. Hampered by a semicompetent rhythm section consisting of Margot Olaverra (bass) and Elissa Bello (drums) and a look consisting of thrift-shop clothing, excessive makeup, and garishly dyed hair, the Go-Go's appeared content to remain a punk novelty.

By 1980, however, the musically experienced rhythm section of Kathy Valentine and Gina Schock had replaced Olaverra and Bello, expediting the group's transition from punk to new wave—a briefly fashionable term applied mainly to rock and pop groups whose punk tendencies were primarily cosmetic. The new Go-Go's received their first high-profile exposure when footage of them performing "We Got the Beat," which they had released as a single in 1980 on the British punk label Stiff Records, was included in the 1981 punk documentary film *Urgh! A Music War* and its sound-track album.

Although largely unknown at the time of the

film's release, the Go-Go's benefited from appearing alongside groups such as XTC, the Police, and the Cramps. They also benefited from the attention shown them by the "Prince of the Sunset Strip," Rodney Bingenheimer, the legendary Hollywood disc jockey, who on his "Rodney on the ROQ" show became the first disc jockey to play one of their songs.

Cover of "Rolling Stone." In the fall of 1981, the Go-Go's released their debut album, *Beauty and the Beat.* In addition to yielding the million-selling single "We Got the Beat," the album sat atop the *Billboard* album chart for six weeks, eventually going double platinum. Filled with catchy, hard-driving songs about the bittersweet nature of romance, *Beauty and the Beat* proved that an all-female band could deliver an album that was more than a collection of singles. While due credit went to the album's producer, Richard Gottehrer, the album's songs and performances stood on their own. A major tour with A Flock of Seagulls as the opening act and an appearance on the cover of *Rolling Stone* magazine in their underwear established the Go-Go's as genuine stars.

Following such an act would not be easy, and the Go-Go's 1982 *Vacation* album was, relatively speaking, a disappointment. Yielding only one hit single (the title song) and selling only half a million copies, it inspired talk of a sophomore slump and had some of the group's more serious supporters wondering if perhaps they had overrated the Go-Go's.

Sensing that their moment might have passed, the group took two years to compose and record their 1984 album, *Talk Show.* A solid and enjoyable collection of songs, the album generated positive reviews, respectable sales, and a heavy-rotation MTV video in "Head over Heels," but it was ultimately overshadowed by such 1984 blockbusters as Bruce Springsteen's *Born in the U.S.A.*, Huey Lewis and the News' *Sports,* Prince and the Revolution's *Purple Rain,* and Tina Turner's *Private Dancer.* Shortly afterward, Wiedlin left the group to pursue a solo career, and in early 1985 they broke up. Wiedlin is more likely to be remembered for her appearance as Joan of Arc in the 1989 film *Bill and Ted's Excellent Adventure* than for any of her solo recordings, none of which sold particularly well.

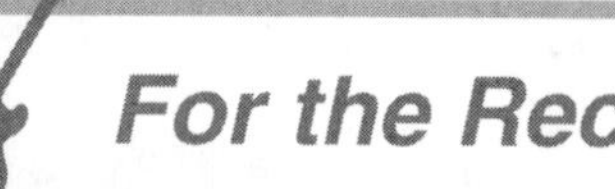

For the Record

The Bangles were the only serious competition of the Go-Go's during the early 1980's for the unofficial title of Best All-Female Rock Band. Ironically, for the Go-Go's' 1994 reunion tour, the pregnant Charlotte Caffey was replaced by Vicki Peterson, the former Bangles guitarist who later joined the New Orleans rock-and-roll band Continental Drifters.

§

Despite the Go-Go's enduring fame as rock and roll's last genuine girl group, the quantity (and some would say the quality) of the solo projects by the group's various members exceeds that of the group itself. Two of Belinda Carlisle's seven solo albums (*Belinda,* 1986; *Runaway Horses,* 1989) have gone gold, and one (*Heaven on Earth,* 1987) has gone platinum. In addition, Carlisle has hit the charts with more Top-40 singles (six) than the Go-Go's (with five). Jane Wiedlin has released three solo albums, and her single "Rush Hour" was a Top-10 hit in 1988. In 1997, her latest band, froSTed, released an album on Geffen Records.

The group continued to work together occasionally in loose configurations. Caffey contributed songs to Carlisle's solo albums, cowriting nine of the ten songs on Carlisle's 1993 album, *Real.* In addition, Caffey, Valentine, Schock, and Wiedlin have each contributed background vocals to Carlisle's recordings. In 1998, shortly after the breakup of Wiedlin's band froSTed, Wiedlin and Caffey announced plans to work together on other various projects.

Makeup to Breakup. The group's first compilation, *Go-Go's Greatest,* appeared in 1990, prompting a reunion. After completing a successful tour, the group broke up again. In 1994, a double-album compilation called *Return to the Valley of the Go-Go's* served as the occasion for another reunion and tour. Whereas *Go-Go's Greatest* had concentrated on the group's better-known material, *Return to the Valley of the Go-Go's* focused on the group's obscurities, with thirteen of the first album's twenty tracks comprising live, previously unreleased performances such as "Beatnik Beach," "Fashion Seekers," and "Johnny Are You Queer?" Some of the recordings date back to 1979 and include Olaverra on bass.

No sooner had their 1994 tour ended than the Go-Go's disbanded again, this time apparently for good. Not only were Carlisle, Wiedlin, Schock, and Caffey still pursuing their respective solo careers, but they had also begun to argue over songwriting royalties, eventually resorting to intragroup litigation. —*Arsenio Orteza*

SELECT DISCOGRAPHY

■ ALBUMS

Beauty and the Beat, 1981
Vacation, 1982
Talk Show, 1984
Go-Go's Greatest, 1990 (compilation)
Return to the Valley of the Go-Go's, 1994

SEE ALSO: Lauper, Cyndi; Reeves, Martha, and the Vandellas; Ronettes, The; Spice Girls, The.

Grandmaster Flash

(Joseph Sadler)

BORN: The Bronx, New York; January 1, 1958
FIRST ALBUM RELEASE: *The Message,* 1982 (as Grandmaster Flash and the Furious Five)
MUSICAL STYLES: Rap, hip-hop

Grandmaster Flash began his career in music as a mobile disc jockey in the Bronx, New York, in the mid-1970's. After pioneering scratch-mixing techniques to enhance the records he was playing, Grandmaster Flash gathered a group of friends to join him onstage to improvise rhymes to the beat of the music. Naming themselves Grandmaster Flash and the Furious Five, the band became the most important rap group of the early 1980's and popularized many of the techniques upon which later rap and hip-hop groups would build.

Innovation. Born Joseph Sadler, Grandmaster Flash spent his teenage years playing records at parties and in parks in the Bronx section of New York City. While other disc jockeys were content to allow records to play all the way to the end, Grandmaster Flash set out to develop a more creative interaction between himself and the recorded material he played on his turntables. After several years of experimentation, he developed scratch-mixing techniques that allowed him to combine different songs and create entirely new sounds by manipulating the speed and direction of his turntables. Grandmaster Flash unleashed his innovative jockeying style on the streets of the Bronx in the mid-1970's and then took the music to another level by inviting friends to improvise rhymed vocals onstage while he played records. He eventually gathered Cowboy, Melle Mel, Kid Creole, Rahiem, and Scorpio, and the six performers became known as Grandmaster Flash and the Furious Five.

The group played local shows until 1979, when the Sugarhill Gang's single "Rapper's Delight" became a hit record and revealed the mass-market potential of rap music. Grandmaster Flash and the Furious Five released the single "Super Rappin'" later in the same year, which was successful enough to gain the attention of Sylvia Robinson, owner of Sugarhill Records. The group released three consecutive gold records for the label in the next two years, but their biggest success came in 1982 with the release of "The Message," which went platinum in forty-one days. Dealing frankly with the uglier side of life in an urban ghetto, "The Message" was significant because it was the first rap song to delve into current social issues. It would become the blueprint for the harsher lyrics that characterized "gangsta" rap in the 1990's.

Solo Careers. Grandmaster Flash and the Furious Five disbanded during the recording of the "White Lines" single the following year in the midst of a dispute between Grandmaster Flash and Melle Mel concerning royalties from "The Message." In 1985, Grandmaster Flash released his first solo album on Elektra Records, *They Said*

It Couldn't Be Done. Sales were disappointing, as were those of his ensuing Elektra albums, *The Source* (1986) and *Ba-Dop-Boom-Bang* (1987). Melle Mel's attempts at a solo career were likewise unsuccessful, and this mutual failure facilitated the re-formation of the original lineup of Grandmaster Flash and the Furious Five in 1987. After the group played a charity concert at New York's Madison Square Garden, they went into the studio to record *On the Strength* on Elektra Records. The album failed to renew the public's interest, and the six members went their separate ways once again.

After successfully overcoming a cocaine addiction in the late 1980's, Grandmaster Flash reappeared in the 1990's as a producer of rap records. He also toured as a disc jockey in support of such "old-school" rap artists as Whodini and Kurtis Blow. Grandmaster Flash and Melle Mel reunited briefly in 1994 to collaborate with Duran Duran on the English new-wave band's remake of "White Lines." —*Douglas Long*

SELECT DISCOGRAPHY

■ ALBUMS

Grandmaster Flash and the Furious Five

The Message, 1982

On the Strength, 1988

Grandmaster Flash

They Said It Couldn't Be Done, 1985

The Source, 1986

Ba-Dop-Boom-Bang, 1987

SEE ALSO: Duran Duran; Run-D.M.C.

For the Record

Grandmaster Flash has explained why he began to mix excerpts from different records and manipulate the records to change their sounds and rhythms: "Most disc jockeys at parties would simply play a record all the way to the end, but I was too fidgety to just wait for the end of the record. So rather than sit and wait, I would do something to enhance the music."

Amy Grant

BORN: Augusta, Georgia; November 25, 1960

FIRST ALBUM RELEASE: *Amy Grant*, 1977

MUSICAL STYLES: Pop, folk, gospel

The best-known and most commercially successful artist in Christian contemporary music (CCM), singer and songwriter Amy Grant recorded several albums of gospel-oriented pop songs before crossing over in the mid-1980's to the mainstream pop market. Her success as a mainstream artist opened doors for other contemporary Christian artists, although fellow Christians frequently criticized Grant for straying from a strict gospel format.

The Girl Next Door. Grant grew up in a prosperous Christian home in Nashville, Tennessee. She attended a private high school where mandatory attendance at lackluster chapel programs inspired her to write her first songs for a program that would both entertain her classmates and express her Christian faith. Afterward, Grant continued writing songs with Christian themes. A typical teenager, Grant listened to pop radio and was influenced by artists such as James Taylor, Elton John, and Carole King rather than by traditional gospel music.

Grant was working as an errand girl in a Nashville recording studio when recording engineer Brown Bannister (who later became Grant's producer) heard a tape of songs she had made for her parents. Bannister played the tape over the telephone for a senior executive at Word Records and the Christian company offered Grant her first recording contract. Her self-titled debut album was released under the Myrhh imprint in her sophomore year of high school.

Grant recorded for Myrhh through high school and college, releasing *My Father's Eyes* in 1979 and *Never Alone* in 1980. Although she saw her songwriting and recording as hobbies, the success of her 1982 gospel-pop album *Age to Age* convinced her that she could pursue a career in music. *Age to Age* would become the first album by a white solo gospel artist to earn gold-record status. The album eventually went platinum, selling more than one million copies.

Amy Grant (AP/Wide World Photos)

Crossover Success. Her album *Straight Ahead* (1984) crossed over into the secular market, appearing briefly on *Billboard*'s pop album charts. Grant's brother-in-law and manager, Daniel Harrell, had believed early in Grant's career that she would have an appeal beyond the CCM audience and had formed a company to promote her on that basis. Grant, however, had no desire to pursue success in the mainstream market.

By the time her album *Unguarded* was released in 1985, Word Records had hired promoters to pitch Grant's records to Top-40 radio programmers (focusing on the songs that contained no specific references to Jesus). *Unguarded* peaked at number 29 on *Billboard*'s album chart and sold more than one million copies. *Unguarded* gave Grant her first mainstream hit with "Find a Way" and her first Grammy Award for Best Contemporary Gospel Performance. The platinum sales and Grammy recognition led Word Records to sign a contract for Grant with A&M Records. Grant's future albums would be promoted simultaneously by Myrhh as Christian contemporary material and by A&M as mainstream pop.

Grant's music was leaning stylistically toward rock and pop, featuring driving guitars and synthesizers, in contrast to the acoustic arrangements of her earlier material. Her live appearances had also progressed from the acoustic performances she gave as a teen to fully produced rock concerts, although Grant was still noted for the rapport she had with her live audiences and for the intimate atmosphere she could evoke in large venues. Christians noted Grant's changing image. Album art showing Grant as a fresh-faced high school girl had given way to studio photography of Grant dancing in apparent ecstasy, wearing a leopard-print jacket that would become her fashion trademark.

The Collection (1986) showcased Grant's earlier work while she took a hiatus from pursuing her career in order to support her husband, Gary Chapman, who had recently signed his own record deal. Grant had a number 1 single in 1986 with "Next Time I Fall," a duet with Peter Cetera which appeared on his album *Solitude/Solitaire.*

Between the release of *The Collection* and *Lead Me On* (1988), Grant and Chapman had their first child and struggled with marital problems, due in part to Chapman's addiction to narcotics. There were no hit singles from *Lead Me On,* but the album is often cited as Grant's best work; she had returned to quieter, acoustic-based arrangements, and her lyrics addressed more somber, adult themes such as slavery, the Holocaust ("Lead Me On"), temptation to infidelity ("Faithless Heart"), and Christian hypocrisy ("What About the Love").

As Grant moved into the mainstream, both Christian and secular critics counted the number of times the words Jesus or Lord occurred in her

For the Record

Grant's hit single "Baby Baby" was written about her baby daughter. Grant originally wanted lots of diapered babies in the "Baby Baby" video, but her teenage nephew talked her out of it.

lyrics. After several albums that spoke to doctrinal issues (albeit in a light, soft-pop style) Grant was exploring the creative freedom of writing songs about any aspect of life without requiring that every lyric explain the gospel. Grant's Christian fans asked why she wrote and recorded songs that were not specifically calls to believe in Christ, and some accused her of deliberately downplaying her Christian message in pursuit of greater mainstream success. At the same time, pop-radio programmers hesitated to play her records because of their Christian references.

Heart in Motion. In 1990 Grant began writing and recording *Heart in Motion*, concentrating on writing happy songs that would surprise her listeners and win her even greater mainstream success (she had decided by this time to actively pursue the secular market). Released in 1991, *Heart in Motion* sold more than five million copies, spent fifty-two weeks on *Billboard*'s album chart, and generated four Top-5 hits. Grant laughingly noted that its success may have been due to Janet Jackson's departure from A&M Records, which had allowed the label to put more energy into promoting Grant's album. The Grammy Award-nominated number 1 single "Baby Baby," cowritten by Grant and Keith Thomas, became a signature tune for Grant.

Grant's 1994 release, *House of Love*, went platinum and produced the hit title song, a duet with Vince Gill, although it was not a critical success. Following *House of Love*, Grant decided that she had become somewhat removed from the process of creating the music on her albums, and that she had revealed little of herself through her music. She returned to playing acoustic guitar (a skill she had lost since her early recordings) and began writing introspective, emotionally risky songs. The resulting album *Behind the Eyes* (1997) was similar to *Lead Me On* in its exploration of life's struggles and sorrows.

In a 1997 interview with *CCM* magazine, Grant discussed the pressure she had felt throughout her career to represent herself as an ideal Christian. Grant reaffirmed her Christian faith even as she described her struggle to free herself from the expectations of family, fans, and friends: "You know, I am either going to heaven or hell; I am either saved or not saved; I am either acceptable or unacceptable in your book, but this is life as I see it. It is my experience, and no one will ever know it but me." —*Maureen J. Puffer-Rothenberg*

SELECT DISCOGRAPHY

■ ALBUMS

Amy Grant, 1977
My Father's Eyes, 1979
Never Alone, 1980
In Concert, Volume One, 1981
In Concert, Volume Two, 1981
Age to Age, 1982
A Christmas Album, 1983
Straight Ahead, 1984
Unguarded, 1985
The Collection, 1986
Lead Me On, 1988
Heart in Motion, 1991
Home for Christmas, 1992
House of Love, 1994
Behind the Eyes, 1997

SELECT AWARDS

Grammy Award for Best Gospel Performance, Contemporary, for *Age to Age*, 1982
Grammy Award for Best Gospel Performance, Female, for "Ageless Medley," 1983
Grammy Award for Best Gospel Performance, Female, for "Angels," 1984
Grammy Award for Best Gospel Performance, Female, for *Unguarded*, 1985
Grammy Award for Best Gospel Performance, Female, for *Lead Me On*, 1988

SEE ALSO: Patti, Sandi.

The Grateful Dead

ORIGINAL MEMBERS: Jerry Garcia (1942-1995), Phil Lesh (b. 1945), Ron McKernan (1945-1973), Bob Weir (b. 1947), Bill Kreutzmann (b. 1946)
OTHER MEMBERS: Mickey Hart (b. 1943), Donna Godchaux (b. 1947), Keith Godchaux (1948-1980), Bruce Hornsby (b. 1954), Brent Mydland (1952-1990), others
FIRST ALBUM RELEASE: *The Grateful Dead*, 1967
MUSICAL STYLES: psychedelic rock, folk, blues

The Grateful Dead reigned as living legends among rock-and-roll bands for three decades. Followed by intensely loyal fans known as "Deadheads," the group kept alive the spirit of the San Francisco psychedelic movement from which they emerged in the mid-1960's. They were so successful at doing so that the Dead (as they were commonly called) remained one of the top-grossing concert acts more than twenty-five years after the demise of San Francisco's psychedelic scene. The band came to an unexpected end in 1995 with the sudden death of Jerry Garcia, the lead guitarist, artistic foundation, and spiritual center of the band.

The Grateful Dead's story not only ends but also begins with Jerry Garcia. A San Francisco native, he was born Jerome John Garcia in 1942. Garcia's father, a Spanish immigrant and jazz musician, named him for songwriter Jerome Kern. The first years of Garcia's life seem to have been happy ones, but then a life-shaping tragedy struck. When he was nine, his father died in a fishing accident. In the words of novelist Ken Kesey, "He watched his father drown. That has always been in his music—the darkness, the next life." The event also helped turn Garcia into a restless young man. He dropped out of high school after only one year and enlisted in the military, only to be quickly discharged.

Roots in Roots Music. Out of the Army and back in San Francisco, Garcia quickly immersed himself in the city's music scene. In 1962, he formed a bluegrass band with friends David Nelson (who would go on to found the New Riders of the Purple Sage) and Pete Albin (later of Big Brother and the Holding Company). The group started out as the Hart Valley Drifters but were renamed several times. While Garcia did not stay with the band for long, his love for bluegrass and other forms of American roots music would endure, reemerging in his work with the Grateful Dead and side projects with artists such as David Grisman.

In 1964, Garcia formed a new band that would gradually evolve into the Grateful Dead. Called Mother McCree's Uptown Jug Champions, the band included fellow San Franciscans Bob Weir on guitar and Ron "Pigpen" McKernan on keyboards and harmonica. The group, with John Dawson on drums, played in San Francisco Bay-area coffeehouses. Legend has it that the band members abandoned old-time jug-band music in favor of rock after they saw the Beatles in the 1964 motion picture *A Hard Day's Night.* McKernan, who grew up listening to rhythm and blues that his father played as a disc jockey, also deserves credit for steering the band toward electric blues, as does Bob Dylan, who had shown that folk musicians could still find inspiration while playing electric guitars.

Koolaid Acid Tests. The band's new musical direction brought new members and a new name. Now known as the Warlocks, the group added composition student Phil Lesh on bass. Around the same time, Bill Kreutzmann replaced Dawson as drummer. The band's fledgling existence received a sudden boost in 1965 when it began providing the live sound track for Ken Kesey's Electric Koolaid Acid Tests, large LSD parties held in the days before the hallucinogenic drug was declared illegal. The Warlocks' drawn-out, experimental, feedback-soaked improvisations made them the perfect house band for Kesey's events. In return, the band gained notoriety within San Francisco's developing psychedelic movement.

Toward the end of 1965, the Warlocks changed their name to the Grateful Dead. How they selected their new identity is a classic tale, one that reflects the spontaneity that was always at the group's core. As Garcia tells the story, "We were at Phil [Lesh]'s house one day; he had a big Oxford dictionary. I opened it up, and the first thing I saw was the 'grateful dead.' It said that on the page, and it was so astonishing."

For awhile, it appeared as if the Grateful Dead would remain little more than a local phenomenon. Other Bay-area groups had started cashing in on the psychedelic movement's growing popularity by signing record deals with major labels, but the Grateful Dead resisted all overtures. The group refused to commit to the artistic limitations they feared a recording contract would bring. They finally signed with Warner Bros. Records in 1967 and recorded their first album, *The Grateful Dead*, in just three days. While critics have charged that it "sounds about as carefully thought out as a scattershot jam," it did yield a couple of songs the band would play for the next thirty years. The ten-minute "Viola Lee Blues" also hinted at the extended improvisations that would become the group's stock and trade.

Anthem of the Sun. Unhappy with their first album, the Grateful Dead spent six months recording the follow-up, 1968's *Anthem of the Sun.* The long process worried Warner executive Joe Smith, who complained about the band's "lack of professionalism." Perhaps he mistook experimentation for amateurism as McKernan and Lesh rigged up prepared pianos in a manner similar to avant-garde composer John Cage, Kreutzmann and new bandmate Mickey Hart leavened the mix with exotic percussion, and Weir asked the recording engineer to give him "thick air." At any rate, Smith's worries proved unfounded. *Anthem of the Sun* was a successful release, bringing them national recognition and an amount commercial success.

Members of the Grateful Dead soon found themselves being proclaimed the honorary mayors of Haight-Ashbury, the San Francisco neigh-

The Grateful Dead at Red Rocks Amphitheater in Colorado in 1987: in front, Phil Lesh, Bob Weir, and Jerry Garcia; behind, drummers Bill Kreutzmann and Mickey Hart (Archive Photos/Melissa Dehnoke)

borhood that served as ground zero for psychedelic happenings. It was an important position to hold. Along with the related peace and love currents, the psychedelic stream flowed more strongly than any other artistic or cultural movement during the latter part of the 1960's. No musical act, not even Jimi Hendrix, embodied its spirit more fully than the Grateful Dead. The group's performance at Woodstock in 1969, marred as it was by sound reinforcement problems, did not fully attest to this fact, nor did their third studio album, *Aoxomoxoa* (1969). It was their 1969 double album, *Live Dead*, that best revealed the band's greatness during the period. In particular, the live version of "Dark Star" was a masterpiece of psychedelic jamming. It may remind listeners of such jazz improvisation masters as John Coltrane and Ornette Coleman, from whom Garcia and his colleagues took much musical inspiration.

Back to Roots. As the 1960's gave way to the 1970's, the psychedelic movement quickly waned. The Grateful Dead seemed to appreciate this and responded by releasing two albums of a considerably different sort. Both *Workingman's Dead* and *American Beauty* (both released 1970) were folk-rock classics filled with what has been called "hippie country music." The long, free-form improvisations were replaced by tightly structured songs filled with a "sweet lyricism" derived from folk and bluegrass influences. Garcia even played beautifully tender steel-string guitar on a number of the songs. Many consider *Workingman's Dead* and *American Beauty* to be the Grateful Dead's musical high point. The albums certainly marked a return to musical roots for Garcia and reflected a musical trend being popularized at the time by the likes of Crosby, Stills, and Nash and Neil Young. The albums also yielded a number of songs the Grateful Dead would perform in concert until they dissolved, including "Uncle John's Band," "Cumberland Blues," and the classic "Truckin'," with its signature loping rhythm.

The Deadheads. With their psychedelic inclinations now paired with down-home sensibilities, the Grateful Dead had created a formula that would sustain the group for the next twenty-five years as a road band. The psychedelic movement died and folk rock died, but the Grateful Dead kept touring year after year. As they did, an intensely loyal kernel of fans emerged known as Deadheads. Indeed, it is fair to say that no other popular act has enjoyed the same intensity of support. Hardcore Deadheads actually created a subculture that seemed to live for the band and its performances. They followed the group from city to city, as stereotype would have it, in Volkswagen buses from which they sold tie-dyed T-shirts in support of their nomadic quest.

It is also fair to say that the Deadheads were almost as much a part of the Grateful Dead phenomenon as the band itself. A Grateful Dead appearance may not have been Haight-Ashbury in the 1960's, but it seemed to be the next best thing. It was often said that a Grateful Dead show could not be explained to someone who had never seen them live. As poet Hugh "Wavy Gravy" Romney put it, "It's not just music. It's a religion." Deadheads came to performances time and time again. Many attended hundreds of Grateful Dead concerts. A subgroup known as Tapeheads specialized in recording Grateful Dead shows. Unlike many acts, the band approved of this activity, requesting only that Tapeheads share tapes with others rather than sell them. This sort of mutual understanding of needs and desires was the foundation of the Grateful Dead's intimate relationship with fans. It was a bond that crossed many social boundaries.

At times, the band itself seemed almost incidental to the whole Dead gestalt, a mere catalyst that created a chemical reaction by mounting the stage. Garcia once said of their fans, "In a way they've allowed themselves that latitude to enjoy a show for lots of different reasons. I think that's in their favor—no matter what the experience has been, they don't get burned." He went on to add, "When a Grateful Dead show is horrible, it's [still] interesting."

Many critics asserted that the group developed little musically after the release of *Workingman's Dead* and *American Beauty*, that they simply continued to mine veins of musical ore they had already unearthed. Perhaps this is true, but they did mature significantly as artists during the 1970's. In particular, Garcia gained remarkable stature as a soloist during this time. The group's studio albums from the decade, those that followed *Workingman's Dead* and *American Beauty*, presented a mixed bag of varying quality. The best known were *Blues for Allah* (1975), which added a jazz tinge to the Grateful Dead sound, and *Terrapin Station* (1977), which explored a few other musical avenues. Most agreed that such studio efforts did not capture the true essence of the Grateful Dead nearly as well as the numerous live albums the band released over the years.

Losses and Gains. In 1986, the Grateful Dead recorded a studio project, *In the Dark*, that quickly went platinum—a first for the group. It also yielded the Top-10 single "A Touch of Grey"—another first. A line from the song, "I will get by/ I will survive," seemed particularly poignant in light of the week-long diabetic coma Garcia suffered in 1985. While Garcia may have survived, some other Grateful Dead members had been less lucky. McKernan died of a drug-related liver problem in 1973. Replacement pianist Keith Godchaux died in a car accident shortly after leaving the band in 1980. Their keyboard heir, Brent Mydland, succumbed to drugs in 1990. Through it all, the Grateful Dead kept on.

In the Dark restoked the fires for the Grateful Dead, bringing them a legion of new fans (sometimes referred to as neo-Deadheads) too young to remember the psychedelic movement of the 1960's. As a result, the group became one of the top-grossing concert acts of the early 1990's. Band members seemed to relish the renewed lease on life and the artistic fruit that came with it. Several band members became involved in outside projects, such as Hart's forays into world drumming and Garcia's successful line of neckties festooned with his own artwork. Garcia even became the inspiration for Ben and Jerry's Cherry Garcia ice cream.

The Long, Strange Trip Ends. In August, 1995, Garcia checked into a drug rehabilitation clinic to try to overcome his addiction to drugs. Early in the morning of August 8, the literal and figurative heart of the Grateful Dead stopped beating. A stunned world of Deadheads and more casual fans regathered their senses and began to eulogize. Tributes came from all quarters. Even the president and vice president of the United States publicly mourned Garcia's passing.

Many Deadheads, not wanting to admit that the trip was over, clamored for the group to stay together, but, at the end of 1995, the Grateful Dead disbanded. Members went on as individual artists and regrouped in 1998 as the Other Ones. The spirit of the Grateful Dead lived on, however, in newer bands such as Phish, who attempted to continue on where the Grateful Dead left off. Musically, the Grateful Dead leave an important legacy. They demonstrated that musical experimentation can be paired with strong traditional roots, a lesson that artists such as Beck have taken to heart.

—David Lee Fish

For the Record

"The Grateful Dead should be sponsored by the government—a public service. And they should set us up to play at places that need to get high." *—Jerry Garcia*

§

In the late 1990's the surviving members of the Grateful Dead were planning a huge amusement park and museum dedicated to the band and its fans. It would be located in San Francisco and named Terrapin Station, after one of the group's better-known albums.

SELECT DISCOGRAPHY

■ ALBUMS

The Grateful Dead, 1967
Anthem of the Sun, 1968
Aoxomoxoa, 1969
Live Dead, 1969 (live)
Workingman's Dead, 1970
American Beauty, 1970
Blues for Allah, 1975
Terrapin Station, 1977

Go to Heaven, 1980
In the Dark, 1987
Dylan and the Dead, 1989
One from the Vault, 1991
Two from the Vault, 1992
Dick's Picks: Vol. 1, 1993
Dick's Picks: Vol. 2, 1995

SELECT AWARDS
Rock and Roll Hall of Fame, inducted 1997

SEE ALSO: Beck; Jefferson Airplane; Phish.

Al Green

BORN: Forrest City, Arkansas; April 13, 1946
FIRST SINGLE RELEASE: "Back Up Train," 1967
MUSICAL STYLES: Soul, gospel

Al Green is not the only soul singer who started his career in gospel music. With him, though, the friction between sacred and secular music has been especially strong, as he has switched back and forth at various points in his career. His popular hits of the early 1970's, featuring his trademark falsetto singing, remain his most influential contribution to the history of popular music.

The Beginnings. Al Green's father was a minister who taught his son to love gospel music. At the age of nine, young Green began singing with his brothers in the Green Brothers gospel quartet. They performed successfully for a number of years on the gospel circuit before his father kicked Al out of the group for listening to the rhythm-and-blues recordings of Sam Cooke and Jackie Wilson. Al then formed a secular group, the Creations, with whom he performed in the 1960's. Under the name of Al Green and the Soul Mates, they recorded their first pop single, "Back Up Train" (1967). The success of this record encouraged Green to move to Memphis. His career remained stagnant for the next several years, though, until he met Willie Mitchell of Hi Records and signed a contract to record albums for the company. In the years ahead, he and producer Mitchell went on to create a unique sound that made Green an ideal singer of tender soul ballads.

Soul Success. The classic Al Green style emerged on the album *Al Green Gets Next to You* (1970). Here he showed his range from heartsick ballads such as "Tired of Being Alone" to the funky "I'm a Ram for You." The sound that made Green famous features a smooth singing style patterned after Sam Cooke, the falsetto range learned from Claude Jeter of the Swan Silvertones, and ornate embellishments and vocal interjections that are uniquely his own. He seldom grabs the listener's attention with raw power, but instead he impresses with exquisite control. Green demonstrated on this album that it is possible for the male falsetto voice to express strength and masculinity in spite of what some might consider the unnatural quality of this vocal range.

A string of hits followed his 1970 album. *Let's Stay Together* (1972), *I'm Still in Love with You* (1972), and *Call Me* (1973) are all classic Green albums that spun off a series of hit singles. They contain original songs that highlight Green's unique strengths (such as the title songs of all three albums), as well as covers (such as the Temp-

Al Green in 1972 (AP/Wide World Photos)

tations' "I Can't Get Next to You" and the Bee Gees' "How Can You Mend a Broken Heart?") that show his ability to adapt his style to other material. His popularity was remarkable, as four singles from 1971 and 1972 were Top-5 hits on both the pop and rhythm-and-blues charts. Many considered Green the next great soul superstar and the heir to James Brown. The best songs of this glory period are brought together on his *Greatest Hits* album of 1975.

Personal Tragedy and Religious Commitment. Green's success story was derailed in October of 1974 by personal tragedy. After Green had an argument with his girlfriend, she scalded him with a pan of boiling grits and then committed suicide. The horrible experience left Green scarred both physically and emotionally. He had already experienced a religious awakening in 1973, and the 1974 tragedy, along with a serious fall from a Cincinnati stage in 1979, led him to leave pop music to concentrate on gospel.

Al Green had never completely strayed from his gospel roots, even at the height of his fame as a soul artist. Both *Call Me* and *Livin' for You* (1973) had included songs of a religious nature. In "Belle" (1977), though, he expressed the tension between sacred and secular music most clearly by singing, "It's you that I want but it's Him that I need."

In 1976, Green was ordained minister of the Full Gospel Tabernacle in Memphis, a position he would continue to hold for more than twenty years. His new responsibilities also resulted in a new direction for his music. Starting with *The Lord Will Make a Way* (1980), his albums have been almost exclusively gospel recordings. These recordings earned the singer Grammy Awards in 1981, 1982, 1983, 1984, 1986, 1987, and 1989, a distinction he had never won for his pop recordings in the 1970's.

For Al Green, though, the worlds of gospel and pop were not too far apart to keep him from crossing over occasionally. His 1988 single "Put a Little Love in Your Heart," a duet with rock singer Annie Lennox, offended some of his gospel fans. Green recalled, "Church folks said I shouldn't sing with Annie Lennox and my response was they can't tell whether she's a Christian or not so they can't tell me not to sing with her." In 1995 he released his first secular album in nearly two decades, *Your Heart's in Good Hands.* His performances on tour that year confirmed that the master of soul was still alive and well. As if to emphasize the two sides of his musical personality, his stage show included both sensuous love songs and fervent prayers. For Green, it seems that gospel and soul are both essential to his work as an artist, and his long and fruitful career has allowed him to make important contributions to both genres.

—E. Douglas Bomberger

SELECT DISCOGRAPHY

■ ALBUMS

Back Up Train, 1967
Green Is Blues, 1970
Al Green Gets Next to You, 1970
Let's Stay Together, 1972
I'm Still in Love with You, 1972
Call Me, 1973
Livin' for You, 1973
Al Green Explores Your Mind, 1974
Greatest Hits, 1975 (compilation)
The Belle Album, 1977
Truth 'n' Time, 1978
The Lord Will Make a Way, 1980
Precious Lord, 1982
Trust in God, 1984
Soul Survivor, 1987

For the Record

Speaking about his religious awakening and his personal tragedy, Al Green said: "I was born again in 1973. . . . It wasn't an incident that did it. No. People are silly when they write that. Nothing happened to bring me to Christ except coming into the knowledge of Christ and being transformed in mind and spirit on a particular morning. I'm a gospel singer now, and when it happened to me, I was singing rock and roll."

Love Ritual: Rare and Previously Unreleased 1968-1976, 1989
Don't Look Back, 1993
Your Heart's in Good Hands, 1995

SELECT AWARDS

Billboard, named Best Pop and R&B Vocalist, 1972
Record World, named Best Pop and R&B Vocalist, 1972
Rolling Stone, named Best Pop and R&B Vocalist, 1972
Cash Box, named Best R&B Vocalist, 1975
Grammy Award for Best Soul Gospel Performance, Traditional, for *The Lord Will Make a Way*, 1981
Grammy Award for Best Soul Gospel Performance, Contemporary, for *Higher Plane*, 1982
Grammy Award for Best Soul Gospel Performance, Traditional, for *Precious Lord*, 1982
Grammy Award for Best Soul Gospel Performance, Male, for *I'll Rise Again*, 1983
Grammy Award for Best Soul Gospel Performance by a Duo or Group for "Sailin' on the Sea of Your Love," 1984 (with Shirley Caesar)
Grammy Award for Best Soul Gospel Performance, Male, for "Everything's Gonna Be Alright," 1987
Grammy Award for Best Soul Gospel Performance, Male or Female, for "As Long as We're Together," 1989
Grammy Award for Best Pop Vocal Collaboration for "Funny How Time Slips Away," 1995 (with Lyle Lovett)
Rock and Roll Hall of Fame, inducted 1995

SEE ALSO: Bee Gees, The; Cooke, Sam; Temptations, The; Wilson, Jackie.

Green Day

ORIGINAL MEMBERS: Billie Joe Armstrong (b. 1972), Mike Dirnt (b. Michael Pritchard, 1972), Tré Cool (b. Frank Edwin Wright III, 1972)
OTHER MEMBERS: John Kiftmeyer, Al Sobrante
FIRST ALBUM RELEASE: *1000 Hours*, 1989 (EP)
MUSICAL STYLES: Rock and roll, punk rock

For the Record

Billie Joe Armstrong's father, who died when Billie Joe was ten, was a jazz drummer and truck driver. Billie Joe began singing in a choral group when he was five. He entertained in children's wards of hospitals and nursing homes. When asked about his career aspirations, he responded that he would either be a singer or a truck driver.

Billie Joe Armstrong got his first guitar at age eleven and wrote his first song, "Why Do You Want Him?" at age twelve. He met Michael Pritchard, who also played guitar, while attending school in the working-class Northern California town of Rodeo. By the time the two were fourteen, they had formed a band called Sweet Children with Pritchard on bass and Armstrong supplying vocals and guitar. The band recorded one independent EP. In 1989, the duo added drummer Al Sobrante to their lineup and changed the band's name to Green Day, taken from a Sweet Children song of the same name. Pritchard changed his surname to Dirnt, and Green Day recorded two independent EPs, *1,000 Hours* (1989) and *Slappy* (1990), and an album, *39/Smooth* (1990).

Shortly after the album's release, Sobrante left the band and was replaced by Tré Cool. Cool had previously drummed for a punk band called the Lookouts, which was coincidentally helmed by the president of Lookout Records, the independent record label that had released *1,000 Hours* and *39/Smooth.* By now the band was steadily building a following in the university city of Berkeley. Their fan base grew immensely upon the release of the second independent album, *Kerplunk*, in 1992.

Major Label. In 1993, Green Day aggressively pursued major label record company interest and signed with Reprise Records. Green Day released its major-label debut, *Dookie*, on January 11, 1994. Critics raved about this neopunk pop album filled with short, funny, and well-written songs with exu-

Green Day (Reprise/Kentaro Kamata)

berant harmonies and catchy melodies. Though Armstrong was born and raised in California, he sang with an English accent, which some critics thought added to the charm and others thought was hopelessly pretentious. At the same time, the band became popular on MTV for their witty concept videos and ever-changing hair color.

In 1995, *Dookie* proved hard to categorize for the Grammy Nominating Committee. The album won for Best Alternative Music Performance and was nominated for Best New Artist. The song "Basket Case" was nominated for Best Rock Performance by a Duo or Group with Vocal. Most puzzling, the single "Longview" was nominated for Best Hard Rock Performance.

The fourth album, *Insomniac*, was released in 1995. It was a lackluster follow-up to its predecessor. The singles failed to capture sustained excitement, and the album was generally considered a disappointment. In 1996, the band abruptly cancelled an in-progress European tour, claiming exhaustion. The band had been touring nonstop for two years. During this downtime, Armstrong worked on a long-running side project called Pinhead Gunpowder. This group, made up of Bay Area musicians, was formed in 1991. The band's second album, *Goodbye Ellston Avenue*, was released independently in 1996.

Nimrod. With time off to concentrate on songwriting, Green Day allegedly readied forty songs, eighteen of which actually made it onto 1997's *Nimrod*, which marked the departure of the band's reliance on short pop/punk-style songs. Though still recognizably Green Day, the songs were more varied, even incorporating a string section and an instrumental. In some cases, the band reached back to its independent records for subject matter. Videos, always an important outlet for the band's creativity, employed larger casts of characters and were even smarter, funnier, and more high-concept than previous videos.

Perhaps the best indicator that Green Day had made it into the mainstream was the success of the uncharacteristic ballad from *Nimrod*, "Good Riddance (Time of Your Life)," which was featured prominently in the two highest-rated television shows of the 1998 season. In the last episode of *Seinfeld*, it accompanied a nostalgic photo montage. The song was discussed and analyzed during two consecutive episodes of *ER* in which a teenage Green Day fan died of leukemia. The single was rereleased after these appearances, and record sales and airplay soared. —*Deirdre Rockmaker*

SELECT DISCOGRAPHY

■ ALBUMS

1,000 Hours, 1989 (EP)
Slappy, 1990 (EP)
39/Smooth, 1990
Kerplunk, 1992
Dookie, 1994
Insomniac, 1995
Nimrod, 1997

SELECT AWARDS

Grammy Award for Best Alternative Music Performance for *Dookie,* 1994

SEE ALSO: Clash, The.

Nanci Griffith

BORN: Seguin, Texas; July 6, 1954

FIRST ALBUM RELEASE: *There's a Light Beyond These Woods,* 1978

MUSICAL STYLES: Folk, country

Without the benefits of radio airplay or a major label promotional drive, folksinger Nanci Griffith took her music from the small bars of Austin, Texas, to the wide stage of New York's Carnegie Hall. Telling stories in her lilting soprano, Griffith takes inspiration from such twentieth century novelists as Eudora Welty, Larry McMurtry, and Carson McCullers. Her refusal to fit into a slick marketing niche opened the door for the mid-1990's resurgence of such contemporary folk-based artists as Mary Chapin Carpenter, Lyle Lovett, and the Indigo Girls.

The Beginnings. Griffith learned to play the guitar from an old public television series, *Laura Weber's Folk Guitar.* She began writing her own songs because it was easier than learning how to play other people's songs and wrote her first song, "A New Generation," at age twelve. At fourteen, she played her first professional performance at an Austin hotel, earning eleven dollars.

Griffith graduated from the University of Texas with an education degree. Throughout the 1970's, she taught kindergarten and first grade during the day and played at Austin's Hole in the Wall bar at night. There she attracted the attention of now defunct independent record label B. F. Deal Records.

The Independent Years. Her 1978 debut album, *There's a Light Beyond These Woods,* was pure folk. Despite the primitive production, Griffith's strength as a storyteller was already evident. In the pre-alternative radio days, she received little or no airplay, and relentless touring became her stock in trade. Over the next four years, Griffith built a strong following from behind the wheel of her Toyota station wagon and recorded her second album, *Poet in My Window,* in 1982 on another independent label, Featherbed. *Poet* was the first album to feature Griffith's trademark mix of country and folk, a blend she would later call "folkabilly."

Rounder Records, a label long known for its support of traditional music, released her next two albums. 1985's *Once in a Very Blue Moon* covered a wide range of styles and tempos, and in-

Nanci Griffith (AP/Wide World Photos)

cluded her tribute to Houston's Anderson Fair music club, "Spin on a Red Brick Floor." Her breakthrough came in 1986 with *The Last of the True Believers*, an album that featured Lyle Lovett on background vocals and on the cover. Country artist Kathy Mattea saw Griffith perform one of the songs, "Love at the Five and Dime," on the television series *Austin City Limits* and took her version of the song to number 1 on the country charts.

The MCA Years. A 1986 Grammy Award nomination brought Griffith to the attention of the major labels, and her independent days were over. She moved to Nashville, Tennessee, and signed with MCA's country division. Her first recording for the label, *Lone Star State of Mind* (1987), blended traditional folk songs with a more mainstream sound. That trend continued with 1988's *Little Love Affairs*. The title tune was an Irish-style ballad cowritten with James Hooker, her longtime keyboard accompanist. It also featured "Gulf Coast Highway," a poignant ballad later covered by both Emmylou Harris and Willie Nelson.

In 1989, Griffith moved to MCA's West Coast division in Los Angeles and her music took on more of a pop mentality. Her next two albums, *Storms* (1989) and *Late Night Grande Hotel* (1991) nearly lost the familiar country-folk sound that had originally made her so popular. Throughout her years with the label, MCA had provided little promotional support, so when her contract ended she moved to Elektra.

Other Voices, Other Rooms. Griffith has always maintained that the songs of the master songwriters need to be sung by new voices in new places to keep them alive. In that spirit, her first Elektra release in 1993, *Other Voices, Other Rooms*, was a tribute to the artists who were her inspirations. Named after Truman Capote's first novel, the album included songs by Woody Guthrie, Bob Dylan, Kate Wolf, Townes Van Zandt, John Prine, Tom Paxton, Janis Ian, Gordon Lightfoot, Jerry Jeff Walker, and Malvina Reynolds. Helping her pay tribute was an all-star lineup of supporting players, including Chet Atkins, Arlo Guthrie, Bob Dylan, the Indigo Girls, Emmylou Harris, Odetta, and John Prine. *Other Voices, Other Rooms* won the 1993 Grammy Award for Best Contemporary Folk Album and is considered by many to be Griffith's finest work.

After devoting so much time to her folk predecessors, Griffith came to realize why their music touched her so deeply. As she told one interviewer, "In recording *Other Voices*, in going back and listening to the writers that influenced me, it occurred to me that the reason they touched me so much was because their work was so autobiographical." This realization led to 1994's *Flyer*, in which she switched from telling other people's stories to telling her own. Dedicated to a long-lost love, the songs on *Flyer* ranged from hurt to hopeful and featured elements of pop, country, alternative, and traditional folk music.

In 1997 Griffith produced *Blue Roses from the Moons* and employed the considerable talents of Buddy Holly's former backup band, the Crickets, in addition to those of her longtime backup band, the Blue Moon Orchestra. Griffith called the album "Dust Bowl rock and roll" and continued the openly autobiographical style of *Flyer*. Most notable of the songs was "Saint Teresa of Avila," about a childhood friend who had recently committed suicide. The deeply personal song was cowritten by Griffith's sister, Mikki, and Margaret Mary Graham (the subject of "There's a Light Beyond These Woods," which appeared on *Lone Star State of Mind*).

For the Record

Nanci Griffith's major label debut, *Lone Star State of Mind*, featured a ballad written by Julie Gold. Griffith felt this song was a surefire hit, but few heard it because MCA refused to release it as a single. Three years later, Bette Midler had a number 1 hit with the very same song—"From a Distance." Griffith continued to use the song as one of her signature pieces, and her version eventually reached number 1 in Ireland, where she has a devoted following.

From 1976 to 1982, Griffith was married to singer-songwriter Eric Taylor. Taylor appears on her first two albums as well as her 1988 live album *One Fair Summer Evening*. She was later engaged to singer-songwriter Tom Kimmel, but they parted before marrying. Griffith has recorded and toured extensively with the Chieftains, having lived in Ireland for a time. She also contributed a song to John Mellencamp's film *Falling from Grace* in 1992. —*P. S. Ramsey*

SELECT DISCOGRAPHY

■ ALBUMS

There's a Light Beyond These Woods, 1978
Poet in My Window, 1982
Once in a Very Blue Moon, 1985
The Last of the True Believers, 1986
Lone Star State of Mind, 1987
Little Love Affairs, 1988
One Fair Summer Evening, 1988
Storms, 1989
Late Night Grande Hotel, 1991
Other Voices, Other Rooms, 1993
Flyer, 1994
Blue Roses from the Moons, 1997

SELECT AWARDS

Grammy Award for Best Contemporary Folk Album for *Other Voices, Other Rooms*, 1993

SEE ALSO: Baez, Joan; Carpenter, Mary Chapin; Chieftains, The; Collins, Judy; Guthrie, Woody; Harris, Emmylou; Indigo Girls, The; Lovett, Lyle; Mattea, Kathy; Seeger, Pete; Vega, Suzanne; Williams, Hank.

The Guess Who / Bachman-Turner Overdrive

The Guess Who

ORIGINAL MEMBERS: Randy Bachman (b. 1943), Chad Allan (b. Allan Kobel, c. 1945), Jim Kale (b. 1943), Bob Ashley, Garry Peterson (b. 1945)

OTHER MEMBERS: Bruce Decker, Burton Cummings (b. 1947), Kurt Winter (b. 1946), Greg Leskiw (b. 1947), Don McDougall (b. 1947), Billy Wallace (b. 1949), Domenic Troiano (b. 1945)

FIRST SINGLE RELEASE: "Shakin' All Over," 1965

Bachman-Turner Overdrive

ORIGINAL MEMBERS: Randy Bachman, Robbie Bachman (b. 1953), C. F. (Fred) Turner (b. 1943), Tim Bachman

OTHER MEMBERS: Blair Thornton (b. 1950), Jim Clench

FIRST SINGLE RELEASE: "You Ain't Seen Nothing Yet," 1974

MUSICAL STYLES: Rock and roll, rhythm and blues

Both the Guess Who and Bachman-Turner Overdrive were outgrowths of the Winnipeg band Al and the Silvertones, led by vocalist Chad Allan (born Allan Kobel) and guitarist Randy Bachman in 1959. These two organized the first lineup of the Guess Who. Pianist Bob Ashley left the band in 1965, and the group underwent major changes when Allan left to attend college. In 1966, Bruce Decker was temporarily lead vocalist and appeared on the group's first single, "Shakin' All Over." Later that year, he was replaced by Burton Cummings (vocals, keyboards) who completed the most important Guess Who lineup with Jim Kale (bass) and Garry Peterson (drums).

For two years, the group accumulated regional and national support, ultimately hosting their own Canadian television series, *Where It's At*. Producer Jack Richardson then mortgaged his home to finance a New York recording session. The group's first international success came after signing with RCA/Victor, issuing their debut album, *Wheatfield Soul* (1969). The album became a million seller, yielding the group's first Top-10 hit, "These Eyes."

While Cummings was accused of imitating the Doors' lead singer, Jim Morrison, and Bachman was deemed a derivative if effective guitar soloist, the group continued to issue hit singles largely based on the team's compositional skills. Their next outing, the double-sided hit "Laughing" and "Undun," was followed by the group's most adventurous album, *American Woman* (1970). This album featured Bachman's title track, the group's only hit in England. Other singles remixed from album tracks included the number 5 hit "No Time" and "No Sugar Tonight."

Splits and Changes: BTO. Later in 1970, an ill Bachman left the band after playing his final single with the Guess Who, "Albert Flasher." A converted Mormon, he had long objected to the group's rowdy road behavior, but at first the split between him and Cummings was amicable.

Again in Winnipeg, Bachman formed the band Brave Belt, teaming with Guess Who founder Chad Allan and brother Robbie Bachman (drums). This group released two albums, but after C. F. (Fred) Turner replaced Allan and another Bachman brother, Tim, became guitarist, the band became Bachman-Turner Overdrive (BTO), named in part for a truckers' magazine. BTO quickly became competitors with the Guess Who for the top-band distinction in Canada, leading to public feuds between Cummings and Bachman.

BTO's debut, *Bachman-Turner Overdrive* (1973), featured two popular songs, "Welcome Home" and "Let It Ride," as well as their first major single, "Taking Care of Business." But the group's breakthrough came with "You Ain't Seen Nothing Yet" from their 1974 *Not Fragile.* This was followed by *Four Wheel Drive* (1975), their last million seller. Other Top-40 hits, while not gold records, were "Roll on down the Highway" (1975), "Hey You" (1975) and "Take It Like a Man" (1976).

Relationships between the two bands worsened, particularly as the Guess Who's albums continued to sell but never again reached the heights of *American Woman.* Two guitarists replaced Bachman in the Guess Who, Kurt Winter and Greg Leskiw, whose contributions were first demonstrated in "Share the Land" in late 1970. Other hits, "Rain Dance," "Hand Me Down World," and "Hang on to Your Life" followed. In 1972 the personnel changed again when Leskiw and Kale quit, replaced by Don McDougall (guitar) and Billy Wallace (bass). Winter stayed for a short time but also left, to be replaced by Domenic Troiano, former guitarist for the James Gang. The group's image continued to erode, falling to its lowest point with the novelty hit "Clap for the Wolfman," featuring brief raps by gravelly voiced Wolfman Jack, disc jockey and announcer on television's *The Midnight Special.*

In 1973, the group released *Onward,* but the band's fortunes waned as Bachman-Turner Overdrive became Canada's top rock band. Two more singles, "Star Baby" (1974) and "Dancing Fool" (1974), eased into the Top 40, but it was clear the Guess Who no longer had hit potential. After Wallace quit in 1975, Cummings disbanded the group. The Guess Who's last official performance was in Montreal, Canada, on September 2, 1975. BTO continued touring for five more years, officially breaking up in 1980.

Reunions and Reformations. In 1979, Kale, who owned the Guess Who name, reformed the group with McDougall and Peterson, playing in small venues throughout the United States and Canada. BTO also had occasional reunions, and Bachman made guest appearances with both of his former groups.

Both Cummings and Bachman attempted solo careers, ultimately reconciling, with Bachman producing Cummings' albums. Bachman also performed with fellow Canadian Neil Young, and in 1997, Bachman paid homage to both of his

For the Record

Bachman-Turner Overdrive's chart-topping "You Ain't Seen Nothing Yet" began as a gag song that Randy Bachman recorded for his brother, Gary. "He stuttered," Bachman later explained. "We thought, just for fun . . . we'd take this song and I'd stutter and we'd send it to him. He'll have the only copy in the world." Later, as the band finished its *Not Fragile* album, a record company official thought it needed another song. Bachman played "You Ain't Seen Nothing Yet" for him, agreeing to use it if he could re-record its vocals. The re-recording didn't work, so—to Bachman's embarrassment—they went with the original stuttering version.

former bands by performing "No Sugar Tonight" and "You Ain't Seen Nothing Yet" as part of Ringo Starr's All-Stars. —*Wesley Britton*

SELECT DISCOGRAPHY

The Guess Who

■ ALBUMS

Wheatfield Soul, 1969
American Woman, 1970
Share the Land, 1970
The Best of the Guess Who, 1971

Bachman-Turner Overdrive

■ ALBUMS

Bachman-Turner Overdrive, 1973
Not Fragile, 1974
Four Wheel Drive, 1975
Best of BTO (So Far), 1975 (compilation)

Guns n' Roses

ORIGINAL MEMBERS: Axl Rose (b. William Rose, 1962), Slash (b. Saul Hudson, 1965), Izzy Stradlin (b. Jeffrey Isabelle, 1962), Steven Adler (b. 1965), Duff McKagan (b. Michael McKagan, 1964)

OTHER MEMBERS: Gilby Clarke (b. 1962), Matthew Sorum (b. 1960), Dizzy Reed (b. Darren Reed, 1963)

FIRST ALBUM RELEASE: *Appetite for Destruction,* 1987

MUSICAL STYLES: Rock and roll, heavy metal

A series of strange coincidences brought together five transplants to Los Angeles—vocalist W. Axl Rose, guitarists Izzy Stradlin and Slash, bassist Duff McKagan, and drummer Steven Adler—to become Guns n' Roses. As Slash told *Musician* magazine, "We were the only five people . . . that could enjoy what each other did enough to start a band." The five musicians moved into a tiny apartment/rehearsal space with no running water on Sunset Boulevard.

The band fought with promoters to play often, resulting in a large following. By the end of 1985, a record company bidding war had begun, and the band signed with Geffen Records in 1986. While they were recording, Geffen released ten thousand copies of a four-song EP, *Live ?!*@ Like a Suicide,* through the band's own Uzi/Suicide label.

Sudden Success. The full-length album *Appetite for Destruction* was released on July 31, 1987. The album was a graphic depiction of Los Angeles's seedy side, and each song was based on the band members' personal experiences. The original cover art was considered too controversial and was replaced. The band spent one year opening for a variety of top-selling hard rock bands. By the end of the tour, the album was number 1 on the *Billboard* album chart. In February, 1988, the band won Best New Artist at the MTV Video Music Awards.

In December, 1988, Geffen released *GN'R Lies,* which included the four tracks from *Live ?!*@ Like a Suicide* plus four semiacoustic songs. When it entered the *Billboard* album chart at number 2, Guns n' Roses became the only group in the 1980's with two albums in the Top 5 at the same time. Controversy ensued, however, when listeners realized that at least one song contained racial and homophobic slurs. Despite the criticism, Guns n' Roses won an MTV Video Music Award for Best Heavy Metal/Hard Rock Video for the love song "Sweet Child o' Mine." In January, 1990, Slash and McKagan scandalized the American Music Awards when Slash delivered an expletive-filled acceptance speech on live television.

Dizzy Reed, a keyboardist who was a friend of Rose, became the sixth member of the band, while drummer Steven Adler was fired because of drug problems. He was replaced by Matt Sorum, formerly of the Cult. Adler later sued the band for allegedly encouraging his addiction. The suit was settled out of court for $12.5 million. More controversy surrounded a concert in St. Louis at which a destructive riot broke out after Rose allegedly assaulted a fan who was attempting to photograph the band.

Use Your Illusion I and *Use Your Illusion II* were released simultaneously in September, 1991. Packaged as two separate albums, they entered the *Billboard* album chart at number 1 and number 2. Both albums showed a tremendous growth in lyrical content, arrangements, and instrumentation, with Rose exhibiting a full range of raw emotions. The recordings included songs that dated back to the apartment on Sunset Boulevard, piano-led ballads, and angry tirades. The culmination was the ten-minute heart-stopper "Coma."

Just two months later, Stradlin left the band. He had become increasingly uncomfortable with success. Gilby Clarke took over rhythm guitar and was given two weeks to learn forty songs in time for an upcoming tour. For the U.S. dates, Guns n' Roses expanded its lineup with backup singers, a second keyboard player, and a horn section, swelling the onstage ranks to thirteen musicians.

The Spaghetti Incident?, an album of cover songs representing the band's influences, was released in November of 1993. With a heavy emphasis on punk songs, the album also contained an uncredited rendition of Charles Manson's "Look at Your Game Girl," which led to renewed criticism of the band. By 1995, each of the band members except Rose had released a solo album. The sudden lack of Guns n' Roses activity was taking its toll, and the band seemed to be falling apart.

The Next Generation. In late 1996, Rose bought the Guns n' Roses name, which gave him the right to control all musical output, all merchandising, and, most important, which musicians recorded under that name. Shortly afterward, Rose announced that Slash was out of the

Guns n' Roses' Axl Rose and Slash (Paul Natkin)

For the Record

The song "Welcome to the Jungle" (from *Appetite for Destruction*) was featured in Clint Eastwood's 1988 Dirty Harry film, *The Dead Pool.* A then-unknown actor named Jim Carrey played a junkie rock star lip-syncing to Rose's vocals. By the next scene he was dead. Several Guns n' Roses members played mourners at the funeral.

band and that the participation of McKagan and Sorum was "provisional." (Gilby had been fired in 1995.) The musical differences centered on Slash's adherence to the traditional, guitar-heavy Guns n' Roses sound, while Rose was eager to experiment.

Beginning in 1995, many musicians were associated with the "new" Guns n' Roses. Besides Rose, the only holdover from the early years was keyboardist Reed. New members included rhythm guitarist Paul Huge, session drummer Josh Freese, lead guitarist Robin Finck (from Nine Inch Nails), and ex-Replacements bassist Tommy Stimson. Techno star Moby and Guns n' Roses producer Mike Clink were considered as producers, as was ex-Killing Joke bassist Martin Glover Youth, who had produced albums for U2 and the Verve. Despite managing to keep out of the public eye for four years, Rose resurfaced briefly in February, 1998, when he was arrested for disorderly conduct at the Phoenix Sky Harbor Airport.

—Deirdre Rockmaker

SELECT DISCOGRAPHY

■ ALBUMS

Live ?!@ Like a Suicide*, 1986 (EP)
Appetite for Destruction, 1987
GN'R Lies, 1988
Use Your Illusion I, 1991
Use Your Illusion II, 1991
The Spaghetti Incident? 1993

SELECT AWARDS

MTV Video Music Awards Best New Artist, 1988
MTV Video Music Awards Best Heavy Metal/Hard Rock Video, for "Sweet Child o' Mine," 1989

SEE ALSO: Clash, The; Nine Inch Nails; Sex Pistols, The.

Woody Guthrie

BORN: Okemah, Oklahoma; July 14, 1912
DIED: Queens, New York; October 3, 1967
FIRST ALBUM RELEASE: *Dust Bowl Ballads*, 1940
MUSICAL STYLES: Folk, country, rock and roll, blues

Woody Guthrie was more than a bushy-haired man who played guitar and wrote approximately one thousand songs between 1932 and 1952; his life was legendary. His songs are deceptively simple; they helped people to understand and to fight for themselves. He wrote feel-good and humorous songs that made people take pride in themselves and their work. He was an autobiographer (*Bound for Glory*, 1943), artist, balladeer, cartoonist, diarist, illustrator, novelist, painter, folk poet, radio performer, rambling man, and storyteller.

Guthrie is one of the most influential cultural figures of the twentieth century. He inspired a generation of musicians that included Joan Baez, Judy Collins, Bob Dylan, and Phil Ochs. Guthrie virtually created the modern folk tradition and singer-songwriter genre, transforming the folk ballad into a vehicle for social protest and radical politics. He was an early influence on rock and roll. Ironically, Guthrie was a self-taught musician who never learned to read a note of music. By his own admission, he did not have a great singing voice. With just about reasonable talent, he played the guitar, mouth harp, mandolin, mountain fiddle, spoons, tin cans, and an assortment of other instruments. Guthrie was an original folk hero, an American legend. Folklorist Alan Lomax said Guthrie might have been the best folk ballad composer ever known, and critics consider Guthrie's album *Dust Bowl Ballads* (1940) one of the most influential recordings of the twentieth century.

The Beginnings. Of Scottish and Irish ancestry, Woodrow Wilson Guthrie was born on July 14, 1912, in the small frontier town of Okemah, Oklahoma. His parents, Charley and Nora Guthrie, were strong democrats and musically inclined. They named their son after politician Woodrow Wilson, who had just been nominated for U.S. president. Guthrie's father was a real-estate speculator, self-taught prizefighter, and politician who fell on hard times. Guthrie's mother suffered from Huntington's disease, a genetic nerve disorder that led to her death in a state mental hospital. A terrible fire destroyed the family home and killed his sister Clara, and his father was burned in another fire.

Despite the tragedies and the difficulties of his early life, Guthrie was a playful, happy child. He began singing at age two. By age four, he discovered that he could easily make up songs about any subject. He dropped out of school around age thirteen or fourteen. With no home and a broken family, Guthrie set out on his own. He made his living playing the harmonica and guitar at bars, pool halls, barn dances, and revival meetings. He also collected and sold junk, painted signs, sold corn whiskey, delivered milk, shined shoes, washed spittoons, and met night trains to solicit customers for a local hotel. In 1931, he moved to Pampa, Texas, where he founded his first band, the Corncob Trio.

During the 1930's, Guthrie traveled by hopping freight trains and hitchhiking among migrants, hobos, and Dust Bowl refugees. Guthrie was like many other migrants during the Depression; the "Okies" were Oklahomans who found themselves forced out of the life they knew by the coming of the soil erosion and dust storms in the central United States. The Okies immigrated westward to California looking for work, in hopes of a better life. Often, the immigrants were people who had been dispossessed, had lost their belongings and even their dignity, and were trying to find themselves again. Some refugees arrived in the promised land of California only to be exploited and humiliated by powerful landowners and growers. Guthrie was outraged about what had happened to these people and how they were treated.

His first exposure to radicalism came from his discussions in hobo jungles with old "Wobblies," members of the militant union known as the Industrial Workers of the World. These experiences were captured in his songs and other writings. In 1937, Guthrie had his own successful radio show with "Lefty Lou" (Maxine Crissman) on KFVD in Los Angeles. By the decade's end, his Populist convictions led him to embrace Communism, although he was denied membership in the Communist Party because he refused to renounce his religion. He often played at Communist Party meetings, at rallies, and on picket lines. He even wrote columns in Communist newspapers.

Recording Career. Guthrie arrived in New York in 1940. In the city, he met folklorist Alan Lomax and performers Pete Seeger, Cisco Houston, and Leadbelly. Lomax faithfully recorded Guthrie's songs for the Library of Congress' American folksong archive. He was a major promoter of Guthrie's career and preserver of his songs. Lomax's most important contribution was to persuade Victor Records to produce a two-album, twelve-record set of Guthrie's ballads, entitled *Dust Bowl Ballads.*

Guthrie wrote "This Land Is Your Land" on February 23, 1940. For unknown reasons, he forgot about the song until he recorded it in the spring of 1944. Since then, the song has been mentioned as a possible replacement for "The Star-Spangled Banner" as the U.S. national anthem. The song was a favorite of the Civil Rights movement in the 1960's, and United Airlines and the Ford Motor Company used it as an advertising jingle. It was also the theme song for politician George McGovern's 1972 presidential campaign.

Prolific Artist. Guthrie performed on network radio, played at strikes and union rallies, and recorded for the Folkways record label. For ten years, Moses Asch of Folkways Records recorded everything Guthrie brought him and released eleven solo albums and dozens of collaborations with Houston, Seeger, and Leadbelly. Asch was interested in preserving American folk music without any frills. In 1940, Guthrie and Seeger toured the South and Southwest, singing in migrant camps and at union halls. In 1941, the U.S. Department of the Interior commissioned Guthrie to write songs promoting the building of the Bonneville Dam on the Columbia River in Washington. He wrote twenty-six songs in thirty days.

In 1941, Guthrie joined Seeger, Lee Hays, Millard Lampell, and others in the Almanac Singers. The group was named after the *Farmer's Almanac.* Members hoped their music would prove as useful to Americans as the *Almanac* was. The Almanac Singers were the first urban folk-singing group. The members lived and worked communally, sharing the money they received for performing and recording. They sang in union halls and to audiences of farmers and factory workers. Perhaps the Almanac Singers' most famous song was "Talking Union." The song was coauthored by Seeger and Guthrie and described how to start a union. Another of the group's best-known songs was "The Sinking of the Reuben James." The song was a ballad composed in 1942, after a German submarine torpedoed the USS *Reuben James* off the coast of Iceland, killing eighty-six crew members.

Guthrie chronicled and illustrated his cross-country travel odyssey in his 1943 autobiography, *Bound for Glory.* That year, he received a seventeen-hundred dollar fellowship from the Julius Rosenwald Fund to write books, ballads, songs, and novels that would help people to know each other. During World War II, Guthrie joined the National Maritime Union and shipped out as a merchant seaman with Cisco Houston. Guthrie took part in three European invasions and his ship was torpedoed twice. He was then drafted into the Army. After being discharged, he became involved with People's Songs. Seeger had organized this group, which was a loosely knit union of songwriters who would stage occasional hootenannies. During the next few years, Guthrie rambled across the country, giving concerts and writing newspaper and magazine articles on folklore, politics, and other subjects. His second book, *American Folksong,* was published in 1947.

Woody Guthrie in 1944 (AP/Wide World Photos)

Huntington's Disease. By the mid-1940's, Guthrie began experiencing unexplainable bouts of depression and disorientation. These symptoms signaled the onset of the genetic nerve disorder (Huntington's chorea or Huntington's disease) that had afflicted his mother. Huntington's is a hereditary, degenerative disease of the central nervous system that features random, purposeless movements, and mental unbalance. Once, his behavior was interpreted as a result of alcoholism. He developed a lopsided walk and speech problems and eventually was unable to control his movements. His health deteriorating slowly and agonizingly, he was eventually confined to hospitals. Guthrie spent approximately fifteen years of his life in and out of hospitals.

In 1955, Seeger and several Guthrie friends established the Guthrie Children's Trust Fund. The purpose of the fund was to provide for his children and to collect, publish, and safeguard the rights and interests of his musical and literary works. A Guthrie benefit concert was held in New York on March 17, 1956. Seeger and other folk musicians have said the concert was the beginning of the canonization of Woody Guthrie. Guthrie died on October 3, 1967, at age fifty-five. He left behind eight children (including folksinger Arlo) and approximately one thousand songs. He recorded more than twenty albums for Stinson Records, Folkways Records, and the Asch Recording Company.

By the mid-1960's, Guthrie had become a cultural icon. Most of the royalties he or his estate made came from other people's renditions of his songs. Performers who sang "This Land Is Your Land" included Peter, Paul and Mary, Harry Belafonte, Bing Crosby, the Mormon Tabernacle Choir, and later, Bruce Springsteen, among numerous others. While he was alive, Guthrie never made much profit from his songs; much of his financial success came long after Guthrie himself could enjoy it. In the years after his death, he was honored by many memorial concerts, including one at New York's Carnegie Hall. The Guthrie family played a major role in founding the Huntington's Disease Society of America to find a cure for the disease that killed Guthrie.

Legacy. Woody Guthrie's combination of Dust Bowl and Depression grit, on-the-road wonder, anger at injustice, infectious sense of freedom and hope, leftist populism, Okie wit, bitter humor, and songwriting brilliance helped him produce such classic songs as "This Land Is Your Land," "So Long, It's Been Good to Know You," and "Do Re Mi." He was the bridge from the ballads of small-town America to commercial folk music. His hobo's lifestyle gave him credibility in the eyes of the Beat generation, and he was even called a national treasure.

During the mid- to late 1950's and 1960's, a new generation discovered Guthrie. His spirit inspired the folk music revival. Seeger played a significant role in keeping the Guthrie legend alive. Seeger traveled across the country, often performing on college campuses and relating stories about Guthrie. Seeger described Guthrie as an angry man from Oklahoma who rode the boxcars during the Depression, fought against the establishment, and wrote great songs. Guthrie re-created and popularized social commentary music—music that expressed anger and protested against unjust social conditions.

Guthrie said he got the ideas for his songs anywhere he could find them, from books, magazines, daily papers, films, streets, buses , trains, or airplanes. He often put his own words to old tunes. Guthrie was one of the first U.S. songwriters to give a popular voice to the struggles and politi-

For the Record

"I hate a song that makes you think that you're not any good. I hate a song that makes you think that you are just born to lose. No good to nobody. No good for nothing. . . . I am out to fight those kinds of songs to my very last breath of air and my last drop of blood. I am out to sing songs that will prove to you that this is your world and that if it has hit you pretty hard and knocked you for a dozen loops, no matter how hard it's run you down and rolled over you, no matter what color, what size you are, how you are built, I am out to sing the songs that make you take pride in yourself and in your work." —*Woody Guthrie*

cal issues concerning the American people. This style was embraced by such later leading folk and rock-and-roll singer-songwriters as Pete Seeger, Bob Dylan, Bruce Springsteen, Joni Mitchell, Phil Ochs, Suzanne Vega, Tracy Chapman, John Mellencamp, Ramblin' Jack Elliot, and Arlo Guthrie. He was probably one of the first folk guitarists to play with an orchestra. Top performers, bands, and orchestras have recorded his songs, including Willie Nelson, U2, Dolly Parton, Emmylou Harris, Ry Cooder, and the Boston Pops Orchestra. The Weavers' version of "So Long, It's Been Good to Know You" was a hit. The Kingston Trio recorded many of Guthrie's songs, including "Hard, Ain't It Hard," "Pastures of Plenty," "Hard Traveling," and "Deportee." Performers such as Ramblin' Jack Elliot and Bob Dylan remade themselves in Guthrie's image. Reissues of Guthrie's material would continue to appear each decade. In 1998, more than three thousand song lyrics, the vast majority of them never heard or even recorded, were made public by the Woody Guthrie Foundation. These lyrics were put to music and recorded by artists Billy Bragg and Wilco, to much acclaim.

As a balladeer, Guthrie captured the dreams and aspirations of the American people. His music had a profound impact not only on folksingers, but on society, his music mirroring the hopes and aspirations of the American people. He had his finger on the pulse of the working class—the sorrow and laughter, the strife, the hunger and joblessness, the desire for a better life. One of the most important figures in the history of American music, Woody Guthrie was a true American folk poet. *—Fred Buchstein*

SELECT DISCOGRAPHY

■ ALBUMS

Dust Bowl Ballads, 1940
This Land Is Your Land, 1967
A Legendary Performer, 1977
The Greatest Songs of Woody Guthrie, 1988 (compilation)

SELECT AWARDS

U.S. Department of the Interior Conservation Award, 1966
Nashville Songwriters Hall of Fame, inducted 1977
Rock and Roll Hall of Fame, inducted 1988
Grammy Hall of Fame, inducted 1989
North American Folk Music and Dance Alliance Lifetime Achievement Award, 1996

SEE ALSO: Baez, Joan; Chapman, Tracy; Dylan, Bob; Griffith, Nanci; Indigo Girls, The; Mellencamp, John; Mitchell, Joni; Seeger, Pete; Springsteen, Bruce.

Buddy Guy

BORN: Lettsworth, Louisiana; July 30, 1936
FIRST SINGLE RELEASE: "Sit and Cry (The Blues)," 1958
MUSICAL STYLES: Blues, rhythm and blues, rock and roll

Before Jimi Hendrix, Eric Clapton, and Stevie Ray Vaughan, a venerable trinity of rock-and-roll guitar heroes, there was Buddy Guy, the frenetic singer-guitarist whose style captivated Chicago in the mid-1950's. Born of humble origins in rural Baton Rouge, Louisiana, Guy re-emerged in the 1990's as a highly influential artist and a bona fide rock-and-roll guitar legend.

Beginnings. The son of sharecroppers Sam and Isabell (Toliver) Guy, George "Buddy" Guy began teaching himself the rudiments of guitar by fashioning a handmade instrument at age thirteen. Raised in a region of Louisiana more noteworthy for its zydeco tradition, Guy was influenced by the family's meager record collection and the few bluesmen who would appear live in the area, including New Orleans' Guitar Slim (Eddie Jones) and B. B. King.

In his early twenties, Guy was working in Baton Rouge as a janitor at Louisiana State University by day and playing around town in a variety of blues clubs with a variety of bands, including the locally popular Poppa Big John Tilly Band, by night. During this period, Guy came into contact with a number of young and influential Louisiana musicians who would themselves go on to enjoy national success, including harmonica players Lazy Lester (Leslie Johnson), Slim Harpo (James Moore), and guitarist Lightnin' Slim (Otis Hicks), important learning experiences for the guitarist who would later make a name for himself based on both his talent and his versatility.

Buddy Guy in 1970 (Archive Photos)

North to Chicago. The lure of wealth and fame in Chicago's increasingly growing blues scene was too strong a pull, and, like so many other young southern blues artists, Guy left his rural roots in search of the city's blues scene. Most of Chicago's scene had taken shape along the city's South Side, or "Little Mississippi," where most of the early post-World War II rural southern migrants had settled. Overcrowded conditions in the South Side, however, were creating something of a spillover effect by the mid-1950's, and, as a result, newly arrived and primarily black Chicagoans were beginning to populate the city's West Side. It was here, in Chicago's West Side bars and clubs, where a younger, more modern blues sound was beginning to take shape, a style more reliant on heavily amplified instruments and younger artists driven by the careers of older musicians such as Mississippi's Albert King and Texas guitar showman Aaron "T-Bone" Walker. This style came to be called West Side blues.

By the time Guy arrived in Chicago in 1957, two other southern-born guitarists had already begun staking their claims to West Side blues supremacy, Magic Sam Maghett and Otis Rush, both from the Mississippi Delta region. Their sound was significantly more gospel-tinged and considerably less traditional than the blues of older Chicago statesmen such as Muddy Waters (McKinley Morganfield) and Howlin' Wolf (Chester Burnett) and clearly more geared toward Guy's diverse background and youthful exuberance.

Though he nearly starved within his first six months in Chicago, Guy was determined to carve his own niche and gained his first major victory in 1958 in a "Battle of the Blues" contest held at the Blue Flame Club in Chicago, where he defeated both Magic Sam and Otis Rush. Impressed, Magic Sam would later arrange for Buddy Guy's first recording contract with Cobra Records, the West Side's short-lived, yet groundbreaking independent label, which released his first singles "Sit and Cry (The Blues)" and "This Is the End" on its subsidiary Artistic label in 1958 and 1959. He was also championed by Chicago's premier blues figure, the venerable Muddy Waters, who quickly introduced him around town.

After Cobra Records went bankrupt, Guy signed with Chicago's legendary independent blues label Chess Records in 1960 and quickly became an in-demand session guitarist, appearing on recordings from such notable labelmates as Big Willie Dixon, the label's chief songwriter, arranger, and producer; harmonica virtuoso Little Walter Jacobs; and singer Koko Taylor. The Chess brothers were amazed that someone as young as Guy could be at the same time both innovative and traditional—whichever was necessary for the particular recording. The contrast between his hard edged and exceedingly modern sounding Chess solo recordings, such as "Stone Crazy," his first hit single which reached number 12 on the rhythm-and-blues charts in 1962, and his session work, including the 1963 Muddy Waters *Folksinger* album which shows Guy in a very traditional, albeit dated mode, is glaring. As he often reminds his audience during live performances, his repertoire covers many styles, from Delta blues to Chicago blues to rock and roll, a boast which he often backs with an impressive display of instrumental flourishes along with an ever present gold-toothed grin.

Blues Brother. Guy's most productive period as a frontman came primarily as a result of his long-standing partnership with harmonica player Amos "Junior" Wells, a former member of the Muddy Waters Band and longtime Chess artist. Both Guy and Wells found themselves leaving Chess Records for Chicago's Vanguard label in 1967, and in addition to working on each other's solo releases, they also logged a number of important collaborative efforts. More important for each were the national and international tours which would take them as far as Asia and Africa. They also served as opening acts for rock-and-roll artists such as Eric Clapton and the Rolling Stones throughout the 1960's and 1970's. They were critically hailed as blues stars during the 1970's and 1980's, and in something of a testament to their success and influence, they would serve as the models for John Belushi and Dan Ackroyd's fictional characters the Blues Brothers, which were parlayed into improbable commercial recording and motion-picture success.

Reemergence. Guy suffered through the 1970's and 1980's without a recording contract, which made it difficult to find well-paying performance dates, though he continued to perform almost constantly around the world both with and without Junior Wells. He was also hailed by the coming generation of rock guitarists as a founding father of their genre—Jimi Hendrix actually took tape recorders to his 1960's-era performances and bragged to him that he had copied much of his style—but this sort of critical acclaim rarely translated into commercial success.

In 1989, he opened his famous club, Buddy Guy's Legends, a raucous venue on the South Side which is home to many of the best blues and blues-based acts who play in or come through Chicago. In 1991 he received his first recording contract in thirteen years, signing with Silvertone Records, which released first his comeback album, *Damn Right, I've Got the Blues,* in 1991, and his two follow-up albums, *Feels Like Rain* in 1993 and *Slippin' In* in 1994. Additionally, he would appear on the albums of countless other blues artists, including John Lee Hooker, and many of his rock-and-roll guitar disciples, including Eric Clapton and Stevie Ray Vaughan, both of whom would appear on his Silvertone releases. He would also perform before a completely new and enthu-

For the Record

"Buddy Guy is by far and without a doubt the best guitar player alive."

—*Eric Clapton*

siastically appreciative audience of post-baby boomers who, by the late 1990's, would consider Guy to be, ironically, a freshly discovered rock-and-roll phenomenon. *—Joel Nathan Rosen*

SELECT DISCOGRAPHY

■ ALBUMS

Left My Blues in San Francisco, 1967
Hold That Plane, 1972
Stone Crazy! 1981
Damn Right, I've Got the Blues, 1991
Alone & Acoustic, 1991 (with Junior Wells)
The Complete Chess Studio Recordings, 1992
As Good as It Gets, 1998

SELECT AWARDS

Grammy Award for Best Contemporary Blues Album for *Damn Right, I've Got the Blues*, 1991
Grammy Award for Best Contemporary Blues Album for *Feels Like Rain*, 1993
Grammy Award for Best Contemporary Blues Album for *Slippin' In*, 1994
Grammy Award for Best Rock Instrumental Performance for "SRV Shuffle," 1996 (with others)

SEE ALSO: Clapton, Eric; Dixon, Willie; Howlin' Wolf; King, B. B.; Waters, Muddy.

H

Merle Haggard

BORN: Bakersfield, California; April 6, 1937
FIRST SINGLE RELEASE: "Singin' My Heart Out"/"Skid Row," 1962
MUSICAL STYLE: Country

Merle Haggard has made the country music charts with thirty-eight number 1 records in forty years, and ninety of his records have reached the Top 40. He has written the majority of these hits himself. Generally considered one of the best songwriters in modern country music, he has penned many classic lyric songs about the travails of love as well as vivid semiautobiographical and realistic songs about life and hard times in California. He has always stayed true to country music traditions and honored his influences and predecessors.

Merle Haggard (Paul Natkin)

Hardscrabble Youth. Haggard was born in a converted boxcar where his parents lived after trekking over Route 66 from Checotah, Oklahoma, in 1934. Their barn had been burned down by an arsonist, and California seemed to offer a "better" life during the hard times of the Depression. In some ways they were like the other "Okies" depicted by John Steinbeck in his 1939 novel *The Grapes of Wrath.* They, too, settled in the San Joaquin Valley in central California, near Bakersfield. There was music in the family; Haggard's father had been a country fiddler back in Oklahoma. Once they arrived, Haggard's father took a job on the Santa Fe railroad and had to work hard to support his family. His sudden death when Haggard was nine had a devastating effect on his son. With his mother forced to take a bookkeeping job, Haggard soon became footloose and drifted into a life of petty crime and truancy. Sent to several reform schools over the years, he became a drifter, running off with friends by car and train for escapades as far away as Texas.

Haggard's eventual saving grace from his rootless lifestyle was his love of music. In his teens he began to play guitar and came to adore the music of Jimmie Rodgers, Bob Wills, Hank Williams, and Lefty Frizzell. Although Rodgers had died in 1933 and Williams in 1953, their music was kept alive in California, especially by the displaced Okies. In the Bakersfield area there were numerous clubs where local talent and fledgling bands could perform their music. Wills and Frizzell played in the area, and Haggard had a chance to hear them live, not just on records. He liked the jazzy and blues-inflected style of Wills with his big dance band and swinging lineup. Frizzell, whom he came to know briefly, carried on the hard-edged country style of Hank Williams, but with a lazy Texas drawl and an infinitely subtle and pliable voice that broke words and syllables apart with the sort of melismata (using more than one note for a syllable) that could stress the emotive potential of words. These were Haggard's inspirations and the foundation of his own work.

Eventually, Haggard's life of petty crimes and a botched robbery landed him in San Quentin prison in 1958. He had already played in clubs, and his music was an inspiration during his detainment. He served slightly more than two years in San Quentin, receiving a pardon in 1960. He immediately returned to the Bakersfield scene, determined to start a musical career.

For the Record

While he was in San Quentin, Merle Haggard witnessed a situation that inspired "Sing Me Back Home." He befriended a convict named Rabbit who had a plan for a foolproof escape. Rabbit told Haggard that he was welcome to come along but also noted that Haggard, unlike Rabbit, had a chance to succeed with his music and could ruin his chances if he chose to join the escape. Rabbit indicated that if caught, he was going to "hold court in the streets." Haggard declined the escape. Rabbit did escape, but two weeks later he was caught and killed a state trooper before being pinned down. He was returned to San Quentin and was executed while Haggard was still there. Years later, Haggard wrote the song to express how Rabbit must have felt as he went to his death.

Bakersfield Country. Haggard soon began recording for the local Tally label and formed a band that, in a few years, became one of the tightest and most popular in country music, the Strangers. His first recordings received some notice, especially "Sing a Sad Song," which made the charts. Capitol Records signed him in 1965 with "(My Friends Are Gonna Be) Strangers" in 1965, the real beginning of his success. There followed a string of songs, many of them his own, that made him a national country star: "Swinging Doors," "The Bottle Let Me Down," "The Fugitive," "Branded Man," "Sing Me Back Home," "Mama Tried," "I Take a Lot of Pride in What I Am," "Hungry Eyes," "Okie from Muskogee," "The Fightin' Side of Me," "Someday We'll Look Back," "Today I Started Loving You Again," "It's Not Love (But It's Not Bad)," "Ramblin' Fever," and "Big City," to name only a few. These songs treated the themes and topics Haggard would become best known for: There are barroom laments, songs of broken love relationships, memories of hard-scrabble times in California, complaints about freer lifestyles and eroding standards in the late 1960's, and evocations of freedom on the road.

Songs like the immensely popular, and in some circles controversial, "Okie from Muskogee" and "The Fightin' Side of Me" reflected Haggard's worry over the national tensions (especially among hippies) at the time of the increasingly unpopular Vietnam War in the late 1960's and early 1970's. These two songs, which helped make Haggard a national icon even outside country music, take on an aspect of period pieces that do reflect—in however exaggerated a form—real issues in the country at the time.

Poet of the Common Man. Haggard's songwriting has been complemented by his warm baritone voice, which has deepened over the years. Like his idol Frizzell, he can bend notes and put a hard edge on songs, yet do a bit of straightforward crooning (he was also influenced by Bing Crosby) as his backup musicians nicely accompany his quieter moods and attention to individual words. Many of his songs depict life's harsh realities. He has written several prison songs such as "Branded Man," "Sing Me Back Home,"

"Huntsville," and the Vietnam prisoner-of-war song, "I Wonder If They Ever Think of Me." Songs such as "Mama Tried" and "Hungry Eyes" are chilling evocations of a barely disguised rough youth. "California Cottonfields" (although not his own song), "Tulare Dust," "Daddy Frank (The Guitar Man)," and "Grandma Harp" are songs about the early days of Okie life in California in the 1930's and 1940's. "Tulare Dust," in particular, describes the tearing down of the federal labor camps set up to house displaced migrants during the Depression. These songs keep the past's memories alive in song. "Irma Jackson" depicts an interracial romance, and "Workin' Man Blues," "If We Make It Through December," and "Are the Good Times Really Over (I Wish a Buck Was Still Silver)" speak of the woes of job losses and hard economic times that ring true in any era. In all of these, Haggard reveals his respect for his roots and his unrelenting sense of the folk roots of country music.

Legacy of a Legend. Haggard's recording and live performance career would continue into the 1990's. Although he did not find much success at the top of the charts after the late 1980's, he would still draw and inspire a legion of younger singers, such as George Strait and Garth Brooks, to try to keep the music down to earth and real. His greatest honor, perhaps, was to be elected to the Country Music Hall of Fame in 1994. Like his fellow Okie who was transplanted to California, Woody Guthrie, Haggard indelibly etched the concerns of working-class people in a body of songs, another testament to the redeeming power of music.

—Frederick E. Danker

SELECT DISCOGRAPHY

■ SINGLES

"Branded Man," 1967
"Sing Me Back Home," 1967
"Mama Tried," 1968
"Hungry Eyes," 1969
"Workin' Man Blues," 1969
"Okie from Muskogee," 1969
"The Fightin' Side of Me," 1970
"It's Not Love (but It's Not Bad)," 1972
"I Wonder If They Ever Think of Me," 1972
"If We Make It Through December," 1973
"Big City," 1981

■ ALBUMS

Same Train, Different Time: Merle Haggard Sings the Great Songs of Jimmie Rodgers, 1969
Tribute to the Best Damn Fiddle Player in the World, 1970
Down Every Road, 1996 (3-CD boxed set, compilation)

SELECT AWARDS

Country Music Association Entertainer of the Year, Album of the Year for *Okie from Muskogee*, Single of the Year for "Okie from Muskogee," and Male Vocalist of the Year Awards, 1970
Grammy Award for Best Country Vocal Performance for "That's the Way Love Goes," 1984
Country Music Hall of Fame, inducted 1994

SEE ALSO: Frizzell, Lefty; Owens, Buck; Rodgers, Jimmie; Williams, Hank; Wills, Bob, and His Texas Playboys.

Bill Haley

BORN: Highland Park, Michigan; July 6, 1925
DIED: Harlingen, Texas; February 9, 1981
FIRST ALBUM RELEASE: *Rock with Bill Haley and the Comets*, 1954
MUSICAL STYLES: Western swing, rhythm and blues, rockabilly, rock and roll

Bill Haley is universally recognized as a pioneer of rock-and-roll music; however, the extent to which he helped create the genre has been hotly debated. Haley himself wanted to be remembered as the "father" of rock and roll, but it might be more accurate to call him its "midwife," for there can be no doubt that he assisted mightily at its birth. At the very least, he can be credited with establishing rock and roll as a loud, boisterous party music.

Haley is remembered as the leader of Bill Haley and His Comets, the band with which he recorded his most important hits and sold about sixty million records. The band itself, however, was little more than an extension of his own musical personality. It contained several outstanding musicians, but Haley owned it outright and exercised dictatorial control over its members, many of whom left him because of disagreements about money.

Musical Roots. Though born and raised in a suburb of Detroit, Michigan, Haley grew up amid country-and-western music. His father played country banjo, and his mother was a church organist. He received his first guitar while in grade school, began playing with local country groups at age thirteen, organized his first band at age fifteen, and recorded a single, "Candy Kisses," when he was only eighteen. After high school he toured with his own band. In the late 1940's, he worked as a disc jockey in a Chester, Pennsylvania, radio station. Styling himself the Ramblin' Yodeler, he formed the Four Aces of Western Swing to perform on his show.

Another Haley band, the Down Homers, became the Saddlemen, with whom he recorded a string of country songs that were unsuccessful. The band played tunes by Red Foley and Hank Williams in a mixed repertoire of western swing and polka music. Around 1951 Haley began covering rhythm-and-blues hits and had a minor success with "Rocket 88," which Jackie Brenston had made a hit that year. Haley's arrangement fused country and rhythm and blues with the kind of steady drum beat that would later characterize rock and roll. According to the producer with whom Haley later worked at Decca, Haley could not read music; he had riffs hummed to him until he learned them by rote.

The Birth of Rock and Roll. The Saddlemen's modest success with "Rocket 88" convinced Haley to shift toward more energetic music that would attract young people. In 1952 he finally abandoned his original cowboy image and renamed the Saddlemen Bill Haley and His Comets. The group then scored another minor success with a cover of the rhythm-and-blues tune "Rock the Joint." The Comets followed it with an original Haley composition, "Crazy Man Crazy," which in 1953 became the first rock-and-roll song to make the *Billboard* charts. The following year Haley left the tiny Essex label to sign with Decca.

For the Record

Bill Haley called his band "Comets" because of the similarity of his surname with that of English astronomer Edmund Halley (1656-1742), after whom Halley's Comet is named. Vastly more familiar with rock-and-roll music than astronomy, most Americans have grown up mispronouncing "Halley's Comet," using the pronunciation of Haley's name (hay-lee), rather than that of Halley (hal-lee).

Haley himself later admitted that during those years he and his band did not fully understand what they were doing. He saw his band as having started out as a "country-western" group that added a "touch of rhythm and blues," evolving until they reached a point where they "weren't accepted as country western or rhythm and blues. . . . We were something different, something new." That something new was modern rock and roll. With Milt Gabler as his producer, Haley recorded a string of hit records for Decca that helped make rock and roll a worldwide cultural phenomenon.

A defining moment in rock history came in early 1954 with the Comets' recording of a rockabilly song that Max Freedman and Jimmy DeKnight (Jim Myers) wrote especially for Haley, "Rock Around the Clock." With lines such as "Put your glad rags on, join me, Hon/ We'll have some fun when the clock strikes one," the song was tame by the standards of a later rock-and-roll generation. Nevertheless, it had a revolutionary impact on the youth of its era. Its pulsating beat drove simple lyrics that urged dropping everything in order to rock forever. Its simple, almost mathematically logical message was reinforced by immaculate timing, catchy vocal and guitar breaks, and a driving drumbeat.

Like many pioneers, neither Haley nor his producers sensed anything special in "Rock Around the Clock" when they released it as a B-side recording. Indeed, its initial sales were so modest that it might have died, were it not for a lucky break that led to a seminal moment in rock-and-roll history. In 1955 the producers of *The Blackboard Jungle* made a last-minute decision to add a rock-and-roll song to the film's sound track and accepted Jimmy DeKnight's suggestion to use Haley's recording of his own "Rock Around the Clock."

A tense melodrama starring Glenn Ford as a teacher in a violent inner-city high school, *The Blackboard Jungle* captured the imaginations of American teenagers, who adopted "Rock Around the Clock" as a rallying cry for their rebelliousness. Reissued as a single, the song shot to the top of the charts, where it remained for eight weeks. The song later was featured in at least fourteen other films and used in the television series *Happy Days*; it eventually sold 25 million records, making it the best-selling rock single of all time.

In 1956 Haley capitalized on the popularity of his first major hit by appearing in a film titled *Rock Around the Clock*, in which he lip-synched nine of his songs. This production featured Haley's Comets as a band playing a revolutionary new music that sweeps the country—a none-too-subtle affirmation of Haley's own place in the rock revolution. Other acts appearing in the film included the Platters, Little Richard, Freddie Bell and the Bellboys, and Tony Martinez and His Band. Disc jockey Alan Freed was also in the film. In response to growing public criticism of rock and roll, Haley wrote "Don't Knock the Rock," and this became Alan Freed's byword in Haley's second and last film, *Don't Knock the Rock* (1956).

Haley's star rose as he released more hit songs, such as "Shake, Rattle and Roll," a sanitized version of a popular rhythm-and-blues tune by an African American blues shouter named Big Joe Turner. Haley made the song notable for its jive lyrics and innovative use of the saxophone and the upright bass. Other innovative hits included "Rudy's Rock," an instrumental piece that featured Rudy Pompilli's jump-band saxophone style; "Burn That Candle"; "Dim, Dim the Lights"; "Razzle-Dazzle"; and "See You Later Alligator." Through 1955 and 1956, Haley reigned the pop charts. With twelve Top-40 hits during those years alone, he was, indeed, the unchallenged king of rock and roll.

Ironically, "Rock Around the Clock," the song that made Haley the king of rock and roll, also contributed to the shortness of his reign. The song's close identification with the youthful violence of *The Blackboard Jungle* helped give rock and roll a wild public image to which Haley himself could not live up. Haley's music continued to excite the young generation, but his physical appearance, which his films revealed to the world, worked against him. In 1957, when his fame had peaked, he was thirty-two years old and looked plump and balding, not an icon of youth and rebellion. Younger, more flamboyant performers, such as Elvis Presley and Jerry Lee Lewis, soon displaced him in the rock hierarchy.

On the Road. While Presley and others were displacing Haley as the leaders of rock and roll, Haley retained his fans by keeping his band constantly on the road. Despite his own limited charisma, his band electrified audiences with an energetic stage act built around Haley's vocals, Rudy Pompilli's bravura saxophone, and Al Pompilli's acrobatic handling of his standup bass. The often hysterical reactions of young audiences added to the alarmed public perceptions of rock and roll.

In early 1957 Haley scored another first by becoming the first rock-and-roll star to tour abroad when he took his band to Great Britain, where fans mobbed him and went wild at his concerts. His popularity there was partly due to the fact that because his mother was English, he was half-English.

Haley released his last U.S. Top-40 hit, "Skinny Minnie," in 1958. Afterward, he did little to change his music or his public image. Though membership in his band changed constantly, he kept the Comets together through the 1960's by touring Europe and Latin America. Mostly playing his early rock and roll, he and the Comets joined Richard Nader's traveling "Rock 'n' Roll Revival" shows that toured the United States during the early 1970's.

After the mid-1970's, Haley worked much less because of personal and tax problems. A new album he released in 1979, *Everyone Can Rock 'n' Roll*, attracted little attention but gave him an excuse to tour Europe again. He planned another European tour the following year but canceled because of poor health. In early 1981 he was found dead at his Texas home, the victim of a heart attack. In later years, several original members of his band went back on the road together as the Comets. —*R. Kent Rasmussen*

SELECT DISCOGRAPHY

■ SINGLES

"Rock Around the Clock," 1955
"Burn That Candle," 1955
"See You Later, Alligator," 1956

■ ALBUMS

Rock Around the Clock, 1955
Everyone Can Rock 'n' Roll, 1979
From the Original Master Tapes, 1985

SELECT AWARDS

Rock and Roll Hall of Fame, inducted 1986

SEE ALSO: Lewis, Jerry Lee; Presley, Elvis; Williams, Hank.

Hall and Oates

ORIGINAL MEMBERS: Daryl Hall (b. Daryl Hohl, 1949), John Oates (b. 1949)
FIRST ALBUM RELEASE: *Whole Oates*, 1972
MUSICAL STYLES: Rock and roll, rhythm and blues, soul

Formed in 1969 in Philadelphia, Pennsylvania, Hall and Oates found moderate success during the 1970's, then became the most successful white soul group of the 1980's. With Daryl Hall on keyboards and mandolin and John Oates on acoustic guitar, the duo has written most of their own songs, as well as songs for other artists.

The Beginnings. Although they did not meet until the late 1960's, Daryl Hall and John Oates grew up in the suburbs of Philadelphia. Both attended Temple University, where Oates earned a degree in journalism; Hall studied music but dropped out during his senior year.

While a student at Temple, Hall was lead singer of the Temptones, a white group inspired by the Temptations, who recorded the single "Girl I Love You" in 1966. He also made solo records for Amy and Parallax. Oates, a member of a soul band called the Masters, met Hall in 1967 when the Temptones competed against the Masters in a "Battle of the Bands" at the Adelphi Ballroom in Philadelphia. Hall then formed the soft-rock band Gulliver, recording one album for Elektra in 1969. Later that year, Oates joined Gulliver, shortly before the group disbanded.

Oates went to Europe, while Hall became a studio musician, singing backup for the Delfonics, the Stylistics, and the Intruders. When Oates returned to the United States, the two began writing songs together and signed a contract with Atlantic Records. Although their first album, the folk-inspired *Whole Oates* (1972), attracted little attention, the second, *Abandoned Luncheonette* (1973), was better received. It included "She's Gone," which would eventually become a classic soul ballad and a Top-10 record for Hall and Oates when it was reissued in 1976. Todd Rundgren produced their third album, *War Babies* (1974), but it was even less successful than the previous two, and Hall and Oates were dropped by Atlantic.

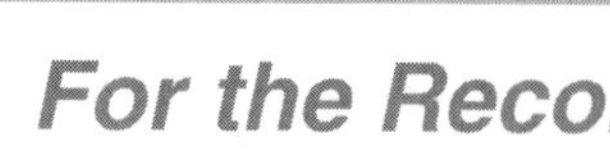

For the Record

Although Hall and Oates's "Kiss on My List" was number 1 on the charts three weeks in a row in April, 1981, many listeners thought its title was "Kiss on My *Lips*." "People heard kiss on my lips instead of kiss on my list," Oates complained to *Creem* magazine, "because they didn't listen carefully." He also noted that the song's contents were misunderstood: "It means that your kiss is only on the list of the best things, it's not the only thing. Everyone thinks it's 'I love you and without you I would die.' It's exactly the opposite of that."

Recording Classics. They soon signed with RCA, which issued *Daryl Hall/John Oates* in 1975. A single from this album, "Sara Smile," sold more than one million copies, bringing the duo into the national spotlight for the first time. Their next album, *Bigger Than Both of Us* (1976), became the duo's first platinum album and contained their first number 1 single, "Rich Girl." After several unimpressive albums, including an experiment with disco on *X-Static* (1979), Hall and Oates returned to the charts in 1980 with *Voices.* With four hit singles, including the number 1 hit "Kiss on My List" and a cover of the Righteous Brothers' "You've Lost That Lovin' Feelin'," *Voices* went platinum and marked a turning point in the group's career. Two singles from their next album, *Private Eyes* (1981), the title song and "I Can't Go for That (No Can Do)," were both number 1 hits. From 1982 through 1985, Hall and Oates had several successful albums and numerous hit singles. On *Live at the Apollo* in 1985 they were joined by Eddie Kendricks and David Ruffin of the Temptations.

Hall and Oates separated briefly during the mid-1980's, and in 1986 Hall released a solo album (his second), *Three Hearts in the Happy Ending Machine,* on which Joni Mitchell was a guest vocalist. Reunited in 1988, Hall and Oates recorded *Ooh Yeah!,* featuring the hit "Everything Your Heart Desires." With *Change of Season* in 1990, produced by Jon Bon Jovi, they added more rock features to their style. *Marigold Sky* (1997) is an eclectic album of rock and soul.

Although they owe a debt to the Righteous Brothers, as well as to many black doo-wop, soul, and Motown groups, notably the Temptations, Hall and Oates's style is distinctive. Influencing other artists, such as Michael Bolton, the duo confirms the continuing popularity of white, or blue-eyed, soul music. —*Mary A. Wischusen*

Hall and Oates (Paul Natkin)

SELECT DISCOGRAPHY

■ ALBUMS

Whole Oates, 1972
Abandoned Luncheonette, 1973
War Babies, 1974
Daryl Hall/John Oates, 1975
Bigger Than Both of Us, 1976
X-Static, 1979
Sacred Songs, 1980 (Hall solo)
Voices, 1980
Private Eyes, 1981
H_2O, 1982
Big Bam Boom, 1984
Live at the Apollo with David Ruffin & Eddie Kendrick, 1985
Three Hearts in the Happy Ending Machine, 1986 (Hall solo)
Ooh Yeah!, 1988
Change of Season, 1990
Soul Alone, 1993 (Hall solo)
Can't Stop Dreaming, 1996 (Hall solo)
Marigold Sky, 1997

SEE ALSO: Bolton, Michael; Bon Jovi; Mitchell, Joni; Righteous Brothers, The; Rundgren, Todd; Temptations, The.

Hammer

(Stanley Kirk Burrell)

BORN: Oakland, California; March 30, 1963
FIRST ALBUM RELEASE: *Feel My Power*, 1988
MUSICAL STYLES: Rap, hip-hop

Hammer, rap's top-selling artist in 1990, earned a reputation as one of popular music's flashiest, slickest performers. Overexposure and a drastic change from his clean-cut hip-hop style to gangsta rap caused him to lose many of his fans. By 1996, Hammer had lost his record contract and the fortune he had amassed only a few years before.

Beginnings. Growing up in tough East Oakland as one of six children in a single-parent family, Stanley Kirk Burrell's early passions were baseball and entertainment. He landed a job as a batboy with the Oakland Athletics baseball team after owner Charlie Finley spotted him dancing in the parking lot. The players nicknamed him "Little Hammer" because he resembled "Hammerin'" Hank Aaron of the Atlanta Braves. With a $20,000 investment from two players, Dwayne Murphy and Mike Davis, Hammer launched Bust It Records and recorded a single, "Ring 'Em," which became a local hit. His first album, *Feel My Power* (1988), sold sixty thousand copies and led to a contract with Capitol Records.

At the Top. By 1990, Hammer sat unchallenged atop the rap music mountain. His second Capitol album, *Please Hammer Don't Hurt 'Em*, sold more than ten million copies, making Hammer hip-hop's most successful artist. He was blasted by critics, however, for his heavy use of digital samples of previous hits by Prince, the Jacksons, and the Chi-Lites. These formed the basis of the album's smash hits: "Pray," "Dancin' Machine," "Have You Seen Her," and what became his signature song, "U Can't Touch This," which borrowed its bass line from Rick James' hit "Superfreak." The infraction prompted James to file a lawsuit, which was eventually settled out of court after it was agreed that James would receive cowriting credit. Critics also sneered at Hammer's easy hooks, shiny suits, and slippery dance moves. Rapper Dr. Dre slammed Hammer as "the John Travolta of rap."

For the Record

In 1991, Hammer launched a publicity stunt in which he offered $50,000 for the return of Michael Jackson's stolen rhinestone-covered glove. "I am the one," Hammer boasted to the magazine *Entertainment Weekly*, "who's going to take the thing from him."

Despite the backlash, Hammer pounded his image into the consciousness of U.S. audiences even harder. For his 1991 album *Too Legit to Quit*, he shortened his moniker from M.C. Hammer to Hammer and unleashed a multimedia marketing bombardment worthy of a Beatles reunion: A dozen videos, a four-song tie-in with *The Addams Family* movie, a Pepsi commercial, a laserdisc, a television special, a Hammer doll, and the *Hammerman* cartoon show. The campaign was sealed with a monster tour that included three dozen backup musicians and dancers.

The hype overshadowed some fine songs on *Too Legit to Quit*, including "Street Soldiers," a song about black-on-black crime, and the gospel track "Do Not Pass Me By." *Too Legit to Quit* sold 3.5 million records, a triumph for most acts but a failure considering the energy that went into promoting it. Soon after, Hammer and Capitol Records—the label that had once called Hammer "the most valuable franchise in music"—parted ways.

Hammer the Gangsta. After leaving Capitol, Hammer switched to Giant Records, a Warner Bros. Records label that eventually changed its name to Revolution Records. With the new label came an abrupt change in style that many perceived as an attempt to conform with the times. On 1994's *The Funky Headhunter*, the Hammer once adored by everyone from kids to grandmas unveiled himself afresh as a stocking-capped gangsta rapper. The man who once rapped about salvation, self-respect, and the drug-free life was now serving up lyrics about pimp fantasies and savaging his critics on disc. Hammer's new gangsta image only fueled the criticism of him as an opportunist ready to jump on the next musical trend. *The Funky Headhunter* sold close to one million copies—still a respectable number but nowhere near his past success.

By January, 1996, Hammer had left the Giant/Revolution label. The bottom fell out three months later when Hammer and his wife filed for bankruptcy. Because he worked so hard at promoting his image, Hammer may be less remembered for his music than his shiny purple suits and catchphrases such as "you can't touch this" and "proper!" —*Louis R. Carlozo*

SELECT DISCOGRAPHY

■ ALBUMS

Feel My Power, 1988
Let's Get It Started, 1988
Please Hammer Don't Hurt 'Em, 1990
Too Legit to Quit, 1991
The Funky Headhunter, 1994

SELECT AWARDS

Grammy Awards for Best R&B Song (with Rick James and Alonzo Miller) and Best Rap Solo Performance for "U Can't Touch This," 1990

SEE ALSO: James, Rick; Prince.

Herbie Hancock

BORN: Chicago, Illinois; April 12, 1940
FIRST ALBUM RELEASE: *Takin' Off*, 1962
MUSICAL STYLES: Jazz, jazz fusion

Herbie Hancock has achieved a balance of commercial and artistic success in his career as a musician that is rare in the world of jazz. He also has the distinction of having been a member of one of the most famous and innovative jazz quintets in the history of jazz. Formed by Miles Davis, the legendary jazz trumpeter, in the 1960's, the group included Wayne Shorter on saxophone, Ron Carter on bass, and Tony Williams on drums.

The Early Years. Born in Chicago in 1940, Hancock began taking piano lessons at age seven, focusing, as do most beginning students, on the traditional classical repertoire. By the time he was eleven, he was performing Mozart with the Chicago Symphony. An awareness of jazz came later, in high school. Listening to his favorite rhythm-and-blues station, he heard music that he did not understand but knew it was jazz. Then, when he became friends with a student in his high school who played jazz piano in a trio, he began listening to George Shearing, Erroll Garner, and Oscar Peterson.

Although Hancock's interest in jazz was growing, he did not think of pursuing jazz as a career. He attended Grinnell College in Iowa, planning to get a degree in engineering. Later he did switch to music, but maintained his interest in electronic science, which continued into his adult years. These interests were to merge later in his career at the height of the fusion revolution in jazz.

Watermelon Man. Hancock was twenty when jazz trumpeter Donald Byrd heard him playing in Chicago and brought him to New York. Byrd was recording for Blue Note records at the time and introduced him to the record company's executives. For two years, Hancock developed his repertoire and skill at the keyboard while doing recording session work with such jazz greats as saxophonist Phil Woods and well-known arranger Oliver Nelson. After two years, and at the young age of twenty-three, Hancock recorded his first album for Blue Note as a leader, *Takin' Off* (1962). It featured guest musicians Freddie Hubbard and Dexter Gordon. This album included Hancock's first Top-10 hit—another rarity in the jazz world—"Watermelon Man." This tune gave Hancock access to an audience far wider than that reached by most jazz musicians. It put him in the "popular" category, which led to many other opportunities to compose music for other artists, television shows, and films.

Hancock's reputation as a forward-thinking artist came to the attention of Miles Davis, who asked him to join what was to become the legendary group of Davis, Hancock, Shorter, Williams, and Carter. During that time Hancock's work with bassist Carter and drummer Williams set a new standard for inventive and progressive rhythm-section playing. Hancock stayed with Davis from

1963 to 1968. For many musicians, performing with Miles Davis would have been enough, but Hancock was also recording on his own sessions with Blue Note, creating such classic works as *Maiden Voyage* (1966) and *Speak Like a Child* (1968). He wrote his first film score for director Michelangelo Antonioni's *Blow-Up* (1967). Three years later he composed the music for Bill Cosby's television special, "Hey, Hey, Hey, It's Fat Albert."

Exploration. Miles Davis could be said to have launched "fusion" music in the late 1960's by combining improvisational elements of jazz with the louder volume and solid rhythms of rock. Hancock and a few others—such as Weather Report, John McLaughlin, and Chick Corea—took the concept in their own directions and expanded its audience in the 1970's. In 1971 Hancock formed a band that would explore the outer limits of electronic jazz. Its first release was the spacy 1971 *Mwandishi* album. In 1973 Hancock put together a new group, the Headhunters, to play what might be termed a funk-jazz fusion. Previously Hancock had mostly played piano and electric piano, but now he increasingly employed synthesizers as well. The *Headhunters* album became the largest-selling jazz album in history. It contained another hit that has become standard repertoire for jazz and fusion artists, "Chameleon."

Herbie Hancock and his keyboard-playing robot (Paul Natkin)

Not one to be pigeonholed or to ride the waves of success, Hancock continued to explore a variety of artistic possibilities and returned to his roots as an acoustic pianist. He formed a quartet with old friends and musical colleagues Carter, Williams, and Shorter. (Shorter had gone on to found Weather Report with Joe Zawinul, another Davis alumnus.) He also recorded and performed with jazz pianist Chick Corea and an earlier influence on piano, Oscar Peterson. In addition to pursuing his own career, Hancock produced Wynton Marsalis's debut album and introduced him on a worldwide tour.

Always current and demonstrating his wide musical interests, Hancock topped the rhythm-and-blues dance charts with his 1983 hit *Future Shock*, an album that included "Rockit," which won a Grammy Award. The video of that track, produced by the award-winning team of Kevin Godley and Lol

For the Record

Trained in both classical and jazz music, Herbie Hancock resisted taking up electronic instruments until he worked with Miles Davis. One day he reported to Davis in a recording studio and was surprised to find an electronic, instead of acoustic, piano waiting for him. Davis told him to play it. Hancock later recalled that he "went over to it, hit a chord, and it sounded so good! It blew my mind. It was rich and full with that round sound that's halfway between a guitar and vibes and a piano. I liked it right away."

Creme, was one of the most inventive and entertaining in music-video history.

Hancock continued his work in film, winning an Oscar for best score in 1986 for *'Round Midnight*, the highly acclaimed film by French director Bertand Tavernier. Hancock also appeared in an acting role, along with jazz saxophonist Dexter Gordon. Other film scores followed: *A Soldier's Story*, *Jo Jo Dancer, Your Life is Calling*, *Action Jackson*, *Harlem Nights*, and the controversial *Colors*, directed by Dennis Hopper.

From 1989 to 1991 Hancock hosted a series of specials entitled *Coast-to-Coast* on the cable channel Showtime. This program featured a unique cross section of musical personalities in concerts and interviews. Hancock continued to record and tour extensively in the 1990's, spending half the year in his Los Angeles home and the other half on the road. Hancock has, as he puts it, "his fingers into a lot of things besides a piano, from multimedia projects and cutting-edge Internet audio productions to up-to-the-minute advances in technology." *—Jo Ann Collins*

SELECT DISCOGRAPHY

■ ALBUMS

Takin' Off, 1962
Empyrean Isles, 1964
E.S.P., 1965 (with Miles Davis)
Maiden Voyage, 1966
Speak Like a Child, 1968
Headhunters, 1973
V.S.O.P. Quintet, 1977
Future Shock, 1983
The New Standard, 1996
Gershwin's World, 1998

SELECT AWARDS

Grammy Award for Best Rhythm and Blues Instrumental Performance for "Rockit," 1983
Academy Award for Best Original Score, *'Round Midnight*, 1986
Grammy Award for Best Jazz Instrumental Performance for *A Tribute to Miles*, 1994 (with others)

SEE ALSO: Davis, Miles; McLaughlin, John; Weather Report.

Hanson

ORIGINAL MEMBERS: Isaac Hanson (b. 1980), Taylor Hanson (b. 1983), Zachary Hanson (b. 1985)
FIRST ALBUM RELEASE: *Middle of Nowhere*, 1997
MUSICAL STYLE: Pop

Hanson became one of the great stories of popular music in 1997, bursting on the scene with the infectious hit "MMMBop." The trio of young brothers from Tulsa, Oklahoma, were reminiscent of the young Jackson 5 and the Osmonds of the 1970's, passable musicians with strong vocals and energetic acts, known for attracting large numbers of young teens.

Musical Influences. Isaac, Taylor, and Zachary Hanson began singing in their home, with much encouragement from their parents. Before their father took them to South America for one year (where he was working as an oil-industry consultant), he purchased a rock-and-roll anthology that covered the years 1957 to 1969, which the boys listened to incessantly. They learned to harmonize by singing along with songs such as "Good Golly Miss Molly" and "Rockin' Robin."

When the Hanson family returned to the United States, eleven-year-old Isaac began writing songs, and the brothers performed anywhere they could, from company picnics to state fairs. They were finally discovered by Christopher Sabec, an attorney with a music law background, who agreed to manage the band. In a music climate not friendly to a teenybop band, Hanson was turned down by at least five record labels. They released two self-produced albums, including *Boomerang* (1995). On the strength of an early version of "MMMBop," Steve Greenberg of Mercury Records finally signed them to a record deal in 1996.

Hanson: Isaac, Taylor, and Zac (AP/Wide World Photos)

According to Greenburg, "Their knowledge of rock and roll stops cold at 1970 and doesn't pick up again till about Hootie [and the Blowfish]. They loved the Beach Boys but had never heard of the Eagles. I realized this was a chance to make the great lost record of my youth." Greenburg marshaled all his forces, bringing in veteran songwriters and experienced producers (including Black Grape producer Steve Lironi and the Dust Brothers, who produced the Beastie Boys and Beck). Four songs, including "MMMBop," were written entirely by Hanson, while the others were penned in conjunction with Mark Hudson (Aerosmith), Ellen Shipley (Belinda Carlisle), and Barry Mann and Cynthia Weil (the Righteous Brothers, the Crystals, the Animals).

For the Record

Hanson appeared in Ringo Starr's video for "La De Da" (1998). In the video, as soon as Isaac, Taylor, and Zachary join Starr on a bench in New York's Times Square, a group of teenage girls sends them running, leaving Starr alone again.

Instant Popularity. The result was their debut major release, *Middle of Nowhere* (1997), which sold four million copies in its first year. Mercury invested heavily in advance publicity and hired Tamara Davis to direct the video for the first single, "MMMBop," which debuted at number 13 and eventually went to number 1. At the peak of "Hansonmania," Hanson received almost 25,000 fan letters each week, and their Website drew over 100,000 hits a day. Becoming major teen idols, they quickly followed *Middle of Nowhere* with *Snowed In* (1997) a Christmas album, and *3 Car Garage: The Indie Recordings, 1995-96,* which included much of the demo material that was turned down by a dozen record executives, including an early version of "MMMBop." It rose to number 6 on the album charts in the United States and was popular in many foreign countries as well.

—John Powell

SELECT DISCOGRAPHY

■ ALBUMS

Middle of Nowhere, 1997

Snowed In, 1997

3 Car Garage: The Indie Recordings, 1995-96, 1998 (compilation)

Live, 1998

SEE ALSO: Beach Boys, The; New Kids on the Block; Osmonds, The.

Emmylou Harris

BORN: Birmingham, Alabama; April 2, 1947
FIRST ALBUM RELEASE: *Gliding Bird*, 1970
MUSICAL STYLES: Country, country rock, folk

Born April 2, 1947 to a military family stationed in Birmingham, Alabama, Emmylou Harris spent her adolescence in North Carolina and moved to Woolbridge, Virginia, in her teens where she graduated from high school as valedictorian of her class. She was awarded a dramatic scholarship to the University of North Carolina, where she came under the musical influence of such notables as Bob Dylan and Joan Baez, which inspired her to form a duo with her classmate, Mike Williams. Drawn by the lure of music, she dropped out of school and moved to New York City only to find that the folk music scene there was dying. She chose to stay in Greenwich Village, playing the folk clubs and occasionally sharing the stage with Jerry Jeff Walker and David Bromberg. While living in New York City, she met and married songwriter Tom Slocum in 1969 and recorded her first album, *Gliding Bird*, in 1970. After a brief relocation to Nashville, Tennessee, her marriage broke up, so Harris, along with daughter Hallie, moved to the Washington, D.C., area to live on a farm with her parents.

Early Bands. Little did Harris realize in 1971 when she was performing with Gerry Mule and Tom Guidera at a local Washington, D.C., club called Clyde's, that her musical career was about to change. In the audience was former Byrd member Chris Hillman, who was then with the pioneer country-rock band the Flying Burrito Brothers. Already familiar with Harris's talents, Hillman insisted that his friend and former leader of the Flying Burrito Brothers, Gram Parsons, listen to her. Parsons had, since leaving the Flying Burrito Brothers, returned to his California home and was creating a new form of country music that he called "Cosmic American Music," and he was looking for a female vocalist to sing harmony. Parsons was immediately impressed with the expressive qualities of Harris's voice and, about one year after their first meeting, Parsons sent Harris an

Emmylou Harris (Paul Natkin)

airline ticket, inviting her to sing on his solo debut, *GP* (1972). Although their union was to be brief, Parsons was in many ways Harris's musical mentor. She became part of Parsons's tour band, the Fallen Angels, formed to promote the album; in the summer of 1973, Harris joined Parsons in the studio to participate in the recording of his celebrated album *Grievous Angel*. Unfortunately, just months after completing the recording, Parsons met an untimely death brought on by drug and alcohol abuse. During her tenure as one of the Fallen Angels, Harris observed first-hand the creative genius of Parsons and began to establish her reputation as an accomplished vocalist.

Upon Parsons's death, Harris returned to Washington, D.C., and, along with former bandmate Tom Guidera, formed the Angel Band. In 1974, Mary Martin of Warner Bros. introduced Harris to producer Brian Ahern and offered to sign her to a contract, provided that Ahern could produce the recording. The band signed with Warner Bros./Reprise Records and relocated to Los Angeles where, with the assistance of musicians from the Parsons albums, they recorded Harris's highly acclaimed major label debut, *Pieces of the Sky* (1975). The centerpiece of this project was Harris's original composition, "Boulder to Birmingham," her tribute to fallen mentor Parsons. The second single release of this project, her arrangement of the Louvin Brothers' "If I Could Only Win Your Love," became her first Top-5 hit. Harris and Ahern were married, and Ahern produced her next ten albums.

Ladder of Success. With the success of her first major label recording, Warner Bros./Reprise Records recommended that she get herself a "really hot band." She did just that, even going so far as to name them the Hot Band. Original members included legendary Elvis Presley sidemen James Burton and Glen Hardin, along with young songwriter Rodney Crowell, Hank de Vito, John Ware, and Emory Gordon, Jr. Tradition has it that Parsons once told her, "always pay for the best and then you will play with the best." While the story itself may be apocryphal, the truth of the maxim is not; Harris's success has resulted, in part, from the outstanding talent with which she has consistently surrounded herself. Regardless of the makeup, the Hot Band was always in a league of its own and became the standard against which other country bands were measured. With the Hot Band in place, her next project, *Elite Hotel* (1976), advanced her measurably up the ladder of success. Two of the singles from the project, Buck Owens's "Together Again" and Patsy Cline's "Sweet Dreams," became Harris's first two number-1 chart hits. On this album, Harris once again paid homage to Parsons as she included covers of the Flying Burrito Brothers' "Sin City" and "Wheels," along with "Ooh Las Vegas" from the *Grievous Angel* album.

Harris moved to Asylum Records in 1993, recording *Cowgirls Prayer*, and in 1995 she recorded *Wrecking Ball* for Grapevine Records. At a stage in her career when most artists take refuge in the safety of rereleasing their greatest hits, Harris continued to engage in adventurous projects such as *Wrecking Ball*, which received the 1996 Grammy for Best Contemporary Folk Album. On receiving her eighth Grammy, Harris said, "I feel like I've had sort of a musical renaissance with *Wrecking Ball*, and I'm ready for another twenty years."

—*Wayne M. Bledsoe*

SELECT DISCOGRAPHY

■ ALBUMS

Gliding Bird, 1970
Pieces of the Sky, 1975
Elite Hotel, 1975
Luxury Liner, 1977
Blue Kentucky Girl, 1979
Last Date, 1982
White Shoes, 1983
The Ballad of Sally Rose, 1985
Thirteen, 1986
Angel Band, 1987
Trio, 1987 (with Dolly Parton and Linda Ronstadt)
Duets, 1990
At the Ryman, 1992
Cowgirl's Prayer, 1993
Wrecking Ball, 1995
Portraits, 1996

SELECT AWARDS

Grammy for Best Country Vocal Performance, Female, for *Elite Hotel*, 1976

Grammy for Best Country Vocal Performance, Female, for *Blue Kentucky Girl*, 1979

Country Music Association Female Vocalist of the Year Award, 1980

Grammy for Best Country Performance by a Duo or Group with Vocal, for "That Lovin' You Feelin' Again" (with Roy Orbison), 1980

Grammy for Best Country Vocal Performance, Female, for "In My Dreams," 1984

Academy of Country Music Album of the Year Award, for *Trio* (with Dolly Parton, Linda Ronstadt, and George Massenburg), 1987

Grammy for Best Country Performance by a Duo or Group with Vocal, for *Trio* (with Dolly Parton and Linda Ronstadt), 1987

Country Music Association Vocal Event of the Year Award, for *Trio* (with Dolly Parton and Linda Ronstadt), 1988

Grammy for Best Country Performance by a Duo or Group with Vocal, for *Emmylou Harris and the Nash Ramblers at the Ryman* (Emmylou Harris and the Nash Ramblers), 1992

Grand Ole Opry, became member 1992

Academy of Country Music Minnie Pearl Humanitarian Award, 1992

SEE ALSO: Gill, Vince; Monroe, Bill, and the Blue Grass Boys; Parsons, Gram; Ronstadt, Linda; Skaggs, Ricky.

George Harrison

BORN: Liverpool, England; February 25, 1943

FIRST SOLO ALBUM RELEASE: *Wonderwall Music*, 1968

MUSICAL STYLES: Rock and roll, pop

Known as the "quiet Beatle," guitarist George Harrison surprised the recording industry and the listening public with his early post-Beatles work. During the late 1960's, he was frustrated by his lack of opportunity to include more of his songs on Beatles albums. With the breakup of the Beatles in 1970, Harrison made up for lost time by releasing a hefty backlog of songs that he had written during his Beatle years. While his solo career has to be considered uneven, Harrison has recorded a number of popular and critically acclaimed songs.

The Beginnings. George Harold Harrison, the youngest of four children of Harold and Louise Harrison, began listening to rock and roll during the mid-1950's. Fascinated with the guitar, he convinced his mother to give him three pounds in order to purchase one. With his mother's encouragement, he methodically learned some basic chords. Idolizing such American guitarists as Carl Perkins, Chet Atkins, Buddy Holly, and Duane Eddy, Harrison was determined to master the instrument. In 1957, Paul McCartney introduced him to John Lennon. By 1958, Harrison had become a member of Lennon's band, the Quarry Men, of which McCartney was already a member; the group soon evolved into the Beatles. After revolutionizing popular music during the 1960's, the Beatles disbanded in 1970.

With the Beatles, Harrison demonstrated his prowess as the band's lead guitarist and also served as lead singer on a number of songs, although he more commonly provided harmony for Lennon and McCartney's lead vocals. In the mid-1960's, he became deeply interested in Eastern religion and music, and he played a principal role in introducing the sitar and other Indian instruments into rock music. He also showed that he could write excellent songs. At a minimum, his "Taxman" (from 1966's *Revolver*) and "While My Guitar Gently Weeps" (from 1968's *The Beatles*, commonly known as the "White Album") rank among the group's stronger efforts; his compositions "Something" and "Here Comes the Sun" (both from the 1969 release *Abbey Road*) rank even higher, both having achieved standard status. Nevertheless, with the astonishingly prolific Lennon and McCartney entrenched as the band's principal writers (and with the late 1960's emergence of drummer Ringo Starr as a contributor of occasional tunes), little space could be allotted for Harrison's compositions on Beatles albums. He argued repeatedly with Lennon and McCartney in

For the Record

George Harrison married his first wife, Pattie Boyd, in 1966. Unfortunately, a few years later Harrison's friend Eric Clapton fell in love with Pattie; he wrote the classic song "Layla" about her. Eventually George and Pattie divorced, and Eric and Pattie were married. Harrison and Clapton managed to remain friends through it all, and Harrison was quoted as saying that if anyone had to fall in love with his wife, it might as well be a close friend.

an effort to have more of his songs represented on Beatles releases, but to little avail.

In the wake of the band's breakup, therefore, Harrison decided to record the large backlog of songs he had accumulated. While his first solo project was the electronic instrumental music he wrote for a 1968 soundtrack album, *Wonderwall Music*, his 1970 release *All Things Must Pass* represented his first true attempt at showing what he could do as a songwriter and vocalist away from the Beatles. A three-record set produced by Harrison and the legendary Phil Spector, *All Things Must Pass* was both a critical and commercial success. Released in November, 1970, the album included such spiritual—and popular—songs as "My Sweet Lord," "What Is Life," and "Awaiting on You All"; many of the album's lyrics reflected Harrison's devotion to the Eastern spiritualism of the Maharishi Mahesh Yogi. *All Things Must Pass* went to number 1 on the U.S. pop charts and sold millions of copies, and "My Sweet Lord" was a number 1 hit as a single. (In 1976, Harrison was successfully sued for copyright infringement over "My Sweet Lord"; a judge ruled that he had unintentionally plagiarized the melody from the Chiffons' early 1960's hit "He's So Fine.")

After the success of *All Things Must Pass*, Harrison organized a charity benefit for the starving people of Bangladesh. Held at New York's Madison Square Garden in 1971, the two-concert event featured an all-star cast of performers that included Eric Clapton, Bob Dylan, Leon Russell, Ringo Starr, Ravi Shankar, and Harrison himself. As a result of the benefit, a successful film and a Grammy-winning three-record album, both entitled *The Concert for Bangla Desh*, were released. Harrison's 1973 release *Living in the Material World* was also well received, and a single from the album, "Give Me Love (Give Me Peace on Earth)," became another number 1 hit.

New Directions. In 1974, Harrison released *Dark Horse* and embarked on his first solo tour of North America. Neither the album nor the tour was an unqualified success, and it became evident that Harrison's popular appeal was waning. While his 1976 album *33 & 1/3* contained some strong material (including the minor hits "Crackerbox Palace" and "This Song," a sly commentary on the "My Sweet Lord" litigation), Harrison's other recordings during the late 1970's and most of the 1980's were uneven. In 1977, moreover, Harrison and his wife, the former model Pattie Boyd, were divorced after eleven years of marriage. In 1978, he was remarried to Olivia Arias.

With his music career in decline, Harrison became increasingly involved in producing films, and he and business partner Denis O'Brien formed HandMade Film Productions. The company produced such successful films as *Monty Python's Life of Brian* (1979), *Time Bandits* (1981), and *Mona Lisa* (1986). In 1981, his nostalgic single "All Those Years Ago," a tribute to the recently slain Lennon that included appearances by Starr, McCartney, and McCartney's wife Linda, reached number 2. In 1987, Harrison made a strong musical comeback with the album *Cloud Nine*, which climbed to number 8 on the U.S. pop charts and included a hit cover version of Ruby Clarke's "Got My Mind Set on You."

After the success of *Cloud Nine*, Harrison joined Bob Dylan, Roy Orbison, Tom Petty, and Jeff Lynne to form the Traveling Wilburys. In 1988, this "supergroup" released *Traveling Wilburys, Volume One*, which reached number 3 on the U.S. pop charts. After the death of Orbison, the Wilburys released *Vol. 3* in 1990. During the 1990's, Harrison worked with the remaining Beatles on the

Anthology project. On June 28, 1998, Harrison revealed that he had been receiving treatment for throat cancer that had been diagnosed in July, 1997. Doctors told Harrison that they had stopped the spread of the cancer and that he was healthy.

—Jeffry Jensen

SELECT DISCOGRAPHY

■ ALBUMS

Wonderwall Music, 1968
All Things Must Pass, 1970
Living in the Material World, 1973
Dark Horse, 1974
33 & 1/3, 1976
Cloud Nine, 1987
Traveling Wilburys, Volume One, 1988 (with the Traveling Wilburys)
Vol. 3, 1990 (with the Traveling Wilburys)

SELECT AWARDS

Grammy Award for Album of the Year for *The Concert for Bangla Desh*, 1972 (with others)
for Best Rock Performance by a Duo or Group with Vocal for *Traveling Wilburys, Volume One*, 1989 (with the Traveling Wilburys)

SEE ALSO: Beatles, The; Clapton, Eric; Dylan, Bob; Lennon, John; McCartney, Paul; Petty, Tom, and the Heartbreakers.

P. J. Harvey

BORN: Yeovil, England; October 9, 1969
FIRST ALBUM RELEASE: *Dry*, 1992 (PJ Harvey band)
MUSICAL STYLES: Rock and roll, pop

The alternative power trio PJ Harvey, led by the talented singer-songwriter and guitarist Polly Jean "P. J." Harvey, emerged from the small English town of Yeovil to take the London music world by storm in 1991. With darkly humorous songs about sex, love, and hate, Harvey's music jolted listeners with its raw emotion and punk-influenced aggression.

The Beginnings. The daughter of a sculptor mother and quarryman father, Harvey grew up on a secluded sheep farm and was exposed to music at a young age. While still in her teens, Harvey performed in two bands, Bologna and Automatic Dlamini, playing saxophone and occasionally contributing a song. When she met bassist Stephen Vaughn and drummer Robert Ellis, the band PJ Harvey was born, and the trio released two well-received singles, "Dress" and "Sheela Na Gig," in 1991. From the start, Harvey, as a singer and writer, concerned herself with the intricacies of male-female relationships. Her songwriting has often been abstract, focusing on women's sexual desire and power as well as their strengths and weaknesses. Men in Harvey's musical world exist as a vantage point for her to discuss their impact on her life.

Ambiguous Look and Image. Harvey's image has always been hard to define. She has portrayed herself as powerful and proud—"Look at these, my childbearing hips," she sang on one song—and desirous of male attention and validation. The ambiguity seemed to only make her and her music more intriguing to the public, and the intense media attention reportedly brought her to the brink of a nervous breakdown in 1992, shortly after playing at the massive Reading Music Festival in England.

The first PJ Harvey album, the bristling, deeply personal *Dry* (1992), was jolting in its sexual imagery and raw, stripped-down sound. On songs like "Dress" and "Happy and Bleeding," Harvey sang about her love-hate relationship with her body—and with men—and the album cover featured a photo of the androgynous singer barechested.

For the band's second album, 1993's *Rid of Me*, Harvey chose Chicago-based producer Steven Albini to man the recording helm. The end product

For the Record

A confirmed tomboy, P. J. Harvey as a child spent most of her time with boys, wore pants, had short hair, and demanded to be called "Paul."

was noisier and harder-edged than the debut, and again, Harvey concerned herself with sexuality and relationships. *Rid of Me* was Harvey's musical mood swing, with songs jumping between dominance and submission, attraction and repulsion, sexual need and detachment. In interviews with the press, Harvey's ambiguity continued: She baffled fans by denouncing feminism, while many of her songs seemed to embrace its concepts.

Polly Jean Goes Solo. In the summer of 1993, Ellis left the band. A release of the demos of *Rid of Me,* titled *4-Track Demos,* showed that Harvey's powerful gut-wrenching voice had been all but buried under layers of production, and the record included five new tracks as well, including the catchy "Reeling." Many critics noted that the record, which highlighted Harvey's self-sufficiency as a musician, confirmed what they'd suspected: that PJ Harvey, the band, was actually P. J. Harvey, the solo act.

P. J. Harvey (Paul Natkin)

Thus it came as little surprise when, in 1995, Harvey disbanded the PJ Harvey band completely and released *To Bring You My Love* as a solo artist. This was an ambitious, bluesy, confident collection of songs, coproduced by Harvey, guitarist John Parish, and Flood, best known for his production work with U2. The following year, Harvey and Parish released a collaborative effort, *Dance Hall at Louse Point,* which featured eleven new, jointly written songs and a cover version of the Peggy Lee standard "Is That All There Is?" To promote the record, Harvey and Parish did a brief U.K. tour with a five-piece band that included original PJ Harvey band member Ellis.

In early 1997, it was announced that British choreographer Mark Bruce would use the music of *Dance Hall at Louse Point* for a contemporary dance piece to be commissioned by the Performing Arts South Bank Centre in London. While Harvey kept a low public profile in 1997, she began recording a new album, intended for release in the fall of 1998, entitled *Is This Desire?*

—Nicole Pensiero

SELECT DISCOGRAPHY

■ ALBUMS

Dry, 1992 (PJ Harvey band)
4-Track Demos, 1993 (PJ Harvey band)
Rid of Me, 1993 (PJ Harvey band)
To Bring You My Love, 1995 (Harvey solo)
Dance Hall at Louse Point, 1996 (Harvey with John Parish)
Is This Desire?, 1998

SELECT AWARDS

Rolling Stone, named Best Songwriter and Best New Female Singer, 1993

SEE ALSO: Smith, Patti.

Isaac Hayes

BORN: Covington, Tennessee; August 20, 1942
FIRST ALBUM RELEASE: *Presenting Isaac Hayes,* 1967
MUSICAL STYLE: Rhythm and blues

Often considered to be the first African American rock superstar, Isaac Hayes was raised as an orphan on his grandparents' sharecropper farm forty miles north of Memphis, Tennessee. As a youth, he worked manual labor jobs and taught himself the piano and organ while singing in church choirs. In the late 1950's, he played with his first band, Sir Isaac and the Doo-Dads.

Rise to Stardom. After moving to Memphis, Hayes became an important saxophonist and keyboard session player for Stax-Volt Records, performing on albums by Booker T. and the MG's, Carla Thomas, and Otis Redding. Hayes and David Porter cowrote the majority of the Sam and Dave catalog of songs, including the hits "You Don't Know Like I Know," "Hold On! I'm Comin,'" and "Soul Man." As a producer, Hayes began work on his first solo album, *Presenting Isaac Hayes*, in 1967, which turned out to be a critical and commercial failure.

Hayes's breakthrough came in 1969 with *Hot Buttered Soul*, an album produced at Stax-Volt Records on Hayes's own time. The record's immediate success caught Jim Stewart, the record company's owner, off guard as the label had not yet signed a performance agreement with Hayes. The platinum-selling album was the first of a series of bombastic collections of reworkings of popular songs, such as the million-selling single "By the Time I Get to Phoenix," and Hayes's original songs, such as "Hyperbolicsyllabicsesquedalymistic." His next single, "Walk on By," also went gold in 1969, as did *Live at the Sahara Tahoe* (1973), which went to number 8 on the *Billboard* album charts.

Hayes's next four albums continued his chart-topping streak of success. Each album featured Hayes's raspy, deep-bass vocal delivery and built on his public image of imposing arrogance. For live performances, he formed the Isaac Hayes Movement, which featured a forty-piece orchestra, highly visible bodyguards, and an entourage of beautiful women. Hayes's trademark shaved head, sunglasses, and gold chains established his personal stage presence.

Sound Tracks. In 1971, along with Curtis Mayfield and Marvin Gaye, Hayes became associated with black exploitation films when he released the theme from *Shaft*, a double-album sound track that became the prototype for 1970's guitar-based funk. The title song's popularity led to Hayes becoming the first African American composer to be honored with an Academy Award for a film score. The album reached number 1 on the charts and earned a Grammy, and Hayes's performance at the Grammy ceremonies created an international sensation. His trendsetting fashion sense earned him the nickname "Black Moses," which became the title for his next Grammy-winning album later that year.

Hayes issued nine albums from 1969 through 1973, but each became more extravagant until they reached the point of self-parody. However, he continued to produce successful hits, including "Never Say Goodbye" (1971), "Do Your Thing" (1972), "Theme from *The Men*" (1972), and "Joy (Part 1)" in 1974. In that year, he acted in and composed two movie scores for *Three Tough Guys* and *Truck Turner*, each earning lackluster critical and commercial response. After a royalty disagreement with Stax-Volt Records in 1975, Hayes created his own record company, Hot Buttered Soul (HBS), and issued *Chocolate Chip*, which clearly demonstrated that his streak of influence and musical popularity had waned.

Occasional releases returned him to the charts, such as his 1976 "Disco Connection," which was a minor hit in England. He recorded "A Man and a Woman," a duet with Dionne Warwick for whom he had produced the single "Déjà Vu." After a nine-million-dollar bankruptcy debt, Hayes

For the Record

Although he won multiple awards for composing, Isaac Hayes could neither read nor write music through most of his musical career. He composed by recording his tunes and rhythms on tapes, from which professional arrangers wrote the scores.

moved through a series of record labels, issuing the million-selling *Don't Let Go* (1979) as well as *Branded* (1995). In 1981 he hosted a two-hour radio show, "Black Music Countdown Featuring Isaac Hayes," but worked on no musical projects between 1981 and 1985.

Before and after this hiatus, Hayes continued to write scores for motion pictures, including *Robin Hood: Men in Tights* (1993) and *Escape from New York* (1981), and television shows, including *The Rockford Files, The A-Team,* and *Miami Vice.* He also guest-starred on such television shows as *The Rockford Files, Sliders,* and *The Fresh Prince of Bel-Air.* In the late 1990's, Hayes's career took another turn when he provided the voice for the character Chef on the animated series *South Park.* He sang a number of humorous and risqué songs for the series and was featured in the 1998 album *Chef Aid.*

Wesley Britton

SELECT DISCOGRAPHY

■ ALBUMS

Presenting Isaac Hayes, 1967
Shaft, 1971 (sound track)
Black Moses, 1971
Chocolate Chip, 1975

SEE ALSO: Gaye, Marvin; Mayfield, Curtis; Sam and Dave; White, Barry.

Heart

ORIGINAL MEMBERS: Ann Wilson (b. 1951), Nancy Wilson (b. 1954), Roger Fisher (b. 1950), Steve Fossen (b. 1949)

OTHER MEMBERS: Howard Leese (b. 1952), Michael Derosier (b. 1951), Mark Andes (b. 1948), Denny Carmassi

FIRST ALBUM RELEASE: *Dreamboat Annie,* 1976

MUSICAL STYLES: Rock and roll, pop

Sisters Ann and Nancy Wilson grew up in a suburb of Seattle, Washington, and formed a folk duo in the 1960's. In Seattle, Ann met guitarist Roger Fisher and bassist Steve Fossen to form Heart (originally called White Heart) in the early 1970's. Ann and the band moved to Canada to be with Mike Fisher, Roger's older brother. Mike became Heart's road manager, and Nancy moved to Canada to join the group. The group survived hard times until their first album lifted them to stardom with the Wilson sisters as two of the early hard-hitting women of rock and roll.

A Rocking Concept. Heart's first album, *Dreamboat Annie* (1976), was recorded for Mushroom Records, a small, independent label based in Vancouver. The album is organized somewhat like a concept album, where there is a continual flow from one song to the next, rather than merely a collection of separate, unrelated songs. The connections between the songs give a sense of unity to the album.

The album contains dramatic changes in style, from the soft, lyric style of "Dreamboat Annie" and its following acoustic guitar solo, to the heavy-metal sound of "Crazy on You." Although this style was similar to the sound of Led Zeppelin, Ann's singing was unique. Heart's hard-rock style helped make their debut album a success, and it sold more than one million copies, going platinum in less than seven months. "Crazy on You" and "Magic Man," released as singles, became hits.

Rocking Ladies. A significant aspect of Heart's style is the hard-rock singing of Ann Wilson and guitar playing of Nancy Wilson. In a 1980 *Rolling Stone* story, it is noted that Ann "can belt and screech the hardest rock tune, then slide through every delicate nuance of a tender folk ballad." Ann's strong belting was unique at the time of *Dreamboat Annie.* Before the 1970's, most female singers, guided by the media's image of well-behaved women, sang with very soft, pleasing voices and did not shout (Tina Turner, Grace Slick of Jefferson Airplane, and Janis Joplin are notable exceptions), despite the fact that their male counterparts often distorted their voices to near-shouting levels, a characteristic that is one of the defining features of rock and roll.

In addition to Ann's strong voice, Heart featured a superb guitarist in Nancy Wilson. Nancy could match Ann's emotional contrasts by playing gentle folk-based acoustic solos or aggressive heavy metal. Female instrumentalists were also rare in rock bands before the 1970's, so to have two musically powerful women (sisters, no less) in the same band during this time was truly significant to the world of rock and roll.

Into the Courts. In early 1977 Heart left the Mushroom label and signed to Portrait, but had to go to court to be released from Mushroom, which had sued them. *Little Queen* was released in 1977 by Portrait, while Mushroom released *Magazine*, an album started before Heart left for Portrait, from the raw tracks and an older tape from the band. A court order stopped production of *Magazine*, and eventually Heart won the right to rerelease the album in 1978 with their own updates (the case was settled out of court).

"Heartless," which became a hit from *Magazine*, shows Ann's powerful range as lead vocalist as she switches between near-speaking to her trademark shout. Her ability to switch between ballad and rock singing is evident in the song "Without You." *Magazine* went on to sell more than one million copies.

For the 1978 album *Dog and Butterfly*, Ann and Nancy teamed up with childhood friend Sue Ennis to cowrite all of the new songs. The album was conceptually more advanced (Ennis was a doctoral candidate in German literature at the University of California at Berkeley at the time) and included the hit "Straight On," although the album was not as commercially successful as previous ones.

1980's and 1990's. After *Dog and Butterfly*, Fisher left Heart to form his own band (he and Nancy split romantically as well). Nancy moved to lead guitar, and Heart's next album, *Bébé le Strange* (1980), became a Top-10 album. By 1983 Heart's personnel consisted of Ann and Nancy, Howard Leese (who had been with Heart since their first album) on guitars and background vocals, and

Heart (Fotos International/Archive Photos)

newcomers Mark Andes on bass guitars and Denny Carmassi on drums. After Heart's move to the Capitol label in 1985, they had two more successful albums before the decade was out: *Heart* (1985) and *Bad Animals* (1987). *Heart* included the major hits "What About Love," "Never," and the number 1 hit "These Dreams." *Bad Animals* included "Alone" (written by Tom Kelly and Billy Steinberg), which was Heart's first British Top-10 hit as well as their second American number 1 song.

Heart's 1990 album *Brigade* was billed as a return to the band's 1970's roots. The album includes some more exotic textures with Nancy playing on Dobro, mandolin, and blues harp. Heart continued to record in the 1990's, although later albums were compilations (including *The Road Home* from 1995 and *Greatest Hits* from 1997). Ann and Nancy Wilson would continue to perform and record with the group Lovemongers, releasing the 1992 album *Lovemongers—Battle of Evermore.* Although personnel changed over the years, the heart of Heart was the Wilson sisters, and they helped discard old cliches and establish a new level of exitement for women performers in rock and roll. *—Mark J. Spicer*

SELECT DISCOGRAPHY

■ ALBUMS

Dreamboat Annie, 1976
Little Queen, 1977
Magazine, 1978
Dog and Butterfly, 1978
Bébé le Strange, 1980
Greatest Hits Live, 1980
Private Audition, 1982
Passionworks, 1983
Heart, 1985
Bad Animals, 1987
Brigade, 1990
Rock the House Live, 1991
Desire Walks On, 1993
The Road Home, 1995
Greatest Hits, 1997

SEE ALSO: Jefferson Airplane / Jefferson Starship; Joplin, Janis; Led Zeppelin; Turner, Ike and Tina / Tina Turner.

Jimi Hendrix

BORN: Seattle, Washington; November 27, 1942
DIED: London, England; September 18, 1970
FIRST ALBUM RELEASE: *Are You Experienced?* 1967
MUSICAL STYLES: Blues, rock and roll, rhythm and blues

Jimi Hendrix was a revolutionary musician. A gifted and skilled guitarist, he awed not only the crowds who flocked to see him but also his peers in various musical genres. Hendrix literally redefined how to play the electric guitar. He also epitomized the late 1960's image of flamboyant rock and roll, sexuality, and drug use.

Background. Born Johnny Allen Hendrix (later renamed James Marshall Hendrix) in Seattle, Jimi Hendrix emerged from a modest African American background to become the most innovative and influential rock guitarist of the 1960's, perhaps of all time. At a young age he listened to blues guitarists Muddy Waters and B. B. King, early rockers such as Chuck Berry, and white performers such as Eddie Cochran. He learned guitar at the age of twelve, playing in local bands for soft drinks and hamburgers. As a teenager Hendrix sometimes dated white girls and often got into trouble because of it in the conservative 1950's. After performing with high school bands, Hendrix joined the U.S. army after finishing high school in 1959 at the age of seventeen. He became a paratrooper. He also performed in military clubs, where he met bassist Billy Cox, whose friendship and musical talent Hendrix revived years later when under great stress at the apex of his astonishing career. Discharged after parachuting injuries in 1961, Hendrix began working as a guitarist under the name Jimmy James. He worked on various southern tours, backing up his idol B. B. King, Sam Cooke, and many others after a short fling in a band known as the Flames. Afterward, Hendrix played behind Little Richard and Ike and Tina Turner before moving to New York City.

While in New York, Hendrix made adjustments that became characteristic of his style. After listening to Bob Dylan sing, Hendrix concluded that

The Jimi Hendrix Experience: Mitch Mitchell, Hendrix, Noel Redding (MCA)

having a voice that was subpar by traditional pop standards was not a drawback. He set aside his doubts about his singing voice, and he became known in Greenwich Village clubs for his skill as a blues performer. More important, Hendrix began experimenting with feedback and distortion-producing "fuzz box" devices, producing unusual sounds from his Fender Stratocaster guitar. The extreme volume that Hendrix used enabled him to obtain the feedback and added to the excitement of his performances. After attempting to support himself by working with the Isley Brothers, King Curtis, and others, Hendrix met entrepreneur Ed Chapin, who signed him to a management and recording contract. With the help of Chapin, Hendrix became the lead guitarist in Curtis Knight's band. His incredible ability as a guitarist soon began catching people's attention, including Chas Chandler, the original bassist for the English group the Animals. Chandler brought Hendrix to London and promised to make him a star.

Initial Impact. It did not take long for Hendrix to became a recognized celebrity. Chandler and his partner persuaded Hendrix to adopt his surname again, and they introduced him to a pair of British musicians, bassist Noel Redding and drummer Mitch Mitchell. Hendrix and his two sidemen frizzed their hair and dressed in the wildest clothes that they could find. The Jimi Hendrix Experience, as they were now called, quickly developed into a powerful band. Often playing soul tunes such as "Land of a Thousand Dances" and "In the Midnight Hour," Hendrix also performed contemporary songs such as "Like a Rolling Stone" and "Hey Jude." Musical peers such as Eric Clapton and Pete Townshend attended as many Hendrix shows as possible. The Jimi Hendrix Experience soon astonished Great Britain and the rest of Europe. The band's first single, "Hey Joe," reached number 6 on the British charts in early 1967, followed shortly by their signature piece, "Purple Haze." Even more stunning was their initial album, *Are You Experienced?* (1967), which included "Foxy Lady." By the summer of 1967 Hendrix and his band had completed a successful tour of Britain, Germany, and Scandinavia.

A Star Is Born. Rumors of the Hendrix phenomenon had spread to the United States, and the release of *Are You Experienced?* set the stage for the band's U.S. appearance at a pop festival in Monterey, California. At Paul McCartney's insistence, the Jimi Hendrix Experience was lined up for the Monterey Pop Festival in June, 1967. Their appearance there made Hendrix a pop icon. Appearing as the last act of the night, Hendrix went on stage after the Who's flashy set. The Who's driving music, mod clothes, and wild destructiveness presented a hard act to follow, but Hendrix rose to the challenge. The band played a strong set, and Hendrix dazzled the audience. He played his guitar with his teeth, and he played it behind his back. Finally, after caressing and seeming to make love to his guitar, Hendrix concluded his set by squirting lighter fluid onto it and burning it. His flamboyant approach immediately thrust Hendrix into center stage in the rock world, but it also locked him into a role that soon frustrated him. Audiences often seemed to be more excited about the outlandish aspects of the show than about the music. There was no doubt that Hendrix was a dramatic performer, but he considered himself primarily a musician.

The Jimi Hendrix Experience first toured the United States as an opening act for the pop group the Monkees. Their very young audience did not respond well to Hendrix. His managers rescued him from the situation by announcing falsely that the Daughters of the American Revolution had demanded that Hendrix be taken off the tour. This story became part of the Hendrix legend—Hendrix as a rebellious, wild, African American antihero.

In 1968 Hendrix reached the height of his success. Two gold albums came out that year, *Axis: Bold as Love* and *Electric Ladyland.* On both albums, relentless rock and blues rhythms mixed with surreal, sometimes delicate, lyrics, dazzling guitar work, distortion, and feedback. Hendrix consolidated seemingly diverse elements and styles and made them his own. *Axis: Bold as Love* showed an artist who could play tender, wistful ballads such as "Little Wing" (a song since recorded by many others), the jazzy "Up from the Skies," heavy rock, and psychedelic guitar sound effects never heard before. In "Spanish Castle Magic" Hendrix pays homage to a music hall in Tacoma, Washington, from his younger days. On the double album *Electric Ladyland* Hendrix took recording studio techniques even further. This album included his version of Dylan's "All Along the Watchtower" and such improvisational showcases as "Voodoo Chile." The contributions of bassist Redding and, particularly, drummer Mitchell to the first three Hendrix albums should not be overlooked. Both added significantly to the range and style of the music, and Mitchell's exuberant and inventive drumming influenced a generation of players.

Despite his success, Hendrix was restless. He fretted over his image as a flashily dressed, outrageous entertainer, and he set high standards for himself that his fans often did not understand. Shortly after the beginning of his second U.S. tour, early in 1968, Hendrix dropped the more extravagant aspects of his performance and usually performed his music straight. Audience re-

For the Record

The Monkees caught Jimi Hendrix's act in London in 1967 and brought him back to open their U.S. tour. Hendrix's wild, sexually charged performing style did not fit in well with the Monkees' squeaky clean image, however. Writer Lillian Roxon recalled how Hendrix did "things to his guitar so passionate, so concentrated, and so intense that anyone with halfway decent manners had to look away."

ception to this approach was occasionally hostile. Hendrix's attempt to prevail and ride out this response was not helped by having to fulfill a tough schedule of fifty-four dates in forty-seven days while living a chaotic round of encounters with groupies and drugs. Hendrix lost weight and became convinced that his managers had mishandled his earnings. As 1968 came to a close, disagreements broke out between Chas Chandler and co-manager Michael Jeffery. Jeffery gradually won the upper hand. Also in 1968, Hendrix spent the night in jail after a nasty dispute with Noel Redding—a clear sign that their working relationship was beginning to break down.

New Directions. Hendrix had begun to feel that his best music emerged from informal settings. Previously, Hendrix had liked to work out his material very carefully in a studio environment; now he preferred a situation in which musical ideas appeared spontaneously. Eager to experiment, Hendrix jammed with guitarists John McLaughlin and Larry Coryell, Jefferson Airplane bassist Jack Casady, and members of Traffic. Miles Davis admired the inventiveness of Hendrix and planned a recording session with him. The usually aloof Davis believed that Hendrix could become a legendary jazz artist because of the experimental width of his music. Davis even stated that Hendrix had passed him by in musical terms. Hendrix continued to jam with musicians in New York whenever the opportunity arose to sit in with others who interested him. The jam sessions with other artists led to some of the tracks on *Electric Ladyland.* Sensing a new burst of creativity, Hendrix, along with manager Jeffery, planned construction of his own recording studio, in New York.

By the beginning of 1969 Hendrix was uneasy with his popularity and unsure of his future direction. He became increasingly introverted. Hendrix had a reputation for heavy drug use and was arrested for drug possession in Toronto in May, 1969. He was also under pressure from Black Power advocates to play to African American audiences. Hendrix claimed that he wanted no part of politics, but as a famous black musician whose audiences were overwhelmingly white, he was caught in an uneasy situation. These problems increased the tension in the band. The Experience played at the Newport Pop Festival in late June and at a festival in Denver a week later. There Hendrix abruptly announced that it would be the last performance of the Experience. Redding departed for England, and Hendrix replaced him with old army friend Billy Cox. Mitchell stayed on briefly, but by August the Experience no longer existed.

Most of the summer was spent in New York, where Hendrix assembled a group of primarily blues musicians that he referred to as his "electric sky church." Part of this group appeared with Hendrix at the Woodstock festival in August, 1969. This casual and relatively large ensemble backed Hendrix effectively, and he put on a stunning performance. Particularly notable were a riveting rendition of "Purple Haze," in which Hendrix demonstrated yet again his ability to improvise, and his overwhelming version of "The Star Spangled Banner."

The solution to the various pressures that tormented Hendrix was the creation of the Band of Gypsys in December, 1969. Among this trio was bassist Billy Cox and drummer Buddy Miles, who had previously played soul venues as well as the rock circuit with the Electric Flag. The Band of Gypsys' debut concert at New York's Fillmore East on New Year's Eve, 1969, resulted in the only album from this group. Hendrix was disappointed with the band's abilities. At their follow-up concert at Madison Square Garden in January, 1970, Hendrix walked out in the middle of the second song. Band of Gypsys received a mixed response from Hendrix fans.

Hendrix attempted to reunite the original Experience band, but after only a few weeks the effort collapsed. Performing his final appearances with Mitchell and Cox left the notion that Hendrix could not decide what to play. With Mitchell and Cox, he recorded *The Cry of Love* (1971), his last self-authorized album. At last work was completed on the new Hendrix studio, Electric Lady. There Hendrix recorded new material and jammed with friends after its August, 1970, opening. Hendrix later departed for the Isle of

Wight festival, his last concert appearance, in August, 1970. His performance was greeted with a lukewarm reception. Afterwards, Hendrix toured continental Europe despite his fears that Europeans had forgotten him since he had spent most of the last two years in the United States. The European tour was cut short and Hendrix returned to London alone in mid-September.

Death and Legacy. On September 18, 1970, Hendrix died in London, suffocating on his own vomit following barbiturate intoxication. Suicide was not ruled out, but evidence seems to point toward his death being an accident. The coroner released a noncommittal report, claiming that the evidence was insufficient for a finding of either suicide or carelessness.

Hendrix's state of mind during the days before his death is not known. Some acquaintances asserted that Hendrix had finally put his musical and business affairs in order. Others suggested that he had been more depressed than usual. Hendrix had very few close friends, but rather a large entourage to whom he did not confide. As a result, few have been in a position to detail Hendrix's attitudes about drugs, his feelings about being African American, or his sexual relations. His death only reinforced the mystery and confusion about his career and his personal life. It is clear that Hendrix was a modest person who did not understand, until very late in life, that famous musicians need to defend themselves against the decimation of their profession. Hendrix never learned how to construct a sound defensive strategy.

Since Hendrix's death, a huge volume of his recorded material has been released in a variety of repackaged formats. These attest the scope of his musicianship and indicate how strong interest in Hendrix remains among musicians and fans. He was a left-handed guitarist who played a right-handed guitar upside-down. Hendrix had the ability to play lead on most of his guitar strings while unleashing feedback on others. By these means, he could produce the effect of two guitarists playing at the same time. His influence on other guitarists—and on the use of studio recording techniques—is hard to measure. Innumerable guitarists have copied his techniques; some have tried to re-create his sounds and playing, with little success. Texas blues guitarist Stevie Ray Vaughan, who acknowledged his debt to Hendrix by recording two of his songs, was perhaps the most adept at incorporating Hendrix touches into his own playing. —*Douglas W. Richmond*

SELECT DISCOGRAPHY

■ ALBUMS

Are You Experienced? 1967
Axis: Bold as Love, 1968
Electric Ladyland, 1968
Smash Hits, 1969
Band of Gypsys, 1970
The Cry of Love, 1971
Hendrix in the West, 1972
Soundtrack Recordings from the Film "Jimi Hendrix," 1973
The Essential Jimi Hendrix, 1978
The Jimi Hendrix Concerts, 1982
Live at Winterland, 1987

SELECT AWARDS

Rock and Roll Hall of Fame, inducted 1992

SEE ALSO: Berry, Chuck; Clapton, Eric; Cooke, Sam; Davis, Miles; Dylan, Bob; King, B. B.; Little Richard; McLaughlin, John; Traffic; Turner, Ike and Tina / Tina Turner; Vaughan, Stevie Ray; Waters, Muddy.

Don Henley

BORN: Gilmer, Texas; July 22, 1947
FIRST SOLO ALBUM RELEASE: *I Can't Stand Still*, 1982
MUSICAL STYLES: Pop, rock and roll, country

Don Henley was a founding member of the Eagles, one of the most popular rock groups of all time. After the group's breakup, his solo writing would abandon the country-rock feel of the early Eagles albums completely for a pop-rock sound with lyrics that often addressed difficult social issues. While important, influential, and award-winning, Henley's musical output since leaving the band has been sparse: only three albums, plus a greatest-hits compilation, in fifteen years. By the late 1990's, his name was associated as much with social activism as with music.

From Texan to Troubadour. On the advice of an English teacher, Henley dropped out of college in Texas and moved his band Shiloh to Los Angeles in 1969. He met musician Glenn Frey at the popular nightclub the Troubadour soon after. Befriending Henley, Frey found him a job playing drums for Linda Ronstadt for two hundred dollars per week. Six months later, with Ronstadt's blessing, the two left to form their own band. "[Frey] told me about Randy Meisner and Bernie Leadon, who had been with Poco and the [Flying] Burritos, respectively," Henley said. "Glenn said we needed to get those guys because they could play the kind of country rock we were all so interested in." After that, with the help of future music industry giant David Geffen, the Eagles were born.

The quartet went to England and recorded their self-titled album in 1972. Between 1972 and 1979 the Eagles had a phenomenal career, releasing seven successful albums. Their 1975 *Greatest Hits* album sold over twenty-two million copies. Their artistic and popular peak was the next album, *Hotel California* (1976), which was their third consecutive number 1 album. Over the course of their 1970's albums the Eagles steadily moved from country rock to a more straight rock sound, and there were a few key personnel changes along the way. Through it all, Henley and Frey wrote most of the songs, steered and dominated the band, and eventually squabbled between themselves.

Three years went by between *Hotel California* and *The Long Run.* The fights between Frey and Henley were becoming more difficult to overcome. In 1980, when the group finally broke up, Henley said that they would play together again only "when hell freezes over." In 1981 Henley recorded a duet with former girlfriend Stevie Nicks called "Leather and Lace" that hit number 6 on the charts.

Solo Bird. In 1982 Henley released his first solo album, *I Can't Stand Still,* on his old friend Geffen's new label, Geffen Records. It was well received by critics, who responded especially well to his lyrics that reflected his concern with social and political issues.

Don Henley (Ken Settle)

The album featured the song "Dirty Laundry," which made it to number 3 on the charts. The song was inspired by bad press Henley had received when some underaged women were allegedly found unconscious in his house, possibly from intoxication, after a party. The tabloid press exploited the incident, presenting Henley as an excessive, out-of-control rock star. Henley's side of the story went unheard, and "Dirty Laundry" was his response to the media. Containing the chant "Kick 'em when they're up/ Kick 'em when they're down" in the chorus, the lyrics of the song portrayed the media as a ruthless, shallow group.

For the Record

"I think in all great groups there is tension between two or more of the members," Don Henley said in an Internet interview. "That tension is a double-edged sword, because it is the thing that makes the creativity work, and it also the same thing that destroys the group eventually."

Building the Perfect Beast (1984) was a great success for Henley and showed his more mature side. Videos from the album received much play on MTV, and the album reached number 2. Two singles reached the Top 10 in 1985: "The Boys of Summer" and "All She Wants to Do Is Dance." The album appeared on many Best Albums of the Year lists and earned Henley a Grammy Award for Best Rock Vocal Performance.

It would take Henley five years to record his next album, the equally successful *The End of the Innocence* (1989). The title track was a number 8 hit, and the album earned for him yet another Grammy in the same category as his first, Best Rock Vocal Performance. By then, what would be a long and public fight with Geffen and his record company had begun, and Henley desperately tried to break the contract with the man who had given the Eagles their start. It would be years before the legal battle was resolved, and before it was, against Henley's wishes, a greatest-hits album of Henley's solo material would be released.

Actual Miles (1995) contained hits of the prior three albums in addition to a few new songs. "Garden of Allah," similar to "Hotel California," was about a once grand place that was neglected, ruined, and then turned into another Southern California strip mall. Another new song, "You Don't Know Me at All," was written as a farewell to California, as Henley moved his wife and child back to his home state of Texas.

In 1994, the Eagles reunited in one of the most successful and profitable tours in history. They also made a popular MTV *Unplugged* appearance and a live album. The tour and album, self-mockingly titled *Hell Freezes Over*, contained several new songs by Henley and Frey, including "Get Over It," a modest hit. Yet despite the great success, old rivalries reappeared, and after a year and a half, the band broke up once again.

Saving Walden. While a college student in the 1960's, Henley said he discovered the writings of nineteenth century American philosopher Henry David Thoreau. Thoreau's 1854 collection of essays, *Walden*, about his life in a wooded area in Massachusetts, proclaimed his belief that spirituality was found in nature. By the late 1980's, the place known as Walden Pond had become neglected—overused, littered with trash, and slated for the building of an office park. In 1990, Henley launched his "Walden Woods Project" to preserve the treasured area.

Through concerts starring many like-minded musician-activists, such as Jackson Browne and Joni Mitchell, and benefit dinners featuring actors such as Jerry Seinfeld, by 1998 Henley had raised eighteen million dollars to acquire the ninety-six acres of Walden land. That year, the institute he created was dedicated; it would serve as a center for research and education about Thoreau as well as preserve the land. The dedication ceremony was attended by many activists, musicians, and politicians, including President Bill Clinton, who praised Henley for his work.

—Kevin M. Mitchell

SELECT DISCOGRAPHY

■ ALBUMS

I Can't Stand Still, 1982
Building the Perfect Beast, 1984
The End of the Innocence, 1989
Actual Miles: Henley's Greatest Hits, 1995 (compilation)

SELECT AWARDS

Grammy Award for Best Rock Vocal Performance, Male, for "The Boys of Summer," 1985
Grammy Award for Best Rock Vocal Performance, Male, for *The End of the Innocence*, 1989

SEE ALSO: Browne, Jackson; Eagles, The; Nicks, Stevie; Rondstadt, Linda.

John Hiatt

BORN: Indianapolis, Indiana; August 20, 1952
FIRST ALBUM RELEASE: *Hangin' Around the Observatory*, 1974
MUSICAL STYLES: Alternative, rhythm and blues

In the late 1980's and early 1990's, John Hiatt became a popular and successful singer-songwriter. He was benefiting from the growing popularity of crossover country music and the record-buying baby boomers' concern with more mature themes such as children, divorce, and confronting the past. Hiatt was not merely the latest entrant into a musical genre attractive to aging baby boomers, however; he was an experienced songwriter, singer, and musician who had been in the music business for two decades. His music draws upon a combination of wit, talent, and some very painful experiences. Hiatt's songs have been recorded by numerous other rock and country artists.

Difficult Beginnings. From his earliest years, John Hiatt's life was filled with obstacles, tragedy, and pain. His father became too ill to work when John was only a child. The eldest of the seven children in Hiatt's family, John's brother Michael had to support the family at age eighteen. The burdens of responsibility drove Michael to commit suicide three years later, when John was only nine years old. Two years later, John's father died from his extended illness.

As a young teenager John Hiatt was severely overweight, weighing as much as three hundred pounds. He tended not to be popular or successful in school and eventually dropped out. His main interest and source of escape from the negative aspects of his life proved to be music. He took guitar lessons, wrote his own songs, and formed a number of bands. In 1971 he decided to move to Nashville, and he soon secured a job writing music for a major country music publisher. Hiatt had some moderate success with his music writing, including his "Sure as I'm Sittin' Here," which was recorded by Three Dog Night and made the Top 20 in 1974.

For the Record

When John Hiatt was touring in the late 1970's, he used to perform his entire set sitting down. One night George Thorogood and the Delaware Destroyers filled in for a show Hiatt was unable to perform, and the band played their entire set sitting down in deference to Hiatt.

That same year Hiatt recorded his first solo album, *Hangin' Around the Observatory*, for Epic Records. The music was an unusual blend of country and rock, far different from the day's mainstream country-rock acts such as the Charlie Daniels Band. Hiatt's music incorporated unexpected chord changes, variegated rhythms, pleasing harmonies, and frequent hooks. It was his lyrics, however, that made Hiatt's songs so unique. His blend of biting wit, wordplay, and sense of the absurd provided an engaging, even arresting narrative atop the catchy but quirky melodies. The next year, Hiatt released a second album entitled *Overcoats*, which essentially followed the format of his first album. Both albums earned some critical praise, but commercially they were not successful. Epic subsequently dropped Hiatt from the label.

The New-Wave Phase. Hiatt's troubles were compounded by alcohol and drug abuse. He spent the next several years on the road, opening for more established acts, but much of his money went to support his habits. He also got married during this time and divorced after a month. Then he got another break: In 1979, Hiatt secured a contract with MCA Records and released two new albums. *Slug Line* (1979) and *Two Bit Monsters* (1980) were a musical departure from Hiatt's earlier work, with his new albums incorporating faster rock tempos, more sophisticated mixing, and wider instrumentation. The country influence apparent in the previous albums was almost entirely absent. Hiatt's new albums were generally categorized as new wave, and critics began to compare his work favorably to that of Elvis Costello and other major names of the day. Still, the albums were not popular with the buying public. Hiatt also continued to suffer from personal problems, including a second bad marriage and continuing drug and alcohol abuse.

Hiatt recorded his next three albums for Geffen, and these demonstrated a continuing sophistication in Hiatt's songwriting. *All of a Sudden* (1982) represented the peak of Hiatt's new-wave phase, with heavy use of electronic instrumentation and lyrics about alienation. *Riding with the King* (1983) began Hiatt's slow and subtle return to country influences, evident both in some of the musical arrangements and even in Hiatt's decidedly more twangy accentuation ("The Love That Harms"). The album also marked a deepening cynicism and bitterness, with songs about manipulation, suicide, lost love, revenge, cheating, spousal abuse, and failure. *Warming Up to the Ice Age* (1985) included Hiatt's strongest material, utilizing horns, driving rhythms, heartfelt lyrics, and a duet with Elvis Costello. Not only had Hiatt been compared with Costello, but Costello became a genuine fan of Hiatt's music. The two's rendition of "Living a Little, Laughing a Little" (originally recorded by the Spinners) reflects a soulful intensity that seems to bind the two artists. "The Crush" charted new territory for Hiatt in bluesy rock, and "When We Ran" emphasized Hiatt's more sensitive side as a songwriter and singer.

Ironically, just as Hiatt was producing his best work, his personal life was at its worst. Hiatt was increasingly controlled by his drug habits. Meanwhile, his second wife gave birth to a daughter and Hiatt, unable to cope with this new complication in their problem-ridden marriage, left the two of them. He entered a drug treatment program, which he successfully completed in four weeks.

John Hiatt rehearsing as producer Don Was looks on (Paul Natkin)

Several months later, however, Hiatt's estranged wife committed suicide, and Hiatt found himself raising their daughter. One year later Geffen dropped Hiatt from its label.

Maturity, Stability, and Happiness. Hiatt, now married to his third wife, Nancy, set about supporting her and the two children they brought from their previous marriages. His next album, entitled *Bring the Family*, brought together some of the biggest names in music: Ry Cooder on guitar, Nick Lowe on bass, and Jim Keltner on drums. Initially recorded without a label, the album was released by A&M in 1987. *Bring the Family* marked Hiatt's emotional coming-of-age, the softening of his bitterness, and his triumph over adversity. Songs such as "Thing Called Love," "Have a Little Faith in Me," "Thank You Girl," and "Learning How to Love You" express Hiatt's newfound positive attitudes about love and relationships, while "Your Dad Did" celebrates family life. Notwithstanding the more positive attitude, the songs still showcased Hiatt's trademark wit and senses of irony and humor. The album also marked Hiatt's continuing move back to country influences. The album constituted Hiatt's first reasonably successful album, selling more than 200,000 copies. "Thing Called Love" was subsequently covered by Bonnie Raitt, who turned out to be another fan of John Hiatt's music. (She would later contribute vocals on "I Can't Wait" for Hiatt's *Walk On* in 1995.)

Slow Turning (1988) continued in the same genre as *Bring the Family*. The themes extended a bit further beyond family and love, and the country influence was more pronounced. Hiatt seemed to have settled on a more mature, slower, guitar-based music. He included the occasional song of retrospection, such as "Paper Thin." These themes and styles extended to his next album, *Stolen Moments* (1990).

By the early 1990's Hiatt had achieved commercial success, emotional stability, and family happiness. With Nancy he now had another daughter (the subject of "Georgia Rae" on *Slow Turning*). He had developed the confidence and perspective to write beyond the themes of personal epiphany and redemption that had influenced so much of his previous two albums. Still, his next albums, including *Perfectly Good Guitar* (1993) and *Walk On* (1995), were focused primarily on the frailties of human lives and relationships. Although Hiatt may not be an authority, he speaks from experience. The combination of his ability to express feelings through lyrics and his soulful voice makes him a compelling artist indeed. —*Steve D. Boilard*

SELECT DISCOGRAPHY

■ ALBUMS

Hangin' Around the Observatory, 1974
Overcoats, 1975
Slug Line, 1979
Two Bit Monsters, 1980
All of a Sudden, 1982
Riding with the King, 1983
Warming Up to the Ice Age, 1985
Bring the Family, 1987
Slow Turning, 1988
Stolen Moments, 1990
Perfectly Good Guitar, 1993
Walk On, 1995
Little Head, 1997

SEE ALSO: Costello, Elvis; Raitt, Bonnie.

Hole

ORIGINAL MEMBERS: Courtney Love (b. Michelle Harrison, 1965), Eric Erlandson (b. 1963), Jill Emery, Caroline Rue

OTHER MEMBERS: Melissa Auf Der Maur (b. 1972), Patty Schemel (b. 1967), Kristen Pfaff (1967-1994)

FIRST ALBUM RELEASE: *Pretty on the Inside*, 1991

MUSICAL STYLES: Alternative, grunge

Formed in 1989, Hole was considered part of the alternative rock and grunge movement that emerged in Seattle in the early 1990's. Much of Hole's popularity has been attributed to lead singer Courtney Love's marriage to grunge legend Kurt Cobain of Nirvana. The two were married in 1992 at the height of the Seattle music scene and the floodtide of Nirvana's fame. The band has also received attention as a result of

Hole: Melissa Auf Der Maur, Courtney Love, Patty Schemel, Eric Erlandson (Geffen Records/Guzman)

Love's notorious public image: her self-described "kinderwhore" look, her reputation for violence and angry outbursts, her drug use, and her fledgling acting career. However, Hole has also merited public attention legitimately, on the strength of their music. Their harsh, angst-filled sound, a unique mixture of punk-influenced grunge rock and poetic lyricism, has earned the band commercial success and critical acclaim that have outlasted the fervor over Love's marriage and public persona.

The Beginnings. Courtney Love assembled the original lineup of Hole in 1989. Prior to this time, however, she was already heavily involved in the music scene. She became acquainted with punk rock when she was sent away to school as a teenager. After experimenting with exotic dancing and rock photography, she found her way to music—first as a fan and then as an aspiring performer. For a short time, Love joined Kate Bjelland in a band that would later become Babes in Toyland. Love also did a brief stint as a singer for the rock band Faith No More in 1989. Later that year, she moved to Seattle and began to assemble her own band, Hole.

Love acquired guitarist Eric Erlandson when he answered an advertisement she placed in a Seattle newspaper. The music they began to create together reflected a merging of Love's traditional punk-influenced vocals and the loud, plaintive wail of Erlandson's guitar stylings. Love invited

For the Record

Despite its apparent off-color connotations, Hole's name was taken from an ancient Greek play written by Euripides.

bassist Jill Emery and drummer Caroline Rue into the group, and the band Hole emerged from the Seattle grunge scene. Their first singles, "Retard Girl" (1990) and "Dicknail" (1991), were both released by Sub Pop, a prestigious independent label in Seattle. Later that year, Hole's first album, *Pretty on the Inside*, was released by Caroline Records to modest commercial success. Like many of the band's like-minded peers in Seattle, Hole articulated the anguish of teenagers living in the early 1990's. In their first album, Hole created the sound that would become their trademark: classic, full-bore rock chords alternating with mournful guitar riffs and spiked by lyrics that were poetic even when Love sang them in screech mode.

Changing of the Guard. In 1992, Love fired Hole's rhythm section—Emery and Rue—and replaced them with bassist Kristen Pfaff and drummer Patty Schemel. In its original incarnation, Hole was one of the noisiest, most abrasive bands performing in the early 1990's, but with a new lineup came a smoother sound. The music produced by Hole in this period was still powerful and harsh, but more complex musical ideas had begun to emerge as exemplified by the band's second album, *Live Through This* (released by Geffen Records in 1994). The release of *Live Through This* was initially overshadowed by the death of Love's famous husband, Cobain, which occurred only four days before the album's release. As the impact of Cobain's suicide lessened, however, the actual music and message of the album continued to bring in new fans. Two songs off the album, "Doll Parts" and "Violet," became hits. The album itself went platinum and was named record of the year in 1994 by *Rolling Stone*, *Spin*, and *The Village Voice*. Press coverage of Hole continued throughout 1994 with the death of bassist Pfaff to drug overdose and other controversies involving Love. Pfaff was eventually replaced by Melissa Auf Der Maur, and Hole continued to record, releasing the EP *Ask for It* in 1995 and a cover version of Fleetwood Mac's "Gold Dust Woman" the following year.

Hole and Nirvana. Hole was in the midst of establishing itself as a force in the Seattle grunge movement when Love met and married grunge icon Cobain of the band Nirvana. The two were married in 1992, at the apex of Nirvana's phenomenal popularity. Love's marriage and subsequent widowhood—Cobain took his own life in 1994—largely obscured her musical achievements and those of her band. The public received the impression that Hole was merely a Nirvana imitator. Though Love and her music could certainly be said to have a lyrical affinity with the work of Nirvana and punk poet of teenage angst Cobain, the album *Live Through This* showed that Love also had, according to *The Rough Guide to Rock* (1998), "her own well of distinctive images, and a band with sufficient musical resources to realize them." —*Amanda Walzer Scott*

SELECT DISCOGRAPHY

■ ALBUMS

Pretty on the Inside, 1991
Live Through This, 1994
Ask for It, 1995 (EP)
Gold Dust Woman, 1996 (EP)
My Body, the Hand Grenade, 1997 (previously released material)
Celebrity Skin, 1998

SELECT AWARDS

Rolling Stone Record of the Year, for *Live Through This*, 1994
Spin Record of the Year, for *Live Through This*, 1994
The Village Voice Record of the Year, for *Live Through This*, 1994

SEE ALSO: Nirvana.

The Hollies

ORIGINAL MEMBERS: Graham Nash (b. 1942), Allan Clarke (b. 1942), Anthony Hicks (b. 1943), Donald Rathbone, Eric Haydock (b. 1943)
OTHER MEMBERS: Robert Elliot (b. 1942), Bernard Calvert (b. 1943), Terry Sylvester (b. 1945), Mikael Rickfors (b. 1948)
FIRST ALBUM RELEASE: *Here I Go Again*, 1965
MUSICAL STYLE: Pop

While they never had much prestige, the Hollies remain, after the Beatles, England's most consistently successful singles band. This is the group that gave the world Graham Nash, who went on to find greater fame with the group Crosby, Stills, and Nash. While they are associated heavily with the 1960's, the Hollies had several hits in the 1970's as well, including their biggest U.S. hit, 1972's "Long Cool Woman (in a Black Dress)" and a successful follow-up two years later with "The Air That I Breathe." The Beatles, it has been said, never considered the Hollies much of a threat, but the Manchester-based Hollies certainly challenged their fellow northern England artists on the charts.

The Beginnings. The Hollies were founded by childhood buddies Graham Nash and Allan Clarke, who had spent their teen years in various duo incarnations; the Two Teens, Ricky and Dane, and the Guytones were a few of their names. After adding Don Rathbone and Eric Haydock to their lineup, they called themselves the Deltas, and then, after guitarist Tony Hicks came onboard, the Hollies (for either the plant or for Buddy Holly).

By late 1963, they had reached the British Top 20 twice with cover versions of the Coasters' "Searchin'" and the Zodiacs' "Stay." Clarke handled lead vocals, with Nash singing harmonies. The band's first British chart-topping single was 1965's "I'm Alive." The following year, the Hollies cracked the U.S. Top 10 with "Bus Stop" (number 5). Over the next few months, the band continued producing hit after hit, including "Stop Stop Stop" (number 7, 1966), "Carrie-Anne" (number 9, 1967), and "On a Carousel" (number 11, 1967).

The Hollies in 1964: Graham Nash, Tony Hicks, Bobby Elliot, Allan Clarke, Eric Haydock (Archive Photos/John Platt Collection)

In keeping with the times, the Hollies decided to become more experimental with their music in the late 1960's. The resulting albums, *Stop Stop Stop* (1967), *Dear Eloise/King Midas in Reverse* (1967), and *Evolution* (1967), confirmed what the critics suspected all along: The Hollies were truly a singles band, and there were not going to be any successful conceptual albums for this group.

Nash, who wrote (or cowrote) many of the Hollies' hits, left the band in 1968, reportedly frustrated that the band decided to make an album of Bob Dylan covers (*Words and Music by Bob Dylan*, 1969) while refusing to record some of his original tunes, including "Marrakesh Express" and "Lady of the Island" (which he recorded the following year on the debut Crosby, Stills, and Nash album). The band, via a trade paper advertisement, found a replacement for Nash in Terry Sylvester, who stayed with the group until 1981.

The 1970's started promisingly for the Hollies with "He Ain't Heavy, He's My Brother," which reached the number 7 spot on the U.S. charts. However, that year, Clarke, the band's other founding member, was fired, allegedly because of personality conflicts with the other band members. Swedish vocalist Mikael Rickfors was hired as a replacement, and after he was forced out because of his thickly accented vocals, Clarke rejoined the band in 1973.

The Hollies had their biggest U.S. hits with "Long Cool Woman (in a Black Dress)," which reached the number 2 spot on the charts, and peaked again with "The Air That I Breathe" two years later (number 6). In 1977, Clarke again left the band, recorded a second solo album, *I Wasn't Born Yesterday,* and then again came back to the Hollies for 1978's *A Crazy Steal,* which did not make much of an impact on the charts.

Together Again. In 1983, Nash (experiencing one of many breaks in his Crosby, Stills, and Nash career), Clarke, Hicks, and Robert Elliot reformed to record *What Goes Around* . . . . This reformed version of the Hollies, minus Nash, continued to tour together on and off, and in 1988 a reissued version of "He Ain't Heavy, He's My Brother" surprised everyone by hitting the top of the British charts, proving a good singles band can always make a comeback. —*Nicole Pensiero*

SELECT DISCOGRAPHY

■ SINGLES

"Look Through Any Window," 1966
"Bus Stop," 1966
"Stop Stop Stop," 1966
"Carrie-Anne," 1967
"He Ain't Heavy, He's My Brother," 1970
"Long Cool Woman (in a Black Dress)," 1972
"The Air That I Breathe," 1974

■ ALBUMS

Here I Go Again, 1964
Hear! Here! 1965
Beat Group! 1966
Bus Stop, 1966
Stop Stop Stop, 1967
The Hollies' Greatest Hits, 1967
Evolution, 1967
Dear Eloise/King Midas in Reverse, 1967
Words and Music by Bob Dylan, 1969
He Ain't Heavy, He's My Brother, 1969
Moving Finger, 1970
Distant Light, 1971
Romany, 1972
Hollies, 1974
Another Night, 1975
A Crazy Steal, 1978
What Goes Around . . . , 1983
30th Anniversary Collection, 1993

SEE ALSO: Beatles, The; Crosby, Stills, Nash, and Young.

Buddy Holly / The Crickets

Buddy Holly
(Charles Hardin Holley)

BORN: Lubbock, Texas; September 7, 1936
DIED: Near Clear Lake, Iowa, February 3, 1959

The Crickets

ORIGINAL MEMBERS: Buddy Holly, Jerry Allison (b. 1938), Joe B. Mauldin (b. 1940), Niki Sullivan (b. 1937)
FIRST SINGLE RELEASE: "Blue Days, Black Nights," 1956
MUSICAL STYLES: Country rock, country, rock and roll, rockabilly

A singer, songwriter, performer, and producer of legendary status, Buddy Holly's influence is still heard and felt in many of today's recording artists. Holly was a musical free spirit, being one of the first artists to use the new solid-body Fender Stratocaster guitar in recordings and performances. He always played with powerful downstrokes only. His group consisted of lead and rhythm guitars, bass, and drums, a line-up nearly unique at the time but one that became the standard for such

Buddy Holly (AP/Wide World Photos)

while accompanying himself on a miniature violin. His mother and a piano teacher taught him how to play rudimentary piano; he also learned, through trial and error, how to be a competent drummer. Buddy mastered the mandolin and banjo as well, but his favorite instrument was the guitar. At first his parents encouraged him to play the horizontally mounted steel guitar, but by the age of thirteen he was a competent and capable six-string guitarist.

His earliest musical influence was the traditional gospel music he grew up listening to Sunday mornings at the local Baptist church. The performing artist who had the strongest impact on him was the legendary Hank Williams. Williams was a highly gifted songwriter and a mesmerizing performer who sang sad stories of hard nights and mean women. Holly was particularly impressed by Williams's composing talent and guitar playing.

1960's groups as the Beatles. He also wrote a number of hit songs that are still played and have been covered by many other artists. He accomplished all this in a professional career of a few years—before his twenty-third birthday.

The Beginnings. The members of the Crickets—Buddy Holly, Jerry Allison, Joe B. Mauldin, and Niki Sullivan—all were natives of the west Texas town of Lubbock, a very conservative and fundamentalist community. Buddy Holly, born Charles Hardin Holley on September 7, 1936, in Lubbock, was the youngest child of an industrious but poverty-stricken family. Buddy's mother and two older brothers were musically talented, but the last-born demonstrated especially precocious abilities. At the age of five, he won a talent show in the nearby city of County Line by singing an old sentimental song, "Down the River of Memories,"

While still in high school, Holly formed a group with a friend, Bob Montgomery. This group, Buddy and Bob, performed locally wherever a willing audience could be found. Most listeners wanted to hear country-and-western swing music, and even though Buddy could perform this genre well, he soon wanted to stretch in different musical directions. Accordingly, while still performing with Montgomery, Holly would often sit in with other performers and groups. These varied musical experiences helped him develop an engaging stage persona and expertise in several types of popular music.

Shooting for the Stars. In the fall of 1953, Holly and Montgomery appeared on the radio, performing regularly on the new station KDAV, the first purely country station in the nation. In 1954 they began appearing regularly on the Big D

Jamboree, a country-music program broadcast live over the powerful Dallas station KRLD. In Lubbock, Holly was now performing at the Cotton Club, a venue that attracted such traveling performers as Marty Robbins, Carl Perkins, and Johnny Cash. When such acts would appear at the club, Holly could sometimes persuade the local promoter to let him open the show. Holly could thereby meet the star performers and make needed business contacts. On October 14, 1955, early rock-and-roll act Bill Haley and His Comets appeared at the club. KDAV owner and promoter Dave Stone believed that putting Holly on the same show might impress Nashville talent scout Eddie Crandall, present that evening, with Holly's talent and versatility.

Crandall definitely believed that Buddy Holly had commercial potential and thought the Texan could be marketed as a rock-influenced country artist, not unlike the increasingly popular Elvis Presley. Decca Records signed Holly to a contract in January, 1956, and later that month he made his first professional studio recordings. Buddy's partner, Bob Montgomery, preferred to stay in the Lubbock area, so a new band was needed. Guitarist Sonny Curtis, bassist Don Guess, and drummer Jerry Allison were recruited to accompany Holly to the Nashville Decca studio, where four songs were recorded January 26, 1956. Unfortunately, the session's producer, Owen Bradley, tried to coerce Holly into the formulaic conventionality of the Nashville recording industry. The young artist's ideas, methods, and style were disregarded. What resulted was, unsurprisingly, an aesthetic and market failure. At the end of 1956 Decca failed to exercise its option, and Holly was released from his contract. Better days, however, were immediately at hand.

Norman Petty was an independent record producer who owned his own studio in Clovis, New Mexico, only a hundred miles west of Lubbock. Holly had known Petty for some time and had even recorded some demo tapes at the facility. Beginning in early 1957, Holly recorded nearly exclusively at Petty's Clovis studio. Although the artist would later claim that Petty cheated him out of royalties, in the studio for the next two years they had an ideal musical relationship.

Music History. Petty allowed Holly almost total artistic control, and the budding star responded accordingly. He experimented—recording (overdubbing) double vocal tracks, playing exotic instruments, and developing a vocal style that involved yodeling and a unique "hiccuping" sound. By this time, Holly was recording and performing with the classic Crickets lineup of Jerry Allison on drums, Joe B. Mauldin on bass, and Niki Sullivan on rhythm guitar. At Clovis the group recorded a version of "That'll Be the Day" that was faster and louder, and had a more driving beat, than the earlier Decca version. This newer version entered the national charts in August, 1957, and soared to the top position. Other Clovis recordings that soon made the Top 25 included "Peggy Sue," "Oh, Boy!," and "Maybe Baby." The Crickets toured extensively and made several appearances on national television.

On August 15, 1958, Holly married Maria Elena Santiago. Personal animosity between Maria Elena and Norman Petty, as well as Holly's growing belief that Petty was mismanaging his finances, led to the newlyweds leaving Petty, the Clovis recording studio, and the other

For the Record

According to Niki Sullivan, the Crickets originally considered calling itself the "Beetles" until Jerry Allison complained, "Aw, that's just a bug you'd want to step on."

§

The spelling of Buddy Holly's last name is said to have been changed from "Holley" to "Holly" when it was typed wrongly on a recording contract and Buddy did not bother to make the correction. This mistake was by no means the only problem in Holly's business dealings—the confused state of his affairs is indicated by the fact that he recorded for at least five different companies.

Crickets and moving to Greenwich Village in New York City. In his final recordings, produced in New York, Holly experimented with a substantially different sound that included orchestral backing.

Tragedy. Because his income from royalties was tied up in litigation with Petty, Holly had to tour to earn money. He was forced to participate in a tour package traveling through the upper Midwest. The "Winter Dance Party '59" proved to be a poorly managed fiasco. The tour bus frequently broke down, and the performers were often extremely cold, overcrowded, and exhausted. While appearing at frozen Clear Lake, Iowa, Holly made arrangements to fly ahead to the next stop to escape the dreadful bus, get a good night's sleep, and have the chance to get his clothes clean. Originally, Holly's new band members Waylon Jennings and Tommy Allsup were to also ride on the plane, but fellow tour members J. P. Richardson (the Big Bopper) and Ritchie Valens persuaded them to surrender their seats. A combination of terrible weather and pilot inexperience proved deadly. The small single-engine plane crashed near Mason City, Iowa, shortly after 1:00 A.M. on February 3, 1959. There were no survivors. *—Thomas W. Buchanan*

SELECT DISCOGRAPHY

■ SINGLES

"That'll Be the Day," 1957
"Peggy Sue," 1957
"Oh, Boy!" 1957
"Maybe Baby," 1958
"It Doesn't Matter Anymore," 1959

SELECT AWARDS

Rock and Roll Hall of Fame, inducted 1986

SEE ALSO: Everly Brothers, The; Little Richard; Presley, Elvis; Valens, Ritchie.

John Lee Hooker

BORN: Clarksdale, Missipppi; August 22, 1917
FIRST ALBUM RELEASE: *I'm John Lee Hooker*, 1959
MUSICAL STYLES: Blues, folk

Along with Muddy Waters and B. B. King, John Lee Hooker has had one of the longest and most influential careers of any traditional blues singer-guitarist. Hooker is one of those performers who seems to be newly discovered by each generation of blues enthusiasts. While his audiences may grow younger and whiter, Hooker still sings and plays essentially as he did in the 1940's.

The Beginnings. The exact date of Hooker's birth is not clear; sources disagree about the year, often given as 1920, and the specific day. He was the fourth of the eleven children of William and Minnie Hooker, and after his parents divorced, his mother married blues musician Will Moore, who became the boy's mentor. Moore, who performed with such legends as "Blind" Lemon Jefferson and Charley Patton, taught his stepson his inimitable guitar style: heavily rhythmic with few chord progressions, unlike standard Delta blues. Young Hooker grew up listening to recordings by Jefferson and Lonnie Johnson and heard the young Aaron Thibeaux "T-Bone" Walker, another of his idols, in person, but he developed his minimalist style through Moore. Hooker pays tribute to what he learned from his stepfather in "Teachin' the Blues."

Hooker left home for Memphis at age fourteen and began performing with such fellow bluesmen as Robert Lockwood. Moving on to Cincinnati, he sang with several gospel groups. (Ironically, Hooker would years later sing in "Burning Hell," one of his most powerful songs, "Ain't no Heaven/ Ain't no burning Hell.") He moved to Detroit in 1943, worked as a janitor in a Chrysler plant, and soon became a regular performer at black nightclubs, switching from acoustic to electric guitar, progressively moving from country blues, a genre similar to folk music, to a more intense urban style.

Modern Records. In 1948, Hooker made some demonstration recordings for Bernie Besman of the Pan American Record Company. Besman sent one song, "Boogie Chillun," to Modern Records in Los Angeles, and the song, still one of Hooker's best, reached number 1 on the rhythm-and-blues charts in 1949. The emphasis on beat, accompanied by Hooker's tapping foot, rather than chord

John Lee Hooker (Archive Photos/Frank Driggs Collection)

changes, along with his rich baritone, helped make "Boogie Chillun" and other early hits such as "Crawlin' Kingsnake" and "I'm in the Mood" predecessors of the rhythms of rock and roll. Because of his singular approach to the blues, most of these early recordings are solos or occasional duets with singer-guitarist Eddie Kirkland. Despite the surprising sales of these records, Hooker was not paid regularly by Modern Records and recorded, between 1949 and 1953, for as many as twenty-four other labels under such pseudonyms as Johnny Williams, Delta John, Texas Slim, Birmingham Sam, and the Boogie Man. (He did not leave his Chrysler job until 1951.) He moved to Vee Jay Records in 1955, and some of that label's artists, notably Jimmy Reed, performed on Hooker's recordings.

New Audience. As the 1950's progressed, the basic audience for the blues began to change, as young African Americans discovered rhythm and blues and rock and roll. Many of Hooker's recordings, such as the classic "Dimples," began selling better in Europe, particularly the United Kingdom. He was surprised at his fame in Europe when he first toured there in 1962. Unlike American teenagers, Europeans were willing to listen to and appreciate music rather than merely dance to it.

The growing popularity of folk music in the early 1960's introduced blues artists to new listeners. Hooker first performed at the Newport Folk Festival in 1960 and began playing at coffeehouses and on college campuses, often turning down the amplification on his guitar or even playing an acoustic guitar to better fit the folk mode. When the rock "British invasion" began in 1964, many more Americans were introduced to the blues through such groups as the Animals, who had a hit with Hooker's "Boom Boom," the Rolling Stones, and the Yardbirds. Hooker recorded an album in 1965 with John Mayall and the British

For the Record

"The blues is the only music. Everything else they're doing—rock and roll, pop—it all comes from there. Something about a woman. Something about a man. Something about a man and a woman. That's the blues. I don't try to figure it out too much, though. Just is." —*John Lee Hooker*

§

Bob Dylan made his first New York appearance at Gerde's Folk City in 1961 as Hooker's opening act.

group the Groundhogs, the first of many collaborations with rock performers. Pete Townshend of the Who has credited Hooker as the major influence on his sound.

Hooker and Heat. During the 1960's, Hooker turned his focus from singles to albums and released dozens of recordings of new and old material, recording with a variety of artists, including his cousin Earl Hooker. One of his biggest successes and best albums, *Hooker 'n' Heat,* released in 1971, teamed him with the Los Angeles blues rock band Canned Heat. One of the problems with many of Hooker's early recordings is that his style does not always blend with that of his fellow musicians. Hooker often plays at a rhythm only he seems to understand, leaving the other instrumentalists charging ahead of him or shifting gears to try to let him catch up. Canned Heat, made up of authentic blues enthusiasts, perfectly complements his idiosyncratic approach to the blues. The harmonica playing of Bob "The Bear" Hite particularly blends well with Hooker's style. As he grew older, however, Hooker was sometimes criticized for letting his musicians do too much of the work for him.

New Fame. The 1980's and 1990's saw new awareness of and appreciation for Hooker. He appeared in the 1980 film *The Blues Brothers* and recorded "Don't Make Me No Never Mind" for the 1985 Steven Spielberg film *The Color Purple.* Hooker performed, with Miles Davis, the sound track for Dennis Hopper's *The Hot Spot* (1990), and his music is featured in several other films, including Bernardo Bertolucci's *Stealing Beauty* (1996). "Boom Boom" was featured in a Lee Jeans commercial in the early 1990's, and Hooker himself appeared in a Pepsi-Cola television commercial in the middle of that decade.

More important, Hooker began producing critically and commercially successful albums, beginning with 1989's *The Healer,* produced by Roy Rogers, his former guitarist, and featuring a diverse group of collaborators including Carlos Santana, Robert Cray, Bonnie Raitt, Los Lobos, and George Thorogood. His duet with Raitt on "I'm in the Mood" won a Grammy Award for Best Traditional Blues Recording. *The Healer* became one of the best-selling blues albums of all time. Rogers produced another all-star Hooker collaboration with 1991's *Mr. Lucky,* featuring Albert Collins, Ry Cooder, Van Morrison, Booker T. Jones, John Hammond, Johnny Winter, Keith Richards, Cray, and Santana. In 1997, Morrison, who had worked with Hooker several times beginning in 1972, produced *Don't Look Back,* with the two performing four duets. Following Hooker's induction into the Rock and Roll Hall of Fame in 1990, a tribute concert was held at New York's Madison Square Garden, featuring Collins, Cooder, Raitt, Winter, Willie Dixon, Bo Diddley, Joe Cocker, Greg Allman, and others. After a 1994 hernia operation, Hooker began making only a handful of public performances each year. Some take place in the Boom Boom Room, the San Francisco blues club he opened in 1997.

Hooker's Work. According to some authorities, Hooker may be the most recorded blues musician, with more than five hundred tracks to his credit. There are often ten or more versions of the same songs with different arrangements and collaborators and sometimes even slightly different titles. Sorting through all these recordings for the best versions of songs such as "Boogie Chillun," "Crawlin' Kingsnake," "I'm in the Mood," "Burning Hell," "Dimples," "Maudie," "Boom Boom," "Big Legs, Tight Skirt," "One Bourbon, One Scotch, and One Beer," "I'm Bad Like Jesse

James," and "Bottle Up and Go" is difficult, since they vary greatly in quality. To encompass the scope of his achievement, any compilation would have to include several versions of each of the hits of his early and middle periods.

Hooker may be inferior to many of his contemporaries as a guitarist and lyricist, but few can match him for the enormous body of his work and the distinctive quality of his voice. The raw unsentimentality of his primitive, timeless blues and his booming, droning voice are captured by the title of one of his best songs, "Serves Me Right to Suffer." —*Michael Adams*

SELECT DISCOGRAPHY

■ ALBUMS

The Country Blues of John Lee Hooker, 1959
Burning Hell, 1964
John Lee Hooker at Newport, 1964
Urban Blues, 1967
Get Back Home, 1969
Hooker 'n' Heat, 1971 (with Canned Heat)
Chess Masters, 1982 (compilation)
The Healer, 1989
Mr. Lucky, 1991
The Ultimate Collection (1948-1990), 1991 (compilation)
The Legendary Modern Recordings, 1948-1954, 1993 (compilation)
On Vee Jay, 1955-1958, 1993 (compilation)
Chill Out, 1995
Don't Look Back, 1997

SELECT AWARDS

Blues Foundation Hall of Fame, inducted 1980
Smithsonian Institution's Folk Heritage Award, 1983
Grammy Award for Best Traditional Blues Recording for "I'm in the Mood," 1990 (with Bonnie Raitt)
Rock and Roll Hall of Fame, inducted 1990
Blues Foundation Lifetime Achievement Award, 1996

SEE ALSO: Cray, Robert; Dixon, Willie; Guy, Buddy; Howlin' Wolf; Johnson, Robert; King, Albert; King, B. B.; Morrison, Van; Raitt, Bonnie; Santana, Carlos; Waters, Muddy.

Hootie and the Blowfish

ORIGINAL MEMBERS: Darius Rucker (b. 1966), Mark Bryan (b. 1967), Dean Felber (b. 1967), Jim "Soni" Sonefeld (b. 1964)
FIRST ALBUM RELEASE: *Cracked Rear View*, 1994
MUSICAL STYLES: Rock and roll, pop, soft rock

With the second best-selling debut album of all time, Hootie and the Blowfish became a band that audiences loved and critics hated. Ironically, initial reviews of the album *Cracked Rear View* were positive, but as the album went on to sell over thirteen million copies, critics began commenting that the band did not deserve such lavish attention.

South Carolina. Hootie and the Blowfish originated as a college fraternity band who stayed together after their college days were over. All four members were students at the University of South Carolina in Columbia, where guitarist Mark Bryan heard Darius Rucker singing in the dormitory shower and persuaded him to form a duo called the Wolf Brothers. Next, the two recruited Dean Felber, with whom Bryan had played music in high school, and Jim "Soni" Sonefeld. The group adopted the name Hootie and the Blowfish based on the nicknames Rucker had given two friends, one with owl-like eyeglasses and the other with full cheeks. They played at fraternities and local bars, performing cover songs by groups such as R.E.M. and U2.

For the Record

Constantly asked what it is like to have a black lead singer in an otherwise white band, Hootie and the Blowfish have tried to show that race is simply not an issue for them. In a 1995 Rolling Stone interview, drummer Jim "Soni" Sonefeld said, "I never did understand this discussion. Everyone says we're one black guy in an all-white band, but that's not true—we're actually three white guys in an all-black band."

When Bryan, Felber, and Sonefeld graduated, the group decided to take their act on the road. They traveled the southeastern United States circuit with other country and rock groups, and they began to write their own songs. Felber, who had majored in finance, managed the group. He formed a partnership corporation and saw to it that the band treated their modest earnings as a serious living rather than quick spending money. After a record deal fell through in 1992, the group financed their own extended-play single titled *Kootchypop*; its six tracks included an early version of "Hold My Hand," which would become the group's first hit a few years later. *Kootchypop* sold an impressive fifty thousand copies at the group's shows and through mail order, but more importantly, the record convinced Atlantic Records to sign the group to a contract.

A Surprise Hit. When Hootie and the Blowfish's first full-length album, *Cracked Rear View* (1994), began to sell beyond the group's expectations, even Atlantic Records was surprised. Two years after its release, the album was still on the *Billboard* Top-20 chart. The album's success can be traced in part to a well-established fan base in the southeastern United States and to a great deal of airplay on the music video channel VH1, which adopted the group in an effort to attract a younger audience. The album contained a large number of hits, including "Hold My Hand," "I Only Want to Be with You," and "Time." Audiences seemed to relate to Rucker's heartfelt rendering of his lyrics, many of which were semi-autobiographical. They also seemed to appreciate the roots-rock style which other acts such as the Counting Crows and Sheryl Crow were helping to popularize.

Hootie and the Blowfish: Mark Bryan, Dean Felber, Jim Sonefeld, Darius Rucker (Paul Natkin)

After receiving so much attention over their debut album, the group knew that their next effort, *Fairweather Johnson* (1996), was unlikely to sell as well, but they felt the new album showed their musical maturity and hoped the critics would be more receptive. However, the band's success seemed to make them a target for critical abuses, and some critics contended that Rucker had not yet learned to control his voice. The band was also called dull and conservative, which the members attributed to the fact that they have been more down to earth than most rock stars. After *Fairweather Johnson* it was clear that a third album would be critical in determining whether Hootie and the Blowfish could sustain their popularity or whether the impressive success of their first album was an aberration. —*Amy Sisson*

SELECT DISCOGRAPHY

■ SINGLES

"I Go Blind," 1995 (from *Friends* sound track)

■ ALBUMS

Kootchypop, 1992 (EP)
Cracked Rear View, 1994
Fairweather Johnson, 1996
Musical Chairs, 1998

SEE ALSO: Counting Crows; Crow, Sheryl; Lewis, Huey, and the News; R.E.M.; U2.

Whitney Houston

BORN: Newark, New Jersey; August 9, 1963
FIRST ALBUM RELEASE: *Whitney Houston*, 1985
MUSICAL STYLES: Pop, rhythm and blues, gospel

Whitney Houston was born on August 9, 1963, in Newark, New Jersey, to John and Emily Houston. Her mother, who is better known as Cissy, was the director of the choir at the New Hope Baptist Church in Newark. A veteran gospel and rhythm-and-blues (R&B) singer, Cissy had been the lead singer of the R&B group the Sweet Inspirations, who sang background vocals for several noted recording artists including Elvis Presley and Aretha Franklin. She was also a member of the Drinkard Sisters, a gospel trio, with her nieces Dionne and Dee Dee Warwick. From infancy, Houston was immersed in the black gospel music of the church and the best R&B and soul artists of the late 1960's and early 1970's, all of which she absorbed like a musical sponge. At an early age, Houston sang in the New Hope Baptist Church choirs, began performing occasionally in concerts with the Drinkard Sisters, and put down strong musical roots in gospel, R&B, and soul music. Those stylistic roots became the foundation for her career.

Early Career. Soul singer, songwriter, and producer Luther Vandross offered to produce Houston as a solo artist when she was only fifteen years old, but her parents insisted that she finish high school first. She did, however, make her recording debut in 1979 at the age of fifteen, singing lead vocals on "Life's a Party," the title track for the Michael Zager Band's second album for the Private Stock label.

After her 1981 graduation from Mount St. Dominic Academy in Caldwell, New Jersey, Houston signed a management contract with Gene Harvey and Seymour Flics. There were several labels that expressed interest in signing her to a recording contract, but Harvey declined their offers, preferring to allow Houston to develop artistically without having the pressure of producing hits immediately.

Houston's first career was not in music, but as a fashion model, appearing in magazines such as *Essence*, *Harper's Bazaar*, *Seventeen*, *Glamour*, and *Cosmopolitan*. She also took acting lessons and won small roles in television series such as *Silver Spoons* and *Gimme a Break*. She sang on some commercials, sang background vocals on recording sessions for the Neville Brothers and the funk band Material, sang "Eternal Love" with Paul Jabara and Jay Asher on the album *Paul Jabara and Friends*, and continued to perform occasionally during her mother's live performances. One of the first solos she performed in her mother's show was "Greatest Love of All," from the motion picture *The Greatest* (1977), the story of Muhammad Ali, which would become one of her first number 1 recordings years later.

In 1983, Houston auditioned for and was signed by Clive Davis, the founder and president of Arista Records. Davis and Arista spent the next two years and several hundred thousand dollars grooming Houston, preparing her debut album, looking for the right songs from the best songwriters, and marketing her to the public through guest appearances on television and duets with Teddy Pendergrass and Jermaine Jackson.

Debut Album. Houston's debut album, *Whitney Houston,* appeared in 1985. The first single released from the album was the R&B-flavored "You Give Good Love," which went to number 3 on *Billboard*'s Hot 100. The next single release, the ballad "Saving All My Love for You," which had originally been recorded by Marilyn McCoo and Billy Davis, Jr., became her first number 1 hit in late October, 1985. Two more singles from the album reached number 1 as well: "How Will I Know" (number 1 for two weeks in February, 1986) and "Greatest Love of All" (number 1 for three weeks beginning in mid-May, 1986), establishing her as a major force in the popular music industry. The three number 1 hits from her debut album were a first: No female artist had ever managed three number 1 songs from one album, much less a debut album. The album sold twelve million copies in the United States, making it the biggest-selling debut album by a female artist until Alanis Morissette's *Jagged Little Pill* (1996) album broke the record with fourteen million in sales in the United States.

Houston's second album, *Whitney* (1987), was the first album by a female artist to enter the chart at number 1. It produced four number 1 hits: "I Wanna Dance with Somebody (Who Loves Me)" (number 1 for two weeks beginning in late June, 1987), "Didn't We Almost Have It All" (number 1 for two weeks beginning in late September, 1987), "So Emotional" (number 1 for one week in January, 1988), and "Where Do Broken Hearts Go" (number 1 for two weeks in April, 1988). "Where Do Broken Hearts Go" was her seventh consecutive chart single to go number 1, breaking the record of six that had been held jointly by the Bee Gees and the Beatles.

Whitney Houston performing at the White House in 1994 (AP/Wide World Photos)

There was an unusually long break between Houston's second and third albums: three years. The third album, *I'm Your Baby Tonight,* debuted in 1990 when the title track and "All the Man That I Need" reached number 1 on the singles chart.

Motion Pictures. *The Bodyguard,* a 1992 motion picture costarring Oscar-winning actor-director Kevin Costner and Houston (in her first major acting role), was an overwhelming success, grossing over $400 million worldwide. The sound track album from the motion picture was also incredibly successful, selling 33 million copies around the world, becoming the biggest-selling motion picture sound track to date. The first single, a cover of Dolly Parton's "I Will Always Love You," sold eight million copies worldwide and established a new record of fourteen weeks at number 1 on *Billboard*'s Hot 100. Houston was a big winner at the Grammy Awards that year, claiming the Album of the Year award for *The Bodyguard* and

Record of the Year and Best Pop Female Vocal Performance for "I Will Always Love You."

Houston took another break after *The Bodyguard*, giving birth to a baby girl, Bobbi Kristina, after having married fellow performer Bobby Brown in 1992.

Waiting to Exhale (1995), a motion picture about four women who share the joys and frustrations of romance while looking for career success, was Houston's second acting role. She performed three songs for the sound track, while the other songs were sung by various female singers including Mary J. Blige, Brandy, Faith Hill, Aretha Franklin, and Chaka Khan. Houston's "Exhale (Shoop Shoop)" climbed to the top of the chart, becoming her eleventh number 1 single.

In 1996, Houston returned to her black gospel roots. She starred opposite Denzel Washington in the motion picture *The Preacher's Wife*, in which she performed several gospel numbers, including "Joy," "I Go to the Rock," and "Step by Step." The motion picture and the sound track album were not the most commercially successful projects of Houston's career, but they clearly illustrated her incredible vocal facility with the black gospel style of her childhood and youth. Gospel music has always been much more than just a musical style to Houston. She has remained committed to her faith through all of her success.

In November, 1997, Houston served as executive producer and played the role of the fairy godmother in an all-star, interracial television production of Richard Rodgers's and Oscar Hammerstein's *Cinderella*. The two-hour American Broadcasting Companies (ABC) special was estimated to have been watched by sixty million viewers.

Whitney Houston has become an international superstar in two fields: music and motion pictures. Her first four albums collected global sales of 86 million copies. She has become an international household name, amassing countless awards and breaking box-office records with her concerts worldwide. Like some of the other musical superstars, Houston has not turned her back on the needs of the world. In 1989, she formed the Whitney Houston Foundation for Children. She has also given her time and energy to numerous other worthwhile causes, including the United Negro College Fund, the Children's Diabetes Fund, St. Jude's Children's Hospital, and several AIDS–related charities.

—Don Tyler

SELECT DISCOGRAPHY

■ SINGLES

"You Give Good Love," 1985
"Saving All My Love for You," 1985
"How Will I Know," 1985
"Greatest Love of All," 1986
"I Wanna Dance with Somebody (Who Loves Me)," 1987
"Didn't We Almost Have It All," 1987
"So Emotional," 1987
"Where Do Broken Hearts Go," 1987
"I'm Your Baby Tonight," 1990
"All the Man That I Need," 1990
"I Will Always Love You," 1992
"Exhale (Shoop Shoop)," 1995
"I Believe in You and Me," 1996

■ ALBUM

Whitney Houston, 1985
Whitney, 1987
I'm Your Baby Tonight, 1990
The Bodyguard, 1992
Waiting to Exhale, 1995 (with various other artists)
Preacher's Wife, 1996
my love is your love, 1998

SELECT AWARDS

Grammy Award for Best Pop Vocal Performance, Female, for "Saving All My Love for You," 1985
Grammy Award for Best Pop Vocal Performance, Female, for "I Wanna Dance with Somebody (Who Loves Me)," 1987
Grammy Awards for Record of the Year (with David Foster) and Best Pop Vocal Performance, Female, for "I Will Always Love You"; for Album of the Year for *The Bodyguard* sound track (with others), all 1993

SEE ALSO: Carey, Mariah; Franklin, Aretha; Khan, Chaka; Morissette, Alanis; Parton, Dolly; Pendergrass, Teddy; Presley, Elvis; Vandross, Luther; Warwick, Dionne.

Howlin' Wolf

(Chester Arthur Burnett)

BORN: West Point, Mississippi; June 10, 1910
DIED: Hines, Illinois; January 10, 1976
FIRST SINGLE RELEASE: "Moanin' at Midnight," 1951
MUSICAL STYLES: Blues, rhythm and blues

Chester Burnett, known as Howlin' Wolf, was one of the most influential and electrifying performers in the postwar Chicago blues tradition. Wolf's music, with its gritty vocals and earthy rhythms, has its roots in the blues of the rural Mississippi Delta.

Early Influences. Burnett was born in West Point, Mississippi, but he soon moved to Ruleville in the Delta region. It was here in 1928 that he started playing the guitar his father bought him. More important, though, was his contact with one of the legendary blues performers in the Delta, Charley Patton. Burnett's family lived on a local plantation when he met Patton, a traveling musician who played in the area. Burnett credits Patton with teaching him many traditional blues songs, such as "Spoonful" and "Banty Rooster," and showing him the rudiments of guitar in the evenings after the work in the fields was done.

Patton's influence remained evident throughout Burnett's musical career. Burnett also remembered the songs of the farm workers in the fields. In a 1967 *Down Beat* interview he recalls: "There was a lot of music around there. Work songs. Some of the fellows was [sic] making songs like 'I worked old Maude, and I worked old Belle'—things like that. They'd just get out there and sing as they worked. Plowing songs, songs to call mules by."

It was during this time that Burnett began to play music professionally. He called himself Howlin' Wolf, a nickname given to him by his grandfather. Although Wolf admired Patton's music a great deal, he preferred the music of a band from the area, the Mississippi Sheiks. In contrast to Patton's slow, hypnotic music, the Mississippi Sheiks played an up-tempo style that appealed to Wolf. Other famous bluesmen in the area also influenced the young performer. Sonny Boy Williamson (Rice Miller) taught him how to play harmonica, and Wolf mentions meeting another Delta great, Robert Johnson, during this time in his life.

King Biscuit Time. Wolf moved to Memphis in the 1930's, which was around the time Williamson began a series of live broadcasts, the *King Biscuit Time,* from a Helena, Arkansas, radio station. These broadcasts featured live performances of blues and were quite popular throughout the area. The success of these broadcasts prompted other stations to follow suit. In West Memphis, for example, radio station KWEM began selling blocks of time to live performers.

Wolf's efforts to continue his playing in Memphis were interrupted when he was drafted into the Army in 1941. When he returned to Memphis in the mid-1940's, he took advantage of the trend toward live broadcasts and produced his own radio show, on which he performed his music and presented advertising for local merchants. The show was very successful, and he continued it for five years. These were fruitful years for Wolf, and it was around this time that he formed his first band, the House Rockers. They played throughout the Arkansas, Alabama, Mississippi, and Missouri area, and they used only electric instruments.

In 1948 Wolf recorded his first single, "Saddle My Pony," backed with "Worried All the Time," for Sun Records in Memphis. A few years later, in 1951, Wolf recorded his first hit, "Moanin' at Midnight" for Sun Records, who eventually sold it to Chess Records in Chicago. The success of the record—number 8 on the *Billboard* rhythm-and-blues chart—prompted Chess and a Los Angeles

For the Record

"When I go out, I sing for the people. . . . I just watch people, their ways. I play by the movement of the people, the way they live." —*Howlin' Wolf*

company to fight over who would secure the right to record this dynamic young blues singer. Chess eventually prevailed, and virtually all of Wolf's records for the remainder of his career would be recorded with Chess Records.

In Chicago. In 1953, Wolf moved to the Chicago area to continue his recording and performing career. His gritty vocals and rhythmic blues, which expressed so well the lives of southern African Americans, quickly dominated the blues scene in the Windy City. The only other blues performer of Wolf's stature in Chicago during this time was his chief rival, Muddy Waters.

Wolf's performing style, with its growling vocals, eerie falsettos, and biting harmonica, was almost fearsome in its intensity. He was a big man, and his size and unique stage presence proved to be a formidable combination in the clubs of Chicago. His personality was equally forceful, although there are differing opinions about his nature. Wolf was known by many as a suspicious and mistrustful man, and some say he was prone to violence toward bandmates. To others he was soft-spoken and thoughtful. Wolf seemed to agree with the latter opinion. He once said: "I'm not a smart man. See, I got a little head and a big heart. That's all I need."

Two other Chicago bluesmen were to have a profound influence on Wolf's career. The first was Willie Dixon, another transplant from the Delta region. Dixon wrote many songs for Wolf, and his unique lyrics fit Wolf's dynamic stage presence perfectly. The other was Hubert Sumlin, a guitarist whom Wolf brought up from the South. Sumlin was much younger than Wolf, but the two remained together, in a sometimes stormy relationship, for the rest of Wolf's career. Sumlin's guitar work was featured on almost all of Wolf's records, but it was not until Wolf's later recordings that Sumlin developed into one of the most unique and dynamic blues guitarists in the world.

"Evil." In 1954 Wolf recorded one of his best-known songs, "Evil." This was his first recording in Chicago and combined the lyrics of Dixon with the distinctive guitar of Sumlin. It was a formula that Wolf was to exploit many times, although he admitted that he sang his own songs

Howlin' Wolf (Archive Photos)

much better than those of Dixon. In 1956, Wolf's "Smokestack Lightnin'," again with Sumlin on guitar, made it to number 11 on the rhythm-and-blues charts. Wolf would turn more toward recording his own songs rather than Dixon's in the later years of his career.

The success Wolf enjoyed was modest by later standards, but his influence began to spread when young rock musicians in the United States and

England began to listen to and emulate the Chicago blues style that Wolf helped create. His songs were recorded by such artists as Cream, Led Zeppelin, and John Mayall, and in 1971 Wolf went to London to record an album with his young admirers. No other artist better expresses the raw, earthy blues that sprang from the plantations and farms of the Mississippi Delta—not only the songs of traveling musicians such as Patton, but the soulful laments of the field workers as well.

—*Robert Clifford*

SELECT DISCOGRAPHY

■ SINGLES

"Evil," 1954

"Who's Been Talking," 1957

■ ALBUMS

Howlin' Wolf, 1958

Moanin' in the Moonlight, 1964 (compilation)

The Real Folk Blues, 1966

The London Sessions, 1971

Change My Way, 1975 (compilation)

Cadillac Daddy: Memphis Recordings, 1952, 1987

The Chess Box, 1991

SELECT AWARDS

Rock and Roll Hall of Fame, inducted 1991

SEE ALSO: Allman Brothers Band, The; Clapton, Eric; Cray, Robert; Cream; Dixon, Willie; Guy, Buddy; Hooker, John Lee; King, Albert; King, B. B.; Led Zeppelin; Raitt, Bonnie; Rolling Stones, The; Waters, Muddy.

I

Ice Cube

(O'Shea Jackson)

BORN: Los Angeles, California; June 15, 1969
FIRST ALBUM RELEASE: *AmeriKKKa's Most Wanted*, 1990
MUSICAL STYLES: Rap, hip-hop

Ice Cube was the first member of the notorious "gangsta" rap band N.W.A. to quit the group to start his own career. His first solo album, 1990's *AmeriKKKa's Most Wanted*, set off a firestorm of protest over the controversial lyrics. The music overpowered the criticism, however, and Ice Cube's debut and several subsequent albums became hip-hop classics.

Ice Cube (Archive Photos/Nicola Goode)

From N.W.A. to a Solo Career. Born O'Shea Jackson, Ice Cube wrote his first rap song in a high school typing class after he heard the Sugarhill Gang's single "Rapper's Delight." After making several recordings with friends, he joined Eric "Eazy E" Wright and Dr. Dre to form Niggaz With Attitude (N.W.A.). After the group released the seminal "gangsta" rap album *Straight Outta Compton* (1989) and completed a fifty-city tour, Ice Cube quit in the midst of a dispute with the band's manager, Jerry Heller, about money.

Ice Cube immediately moved to New York and formed a backing band called Da Lench Mob. In 1990, he released his debut solo album, *AmeriKKKa's Most Wanted.* The violent and obscenity-laden lyrics drew intense criticism from parents and moral watchdog groups. The inclusion of the song "It's a Man's World," in which female rapper Yo-Yo provided pointed responses to Ice Cube's sexist lyrics, did little to allay charges that Ice Cube was an unrepentant misogynist. Despite these criticisms, the album was considered a masterpiece by the rock media and went platinum in three weeks. Later that year, Ice Cube released *Kill at Will*, which also received strong reviews. In the summer of 1991, Ice Cube made his acting debut to favorable reviews in John Singleton's motion picture *Boyz N the Hood.*

More Controversy. Ice Cube's next album, 1991's *Death Certificate*, raised even more criticism than his debut. Critics pointed to two songs in particular: "No Vaseline," an anti-Semitic rant against N.W.A. manager Jerry Heller, and "Black Korea," which called for the razing of grocery stores owned by Koreans. (The targeting of Korean-owned businesses by African Americans during the Los Angeles riots the following year made the song seem disturbingly prophetic.) The lyrics prompted *Billboard* magazine to publish a condemnation of the album, the first time the long-running trade publication had ever targeted a single artist. Ice Cube was quick to point out, however, that no one seemed to be bothered by the songs dealing with the problem of black-on-black violence that plagued urban ghettos. In the midst of the controversy, the album climbed to number 2 on the album charts.

Ice Cube expanded his audience in 1992 when he toured with the Lollapalooza rock festival along with the Red Hot Chili Peppers, Soundgarden, and Pearl Jam. Later in year, he released *The Predator* in the wake of the Los Angeles riots. The album received excellent reviews and became the first recording to debut on both the pop and rhythm-and-blues charts at number 1. By the time the follow-up album, *Lethal Injection*, was released in 1993, Ice Cube had converted to the Nation of Islam and settled into a happy family life. The album drew inspiration from Dr. Dre's "gangsta" funk sound, and Ice Cube seemed to be heading away from controversy and toward mainstream acceptance.

Moving On. Ice Cube spent the next several years producing albums for other rap performers such as Da Lench Mob and Kam. In 1994, he released a collection of outtakes titled *Bootlegs and B-Sides*. The following year he appeared in John Singleton's film *Higher Learning* and released the single "Natural Born Killaz," a duet with Dr. Dre. In 1997, Ice Cube released the album *Featuring . . . Ice Cube*, a collection of previously released material, and continued his acting career by starring in the horror movie *Anaconda*. —*Douglas Long*

For the Record

During an interview for *Spin* magazine conducted by bell hooks, an African American feminist theorist, Ice Cube said, "I do records for black kids, and white kids are basically eavesdropping. White kids need to hear what we got to say about them, and their forefathers, and uncles, and everybody that's done us wrong."

SELECT DISCOGRAPHY

■ ALBUMS

AmeriKKKa's Most Wanted, 1990
Death Certificate, 1991
The Predator, 1992
Lethal Injection, 1993
Bootlegs and B-Sides, 1994
Featuring . . . Ice Cube, 1997 (compilation)
War and Peace, Vol. 1, 1998

SEE ALSO: Dr. Dre; N.W.A.

Ice-T

(Tracy Marrow)

BORN: Newark, New Jersey; February 16, 1958
FIRST ALBUM RELEASE: *Rhyme Pays*, 1987
MUSICAL STYLES: Hip-hop, rap, heavy metal

Although a native of New Jersey, Tracy Marrow moved to California at a young age after his parents died in an automobile accident. In 1983, Marrow changed his name to Ice-T (after Iceberg Slim, a 1930's pimp turned poet and writer) and became one of the leading figures of California hip-hop.

Early Recordings. After spending his teenage years involved in gang activity in Los Angeles, Ice-T recorded several undistinguished singles in the early 1980's on an independent label, for which he earned twenty dollars. In 1987, Ice-T signed with Sire Records, an affiliate of Warner Bros. Records, and released his debut album, *Rhyme Pays*. DJ Aladdin and producer Afrika Islam helped provide the rolling, spare beats and samples to support Ice-T's charismatic rhymes. *Rhyme Pays*, which was primarily a party-oriented album, went gold soon after it was released.

Following his debut album, Ice-T recorded the theme song for Dennis Hopper's gang-culture motion picture, *Colors* (1988). This single, also called "Colors," was more incisive, both musically and lyrically, then previous recordings. In 1988, Ice-T released *Power*, his second album, which also went gold, and formed Rhyme Syndicate Records the following year. Although it was Ice-T's own label, it was still an affiliate of Sire/Warner Bros. Records. Under the name of his new recording label, Ice-T released a number of groundbreaking hits, including 1989's *The Iceberg/Freedom of Speech . . . Just Watch What You Say*, which firmly established him as a hip-hop superstar.

The year 1991 marked the beginning of Ice-T's acting career. He costarred with Wesley Snipes in the Mario Van Peeples film *New Jack City* and recorded the single "New Jack Hustler" for the film's sound track (the song became one of the centerpieces for Ice-T's 1991 album *O.G. Original Gangster*). Other acting roles for motion pictures followed, and Ice-T also appeared on the television show *New York Undercover* and in *Players* (1997), his own made-for-television film. In addition to acting, Ice-T published his best-selling book *The Ice Opinion* in 1994, which was translated into four different languages and led to a lecture tour of such prestigious universities as Harvard, Stanford, and the University of California at Berkeley.

Body Count. In 1991, Ice-T formed a heavy metal band called Body Count, named after his own heavy metal song on the album *O.G. Original Gangster.* The band's 1991 tour increased Ice-T's appeal among heavy metal listeners and middle-class white teenagers. In 1992, the band released *Body Count*, their debut album, which included the song "Cop Killer." The song was written from the perspective of a would-be executioner of law enforcement officers. Vice President Dan Quayle, President George Bush, the National Rifle Association, and law enforcement activists all claimed that the song was a threat to law enforcement officers. Although Sire/Warner Bros. Records supported Ice-T and Body Count during the controversy, the label refused to release Ice-T's *Home Invasion* in 1993, claiming that the rap album's cover was unsuitable for the public. Ice-T left Sire/Warner Bros. and released *Home Invasion* on Priority Records in the spring of 1993. Unfortunately, the album received lukewarm sales, a sign that Ice-T was losing most of his hip-hop and rap audience.

Body Count released *Born Dead* in 1994. Even though they failed to stir up the same controversy as the previous album, *Born Dead* was successful in night clubs and on tour. Ice-T released *Return of the Real* in the summer of 1996, which was his first rap album since *Home Invasion* in 1993. *Return of the Real* did not live up to its commercial expectations and received mixed reviews by critics.

—Alyson C. Allison

SELECT DISCOGRAPHY

■ ALBUMS

Rhyme Pays, 1987
Power, 1988
The Iceberg/Freedom of Speech . . . Just Watch What You Say, 1989
O.G. Original Gangster, 1991
Body Count, 1992
Home Invasion, 1993
Return of the Real, 1996

SELECT AWARDS

Grammy Award for Best Rap Performance by a Duo or Group for *Back on the Block*, 1990 (with others)

SEE ALSO: Cypress Hill; Ice Cube; Kool Moe Dee; N.W.A.; Run-D.M.C.

Billy Idol

(William Broad)

BORN: Stanmore, Middlesex, England; November 30, 1955
FIRST ALBUM RELEASE: *Generation X*, 1978 (with Generation X)
FIRST SOLO ALBUM RELEASE: *Don't Stop*, 1981
MUSICAL STYLES: Punk rock, pop rock

Of all of the young British punks who adulated the Sex Pistols in the late 1970's—the Bromley Contingent, as they were called—only Billy Idol found mainstream pop stardom. His trademark sneer, platinum hair, and tough image helped him sell millions of albums.

Early Days. William Broad, a middle-class, chubby child with dull brown hair and thick glasses, wanted to be David Bowie. He became a vegetarian in order to lose weight, replaced his

Billy Idol (AP/Wide World Photos)

glasses with contact lenses, and dyed his hair platinum. He dropped out of Sussex University and moved to London, taking the name Billy Idol.

In 1975, punk rock was becoming fashionable. Groups such as the Sex Pistols, the Clash, and the Damned were responsible for London's burgeoning punk scene. Idol and his friends Susan Dallion and Tony James began following the Sex Pistols to all of their shows, emulating the punk rockers by composing their own songs and occasionally jumping on stage. "They can't get rid of you if you write your own songs," was Idol's credo. Dallion renamed herself Siouxsie Sioux and formed her own band, the Banshees. James and Idol joined Mick Jones (later of the Clash) and Brian James (later of the Damned) and started a dance-punk group called Chelsea.

Chelsea performed throughout 1976, but soon Jones and Brian James broke away, leaving Idol, Tony James, and guitarist Bob Andrews to form Generation X, named after the Douglas Copeland novel. Most important, the group brought in Keith Forsey as producer, and it was he who shaped the power-pop-punk-dance hybrid that was Generation X. With the hit club tune "Dancing with Myself," Gen X, as they were known, rode to the top of the British charts and went on to record three albums (plus a few greatest-hits collections) before their demise in 1981.

Idol Solo. Tony James went on to form Sigue Sigue Sputnik, while Idol went to New York City to start a solo career. His timing was perfect. With his cover-boy cheekbones, his Elvis Presley sneer, his Jim Morrison baritone, and his black leather jacket, he was perfect for the nascent music video business. He first attracted attention with an extended-play single, *Don't Stop*, in which he rerecorded the Generation X hits "Dancing with Myself" and "Mony Mony."

In New York, Idol signed with manager Bill Aucoin, who had previously steered Kiss to stardom. Utilizing that same sense of cartoonish exaggeration, Idol snarled more and became blonder and more punk. He draped his leather jacket with rosaries: "I'm making fun of religion," he said, "but I'm also making people think. Of course, they also look good." Next, Idol got together with hard-rock guitarist Steve Stevens, who would help shape his rough, tough, danceable sound. By the time the Chrysalis debut, *Billy Idol*, was released in the United States in 1982, Idol had a distinctive, eye-catching style. Thanks to video hits such as "White Wedding" and "Hot in the City," *Billy Idol* spent two years at the top of the charts. Idol's touring schedule was erratic, marred by missed dates caused by his drug and alcohol habits.

Rebel Yell (1983) was an even bigger hit for Idol, yielding the power ballad "Eyes Without a Face" and enabling him to cross over to mainstream radio. "Eyes Without a Face" even won an American Society of Composers, Authors and Publishers (ASCAP) Award as a Most Played Song in 1984.

Charmed Life. Idol spent the 1980's living his dream, being a famous rock star. *Whiplash Smile* (1986) continued his string of album successes. He had a child, Willem Wolfe, with actress and singer Perri Lister. He graced the cover of numerous fan magazines. In 1990 he released the album *Charmed Life* and had a small role in the Oliver Stone film *The Doors*. Although *Charmed Life* was successful, Idol's heyday as a rock star was over. Years of hard living had marred the poster-boy features. Plaid shirts and well-worn skateboarding shoes had replaced studded leather jackets and boots. Idol's 1993 attempt to capitalize on the multimedia revolution, *Cyberpunk*, was a failure.

Idol's songs would continue to receive airplay throughout the late 1990's, but Idol himself remained out of the spotlight. He did appear briefly with the Who in a stage revival of *Quadrophenia*, and he portrayed himself in the 1998 film *The Wedding Singer*. Billy Idol remains an exemplar of the 1980's, a monument to self-obsession and excess. —*Ethlie Ann Vare*

SELECT DISCOGRAPHY

with Generation X

■ ALBUMS

Generation X, 1978
Valley of the Dolls, 1979
Kiss Me Deadly, 1981

solo

■ ALBUMS

Billy Idol, 1982
Rebel Yell, 1983
Whiplash Smile, 1986
Charmed Life, 1990
Cyberpunk, 1993

SEE ALSO: Clash, The; Sex Pistols, The.

For the Record

Film director Oliver Stone asked Billy Idol to appear in a major studio motion picture, *The Doors*. However, just before filming started in February, 1990, Idol was racing his Harley-Davidson motorcycle home from a mixing session on the (ironically named) *Charmed Life* album and suffered injuries in an accident. Idol fractured his left forearm and injured his right leg. He ended up performing in *The Doors* film after all, in a smaller role and on crutches.

Julio Iglesias

BORN: Madrid, Spain; September 23, 1943
FIRST ALBUM RELEASE: *Yo Canto*, 1969
MUSICAL STYLE: Pop

Julio Iglesias, whose full name is Julio Jose Iglesias de la Cueva, is related to Spanish nobility on his mother's side. He grew up in Madrid, Spain, and developed a love of soccer, although his father, Julio Iglesias Puga, wanted him to study law. After studying at Sagrados Corazones, he began the study of law at the Colegio Mayor de San Pablo in Spain. Iglesias was very talented as an athlete, and he served as the goalkeeper for the Real Madrid soccer team. He dreamed of becoming a professional soccer player, and his future in athletics looked promising.

Shattered Dreams. His vision of soccer stardom was shattered on the night before his twentieth birthday, when he was almost killed in a automobile crash. After the accident, he was partially paralyzed and had to use a wheelchair for more than one year. There were doubts that he would be able to walk again. Iglesias passed his time at the Eloy Gonzalo Hospital in Madrid by writing poetry and listening to the radio. He became friendly with Eladio Magdaleno, a staff member at the hospital who gave him a guitar.

With this thoughtful gift, Iglesias's poems could be given a musical setting. He applied himself to the instrument and learned how to play chords. He began to find melodies for the sad poems he had written and sing them. After his recovery, he went to Murcia University to resume his studies. He was interested in languages, and he traveled to England to study English in Cambrige. For recreation, he began to sing in local English pubs. His material consisted of popular songs of the time, including pieces by the Beatles, Engelbert Humperdinck, and Tom Jones.

In addition to his first musical performances, he met Gwendolyne Bollore, for whom he composed a song.

Upon his return trip to Spain, he visited a recording studio in Madrid with hope of finding a singer who could record his material. After it was suggested that he sing it himself, Iglesias entered the 1968 Spanish Song Festival, a national competition, and sang his own composition, "La Vida Sigue Igual" ("Life Goes On"). He won the contest and was awarded a recording contract with Columbia Records.

Stardom. The year 1969 was busy for the newly discovered artist. Iglesias recorded his first album at the Decca studios in London, toured Spain, and sang at festivals in Romania, Chile, and Italy. He was also involved in his first film, which had the name of his winning song, *La Vida Sigue Igual.*

His international reputation grew quickly. This was aided by his flair for languages, since he recorded and performed in English, Spanish, Italian, French, German, and Portuguese. By 1971, his linguistic challenges even included a venture into Japanese with another of his songs, "Como el Lamo al Camino." In the same year, he sang "Gwendolyne," (the piece he had written for his English girlfriend just before he become famous) at the Eurovision Song Contest.

Iglesias was married to Isabel Preysler Arrastria in 1971 in the Spanish city of Toledo. They had three children, "Chabeli" Mara Isabel (b. 1971), Julio Jos (b. 1973), and Enrique Miguel (b. 1975). They were separated in 1978, and the marriage was annulled in 1979.

Having achieved major success in Europe and the entire Spanish-speaking world, fame in the English-speaking world eluded him until his 1981 cover of "Begin the Beguine" became popular in England, and in 1984, two duets with U.S. artists, Willie Nelson ("To All the Girls I've Loved Before") and Diana Ross ("All of You"), became hit singles in the United States. These U.S. collaborations appeared on the album *1100 Bel Air Place* (1984), which went triple platinum. *Crazy,* recorded in 1994, included guest vocals by Art Garfunkel and Dolly Parton. Other recording collaborations have been with Paul Anka, Placido Domingo, and Frank Sinatra. Continuing to develop new audiences in Asia, in 1995 Iglesias became the first foreigner to be given China's Golden Record Award.

Also in 1995, he began work on a special project that was in some ways a departure from his usual focus on mainstream popular styles, but in other ways an exploration of his romantic essence. As a child, he had heard his parents play recordings of their beloved tango music, especially the work of Carlos Gardel, whom Iglesias considered one of the best lyricists of the twentieth century. Iglesias and his producer Robert Livi carefully studied Gardel's recordings and selected twelve of the best for Iglesias's album *Tango,* which was completed in 1996. The recording was extremely successful.

Accolades. Iglesias eventually moved to Miami, Florida. On September 7, 1997, Iglesias's fourth child, Miguel Alejandro, was born in Miami Beach to Iglesias and his companion, Dutch model Miranda Rinjsburguer. The next day, he became the first Spaniard to receive the American Society of Composers, Authors, and Publishers (ASCAP) Pied Piper Award, the society's highest award to an entertainer. Previous recipients included Ella Fitzgerald, Barbra Streisand, and Frank Sinatra. Miami Mayor Joe Carrollo was also there to announce a special "Julio Iglesias day" in Miami.

Although he prefers love songs to politics, Iglesias has concertized for charitable causes, and he has remained concerned with world events as well as with developments in his native country. In 1989, Iglesias was appointed Ambassador of the World for United Nations International Children's Emergency Fund (UNICEF).

For the Record

In 1998 *Billboard* confirmed that Julio Iglesias has sold more records than any other artist in history. He holds the *Guinness World Book of Records* world record for record sales, over 220 million.

Iglesias's 1998 world tour schedule included concerts all over the world, including Australia, Brazil, Chile, Argentina, the United States, Russia, and Lebanon. As of March, 1998, he had sold over 200 million records internationally, receiving more than 1,000 gold and 500 platinum awards worldwide.

Style. Most of Iglesias's famous recordings are of soft, romantic songs taken at a medium or slow tempo. His vocal style is very expressive, with a subtle, rapid vibrato that conveys a trembling excitement, barely held in control. In louder passages, his voice has a touch of operatic strength and drama. His distinctive sound is delivered with a flair for gesture, and his stage presence has made him especially popular as a live performer.

—Alice Myers

SELECT DISCOGRAPHY

■ ALBUMS

Soy, 1970
Gwendolyne, 1970
A Mexico, 1975
Hey! 1980
From a Child to a Woman, 1981
Moments, 1982
In Concert, 1983
1100 Bel Air Place, 1984
Libra, 1985
Starry Night, 1990
Crazy, 1994
Tango, 1996

SELECT AWARDS

Hollywood Walk of Fame, star awarded 1984
Grammy Award for Best Latin Pop Performance for *Un Hombre Solo*, 1987
Monaco World Music Best Latin Singer Award, 1997
American Music Award for Best Latin Artist, 1998

SEE ALSO: Nelson, Willie; Ross, Diana.

The Impressions. *See* Curtis Mayfield

Indigo Girls

MEMBERS: Amy Ray (b. 1964), Emily Saliers (b. 1963)
FIRST ALBUM RELEASE: *Strange Fire*, 1987
MUSICAL STYLES: Folk rock, alternative

Amy Ray and Emily Saliers, collectively billed as the Indigo Girls, first performed together as high school students for their Parent-Teacher Association (PTA) in Decatur, Georgia. Since that time, the duo, famous for their moving melodies, rich harmonies, and complex, thought-provoking lyrics, has moved from Atlanta nightclub act to cult status to worldwide fame.

Early Days. While they knew each other during their grade school years in Decatur, Saliers and Ray did not begin to sing their now legendary harmonies until mutual friends brought them together in high school. Their partnership continued while they were students in the early 1980's at Atlanta's Emory University, where Saliers majored in English, and Ray majored in English and religion. Billing themselves as Saliers and Ray, they began to perform at local clubs. As their popularity grew, they recognized the need for a new name and chose "indigo" from the dictionary, simply because they liked the way it sounded. On the Atlanta club circuit the Indigo Girls became a local sensation, their loyal fans following them from performance to performance. They also opened for many acts, including John Sebastian, Donovan, and Janis Ian. Originally they managed their own careers, independently releasing their first singles, "Crazy Game" and "Someone to Come Home," on their own label in 1985. The following year they released a self-titled, six-song extended-play single, and in 1987 they released their first full album, *Strange Fire*, again on Indigo Records.

National Renown. Some of the songs from *Strange Fire*, most notably "Blood and Fire" and "Land of Canaan," attracted enough national radio airplay to bring the Indigo Girls to the attention of at least one major recording company, Epic Records. In 1988, under the direction of their new manager Russell Carter, they signed a recording contract with Epic, and in 1989 they released their first album, *Indigo Girls*, for the label. Their efforts were successful. *Time* magazine welcomed the Indigo Girls' arrival on the national scene, calling them "two gifted writer-performers." That self-titled national debut was certified gold in September of 1989 with such songs as "Closer to Fine" and "Land of Canaan" propelling it to a Grammy Award as Best Contemporary Folk Recording of that year.

Indigo Girls (Paul Natkin)

For the next several years the Indigo Girls released a number of albums and toured extensively throughout the United States, attracting an increasingly larger audience. Both their music and their intensely personal performing style, a standout for its lack of pop-star glitz, were particularly popular on college campuses. Their 1991 extended-play single, "Back on the Bus Y'All," recorded live at the University of Notre Dame, West Georgia College, and the Uptown Lounge in Athens, Georgia, showcased their rapport with their audiences. By 1995, after they released their sixth album, it was clear that they had moved beyond the niche of the college audience to the mainstream. *Swamp Ophelia* (1994), debuted at number 9 on the *Billboard* pop album chart and was certified gold within six weeks.

As they had in their early days, the Indigo Girls frequently used their music to support various political or social movements. Before they signed with Epic, they had often played club benefits in Atlanta for the homeless. In their newer, more national arena, they continued to promote the causes they espoused. In 1990, for example, they headlined a gala fundraiser for the Children's Health Fund, and in 1995, on the twenty-one date "Honor the Earth" tour, they helped raise money and support for grassroots Native American activists. Other causes they have supported include acquired immunodeficiency syndrome (AIDS) research, Greenpeace and other environmental organizations, and Habitat for Humanity. While both women are openly gay, they rarely make an issue of their sexuality in their music, preferring to focus instead on the spiritual, political, and social issues for which their lyrics have become known.

Their Music. The Indigo Girls' signature style is music with a heart, a mind, and a conscience. Since their early club days their songs have been primarily original. Each member of the duo usually writes her own material, collaborating with the other only on the vocal and instrumental arrangements. Their academic background is evident in their music. Titles such as "Virginia Woolf," "Hey Jesus," and "Prince of Darkness" are clues to the depth of their lyrics, which often include biblical or literary imagery. These lyrics, which range from mystical to confrontational, tackle such diverse subjects as reincarnation, racism, and privacy issues. Often intensely personal, their songs are frequently inspired by various events in their lives. Ray wrote "This Train Revised," as recorded on *Swamp Ophelia,* for example, after a visit to the Holocaust Museum in Washington, D.C. It evokes the tragedy of Nazism in World War II: "Measure the bones/ count the face/ pull out the teeth/ do you belong to the human race?" Such sharp-edged, impassioned lyrics have often led to comparisons between the Indigo Girls and other socially conscious musicians including Bob Dylan and Bruce Springsteen.

Saliers usually plays lead guitar for the Indigo Girls. Ray, who plays rhythm guitar, blends her haunting alto seamlessly with her partner's soaring soprano in harmonies that even their critics praise. Ray's compositions tend to be rougher, synthesizing rock with folk; Saliers incorporates more jazz and soul into her songs. Nevertheless, their musical styles mesh, and their later albums strive for an even greater musical diversity. *Shaming of the Sun,* released in 1997, relies on various instrumental accompaniments, from strings to mandolin, and includes backup vocals by a Native American ensemble. The Indigo Girls have collaborated throughout their career with various musicians, including Luka Bloom, Michelle Malone, Jackson Browne, David Crosby, and various members of R.E.M. In 1997 they performed for one month with Sarah McLachlan's all-female Lilith Fair tour.

The Indigo Girls first emerged during the heavily commercial, video-oriented 1980's music scene. While they were in many ways the antithesis to this scene, they found their niche and flourished. By the mid-1990's, when female and alternative voices were gaining a larger share of the music industry, the Indigo Girls maintained their originality while becoming part of the mainstream. —*Jane Marie Smith*

For the Record

The Indigo Girls have done some acting. They appeared in the 1995 film *Boys on the Side* with Whoopi Goldberg and Drew Barrymore and starred in a revival of Andrew Lloyd Webber's *Jesus Christ Superstar,* in which Saliers played Mary Magdalene and Ray portrayed Jesus. While working on *Boys on the Side,* Ray dropped her 1947 Martin guitar and cracked it. Goldberg managed to find a duplicate and presented it to her on the set as a replacement.

SELECT DISCOGRAPHY

■ SINGLES

Indigo Girls, 1986 (extended-play single)
Back on the Bus Y'All, 1991 (extended-play single)

■ ALBUMS

Strange Fire, 1987 (rereleased in 1989)
Indigo Girls, 1989
Nomads Indians Saints, 1990
Rites of Passage, 1992
Swamp Ophelia, 1994
1200 Curfews, 1995
Shaming of the Sun, 1997

SELECT AWARDS

Grammy Award for Best Contemporary Folk Recording for *Indigo Girls,* 1989

SEE ALSO: McLachlan, Sarah; R.E.M.

James Ingram

BORN: Akron, Ohio; February 16, 1956
FIRST ALBUM RELEASE: *It's Your Night,* 1983
MUSICAL STYLES: Soul, pop

James Ingram broke into the 1980's as the freshest fireside balladeer in the music business. With a smooth, deep voice and an unerring touch in performing duets, he became one of the best-known singers who never had an album make the Top 40.

Breaking In. When Ingram's band Revelation Funk broke up after a move to Los Angeles in the mid-1970's, he began singing demo tapes for a music publishing company and playing keyboards, producing, and writing for Ray Charles. Producer Quincy Jones was impressed by what he heard and featured Ingram on two songs from his 1981 platinum album, *The Dude.* Ingram entered the charts with "Just Once" (number 17) in August, 1981. The follow-up, "One Hundred Ways," went to number 14 the following year and earned Ingram a Grammy Award for Best Male R&B Vocal Performance.

His association with Jones led to other opportunities. As a favor, Ingram agreed to sing a duet with Patty Austin, Jones's goddaughter who also had performed on *The Dude.* "Baby, Come to Me" seemed a failure, peaking at number 73 early in 1982. Yet when the song was included as background music for a steamy love scene on the soap opera *General Hospital,* outpourings of letters and phone calls demanded to know who the vocalist was. Having been off the charts since May, "Baby, Come to Me" was rereleased in October and climbed to number 1 in February of 1983. Jones, who was also producing Michael Jackson's *Thriller,* included "P.Y.T. (Pretty Young Thing)," co-authored by Ingram, on Jackson's hit album. Before he had ever released an album, Ingram had 3 Top-20 hits, one of them number 1, and a hand in the world's biggest-selling album of all time.

James Ingram (Archive Newsphotos/Lee)

Ingram's debut album, *It's Your Night* (1983), was certified gold more than one year after its release but never reached higher than number 46 on the charts. It featured Ingram at his smooth, middle-of-the-road best but gained little acclaim except for his Grammy Award-winning duet with Michael McDonald,"Yah Mo B There," in 1984. This would be typical of his career, as none of his albums reached the Top 40. He became known as the consummate singles artist, with a special talent for group efforts.

Duets. Ingram and Patty Austin followed their chart-topping "Baby, Come to Me" with "How Do You Keep the Music Playing" in 1983 (number 45). In 1984 he teamed with Kenny Rogers and Kim Carnes on "What About Me?," which rose to number 15. Two years later Ingram and Linda Ronstadt paired to take "Somewhere out There," from the 1986 film *An American Tail,* to number 2 on the charts.

Quincy Jones continued to include Ingram in his projects. In 1985 Jones brought him in to work on the film *The Color Purple* and invited him to sing on the number 1 group effort to aid victims of African famine, "We Are the World." Finally, Ingram joined Jones, Al B. Sure!, El DeBarge, and Barry White to produce the number 1 rhythm-and-blues hit "The Secret Garden (Sweet Seduction Suite)" (1990), the sensual melodic tale of four men courting the same woman.

Solo Stardom. Only in 1990 did Ingram finally have a solo hit. In October, almost nine years after his chart debut and more than one year after the release of *It's Real,* "I Don't Have the Heart" reached the top of the pop charts. —*John Powell*

For the Record

In the 1970's, James Ingram played keyboards for the Coasters on the Dick Clark "oldies" tour.

SELECT DISCOGRAPHY

■ ALBUMS

It's Your Night, 1983
Never Felt So Good, 1988
It's Real, 1989
The Power of Great Music: The Best of James Ingram, 1991 (compilation)
Always You, 1993

SELECT AWARDS

Grammy Award for Best R&B Vocal Performance, Male, for "One Hundred Ways," 1981
Grammy Award for Best R&B Performance by a Duo or Group with Vocal for "Yah Mo B There," 1984 (with Michael McDonald)

SEE ALSO: Doobie Brothers / Michael McDonald; Ronstadt, Linda.

INXS

ORIGINAL MEMBERS: Michael Hutchence (1960-1997), Andrew Farriss (b. 1959), Tim Farriss (b. 1957), Jon Farriss (b. 1961), Kirk Pengilly (b. 1958), Garry Gary Beers (b. 1957)
FIRST ALBUM RELEASE: *INXS*, 1980
MUSICAL STYLES: Rock and roll, pop

INXS rose from moderate success in their native Australia in the early 1980's to international fame in the late 1980's and 1990's. The band paved the way for later Australian rock bands such as Midnight Oil. Much of INXS's success can be attributed to the charisma of lead singer Michael Hutchence, whose death in 1997 brought the band's twenty-year career to a sudden end.

Early Years in Australia. Michael Hutchence and the three Farriss brothers, Tim, Andrew, and Jon, together with Kirk Pengilly and Garry Gary Beers, formed a band in Sydney, Australia, in 1977. Originally known as the Farriss Brothers, the group soon changed their name to INXS (pronounced "in excess") and moved to the city of Perth in western Australia.

Unlike many rock bands, INXS's lineup remained unchanged throughout their career. In addition to Hutchence as lead vocalist, the group featured Andrew Farriss on keyboards, Tim Farriss on guitar, Jon Farriss on drums, Pengilly on guitar and saxophone, and Beers on bass.

INXS was influenced by dance music and soul music to develop its own blend of pop and rock that resembled the so-called "new romanticism" of early 1980's bands such as Duran Duran. The first single by INXS, containing the songs "Simple Simon" and "We Are the Vegetables," was released by the small independent company Deluxe in 1980. Their self-titled debut album appeared the same year.

Over the next three years, INXS was fairly popular in Australia, placing six songs in the Australian Top 40. Their second album, *Underneath the Colours*, sold well in 1981, and their third album, *Shabooh Shoobah*, reached the Australian Top 5 in 1982. In the United States, INXS achieved moderate success with the single "The One Thing" (1982), which sounded like a Roxy Music tribute. INXS finally reached number 1 in Australia with the album *The Swing* and the single "Original Sin" in 1984.

Reaching the World. The success of "Original Sin" and *The Swing* led to the worldwide success of the next album, *Listen Like Thieves*, in 1985. With this album, INXS developed their distinctive, harder sound, featuring strong guitar melodies and grittier vocals, most notably in the title hit and the hit single "What You Need." In 1987 Hutchence appeared in the motion picture *Dogs in Space*. "Rooms for the Memory," a song from this film, gave Hutchence a solo Top-10 hit in Australia.

During the late 1980's INXS toured constantly in the United States and Europe. The band had their greatest success in 1987 with the album *Kick*, which sold nine million copies around the world.

For the Record

"People lead really flat lives. They need a sort of peak. I like to be that peak."

—*Michael Hutchence*

The album included "Need You Tonight," which reached number 1 in the United States in January of 1988. *Kick* featured softer, more melodic sounds, such as the single "Never Tear Us Apart." The video for "Need You Tonight" included the novelty song "Mediate," which consisted of a man flipping cardboard one- or two-word lyrics that all rhymed with the title, followed by a saxophone solo. Despite any political message INXS might have had in mind for the song, the video was frequently parodied.

The members of INXS took a yearlong break after *Kick* and worked on other projects. Hutchence appeared with Max Q on the album *Max Q* in 1989, and Beers appeared with Absent Friends on the album *Here's Looking up Your Address* in 1990. INXS was not as popular in the 1990's as in the late 1980's but continued to release albums and appear in concert.

A Tragic End. On November 22, 1997, just before INXS was to begin a twentieth-anniversary Australian tour, Hutchence was found dead in his hotel room in Sydney. The cause of death was suicide by hanging. Hutchence was two months short of reaching his thirty-eighth birthday.

—*Rose Secrest*

SELECT DISCOGRAPHY

■ ALBUMS

INXS, 1980
Underneath the Colours, 1981
Shabooh Shoobah, 1982
The Swing, 1984
Listen Like Thieves, 1985
Kick, 1987
X, 1990
Live Baby Live, 1991 (compilation)
Welcome to Wherever You Are, 1992
Full Moon, Dirty Hearts, 1993
The Greatest Hits, 1994 (compilation)
Elegantly Wasted, 1997

SEE ALSO: Duran Duran; Midnight Oil; Roxy Music.

Iron Maiden

ORIGINAL MEMBERS: Steve Harris (b. 1957), Dave Murray (b. 1958), Paul Di'anno (b. 1959), Doug Sampson

OTHER MEMBERS: Bruce Dickinson (b. 1958), Adrian Smith (b. 1957), Nicko McBrain (b. 1954), Dennis Stratton (b. 1954), Clive Burr (b. 1957), Janick Gers, Blaze Bayley

FIRST ALBUM RELEASE: *Iron Maiden*, 1980

MUSICAL STYLE: Heavy metal

Iron Maiden formed in 1976, but they had trouble getting a record contract, even after they released a demo in 1978. After the release of two songs on the compilation *Metal for Muthas* in 1979, Iron Maiden finally signed with EMI records and began to tour with Judas Priest.

Fun with Eddie. A significant member of the new wave of British heavy metal, Iron Maiden quickly gained a following in their native country. Although their music was hard-core heavy metal with a requisite screaming lead singer, Iron Maiden distinguished themselves with intelligent lyrics, vivid, gross imagery, obsession with death, and themes taken from horror films (such as 1978's *Omen II*) and ancient mythology (as in "Flight of Icarus," 1983). The name of the band comes from a medieval torture device in which the victim was housed in a iron coffin and pierced with spikes. Their music was appropriate to this dark moniker.

The band's albums were noteworthy for their cover art, which featured Eddie, a monster that came to be a popular attraction at their concerts. At first a backdrop painting, Eddie metamorphosed into a ten-foot-tall robot that could be animated by a road crew member. While popular at concerts, Eddie became the center of controversy in England in the 1980's, when he was depicted slashing the current British prime minister Margaret Thatcher. The cover of a single showed Margaret Thatcher again, this time with a machine gun. Threatened with a lawsuit, Iron Maiden resorted to blacking out her eyes to preserve anonymity. On stage, Eddie also waved a replica of Ozzy Osbourne's head that looked as if it had been bitten off, in reference to Osbourne's propensity for biting the heads off of doves and bats.

Fame. Iron Maiden's first album went to number 4 in England, but it was not until 1982 that they had a number 1 hit with *The Number of the Beast.* In the United States, it went gold, and their next album, *Piece of Mind* (1983), went platinum, despite limited airplay of singles. Iron Maiden toured constantly during the 1980's, pausing to play soccer matches with other rock groups such as the Scorpions and Def Leppard. In England, they would occasionally play small shows under other names, such as the Entire Population of Hackney. Their popularity was confirmed in 1983 when readers of the British heavy metal magazine *Kerrang* voted *Piece of Mind* and *The Number of the Beast* as the top two heavy metal albums of all time.

New Era. Iron Maiden kept to their reputation for fast, loud heavy metal on tour, with forty tons of light and sound equipment that could blare 152,000 watts. After a break in 1989, however, it was clear that their popularity had faded somewhat. Lead singer Bruce Dickinson left the band for a solo career, and bands such as Anthrax and Metallica were captivating audiences in the new speed-metal era. In England, however, Iron Maiden continued to have numerous fans and respectable record sales. —*Rose Secrest*

For the Record

Iron Maiden won the 1989 Golden Raspberry Award for worst original song, "Take Your Daughter to the Slaughter," from *A Nightmare on Elm Street 5: The Dream Child.*

§

In response to conservatives who claimed that heavy metal records reveal satanic messages when played backwards, Iron Maiden intentionally put a backwards message on their single "The Trooper" in 1983. In essence, it told listeners not to be concerned with what they do not understand.

§

Iron Maiden's lead singer, Bruce Dickinson, became a novelist in 1990 with *The Adventures of Lord Iffy Boatrace.* An expert swordsman, he placed seventh in Great Britain's fencing contest, the Men's Foil, in 1989.

SELECT DISCOGRAPHY

■ ALBUMS

Iron Maiden, 1980
Killers, 1981
The Number of the Beast, 1982
Piece of Mind, 1983
Powerslave, 1984
Live After Death, 1985
Somewhere in Time, 1986
Seventh Son of a Seventh Son, 1988
No Prayer for the Dying, 1990
Fear of the Dark, 1992
A Real Live One, 1993
A Real Dead One, 1993
Live at Donington, 1993
The X Factor, 1995
Best of the Beast, 1996 (compilation)

SEE ALSO: Black Sabbath; Def Leppard; Led Zeppelin; Metallica.

Chris Isaak

BORN: Stockton, California; June 26, 1956
FIRST ALBUM RELEASE: *Silvertone,* 1985
MUSICAL STYLES: Rock and roll, rhythm and blues, rockabilly

Chris Isaak has enjoyed a career as a crooner in the tradition of Roy Orbison and Elvis Presley. Armed with a wide vocal range and an ominous falsetto, Isaak built a following around his heartfelt retrospective music. With his excellent backup band, Silvertone, Isaak made several successful albums and one hit single during the 1980's and 1990's.

A Long Road. Chris Isaak's rise to a position of recognition in the world of popular music was long in coming. His teen years saw Isaak attempting an amateur boxing career. His twenties led to different interests. Isaak studied English and communication arts in college. All the while, Isaak was interested in music and singing. He formed the band Silvertone to assist him in crafting a rockabilly revival. Silvertone consisted of Kenny Dale Johnson (drums), Rowland Salley (bass), and James Calvin Wilsey (guitar). While all solid musicians, Wilsey's imaginative and haunting guitar especially provides an excellent foil for Isaak's vocal stylings.

The First Recordings. In 1985, Isaak secured a recording contract with Warner Bros. His debut album, *Silvertone*, earned generally favorable reviews, although some speculated that Isaak's evocations of bygone styles were more retro stylizations than the articulation of an original voice. The album owed much to the rockabilly-and country-influenced ballads of Elvis Presley and especially Roy Orbison.

Isaak's second album, *Chris Isaak* (1987), confirmed Isaak's commitment to rock's impassioned past, although rhythm and blues shared center stage with the previous album's rockabilly emphasis. Only the song "Blue Hotel" achieved much success from these first two albums, and that success was mostly limited to France, where Isaak's popularity soared. Later in his career, a rerelease of "Blue Hotel" would make the charts in the United States.

"Wicked Game." In 1990, Isaak exploded onto the music scene with a hit single, "Wicked Game," from his third album, *Heart Shaped World.* The album was released in 1989 to little fanfare, but the inclusion of "Wicked Game" and "Blue Spanish Sky" in David Lynch's 1990 film *Wild at Heart*

Chris Isaak (Reprise/Aaron Chang)

(winner of the 1990 Palme d'Or at the Cannes Film Festival) brought Isaak international attention. "Wicked Game" reached number 6 on the U.S. charts and formed the backbone of Isaak's growing popularity.

Isaak's vocals on "Wicked Game" rank among the most memorable in the history of rock ballads. He opens with breathy and anguished speechlike material in his low register. On the refrain, Isaak launches into an unforgettable melodic line dexterously employing falsetto in a manner worthy of Roy Orbison at his best. Wilsey supports with haunting guitar slides. The lyrics, full of doom-laden love, are reminiscent of Orbison's ballads of the early 1960's.

Some of the song's success must be credited to its outstanding music video directed by David Lynch, who had previously been instrumental in an international revival of interest in Roy Orbison. Isaak has also pursued a film career with small roles in *Married to the Mob* (1988) and *The Silence*

For the Record

Isaak's looks are distinctive. In an effort to clarify his relationship to the past, he wears his hair in a pompadour much like that worn by Elvis Presley around 1960. Perhaps his most distinctive feature is his flattened nose, the product of a failed boxing career.

of the Lambs (1991), both directed by Jonathan Demme. He had a substantial role in Lynch's controversial *Twin Peaks: Fire Walk with Me* (1992), in which Isaak played a Federal Bureau of Investigation agent investigating a murder. His talent for understatement and his awkward earnestness earned him good notices for his role.

Isaak's career stands as a monument to tradition during the 1990's, a decade that saw a general trend toward increased reliance on technology and conscious attempts to break with rock's past. Isaak's respect for the past is perhaps best exemplified by his lively cover of Bo Diddley's "Diddley Daddy" on the album *Heart Shaped World.* While so many acts were trying to cut ties with tradition, Isaak nurtured ties to rock's past. —*Michael Lee*

SELECT DISCOGRAPHY

■ ALBUMS

Silvertone, 1985
Chris Isaak, 1987
Heart Shaped World, 1989
San Francisco Days, 1993
Forever Blue, 1995
Speak of the Devil, 1998

SEE ALSO: Orbison, Roy; Presley, Elvis.

The Isley Brothers

ORIGINAL MEMBERS: Ron Isley (b. 1941), Kelly Isley (1937-1986), Rudolf Isley (b. 1939)

OTHER MEMBERS: Jimi Hendrix, Marvin Isley, Ernie Isley, Chris Jasper

FIRST SINGLE RELEASE: "Shout," 1959

MUSICAL STYLES: Rock and roll, rhythm and blues

For nearly three decades, the three Isley Brothers led a rock and soul act that was uneven in terms of their own recorded hits, but throughout their careers they remained important influences on succeeding generations of rock and soul artists from the Beatles to Sly and the Family Stone. Their inconsistency in style and frequent label changes kept them from sustaining a presence on the record charts, but they remained a vital and original stage act from the 1950's through the 1970's.

Opening Doors. Raised in Cincinnati, Ohio, Ron, Kelly (born O'Kelly), and Rudolf Isley were originally part of a gospel quartet with brother Vernon. After Vernon's death due to a bicycle accident in 1955, the trio left for New York City to begin their recording careers in 1957. For the Teenage and Gone labels, they released rock and doo-wop ballads without commercial success.

In 1959, they received their first major break when RCA Victor producers Hugo Peritti and Luigi Creatore helped shape "Shout," a call-and-response gospel-flavored hit featuring the brothers' church organist. The song is considered a major rock milestone that opened doors for the soul and rock fusion of the following decade. While the Isleys' version only reached the Top 50, cover versions by Joey Dee and the Starliters in the United States and Lulu and the Luvvers in the United Kingdom were more successful. The Beatles performed one version of the song on British television's *Ready, Steady, Go,* but did not release the song until 1995 in their *Anthology* series.

False Starts and Chart Toppers. Briefly working with production and songwriting team Jerry Leiber and Mike Stoller at Atlantic Records, the Isley Brothers' next major hit was for Wand Records in 1962. Under the direction of hitmaker Bert Berns in the heyday of twist dances, "Twist and Shout," the Isleys' cover of a Topnotes single, became another song defined by the Isleys that found greater commercial success for other groups. In particular, "Twist and Shout" became one of the Beatles' early hits.

The Isleys then formed their own record label, T-Neck Records, and in 1964 hired the then-unknown guitar wizard Jimi Hendrix. While Hendrix stayed with the Isleys only a short period, he helped shape their career by providing a guitar style they continued to use after his departure. After Hendrix became an important rock force in the late 1960's, the group rereleased material recorded with him, *In the Beginning . . . with Jimi Hendrix* (1972), with Hendrix's guitar work remixed to emphasize his playing.

In 1965, Motown founder Berry Gordy, Jr., signed the group and put them under the creative direction of producers and songwriters Brian Holland, Lamont Dozier, and Eddie Holland. This team produced the Isleys' next hit, "This Old Heart of Mine." In March, 1966, the song moved quickly up the U.S. charts, and in November, 1968, it reappeared as a hit in England.

The group released two other hits for Motown, "Behind a Painted Smile" and "I Guess I'll Always Love You," but the group ended the decade known more for its energetic stage act built around Ronald's vocals than their on-again, off-again recording career.

In 1969, they reactivated T-Neck records and created one of the earliest funk hits with the lengthy jam "It's Your Thing," which also won them a Grammy Award for Best R&B Vocal Performance. With the addition of cousin Chris Jasper and younger brothers Ernie and Marvin Isley, the group became entirely a self-contained family unit and moved from the soul styles of their past into the Stevie Wonder-inspired synthesizer sounds of the 1970's. In 1973, they signed a new distribution arrangement with yet another label, Columbia Records, and issued the critically-acclaimed *3+3*. From this album, they enjoyed two hits, their own composition, "That Lady," and their cover of Seals and Crofts' "Summer Breeze." This album was considered the Isleys' breakthrough to the mass market, but the followup, *Live It Up*, failed to continue the group's fortunes. *The Heat Is On* (1975), however, contained the single "Fight the Power," which was well received on black radio stations.

The Isley Brothers (Fotos International/Archive Photos)

The 1980's. In the 1980's, the group split, with the two younger Isleys and Jasper forming Isley-Jasper-Isley. Kelly Isley died on March 31, 1986. Later, the group successfully sued singer Michael Bolton for plagiarizing their song "Love Is a Wonderful Thing."

—*Wesley Britton*

SELECT DISCOGRAPHY

■ SINGLES

"Twist and Shout," 1962
"This Old Heart of Mine (Is Weak for You)," 1966
"It's Your Thing," 1969
"That Lady," 1973
"Fight the Power," 1975

■ ALBUMS

3+3, 1973
The Heat Is On, 1975
Harvest for the World, 1976
Winner Takes All, 1979
Go All the Way, 1980
Between the Sheets, 1983

SELECT AWARDS

Grammy Award for Best R&B Vocal Performance by a Group or Duo for "It's Your Thing," 1969

SEE ALSO: Beatles, The; Jimi Hendrix.

J

Alan Jackson

BORN: Newnan, Georgia; October 17, 1958
FIRST SINGLE RELEASE: "Here in the Real World," 1990
MUSICAL STYLE: Country

Alan Jackson's first hit, "Here in the Real World," reached number 1 on the *Billboard* charts in April, 1990. Eight years later Jackson had recorded twenty number 1 hits and had sold more than twenty million albums.

Beginnings. Most of Alan Jackson's fans would say that his appeal lies in the fact that the subject matter of his songs illustrates that he lives in the real world. In fact, Jackson is from his fans' world; the titles and subject matter of his recordings reflect that world. His lifestyle reflects the fact that he holds his fans' values, which he discusses in his songs.

Born in Newnan, Georgia, Jackson graduated from high school there and spent one year at West Georgia College. He married in 1979. Two decades later Denise Jackson was still his wife, and she and Alan were the parents of three children. Prior to becoming a recording star and country music performer, Jackson was a writer for Seven Sun Music, Glen Campbell's recording company. However, before Jackson became involved in the professional music business, he held jobs which many of his fans could readily understand and identify with. Jackson supported himself, after coming to Nashville to establish a music career, by working in the mailroom at The Nashville Network (TNN). Before moving from Georgia to Nashville, he held various blue-collar and white-collar positions: He worked as a forklift operator for Kmart, as a construction worker, and as a car salesperson.

Produced by Keith Stegall and written primarily by Jackson himself, Jackson's repertoire during the 1990's was one of the most popular in country music. Songs such as "Here in the Real World" (from *Here in the Real World,* 1990) and "Working Class Hero" (from *Don't Rock the Jukebox,* 1991) led Jackson's fans to believe that he was singing about the lives which they were living. Songs such as "Chasin' That Neon Rainbow" (from *Here in the Real World*), "Don't Rock the Jukebox," and "Midnight in Montgomery" (both from *Don't Rock the Jukebox*) caused his fans to think that he loved the honky-tonk music which they loved, and that he revered the same country music legends which they revered. "I Only Want You for Christmas," "Please Daddy (Don't Drink This Christmas)," and "If We Make It Through Christmas" (all from *Honky Tonk Christmas,* 1993) are examples of recordings which led Jackson's fans to think that he had the same understanding of family and romantic relationships that they had. Jackson's fans have always believed that he understood them well.

The topics about which Jackson writes and the themes which he explores are the same topics and themes which country music had examined for more than fifty years before Jackson began recording. Jackson, however, is special in that he chose to continue developing those topics and themes at a time when most new country entertainers were turning away from the traditional subject matter and presentation of country music in order to develop themes and styles which generally had been associated with pop or rock music. Jack-

For the Record

"Of all the things I've been and the awards I've won . . . I still get more excited when I sit on the bus and write a good song. It's a whole rush to do something you just created and have people like it."

—*Alan Jackson*

son has developed those traditional country themes and topics and has presented his music, both in recordings and in live performances, in a style and voice which have generally been associated with the performers of traditional country music. His recordings and performances offer his fans a down-home feeling.

Career Development. Not only did Jackson become popular with country music fans because of the themes of his music but also because of the way in which he performed. In the 1990's, when performers such as Garth Brooks made recordings which were as slick and smooth as any pop performance, Jackson, through his style and use of voice, retained the persona and sounds of a traditional country performer. Jackson's performances eschewed much of the dancing, theatrics, and light shows made popular by other country performers who came of age in the early 1990's.

It has been said that the 1950's had Hank Williams, the 1960's had Merle Haggard, the 1970's had John Anderson, the 1980's had Randy Travis, and the 1990's had Alan Jackson. For his part, Jackson has said that his favorite performers are George Jones, Merle Haggard, and Hank Williams, with Jones's classic "He Stopped Loving Her Today" being his all-time favorite country song. Jackson paid homage to earlier traditional country performers in his 1992 number 1 single "Midnight in Montgomery." He has also associated himself with his country music heroes in other ways. In 1993 Alan Jackson and George Jones's performance of "I Don't Need Your Rocking Chair" (from the *Walls Can Fall* album) was named by the Country Music Association as the Vocal Event of the Year. (*Walls Can Fall* was a cooperative effort by various country music artists.) In 1995 The Nashville Network/Music City News named Jackson and Jones's performance of "A Good Year for the Roses" (from *The Bradley Barn Sessions with George Jones* album) as the Vocal Event of the Year. Jackson and Jones filmed videos for both "I Don't Need Your Rocking Chair" and "A Good Year for the Roses." Jackson has also performed Merle Haggard songs on a tribute album to Haggard that featured various artists.

Jackson as a Songwriter. Jackson has said that he is happiest when he is writing music. When choosing subjects for his songs, Jackson looked to his roots; "Chattahoochee," a 1992 number 1 single on the *Billboard* country charts, was written about his home state of Georgia. He also looked to his heroes in songs such as "Midnight in Montgomery," another number 1 song, and to his love of honky-tonk as illustrated in songs such as "Chasin' That Neon Rainbow" (1991). Jackson's greatest source of subject matter was everyday life, illustrated in the songs found on *Here in the Real World* and *A Lot About Livin' (and a Little 'Bout Love)*, from 1992.

In addition to writing much of the music for his own recordings, Jackson has written for other artists and collaborated with them. Both Faith Hill and Randy Travis have performed songs written bv Jackson, and Jackson and Travis have been collaborators on various songs.

Jackson has been lauded by his peers for his songwriting. In 1991 The Nashville Songwriters Association International named Jackson Songwriter/Artist of the Year. He has received songwriting awards from Music City News: In 1990 he received the Country Songwriter of the Year Award for "Here in the Real World" and in 1993, the Country Songwriter of the Year Award for "Chattahoochee." —*Annita Marie Ward*

SELECT DISCOGRAPHY

■ ALBUMS

Here in the Real World, 1990
Don't Rock the Jukebox, 1991
A Lot About Livin' (and a Little 'Bout Love), 1992
Honky Tonk Christmas, 1993
Who I Am, 1994
Greatest Hits, 1995 (compilation)
Everything I Love, 1996
High Mileage, 1998

SELECT AWARDS

Academy of Country Music New Male Vocalist of the Year Award, 1990
Country Music Association Single of the Year and Music Video of the Year Awards for "Chattahoochee"; Vocal Event of the Year

Award for "I Don't Need Your Rocking Chair" (with George Jones and others), 1993
Academy of Country Music Male Vocalist of the Year Award, 1994, 1995
Country Music Association Entertainer of the Year Award, 1995

SEE ALSO: Jones, George; Travis, Randy.

Janet Jackson

BORN: Gary, Indiana; May 16, 1966
FIRST ALBUM RELEASE: *Janet Jackson,* 1982
MUSICAL STYLES: Pop, soul, rhythm and blues

There was a time when Janet Jackson was most famous for being Michael Jackson's little sister. Later, with only six studio albums under her belt, the youngest Jackson sibling could boast more than forty million albums sold worldwide and sixteen gold singles. Working hard to distance herself from her family's show business dynasty, Jackson has distinguished herself as a strong, independent woman who is not afraid to take control of her career and her life.

The Beginnings. Janet Damita Jo Jackson was the youngest of nine children born to Joe and Katherine Jackson. Music ran in the family; five of her six older brothers enjoyed a string of Motown hits in the early 1970's as the Jackson 5. By the time she was seven, Jackson was appearing onstage with her brothers, imitating Mae West and Cher, with twelve-year-old brother Randy filling in as Sonny Bono.

Her initial show business success came not in music, but on television. At age eleven, she joined the cast of the prime-time show *Good Times* in 1977 as abused runaway Penny Gordon. At age fifteen, she joined the cast of *Diff'rent Strokes,* playing Charlene, the girlfriend of Willis Jackson (Todd Bridges).

First Album. As with her brothers, Jackson's father managed her career. Joe Jackson won his daughter a recording contract with A&M Records in 1982, and at age sixteen, she released her self-titled debut. The package was essentially an extension of her cute, little-sister television persona and was perceived as little more than an attempt to capitalize on the Jackson family name.

Janet Jackson (Ken Settle)

Jackson graduated from high school in 1983 with one album and two television series to her name. She wanted to go to college; her manager-father wanted her to go to work. She relented, accepting the role of shy, insecure Cleo on the critically acclaimed series *Fame.* Her unhappiness grew, both with her career and her home life. In 1984, eighteen-year-old Jackson eloped with singer James DeBarge while the rest of the family was involved with the Jacksons' "Victory" tour. The marriage was more about escape than love, and by the following March, the union was annulled, and Jackson had moved back home.

It was during this time that Jackson released her

second album, *Dreamstreet* (1984). This album was coproduced by Giorgio Moroder (of "Flashdance" fame) and featured a more mature, mid-1980's dance-pop sound. Though one single, "You Don't Stand Another Chance," received some airplay, *Dreamstreet* followed its predecessor into obscurity.

Control. With the dismal performance of her first two albums, Jackson clearly needed a new direction. On the recommendation of a family friend, she traveled to Minneapolis, Minnesota, to meet producers Jimmy Jam and Terry Lewis (formerly of the Time, then one of the top production and songwriting teams of the 1980's and 1990's). Jam and Lewis gave the nineteen-year-old Jackson something her family had never given her: personal and artistic freedom. The result was *Control*, Jackson's 1986 breakthrough third album. *Control* stood for more than just the title, it was an attitude—little Janet Jackson declaring her musical independence. "In the past," she told an interviewer, "I'd just been given a tape of a song, learned it, and then gone into the studio and sung to a completed instrumental track. But I wanted to be completely involved in the recording process, from the songwriting to the playing to the production." *Control* produced six number 1 singles, including "Nasty" and "What Have You Done for Me Lately," as well was a series of highly successful videos.

Not content to rest on her success, Jackson continued to move forward. In 1987, she finally broke free from her manager-father and went to work on her fourth album, 1989's *Rhythm Nation 1814*. Coproduced with Jam and Lewis, the ambitious concept album showcased Jackson's evolution as a songwriter, tackling controversial subjects such as racism, violence, and empowerment. *Rhythm Nation 1814* spawned four number 1 singles, with total sales topping eight million. Continuing the spirit of social consciousness, Jackson donated 400,000 dollars from the "Rhythm Nation" tour to the Cities in Schools program.

Breaking Records. In 1993, Jackson left A&M and signed a forty-million-dollar deal with Virgin Records, at that time the largest contract ever offered to a pop singer. Her first release on the new label was *janet*, a frank celebration of sexuality that obliterated all remaining traces of her cute, chubby, little-girl image. The album debuted at number 1 on the *Billboard* charts, making Jackson the first female artist to ever send an album straight to the top, and produced four Top-5 singles, including "That's the Way Love Goes" and "Again." In celebration of her newfound sexuality, Jackson posed for a famous *Rolling Stone* cover, wearing nothing above the waist except the strategically placed hands of her longtime boyfriend, Rene Elizondo, Jr.

In 1995, Jackson joined her brother Michael on a new single for his greatest hits package, *HIStory: Past, Present and Future Book I.* The single, "Scream," entered the charts at number 1 and filled the MTV airwaves with a stunning dance video set in outer space. Her own greatest-hits collection, *Design of a Decade 1986/1996*, soon followed. The compilation fulfilled her obligation to A&M and produced the hit "Runaway," which became her sixteenth gold single. That same year, she renegotiated her contract with Virgin for a reported eighty million dollars.

In 1997, Jackson reunited with producers Jam and Lewis for *The Velvet Rope.* In interviews, she called the concept album her most personal to date. Following current trends in hip-hop, Jam and

For the Record

Janet Jackson has said that Sly and the Family Stone's 'Hot Fun in the Summertime' was a big musical influence: "I was only three years old when that song had me jumping up and down."

§

In 1990, Janet Jackson became the first artist to place seven Top-5 singles from an album on *Billboard*'s pop singles chart. The album was *Rhythm Nation 1814*; the singles, were "Miss You Much," "Rhythm Nation," "Escapade," "Alright," "Come Back to Me," "Black Cat," and "Love Will Never Do (Without You)."

Lewis relied heavily on rap dubbed over samples. Many of the tracks used melodies from a diverse group of artists, such as Joni Mitchell, War, and Archie Bell and the Drells as the background for Jackson's ongoing sexual exploration. Though well received by fans, *The Velvet Rope* did not match the sales or critical acclaim of its predecessors.

The 1998 tour in support of *The Velvet Rope* kicked off Jackson's affiliation with America's Promise—the Alliance for Youth, led by General Colin Powell. A portion of the tour proceeds were donated to the nationwide nonprofit organization dedicated to children's mentoring programs throughout the United States. —*P. S. Ramsey*

SELECT DISCOGRAPHY

■ ALBUMS

Janet Jackson, 1982
Dream Street, 1984
Control, 1986
Rhythm Nation 1814, 1989
janet, 1993
Design of a Decade 1986/1996, 1995
The Velvet Rope, 1997

SELECT AWARDS

Grammy Award for Best Music Video, Long Form, for *Rhythm Nation 1814*, 1989
Broadcast Music Incorporated (BMI) Songwriter of the Year Award, 1990
Hollywood Walk of Fame, star awarded 1990
Grammy Award for Best R&B Song for "That's the Way Love Goes," 1993 (with James Harris III and Terry Lewis)
Grammy Award for Best Music Video, Short Form, for "Scream," 1995 (with Michael Jackson)

SEE ALSO: Jackson, Michael; Jackson 5, The; Mitchell, Joni; Prince; Shakur, Tupac.

Joe Jackson

BORN: Burton-on-Trent, Staffordshire, England; August 11, 1954
FIRST ALBUM RELEASE: *Look Sharp*, 1979
MUSICAL STYLES: New wave, rock, swing

Joe Jackson's music is difficult to categorize. After his debut as a new-wave pioneer in 1978, Jackson has experimented with swing, jazz, classical, rock, Latin, reggae, and other styles of music. Notwithstanding his eclecticism, Joe Jackson has a musical and lyrical style marked by a combination of euphony, wryness, and wittiness. Although he would continue to attract critical commendation, his greatest influence on popular music had passed by the time of his third album in 1980.

Early Musical Interests. Joe Jackson was born in northern England in 1954 and moved with his family to the southern coastal town of Portsmouth when he was one year old. During his childhood in Portsmouth, Jackson took music lessons for violin, piano, woodwinds, and percussion. His greatest musical passion as a teenager was classical music, which he even tried his hand at composing. Between the ages of seventeen and twenty, Jackson studied musical composition and theory at London's Royal Academy of Music. He also supplemented his more classical musical foundation with a continuing interest in popular and experimental music, from the Beatles and the Rolling Stones to the Damned and the Clash.

After earning his degree from the Royal Academy of Music, Jackson played piano with various bands in the Portsmouth area. Sometimes those bands played original songs he had written. One of those bands, Arms and Legs, released two unremarkable singles in 1976, but Jackson soon went out on his own. After selling some demonstration tapes, Jackson was able to secure a recording contract with A&M records. The single "Is She Really Going out with Him?" was released in 1978. The album *Look Sharp*, which included "Is She Really Going out with Him?," was released early in 1979. It was soon difficult to listen to a Top-40 music station in the United States without hearing Joe Jackson.

New-Wave Phase. Joe Jackson is probably best known for his contributions to the burgeoning new-wave music of the mid- and late 1970's. He did not define the genre, but it would be fair to say that he refined it. With only four musicians (Jackson's piano and vocals were backed by a bass, drums, and guitar), *Look Sharp* followed new

For the Record

Big World is a "three-sided" album. It was released on two LP disks, but the label on side 4 says simply, "There Is No Music on This Side." Although A&M wanted to price the album as a two-record set, Joe Jackson insisted that the absence of a side 4 would make buyers feel cheated. The album was therefore priced the same as A&M's single albums.

wave's (and punk's) minimalism, which intentionally protested the vapidity and synthetic orchestration of disco. Furthermore, Jackson's singing voice was (and would remain) unpolished, somewhat strained, and occasionally whiny. However, Jackson was not simply imitating the new-wave/punk style that had caught his interest. Most of the cuts were catchy, and though the lyrics were frequently sardonic, they were softened with humor and self-deprecation. The refrain from "Fools in Love" is illustrative: "Fools in love, they think they're heroes/ 'Cause they get to feel no pain/ I think fools in love are zeroes/ I should know . . . because this fool's in love again." Jackson's debut was well received. "Is She Really Going out with Him?" made it to the Top 10. The album itself reached number 20.

In late 1979, A&M released Jackson's second album, *I'm the Man*. The album continued very much in the same vein as *Look Sharp*. The title cut in particular received considerable airplay. "I'm the Man" reached number 22 in the United States and went all the way to number 12 in Britain. An increasing number of critics found Joe Jackson to be an intriguing and refreshing musical artist, and he began to develop a loyal following of listeners.

Jackson's third album, *Beat Crazy*, was released in 1980. Its music was infused with a distinct reggae influence, but the basic musical and lyrical format of the first two albums remained. The album did not break much new ground for Jackson, and it failed to enter the Top 40. Reflecting back a number of years later, Jackson would remark that those first new-wave albums were not especially serious work and that he did not wish for his musical contributions to be defined by them. After recording *Beat Crazy*, Jackson made the first of several major changes in his style of music.

Jazz and Swing Phase. In 1981 Joe Jackson recorded an entirely different kind of album. *Jumpin' Jive* was conceived as a tribute to musician Louis Jordan, with a dozen classic swing songs from the 1940's. Jackson's band, now augmented with saxophones, trumpet, and clarinet, produced energetic, fairly authentic 1940's music. The album did not sell well, but Jackson was uninterested in turning back from his foray into loosely interpreted jazz. *Night and Day* (1982) was an eclectic mix of music said to be inspired by Jackson's recent move to New York City. Notwithstanding its diversity of musical styles, a distinct feel of jazz and Latin rhythms pervades the music. The album earned critical praise, including Grammy Award nominations for Best Male Pop Vocal Performance and for Record of the Year. The album's upbeat yet silky "Steppin' Out" reached the Top-10 singles charts, and the album itself reached number 4 on American charts.

Jackson clearly enjoyed working in jazz, and contributed a rendition of "Round Midnight" to Hal Wilner's tribute album to Thelonious Monk, *That's the Way I Feel Now*. In Jackson's next album, *Body and Soul* (1984), he continued to explore jazz themes and to incorporate a number of wind instruments (including saxophones, flute, trumpet, and fluegelhorn). Jackson recorded the album in an old wood-and-stone Masonic lodge in New York City. Evidently pleased with the result of a nonstudio venue, Jackson recorded his next album, *Big World* (1986), during five live performances at New York's Roundabout Theatre. *Big World* included fifteen songs about different countries and cultures, reflecting an international range of musical styles. Jackson's work was no longer making the Top 20, but he continued his pursuit of experimenting with and combining different musical styles. In *Will Power* (1987) Jackson returned to his earlier love of composing classical music, and he utilized a fifty-piece orchestra (supplemented with several rock musicians) for the recording.

Return to Rock. In 1989 Jackson released *Blaze of Glory,* which marked his return back to more mainstream pop music. The album reflected some of Jackson's earlier musical qualities, including rock tempos, biting lyrics (especially in "Nineteen Forever"), and political commentary (in "Evil Empire"). Jackson was not simply moving back to his musical beginnings; he had clearly matured. His instrumentation was more sophisticated, continuing to include a range of percussive, wind, and electronic instruments. His lyrics were more reflective and sophisticated. Still, Jackson's music was not becoming more popular. *Blaze of Glory* rose no higher than number 61 on the charts. *Laughter and Lust* (1991) followed very much in the style of *Blaze of Glory* and despite favorable reviews did as poorly in the stores.

Jackson again turned away from mainstream pop music in 1994 with *Night Music,* a collection of show tunes and classical music. Three years later he released *Heaven and Hell,* with tracks representing each of the seven deadly sins. Although his influence on pop music has been limited since his success in the late 1970's, Joe Jackson has proven to be a versatile, talented, and accomplished musician and composer.

—*Steve D. Boilard*

SELECT DISCOGRAPHY

■ ALBUMS

Look Sharp, 1979
I'm the Man, 1979
Beat Crazy, 1980
Jumpin' Jive, 1981
Night and Day, 1982
Mike's Murder, 1983 (sound track)
Body and Soul, 1984
Big World, 1986
Will Power, 1987
Blaze of Glory, 1989
Laughter and Lust, 1991
Night Music, 1994
Heaven and Hell, 1997

SEE ALSO: Costello, Elvis.

Mahalia Jackson

BORN: New Orleans, Louisiana; October 26, 1911
DIED: Evergreen Park, Illinois; January 27, 1972
FIRST SINGLE RELEASE: "God's Gonna Separate the Wheat from the Tares," 1934
MUSICAL STYLES: Gospel, spirituals

Mahalia Jackson, who became known as the "Gospel Queen," was born to poor parents. She was the daughter of John A. Jackson, a longshoreman, barber, and preacher, and Charity Clark, a laundress and maid. Mahalia's mother, a pious Baptist, died at about age twenty-five, when Mahalia was five. Then Mahalia and her eight-year-old brother, Peter, went to live with their Aunt Duke (Mahalia Paul), a sternly religious woman who forced Mahalia to work diligently and caused her to quit school to work as a laundress after completing the eighth grade.

Musical Influence. Jackson was always surrounded by music. She sang in the congregation of her family's Mount Moriah Baptist Church, where services were held every evening as well as on Sundays. Jackson especially liked the way the preacher delivered his messages in a kind of singing voice. She also listened to the music coming from the Sanctified church located next door to her house, where the people clapped, stomped, danced, and used instruments as they sang. However, Jackson's musical influence was not exclusively restricted to the church. She was affected by the music she heard on the streets of New Orleans: brass bands, jazz bands, and local musicians such as Jelly Roll Morton and King Oliver. She enjoyed listening to the music during the annual festival of Mardi Gras and other parades. Additionally, when Aunt Duke was not home, she listened to some of her cousin Fred's blues recordings of Ma Rainey, Mamie Smith, and Bessie Smith. She particularly liked Bessie Smith's renditions of "Careless Love" and "St. Louis Blues." All of these musical styles, secular and nonsecular, helped Jackson to create her own style of gospel singing.

Despite the fact that Jackson was fascinated by the blues, she knew that her immediate relatives were opposed to the blues, considering it inappropriate for Christians. Her relatives believed that Christians should sing gospels, not blasphemous blues tunes. Consequently, Jackson decided to audition for the Baptist choir. After singing "I'm so glad, I'm so glad, I'm so glad I've been in the grave an' rose again . . . ," she won a place in the choir, and people came to recognize her powerful voice.

Chicago. In 1927 when Jackson was sixteen, she moved to Chicago, hoping to become a nurse. She resided with her Aunt Hannah Robinson while working several odd jobs such as laundress, hotel maid, and date packer. Later she joined her aunt's Greater Salem Baptist Church. Jackson did not know how to read music, nor had she ever sung with a pianist. Nevertheless, she, possessing a majestic contralto voice, decided to try out for the choir. When she sang "Hand Me down My Silver Trumpet, Gabriel," her electrifying voice demanded the attention of people inside the church as well as some from the street. As a result, she became a member of the choir and later a soloist. Then in 1930 she joined a quintet, the Johnson Gospel Singers, which consisted of the minister's three sons and another female teenager. She traveled and sang with the group, performing at many church activities.

Even though Jackson realized that she could make more money singing the blues, she was determined not to sing any songs that her relatives did not approve of, especially her grandfather, Paul Clark, who had suffered a stroke and was in a coma. She said that if her grandfather recuperated, she would not set foot into a theater again, nor would she sing any songs which did not meet with his approval. Her grandfather soon recovered, and Jackson kept her vow. She rejected many lucrative offers to perform in nightclubs; she even refused an offer of ten thousand dollars per week for her performances.

Jackson encountered many hardships in her private life, including two unsuccessful marriages. In 1936 Jackson married Isaac Hockenhull, an educated man with a degree in chemistry, whom she later divorced. In 1964 she married Sigmund Galloway, a businessman and musician, but in 1967 that marriage also ended in divorce.

Recognition. During the late 1930's, Jackson attracted the attention of Thomas A. Dorsey, a renowned gospel composer and publisher, who became known as the "Father of Gospel Music." Jackson and Dorsey, who served as Jackson's mentor, toured various churches together from 1939 to 1944. During this time, Jackson performed many of Dorsey's songs. After five years of touring, Jackson returned to Chicago, where she opened Mahalia's Beauty Parlor and later Mahalia's House of Flowers. She received the patronage of many of her gospel followers.

When Jackson began another tour, she did so in high style. She purchased a lavender Cadillac with adequate space for sleeping and dining accommodations so that she would not have to be concerned about negative treatment in segregated southern areas. During this time, she started appealing to both white and black listeners. She appeared often on radio shows, especially on Chicagoan Studs Terkel's radio show, and later on her own radio and television programs. Also, she traveled and performed exten-

Mahalia Jackson (Frank Driggs/Archive Photos)

sively in such places as France, England, Germany, Denmark, Japan, and Israel. Mildred Falls, a close friend, was usually her full-time accompanist at the piano.

The Gospel Queen's musical style was not without criticism. Many of her critics said that her style, which included hand clapping, stomping, and bouncing as she sang, lacked dignity. However, she usually justified her behavior with one of her favorite scriptural passages: "Oh clap your hands, all ye people! Shout unto the Lord with the voice of triumph!" She believed in making a joyful noise and praising the Lord with her whole body.

Civil Rights Movement. During the mid-1950's and early 1960's, Jackson was active in the Civil Rights movement. She honored the request of Reverend Martin Luther King, Jr., by taking part in the Montgomery bus boycott; and she was present at many of King's rallies, singing such inspirational songs as "We Shall Overcome" and "If I Can Help Somebody." In addition, in 1963 Jackson sang the slave spiritual "I Been 'Buked and I Been Scorned" shortly before Dr. King gave his "I Have a Dream" speech at the Lincoln Memorial.

During Jackson's final years, she encountered several illnesses which resulted in a heart condition. Having achieved international acclaim, she died of heart failure in 1972 in Evergreen Park, Illinois. After funerals in Chicago and New Orleans, her body was laid to rest in Providence Memorial Park in Metairie, Louisiana.

—*Nila M. Bowden*

For the Record

In 1947 Mahalia Jackson recorded "Move on Up" for Apollo Records, and it sold 100,000 copies nearly overnight. Later sales in the United States soared to more than two million copies.

§

Jackson was the first gospel singer to perform at Carnegie Hall in New York City—on October 4, 1950. She also sang at President John F. Kennedy's inauguration in 1961.

SELECT DISCOGRAPHY

■ ALBUMS

Live at Newport, 1958
Silent Night—Songs for Christmas, 1962
Gospels, Spirituals, and Hymns, 1991 (compilation)
The Apollo Sessions, 1946-1951, 1994 (compilation)

SELECT AWARDS

Grammy Award for Best Gospel or Other Religious Recording for "Every Time I Feel the Spirit," 1961
Grammy Award for Best Gospel or Other Religious Recording for *Great Songs of Love and Faith*, 1962
Grammy Award for Lifetime Achievement, 1971
Grammy Award for Best Soul Gospel Performance for *How I Got Over*, 1976

SEE ALSO: Green, Al; Staple Singers, The; Winans, The.

Michael Jackson

BORN: Gary, Indiana; August 29, 1958
FIRST SINGLE RELEASE: "Big Boy," 1968 (with the Jackson 5)
FIRST SOLO SINGLE RELEASE: "Got to Be There," 1971
MUSICAL STYLES: Rhythm and blues, soul, disco, pop

One of the most popular entertainers of all time, Michael Jackson reinvigorated a struggling record industry in the early 1980's with the release of *Thriller*, an album which would eventually sell nearly fifty million copies worldwide. His skillful blend of pop, rhythm and blues, and disco appealed to a wide audience who also appreciated his extraordinary gifts as a dancer. However, Jackson's reputation was tarnished by an eccentric personal life that alienated many fans.

The Jackson 5. The seventh of nine children, Jackson was exposed to a variety of musical influences at an early age. His father Joseph performed in a local rhythm-and-blues group, and his mother Katherine sang country-and-western standards to her children. Viewing musical success as the key to escaping a dreary lower-middle-class existence that offered few opportunities other than work in the nearby steel mills, Joseph taught his sons Tito, Jackie, and Jermaine to sing, dance, and play musical instruments. With their brother Marlon on bongos, the Jacksons practiced in the family living room. When Michael, who was only four years old, joined in the rehearsals, his remarkable talents as a singer and dancer prompted Joe to make him the lead vocalist.

Billed as the Ripples and Waves Plus Michael, the Jackson brothers performed publicly, appearing in local talent contests, department stores, and nightclubs. Renamed the Jackson 5, the brothers were soon appearing in clubs and amateur talent shows in nearby Chicago. On weekends they toured the "chitlin' circuit," a network of theaters in major cities in which African American acts performed during the era of racial segregation. When the Jackson 5 opened for artists including James Brown, Gladys Knight and the Pips, and Jackie Wilson, Michael watched these stars from the wings, learning the tricks of the trade from some of the greatest performers of the day. The group's hard work paid off in 1969, when Motown Records signed the Jackson 5 to a recording contract.

Michael Jackson (Paul Natkin)

However, success came at a cost. Joseph Jackson was physically and emotionally abusive, beating and berating his sons when their performances did not meet his standards. Michael and his brothers spent most of their time rehearsing and touring, leaving little opportunity for typical childhood activities. Working in nightclubs exposed Michael to adult behaviors that most children rarely witness. These experiences had a profound impact on Michael, and in later years he would struggle to recreate the childhood that he had lost.

Fame. Michael and his brothers moved to California in 1969 in order to record at Motown's Hollywood studios. Their first single, the bouncy "I Want You Back," reached number 1 on the *Billboard* charts in January, 1970. The Jackson 5 quickly became one of the most popular groups in the United States. Their success stemmed in part from the upbeat, positive tone of their music, which provided a welcome contrast to the social turmoil (from the Vietnam War and the Civil Rights movement) Americans experienced during the early 1970's. In addition, the group held a special attraction for young African Americans, a group which record marketers had long ignored. However, it was Michael's youthful charm and his gifts as a performer that made the group popular with Americans of all races and ages. Recognizing Michael's potential, Berry Gordy, Jr., marketed him as a solo artist as well as a member of the Jackson 5. In 1971, he released his first solo single, "Got to Be There." It sold more than one million copies. His next single, "Rockin' Robin," reached number 2 on the charts, and in 1972 he had his first number 1 solo single, "Ben." Michael Jackson was a full-fledged teen idol, regularly featured in *16*, *Soul*, and *Right On!* magazines, which catered to teenage fans, and appearing on the cover of *Rolling Stone* magazine in 1971.

Despite his popularity, Michael's solo record sales and those of the Jackson 5 fell during the mid-1970's. The Jackson family blamed the declining sales on Motown, which they left for Epic Records, a subsidiary of CBS, in 1976. (With their departure from Motown they lost the rights to the name Jackson 5, so they billed themselves as the Jacksons.) Michael used the label change as a means to write his own songs and to develop artistically. He wrote "Different Kind of Lady," which appeared on the Jacksons album *Goin' Places* (1977). Although the song was never released as a single, it was a big hit in dance clubs, which bolstered his confidence in his songwriting abilities. The Jacksons' third Epic album, *Destiny* (1978), went platinum, partly on the strength of the single "Shake Your Body," which Michael cowrote with his younger brother Randy. That same year Jackson tried his hand at acting, playing the role of the Scarecrow in the motion picture *The Wiz*, a modern adaptation of *The Wizard of Oz*. The most expensive musical film to that date, *The Wiz* was a commercial and critical failure, but Jackson admired the film's musical director, Quincy Jones. Their professional relationship would change Jackson's career and make him a superstar.

Jones produced Jackson's first solo album with Epic, *Off the Wall* (1979). Heavily influenced by disco, *Off the Wall* sold more than five million copies in the United States, another two million abroad, and yielded four singles that each sold more than one million copies and reached the Top 10. Jackson wrote one of the singles, "Don't Stop 'Til You Get Enough." Another single, "Rock with You," received airplay on radio stations that usually ignored African American artists. However, Jackson was not satisfied with his achievements. He was especially disappointed that *Off the Wall* received only one Grammy Award (for Best R&B Vocal Performance). He set his sights on an incredible goal, that of creating the biggest-selling album in history.

For the Record

Few people in any field have enjoyed the kind of success that Michael Jackson had in 1983. That year he released *Thriller*, an album that ranked number 1 on *Billboard*'s album chart for a record-setting 37 weeks and eventually sold more than 40 million copies to become the best-selling album of all time. The same album contained seven songs that made it to the top-10 in the singles chart. When Jackson's "Billie Jean" hit number 1, he became the first artist to have both singles and albums topping the pop and black music charts at the same time. *Thriller* also topped the dance/disco chart, and both it and "Billie Jean" topped the charts in Great Britain.

Thriller. Jackson returned to the studio in August, 1982, again calling upon Quincy Jones to serve as producer. He also used Rod Temperton, a songwriter with whom he had worked on *Off the Wall*. Guest artists included rock guitarist Eddie Van Halen, former Beatle Paul McCartney, and horror-film star Vincent Price. Because the record company wanted to release the record before the Christmas retail season, Jackson had only three months to complete the project. To complicate matters, he was also hurrying to complete narration on *E.T. the Extra-Terrestrial*, a children's album based on the 1982 motion picture of the same name.

***Thriller* Success.** After weeks of arduous work, the first playback of the new material was so disappointing that Jackson broke down in tears. However, remixing solved the problems and the final product met his high standards. Originally called *Starlight,* the album *Thriller* was a mixture of heartfelt ballads such as "The Lady in My Life," dance songs such as "P.Y.T. (Pretty Young Thing)" and "Wanna Be Startin' Something," and the pop tune "The Girl Is Mine." Critics and fans agreed that "Beat It" and "Billie Jean," both written by Jackson, were the best songs on the album. The hard-rock tinged "Beat It" featured an Eddie Van Halen guitar solo. Jackson later explained that "Billie Jean," in which the singer denies that he is the father of the title character's child, was not based on a true story.

Its diversity of musical styles made *Thriller* accessible to a wide range of listeners, and the album, which was released in December, 1982, quickly shot up the charts, reaching number 1 and remaining there for a record thirty-seven weeks. Seven singles from the album reached the Top 10. When the single "Billie Jean," reached number 1, Jackson held the top spot on the pop single, pop album, rhythm-and-blues single, and rhythm-and-blues album charts, another unprecedented achievement. The album collected seven Grammy Awards and eventually sold nearly fifty million copies, securing a place in the *Guinness Book of Records* as the best-selling album of all time.

Jackson's success extended into the new medium of music videos. The first video channel, MTV, had been in operation for less than one year when *Thriller* was released. Critics noted that MTV's format largely excluded African American artists. The channel initially refused to air the "Billie Jean" video, but when CBS Records threatened to pull all of its artists from the station, MTV reluctantly agreed to put "Billie Jean" into heavy rotation. The video, which featured Jackson's remarkable dancing, furthered sales of the already popular *Thriller.* In addition, it brought a new level of professionalism to the fledging art of music videos. Two other videos from the album, "Beat It" and a fourteen-minute video based on the title track, aired on MTV. Both videos received popular and critical acclaim ("Thriller" would long stand as MTV's number one video).

Dancing Sensation. Jackson was now an international superstar, a status confirmed by his performance at an anniversary celebration for Motown held in March, 1983. Michael lip-synched "Billie Jean," (the only song performed that night which was not a Motown release). His dance included the moonwalk, in which the performer appears to be walking forward but actually glides backward. Although Jackson did not originate the move—street dancers called it the backward slide—he brought it to the attention of an estimated forty-seven million Americans who watched a television broadcast of the show which aired in May. Jackson's performance was stunning, receiving praise from dancer Fred Astaire, a longtime Jackson idol.

Jackson received recognition from his peers in the music industry at the 1983 Grammy Awards presentation in February, 1984. Although he had received second-degree burns on his head while filming a television commercial only weeks before, he appeared at the awards show in a uniform with epaulets and a sash, his trademark white glove on his right hand. The crowd roared in appreciation as Jackson received seven Grammy Awards and shared an eighth with Quincy Jones for Best Producer.

Decline. The spring of 1984 marked the pinnacle of Michael Jackson's success. He had the best-selling record of all time, numerous awards, and the adoration of millions of fans across the world. In May, he met President Ronald Reagan at a White House ceremony. However, professional and personal errors would soon begin to erode Jackson's popularity and raise doubts about his suitability as a hero to young children.

The first public relations misstep occurred in July, 1984, when the Jacksons announced that Michael and his brothers would undertake the "Victory" tour. Fans complained that the tickets were overpriced, prompting Michael to change the ticket policy. Although the "Victory" tour drew hundreds of thousands of fans and made millions of dollars, critics charged that the tour lacked feeling and soul. Given that Michael had only agreed to tour as a favor to his family, the uninspired performances were not really that surprising.

Personal Eccentricities. Yet Michael Jackson remained incredibly popular. In 1985, "We Are the World," which he cowrote with Lionel Richie to benefit famine victims in Africa, topped the charts. His 1987 album, *Bad*, sold more than twenty-five million copies, a great success by any standards but Jackson's own—he had hoped to top the sales of *Thriller.* However, speculation regarding Jackson's personal life, especially his sexual orientation, also gained attention. Many people were curious about his altered appearance. Jackson had obviously undergone plastic surgery, and he acknowledged two rhinoplasty operations ("nose jobs"), which he claimed were necessary after a dancing accident. However, some reporters claimed that he had had more surgery in an effort to look Caucasian. Jackson's skin also became noticeably lighter over the years, prompting critics to charge that he bleached his skin as a means of rejecting his African American heritage. Although he eventually claimed that he suffered from a skin disorder, many people did not accept the explanation.

His eccentric habits, which at first had seemed charming, also began to alienate the public. Jackson reportedly traveled everywhere with his pet chimpanzee; he was obsessed with the Elephant Man, a nineteenth-century English man who suffered from a disfiguring disease, whose remains Jackson wanted to purchase; he slept in an oxygen chamber so that he could live to be 150 years old. The British press took to calling him "Wacko Jacko." It was later revealed that Jackson and his public relations agents planted these stories to gain media attention, a ploy which backfired because some fans decided that their hero was simply too strange.

Despite the bad press, in 1991 Sony signed Jackson to a contract that was hailed as the first billion-dollar entertainer contract. The 1991 release *Dangerous* did not do as well as earlier albums but still sold millions. He remained a favorite performer with audiences, selling out concerts, singing at the inaugural ball for President Bill Clinton, and performing before a television audience estimated at 133 million people during the half-time show of the 1993 Super Bowl. During a live television interview with talk-show host Oprah Winfrey in February, 1993, which drew ninety million viewers, Jackson dismissed claims that he was bleaching his skin.

It appeared that Jackson's standing with the public was on the mend when allegations that Jackson had sexually molested a young boy became public in August, 1993. Jackson denied the accusations, but he settled the civil lawsuit out of court with a multimillion dollar payment, a decision which led many Americans to suspect that he was guilty of the charges. His 1994 marriage to Lisa Marie Presley, which later ended in divorce, prompted critics to charge that the marriage was a sham intended to deceive the public about Jackson's sexual habits. The 1996 announcement of his second marriage, this time to a woman carrying his child, was treated as yet another bizarre turn in the life of Michael Jackson. The child, who was born in February, 1997, was named Prince Michael Jackson.

His personal life mired in controversy, Jackson also began receiving negative reviews of his artistic endeavors. The 1995 album *HIStory: Past, Present and Future Book I*, a mix of hits and new songs, debuted at number 1 on the U.S. charts, but it did not sell as well as expected. Critics complained that the album revealed a paranoid mentality, and record reviews made frequent use of terms such as "weird" when discussing Jackson. They also pointed out that the song "They Don't Care About Us" contained lyrics that seemed anti-Semitic; Jackson denied that he had intended them that way. As the 1990's drew to a close, the public's fascination with Michael Jackson rested as much on his personal life as it did on his musical achievements. *—Thomas Clarkin*

select discography

■ albums

Got to Be There, 1971
Ben, 1972
Music and Me, 1973
The Best of Michael Jackson, 1975 (compilation)
Off the Wall, 1979
Thriller, 1982
Bad, 1987
Dangerous, 1991
HIStory: Past, Present and Future Book I, 1995

SELECT AWARDS

Grammy Award for Best R&B Vocal Performance, Male, for "Don't Stop 'Til You Get Enough," 1979

Grammy Awards for Record of the Year and Best Rock Vocal Performance, Male, for "Beat It"; for Album of the Year and Best Pop Vocal Performance, Male, for *Thriller*; for Best R&B Vocal Performance, Male, for "Billie Jean"; for Best Recording for Children for *E.T. the Extra-Terrestrial*; for Producer of the Year, Nonclassical (with Quincy Jones), all 1983

Grammy Award for Song of the Year for "We Are the World," 1985 (with Lionel Richie)

Grammy Legend Award, 1993

Soul Train Hall of Fame, inducted 1995

SEE ALSO: Brown, James; Jackson 5, The; Knight, Gladys, and the Pips; Richie, Lionel; Wilson, Jackie.

The Jackson 5

ORIGINAL MEMBERS: Sigmund "Jackie" Jackson (b. 1951), Toriano "Tito" Jackson II (b. 1953), Jermaine Jackson (b. 1954), Marlon Jackson (b. 1957), Michael Jackson (b. 1958)

FIRST SINGLE RELEASE: "Big Boy"/"You've Changed," 1968

MUSICAL STYLES: Pop, soul, disco, rhythm and blues

The Jackson 5 were an enormously popular family singing group in the 1970's. The five brothers were the last great act from Motown Records' famed hit factory as it moved operations from its base in Detroit, Michigan, to the glamour of Hollywood, California. Packaged as a wholesome, boys-next-door teen act, Jackson 5 gave testimony to Motown's credo of making danceable crossover music able to make the top of the pop charts.

Gary's Favorite Musical Family. Six Jackson brothers and three sisters were born and reared in industrial Gary, Indiana. Joe Jackson, their father, worked in a steel mill but was also a guitarist and a one-time member of a rhythm-and-blues group. He saw talent in the three older male children (Jackie, Tito, and Jermaine) and as early as 1963 had them performing. Soon he added younger brothers Marlon and Michael, making them the Jackson 5. A self-contained band with Tito on electric guitar, Jermaine on electric bass, and a couple of friends on drums and keyboards, they toured regionally and, in 1968, finally went as far as Harlem's premier showcase for African American performers, the Apollo Theatre. At that time they recorded their first song, "Big Boy," for a local Gary label, Steeltown. Their success, however, was in live performances, with Michael quickly learning all the moves and singing mannerisms of his heroes James Brown and Jackie Wilson. Touring the Midwest in a van, they began to open for star acts and soon became known as teenage sensations in an up-and-coming rhythm-and-blues or soul act.

The Sound of Young America. After watching the Jacksons' act, Motown Records owner Berry Gordy, Jr., signed them to a contract at the end of 1969, just as he was planning to move the center of Motown operations to California. Having grown up in the tough, grimy industrial city of Gary, the Jackson 5 found the clearer skies and sunshine of Los Angeles and Hollywood to be a new world. The family enjoyed the attention and excitement of having five of them about to take off in a career as superstars with the most successful black-owned record company in history.

A Detroit native, Berry Gordy had been a boxer, an autoworker, and a songwriter for Jackie Wilson before deciding to start his own record company in 1959. Motown soon became a great success with black recordings aimed to cross over to the more lucrative mainstream of white pop. Gordy's instincts reflected the push for civil rights and black pride of the 1960's. He set up headquarters in Detroit in a combination studio-office complex that came to be named Hitsville. He hired a largely black staff of songwriters, producers, and musicians who would handle everything.

For a decade, Motown artists reigned on the rhythm-and-blues charts and shared top hits on the pop charts with British rock acts such as the

The Jackson 5 in 1972 (Archive Photos)

Beatles. Performers such as Diana Ross and the Supremes, the Temptations, Smokey Robinson and the Miracles, Stevie Wonder, Mary Wells, and Marvin Gaye became national and international figures. Even the Beatles covered Motown songs. The label, along with Stax in Memphis, Tennessee, defined soul music for millions.

Many of Gordy's artists were just out of high school when they first recorded and had no experience on the stage as professionals. Gordy inaugurated his famous artist development department to groom them for upscale venues so that they could compete with the best of pop singers. He hired Cholly Atkins, an expert on African American popular dance, to help develop "vocal choreography." The Motown acts came to epitomize this integration of singing and dancing with words and rhythms flowing together to express meaning and feeling.

Superstars for the 1970's. The Jackson 5 came aboard at Motown with several years of professional experience under the demanding discipline of their father and Michael's own study of the vocal choreography of James Brown and Jackie Wilson. They needed less grooming, but they did need a strong commercial direction. They had been essentially a rhythm-and-blues act. Gordy wanted them to aim more at a both black and white teen market. He decided to have them specialize in up-tempo teen love songs with a heavy dance beat, especially with a prominent bass guitar underpinning. The formula worked wonders immediately with their first Motown release in the fall of 1969, "I Want You Back." It began a string of four number 1 rhythm-and-blues and pop hits in 1970, followed by "ABC," "The Love You Save," and "I'll Be There." In 1971 they scored a number 1 rhythm-and-blues hit (number 2, pop) with "Never Can Say Goodbye," and went to number 2 on both charts with "Mama's Pearl." Several other hits followed in the 1970's, most notably "Dancing Machine" in 1974, a number 1 rhythm-and-blues and number 2 pop hit. The Jackson 5 were favorites on national television shows and even had a cartoon series based on them.

Jackson 5 recordings are usually rhythmic pop dance songs about romance. With Michael alone dominating the vocal leads or in tandem with his older brother Jermaine, the records have a balance of voices and instruments, while the lyrics are shouted out and phrases repeated over and over. "I'll Be There" is one of the few balladic and serious pieces done in a more restrained manner. As a teenager, Michael's voice was high-pitched and without much heft, while Jermaine's was decidedly richer and more distinctly articulated. With their engaging vocal choreography and cute appeal, they had little competition as Motown's youth act of the era.

After the 1970's. At the same time that the group was amassing hits, both Michael and Jermaine started solo careers. As early as 1972, Michael had a number 1 pop hit with the gentle and touching "Ben." He soon became a superstar in his own right. When the Jackson 5 shifted to the Epic label in 1976, Jermaine stayed with Motown. Then called the Jacksons, the group enlisted brother Randy as a member and continued to have hits late in the decade and into the early 1980's. However, their time had passed as they grew into their twenties and thirties, having been essentially a teen-idol band for the 1970's. Yet they proved much of Berry Gordy's dream true. Black artists recording for a black-owned label could, with the right material and presentation, conquer the world. *—Frederick E. Danker*

SELECT DISCOGRAPHY

■ SINGLES

"I Want You Back," 1969
"ABC," 1970
"The Love You Save," 1970
"I'll Be There," 1970
"Never Can Say Goodbye," 1971
"Dancing Machine," 1974

■ ALBUMS

ABC, 1970
The Jacksons, 1976
Victory, 1984
The Jackson Five, Soulsation: 25th Anniversary Collection, 1995 (4-CD compilation)

SEE ALSO: Brown, James; Jackson, Janet; Jackson, Michael; Wilson, Jackie.

Etta James

(Jamesetta Hawkins)

BORN: Los Angeles, California; January 25, 1938
FIRST ALBUM RELEASE: *At Last*, 1961
MUSICAL STYLES: Blues, rhythm and blues, rock and roll, soul, pop

Etta James's long career has seen many ups and downs, in part because of her well-publicized drug habit, but more important, it has offered an impressive body of recordings in several styles. James, usually characterized as a blues singer, though she cannot be limited to any single category, has also recorded rhythm and blues, rock, jazz standards, and even a few country numbers. This highly versatile performer has received her greatest recognition since turning fifty.

The Beginnings. Jamesetta Hawkins was the illegitimate daughter of a fourteen-year-old mother unable to care for her. The child was turned over to the care of Dorothy Hawkins's landlady, Lula Rogers, and became, under the tutelage of James Earle Hines, a gospel prodigy, performing in the choir at the Saint Paul Baptist Church and on local radio in Los Angeles. After Rogers's death, mother and daughter moved to San Francisco in 1950, where Hawkins formed a singing group with two other girls. Bandleader Johnny Otis gave the trio an audition, and they recorded, as the Peaches (from Hawkins's nickname), "Roll with Me, Henry" for Modern Records in 1954 as an answer to "Work with Me, Annie," a hit for Hank Ballard and the Midnighters. Because of the suggestiveness of the title, the song was called "The Wallflower" by some radio stations. (Georgia Gibbs had a much bigger hit the following year with a sanitized version entitled "Dance with Me, Henry.") Although the Peaches broke up shortly thereafter, James, who had been given her new name by Otis, stayed with Modern for the remainder of the 1950's, recording such songs as "Good Rockin' Daddy," "Tough Lover," and "W-O-M-A-N." Some of these early recordings show signs of James's talent for phrasing, but the lyrics are generally too lightweight to elicit much emotion.

Chess Period. James moved to Chess Records' Argo subsidiary in 1960, recording duets with her boyfriend, Harvey Fuqua, lead singer for the Moonglows. Seeing her as a classy ballad singer with appeal beyond the rhythm-and-blues audience, Leonard Chess provided lush orchestra arrangements for such songs as "At Last," one of her biggest hits. James moved easily between such love songs in a style reminiscent of Billie Holiday and Dinah Washington, harder-edged material such as "Something's Got a Hold on Me," a raucous rocker that called upon the shouting style associated with her gospel roots, and more mainstream songs such as "Pushover," which resembled the bouncy girl-group songs of the early 1960's. Her breakup with Fuqua may have contributed to the increased melancholy tone of her songs.

In 1967, James recorded two of her signature tunes, "Tell Mama" and "I'd Rather Go Blind," at Rick Hall's legendary Fame Recording Studio in Muscle Shoals, Alabama, where Wilson Pickett and Aretha Franklin had done some of their best work. While "At Last" and "Tell Mama" are her best-known songs, some critics consider "I'd Rather Go Blind," a soulful blues ballad, the recording which best captures her distinctive style. James stayed at Chess until 1975, moving gradually into more rock-inflected material.

Rehabilitation. The middle period of James's career was hampered severely by her twenty-year addiction to heroin that began around 1963. This travail is recounted in detail in *Rage to Survive: The Etta James Story*, written with David Ritz and published in 1995. James recalls meeting Holiday, one of her idols, when they and Count Basie performed on a radio program in the late 1950's. The drug-ravaged Holiday, whose hands and feet were horribly swollen, warned her young colleague not to allow the same to happen to her. James, unfortunately, paid little attention to this advice, getting into relationships with men who beat her and serving jail time in the 1970's in New York, Illinois, and California for writing bad checks and forging prescriptions. A California judge sent her to a rehabilitation program at the Tarzana Psychiatric Hospital, where she spent seventeen months. One year later, she was using drugs again. After more rehabilitation at the Betty Ford Clinic and with the help of her husband Artis Mills and her sons, Donto and Sametto, she stopped abusing drugs.

Etta James (Archive Photos/Frank Driggs Collection)

During all this chaos, James still managed to record some good work. *Come a Little Closer* (1974), produced by Gabriel Meckler during her rehabilitation, features Randy Newman's "Let's Burn down the Cornfield," one of James's favorites because of its aggressive sexuality, and an interpretation of W. C. Handy's immortal "St. Louis Blues," which was nominated for a Grammy Award. *Deep in the Night* (1978), produced by the legendary Jerry Wexler and featuring Bonnie Raitt and Merry Clayton among its backup singers, includes a soulful version of the Eagles' "Take It to the Limit." (Like Ray Charles, another of her idols, James had a strong affinity for country-tinged music.) The album's highlight is "Only Women Bleed," which seems almost a catharsis.

Back on Track. After her recovery, James recorded several albums which mixed blues, rock, and soul styles. *The Right Time* (1992), another Wexler production with Steve Cropper, formerly of Booker T. and the MG's, includes stylish versions of Al Green's "Love and Happiness" and Pickett's "Ninety-Nine and a Half (Won't Do)" as well as a duet with Steve Winwood on Allen Toussaint's "Give It Up." The album is a showcase for the diverse styles, including gospel, in which James excels. *Rolling Stone* called it "a masterpiece."

James's greatest triumphs during the 1990's resulted from the biggest stylistic departure of her career. While she had recorded several pop standards over the years, she had never devoted an entire album to them until *Mystery Lady: Songs of Billie Holiday* (1994), produced by John Snyder, for which she earned a Grammy Award for Best Jazz Vocal Performance. (James credits blues singer Johnny "Guitar" Watson with showing her how to phrase the standards.) While her bluesy takes on such songs as George and Ira Gershwin's "Embraceable You" clash occasionally with the more conventional approaches of her instrumentalists, the album proves once again that James can conquer any singing style and give a distinctive twist to almost any song. She followed this triumph with *Time After Time* (1995), another collection of standards, notably the Gershwins' "Love Is Here to Stay" and Hoagy Carmichael's "The Nearness of You."

For the Record

"No matter how much respect I have for a tune, I still put my own hurtin' on it. I don't think straight, so why should I sing straight? All I can do is be honest."

—*Etta James*

§

While at Chess Records, Etta James occasionally sang backup on others' recordings, including Chuck Berry's "Almost Grown" and "Back in the USA."

Legacy. Diana Ross has called James her first inspiration, and the singer has been a favorite of such performers as Otis Redding, Mick Jagger, Janis Joplin, and Joan Osborne. Artists such as Joplin and Rod Stewart have recorded songs originated by James. She was also at the center of the creation of what can broadly be called rock and roll, having known Chuck Berry, Little Richard, Bo Diddley, B. B. King, Ike and Tina Turner, Sam Cooke, James Brown, Jackie Wilson, Marvin Gaye, Aretha Franklin, and the Rolling Stones, performing with many of them, staying at the peak of her talent longer than most. Her voice deepened and coarsened somewhat with age, making it even more suitable for wailing about life's disappointments. Throughout her career, James has been able to take familiar rock, blues, and pop songs and reinvent them, turning them, in the words of David Ritz, into "psychodramas of great depth and anguish." —*Michael Adams*

SELECT DISCOGRAPHY

■ ALBUMS

Rocks the House, 1963
Tell Mama, 1968
Come a Little Closer, 1974
Deep in the Night, 1978
The Right Time, 1992
How Strong Is a Woman: The Island Sessions, 1993 (compilation)
The Essential Etta James, 1994 (compilation)

Mystery Lady: Songs of Billie Holiday, 1994
These Foolish Things: The Classic Balladry of Etta James, 1995 (compilation)
Time After Time, 1995

SELECT AWARDS
Rock and Roll Hall of Fame, inducted 1993
Grammy Award for Best Jazz Vocal Performance for *Mystery Lady: Songs of Billie Holiday*, 1994

SEE ALSO: Charles, Ray; Franklin, Aretha; Joplin, Janis; Newman, Randy; Pickett, Wilson; Raitt, Bonnie; Redding, Otis; Turner, Ike and Tina / Tina Turner.

Rick James

(James Johnson)

BORN: Buffalo, New York; February 1, 1952
FIRST ALBUM RELEASE: *Come Get It*, 1978
MUSICAL STYLES: Rock and roll, rhythm and blues, funk

One of eight children raised by his mother Betty in Buffalo, New York, Rick James was sent to two juvenile homes for stealing cars while a teenager. After being expelled from Bennett High School in 1964, James enlisted in the U.S. Naval Reserves for one year. Soon after, however, he deserted his post without leave and eluded U.S. authorities by fleeing to Toronto, Canada.

While in Canada, he and Canadian singer-guitarist Neil Young formed the rock group the Mynah Birds. In 1965, this group moved to Detroit, Michigan, where they recorded demo tapes for Motown Records. After a tip from James's estranged manager, the Federal Bureau of Investigation (FBI) arrested James for desertion and returned him to New York. As a result, Motown Records dropped the band from its roster, which prompted Young to relocate to California to help form Buffalo Springfield.

Motown. James spent one year in jail, then traveled throughout England, India, and Sweden from 1966 through 1976. After returning to the United States, James formed the first Stone City Band in 1977 and sent demo tapes to Motown Records, who signed the group in that year. In 1978, James released *Come Get It*, which included his first hit, "You and I," and sold over one million copies. At that time, he told interviewers that his sound was influenced by funk performers such as Parliament and Bootsy Collins, as well as other black rock artists known for their ostentatious stage shows, notably Jimi Hendrix and James Brown. He claimed that he intended to supersede these acts with his own onstage performances. Becoming known for his trademark dreadlock hairstyle, he also began an ongoing addiction to cocaine.

His recording breakthrough came in 1981 with the release of *Street Songs*, which quickly went double platinum, won an Academy of Music Award, and was nominated for a Grammy. A series of singles from the album became hits, including "Come Give It to Me Baby," "Mary Jane," "Bustin' Out," and his biggest seller, "Super Freak." These songs established his reputation as a songwriter interested in the twin themes of sex and drugs.

James also began to build a reputation as a record producer. He wrote and produced comedian Eddie Murphy's first musical album and organized and produced the Mary Jane Girls, who had a hit with "In My House." He also produced albums for Teena Marie, the Temptations, Smokey Robinson, and Chaka Khan. From 1982 to 1984, James dated actress Linda Blair, for whom he composed the 1983 gold record "Cold Blooded." Other successes in this period included his own million-selling album *Throwin' Down* (1982) and the single "17" (1984). However, his drug dependency began to drain his talent, and he became isolated from friends and family. In 1986 the Stone City Band broke up. In 1990, James sued Hammer after the release of Hammer's hit song "U Can't Touch This," which contained material that had been blatantly appropriated from James's "Super Freak." James eventually received cowriting credit after the case was settled out of court.

Jail Time. In 1991, seventeen-year-old dancer Tanya Hijazi moved in with James to act as his caretaker. Later that year, the couple was arrested for drug trafficking and the assault, kidnapping, torture, and false imprisonment of Frances Alley. After the death of James's mother the following month, a second set of charges for the kidnapping, assault, and torture of music executive Mary Sauger in a Hollywood hotel room was added to his indictment. Convicted of most charges, James was sentenced to five years in prison. In 1994, Sauger was awarded two million dollars in a civil action that left James bankrupt.

After converting to Islam, James was released in August, 1996, married Hijazi, and established a home for his son Tazman and daughter Tyenza. In 1997, he reformed the Stone City Band and issued the critically favored *Urban Rhapsody*, which featured guest appearances by Snoop Doggy Dogg and Bobby Womack. The reformed Stone City Band conducted a sold-out twenty-five-city U.S. tour. Among the album's autobiographical songs, many written in prison and reflecting the influence of rap music, was "Mama's Eyes," a tribute to the singer's deceased mother. In 1998, James and his brother Carmine established a drug-outreach program in Buffalo. —*Wesley Britton*

SELECT DISCOGRAPHY

■ ALBUMS

Come Get It, 1978
Street Songs, 1981
Urban Rhapsody, 1997

SEE ALSO: Brown, James; Clinton, George / Parliament / Funkadelic; Hammer; Hendrix, Jimi; Khan, Chaka; Robinson, Smokey; Temptations, The; Young, Neil.

Jan and Dean

MEMBERS: William Jan Berry (b. 1941), Dean Ormsby Torrence (b. 1940)
FIRST SINGLE RELEASE: "Baby Talk," 1959
MUSICAL STYLES: Rock and roll, doo-wop

Jan and Dean are best known for their surf music recordings. They began their musical careers, however, as West Coast doo-wop artists. William Jan Berry and Dean Ormsby Torrence first met as football teammates at Emerson Junior High in Los Angeles, California, where they formed a band called the Barons. Their band later included future Beach Boy Bruce Johnston on piano and Sandy Nelson, whose song "Teen Beat" would rise to number 4 on the pop charts in 1959, on drums. In 1958, Jan, Dean, and Arnie Ginsburg used Jan's garage studio to record "Jenny Lee," a tribute to a local stripper. When Jan went to Western Recorders to have a disc made, he encountered Joe Lubin of Arwin Records, a label owned by Doris Day and her husband Marty Melcher. The label bought the rights to the song, which became a Top-10 hit. The recording was released as Jan and Arnie because Dean was serving a six-month tour of duty in the Army; Arnie quit the band to join the Navy when Dean returned.

Doo-Wop Years. In 1959, Jan and Dean met Herb Alpert and Lou Adler of Dore Records, who had recently had a hit with the Teddy Bear's "To Know Him Is to Love Him." Alpert and Adler produced Jan and Dean's first hit, "Baby Talk," which reached number 7 on the charts. Between July, 1959, and July, 1961, the duo released eight records on the Dore label, and, although they reached only the lower end of the charts, their careers gained enough momentum to attract a larger record label. In 1961, they recorded a doo-wop version of "Heart and Soul." Liberty Records was interested in Jan and Dean but did not like "Heart and Soul," so Adler arranged to have the song released on Gene Autrey's Challenge Records. "Heart and Soul" became their biggest hit in two years, reaching number 25 on the pop charts.

Surf Years. In 1961, Jan and Dean signed with Liberty Records and experienced some success with a doo-wop version of "Linda," a song written in 1947 by Jack Lawrence honoring George Eastman's daughter Linda, the future wife of Paul McCartney. Jan and Dean first encountered the Beach Boys in August, 1962, when the two bands performed together on a show several months after the Beach Boys' first hit, "Surfin'." The two bands became friendly and often worked together. In early 1963, Jan and Dean invited the Beach Boys to a recording session for an album called *Jan and Dean Take Linda Surfin'*, the duo's first venture into surf music. At the session, they recorded the Beach Boys' "Surfin'" and "Surfin' Safari" and asked Brian Wilson if he had any other surf songs they could record. Wilson gave them a song he was working on called "Two Girls for Every Boy," which, after rewriting, became "Surf City." Jan and Dean recorded "Surf City" with the Beach Boys singing background, and it became their first number 1 hit. Wilson and Jan continued working together on songwriting and developing the vocal overdubbing techniques Wilson used with the Beach Boys.

Jan and Dean followed this success with other surf songs such as "Honolulu Lulu," "Ride the Wild Surf," and "Sidewalk Surfin'," which celebrated the new sport of skateboarding that was designed to take the place of surfing for teens who could not get to the beach. Jan and Dean also added several car songs to their repertoire, such as "Drag City," "Dead Man's Curve," and "The Little Old Lady (from Pasadena)." "Dead Man's Curve" told the story of a drag-racing accident, and "The Little Old Lady (from Pasadena)" played upon a phrase made popular by *Tonight Show* host Johnny Carson in a skit about a used car salesman who described a vehicle as "used by a little old lady from Pasadena to drive to church on Sundays."

In 1964, Jan and Dean hosted the *TAMI Show*, one of the most famous rock-and-roll music films of the 1960's. The film included live performances by some of the most popular artists of the period, including Chuck Berry, James Brown, the Supremes, Smokey Robinson and the Miracles, Marvin Gaye, the Beach Boys, and the Rolling Stones.

The Music. "Surf City" was a simple song that was typical of the songs written for teenage record buyers. Just as Bill Haley consciously used teenage slang for his songs "Crazy Man, Crazy" and "See You Later Alligator," Wilson and Jan aimed their songs at the interests of California teens. Examining Jan and Dean's recorded output illustrates their conscious effort to write for that audience: "Gas Money" (Jan and Arnie, 1958), "Baby Talk" (1959), "White Tennis Sneakers" (1960), "Baggy Pants" (1961), "Surf City" (1963), "Drag City" (1963), and "Sidewalk Surfin'," (1964). Additionally, they modernized older songs that had instant audience recognition such as "Clementine" and "Heart and Soul."

Musically, their songs were based on forms and chord progressions popular in the 1950's coupled with the falsetto voice that was characteristic of doo-wop. "Surf City" was based on an adapted twelve-bar blues form: The chorus was standard twelve-bar blues, and the verse was twelve bars long (plus a one-bar drum fill) but used a different chord progression than the blues. The lyrics employed surf jargon, and their car songs used slang words and phrases associated with auto racing.

The Crash. The end of Jan and Dean came on April 12, 1966, when Jan, having just received his Army draft notice, hit a truck parked on Whittier Boulevard with his white Corvette Stingray, killing three passengers and leaving him in a coma. The eerie foreshadowing of "Dead Man's Curve" was not lost on their fans. Jan emerged from the coma with brain damage that affected his speech and motor skills.

Dean and Liberty Records tried to keep their name alive by releasing and repackaging older recordings. Later, Dean formed J&D Records to continue to work under the Jan and Dean name, but Jan refused to be a silent partner. Dean eventually formed Kittyhawk Graphics and designed album covers for the record industry, including the Turtles' *Golden Hits* album. In 1978, a television movie, *Dead Man's Curve*, sparked a renewed interest in their music, which led to successful appearances on the oldies circuit. —*G. W. Sandy Schaefer*

SELECT DISCOGRAPHY

■ SINGLES

"Baby Talk," 1959

"Heart and Soul," 1961

"Linda," 1963

"Surf City," 1963

"Honolulu Lulu," 1963

"Drag City," 1963

"Dead Man's Curve," 1964

"The Little Old Lady (from Pasadena)," 1964

"Ride the Wild Surf," 1964

"Sidewalk Surfin'," 1964

SEE ALSO: Beach Boys, The.

Jane's Addiction / Porno for Pyros

Jane's Addiction

ORIGINAL MEMBERS: Perry Farrell (b. Perry Bernstein, 1959), Dave Navarro (b. 1967), Steven Perkins (b. 1967), Eric Avery (b. 1965)

FIRST ALBUM RELEASE: *XXX* (also known as *Jane's Addiction*), 1987

Porno for Pyros

ORIGINAL MEMBERS: Perry Farrell, Steven Perkins, Martyn Le Noble (b. 1969), Peter DiStefano (b. 1965)

FIRST ALBUM RELEASE: *Porno for Pyros*, 1993

MUSICAL STYLES: Alternative, grunge, punk rock, rock and roll

Formed in 1986, Jane's Addiction developed into one of the most influential bands in the history of alternative rock. With gold and platinum sales of their first two major-label releases and a video that received heavy rotation on MTV, Jane's Addiction became the first act recognized as alternative to capture mainstream attention. With the formation of the Lollapalooza tour by frontman Perry Farrell, the eventual formation of Porno for Pyros by Farrell and drummer Steven Perkins, and the induction of Jane's Addiction guitarist Dave Navarro into the Red Hot Chili Peppers, Jane's Addiction permeated the popular music scene of the 1990's. Their success allowed groups such as Nirvana, Pearl Jam, Soundgarden, and the Smashing Pumpkins to bring the alternative-rock genre to the public's ears and hearts.

For the Record

According to the band's story, a prostitute named Jane liked the band so much when Perry Farrell was forming it that she helped finance it until it was making money. In gratitude for her help, the band's members named their group after her. Farrell himself is really named Simon Bernstein; his stage name is reportedly a pun on the word "peripheral."

In the Beginning. In the summer of 1986, Perry Farrell was the lead vocalist of the Los Angeles group Psi Com. Farrell was becoming disenchanted with his fellow bandmates and the direction of the group. It was at this time that Farrell met Eric Avery. After a couple of months and several different drummers and guitarists, Stephen Perkins, the then-boyfriend of Avery's sister, was allowed an audition. Upon his acceptance into the band, he recommended Dave Navarro, whom Perkins had played with in high school in the hard-rock band Disaster.

The End . . . Maybe. The rise and fall of Jane's Addiction was brief. In June, 1987, the quartet released their self-titled debut album on Triple X Records. The predominantly live album catapulted Jane's Addiction from one of L.A.'s most popular groups into the view of the record industry. Warner Bros. acted quickly, signing the band later that summer.

One year later, Jane's Addiction released their Warner Bros. debut, *Nothing's Shocking* (1988). The album garnered a Grammy Award nomination for Best Hard Rock/Metal Performance. The band then made their popular splash in August, 1990, with their third album, *Ritual de lo Habitual*. About three months later, *Ritual de lo Habitual* was certified gold, followed in June of 1991 with *Nothing's Shocking*'s gold certification.

The summer brought continued success for Jane's Addiction. The group headlined Farrell's first Lollapalooza tour. The multiact bill, which included Siouxsie and the Banshees, Living Colour, Nine Inch Nails, Ice-T, and the Henry Rollins Band, was the first attempt by concert promoters to assemble a primarily underground lineup to launch a major tour and to cross pop genres, such as rap, heavy metal, gothic, and industrial, all in one show. It was a rousing success, one which became the precursor to festivals such as HORDE and Lilith Fair.

But despite the success of Lollapalooza and the two Warner Bros. albums, the band's tenure together was coming to an end. Increasing prob-

Jane's Addiction (Paul Natkin)

lems with certain members' drug habits, as well as conflict concerning the band's management and onstage fights, led the group to dissolve on September 27, 1991, just three days after *Ritual de lo Habitual* was certified platinum.

Starting over Again. Jane's Addiction split into two factions upon their breakup. Farrell and Perkins joined Martyn Le Noble and Peter DiStefano to form Porno for Pyros. Avery and Navarro stayed together for one album after forming the band Deconstruction. Navarro then went on to join the Red Hot Chili Peppers to fill their revolving-door guitar slot. Farrell continued his sometimes relationship with Lollapalooza and formed another tour, "Enit," dedicated to lesser-known bands and dance-oriented music. He also released his feature film, *Gift*.

It was not long before some of Jane's Addiction's members began to gather again. In the summer of 1994, Dave Navarro and Red Hot Chili Peppers bassist Flea (who played horn on "Idiot's Rule" from *Nothing's Shocking*) joined Porno for Pyros in the studio on the track "Freeway," which appeared on the album *Good God's Urge* (1996). The group got together again in the studio in December of 1996, this time to record the track "Hard Charger" for the 1996 film *Private Parts*. The relapse came full circle in February of 1997. Navarro and Flea joined the members of Porno for Pyros once again, this time onstage at the *Private Parts* MTV premiere, to play "Hard Charger" and the Jane's Addiction tune "Mountain Song."

On July 14, 1997, Jane's Addiction officially announced they had "relapsed" and would once again tour together and release an album, the rarities/live music project *Kettle Whistle*. One member, Avery, refused the opportunity, preferring to work with his band, Polar Bear. Flea stepped in to play bass guitar, and a revamped Jane's Addiction started touring after an almost six-year lapse.

Sounds. Jane's Addiction and Porno for Pyros are part of a continuous line of musical evolution. With *XXX*, Jane's Addiction staked a claim to rock's past, working with acoustic arrangements and long-form jams reminiscent of bands such as Crosby, Stills, Nash, and Young and Creedence Clearwater Revival.

Jane's Addiction even went one step further on their major-label debut, *Nothing's Shocking*. The punk-rock sensibility of Farrell's lyrics, a grasp of the underside of Los Angeles culture (similar to the art-rock stylings of the Velvet Underground), and the epic Led Zeppelin-type rock anthems were rolled together to form the album that catapulted Jane's Addiction to the forefront of the alternative-rock movement. Their penchant for heavy-metal stylings, influenced by Guns n' Roses, and their third album, *Ritual de lo Habitual*, further proved the band's versatility and varied tastes.

From its inception, Porno for Pyros was a departure from the rock tradition. *Porno for Pyros* indicated more of a pop aesthetic, leaving behind the six-minute tracks from typical Jane's Addiction fare in favor of more radio-friendly four minute tracks. Lyrically, Porno for Pyros maintained an angry tone. Most of the tracks from their debut album were written during and in the wake of the 1992 Los Angeles riots after the Rodney King trial. The songs represent Farrell's, and L.A.'s, turmoil during a chaotic time.

Good God's Urge, Porno for Pyros' second album, was a complete turnaround. This album was influenced by Farrell's interest in techno (heavily electronic) music, as well as time he spent in seclusion surfing near small islands around the world. Tribal drumming, sampling, and an acoustic-electric mix constitute an album that may have been released a year or two ahead of its time.

Kettle Whistle, the live/rarities album released at the beginning of Jane's Addictions' regrouping, is a combination of all styles used by the band. Acoustic, rock, punk, alternative, electronic, and industrial, *Kettle Whistle* is a glimpse of all that is Jane's Addiction. —*Benji L. Kreider*

SELECT DISCOGRAPHY

■ ALBUMS

Jane's Addiction

XXX (also known as *Jane's Addiction*), 1987

Nothing's Shocking, 1988

Ritual de lo Habitual, 1990

Porno for Pyros

Porno for Pyros, 1993

Good God's Urge, 1996

SELECT AWARDS

MTV Video Award for Best Alternative Video for "Been Caught Stealing," 1991

SEE ALSO: Red Hot Chili Peppers, The.

Jazzy Jeff and the Fresh Prince. *See* DJ Jazzy Jeff and the Fresh Prince

Jefferson Airplane / Jefferson Starship

Jefferson Airplane

ORIGINAL MEMBERS: Marty Balin (b. 1942), Signe Anderson (b. 1941), Paul Kantner (b. 1941), Jorma Kaukonen (b. 1940), Jack Casady (b. 1944), Alex "Skip" Spence (b. 1946)

BEST-KNOWN LINEUP: Balin, Grace Slick (b. 1939), Kantner, Kaukonen, Casady, Spencer Dryden (b. 1938)

OTHER MEMBERS: Papa John Creach (1917-1994), Joey Covington, others

FIRST ALBUM RELEASE: *Jefferson Airplane Takes Off*, 1966

MUSICAL STYLES: Psychedelic rock, rock and roll, folk rock

Jefferson Starship

ORIGINAL MEMBERS: Kantner, Slick, Creach, John Barbata (b. 1945), David Freiberg (b. 1938), Peter Kangaroo (b. Peter Kaukonen), Craig Chaquico (b. 1954)

OTHER MEMBERS: Mickey Thomas (b. 1950), Pete Sears (b. 1948), Aynsley Dunbar (b. 1946), others

FIRST ALBUM RELEASE: *Dragon Fly*, 1974

MUSICAL STYLES: Rock and roll, pop

Marty Balin formed the Jefferson Airplane in 1965 to provide a band for a nightclub he had recently opened. The band went on to become one of the premier groups in late 1960's rock and roll. The Airplane epitomized Haight-Ashbury and the San Francisco hippie scene and became international stars. When they disbanded in 1974, Jorma Kaukonen and Jack Casady went on to form Hot Tuna, and Paul Kantner, Marty Balin, and Grace Slick combined forces in Jefferson Starship.

The Beginnings. In the mid-1960's San Francisco was home to the last vestiges of Beatnik culture and a few popular folk bands. Marty Balin, an aspiring singer, bought an abandoned club, which he renamed the Matrix, and began searching for musicians around whom to build a house band. He met Paul Kantner, a folk guitarist and banjo player, in 1965. Kantner brought a friend of his from college, blues guitarist Jorma Kaukonen. Balin heard Signe Anderson singing folk music in a club and persuaded her to join the group.

Neither the original drummer nor bassist proved satisfactory. The drummer was replaced by Skip Spence, a Canadian guitarist whom Balin recruited largely for his appearance; the new bassist was Jack Casady, a bass player Kaukonen had known since childhood. The band's name was an abbreviated version of "Blind Thomas Jefferson Airplane," a nickname Kaukonen had acquired. They became instantly popular in San Francisco and began playing gigs for entrepreneur Bill Graham, including shows at his burgeoning Fillmore Auditorium.

Initial Recording. The band drew the approving attention of the local press, secured a major recording contract, and released their first album in early 1966. It was an uptempo folk-rock sampling of Balin's songwriting. When the original pressings sold far beyond expectation, RCA released a slightly altered version of the album (deleting "Runnin' Round This World" for using the word "trips," which was deemed a drug reference). The selections were ballads and love songs, and the sound was smooth and accomplished but hardly revolutionary.

Spence, never comfortable in his role as drummer, left to start Moby Grape, another influential San Francisco band, and was replaced by Spencer Dryden, a jazz drummer from Los Angeles. In the fall of 1966 Signe Anderson reluctantly retired in order to raise a newborn child. She was replaced by Grace Slick, a singer in another San Francisco band, the Great Society. Thus began the lineup that produced the band's most successful recordings.

Somebody to Love. Slick brought an infusion of talent, sass, and energy to the band, but the most immediate effect of her joining were two songs that she brought with her—they became the group's first big hits. "White Rabbit" interwove images from *Alice's Adventures in Wonderland* and psychedelic drug references, and "Somebody to Love" was a roaring song about the need for love that the Jefferson Airplane played throughout their career. The album on which the songs appeared, *Surrealistic Pillow* (1967), also featured strong numbers by Marty Balin—"Plastic Fantastic Lover" and "3/5 of a Mile in 10 Seconds"—and a haunting acoustic guitar piece by Jorma Kaukonen, "Embryonic Journey," which he had been playing since his days as a solo guitarist. During this time the Airplane fired their manager and hired Bill Graham in that capacity and were playing concerts constantly, one of the most important of which was an appearance at the 1967 Monterey Pop Festival. (Two of their numbers are featured in the D. A. Pennebaker film of the festival.)

After Bathing at Baxter's (1967) was the first album to give some idea of the band's concert sound, and it took an unprecedented seven months to complete. Songs often blend from one into another, and all members of the band, including Dryden, are given songwriting credits. Balin, however, the dominant composer and singer on the first two records, was relegated to the slimmest of supporting roles. In many ways, the album was both a harbinger of music to come and a reflection of the character of the band. In place of the uniform sound of the first album, this was a collection of separate songs that reflected different sensibilities—Balin continued with love songs, Kantner contributed a solid group of folk-rock songs, Slick continued to explore literature (writing about James Joyce's *Ulysses* in "rejoyce"), and Kaukonen and Casady gave a preview of Hot Tuna in the loose jamming on "Spare Chaynge."

Crown of Creation (1968) was a bridge between the smooth professionalism of *Surrealistic Pillow* and the loose experimentation of *After Bathing at Baxter's*. Slick continued writing elusive, provocative songs such as "Lather," an ironic tune for Dryden's thirtieth birthday, and "Greasy Heart." She sang "Triad," a David Crosby song that had been rejected by the Byrds because of its controversial subject matter. During this time the band's new manager, Bill Thompson, an old friend of Balin's, convinced them to buy a Victorian mansion across the street from Golden Gate Park that became both a home and the base of the band's operations.

Jefferson Airplane, late 1967: Marty Balin (top left), Spencer Dryden, Jorma Kaukonen, Grace Slick, Paul Kantner, Jack Casady (AP/Wide World Photos)

Flying High. In the next year a dynamic collection of live material, *Bless Its Pointed Little Head,* featured some of their best songs as well as a sampling of blues standards, a Donovan song, and some extended jams. That summer the band toured extensively and made a prominent appearance at the Woodstock festival in August. Late in 1969 *Volunteers* was released, arguably their best studio effort.

Volunteers was challenging in many respects. It challenged the patience of the band's record company, RCA, with its use of profanity. It challenged the political and cultural establishment with its theme of revolution, and producing it had challenged the fragmenting allegiance of the band members themselves. The band's version of "Wooden Ships" (which Crosby, Stills, and Nash had recorded previously) is a standout cut. The title song, which emerged from Balin's spotting a "Volunteers of America" logo on a truck, became a revolutionary anthem (drawing ire from the actual Volunteers of America organization) and a mainstay of their stage shows. After the album's successful rise up the charts, Dryden retired, later to appear with New Riders of the Purple Sage and the Dinosaurs. The year ended with the Jefferson Airplane's appearance at the disastrous Altamont Festival in California, at which Balin was knocked unconscious by a Hell's Angel when he attempted to intervene on behalf of a fan being beaten by the motorcyclists.

Starship and Beyond. In 1971 Balin left and a middle-aged jazz violinist, Papa John Creach, joined the band. The next two albums—*Bark* (1971) and *Long John Silver* (1972)—although they had a few memorable songs, were largely hollow efforts. Highlights from the Jefferson Airplane's last tour with this lineup appeared on *Thirty Seconds over Winterland* (1973). After that record they disbanded, with Kaukonen and Casady heading off to Hot Tuna, and Kantner, Slick, David Freiberg (formerly of another Bay Area band, Quicksilver Messenger Service) collaborating on some solo efforts and then continuing as Jefferson Starship. That band's first album, *Dragon Fly* (1974), featured a guest appearance by Marty Balin on "Caroline," a soaring, impassioned love song. The tune was such a success that Balin officially joined for the next album and contributed "Miracles," the band's most commercially successful song. The Starship toured extensively and produced a series of popular albums in the 1970's.

Eventually, though, the same problems that plagued the Jefferson Airplane undid the Jefferson Starship. Egos, competition, and success led to short tempers and frayed nerves. Excessive use of mind-altering chemicals did not help matters. Balin left, then Slick. Slick returned, and next Kantner called it quits. Kantner created some hard feelings by suing former band members for rights to the group's name and then went off to play solo. The band continued without Kantner, now calling itself Starship. With singer Mickey Thomas (who had joined in 1979) and original guitarist Craig Chaquico, the Starship had major commercial successes in the 1980's. The 1985 album *Knee Deep in the Hoopla* contained two number 1 hits, "Sara" and "We Built This City." (By now the music—slickly produced commercial pop rock—had nothing in common with the music of the original Jefferson Airplane or earliest Jefferson Starship releases.)

The discographies of Jefferson Airplane, Jefferson Starship, and all the solo and combination albums produced by various band members since 1970 are complicated. The first Hot Tuna album, for example, was a bluesy acoustic album recorded and released as a Kaukonen-Casady side project in 1970. Subsequently they added a drummer and violinist Creach. Hot Tuna recorded and toured until disbanding in 1978, then reformed in 1986. The first album to bear the name Jefferson Starship was actually a 1970 Kantner solo album, *Blows Against the Empire.* Many of the musicians involved with the Airplane or Starship have put out at least one solo album, sometimes with other members guesting. The personnel of the Jefferson Starship and Starship bands changed a number of times, with the revolving door of Slick and Balin departures and arrivals being only the most visible example.

Balin had a somewhat successful solo career, his song "Hearts" reaching number 8 in 1981, and wrote a rock opera. Kantner, Balin, and Casady formed the KBC Band and cut one record in 1986. In 1988 all the original Jefferson Airplane members except Dryden reformed to record *Jefferson Airplane* and toured briefly. In the early 1990's Kantner, Casady, and other musicians carried on as the Jefferson Starship, calling it "the next generation." Balin joined, and Creach was briefly involved. Eventually Slick signed on long enough to appear on the album *Deep Space/Virgin Sky* (1995).

—David W. Madden

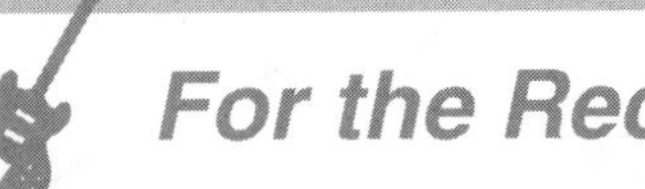

For the Record

In 1967, after recording their second album, the Jefferson Airplane were featured in a series of surreal radio commercials for Levi's jeans.

§

Despite their popularity and various gold records, the Jefferson Airplane never charted either a number 1 single or album. It was the later versions of the band that would: Jefferson Starship with *Red Octopus,* and *Spitfire* and the Starship with "We Built This City" and "Nothing's Gonna Stop Us Now."

SELECT DISCOGRAPHY

Jefferson Airplane

■ ALBUMS

Takes Off, 1966

Surrealistic Pillow, 1967

After Bathing at Baxter's, 1967
Crown of Creation, 1968
Bless Its Pointed Little Head, 1969
Volunteers, 1969
Bark, 1971
Long John Silver, 1972
Thirty Seconds over Winterland, 1973
Early Flight, 1974

Jefferson Starship

■ ALBUMS

Dragon Fly, 1974
Red Octopus, 1975
Spitfire, 1976
Earth, 1978
Freedom at Point Zero, 1979
Modern Times, 1981
Winds of Change, 1982

Starship

■ ALBUMS

Knee Deep in the Hoopla, 1985
No Protection, 1987

SELECT AWARDS

Rock and Roll Hall of Fame, Jefferson Airplane inducted 1996

SEE ALSO: Byrds, The; Crosby, Stills, Nash, and Young; Donovan; Grateful Dead, The.

Waylon Jennings

BORN: Littlefield, Texas; June 15, 1937
FIRST SINGLE RELEASE: "Jolé Blon," 1958
MUSICAL STYLES: Country, country rock, progressive country

From the time Waylon Jennings's mother taught him his first guitar chords in Littlefield, Texas, at eight years old, until his most recent album, country music has been ingrained in the very fiber of his being. Holding fast to his belief that music should have no barriers, Jennings was a pioneer in the pivotal developments in country music. Because of his uncompromising commitment to his musical principles, he was labeled an outlaw. After four decades of influencing instrumental and vocal styles and unifying the various social classes through music, he is one of the industry's true legends.

Early Influences. Waylon Jennings began laying ground for his musical career when he took a job as a deejay at his hometown radio station at age twelve. By the time he was seventeen, he had moved to Lubbock, Texas, where he eventually met Buddy Holly, who proved to be a positive influence on Jennings and taught him various guitar rhythm patterns. Holly financed and produced Jennings's first single record, "Jolé Blon," a cover of Harry Choates's Cajun classic. Impressed by Jennings's musical abilities, Holly invited him to join with him and his band the Crickets on what would turn out to be Holly's final tour. In 1959, when the group headed for an engagement—some by private plane and some by bus—Jennings gave up his seat on the plane to J. P. Richardson (the Big Bopper), who was suffering from a cold. The plane crashed near Fargo, North Dakota, killing all aboard, including Holly and Ritchie Valens. Devastated by Holly's death, Jennings headed back to Lubbock and eventually moved to Phoenix, Arizona, where he started his own band, the Waylors.

Talents Recognized. Recording artist Bobby Bare saw Jennings's performance at J. D.'s, one of the largest nightclubs in Phoenix, and immediately advised Chet Atkins of RCA Records of Jennings's unique vocal sound and style. Atkins agreed with Bare's opinion and signed Jennings to an RCA recording contract in 1965.

As his career began to unfold, Jennings moved to Nashville, Tennessee, in 1966, where he became roommates with Johnny Cash, with whom he developed a lasting friendship. His first Nashville single, "That's the Chance I'll Have to Take" (1965), entered the Top 50. His potential for stardom was evident when, from 1966 to 1968, he scored hits such as "Anita, You're Dreaming" (1966), "The Chokin' Kind"/"Love of the Common People" (1967), and "Only Daddy That'll Walk the Line" (1968). In 1969 he earned a Grammy Award for Best Country Performance by a Duo or Group for his recording of "MacArthur Park" with the Kimberleys. In 1970, his single "The Taker," written by Kris Kristofferson, was a Top-5 hit.

Struggle for Individuality. By the 1970's Jennings was becoming disillusioned with the Nashville establishment. He did not want to be stamped with ideas and styles imposed by bureaucratic producers. He wanted more control over production and, subsequently, the control over his own destiny. On the verge of quitting the business, he met Neil Reshen, who was instrumental in advising both Jennings and Willie Nelson. In 1971 Jennings had a Top-15 hit with "Mississippi Woman," and by 1972 he took over his own production duties and could express his artistic freedom by writing and performing as he wished, without bending to the Nashville bureaucracy. He had three Top-10 singles, "Good Hearted Woman," "Sweet Dream Woman," and "Pretend I Never Happened," and he and Nelson began collaborating on music projects. The solo single "You Can Have Her" proved to be a Top-10 hit in 1973. By 1974 his popularity was soaring, and he was producing back-to-back number 1 hits: "This Time" and "I'm a Ramblin' Man," which crossed over to the pop chart's Top 75.

Waylon Jennings (Lissa Wales)

Award-Winning Years. Continued success followed him in 1975. His duet with Nelson, "Good Hearted Woman," became a number 1 hit single and a Top-25 pop hit, as well as earning the Country Music Association (CMA) Single of the Year Award. It was another banner year when his landmark album of 1976, *Wanted: The Outlaws,* was the CMA Album of the Year and the first country album to achieve multi-platinum status. In addition, Jennings and Nelson earned the CMA Duo of the Year Award. Because of his success and recognition, only his first name was necessary on his records. Two of his singles, "Luckenbach, Texas" and "The Wurlitzer Prize," reached number 1 on the charts in 1977. His album *Ol' Waylon* (1977) was the first country album by a solo artist to go platinum, and *Billboard* magazine named him Country Artist of the Year for 1977. Consistent success was apparent when "Mamas Don't Let Your Babies Grow Up to Be Cowboys," his 1978 duet with Nelson, reached number 1 on the country charts and the Top 10 on the pop charts. The song also earned them a Grammy Award for Best Country Performance by a Duo or a Group. Other hits in 1978 were "There Ain't No Good Chain Gang" with Johnny Cash, "I've Always Been Crazy," and "Don't You Think This Outlaw Bit's Done Got Out of Hand." Not only did Jennings make records; he became successful at breaking records. His 1979 album, *Greatest Hits,* was the first country-and-western album to go quadruple-platinum, and it included the number 1 hit "Amanda." The "Theme from the *Dukes of Hazzard* (Good Ol' Boys)," which Jennings wrote for the television comedy series, was a hit single in 1980. The complementary voices of Jennings and Nelson took "Just to Satisfy You" to number 1 in 1982. Considered one of the finest among fine albums, *Waylon & Company* produced the number 1 solo single "Lucille" in 1983. The single "I May Be Used" made the Top 5 in 1984. In 1985, Jennings, Nelson, Cash, and Kris Kristofferson teamed up to record *Highwayman,* whose title track became a number 1 hit. This foursome of innovative superstar performers went on to record other hit albums together. After signing with a new record label, MCA, Jennings recorded three solo hits in 1986. The autobiographical album *A Man Called Hoss* (1987) was his assurance that his life story would be reflected in truth. Though triple-bypass heart surgery in 1988 slowed Jennings down, he surged back, continuing to produce hit songs.

In 1990, the single "Wrong," from his Top-10 album *The Eagle,* made the Top 5. His children's album, *Cowboys, Sisters, Rascals & Dirt,* was released in 1993 on the Ode 2 Kids label. In Jennings's 1996 album, *Right for the Time,* his deep, powerful, yet mellow voice embraces the words from the cut "The Most Sensible Thing": "I've taken chances . . . against all the odds." This determination has enabled him to succeed on his own terms and has earned him the respect he richly deserves.

—Elizabeth B. Graham

SELECT DISCOGRAPHY

■ SINGLES

"That's the Chance I'll Have to Take," 1965
"MacArthur Park," 1969 (with the Kimberleys)
"This Time," 1974
"I'm a Ramblin' Man," 1974
"Just to Satisfy You," 1982 (with Willie Nelson)

■ ALBUMS

Waylon Jennings Sings Ol' Harlan, 1967
Waylon Jennings, 1969
Wanted: The Outlaws, 1976 (with Willie Nelson, Tompall Glaser, and Jessi Colter)
Ol' Waylon, 1977
Waylon and Willie, 1978 (with Willie Nelson)
Greatest Hits, 1979 (compilation)
What Goes Around Comes Around, 1979
Leather and Lace, 1981 (with Jessi Colter)
Highwayman, 1985 (with Willie Nelson, Johnny Cash, and Kris Kristofferson)
A Man Called Hoss, 1987
The Eagle, 1989
Too Dumb for New York City, Too Ugly for L.A., 1992
Cowboys, Sisters, Rascals & Dirt, 1993
Right for the Time, 1996

SELECT AWARDS

Grammy Award for Best Country Vocal Performance by a Duo or Group for "MacArthur Park," 1969 (with the Kimberleys)
Country Music Association Male Vocalist of the Year Award, 1975
Country Music Association Album of the Year Award for *Wanted: The Outlaws* (with Willie Nelson, Tompall Glaser, and Jessi Colter), Single of the Year Award for "Good Hearted Woman" (with Willie Nelson), and Vocal Duo of the Year Award (with Willie Nelson), 1976
Grammy Award for Best Country Vocal Performance by a Duo or Group for "Mamas Don't Let Your Babies Grow Up to Be Cowboys," 1978 (with Willie Nelson)
Nashville Songwriters Hall of Fame, inducted 1995

SEE ALSO: Atkins, Chet; Cash, Johnny; Holly, Buddy / The Crickets; Kristofferson, Kris; Nelson, Willie; Valens, Ritchie.

For the Record

In 1991, Waylon Jennings's single "The Eagle" was adopted as the unofficial anthem for the troops of Operation Desert Storm in the Persian Gulf.

Jethro Tull

ORIGINAL MEMBERS: Ian Anderson (b. 1947), Mick Abrahams (b. 1943), Glenn Cornick (b. 1947), Clive Bunker (b. 1946)

OTHER MEMBERS: Martin Barre (b. 1946), Jeffrey Hammond-Hammond (b. 1946), John Evan (b. 1948), Barriemore Barlow (b. 1949), John Glascock (1953-1979), Dave Pegg (b. 1947), others

FIRST ALBUM RELEASE: *This Was*, 1968
MUSICAL STYLES: Rock and roll, progressive rock, folk rock, blues

Formed in 1967 in Blackpool, England, Jethro Tull took their name from the eighteenth century English agriculturalist who revolutionized farming with his invention of a mechanical seed drill. Although Jethro Tull started out as more of a blues band than anything else, the band evolved into a progressive rock outfit that incorporated elements of classical, jazz, and English folk music into their repertoire. An eccentric band, Jethro Tull were led by the charismatic front man Ian Anderson. With Anderson at the helm as both singer and songwriter, Jethro Tull—surprisingly—became extremely popular during the 1970's. Anderson wrote eclectic songs and played the flute. Before Jethro Tull, no rock band had employed the flute as one of their principal instruments. The band's musical experimentation and parable-like songs reached their zenith in 1971 with the release of the album *Aqualung*. Constantly reinventing themselves, Jethro Tull remained active for more than thirty years.

The Beginnings. Born in Scotland, Ian Anderson moved with his family to the northwestern English town of Blackpool when he was twelve. In 1963, Anderson formed a blues band called the Blades with Jeffrey Hammond-Hammond and John Evan. The band toured the north of England. By 1965, the band was playing a combination of jazz, blues, and soul music, and had changed their name to the John Evan Band and then to John Evan's Smash. In 1967, Hammond-Hammond left the band and was replaced by Glenn Cornick. The band moved to London in order to be a part of the blues revival that was taking place. Before John Evan's Smash could get a foothold in London, the band broke up. In late 1967, Anderson and Cornick joined forces with blues guitarist Mick Abrahams and drummer Clive Bunker. The new band performed under various names, including Bag of Blues, Navy Blue, and Jethro Tull. They received their most enthusiastic audience response while playing as Jethro Tull, so it became their permanent name.

Jethro Tull leader Ian Anderson (Paul Natkin)

During the summer of 1968, Island Records offered Jethro Tull a recording contract after the band had received glowing notices for their performance at the Sunbury Jazz and Blues Festival. The band's debut album, *This Was*, reached number 10 on the British pop charts by the end of 1968. While *This Was* was primarily a blues-flavored album, there was friction building between Anderson and Abrahams over the direction of the band. The conflict came to a head, and Abrahams left the band to form Blodwyn Pig prior to Jethro Tull's first tour of the United States. Martin Barre was brought in to take Abrahams's place.

The 1969 U.S. tour was a success and helped promote Jethro Tull's second album, *Stand Up* (1969). In addition to being a bold performer, Anderson proved to be a strong songwriter, and the group's distinctive sound was born with this album. Although Anderson wrote some classic irreverent songs for the album, it was his flute arrangement of Johann Sebastian Bach's

"Bouree" that became instantly popular with audiences. The self-taught Anderson had created a unique style of flute playing that took inspiration from the legendary jazz musician Rahsaan Roland Kirk. Wearing a ragged coat, Anderson employed an almost histrionic approach to playing the flute. At times standing on one leg, he would sing into or "flutter-tongue" the flute. Anderson had learned these techniques from Kirk.

Stand Up went to number 1 on the British pop charts and number 20 on the U.S. pop charts. With the success of Jethro Tull's second album, the group was gaining international recognition. In 1969, the group signed a new recording contract with Chrysalis Records. During the spring of 1970, Jethro Tull released their third album, *Benefit*, which did very well in England and the United States. John Evan joined the group later that year, but Cornick left to form the band Wild Turkey. He was replaced by Hammond-Hammond.

***Aqualung* and Other Concept Albums.** In 1971, Jethro Tull released what many consider to be their most important album, *Aqualung*. The album reached number 4 on the British pop charts and number 7 on the U.S. pop charts. The songs that Anderson wrote for *Aqualung* were biting and provocative, and "Aqualung," "Locomotive Breath," "Cross-Eyed Mary," and "Hymn 43" were played repeatedly on the radio. This powerful concept album sold more than four million copies worldwide.

Barriemore Barlow joined Jethro Tull after Bunker left to get married. The band's next record, *Thick as a Brick* (1972), was also a concept album. Anderson wrote a forty-five-minute extended song for *Thick as a Brick* that spoke of a boy's maturation. While some critics thought that the album was self-indulgent and contained obscure references, the record went to number 1 on the U.S. pop charts. In 1973, Jethro Tull released an even more complicated concept album, *A Passion Play*. It was almost universally criticized for being overblown and pretentious but still went to number 1 on the U.S. pop charts. Although Jethro Tull had gone out of favor with the critics, the group continued to remain popular with their fans throughout the rest of the 1970's.

The 1980's and Beyond. During the late 1970's, Jethro Tull released the intriguing folk-rock albums *Songs from the Wood* (1977) and *Heavy Horses* (1978). Unfortunately, the band seemed to have lost their bearings by the early 1980's, releasing albums that had little life or purpose to them. Suffering from a throat infection, Anderson was forced to stop performing until 1987, when Jethro Tull released *Crest of a Knave*. The album, which contained such strong songs as "Steel Monkey" and "Raising Steam," signaled a return to form and earned the band a Grammy Award for Best Hard Rock/Metal Performance for 1988. Although Grammy Award officials were criticized for placing Jethro Tull in the Best Hard Rock/Metal category, it still could not diminish the quality of *Crest of a Knave*. While Jethro Tull continued to record and tour into the late 1990's, both Anderson and Barre also involved themselves with solo projects. When not working on Jethro Tull or solo projects, Anderson turned his attentions to the salmon-farming business that he had begun in the 1970's. —*Jeffry Jensen*

SELECT DISCOGRAPHY

■ ALBUMS

This Was, 1968
Stand Up, 1969
Benefit, 1970

For the Record

Ian Anderson's wife, Jennie, mentioned to him that she had come across a street person whose breathing sounds reminded her of the aqualung that was used in the television show *Sea Hunt*. Anderson used "aqualung" as the name of the street person he created for the album *Aqualung*. The American Aqualung Company threatened to sue in order to stop Jethro Tull's unauthorized use of the name, but the company never carried through with a legal challenge.

Aqualung, 1971
Thick as a Brick, 1972
Living in the Past, 1972 (previously released material)
A Passion Play, 1973
Minstrel in the Gallery, 1975
Songs from the Wood, 1977
Heavy Horses, 1978
A, 1980
Crest of a Knave, 1987
Catfish Rising, 1991
Roots to Branches, 1995

SELECT AWARDS
Grammy Award for Best Hard Rock/Metal Performance, Vocal or Instrumental, for *Crest of a Knave*, 1988

SEE ALSO: Cream; Deep Purple; Genesis; King Crimson; Kirk, Rahsaan Roland; Pink Floyd; Procol Harum; Supertramp; Thompson, Richard; Traffic; Yes.

Joan Jett. *See* The Runaways

Jewel

BORN: Payson, Utah; May 23, 1974
FIRST ALBUM RELEASE: *Pieces of You*, 1995
MUSICAL STYLE: Folk rock

Born in Utah, Jewel Kilcher was raised in a log cabin without electricity or running water on an 800-acre homestead just outside Homer, Alaska. Her father, Atz, was the son of a Swiss immigrant. He made his money singing folk songs in local bars and music halls. Her mother, Nedra, also sang and sold handmade crafts. The two were, for a time, a popular folk duo in Alaska.

Beginning at the age of five, Jewel performed in shows with her parents, doing numbers for tourists in nearby Eskimo villages. When she was eight, her parents divorced. Her mother moved to Anchorage, but Jewel remained with her father, often accompanying him to bars where she sometimes helped him sing his songs. She began observing the people in the audience and putting her thoughts down on paper. When Jewel was twelve (some reports say fourteen), she convinced her parents to let her see more of the world by spending some time with an aunt in Hawaii. She soon decided that she did not care for the tropical life, however, so she returned to Alaska to stay with her mother in Anchorage for a while.

She received a scholarship for her junior and senior years of high school at the prestigious Interlochen Fine Arts Institute in Michigan. She hoped she would learn to sing the blues there, but she was required to study opera instead. When she graduated she had no money for train fare to rejoin her mother, who had moved to San Diego, so she sang on street corners until she had earned enough money to buy her ticket.

Hard Times. Once in San Diego, Jewel worked a variety of low-paying, dead-end jobs, including waitressing, but she frequently lost them because of her interest in talking with the customers. Threatened by eviction, Jewel and her mother moved into a Volkswagen van Jewel had bought. They used the bathrooms in local stores, and Jewel would wash her hair in the ladies room at the local Denny's restaurant.

They parked the van next to the beach, and Jewel spent some time learning how to surf. She also settled down with a guitar to write songs. Some of the songs were inspired by events in her life, and others are loosely based on other people's lives. She wrote "Little Sister" about a friend's little brother but did not want to embarrass him (Jewel has no sisters.) The song "Daddy" is not about her own father but a man she knew as a child who would not let his children watch black people on television.

In 1993 she started performing at a coffeehouse called the Innerchange in Pacific Beach. Her mother now had her own van, and they would often park their vans side-by-side along the San Diego beaches. Word about Jewel soon started to spread, and soon she landed a regular Thursday night gig. Her name began to appear in the local entertainment press, and she earned a few opportunities to open shows for more established

Jewel (AP/Wide World Photos)

bands. She took an extended trip back to Homer at the end of the year, and her career really began when she returned to California in early 1994.

A prolific, versatile songwriter, Jewel regularly debuted a handful of new songs at each show. These acoustic shows were showcases for local talent, and Jewel was frequently joined by boyfriend and songwriting collaborator Steve Poltz, the lead singer of a band called the Rugburns. Every week the audience grew, and soon people were being turned away from sold-out shows. Some of the shows were so packed that she had to walk across the tables to get to the stage.

Success. News of the nineteen-year-old singer had reached Los Angeles, and record executives started driving down the coast to San Diego to catch the shows. They immediately recognized the talent of the young performer, with her combination of songwriting ability, a stunning and flexible voice, and blonde good looks. After brief negotiations, she was signed to Atlantic Records and made the journey to Los Angeles, looking for producers and musicians with whom to record. The money she received as an advance on the record allowed Jewel to rent a house for herself and her mother and to buy a used Volvo and a new guitar.

By this time, Jewel had written over a hundred songs. In July, 1994, a recording crew arrived at the Innerchange to record four of Jewel's shows on her home turf. All the live recordings on her first album, *Pieces of You*, come from those sessions. *Pieces of You* was released February 28, 1995. An album release party, which consisted of two sold-out performances, was held at the Hahn Cosmopolitan Theater in her adopted hometown of San Diego.

Before Jewel or the album had garnered any attention nationally, Jewel was selected to play the role of Dorothy in a benefit production of *The Wizard of Oz* in New York in 1995. It aired on Turner Network Television in November. Other performers included Debra Winger as the Wicked Witch, Jackson Browne as the Scarecrow, Roger Daltry as the Tin Man, Nathan Lane as the Cowardly Lion, Natalie Cole as Glinda the Good Witch, Joel Grey as the Wizard, and Lucie Arnaz as Auntie Em. The event benefitted the Children's Defense Fund.

Pieces of You had been released for many months before the album attained sales success; for a time it was virtually ignored. Touring and television appearances, however, brought Jewel to the public's attention, and soon "Who Will Save Your Soul" and *Pieces of You* were hits. In July of 1997 Jewel appeared on the cover of *Time* magazine; by then the album had sold more than five million copies. She was also one of the featured performers at that summer's Lilith Fair tour put together by Sarah McLachlan. Jewel's musical tastes are varied, and her influences are broad. Her most notable influences include Ella Fitzgerald, John Prine, Tracy Chapman, and Yma Sumac. At various times, Jewel has mentioned the poet Pablo Neruda, Dr. Seuss, and classical philosophers.

—David A. Clark

SELECT DISCOGRAPHY

■ ALBUMS

Pieces of You, 1995

Spirit, 1998

SEE ALSO: Chapman, Tracy; Fitzgerald, Ella; McLachlan, Sarah; Prine, John.

Billy Joel

BORN: Bronx, New York; May 9, 1949

FIRST SOLO ALBUM RELEASE: *Cold Spring Harbor*, 1972

MUSICAL STYLES: Pop, rock and roll

To many, Billy Joel is and always will be the "Piano Man." Catering more to fans than to critics, this classically trained individualist has sold nearly a billion albums in the twenty-five years since his first solo release in 1972.

The Beginnings. Joel grew up in the Bronx, New York, where his German-born father encouraged Joel's interest in Mozart with ten years of classical piano lessons. Joel discovered rock and roll in his early teens, and his father's dislike for it only fueled Joel's passion. In 1964, at age fourteen, he joined his first band, the Echoes, later to become known as the Lost Souls. One year later, Joel was doing session work and ultimately dropped out of high school just before graduation.

In 1967, Joel left the Lost Souls to join the Hassles, a popular Long Island, New York, band with a United Artists recording contract. The Hassles released two albums, a self-titled debut and *Hour of the Wolf*, before breaking up in 1969. Undaunted, he and former Hassles drummer Jon Small formed Attila, a psychedelic instrumental duo inspired by the music of Jimi Hendrix. Their self-titled 1970 debut on Epic was unsuccessful.

Going Solo. Joel began devoting more and more time to songwriting, and in 1972 he released a solo album, *Cold Spring Harbor*, on Family Productions. He spent the rest of the year promoting it, but without strong marketing from the record company, it received little airplay or critical notice. Unfortunately, the contract that earned him his first solo album also cost him his publishing and songwriting rights. He and his girlfriend Elizabeth (who would later become his wife) moved to California, where, for legal reasons, he performed in piano bars under the pseudonym Billy Martin.

One of the songs he performed was "Captain Jack," a striking, self-penned indictment of the drug culture. A Philadelphia radio station obtained a live recording of "Captain Jack" and began giving it heavy airplay, which in turn landed Joel a contract at Columbia in 1973. His first album on that label, *Piano Man* (1973), reached number 27 on the album charts. The title single, culled from experiences during his piano-bar years, earned him national airplay and became his signature song. The specter of his first solo contract remained; under the terms of the agreement, Columbia still had to pay Family Productions royalties for every album sold.

Joel's 1974 album, *Streetlight Serenade*, reached number 35 on the album charts. The next year, he and Elizabeth moved from California back to New York, where he signed with Caribou Management, assembled a band, and set to work on his next album, *Turnstiles* (1976). The move was celebrated in the album's lead song, "Say Goodbye to Hollywood." The recording sessions did not go

For the Record

The original version of Billy Joel's first solo album, *Cold Spring Harbor*, was mastered at the wrong speed. A corrected version has since been issued, but at the height of Joel's popularity, mint copies of the original version were in high demand by collectors and selling for more than three hundred dollars.

§

"I don't know what real childbirth is like, but writing songs seems as close as I'm going to come." —*Billy Joel*

well, and Joel wound up firing his original producer and producing the album himself. He also fired his new management company and hired Elizabeth as his manager.

The Stranger. *Turnstiles* did well, but not as well as its predecessors, and the record company began pressuring Joel for another "Piano Man." Joel balked. He returned to the studio with producer Phil Ramone and made *The Stranger* (1977), an album that not only put him back on the radio, but also put him in the public eye. The second single from the album, "Just the Way You Are," spent four months on the charts. Columbia quickly reissued the first single, "Movin' Out (Anthony's Song)," and a third, "Only the Good Die Young," followed, giving Joel three singles in the Top 100. The 1978 follow-up, *52nd Street*, became Joel's first number 1 album, spending eight weeks at the top of the chart, and the single "My Life" reached number 3.

Glass Houses (1980) featured the number 1 single "It's Still Rock and Roll to Me." *Glass Houses* represented a new, harder-edged sound and was the recipient of some critical backlash. Fans accustomed to the softer Joel were disappointed with the new direction, while some rock critics sneered at the faux-new-wave posturing. Nevertheless, the album followed its predecessors up the charts and continued Joel's string of Grammy Award nominations.

Maturity. The 1981 release of *Songs in the Attic*, a live collection of pre-*Stranger* tunes, gave Joel time to work on his next album, with which he intended to make his mark as a serious composer. It was also during this time that he divorced his wife and manager, Elizabeth. The album that emerged from the personal turmoil, 1982's *The Nylon Curtain*, addressed many social concerns, such as unemployment and the Vietnam War, and spawned two Top-20 singles, "Pressure" and "Allentown."

An Innocent Man (1983) took an entirely different direction—a 1950's throwback celebration of love, courtship, and marriage. It was no coincidence that the emotional upswing in Joel's songwriting occurred after he began dating supermodel Christie Brinkley, whom he married in 1985.

Billy Joel (Ken Settle)

After a two-album greatest-hits compilation, also in 1985, Joel released *The Bridge* (1986), an ambitious album that covered everything from rock and roll to Broadway show tunes. The effort produced three Top-40 singles: "Modern Woman," "Matter of Trust," and "This Is the Time." Joel followed with a series of concerts in the former Soviet Union in 1987. These shows were later released as a live double album, *Kohuept* (concert).

Storm Front. In 1989, Joel fired his longtime manager and former brother-in-law and filed a massive lawsuit against him, charging fraud and misappropriation of funds. Seeking a musical change as well, he fired most of his band and found a new producer—Mick Jones of Foreigner. The result was the triple-platinum *Storm Front*, with its driving centerpiece song, "We Didn't Start the Fire."

In 1993, *River of Dreams* reached number 1 in its first week of release, and the upbeat title song made it to the Top 10. Following this, Joel's musical output lessened as he concentrated on other aspects of his life: spending time with his daughter, Alexa Ray (named for Ray Charles), aiding struggling Long Island fishermen, and dabbling in classical composition. In this time, two compilations were released: *Billy Joel: Greatest Hits Vol. III* in 1997 and *The Complete Hits Collection*, a limited edition four-compact-disc boxed set in 1998.

—*P. S. Ramsey*

SELECT DISCOGRAPHY

■ ALBUMS

Cold Spring Harbor, 1972
Piano Man, 1973
Turnstiles, 1976
The Stranger, 1977
52nd Street, 1978
Glass Houses, 1980
The Nylon Curtain, 1982
An Innocent Man, 1983
The Bridge, 1986
Storm Front, 1989
River of Dreams, 1993

SELECT AWARDS

Grammy Awards for Record of the Year and Song of the Year for "Just the Way You Are," 1978
Grammy Awards for Album of the Year and Best Pop Vocal Performance, Male, for *52nd Street*, 1979
Grammy Award for Best Rock Vocal Performance, Male, for *Glass Houses*, 1980
Grammy Legend Award, 1991
Nashville Songwriters Hall of Fame, inducted 1992
Billboard Century Music Award, 1994
Rock and Roll Hall of Fame, inducted 1999

SEE ALSO: Charles, Ray; John, Elton.

Elton John

(Reginald Kenneth Dwight)

BORN: Pinner, Middlesex, England; March 25, 1947
FIRST ALBUM RELEASE: *Empty Sky*, 1969
MUSICAL STYLES: Pop, rock and roll

Born Reginald Kenneth Dwight, Elton John has had a long and varied career spanning several decades. His imprint on pop music is immeasurable. Even at midlife in the 1990's, the pianist and singer still toured and played to packed auditoriums.

The Beginnings. Reginald Dwight showed musical promise at an extremely early age. He began to play by ear at the age of four, and within a few years his talent was so evident that he auditioned for and entered an exhibition for the Royal Academy of Music. He was designated a student of special interest and was put on a weekly routine of classes and training. From the early 1960's, Dwight played the music of other popular artists of the time and gathered a steady following. Most of the songs he played were culled from the top-playing singles in England and America at the time; as yet he composed little original work.

By 1962 he formed a short-lived band called the Corvettes with Stuart Brown and Geoff Dyson. They played for school functions and private parties. After they disbanded, Dwight participated in a band called Bluesology, in which Brown led with vocals modeled after Jimmy Witherspoon. While with this group, Dwight decided to borrow the first names of one-time associate members Elton Dean and John Baldry. By the time the young men parted ways, Elton John had begun to pen songs independently.

In 1967 John answered an advertisement in a paper for musicians placed by Liberty Records. Ray Williams of Liberty handed John a packet of lyrics by Bernie Taupin, another artist answering the ad. The fortunate John/Taupin association began, and the two soon made serious progress. They were employed for a time as staff writers for music publisher Dick James Music. Through 1968 John and Taupin copyrighted many songs, and in

1968 the single "I've Been Loving You" was the first song released by the Elton John/Bernie Taupin collaboration.

John played with various bands as a hireling and performed several gigs on live radio programs. He played on various popular albums that re-recorded the hits of other stars. However, in 1968 he was involved in the first full-length album, *I've Been Loving You,* a Bluesology album released in the United Kingdom. In June of 1969 the solo album *Empty Sky* was released. It contained nine songs, all cowritten with Taupin. The album was well received by critics, though it did not sell well. However, it set the stage for the successful release of his next album a year later.

Elton John (Paul Natkin)

The 1970's. The self-titled album *Elton John* hit the pop charts in mid-1970. Several songs which have remained classics from this album met with instant success, such as "Your Song," "Take Me to the Pilot," and "Border Song." Elton John made his first tour of the United States, beginning at the Troubadour club in Los Angeles. His five-night stand there, introducing audiences to his energetic stage show, won praise from the critics and audiences in general. "Your Song" was a number 8 single in the winter of 1970-1971. With the release of his new album, *Tumbleweed Connection,* in early 1971, John became a favorite new star in America. John's early albums benefited from the production of Gus Dudgeon and well-suited orchestrations of Paul Buckmaster. Regular sidemen Dee Murray on bass and Nigel Olsson on drums were also important in creating the early Elton John sound. (Guitarist Davey Johnstone officially became a member of the band with the album *Honky Chateau.*)

His real impact on the new decade began with the successful late-1971 release *Madman Across the Water,* which gained solid radio play with songs such as "Tiny Dancer" and "Levon." With the subsequent album, *Honky Chateau* (1972), which went to number 1, John began a string of Top-10 single hits; both "Rocket Man" and "Honky Cat" came from this album. The most popular musician of the 1970's, he had twenty-three Top-40 hits, fifteen of which made the Top 10; five were number 1 songs. After *Honky Chateau* came *Don't Shoot Me, I'm Only the Piano Player,* from which "Crocodile Rock" (John's first number 1 single) and "Daniel" (number 2) were released.

The hugely successful double album *Goodbye Yellow Brick Road* (1973) solidified John's success and reputation. It included the famous songs "Candle in the Wind," "Harmony," "Saturday

Night's Alright for Fighting," and "Bennie and the Jets," and an ambitious introductory instrumental, "Funeral for a Friend." The album held the number 1 chart position for eight weeks. (All told, eight John albums went to number 1.) John started his own record label, Rocket Records, in 1973.

In 1974 John did two recordings with John Lennon, Lennon's "Whatever Gets You Thru the Night" (Lennon's first post-Beatles number 1 song) and John's version of the Beatles' "Lucy in the Sky with Diamonds," with Lennon on guitar. Lennon joined John onstage at Madison Square Garden in November of 1974 to perform the songs. It was to be Lennon's last stage appearance. John's first *Greatest Hits* album was also released in 1974. John was now world-famous—as a songwriter (with Taupin), recording artist, singer, and flamboyant performer who delighted in wearing outrageous costumes. If John had never released another album, his place in pop history would have been assured.

The mid to late 1970's brought the hit songs "Philadelphia Freedom," "Someone Saved My Life Tonight," "Island Girl," "Pinball Wizard" (from the 1975 film of the Who's "rock opera" *Tommy*), and "Don't Go Breaking My Heart" (a duet with singer Kiki Dee). *Captain Fantastic and the Brown Dirt Cowboy* (1975), *Blue Moves* (1976), and the second *Greatest Hits* album (1977) are examples of John's work in the latter part of the decade. Exhausted, John announced that he would retire from touring in late 1977, but it was only two years before he felt the call to return to the stage. In 1978 the writing partnership of Elton John and Bernie Taupin split up temporarily.

Elton John had become immeasurably famous and nearly immeasurably wealthy, buying mansions, a fleet of expensive cars, outrageously expensive jeweled glasses and stage clothes, and eventually a soccer team. He was a pop icon, and his appearance as the Pinball Wizard in the Ken Russell *Tommy* film cemented his association with glitter and glitz—oversized platform shoes, huge glasses, and outrageous costumes. At the same time, his personal life was deeply troubled. He had many rocky relationships and struggled to balance his fame as a superstar with the deeply emotional and personal man inside. He struggled continually with alcoholism, cocaine addiction, and a weight problem. In 1976 he admitted his bisexuality in an interview with *Rolling Stone*; years later he noted that he had deliberately not said "homosexuality," fearing that such a confession might destroy his popularity. Even so, the interview probably did some damage to his career at the time. In 1979 John returned to performing; he became the first Western artist to tour the Soviet Union, and soon John and Taupin rekindled their working relationship and continued into the next two decades.

For the Record

Elton John and Bernie Taupin have never composed a song together in the same room. Taupin has always written the lyrics first and then given them to John—often sending them by mail.

The 1980's. A more subtle and subdued Elton John continued to write, record, and perform in the 1980's. Some observers thought that his career was winding down, but after he reunited with Taupin, much more music was yet to come. While the hits were less frequent, the songs tended to be more personal, echoing the reflective tone of his earlier material. His 1982 release of *Love Songs* set the tone for much of this phase of his career. While the albums were greeted with less attention and fanfare, he continued to put songs on the charts with such hits as "Blue Eyes," "I Guess That's Why They Call It the Blues," "I'm Still Standing," "Who Wears These Shoes," "Nikita," and "Sad Songs." In 1987 the *Live in Australia* concert album and video heightened John's popularity.

John's personal life was still in turmoil. His problems with drugs and alcohol worsened in the 1980's. Still struggling with his sexual identity, he surprised everyone by marrying a woman named Renate Blauel in 1984, but in four years the marriage was over and he came to terms with his homosexuality. After bleak years in 1988 and 1989, John finally turned a major corner in 1990. He underwent rehabilitation therapy, managing to become sober and to gain control over his bulimia. In the late 1980's, John had befriended Ryan White, a young hemophiliac AIDS sufferer. Intensely moved by White's suffering—John was at his side when Ryan passed away in 1990—Elton John founded the AIDS foundation that bears White's name in 1992. As of 1998, the organization had raised nearly fifteen million dollars for various AIDS projects worldwide.

The 1990's. This decade began with the release of the four-CD boxed set *To Be Continued . . .*, a major collection of four segments of John's career. By 1992 he was on the charts again. *The One* (1992) featured the hit title cut, "Simple Life," and "The Last Song." His biggest hit of the early half of the decade, however, was one that would move his career in a new direction. Teaming with lyricist Tim Rice, he wrote the songs for the Disney animated film *The Lion King*. The sound track was a smash hit, containing the songs "Circle of Life," "Hakuna Matata," and particularly "Can You Feel the Love Tonight," sung by John himself. After this success John established Rocket Pictures.

In the second half of the 1990's Elton John released *Made in England* (1995), an expanded version of *Love Songs* (1995), and *The Big Picture* (1997). In 1997 tragedy struck as two friends of John's died in separate incidents. In July fashion designer Gianni Versace was murdered outside his home in Miami. Among those at his funeral were John and Princess Diana, who was seen comforting the grieving John. Only six weeks later, Princess Diana herself was killed in an automobile accident. At John's request, Taupin wrote new words to "Candle in the Wind" in her honor. John sang a moving rendition of the song at Diana's funeral service. He also released a studio version of the song, which set a record for first-day CD sales (over 600,000). Money earned from the CD was given to charity. In early December of 1997, John gave the Princess Diana Charities a check for an astounding thirty-two million dollars for the first few months of the song's sales.

—*Marc E. Waddell*

SELECT DISCOGRAPHY

■ ALBUMS

Empty Sky, 1969
Elton John, 1970
Tumbleweed Connection, 1971
Madman Across the Water, 1971
Honky Chateau, 1972
Don't Shoot Me I'm Only the Piano Player, 1973
Goodbye Yellow Brick Road, 1973
Captain Fantastic and the Brown Dirt Cowboy, 1975
Blue Moves, 1976
DJM Box Set, 1979 (five-album set)
21 at 33, 1980
Ice on Fire, 1985
Live in Australia, 1987
To Be Continued . . ., 1990 (4-CD boxed set)
The One, 1992
The Lion King, 1994 (sound track)
Made in England, 1995

SELECT AWARDS

Hollywood Walk of Fame, star awarded 1975
Rock and Roll Hall of Fame, inducted 1994
Grammy Award for Best Male Vocal Performance for "Can You Feel the Love Tonight," 1994
Academy Award for Best Song in a Motion Picture for "Can You Feel the Love Tonight," from *The Lion King*, 1994

SEE ALSO: Joel, Billy; Lennon, John.

Robert Johnson

BORN: Hazelhurst, Mississippi; May 8, 1911
DIED: Greenwood, Mississippi; August 16, 1938
FIRST ALBUM RELEASE: *King of the Delta Blues Singers*, 1961
MUSICAL STYLE: Blues

If a film were ever made of the life of Robert Johnson, it could be accurately entitled *The Phantom of the Delta Blues*. While Johnson's impact on the development and popularity of the blues in the United States is often taken for granted, the precise details of his life, career, and death have always been elusive, mysterious, and even controversial. However, few dispute the greatness and widespread influence of the twenty-nine songs Robert Johnson recorded during his brief lifetime.

The Life. Robert Johnson was born in Hazelhurst, Mississippi, on May 8, 1911, to Julia Major Dodds and Noah Johnson. Shortly after his birth, the family moved to Memphis, Tennessee. Johnson stayed in Memphis until 1918. His next home was Robinsonville, Mississippi, a small community in the north of the state. It was in Robinsonville that Johnson developed an interest in music, particularly in the harmonica. During the late 1920's, Johnson's musical interests expanded to include the guitar. In February, 1929, Johnson married Virginia Travis, who was only sixteen at the time. Soon thereafter, the couple were expecting their first child. Joy turned to tragedy when both mother and child died during childbirth in 1930. Dejected and lacking any interest in a sharecropper's life, Johnson left Robinsonville and returned to Hazelhurst, Mississippi. It was here that Johnson developed his skills as a blues guitarist by constantly playing in clubs, on street corners, and anyplace else people wanted some entertainment.

Delta Blues. Robert Johnson best represents a style of blues known as the Delta blues. The Delta blues is the earliest style of blues to be recorded; it reflects blues at its most expressive and emotional level. More specifically, the Delta blues style refers to a solo performer, usually accompanied only by a guitar, singing very personal songs of pain and joy reflecting the harsh realities of everyday life.

Most African Americans who were raised in the Mississippi Delta during the early decades of the 1900's worked the land as hired farmers or sharecroppers (tenant farmers who paid their landlords a share of the crops produced on the land). In the Delta, musical entertainment was often viewed as a form of relief and relaxation from the daily drudgery of life. It was from his life in the Delta that Robert Johnson derived his musical inspiration.

Because of his constant musical endeavors, Johnson attracted a following in Mississippi. He spent most of his time and energy perfecting his playing style. He traveled and performed at numerous locations, from the Mississippi Delta to New York City, Detroit, Chicago, and St. Louis. Like most wandering musicians of his time, Johnson played not only the blues but also the popular songs of the decade, including tunes recorded by Bing Crosby. Johnson first recorded his songs in November of 1936. A second recording session took place during June of 1937. A total of twenty-nine songs were recorded during the two sessions; only eleven of these were released during Johnson's lifetime.

For the Record

During the 1930's Robert Johnson quickly transformed himself from an embarrassing novice on the guitar into a virtuoso. This rapid transformation gave birth to the legend that Johnson sold his soul to the devil in order to achieve his playing and composing skills. The titles of Robert Johnson's classic compositions "Hellhound on My Trail" and "Me and the Devil Blues" are taken by some as additional evidence verifying the alleged deal with the devil. The legend maintains that around midnight, Johnson arrived at a crossroads in Mississippi. The devil met him there. The devil reached out for his guitar, tuned it, and then returned the guitar to Johnson. By accepting the guitar, Johnson sealed a pact: He would become an accomplished blues guitarist and composer, and the devil would possess his soul for all time.

§

When Columbia Records reissued *Robert Johnson: The Complete Recordings* in 1990, they expected to sell approximately twenty thousand copies of the two-CD boxed set. The set actually sold over a million units—the only blues collection ever to accomplish this feat.

The Recordings. Through the efforts of several people, Johnson was persuaded to record his songs in 1936. The first recording session, for the American Record Company, took place in San Antonio, Texas, at the Gunter Hotel. Johnson recorded sixteen songs in a three-day session that started on Monday, November 23, and ended on Friday, November 27. As was the case with most blues musicians during the 1930's, the recording session involved one microphone that recorded both the artist's voice and the instrument. Robert Johnson, using a six-string guitar, displayed an ability most often associated with piano musicians, where two hands are used to convey two different rhythms. Johnson was able to accomplish the same effect with one hand; his voice added an extra dynamic dimension to the mix. The San Antonio session produced Johnson's only popular hit, "Terraplane Blues," as well as classic versions of "Cross Road Blues," "Last Fair Deal Gone Down," and "If I Had Possession of Judgment Day."

In June of 1937, Johnson returned to a recording studio in Dallas, Texas, where he recorded thirteen additional songs for the American Record Company. The June session turned out to be the last recording made by Robert Johnson, and it produced some of Johnson's most outstanding compositions: "Stones in My Passway," "Hellhound on My Trail," "Love in Vain Blues," and "Me and the Devil Blues."

According to most sources, Johnson's life ended on August 16, 1938. While playing at a club near Greenwood, Mississippi, a jealous husband apparently poisoned Johnson with strychnine-laced whiskey after learning that Johnson had conducted a brief affair with his wife.

The twenty-nine compositions recorded by Robert Johnson between 1936 and 1937, a few photographs, and the fading and questionable memories of fellow blues musicians are the only remains of Robert Johnson available to the public. The most important remains are his music, which defines his life and career.

The Legacy. Without doubt, Robert Johnson influenced the first wave of bluesmen using electric guitars, including Muddy Waters and Elmore James. In the 1960's, Johnson was rediscovered, especially by the British music community. Diverse artists, American and British, such as Bob Dylan, John Mayall, Eric Clapton, Mick Jagger, Keith Richards, and the Red Hot Chili Peppers recorded versions of Robert Johnson's compositions. Johnson's influence is especially noticeable in the generation of British artists that emerged during the 1960's and 1970's; the Rolling Stones recorded Johnson's "Love in Vain," and Eric Clapton sang Johnson's "Crossroads" for the group Cream. *—Ernest Rigney, Jr.*

SELECT DISCOGRAPHY

■ ALBUMS

King of the Delta Blues Singers, 1961
King of the Delta Blues Singers, Volume Two, 1970
Robert Johnson: The Complete Recordings, 1990 (boxed set)

SELECT AWARDS

Blues Foundation Hall of Fame, inducted 1980 (posthumous)
Rock and Roll Hall of Fame, inducted 1986 (posthumous)
Grammy Award for Best Historical Album for *Robert Johnson: The Complete Recordings*, 1990 (posthumous)

SEE ALSO: Clapton, Eric; Cream; Guy, Buddy; Howlin' Wolf; Rolling Stones, The; Waters, Muddy.

George Jones

BORN: Saratoga, Texas; September 12, 1931
FIRST SINGLE RELEASE: "No Money in This Deal," 1954
MUSICAL STYLE: Country

From the time he strummed his Gene Autry guitar on the streets of Beaumont, Texas, to his 1998 album *It Don't Get Any Better Than This*, George Jones's distinctive voice has brought smiles with his country music. He has had hit singles in every decade from the 1950's through the 1990's.

Formative Years. Jones grew up in a musical family. His father played harmonica and guitar,

George Jones in 1977 (AP/Wide World Photos)

and his mother played piano in the Pentecostal Holiness Church every Sunday. His family lived in various small Texas towns, but he would always consider the "big thicket" area of eastern Texas his home.

As a young boy sitting on his mother's lap listening to the gospel songs sung by his family and friends, Jones would try to sing with the music. A continuous source of strength for Jones was Brother Burl and Sister Annie Stephens, Christian evangelists and gospel singers. Along with gospel music, Jones listened intently to the music on the *Grand Ole Opry* radio program. One of the major influences on his musical career was Hank Williams, who advised him to stay true to his own singing style and not try to imitate other singers.

Road to Stardom. Jones quickly mastered the guitar and began playing for people at bus stops and shoeshine stands. He soon began performing on the dance hall circuit, at an amusement park, and on a daily radio show, where he met Hank Williams. Music continued to be a part of Jones's life even when he joined the Marines in 1951. He would perform in his Marine uniform at various functions, billed as Little Georgie Jones, the Forrester Hill Flash. After being discharged, Jones worked briefly as a housepainter while still performing at social events. In 1954, Jack Starnes and Harold W. "Pappy" Daily, the founders of Starday Records, who were familiar with Jones's talents, launched his career as a recording artist. His version of "Why, Baby, Why" reached the number 4 spot on *Billboard*'s country charts in 1955 and earned him an invitation to sing at the Grand Ole Opry in 1956. Jones switched to the Mercury label in 1958 and recorded his first number 1 single, "White Lightning," in 1959, which remained number 1 on the country charts for five weeks and marked his debut on the pop charts.

During the late 1950's, rock and roll was sweeping the nation and threatening to destroy country music sales. Many of the country artists made adjustments in their instrumental and vocal approaches in order to compete. Against his better judgment, Jones agreed to record a few rockabilly songs under the pseudonym Thumper Jones. When the songs failed miserably, Jones insisted he would sing only traditional country music in the future.

True to Country. Continuing the country tradition with top-selling music, he released his second number 1 single, "Tender Years," in 1961. The single "She Thinks I Still Care," released in 1962 on the United Artists label, earned Jones awards for Favorite Male Artist and Best Country Song of the Year at the Annual Disc Jockey Convention in Nashville. He topped the charts again with his 1967 Musicor release "Walk Through This World with Me." Jones continued to demonstrate his voice mastery in songs such as "The Grand Tour" (1974), from the Epic album of the same name, and "A Drunk Can't Be a Man" (1976), from his album *Alone Again*. His single

"He Stopped Loving Her Today" (1980) was an immediate runaway hit, precipitating Country Music Association (CMA) Awards for the Song of the Year and Single of the Year, as well as a Grammy Award for Best Male Country Vocal Performance. That album resulted in another number 1 hit in 1981, "Still Doin' Time."

Since signing with MCA Records in 1991, Jones has released *And Along Came Jones* (1991), *Walls Can Fall* (1992), and *High-Tech Redneck* (1993). His rollicking rendition of "I Don't Need Your Rocking Chair," from the *Walls Can Fall* album, won the CMA Vocal Event of the Year Award in 1993. "The Honky Tonk Song" on the 1996 *I Lived to Tell It All* mirrors one of Jones's personal experiences of driving a lawnmower to a bar after his wife took his car keys away. Much of Jones's music is related to his personal experiences and transforms the listener into a trusted friend and confidant. *It Don't Get Any Better than This* (1998) contains the song "Wild Irish Rose," which Jones was hesitant to include because it tragically describes a Vietnam War veteran who was refused health care. Like his 1980 hit "He Stopped Loving Her Today," he felt that the song was just too sad to sing. Fortunately for his listeners, he was convinced to record the song.

The Legend Lives On. Jones has been married four times and has four children. He and his third wife, Tammy Wynette, were known as "Mr. and Mrs. Country Music," and together they recorded numerous chart-topping duet albums and singles. Over the years, Jones has also recorded duets with Gene Pitney, Melba Montgomery, and Dolly Parton, among others. Some of his duets include "A Few Old Country Boys" (1991) with Randy Travis, "A Good Year for the Roses" (1995) with Alan Jackson, and "You've Got a Friend in Me," from the 1995 film *Toy Story*, with Kathy Mattea. In 1995, Jones and Wynette were reunited for the first time in eighteen years on the album *One*, which was nominated by the CMA for the Vocal Event of the Year Award.

With his steadfast belief in the traditional basics of country music, Jones has been an influence and inspiration to country artists. *The George Jones Show* debuted in February, 1998, on The Nashville Network, featuring country music and country music artists. His book, *I Lived to Tell It All*, written with Tom Carter and published in 1997, reached the sixth position on *The New York Times* best-seller list. A series of thirteen of this prolific artist's albums has been reissued, which includes his 1974 album *The Grand Tour.* Jones has been called the greatest country singer of all time; no matter what the title, George Jones epitomizes country music.

—*Elizabeth B. Graham*

For the Record

The youngest of eight children, George Jones suffered a broken arm at birth when the doctor dropped the twelve-pound newborn.

SELECT DISCOGRAPHY

■ ALBUMS

Grand Ole Opry's New Star, 1957
White Lightning and Other Favorites, 1959
Heartaches and Tears, 1965
George Jones Golden Hits, 1966 (compilation)
Walk Through This World with Me, 1967
The Best of George Jones, 1970 (compilation)
The Grand Tour, 1974
Bartender's Blues, 1978
Still the Same Ole Me, 1981
Who's Gonna Fill Their Shoes, 1985
And Along Came Jones, 1991
The Bradley Barn Sessions, 1994 (with others)
I Lived to Tell It All, 1996
It Don't Get Any Better than This, 1998 (with others)

SELECT AWARDS

Country Music Association Single of the Year for "He Stopped Loving Her Today" and Male Vocalist of the Year Awards, 1980
Grammy Award for Best Country Vocal Performance, Male, for "He Stopped Loving Her Today," 1980
Country Music Association Male Vocalist of the Year Award, 1981

Country Music Hall of Fame, inducted 1992
Country Music Association Vocal Event of the Year Award for "I Don't Need Your Rocking Chair," 1993 (with others)

SEE ALSO: Black, Clint; Gill, Vince; Haggard, Merle; Jackson, Alan; Jennings, Waylon; Mattea, Kathy; Nelson, Willie; Skaggs, Ricky; Williams, Hank; Wynette, Tammy.

Rickie Lee Jones

BORN: Chicago, Illinois; November 8, 1954
FIRST ALBUM RELEASE: *Rickie Lee Jones*, 1979
MUSICAL STYLES: Rock and roll, jazz, pop

Beginning with her 1978 debut, singer-songwriter Rickie Lee Jones has recorded a number of influential albums filled with stylistically eclectic and lyrically enigmatic songs. Jazzy overtones enliven much of her work. In this, she is somewhat like fellow singer-songwriter Joni Mitchell, with whom Jones has often been compared (over Jones's protests). Her interest in jazz has resulted in the occasional covering of standards and in session work with well-known jazz musicians. Jones's career and personal life both suffered during much of the 1980's, but she returned with a well-received album at the end of that decade and continued to record and perform live regularly in the 1990's.

As a child, Jones was unable to call one place home for long. She instead endured frequent uprooting, her family moving almost every year. Most often, they migrated between Jones's birthplace, Chicago, and Phoenix, Arizona. Their relocations also took them to Olympia, Washington, where Jones began drinking heavily. Expelled from high school, she left home and drifted about as a hippie vagabond for several years. By 1973 she had settled in Los Angeles and was working as a waitress and occasional nightclub performer. In these two activities, Jones took after her parents; both waited tables for a living, and her father often sang made-up songs for his family.

Los Angeles. Jones continued to wait on tables and establish herself as a musician through much of the 1970's. While doing so, she struck up a relationship with Tom Waits, gravel-voiced bard of the night, also spending time with other colorful characters who would inspire a number of her songs. Success first came to Jones as a songwriter. Lowell George, formerly of Little Feat, included Jones's "Easy Money" on his 1979 solo album *Thanks I'll Eat It Here.* Jones was also beginning to find some success as a performer. She was playing Los Angeles' Troubadour club, and a demo tape caught the attention of record executives from several labels. Lenny Waronker soon signed Jones to Warner Brothers and coproduced her 1979 debut, *Rickie Lee Jones.*

The album met with considerable success. The jazz-tinged "Chuck E.'s in Love," about musician friend Chuck E. Weiss, placed well on the singles charts and helped Jones win a Grammy Award for Best New Artist in 1980. The album also met with acclaim from many music critics. They liked its fresh sound and the depth they heard in Jones's sometimes perplexing lyrics. The album was also nonchalantly hip and decidedly jazzy, offering

Rickie Lee Jones (Reprise/Lee Cantelon)

welcome relief from the pestilence of late-1970's disco. Comparisons were quickly made with Joni Mitchell, with Jones being touted as the new poet-queen of singer-songwriters. The path ahead looked rosy indeed, but such rapid success quietly sowed the seeds of future disappointment: The commercial and artistic success of *Rickie Lee Jones* and "Chuck E.'s in Love" set high expectations for a follow-up album.

A Troubled Decade. *Pirates* appeared in 1981. Artistically, it was as good as Jones's debut—even better—and still casts an influential shadow upon songwriters. It also sold well enough. However, it did not contain a hit single. Neither did the next two albums Jones released, *Girl at Her Volcano* (actually an EP), in 1983, and *The Magazine*, in 1984. Sales flagged. In part, Jones was a victim of her own artistry. Her lyrically opaque songs with their chimerical themes and complex structures pleased some critics and a devoted core audience, but they also made her music less accessible to the masses. Furthermore, stylistic changes from album to album made it difficult for listeners to keep up with Jones; *Girl at Her Volcano* contained jazz standards, while *The Magazine*, a collaboration with James Newton-Howard, featured slickly produced, synthesizer-oriented arrangements. (The song "It Must Be Love" was later used effectively in the 1991 film *Frankie and Johnnie*.)

By the mid-1980's Jones's career was at a standstill, a situation exacerbated by business problems and an appetite for alcohol and drugs. Jones had always been subject to extreme emotional highs and lows. As a result of her problems, Jones did not record for five years. A lesser artist might have sunk into obscurity at this point, but Jones was to prove stronger than her woes. Her salvation began with a chance encounter in Tahiti with French musician Pascal Nabet-Meyer. A romantic relationship quickly developed, and the pair subsequently married. Jones gave birth to their daughter, Charlotte Rose, in 1988. This familial grounding seems to have been what the singer-songwriter most needed, for she returned to the studio in 1989 to record an album for Geffen Records.

Comeback. The album, *Flying Cowboys*, marked a new beginning for Jones. Produced by Walter Becker of Steely Dan and featuring the Scottish trio the Blue Nile, it revealed a more mature but no less creative lyricist than the Jones of earlier albums. Her hard-fought victory over personal difficulties was evident. Jones also displayed a wider range of musical expression. In addition, while her wonderful, smoky voice and jazzy, Beat-poetry inflections remained, she had toned down some of her musical mannerisms. The album won back for Jones much of the critical attention she had originally enjoyed and brought to a successful close a decade that had started well but taken a significant turn for the worse.

The 1990's began on the same high note as the 1980's had ended. In the first year of the decade, Jones won a Grammy Award for Best Jazz Vocal Performance for her duet with Dr. John on the standard "Makin' Whoopee." (Through the years Jones also made guest appearances on albums by other artists, ranging from Lyle Lovett to John Mellencamp.) She then recorded two more albums for Geffen. Don Was produced 1991's *Pop Pop*, an album of wide-ranging covers—everything from Jimi Hendrix's "Up from the Skies" to "Bye Bye Blackbird." Jones surrounded herself with jazz artists Charlie Haden, Joe Henderson, and Robben Ford for the outing. *Traffic from Paradise*, her 1993 Geffen release, marked another return of Jones the singer-songwriter, although this time in partial collaboration with Leo Kottke and long-time associate Sal Bernardi. Reviews were not as strong as for *Flying Cowboys*, but *Traffic from Paradise* did proclaim that she was back to stay.

Signing with Reprise, Jones released a live acoustic album in 1995, *Naked Songs*. A video of performances from the album was released under the same title. She then took part in the 1996

For the Record

Speaking of her music, Jones has said, "I believe that people can do their work with the intention of bringing good and healing to the world."

HORDE tour. From that experience came her acquaintance with Rick Boston. The two began collaborating to create 1997's hip-hop-inspired *Ghostyhead.* On the face of it, this album's drum loops and structured sound environments may seem like an experimental departure for her, but Jones demonstrates that hip-hop verse is not that far removed from Beat poetry. *Ghostyhead* also reveals the extent of her personal growth since the dark days of a decade earlier and indicates that she remains a creative force in popular music—willing to forge ahead and take chances rather than recycle past achievements. *—David Lee Fish*

SELECT DISCOGRAPHY

■ ALBUMS

Rickie Lee Jones, 1979
Pirates, 1981
The Magazine, 1984
Flying Cowboys, 1989
Pop Pop, 1991
Ghostyhead, 1997

SELECT AWARDS

Grammy Award for Best New Artist, 1980
Grammy Award for Best Jazz Vocal Performance for "Makin' Whoopee," 1990 (with Dr. John)

SEE ALSO: Dr. John; Mitchell, Joni; Waits, Tom.

Tom Jones

(Thomas Jones Woodward)

BORN: Pontypridd, South Wales; June 7, 1940
FIRST SINGLE RELEASE: "Chills and Fever," 1964
MUSICAL STYLES: Pop, easy listening, soul, country

Emerging during the "British invasion" of the mid-1960's, Tom Jones resembled a Welsh Elvis Presley, full of swagger, good looks, and boundless charisma. His husky baritone could be used to turn any kind of song into a showpiece, and Jones easily glided from rock to soul to country to ballads. His music drove the women in his audiences wild.

Style. Jones enjoyed his greatest record sales during the late 1960's and early 1970's, when he had his own television show. He became especially popular by transforming his concert appearances into celebrations of his sex appeal. Although critics often took Jones to task for his Las Vegas-style showmanship and his over-the-top sense of style (he was fond of wearing unbuttoned shirts with long gold chains), they could not deny that his voice was extraordinary.

Unlike Presley, Jones managed to remain successful into middle age and was still a dynamic artist in the 1990's. In fact, having trimmed down the excess in his act and having applied his voice to an even wider range of material, he was still developing artistically when he was in his fifties.

The Beginnings. Thomas Woodward was born into a coal-mining family in Wales, where he began singing at an early age. He taught himself to play the drums, but it was apparent that his voice was going to earn him success, not his drumming skills. At first calling himself Tommy Scott, Woodward started a band called the Senators, who were popular locally. He was then discovered by Gordon Mills, who became his manager. In 1964, Woodward changed his name to Tom Jones, inspired by the film of the same name, and relocated to London, where he signed with Decca Records. (In the United States, his early records came out on the Parrot label.) His first single in the United Kingdom, "Chills and Fever," did not have many buyers, but his second, "It's Not Unusual," was his breakthrough. It became a number 1 hit in England and made it to number 10 in the United States.

For the Record

Tom Jones and Elvis Presley became close friends. On one occasion Jones's female backup singers decided to quit the act right before a show. Presley dispatched two planes to Las Vegas from different parts of the country, each carrying three vocalists, to make sure he would have backing singers. They all arrived on time, so Jones had a six-girl chorus that night.

Elvis with a Ponytail. In 1964 and 1965, a British heritage was a boost to any singer's career, due to the surge of interest caused by the Beatles and other English groups. Jones had very little in common with the so-called beat groups; he did not grow his hair long or comb it down on his forehead, as was the preferred style. In fact, he kept it short and curly on top but let it fall into a ponytail in the back. His vocal delivery was more similar to the great rhythm-and-blues singers of the day than to the rock style that was popular in the United Kingdom. If anything, Jones had more in common with Elvis Presley than with the Beatles.

Jones's voice was full of gusto and bravado, tightly controlled yet prone to bursts and unexpected crescendos. When he appeared in concert or on television, audiences were riveted, sometimes becoming emotionally unwound over him.

Hit Records and Television. Beginning in 1965, Jones began his true climb to superstardom. His single "What's New Pussycat?," from the film of the same name, was a number 3 seller in the United States. He also had a hit with "Thunderball," the title track from a James Bond film. Jones won a Grammy Award for Best New Artist of 1965.

Just as he was establishing himself as a successful singer of pop, rock, and soul, Jones changed course in 1966 and began recording country music. He was equally successful in that style, having hits with "Green, Green Grass of Home," "Detroit City," and others. By the end of the decade, he was moving into a more adult-oriented music style, which would allow him to reach older audiences in nightclubs and on television and records. Hits such as "Delilah," "I'll Never Fall in Love Again," "Daughter of Darkness," and "I (Who Have Nothing)," a remake of a soul hit by Ben E. King, all between 1968 and 1970, appealed mainly to fans who might be more likely to follow Frank Sinatra than the Beatles.

That did not mean that Jones had lost his sex appeal, though. He played his idol image to the hilt—women found him quite appealing and often acted like young girls at his concerts, shrieking and throwing gifts (ranging from flowers to underwear) at him while he performed. From 1969 to 1971, Jones was arguably at the peak of his popularity when he hosted his own television show, where he often sang duets with his other musical guests. In 1969 alone, he had three albums in the Top 10.

The Las Vegas Years. Jones spent most of the 1970's tailoring his act to Las Vegas showrooms. He recorded less during this period, but he became one of the most popular entertainers on the Las Vegas strip. In the late 1970's, Jones began recording country music again. Starting in 1976 and lasting until 1985, first for Epic Records and then Mercury, Jones placed sixteen singles on the country charts, the first, "Say You'll Stay Until Tomorrow," going to number 1.

The New Tom Jones. By the early 1980's, Jones decided he needed a makeover in order to maintain his career. The singer briefly hosted another television variety series, this time in Canada, but

Tom Jones (Fotos International/Archive Photos)

his real comeback did not occur until the end of the decade. In 1988, Jones, who was never afraid to interpret any kind of song if he thought he could make it his own, recorded a cover of Prince's "Kiss," collaborating with the British electronic dance group Art of Noise. It was a moderate hit, and it brought Jones to a new audience who recognized his talent despite his past history as an adult entertainer. He also performed "Unbelievable," which had been a 1991 hit for another young British group, EMF. His appearance on television's *The Simpsons* also brought him to mainstream young audiences.

In the 1990's, Jones toured often with a small, tight band, performing his old hits, classic soul, Motown songs, and new material by rock bands, country singers, and rhythm-and-blues artists. He toned down the theatrics, opting for a more mature approach. Despite his decades-long career, his 1994 album, *The Lead and How to Swing It*, had a very contemporary sound. —*Jeff Tamarkin*

SELECT DISCOGRAPHY

■ SINGLES

"It's Not Unusual," 1965
"What's New Pussycat?" 1965
"Green, Green Grass of Home," 1967
"Delilah," 1968
"She's a Lady," 1971

■ ALBUMS

Help Yourself, 1969
This Is Tom Jones, 1969
Live in Las Vegas, 1969
Tom, 1970
The Lead and How to Swing It, 1994
The Complete Tom Jones, 1995 (compilation)

SELECT AWARDS

Grammy Award for Best New Artist, 1965

SEE ALSO: Beatles, The; Presley, Elvis; Prince; Sinatra, Frank.

Janis Joplin

BORN: Port Arthur, Texas; January 19, 1943
DIED: Hollywood, California; October 4, 1970
FIRST ALBUM RELEASE: *Big Brother and the Holding Company*, 1967
MUSICAL STYLES: Blues, country rock, folk, rock and roll, rhythm and blues, soul

Often called the "Queen of Rock" of the 1960's, Janis Joplin's musical repertoire represented many different styles. Her gritty, sexually-charged vocal performances moved among the genres of folk, blues, soul, and rock and roll. As critical to Joplin's legacy as her music is her image as a hard-drinking, sexually adventurous woman who broke into the male-dominated world of rock and roll.

Early Influences. Janis Joplin grew up in the conservative oil town of Port Arthur, Texas. Her opposition to 1950's racial segregation, her unwillingness or inability to conform to the standards of proper female behavior and appearance, and her affinity for the beatnik lifestyle set her apart from most of her peers. Throughout her career, Joplin often referred to the pain she had felt at being rejected by many of her classmates.

Joplin first made her way to San Francisco in 1963 with Chet Helms, whom she had met while doing some folk singing as a student at the University of Texas, Austin. Joplin returned to Port Arthur in 1965, however, after a frightening bout with speed and heroin. Upon her return to San Francisco in 1966, Helms introduced her to Big Brother and the Holding Company, a band in need of a solid female vocalist.

Joplin thrived in the San Francisco/Haight-Ashbury atmosphere of artistic and sexual freedom and Big Brother's style fit well with the late 1960's San Francisco sound, which was based on live performances of original, socially relevant material by bands such as Jefferson Airplane and Country Joe and the Fish. At a time when the hippie community of Haight-Ashbury had become a media spectacle and many were lamenting the commercialization of the counterculture, Joplin's on-stage abandon and passion were applauded for their authenticity.

The major breakthrough for Joplin and Big Brother occurred at the Monterey International Pop Festival in 1967. Joplin's searing rendition of Willie Mae "Big Mama" Thornton's blues classic

Janis Joplin performing at Woodstock in August, 1969 (Archive Photos)

"Ball and Chain" won the band an invitation to perform at the festival's finale the next day and launched Joplin's ascent to superstardom. During their post-Monterey tour, they entered into a management deal with Bob Dylan's manager, Albert Grossman. Grossman was able to extricate the band from a 1966 recording contract with Mainstream Records, but not before the 1967 release of a self-titled album, which was criticized as haphazardly orchestrated and sloppy. The band eventually signed with Columbia, and in September, 1968, *Cheap Thrills* was released. The album held the number 1 spot on the *Billboard* charts for several weeks in late 1968. "Piece of My Heart," which came to be known as a Joplin classic, appears on the album and was in the Top 40 for eight weeks.

Joplin's performance of "Ball and Chain" on *Cheap Thrills* exemplifies her ability to use vocal and tonal variety to complicate the message of the lyrics. Her wavering tonal dynamics and spoken-word segments disturb the flow of the song and assert some personal will on lyrics which would otherwise make her a passive victim of love gone wrong.

Singin' the Blues. Joplin's reliance on the styles of African American musical traditions led to much discussion in the mainstream press about a white woman's relationship with a black musical tradition. Often hailed as the first true white female blues singer, she claimed Bessie Smith, Odetta, and Leadbelly as among her most significant musical influences. A *Look* article of September, 1968, called her "Big Brother's White Soul." When confronted with the criticism that she lacked the cultural experiences to produce legitimate blues or soul, Joplin countered that "the myth that only black people have soul" was the result of white people's inability or unwillingness to admit to deep feelings. Joplin emphasized that the goal of her music was to express her feelings and to get her audience to express theirs; since she viewed this mission as the essential goal of blues music as well, she saw no problem in adopting the musical style. Biographer Ellis Amburn (*Pearl: The Obsessions and Passions of Janis Joplin*, 1992) suggests that blues-proficient African American audiences were less enamored with her singing style, however.

For the Record

"I'd rather have ten years of superhypermost than live to be seventy by sitting in some . . . chair watching T.V."

—*Janis Joplin*

Solo Career. Though *Cheap Thrills* received mostly favorable attention in the press, many reviewers felt that Big Brother was holding Joplin back from the fullest expression of her abilities. In late 1968, Joplin left Big Brother to pursue a career as a solo artist. Big Brother guitarist Sam Andrew joined her in forming the Kozmic Blues Band in December of 1968. Despite personnel troubles in the band, Joplin and Kozmic Blues made appearances at numerous outdoor rock festivals, including Woodstock in August, 1969. Her performance of a number of songs from the forthcoming album, including "Try," "Summertime," and "Little Girl Blue," was substandard; as a result, manager Grossman would not allow any of her performance to be included in *Woodstock*, the 1970 film of the festival.

I Got Dem Ol' Kozmic Blues Again Mama! was released on the Columbia label in the fall of 1969. Though it received only mediocre critical reviews, it enjoyed popular success and a sixteen-week stay on the charts. "Little Girl Blue," arranged by Gabriel Mekler, is the highlight of the album. Joplin's contemplative and soulful vocals are supported by Andrew's crystal-clear guitar accompaniment. Joplin's tone is soft and melodic as she commiserates, "Baby I know/ just how you feel."

The Kozmic Blues Band broke up at the end of 1969, the same year that saw the disintegration of bands such as the Jimi Hendrix Experience, the Beatles, and Blind Faith. The rigors of life on the road and the exhaustion of life on drugs and alcohol were taking their toll on Joplin and she often complained of exhaustion. Despite her weariness, she was very excited about her new band, Full Tilt Boogie, formed early in the spring of 1970. Joplin managed to abstain from heroin over the summer of 1970 and spent much energy preparing for her ten-year high school reunion in Port Arthur that August. Waffling between a desire for revenge for the mistreatment suffered as a teenager and hope for final acceptance, Joplin returned home with all the fanfare her celebrity required, only to be disappointed by an argument with her parents and an unsatisfying reunion. It was with some relief that she returned to California to record the new album.

Pearl. Joplin had resumed her use of heroin by mid-September, 1970. Saturday, October 3, was spent recording songs for the new album, *Pearl*, including what became known as Joplin's signature song, "Me and Bobby McGee," written by Kris Kristofferson. Overall, Joplin was pleased with the progress she and the band were making on the album. In the early morning of October 4, 1970, the day she was to have recorded the vocals for Nick Gravenites's "Buried Alive in the Blues," Joplin died of an accidental overdose of heroin.

Pearl was released in January, 1971, and both the album and the single "Me and Bobby McGee" made their way to the top of the *Billboard* charts within weeks. The album's title is based on Joplin's alter ego, who embodied the media image of the singer: an eclectic, wild, sexualized party girl. The album received much critical acclaim and has become a rock-and-roll classic. Joplin has been cited as an influence by 1990's women rockers such as Melissa Etheridge and Courtney Love, and, sadly, has joined fellow 1960's rockers Jim Morrison and Jimi Hendrix in the annals of drug-induced rock-and-roll deaths.

—*Kim Heikkila*

SELECT DISCOGRAPHY

■ ALBUMS

Big Brother and the Holding Company, 1967
Cheap Thrills, 1968
I Got Dem Ol' Kozmic Blues Again Mama! 1969
Pearl, 1971
In Concert, 1972
Janis Joplin's Greatest Hits, 1973 (compilation)
Janis, 1974 (sound track, previously released material)
Farewell Song, 1982 (compilation)
Cheap Thrills/ I Got Dem Ol' Kozmic Blues Again Mama!/ Pearl, 1995 (boxed set)

SELECT AWARDS

Rock and Roll Hall of Fame, inducted 1995

SEE ALSO: Doors, The; Hendrix, Jimi; Jefferson Airplane / Jefferson Starship; Kristofferson, Kris; Leadbelly; Midler, Bette.

Journey

ORIGINAL MEMBERS: Neal Schon (b. 1954), Prairie Prince (b. 1950), Gregg Rolie (b. 1947), Ross Valory (b. 1949), George Tickner

OTHER MEMBERS: Jonathan Cain (b. 1950), Steve Perry (b. 1949), Steve Smith (b. 1954), Aynsley Dunbar (b. 1946), Robert Fleischman, Steve Augeri

FIRST ALBUM RELEASE: *Journey*, 1975
MUSICAL STYLE: Rock and roll

In 1972, former Santana production manager Herbie Herbert organized a group of San Francisco musicians, including Ross Valory (bass), Prairie Prince (drums), George Tickner (guitar), and former Santana guitar prodigy Neal Schon. Santana founder Gregg Rolie (keyboards/vocals), who had helped arrange the Latin-rock band's first four albums, also joined the group. Originally named the Golden Gate Rhythm Section, the ensemble of previously successful musicians was intended to be an instrumental jazz-fusion band designed for stadium concerts rather than record sales. The group soon changed its name to Journey.

Prince shortly departed to rejoin the Tubes and was quickly replaced by English drummer Aynsley Dunbar. Dunbar had one of the most impressive résumés in rock, having played with John Mayall, Frank Zappa, Jeff Beck, and David Bowie. This lineup debuted New Year's Eve, 1973, at San Francisco's Winterland Ballroom. The next day, they played at the Sunshine Festival in Diamondhead Crater in Hawaii. Their debut album, *Journey*, was primarily a collection of instrumental tracks with occasional vocals by Rolie. Tickner departed before the group's next albums, *Look into the Future* (1976) and *Next* (1977), each continuations of the instrumental style.

Seeking a lead singer, Journey first hired Robert Fleischman, who was soon fired. Manager Herbert heard a demo tape of singer Steve Perry, whose hiring brought major changes to the band. With Perry, *Infinity* (1978) became the group's first commercial success yielding three hit singles, "Wheel in the Sky," "Anytime," and "Lights." Conflicts with Dunbar lead to his departure and replacement by Steve Smith, who had played with

Journey (Paul Natkin)

Journey's warm-up band, Montrose. Smith drummed on *Evolution* (1979), *Departure* (1980), and the 1981 live album, *Captured.* Rolie, tired of life on the road, helped choose his own replacement, keyboardist Jonathan Cain of the Babies.

Cain's presence was evident in 1981's *Escape,* for which he cowrote all songs, including the singles "Who's Cryin' Now," "Don't Stop Believin'" and their biggest seller, "Open Arms." The album reached number 1, selling more than nine million copies. While not enjoying critical acclaim, the band was given credit for creating the "power ballad" genre of rock, a form emulated by bands such as Styx and Foreigner.

The follow-up album, 1983's *Frontiers,* also went platinum, producing two hits, "Separate Ways (Worlds Apart)" and "Faithfully." However, when the band returned to the studio, personal difficulties arose when Perry wanted to produce the record, which led to the ouster of Valory and Smith. Journey continued as a trio but did not release a new record until 1986, *Raised on Radio,* criticized for largely being a Perry solo effort. On February 1, 1987, the group formally disbanded.

Reformation. From 1989 through 1996, former Journey members worked together with their bandmates in other projects, notably Schon's Hardline, which evolved into Bad English with Cain on keyboards. In 1991, the Storm included Gregg Rolie, Steve Smith, and Ross Valory. Finally, in 1996, Schon, Cain, Valory, Smith, and Perry reunited and released their reunion album, *Trial by Fire.* The single "When You Love a Woman" made the Top 10, but in 1997, Perry broke his hip and was unable to tour. In March of 1998, Perry was ousted, and Steve Augeri of Tall Stories replaced him. —*Wesley Britton*

SELECT DISCOGRAPHY

■ ALBUMS

Journey, 1975
Look into the Future, 1976
Evolution, 1979
Departure, 1980
Journey: Greatest Hits Live, 1998 (compilation)

SEE ALSO: Santana, Carlos; Zappa, Frank / The Mothers of Invention.

The Judds / Wynonna Judd

The Judds

MEMBERS: Naomi Judd (b. Diana Ellen Judd, 1946), Wynonna Judd (b. Christina Ciminella, 1964)

FIRST SINGLE RELEASE: "Had a Dream (for the Heart)," 1983

Wynonna Judd

BORN: Ashland, Kentucky; May 30, 1964

FIRST SINGLE RELEASE: "She Is His Only Need," 1992

MUSICAL STYLE: Country

Mother and daughter duo the Judds was the most successful female country act of the 1980's. Wynonna's strong and flexible voice coupled with her mother Naomi's harmony highlighted a series of number 1 country hits from 1984 through 1989. Diagnosed in 1990 with chronic hepatitis, Naomi announced her retirement from the act. After a yearlong cross-country tour, the Judds gave their final concert to more than twelve thousand fans on December 4, 1991, at Middle Tennessee State University in Murfreesboro, Tennessee, just south of Nashville, the home of modern country music. Broadcast over cable television and later a best-selling home video, this show perfectly captured the beauty and the bright harmonies that always characterized their performances. With their stunning appearance (it was hard to guess who was the mother and who was the daughter), they benefited from the rise of television channel The Nashville Network (TNN) and the age of the music video. After the Judds ruled the charts for eight years, Wynonna went on to a successful solo career in the 1990's.

The Beginnings. Born a city girl in Ashland, Kentucky, in 1946 to a service station manager, Naomi Judd was a vivacious, bright, and attractive girl in high school. Married to Michael Ciminella at age eighteen in 1964 and giving birth to Christina the same year, she and and her husband decided to move to California in 1967. There a second daughter, Ashley (a successful actress), was born in 1968. Soon Naomi's marriage failed, and she and Michael separated and later divorced. As a mother of two young daughters, she had to support herself and spent several years working part-time as a secretary, receptionist, and model.

Wynonna and Naomi Judd in 1984 (AP/Wide World Photos)

Still calling herself Diana, she decided to move back to Kentucky with Christina and Ashley and to study nursing at Eastern Kentucky University. In 1976, the family settled into a sort of back-to-the-earth existence outside Berea. Living in an old house in the country, without television or indoor plumbing, they began to search out their roots. Christina had musical talent and began to study the guitar. Mother and daughter began to sing together and found bluegrass and old-time country music to their taste. Diana began writing songs inspired by the harmonies and downhome themes of duos such as the Delmore Brothers and the Louvin Brothers. Consciously, they wanted to recapture the simpler values that they had lost in California.

California beckoned again, however. This time they moved to northern California to avoid as much as possible the glitz of Los Angeles where they had lived before. Mother and daughter began to perform together casually in public. Diana returned to nursing school and completed her degree at the end of 1977. Completing a process of discovery for herself, Diana legally changed her name to Naomi, and shortly after, Christina became Wynonna. Wynonna pursued her own guitar playing and absorption of all types of popular music. In particular she loved the singing of Bonnie Raitt. By the end of 1978, they decided to move back east to pursue musical careers.

Duo of the 1980's. In 1979 they moved to the Nashville area with a plan to break into the country music business. This period was a troubled one for country artists. The music had become more pop-oriented in recent years, and by the early 1980's, sales had declined when a certain blandness had crept into the music. Something new was needed. What happened in the next decade has been called the resurgence of traditional country music, or new traditionalism. In the 1980's, singers such as Ricky Skaggs (from a bluegrass background that used only acoustic instruments and focused on themes and harmony styles harking back to the 1930's and 1940's), George Strait with his Texas dance hall and hard country roots, Randy Travis, and Reba McEntire became major purveyors of a harder-edged style of country that used basic instrumentations and avoided the gloss of string orchestrations.

The Judds—Naomi and Wynonna as a duo—fit right in. It took a short time for them to make the necessary contacts. Naomi went to work as a nurse in Franklin, just south of Nashville, where they

For the Record

The Judds were asked to do a live audition before top executives at RCA in 1983. This type of live performance test was uncommon. Nervously strumming her acoustic guitar, Wynonna sang lead with her mother on harmony. They sang their favorite old-time song, "The Sweetest Gift," and some of Naomi's own compositions. The executives asked them to leave for a while. Adjourning to a nearby restaurant, the duo waited anxiously. After a few minutes, the executives came in. Expecting a refusal after four years of trying to break through, they were shocked to be offered a contract on the spot.

bought a small old house and where Wynonna went to high school. Singing on an early morning Nashville Network show and sending around a sample tape of their songs, they finally managed an audition with RCA Records and signed a contract in 1983. Their first single, "Had a Dream (for the Heart)," made an impression, but it was with their next release in 1984, "Mama He's Crazy," that they began their string of number 1 country hits. From then through 1989, their number 1 hits included "Why Not Me" (1984), "Girls Night Out" (1985), "Love Is Alive" (1985), "Grandpa (Tell Me 'Bout the Good Old Days)" (1986), "Rockin' with the Rhythm of the Rain" (1986), "Maybe Your Baby's Got the Blues" (1987), and "Turn It Loose" (1988). Numerous other singles also ranked high on the charts.

The Judds' music was distinctive. The first female duo to make a mark, they featured simple arrangements and sparse instrumentation. As suggested by their song titles, they could perform positive love songs, rocking numbers, bluesy songs of complaint, and nostalgic pieces about days gone by. Wynonna sang lead vocals; Naomi added the harmonies, usually on choruses. Early on, Wynonna displayed a remarkable ability to handle different types of material: the bluesy and tough or the sweet and sentimental. With the instrumental textures bright and clear, her voice was the focus of the music and revealed a wide range.

In addition to the influence of Bonnie Raitt, Elvis Presley was a favorite of Wynonna's. The Judds' first single was a cover of a Presley song, and their cover of "Don't Be Cruel" (1987) was a Top-10 country hit. Naomi wrote many songs, a few of which were recorded by the duo, most notably "Guardian Angels," a tribute to her Kentucky kin. A bluesy song such as "One Man Woman" and Carl Perkins's rockabilly "Let Me Tell You About Love" were just as well and convincingly done as the old-time duet song they had sung for years, "The Sweetest Gift."

Wynonna Solo. Beginning in 1992, Wynonna would prove herself a major solo country singer. She has been able to expand on the vocal skills and lead singing role she had with her mother to take on a somewhat more bluesy and assertive singing style. Her first single in 1992, "She Is His Only Need," was a deeply moving story of a man so in love with his wife that he willingly goes into debt to give her the things she needs. The song went to number 1. Her first album produced two other number 1 singles and a number 4 hit with "My Strongest Weakness," a tender song written by Naomi. Both her first album, *Wynonna* (1992), and her second, *Tell Me Why* (1993), went to number 1. Later songs such as the rocking "Girls with Guitars" (1994), written by Mary Chapin Carpenter, slow and tender songs such as "To Be Loved by You" (1996) and "Come Some Rainy Day" (1997), and such a wistful song as "Love by Grace" (1996) testify to Wynonna's ranking as one of the handful of truly major and long-lasting female singers of the twentieth century. Her versatile voice can handle bold and brassy songs and be as soft and introspective as needed on ballads; she is a truly a soulful singer. —*Frederick E. Danker*

SELECT DISCOGRAPHY

■ ALBUMS

The Judds

The Judds: Wynonna & Naomi, 1984

Heart Land, 1987

Love Can Build a Bridge, 1990
The Judds Collection, 1983-1990, 1992

Wynonna Judd

Wynonna, 1992
Tell Me Why, 1993
Collection, 1997 (compilation)
The Other Side, 1997

SELECT AWARDS

Grammy Award for Best Country Performance by a Duo or Group with Vocal for "Mama He's Crazy," 1984
Country Music Association Horizon Award, 1984
Grammy Award for Best Country Performance by a Duo or Group with Vocal for *Why Not Me*, 1985
Country Music Association Vocal Group of the Year Award, 1985, 1986, 1987
Grammy Award for Best Country Performance by a Duo or Group with Vocal for "Grandpa (Tell Me 'Bout the Good Old Days)," 1986
Grammy Award for Best Country Performance by a Duo or Group with Vocal for "Give a Little Love," 1988
Country Music Association Vocal Duo of the Year Award, 1988, 1989, 1990, 1991
Grammy Award for Best Country Performance by a Duo or Group with Vocal and Best Country Song (wr. with John Jarvis and Paul Overstreet) for "Love Can Build a Bridge," 1991

SEE ALSO: McEntire, Reba; Raitt, Bonnie; Skaggs, Ricky; Strait, George; Travis, Randy.

K

Kansas

ORIGINAL MEMBERS: David Hope (b. 1949), Phil Ehart (b. 1951), Kerry Livgren (b. 1949), Robert Steinhardt (b. 1951), Steve Walsh (b. 1951), Richard Williams (b. 1951)
OTHER MEMBERS: John Elefante (b. 1958), Steve Morse (b. 1954), Billy Greer
FIRST ALBUM RELEASE: *Kansas*, 1974
MUSICAL STYLES: Art rock, progressive rock

The 1970's were dominated by many hybrid rock styles. Bands such as the Eagles, the Marshall Tucker band, and Lynyrd Skynyrd successfully fused country and rock. Funk and disco, which incorporated many ideas from African culture into mainstream rock in the United States, were popular in dance clubs. Bands such as Chicago, Tower of Power, and Blood, Sweat and Tears were combining jazz with rock to form yet another blended style. Some bands even tried to bridge the gap between European classical music and American rock. This style, known as art rock, was made popular by bands such as Genesis, Yes, Styx, Jethro Tull, and Kansas.

From White Clover to Kansas. After finding few opportunities as a rock artist in England, Phil Ehart returned to his homestate of Kansas in 1972, determined to put together a band. Ehart first contacted Steve Walsh, a singer-keyboardist with whom he had worked in previous bands. Walsh, who had been washing windows in Missouri, gladly accepted the offer to get back into the music scene. Classically trained violinist Robby Steinhardt became the third member of the band. Although he had spent his early years in Michigan and Ohio, he moved to Lawrence, Kansas, where his musicologist father served on the faculty of the University of Kansas. Dave Hope and Rich Williams, a high school friend of Ehart, had recently left a band following their midwestern tour and asked to be a part of Ehart's group. Ehart was pleased to be working with them again.

Originally known as White Clover, the five-man band set up a concert tour of the Midwest. Although pleased with Walsh's songwriting abilities, Ehart felt that the group would benefit from an additional songwriter. His search led him to contact his friend Kerry Livgren, a keyboard player, guitarist, and vocalist. Livgren had put together several bands of his own—one of them bearing the name Kansas—but they were not financially successful in spite of their good reputation among local fans. With Livgren on board, the band changed its name to Kansas and began their search for a recording contract.

Kansas Conquers the United States. Promoter Don Kirshner, who was starting his own label, signed the young group after hearing their demo tape. In 1973 the band set to work on their debut album, *Kansas,* which was released in March, 1974, and sold 100,000 copies. In that year Kansas quickly rose from playing in clubs to opening for major rock acts on the West Coast. Their two following albums, *Song for America* (1975) and *Masque* (1975) were moderately successful, selling about 250,000 copies each. Kansas finally reached the pinnacle of their success with the release of *Leftoverture* in October, 1976, selling more than two million copies. This album yielded their first hit single, "Carry On Wayward Son" (written by

For the Record

"We are a potpourri of every kind of music we ever heard. We've been called a classical-rock band, told we're hard, heavy metal, that we sound like Marshall Tucker, like Yes, like Jethro Tull. Nobody can put their finger on us—except our fans. They always know." —*Kerry Livgren, 1977*

Livgren). Snappy lyrics such as "Masquerading as a man with a reason/ my charade is the event of the season" combined with two memorable musical hooks gave this song popular appeal. A heartfelt folk sound is created by the acoustic guitar in the song "Cheyenne Anthem." Also given airplay was the song "The Wall," which also boasts very introspective lyrics while incorporating characteristically classical harmonic progressions and modulations. Another song in which classical influences dominate is "Miracles out of Nowhere" with its fugue during the instrumental break. Additional classical features that appear in *Leftoverture* include sudden shifts in tonality and rhythm, extended instrumental breaks, and the use of violin throughout the album. Another characteristic of art rock prevalent in Kansas' music is the increased frequency and classically inspired structure of the instrumental breaks. These solos are often derived from themes previously played in the introduction or musical hook, rather than being purely improvised.

Following the success of *Leftoverture*, the band wished to change their image. Feeling that they had been labeled a progressive or classical-rock band, they sought to simplify their music and pursue a more commercial direction. *Point of Know Return,* their fourth album, was released in September of 1977. This highly popular album yielded two hit singles: the title song (written by Walsh, Ehart, and Steinhardt) and the folk-like "Dust in the Wind" (written by Livgren). This turn to a simpler sound had not affected their philosophically intense lyrics or their craftsmanship in songwriting, as the album went platinum.

The Show Is Over. Uncertain of their artistic direction and victims of the changing times, Kansas began to fall from favor. Their first live release, *Two for the Show* (1978), did not sell as well as their previous albums. The next two releases, *Monolith* (1979) and *Audio-Visions* (1980) went gold but were not as popular as the band's earlier work. In 1981, Steve Walsh left the band as the result of a disagreement with the group's new direction, and he was replaced by John Elefante from Levittown, New York. Kansas' next album, *Vinyl Confessions* (1982) featured four compositions by singer, songwriter, and keyboard player Elefante. This new lineup also released *Drastic Measures* in 1983, but neither release gained critical acclaim. Kansas split up in 1983, with Livgren and Hope going their separate ways and becoming born-again Christians. After leaving Kansas, Livgren released an album titled *Seeds of Change,* based on his religious experiences, which was a complete failure commercially.

The Reformation. In 1986, Kansas was reborn when three of the founding members (Phil Ehart, Rich Williams, and Steve Walsh) recruited bassist Billy Greer, formerly of the band Streets, and guitarist and accomplished solo artist Steve Morse of the Dixie Dregs. Morse had already built a sturdy reputation as one of the most skilled guitarists in the country. This new version of Kansas signed with a new label and went into the studio to record the album *Power,* released in October, 1986. In an attempt to develop a more contemporary image they abandoned their classical roots in favor of a heavier, hard-driving rock sound that earned moderate acclaim, but failed to recapture their fame of years gone by. —*Kimberly Morgan*

SELECT DISCOGRAPHY

■ ALBUMS

Kansas, 1974
Song for America, 1975
Masque, 1975
Leftoverture, 1976
Two for the Show, 1978
Monolith, 1979
Audio-Visions, 1980
Vinyl Confessions, 1982
Drastic Measures, 1983
The Best of Kansas, 1984 (compilation)
Power, 1986
In the Spirit of Things, 1988
Live at the Whisky, 1992
Freaks of Nature, 1995

KC and the Sunshine Band

ORIGINAL MEMBERS: Harry Wayne "KC" Casey (b. 1951), Richard Finch (b. 1954), Jerome

Smith (b. 1953), Robert Johnson (b. 1953), Fermin Coytisolo (b. 1951), Charles Williams (b. 1954), Ronnie Smith (b. 1952), Beverly Champion Foster, Jeanette Williams, Margaret Reynolds, Debra Carter, Whit Sidener, Denvil Liptrot

OTHER MEMBERS: Mike Lewis, Vinnie Tanno, Kenny Faulk

FIRST ALBUM RELEASE: *Do It Good,* 1974

MUSICAL STYLES: Disco, pop

Formed in 1973 in the studios of T.K. Records in Hialeah, Florida, KC and the Sunshine Band were one of the most popular disco acts of the 1970's. Harry Wayne "KC" Casey and Richard Finch perfected a blend of catchy, hedonistic chants and infectious disco rhythms that by 1979 had resulted in seven Top-10 hits, five of which went to number 1. Although Casey did not release an album of new material after 1984, the Miami sound he helped pioneer would live on both on radio (the dance trio K.W.S. made the Top 10 with a remake of "Please Don't Go" in 1992) and television (Budweiser featured "Get Down Tonight" in its well-known Bud Lite commercials in 1995).

Behind the Scenes. Casey and Finch met in Hialeah, Florida, where Casey was working as a record distributor and Finch as an engineer for T.K. Records. Between Casey's experience with other people's hits and Finch's bass playing and studio prowess, the two were able to consistently write songs that sounded equally good on the radio and in the discotheque.

After several minor rhythm-and-blues hits in both the United States and Europe under the names KC and the Junkanoo Sunshine Band and KC and the Sunshine Band, the duo enjoyed a breakthrough in 1974, when George McCrae's recording of their song "Rock Me Baby" went to number 1 on both the pop and rhythm-and-blues charts. The song prefigured what would come to be the Casey-Finch formula: exuberant singing and bright horns punctuating simple lyrics and catchy choruses over a lively disco beat. McCrae returned to the Top 40 once more with another Casey-Finch song, "I Get Lifted," in 1975. Compared, however, to the hugely successful "Rock Me Baby," "I Get Lifted" was a relative failure, and McCrae never returned to the pop charts.

Chart Topping Made Easy. Five months after the second McCrae release, another Casey-Finch composition topped the charts: "Get Down Tonight" hit the Top 40 in August, 1975, where it spent nine weeks, one of them at number 1. This time, though, Casey and Finch, as KC and the Sunshine Band, performed it themselves. No sooner had "Get Down Tonight" fallen off the charts than the follow-up, "That's the Way (I Like It)," also hit the top spot.

On the strength of the singles, *KC and the Sunshine Band* (1975) rose to number 4. As if to demonstrate, however, the extent to which the group would be regarded as a singles band, the album failed to go gold. The group's 1976 *Part 3* album fared no better, peaking at number 13 despite the fact that two of its four hit singles reached number 1 and one of them reached number 2.

Nonetheless, KC and the Sunshine Band's string of Top-40 smashes made it the quintessential disco act. With Casey as the lead-singing, keyboard-playing frontman and a mostly black nine-member band stocked with percussionists, horn players, and background singers, the group symbolized disco's cross-cultural appeal as faithfully as it captured disco's high spirits.

The group had little time to enjoy their moment at the top. As "Keep It Comin' Love," the last of the *Part 3* singles, was falling off the charts, the *Saturday Night Fever* sound-track album was released. Eventually becoming the best-selling sound-track album of all time, it turned the Bee Gees into disco's standard bearers, leaving other acts—KC and the Sunshine Band included—to fend for themselves in the Bee Gees' shadow. The group enjoyed one fringe benefit from the popularity of *Saturday Night Fever:* "Boogie Shoes," which originally appeared on the group's 1975 *KC and the Sunshine Band* album, became the band's seventh Top-40 hit when it was included on the sound track and released as a single in 1978. In 1979 the group returned to the top of the charts with the ballads "Please Don't Go" and "Yes, I'm Ready," a remake of the 1965 Barbara Mason hit.

For the Record

The disco rhythm of "Rock Your Baby," the number 1 hit that Casey and Finch wrote for George McCrae in 1974, inspired Benny Andersson and Bjorn Ulvaeus of the Swedish pop group Abba to write "Dancing Queen," which in 1977 became Abba's only number 1 single in the United States.

As the decade ended, the abundance and stylistic variety of the group's hits suggested that many years of hitmaking lay ahead.

Crashes and Comebacks. With the advent of the 1980's and the decline of disco, the group's hits slowed. When Casey was seriously injured in a 1982 automobile crash, the hits stopped altogether. In 1984 Casey returned with the *KC Ten* album and scored a Top-20 hit with "Give It Up." It was to be the last of his hits. When his father died later that year, Casey turned to alcohol and pills. He was eventually hospitalized and spent the better part of one year in rehabilitation. His half-hearted attempts at comebacks in 1985 and 1986 met with little success, and by 1990 he had retired from show business. His decision in 1991 to attempt yet another comeback stemmed from the renewed popularity of dance-oriented music and the interest shown in the music of KC and the Sunshine Band by late-night talk-show host Arsenio Hall. Casey returned to live performing, supported by a new fifteen-member Sunshine Band. From the original lineup, only the background singer Beverly Champion Foster and the percussionist Fermin Coytisolo remained.

In 1992 the British dance trio K.W.S. earned a gold single with a remake of "Please Don't Go." The album from which it was taken, *Please Don't Go (the Album)*, also included versions of "Keep It Comin' Love" and "Rock Your Baby."

In 1994 the group participated in "A '70's Celebration: The Beat Is Back," a television special that also featured performances by disco-era stars such as the Bee Gees, Donna Summer, Olivia Newton-John, the Spinners, and the Stylistics. Neither that special, however, nor the group's return to performing resulted in new music. With the exception of a James Brown medley and a version of the Patti LaBelle hit "New Attitude," the group's 1995 *Get Down Live!* album consisted largely of the group's old hits. —*Arsenio Orteza*

SELECT DISCOGRAPHY

■ SINGLES

"Get Down Tonight," 1975
"That's the Way (I Like It)," 1975
"(Shake, Shake, Shake) Shake Your Booty," 1976
"I'm Your Boogie Man," 1977
"Keep It Comin' Love," 1977
"Boogie Shoes," 1978

■ ALBUMS

Do It Good, 1974
Who Do Ya (Love), 1978
Do You Wanna Go Party? 1979
All in a Night's Work, 1982
KC Ten, 1984
The Best of KC and the Sunshine Band, 1989 (compilation)
Get Down Live! 1995

SELECT AWARDS

Grammy Award for Best R&B Song for "Where Is the Love," 1975 (Harry Wayne Casey with others)
Grammy Award for Album of the Year for *Saturday Night Fever*, 1978 (with others)

SEE ALSO: Abba; Bee Gees, The.

R. Kelly

(Robert Kelly)

BORN: Chicago, Illinois; January 8, 1968
FIRST ALBUM RELEASE: *Born into the '90's*, 1991
MUSICAL STYLE: Rhythm and blues

One of the most dominant rhythm-and-blues (R&B) performers of the 1990's, R. Kelly built a million-selling reputation with raunchy anthems such as "Your Body's Callin'" and "Sex Me." In 1997, Kelly's career took a startling turn when he

R. Kelly in the studio (Paul Natkin)

announced his conversion to Christianity. Kelly celebrated his newfound faith in the song "I Believe I Can Fly," written for the 1997 film *Space Jam* at basketball star Michael Jordan's request.

Taking It to the Streets. Robert Kelly grew up in the tough housing projects of Chicago's South Side, where his mother exerted a strong influence on him. While other kids joined street gangs for protection, Kelly found a safe haven in music, singing in a Baptist choir. He soon turned to street performance. "It started out as me and my boys just messing around," Kelly said. "Then one of the fellows dropped a hat while I was playing this keyboard and people started putting money in it. That became our thing. I simply made a regular job out of it."

Kelly, who taught himself to play keyboards, was discovered while performing at a barbecue and was signed to Jive Records. His 1991 debut, *Born into the '90's*, presented Kelly as the latest of the "new-jack" singers—the suavest and sexiest in a line that included Keith Sweat and Bobby Brown. The album went platinum on the strength of Kelly's pleading, gospel-tinged vocals and streetwise rhythms. On 1993's *12 Play*, Kelly turned up the sexual heat, loading the album with lewd lyrics and song titles. "Bump n' Grind" became the longest-running number 1 rhythm-and-blues single in three decades. On tour, Kelly capped his encore by dropping his pants. If the year saw Kelly establish himself as a superstar, however, it also delivered a crushing blow when his mother passed away.

Growing Up in Public. In December, 1994, Kelly met contemporary gospel performer Kirk Franklin, and the two struck up a friendship. Kelly was searching for consolation after his mother's death, and Franklin acted as a spiritual mentor. "Losing my mom saddened me and took me through a lot of trauma," Kelly said.

On his 1995 self-titled album, Kelly was still topping the charts with sexually explicit songs such as "You Remind Me of Somethin'," but there were also signs that Kelly was maturing. On "As I Look into My Life," Kelly sang without accompaniment, his voice verging on sobbing: "Oh, Lord, will you help me find me/ Take this crazy, crazy past of mine and put it behind me." The album closed with "Trade in My Life," a powerful, soul-searching track anchored by a gospel chorus.

Two years later, Kelly picked an unusual time and place to announce that he had become a Christian. He made a guest appearance at one

For the Record

R. Kelly is an avid basketball fan and player. Before his performance at the 1998 Grammy Awards, he went out and shot some hoops to calm himself down.

of Franklin's concerts in Chicago, dressed in a conservative grey suit. As he sat down to perform the song "I Believe I Can Fly," he told the audience, "I used to be flying in sin—now I'm flying in Jesus."

Eyes on the Prize. Despite his considerable success, Kelly had never won a Grammy Award prior to 1997. His sex-drenched lyrics likely hurt his standing with voters from the National Academy of Recording Arts and Sciences, the group that awards the Grammys. With "I Believe I Can Fly," however, Kelly took home three Grammy Awards, for Best R&B Song, Best Song Written Specifically for a Motion Picture or for Television, and Best Male R&B Vocal Performance. "Oh, wow," Kelly exclaimed on accepting the Best R&B Male Vocal award, "You know when you pray for something, you get better than what you pray for."

—*Louis R. Carlozo*

SELECT DISCOGRAPHY

■ ALBUMS

Born into the '90's, 1991

12 Play, 1993

R. Kelly, 1995

R., 1998

SELECT AWARDS

Grammy Awards for Best R&B Song, Best Male R&B Vocal Performance, and Best Song Written Specifically for a Motion Picture or for Television, all for "I Believe I Can Fly," 1997

SEE ALSO: Sweat, Keith.

Kenny G. *See under* G

Chaka Khan

(Yvette Marie Stevens)

BORN: Great Lakes, Illinois; March 23, 1953

FIRST ALBUM RELEASE: *Rufus*, 1973 (with Rufus)

FIRST SOLO ALBUM RELEASE: *Chaka*, 1978

MUSICAL STYLES: Rhythm and blues, soul, funk, dance, pop, disco

Born Yvette Marie Stevens, Chaka Khan was raised on the South Side of Chicago where, at age eleven, she started her first singing group, the Crystalettes. At age thirteen she was christened "Chaka," meaning fire, by an African shaman and began performing under that name a few years later. She acquired the last name "Khan" after a brief marriage.

Khan's first big career move came at age eighteen when she joined the then-fledgling group Rufus. As the new vocalist, Khan quickly powered Rufus to its first album, *Rufus* (1973), followed by *Rags to Rufus* (1974), which included the Grammy-winning single "Tell Me Something Good," a song written by Stevie Wonder. Rufus effectively blended pop, rock, funk, and soul influences for a musical hybrid that landed eleven albums on the charts and scored nine Top-40 hits over the next five years. With Khan as lead singer, Rufus

Chaka Khan (Reprise/Albert Sanchez)

amassed one platinum album, five gold albums, five gold singles, five number 1 hits, and two Grammys. Rufus hits included "Sweet Thing" and "Once You Get Started."

Solo Success. In mid-1970's, Khan grew interested in pursuing a solo career. She kicked off this next phase of her career in 1978 with *Chaka*, an album that included the hit single "I'm Every Woman," written by the legendary songwriting team of Nick Ashford and Valerie Simpson. Khan released three more solo albums and then reunited with Rufus to record *Live . . . Stompin' at the Savoy*, released in 1983, which included Khan's signature song "Ain't Nobody."

The following year, Khan returned to her solo work and released *I Feel for You*, earning a Grammy for the title track. "Through the Fire," another Khan classic, first appeared on this album as well. After releasing *C.K.* in 1988 and *The Woman I Am* in 1992, Khan expanded her repertoire by taking a lead role in the London West End production of *Mama I Want to Sing* and earning the 1995 Capitol Radio Listener's Poll Award for London's Best Actress. Throughout her solo career, Khan also engaged in many highly successful collaborations. Her duets with Ray Charles ("I'll Be Good to You") and Steve Winwood ("Higher Love") both earned Grammys. In addition, she collaborated with Michael McDonald and Me'Shell NdegeOcello.

In 1998, Khan marked another milestone when she released *Come 2 My House*, the first release on her newly formed Earth Song Entertainment label. The same year, Khan established the Chaka Khan Foundation to support a variety of social causes. —*Harriet L. Schwartz*

SELECT DISCOGRAPHY

■ SINGLES

"Tell Me Something Good," 1974 (with Rufus)
"I'm Every Woman," 1978
"Ain't Nobody," 1983 (with Rufus)

■ ALBUMS

Rufus, 1973 (with Rufus)
Rags to Rufus, 1974 (with Rufus)
Rufus Featuring Chaka Khan, 1975 (with Rufus)
Chaka, 1978
Naughty, 1980
What Cha' Gonna Do for Me, 1981
Chaka Khan, 1982
Live . . . Stompin' at the Savoy, 1983 (with Rufus)
I Feel for You, 1984
Destiny, 1986
C.K., 1988
Life Is a Dance/The Remix Project, 1989
The Woman I Am, 1992
Epiphany: The Best of Chaka Khan Volume One, 1996 (previously released material)
Come 2 My House, 1998

SELECT AWARDS

Grammy Award for Best R&B Performance by a Duo, Group, or Chorus for "Tell Me Something Good," 1974 (with Rufus)
Grammy Awards for Best R&B Performance by a Duo or Group with Vocal for "Ain't Nobody," 1983 (with Rufus); for Best R&B Vocal Performance, Female, for *Chaka Khan*; for Best Vocal Arrangement for Two or More Voices for "BeBop Medley" (with Arif Mardin), all 1983
Grammy Award for Best R&B Vocal Performance, Female, for "I Feel For You," 1984
Grammy Award for Best R&B Performance by a Duo or Group with Vocal for "I'll Be Good to You," 1990 (with Ray Charles)
Grammy Award for Best R&B Vocal Performance, Female, for *The Woman I Am*, 1992

SEE ALSO: Charles, Ray; Prince; Traffic / Steve Winwood / Dave Mason.

Albert King

(Albert Nelson)

BORN: Indianola, Mississippi; April 25, 1923
DIED: Memphis, Tennessee; December 21, 1992
FIRST ALBUM RELEASE: *The Big Blues*, 1962
MUSICAL STYLES: Blues, soul, rhythm and blues

Albert King was born Albert Nelson, one of thirteen children of an itinerant preacher and gospel singer in rural Mississippi. His childhood was one of hard work on plantations, but he also sang in a gospel group and taught himself to play a homemade guitar. Around 1931, his family moved to the vicinity of Osceola, Arkansas. Osceola was a well-known early center of the rural blues, close to both Memphis, Tennessee, and the Missouri state line. Albert continued chopping and picking cotton, but he also honed his musical skills singing gospel in churches. He bought his first guitar in 1939 in Boyce City, Arkansas, for one dollar and twenty-five cents and eventually began playing and singing in blues clubs. He lived for a short time in St. Louis, Missouri, but returned to the Osceola area. There he joined a local "jump" band called the In the Groove Boys, which played such popular blues clubs as the T-99 and the Dipsy Doodle. He moved again, this time to Gary, Indiana, and lived there in 1952 and 1953. In Gary, King met Jimmy Reed and played drums with Reed's band for a time. He recorded "Bad Luck Blues" and "Be on Your Merry Way" for the Parrot label in 1953, but sales were poor, and he returned to Osceola one more time before moving back to St. Louis in 1956.

Developing a Distinctive Style. King spent the next ten years refining his style. He had been influenced both by the heavy blues style of such early bluesmen as Elmore James, Robert Nighthawk, Howlin' Wolf, and Robert Johnson, and the lighter approach of B. B. King and T-Bone Walker. Albert King, B.B. King, and Freddie King were not related, but the three musicians were the kings of the guitar-driven blues sound that first began to be embraced by white audiences in the United States in the 1960's. Their musical style was adopted, and sometimes copied, by early rock musicians, first in Great Britain and shortly thereafter in the United States.

Albert King's blues style remained closer to his earthy, rural roots than did that of the better-known B. B. King. Many critics have ranked Albert King as the premier guitar stylist of modern blues. He had a solid, straight-ahead style, marked by aggressive phrasing, an ability to twist notes while punching at the rhythm with finesse, a pronounced, driving, rhythmic delivery, and a broad, metallic sound, featuring repetition and enhanced by his talent at pulling vibrations from a single note. He played a Gibson Flying V guitar, which he named Lucy, reminiscent of B. B. King's guitar, Lucille. Few other blues guitarists played the Flying V, a distinctive guitar favored by rock guitarists. Albert King also had a unique style of playing: Never having been taught to play the guitar, he picked it up on his own and taught himself to play on a regular right-handed guitar, although he was left-handed. Because the normal tuning was uncomfortable for him, he also developed an unusual tuning for his guitar.

Albert King (Freddie Patterson Collection/Archive Photos)

The most notable feature of his playing, however, was his exceptional ability to bend the string, pushing the string up or down with the finger to change the string's tension and thus its musical pitch. Using this technique, a player can achieve partial note changes, as well as create a smooth tremolo effect that cannot be achieved by moving from one string to another. The heavyset, six-foot, four-inch tall King was an imposing figure, usually smoking a pipe while he played, and he complemented his guitar stylings with gritty vocals. He had once worked as a bulldozer operator, and his playing reflected his power.

Achieving National Recognition. In 1959, King had a minor hit with "I'm a Lonely Man," and in 1962, "Don't Throw Your Love on Me So Strong" reached number 14 on the national rhythm-and-blues charts. King then slipped from the charts for several years before signing with the Stax label in Memphis in 1966, with which he stayed until 1974. Stax specialized in the soul sound, a gospel-tinged form of African American music just beginning to gain popularity. With Stax, King was backed by one of the best-known soul rhythm groups, Booker T. and the MG's. Recording classic 1930's blues songs of the Mississippi Delta such as "Crosscut Saw," "Laundromat Blues," and "Born Under a Bad Sign," King made the national rhythm-and-blues charts regularly. These three and other similar songs were collected on the 1967 Stax album *Born Under a Bad Sign*. The album became one of the most important blues albums of the 1960's, strongly influencing such rock-and-roll guitarists as Jimi Hendrix, Eric Clapton and his group Cream, Stevie Ray Vaughn, and Johnny Winter.

King's appeal was wide and versatile: In 1968, he opened for Jimi Hendrix and John Mayall at the Fillmore West, one of the first blues performers to play the renowned San Francisco rock venue. King became a popular and frequent performer there. At the other end of the musical spectrum, King was one of the first blues players to record with a symphony orchestra, performing with the St. Louis Symphony in 1969. While he attracted a strong crossover white audience, he also retained a loyal following at black clubs.

Although King retired several times, he always returned to music. In an interview in the late 1960's, he compared music to an addiction, saying it demands that one keeps coming back to it, not letting one out of its grip. In 1992, King suffered a massive heart attack shortly before he was to embark on a major tour of Europe and died in December of that year. —*Irene Struthers*

For the Record

Albert King had a reputation among musicians as a demanding boss. It is said that when he fired a musician from his band, he gave him three things: a bus ticket to get home, a banana to eat on the trip, and a comic book to read.

SELECT DISCOGRAPHY

■ ALBUMS

Born Under a Bad Sign, 1967
Live Wire/Blues Power, 1968
I'll Play the Blues for You, 1972
New Orleans Heat, 1979
Masterworks, 1982
The Best of Albert King, 1986 (compilation)
Live, 1988
Red House, 1996

SELECT AWARDS

Blues Foundation Hall of Fame, inducted 1983
Guitar Player, Editor's Award for Lifetime Achievement, 1993

SEE ALSO: Clapton, Eric; Cream; Guy, Buddy; Hendrix, Jimi; Howlin' Wolf; Johnson, Robert; King, B. B.; Vaughan, Stevie Ray; Waters, Muddy.

B. B. King

BORN: Itta Bena, Mississippi; September 16, 1925
FIRST SINGLE RELEASE: "Three O'Clock Blues," 1951
MUSICAL STYLES: Blues, rhythm and blues

Riley B. "B. B." King, often referred to as the "King of the Blues," can rightfully be regarded as one of the most original and influential musicians in all of popular music. As the most prolific and highly visible recording artist working primarily in the blues genre, King has assumed the role of the style's ambassador and is credited with having brought the blues from the fringes of the U.S.

music scene to a much more diverse and widespread audience.

Early Life. Riley B. King was the son of Albert and Nora Ella King, sharecroppers whose marriage ended in divorce when their boy was barely four. He was sent to nearby Kilmicheal, Mississippi, where he was raised by his maternal grandmother, Elnora Farr, with whom he would live until her death in 1940. It was during this period in his life that young King was first exposed to the church, an institution in his life which would have immeasurable influence on his musical development. It was while singing in the church choir that King developed both the voice and the presence that would later captivate audiences. It was also there that the choir's director, the Reverend Archie Fair, an in-law on his mother's side, taught King his first three guitar chords, E, A, and B, a rudimentary progression in both the sanctified music of the church and the backwoods-sounding blues of the rural Mississippi Delta region.

By 1935 King had formed a gospel vocal trio consisting of his cousin, Birkett Davis, and a friend, Walter Doris, Jr., a group to which he was doggedly committed. Though determined to remain in Kilmicheal after his grandmother's death, King reluctantly accepted an offer to move in with his father, who by now was raising a new family in Lexington, Mississippi. Within two years King would be back in Kilmicheal reforming the gospel trio and building the foundation for a life as both a farmworker and a singer.

He finally settled in the nearby Delta town of Indianola, the place most often associated with King's earliest musical development. Like so many other area musicians forced to negotiate steady work with musical aspirations, King managed to forge a fairly decent career as a tractor driver, but it was music first and foremost which would drive him far beyond the meager wages of the typical southern agricultural laborer.

His skills as a tractor driver would indeed serve him well for a time in his youth, enabling him to gain both a modicum of local respect and a valuable agricultural deferment which ultimately kept him out of World War II. Still, it was music which served as the driving force in young King's life. By 1943 the gospel trio had expanded to five members and began calling themselves the Saint John's Gospel Singers. They were a moderately successful group which could even boast a few local radio spots. By now, however, King had begun to incorporate blues into his musical repertoire, though typically, and by custom, blues and spiritual music do not coexist peaceably.

Early Memphis Career. Memphis, Tennessee, was the center of postwar blues in the Deep South, and King, like many others, soon realized that Memphis was where he could pursue his musical dream. The security of his day job on Johnson Barrett's plantation made his decision to leave a difficult one, but the deciding factor came in May, 1946, when he accidentally damaged a tractor. Fearing Barrett's angry wrath, King, virtually penniless, left for Memphis and the town's burgeoning music scene.

Postwar Memphis was a fast town by any standards, but for a country boy such as King, Memphis was an entirely new world. Initially, King sought the council and shelter of another family member, his mother's cousin Booker T. Washington White, the noted blues artist who recorded under the name Bukka White. Though they never played together publicly, their private jam sessions and the contacts King made during those early days in Memphis had a dramatic effect on his musical development, though he encountered little commercial success. After ten months of quasi apprenticeship under his cousin, King, depressed and homesick, returned to Indianola in 1947 and worked off his debt.

King would quickly grow tired of the agrarian life, and he returned to Memphis in 1948 with a renewed determination. Once there, he took up with blues radio veterans Aleck "Rice" Miller, who was known as Sonny Boy Williamson, and Robert "Junior" Lockwood, the former a renowned harmonica player and the latter a gifted, albeit moody, guitarist whose style consisted of a curious hybrid of big-band jazz and blues. Impressed, they allowed him to perform on their radio program in West Memphis, Arkansas, another blues mecca of sorts just across the Mississippi River. The venerable Miller even touted King as a rising local talent, and based on the success of his radio appearance, and with Miller's recommendation, King found steady employment playing before live audiences at Miss Annie's Saloon in West Memphis.

The music scene was changing all around northwestern Mississippi, eastern Arkansas, and southwestern Tennessee during these early postwar years, and the appearance of radio station WDIA in Memphis, the first station in the South staffed, managed, and formatted by African Americans, marked one of the most dramatic developments of the period. In 1949 King approached WDIA about using their recording facilities and came away with his own live ten-minute radio spot in which he was to promote the health tonic Pepticon, a rival of Miller's sponsor Hadacol. Opening with the familiar "Pepticon, Pepticon, sure is good—You can get it anywhere in your neighborhood," King's show became so popular that it was expanded to a daily program called the "Sepia Swing Club" and King himself was promoted to full-time disc jockey. Initially calling himself the "Pepticon Boy," King would air recordings of black artists and play along on the air with his guitar wired into the radio board. He would take requests for solos as well, and by the end of the year his popularity from the radio show, coupled with his performances in clubs throughout the legendary Beale Street district of Memphis, helped him shed the "Pepticon Boy" moniker for the less commercial title of "Beale Street Blues Boy," which in time was shortened to "Blues Boy" and ultimately B. B.

B. B. King in 1970 (AP/Wide World Photos)

Recording Career. The uniqueness of B. B. King's musical style can be attributed to his multiple influences, both direct and otherwise. In addition to the lessons learned from his cousin Bukka White and many of the other Memphis musicians with whom he crossed paths came the developmental phases of King's sound that were directly related to his days at WDIA radio. By playing along with the records of some of the world's most innovative and gifted musicians, King was able to foster a guitar technique by fusing the styles of many of the artists aired on his radio program. One can hear in King's guitar playing the blues sounds of Texans "Blind" Lemon Jefferson and Aaron "T-Bone" Walker, New Orleans' versatile guitarist

Lonnie Johnson, and the aforementioned Robert "Junior" Lockwood. From the jazz world King borrowed liberally from the styles of such important artists as Charlie Christian, Eddie Lang, and the legendary guitarist Django Reinhardt, who was something of a fascination of King throughout these early days.

In 1949 King's talents were brought to the attention of Jim Bulleit of Nashville-based Bullet Records. Though none of King's Bullet releases fared well nationally, these recordings caused a local sensation which caught the attention of the Bihari brothers, whose Los Angeles-based Modern Records released six King singles on its RPM subsidiary label near the end of 1949 and forged a professional relationship which would last the next ten years.

By 1951 King was back in Memphis recording in Sam Phillips's now-legendary Sun Studios, though his first national hit record, "Three O'Clock Blues," was actually recorded that same year in a local YMCA. The song was a watershed for the young King, thrusting him into the national blues and rhythm-and-blues spotlight. It was soon followed by a host of other hit records, including "You Know I Love You" in 1952, "Please Love Me" in 1953, and "You Upset Me Baby" in 1954. These successes also allowed for King and his band to begin the arduous touring schedule for which they came to be so famous. Playing all around the United States in venues such as New York's fabled Apollo Theatre, throughout the South in what has been deemed the "chitlin' circuit," a loose conglomeration of roadhouses and honky-tonks where many African American artists honed their talents. As far west as Los Angeles, King was recognized throughout the 1950's as a major national rhythm-and-blues star. In 1956 alone, King and his twelve-piece band played an incredible 342 shows.

King's newfound fame had begun to take its toll on his marriage. His wife, the former Martha Denton whom he married in 1944, had remained in Indianola during his earliest days in Memphis but had joined him after his initial success. Once King began touring, they were once again forced to endure long separations, and this time the marriage broke under the strain. While on tour in 1952, King received word that Martha had left Memphis and filed for divorce, a crushing blow which inspired him to write "Woke Up This Morning," his first big hit following "Three O'Clock Blues."

In order to offset the costs and the logistical uncertainties of traveling, King had purchased a Greyhound bus in 1955 which he dubbed "Big Red" and had it refurbished into a touring vehicle for his eighteen-person entourage. In 1958, however, as Big Red's driver, Millard Lee, swerved to avoid hitting a passing car, the bus careened into a bridge embankment and hit an oncoming oil tanker head on. Though none of the passengers in the bus was hurt, both the drivers died in the crash—King's crew reportedly watched in horror as one of the drivers ran toward the water below with his clothes on fire. King was not on the bus that day, but he had allowed the insurance to lapse over the weekend, leaving him personally responsible for damages, which were in excess of $100,000. This situation kept King in debt for many years to come.

Shortly after the Big Red debacle, King married his second wife, Sue Hall, whose mother had managed a club in Indianola where King had played. As was the case before, however, this marriage collapsed under the strain of King's touring regimen, and the couple divorced in 1966,

For the Record

"Music has no prejudice itself; it's the people who make the difference. And when entertainers get together, they don't think in terms of who's old, who's young, who's white, who's black. We think in terms of combining the talents, and making it good and enjoyable to each other."

§

"The blues? It's the mother of American music. That's what it is—the Source."

—*B. B. King*

an experience which led to the recording which ultimately catapulted King to crossover stardom, "The Thrill Is Gone." His lifestyle was seemingly ill-suited for any long lasting relationships, a condition which would plague him throughout his life.

The 1960's. The 1960's marked some very lean years in King's career. Though he left Modern's subsidiary RPM for the more mainstream ABC-Dunhill label, he was unable to crack into the mainstream of American music until "The Thrill Is Gone" began climbing the pop charts in 1970. Oddly enough, it would be the British blues, the English interpretation of the African American art form, which would rescue King and others like him from virtual obscurity in the mid-1960's, bringing them before an entirely new audience.

Committed London-based artists such as Eric Clapton and the Rolling Stones, along with American rockers with an appreciation of the blues such as Johnny Winter and Paul Butterfield and Michael Bloomfield of the Paul Butterfield Blues Band, began championing the causes of many blues artists who had fallen on hard times. While black youth turned primarily to soul music, young white audiences were being exposed for the first time to a host of blues and blues-related artists, many of whom would serve as opening acts for the much more popular rock-and-roll acts.

The effect on King's music was dramatic. Throughout his salad days of the 1950's, King's shows were celebrations of music with an emphasis on eloquent language and audience participation, much like what Riley King had witnessed in church during his youth. The new white audiences, however, had a decidedly different take on live performance. Though they were generally respectful, they were also passively attentive and demanded much more creative instrumentality. Playing such legendary rock-and-roll venues as the Fillmores East and West, King was forced to refashion his stage show to reflect the technical proficiency of the vaunted guitar hero complete with long and often tedious guitar flourishes, a style made popular by the rock-and-roll guitarists who themselves had learned to play from King's and others' recordings. Throughout this period, and ironically so, King was forced to relearn many of the songs he had recorded years earlier in order to present his new audiences with their preconceived images of him.

King grew to become something of an elder statesmen to the young rock-and-roll generation, but like so many others, he was thrilled to find steady work available once again. With the success of "The Thrill Is Gone," which reached as high as number 15 on the pop charts in 1970 (and number 3 on the rhythm-and-blues charts), King found himself in uncharted waters, a darling of the young white rockers who had taken to referring to him as the "King of the Blues."

Legacy. B. B. King has had a profound effect on blues, rhythm and blues, rock and roll, and to some extent even jazz. He is no longer simply an ambassador of the blues, a mantle he once wore proudly. Rather, he has become an ambassador of all American popular music in general.

He has been honored with inductions to both the blues and the Rock and Roll Halls of Fame, and he has also seen his string of blues clubs, including a very popular Memphis Beale Street location, soar to remarkable commercial success. His opening night in the Memphis location in 1992 culminated in an impromptu jam session that included King, another Indianola guitar great, Albert King, expatriate piano artist Champion Jack Dupree, and lap guitarist Jeff Healey.

Having permanently settled in Las Vegas, Nevada, in the late 1980's, King would operate on a much slower pace into the 1990's as age and a host of health concerns, including diabetes, began to take its toll on his schedule. Nonetheless, he would continue to record prolifically with a variety of jazz, rock, blues, and country artists. For example, he recorded with jazz diva Dianne Schurr, rock group U2, and country legend George Jones as part of a "country-and-blues" project for MCA Records released in 1994. *—Joel Nathan Rosen*

SELECT DISCOGRAPHY

■ ALBUMS

Live at the Regal, 1965

Live in Cook County Jail, 1971

Lucille Talks Back, 1975

Blues 'n' Jazz, 1983
Live at San Quentin, 1990
King of the Blues, 1992 (boxed set, compilation)

SELECT AWARDS
Grammy Award for Best R&B Vocal Performance, Male, for "The Thrill Is Gone," 1970
Blues Foundation Hall of Fame, inducted 1980
Grammy Award for Best Ethnic or Traditional Recording for *There Must Be a Better World Somewhere*, 1981
Rock and Roll Hall of Fame, inducted 1987
Grammy Award for Lifetime Achievement, 1987
Grammy Award for Best Traditional Blues Album for *Blues Summit*, 1993

SEE ALSO: Guy, Buddy; Johnson, Robert; King, Albert; Waters, Muddy.

Ben E. King. *See* The Drifters

Carole King

BORN: Brooklyn, New York; February 9, 1942
FIRST ALBUM RELEASE: *Writer*, 1970
MUSICAL STYLES: Rock and roll, pop

Carole King, born Carole Klein, began her career as a prolific and successful songwriter: she and lyricist Gerry Goffin created more than a hundred Top-40 hits, six of which reached number 1. As a solo singer-songwriter, her 1971 *Tapestry* album produced two more number 1 songs and four Grammy Awards. Twenty-five years later, *Tapestry* was still the twenty-fifth best-selling album in rock-and-roll history. With more than seventeen albums to her credit, King is considered one of the most successful female songwriters of all time.

Precocious Talent. King started singing and playing piano at age four. In her early teens she formed a female vocal group (the Co-Sines) and began writing songs (at her usual furious pace). She completed her first single, "The Right Girl," at age sixteen and was soon marketing her songs in Manhattan. By the time she was twenty, she and husband Gerry Goffin were among the hottest songwriting teams in the music industry.

The Brill Building Era. King's first brush with a national audience came when a neighbor wrote a hit song about her: "Oh! Carol" by Neil Sedaka in 1959. Unfortunately, her response, "Oh Neil" (1960), did not do as well on the charts. It was received favorably by Don Kirshner, however, who signed Goffin and King to a contract with his Aldon Music.

These were the years between the birth of rock and roll in the 1950's and the "British invasion" of the 1960's, the era of teen idols and girl groups. The demand for new songs was great, and Aldon hired a stable of writers to supply large record labels, such as Atlantic, with material. Besides Goffin and King, its other most successful teams included Sedaka and Howie Greenfield ("Breaking Up Is Hard to Do," 1962) and Barry Mann and Cynthia Weil ("You've Lost That Lovin' Feelin'," 1964, with Phil Spector). Working in cubicles at the Brill Building on Broadway (or around the corner from it, in the case of King and Goffin), some two hundred of the music company's songs made the charts between 1959 and 1964.

The first Goffin-King number 1 hit was "Will You Still Love Me Tomorrow," recorded by the Shirelles in 1960. Next came "Take Good Care of My Baby" by Bobby Vee in 1961. Steve Lawrence reached the top spot with "Go Away Little Girl" in 1962, as did Donny Osmond in 1971. Similarly, Little Eva (who was Goffin and King's babysitter) hit number 1 with "The Loco-Motion" (1962), which happened again with Grand Funk Railroad's version of the tune in 1974.

Although not reaching number 1, many other key compositions of the era were written by Goffin and King: "Up on the Roof" (the Drifters, 1962), "One Fine Day" (the Chiffons, 1963), "I'm into Something Good" (Herman's Hermits, 1964), "(You Make Me Feel Like) A Natural Woman" (Aretha Franklin, 1967), and "Pleasant Valley Sunday" (the Monkees, 1967).

The team contributed more than songs to Kirshner's empire, with Goffin producing and King arranging for his Dimension label in the

For the Record

On their first trip to New York, the Beatles wanted to meet Gerry Goffin and Carole King, whom John Lennon and Paul McCartney counted among their idols.

early 1960's. "The Loco-Motion" was Dimension's first release. King's single "It Might as Well Rain Until September" (1962) was its second hit. King and Goffin went on to found their own Tomorrow label in the mid-1960's, which foundered when it failed to put a single on the charts.

On Her Own. King divorced Goffin in 1968 and switched coasts, moving to Los Angeles. She withdrew from the industry for a time, tending to two young daughters (Louise and Sherry) but still writing songs. She formed a group, the City, with bass player Charles Larkey (her second husband) and guitarist Danny "Kootch" Kortchmar. They recorded an album in 1969, *Now That Everything's Been Said.* King soon began a solo career. Kortchmar introduced her to another new artist, James Taylor, for whom she played piano in the studio (*Sweet Baby James,* 1970) and eventually on tour. In return, he encouraged her to perform, and he appeared on *Writer,* her 1970 debut album.

It was her next release, *Tapestry* (1971), which brought King mass acclaim. It reached the top spot on the U.S. album charts and sold in excess of ten million copies. King won four Grammy Awards, for Record of the Year, Song of the Year, Best Pop Female Vocalist, and Album of the Year. In addition, King reached number 1 twice more with "It's Too Late"/"I Feel the Earth Move" and with James Taylor's version of "You've Got a Friend."

In *Tapestry*'s Wake. Remarkably, King's next album, *Music,* was released in December of the same year. It too reached number 1. King would go on to complete five more albums with Lou Adler and Ode Records. Her success continued; all but one album (a sound track) went gold or beyond. "Been to Canaan" from 1972's *Rhymes and Reasons* hit number 2, as did "Jazzman" from 1974's *Wrap Around Joy.* She combined her talents with those of author Maurice Sendak to create *Really Rosie,* an animated television special, the following year. Her 1976 *Thoroughbred* album included four songs reuniting Goffin and King; *Rolling Stone*'s Stephen Holden labeled it her finest work since *Tapestry.*

King moved to Capitol Records in 1976. Unfortunately, her luck changed as well. *Rolling Stone* decided to name *Simple Things* the worst album of 1977 (although it too went gold). *Welcome Home* (1978) marked the first time that she did not reach the Top 100. Her collaborator and third husband, Rick Evers, died of a heroin overdose within a year of their wedding. Some interpreted 1980's *Pearls—The Songs of Goffin and King* as a sign that her muse had departed. She did, however, go on to release five more albums, the last two on her own label, King's X.

The Rest of the Story. By this time King had two more children, Molly and Levi, and she lived in Idaho. She married for a fourth time. She was an active environmentalist who has also been politically involved, performing in support of Farm Aid and President Bill Clinton. King scored her first film in 1985 (*Murphy's Romance*) and received an Academy Award nomination in 1992 for "Now and Forever," her contribution to the sound track of the 1992 film *A League of Their Own.* She has acted in motion pictures and on television and has starred on Broadway.

Legacy. Some critics denigrate the music of the Brill Building era as mere "work for hire," music manufactured to fit the singer or group being promoted at the moment. Others argue that, like their predecessors of Tin Pan Alley, songsmiths such as Goffin and King aimed to compose songs that would be popular because they were good. Their induction as nonperformers into the Rock and Roll Hall of Fame suggests that the latter theory is correct.

Given the strength of her later success, Carole King is a name certain to emerge any time the discussion turns to the singer-songwriter genre.

—J. P. Piskulich

SELECT DISCOGRAPHY

■ ALBUMS

Now That Everything's Been Said, 1969 (with the City)

Writer, 1970

Tapestry, 1971

Music, 1971

Rhymes and Reasons, 1972

Fantasy, 1973

Wrap Around Joy, 1974

Thoroughbred, 1976

Simple Things, 1977

Pearls—The Songs of Goffin and King, 1980

Colour of Your Dreams, 1993

SELECT AWARDS

Grammy Awards for Record of the Year for "It's Too Late"; for Album of the Year and Best Pop Vocal Performance, Female, for *Tapestry*; for Song of the Year for "You've Got a Friend," all 1971

Nashville Songwriters Hall of Fame, inducted 1987

National Academy of Songwriters Lifetime Achievement Award, 1988

Rock and Roll Hall of Fame, inducted 1990

SEE ALSO: Animals, The / Eric Burdon; Diamond, Neil; Drifters, The; Dylan, Bob; Everly Brothers, The; Franklin, Aretha; Mitchell, Joni; Monkees, The; Newman, Randy; Righteous Brothers, The; Sedaka, Neil; Simon, Paul; Taylor, James; Young, Neil.

King Crimson

ORIGINAL MEMBERS: Robert Fripp (b. 1946), Greg Lake (b. 1948), Ian McDonald (b. 1946), Michael Giles (b. 1942), Peter Sinfield (b. 1948)

OTHER MEMBERS: Gordon Haskell (b. 1946), Boz Burrell (b. 1946), Bill Bruford (b. 1949), John Wetton (b. 1950), David Cross (b. 1948), Jamie Muir (b. 1944), Adrian Belew (b. 1949), Tony Levin (b. 1946), others

FIRST ALBUM RELEASE: *In the Court of the Crimson King*, 1969

MUSICAL STYLE: Progressive rock

Since forming the group in 1968, guitarist Robert Fripp has led four distinct bands under the name King Crimson. All have hovered around the fringe of the mainstream rock world, holding onto cult band status as a result of a unique, noncommercial musical style and a defiant independence against an industry that primarily promotes images and trends. In spite of many personnel alterations that have taken place through the process of breakups, reformations, and breaks in time during which no King Crimson existed, the group has maintained its status as one of the most consistently interesting and musical "art rock" bands.

The band evolved from a trio consisting of brothers Michael (drums) and Peter (bass, vocals) Giles and Robert Fripp. Following their first recording (*The Cheerful Insanity of Giles, Giles and Fripp*, 1968), the group's lineup began to change: Multi-instrumentalist Ian McDonald and lyricist/lighting designer Peter Sinfield were added, and Peter Giles left. Greg Lake stepped in on bass and vocals, and King Crimson was officially born on January 13, 1969; their name came from Sinfield's lyrics for the song "Court of the Crimson King."

First King Crimson Recordings. For Fripp and his new band 1969 was an eventful year. Spring and summer were spent working the clubs of London, developing their music, and firmly establishing themselves as a top act within the underground scene. A July appearance before 650,000 people at a free Hyde Park concert (headlined by the Rolling Stones) brought much attention, while sessions for a first album were under way. *In the Court of the Crimson King* was released in October, followed by a short U.S. tour. Critics praised the recording and the live performances, noting the obvious influence of the Beatles, Pink Floyd, and the Moody Blues and comparing them to the British power trio Cream. The band captured the ear of the public with a distinctive and powerful symphonic rock sound, with the added dimension of extensive improvisation and Sinfield's foreboding lyrics.

At the brink of success, King Crimson's rise was interrupted by internal personality clashes. Giles and McDonald handed in their resignations at the conclusion of the U.S. trip, and Fripp and Lake were considering other possibilities (Fripp was offered the guitar chair with Yes, and Lake considered forming a group with keyboardist Keith Emerson). Appearances for 1970 were cancelled, but the band recorded a single ("Catfood") and a full-length album (*In the Wake of Poseidon*) before splintering entirely. By mid-year, Fripp and Sinfield were all that remained of 1969's King Crimson. However, they succeeded in replacing departed members with capable musicians, including Gordon Haskell (bass, vocal), Mel Collins (reeds), and Andy McCullough (drums). Still more personnel changes followed the late-1970 release entitled *Lizard*. The next live appearance came in April of 1971, with Fripp fronting a group that included Boz Burrell (bass, vocal), Ian Wallace (drums), and Collins. An extended tour followed, and their fourth album, *Islands*, was released in December of 1971. Definitely a more commercial effort, *Islands* sold well but was not well received by music critics. A poorly recorded sampling of live material was released in England (*Earthbound*, 1972), presumably to fulfill a contractual obligation.

The 1970's. In the summer of 1972, it seemed that the band had finally collapsed under the weight of an unprecedented number of personnel changes, including the departure of Sinfield. However, Fripp emerged in July with a new group of musicians, including former Yes drummer Bill Bruford, singer-bassist John Wetton, violinist David Cross, and auxiliary percussionist Jamie Muir. They recorded an album (*Lark's Tongues in Aspic*), which was comparable in quality to the band's 1969 debut effort. 1973 was spent on the road. Though Muir decided to depart along the way, the remaining quartet played to critical and popular acclaim in Europe and the United States. After months of shows, the band took a break to record. *Starless and Bible Black* was released in early 1974, followed by another tour, marking the first time that a King Crimson lineup had performed on consecutive tours. The new album and relentless performance schedule had King Crimson on the precipice of major success, but once again the group began to disintegrate. *Red* (1974) featured a Fripp-Wetton-Bruford trio with guest appearances by departed members. It was the last studio effort by this group. A live album (*U.S.A.*, 1975) provided postmortem evidence of the quality performance displayed by this edition of King Crimson.

A New Band. Following the 1974 breakup of King Crimson, Fripp remained busy with solo projects and collaborations with other rock notables. His crisp, technically precise style was perfect within the context of late-1970's art rock groups. His experiences in the recording studios with musicians who were creating a new style of rock music led him to form a new group, which eventually took over the name King Crimson.

Guitarist-vocalist Adrian Belew met Fripp during late-1970's collaborations with Talking Heads and David Bowie. Belew brought to the band an assortment of guitar techniques, a willingness to experiment, and a pop sensibility. He also contributed lyrics that were extremely original. Bassist Tony Levin had established himself as a great performer on the electric bass and on an experimental, ten-string instrument called the Chapman Stick (named for its inventor Emmitt Chapman). Bill Bruford, the outstanding drummer from the second version of King Crimson, completed the group.

Three studio albums were produced by this band before they broke up, all arguably among the

For the Record

In 1970, after only one King Crimson album, the band nearly became a footnote of rock history. During rehearsals to replace departed band members, Robert Fripp considered an offer to replace Peter Banks as the guitarist for Yes. He declined; Yes hired Steve Howe and went on to great popular success. Later, in 1972, Bill Bruford defected from Yes and joined King Crimson.

strongest and most groundbreaking rock-oriented records of the 1980's. *Discipline* (1981) was the most focused of the three and was very much the product of a tour that preceded recording sessions. Remarkably complex and precisely executed, this album effectively captured the live sound the band had achieved on the road.

Beat (1982) and *Three of a Perfect Pair* (1984) followed. Neither demonstrated the focus of *Discipline*, but both showed King Crimson expanding commercially and experimentally. While "Heartbeat" and "Sleepless" showed an ability to create quality pop songs, "Dig Me," "Neurotica," and several instrumental tracks pushed the envelope of abstractness.

The "Double Trio." King Crimson reunited during the spring of 1994, this time as a six-piece unit that included Fripp, Belew, Levin, and Bruford along with Trey Gunn (Chapman Stick) and second drummer Pat Mastellotto. They began experimenting with the concept of the band as a "double-trio" with two guitar-bass-drums units. Two studio efforts followed (*Vroom*, 1994, and *Thrak*, 1995), supported by several tours. These albums showed the band breaking new ground while including pieces that recalled earlier versions of the group. A live record (*B'Boom*) was released in 1995. —*Erik Unsworth*

SELECT DISCOGRAPHY

■ ALBUMS

In the Court of the Crimson King, 1969
In the Wake of Poseidon, 1970
Lizard, 1970
Islands, 1971
Lark's Tongues in Aspic, 1973
Starless and Bible Black, 1974
Red, 1974
Discipline, 1981
Beat, 1982
Three of a Perfect Pair, 1984
Vroom, 1994
Thrak, 1995

SEE ALSO: Anderson, Laurie; Asia; Bad Company; Emerson, Lake, and Palmer; Eno, Brian; Foreigner; Gabriel, Peter; Talking Heads; Yes; Zappa, Frank.

The Kingston Trio

ORIGINAL MEMBERS: Dave Guard (1934-1991), Nick Reynolds (b. 1933), Bob Shane (b. 1934)
OTHER MEMBERS: John Stewart (b. 1939), George Grove, Roger Gambill
FIRST SINGLE RELEASE: "Tom Dooley," 1958
MUSICAL STYLES: Blues, country, folk, pop

Kingston Trio members have described themselves as entertainers who sing story songs, have a good sense of humor, and have a great time performing. Their trademarks include striped shirts, banjos, acoustic guitars, and three-part harmonies with a clean, crisp sound. For a few years the trio was the most popular performing and recording group in the United States. They have been nicknamed "the Beatles of folk music." In fact, the Beatles opened for the Kingston Trio in a 1962 performance at Royal Festival Hall in London. The Kingston Trio influenced an entire generation to start playing guitar and primed them for the Beatles and their electric guitars. The Kingston Trio's sales dropped dramatically—and permanently—when the Beatles conquered America in 1964.

The Beginnings. The original Kingston Trio was formed by Dave Guard in 1957. He was a Stanford University graduate student who learned to play the banjo by reading Peter Seeger's 1948 book, *How to Play the 5-String Banjo*. Guard was joined by two friends, Bob Shane and Nick Reynolds, who were students at nearby Menlo College. Shane, who was the trio's lead singer, and Guard were born in Hawaii and had been singing Hawaiian music and playing together since high school. In the beginning, the group sang calypso songs (which Harry Belafonte was popularizing) and Hawaiian and Tahitian tunes. The musicians wanted a name that would sound both prestigious and calypsonian. They took the group's name from a Belafonte song about a young Jamaican woman in Kingston Town. Calypso soon gave way to folk music, and the original trio achieved almost instant success.

Several behind-the-scenes people played key roles in the group's great success. Frank Werber, their business manager, helped launch the group's career. He was the well-connected publicist at the Purple Onion and Hungry i nightclubs in San Francisco. He arranged for the group to have a weeklong fill-in engagement for comedian Phyllis Diller at the Purple Onion. David "Buck" Wheat provided musical arrangements, and Voyle Gilmore was the consummate producer. Comedian Bob Hope's agent, Jimmy Saphier, spotted the group at the Purple Onion and took demo tapes to Capitol Records, which quickly signed the trio to a seven-year contract. In addition, musician Glen Campbell played banjo to augment several trio songs.

"Tom Dooley." In February, 1958, the Kingston Trio recorded its first album, *The Kingston Trio,* which many fans consider to be the group's best. It included such classics as "Three Jolly Coachmen," "Scotch and Soda," "Hard, Ain't It Hard," and "Tom Dooley." The album was not a blockbuster hit until disc jockies Bill Terry and Paul Colburn of KLUB radio in Salt Lake City, Utah, began playing "Tom Dooley." Capitol released it as a single later that year. The song, which is the biggest-selling record the group has ever had, was first recorded in the 1920's by G. B. Grayson. He was a blind fiddler from Mountain City, Tennessee, and a descendant of the man who arrested the murderer in the song. The song is a morbid story about a young man sentenced to hang for murdering his lover. "Tom Dooley" hit the *Billboard* Top 10 in October and stayed there until January, 1959, eventually selling more than three million copies. The trio did much to establish Capitol as a major record label. Capitol, however, lost interest in the trio after signing the Beatles. The Kingston Trio next signed a recording contract with Decca. The trio avoided any political or racial protest in much of its music. However, protest singers such as Bob Dylan, Joan Baez, and Peter, Paul, and Mary were heavily influenced by the Kingston Trio and eventually succeeded in converting trio fans to their own styles of music. Finances, endless touring, personality differences, and disagreements over musical direction soon led Guard to quit, and the original Kingston Trio dissolved in 1961.

For the Record

The Kingston Trio placed fourteen of its albums in the Top 10, with five of them reaching number 1 and seven remaining one year or more on the charts. They had five albums in the Top 10 at the same time. The group was nominated for eight Grammy Awards, winning twice.

Other Trios. Shane and Reynolds formed a second, different Kingston Trio with John Stewart, a singer-songwriter and banjo player who had written music for the original Kingston Trio. The second Trio sang together until 1967, when the three members parted ways. From 1969 to 1976, the group was billed as the New Kingston Trio. In 1972, Shane reformed the group with George Grove and Roger Gambill, who played together to sold-out audiences for the next decade. When Gambill died in 1985, Reynolds returned. Along the way, Jim Connor, Pat Horine, Bill Zorn, and Bob Haworth have performed with the group. The year 1997 marked the fortieth anniversary of the founding of the Kingston Trio. The group was still touring thirty-five weeks per year and performing with major symphony orchestras.

Legacy. The Kingston Trio has given fans such classic songs as "Tom Dooley," "Scotch and Soda," "Greenback Dollar," "A Worried Man," "Where Have All the Flowers Gone?," "M.T.A.," and "Tijuana Jail." No other group has done as much to popularize the acoustic guitar and the five-string banjo than the Kingston Trio. They revolutionized popular music and reawakened United States listeners to their own rich musical heritage. They paved the way for a broader acceptance of bluegrass, blues, country, and other indigenous American music and were a catalyst to an entire social and cultural phenomenon that affected the country's musical tastes, social conscience, even people's dress and language. The release of "Tom Dooley" in 1958 began the folk music revival and set the stage for Bob Dylan, Joan Baez, Peter, Paul, and Mary, and the protest music movement of the 1960's. The group has had many successful imitators: the Cumberland Three, the Chad Mitchell Trio, and the Highwaymen. They influenced the music of the Beach Boys, Buffalo Springfield, the Eagles, Abba, and Fleetwood Mac. They have entertained generations of fans for decades.

—*Fred Buchstein*

SELECT DISCOGRAPHY

■ SINGLES

"Tom Dooley," 1958
"Tijuana Jail," 1959
"Where Have All the Flowers Gone," 1962
"Reverend Mr. Black," 1963

■ ALBUMS

The Kingston Trio, 1958
From the "Hungry i," 1959
The Kingston Trio at Large, 1959
New Frontier, 1963
Time to Think, 1963

SELECT AWARDS

Grammy Award for the Best Country & Western Performance for "Tom Dooley," 1958
Grammy Award for the Best Performance, Folk, for *The Kingston Trio at Large*, 1959
Billboard, named Best Group of the Year, 1959

SEE ALSO: Abba; Baez, Joan; Beach Boys, The; Beatles, The; Belafonte, Harry; Buffalo Springfield; Campbell, Glen; Dylan, Bob; Eagles, The; Fleetwood Mac; Peter, Paul, and Mary; Seeger, Pete.

The Kinks

ORIGINAL MEMBERS: Ray Davies (b. 1944), Dave Davies (b. 1947), Peter Quaife (b. 1943), Mick Avory (b. 1944)
OTHER MEMBERS: John Dalton, John Gosling, Jim Rodford (b. 1945)
FIRST ALBUM RELEASE: *The Kinks*, 1964
MUSICAL STYLES: Rock and roll, pop

Ray (Raymond Douglas) Davies and younger brother Dave grew up playing guitar in their parents' front room and performed in a few bands. When Ray decided to leave art school and devote himself to music, the Kinks became international stars with the release of "You Really Got Me." Along with the Beatles and the Rolling Stones, the Kinks became one of the premier bands of the early 1960's "British invasion."

The Beginnings. The Kinks—a name the band acquired due to their outlandish costumes—were on the verge of extinction when their first single, a cover of "Long Tall Sally," failed to make much impact. Stealing a riff from "Louie, Louie" and relying on the distortion of their guitars, the band gambled and produced one of the most visceral rock songs ever released, "You Really Got Me" (1964). It went to the top of the British charts, followed by a near clone, "All Day and All of the Night," (1965) which rose to number 2 in Britain.

The next year they again scored number 1 with "Tired of Waiting for You" and had considerable success with "Till the End of the Day," "Everybody's Gonna Be Happy," "Set Me Free," "See My Friends," and "A Well Respected Man." In 1966 they had more success with "Dedicated Follower of Fashion" and another chart topper, "Sunny Afternoon." During this period the Kinks released five albums in the United States, but their popularity resulted from their single releases. Ray Davies quickly gained a reputation as a tunesmith capable of creating commercially viable songs and, more important, as an incisive, ironic social critic. For instance, "Well Respected Man" and "Dedicated Follower of Fashion" can be seen as observations from each side of the social spectrum: The first is an ironic vision of an ultra-conservative and the latter shows a conservative sneering at the fashion craze of Carnaby Street. Davies had the ability to see life from multiple points of view, and those perspectives often yielded sharply drawn portraits.

Growing Maturity. The Kinks' first cohesive and artistically successful album, *Face to Face*, which included the services of famous session pianist Nicky Hopkins, was released in 1967. The collection's most popular song was "Sunny Afternoon," but other gems include "Rainy Day in June," "Dandy" (popularized by Herman's Hermits), and "House in the Country." *Something Else* (1967), perhaps the band's finest album, featured songs about an unemployed clerk ("Situation Vacant"), the most popular boy at school ("David Watts"), and an autobiographical look at Ray's relationship with his brother ("Two Sisters"). The album also features Dave Davies's most successful song, "Death of a Clown." By far the highlight is "Waterloo Sunset," a wistful tribute to London life that is one of Dave's most gentle and moving songs.

The band toured extensively, and Ray Davies finally took a break after a case of nervous exhaustion in the late 1960's. Still living in the neighborhood where he was raised, Ray turned his attention to his family and to writing more songs. The rest and introspection led the band to explore more fully the themes they had begun presenting in earlier albums. With *(The Kinks Are) the Village Green Preservation Society* (1969), they were no longer a hard-rocking band but conservators of tradition and a quiet way of life that was quickly vanishing. More and more, Ray's songs would reflect a suspicion of modern, industrial culture. The album was a commercial failure, and the band's defiantly eccentric stance alienated them from critics and many fans. With all the social and political turmoil of the late 1960's, songs about dear old England seemed hopelessly antiquated.

Resurrection. In 1969, a ban on performing in the United States ended. Also that year, *Arthur: Or, the Decline and Fall of the British Empire,* a musical score originally designed for a British Broadcasting Corporation (BBC) production based loosely on the experience of Ray Davies's brother-in-law, was released. Ray and the band continued their social commentary but returned to their rock roots with songs such as "Victoria" and "Brain-

The Kinks on a 1968 television show (Popperfoto/Archive Photos)

washed." By this time bassist Peter Quaife had left and was replaced by John Dalton. In 1970 Ray scored another major hit with "Lola," an ironic song about sexual initiation and gender confusion. The ensuing album, *Lola Versus Powerman and the Moneygoround* (1970), centers on Ray's longstanding battles with his former managers and for his publishing rights (in songs such as "Denmark Street," "Get Back in Line," and "The Moneygoround"), his ambivalence about professional success ("The Contenders," "Top of the Pops," and "This Time Tomorrow"), and his desire to simply be free of all the pressure of being a performer ("Apeman" and "Got to Be Free").

New Record Company. With the expiration of their original contract and Ray Davies's belief that the band had been abused, the Kinks switched record companies (earning a million-dollar advance in the process) to RCA, which released *Muswell Hillbillies* in 1971. The album continued with Ray's ambivalent social commentary on the lives of simple people, which was accentuated by the cover photo of the band, resplendent in hippie regalia, drinking in a working-class bar. By now the group had also been joined by John Gosling on keyboards. In 1972 they released *Everybody's in Show-Biz*, which included the beautiful "Celluloid Heroes," and their former record company issued *The Kink Kronikles*, a collection featuring many singles that had never appeared in America, such as "Days," "Autumn Almanac," "Wonderboy," "Big Black Smoke," and "Mindless Child of Motherhood." The band returned to the Green Preservation themes of tradition and their bitterness over business dealings in a pair of ill-conceived concept albums, *Preservation Act 1* (1973) and *Preservation Act 2* (1974). *Soap Opera* (1975), which depicts a rock star and a suburbanite in reversed roles, is also flawed, though partially redeemed by one delightfully crazy song, "Ducks on the Wall." The best of these 1970's concept albums is *Schoolboys in Disgrace* (1975), which, like its immediate predecessors, provided costumes and a repertoire for stage shows.

Another New Label. With their singles no longer making the charts and their career now in a shambles, the band signed with Clive Davis's new label, Arista Records. Davis quickly ruled out any further indulgences in concept albums, and the band responded with *Sleepwalker* (1977). The title song put them back on the U.S. charts but did little in Britain, revealing that outside of a few loyal fans at home, the Kinks were now more popular in the United States. *Misfits* (1978) produced an even more successful single with "A Rock 'n' Roll Fantasy," and although the album is full of engaging and amusing songs, none stands out. More personnel changes took place, with Jim Rodford joining the band as the bassist and Gosling departing. The Kinks' next effort, *Low Budget* (1979) generated another popular single, the disco-influenced "(Wish I Could Fly Like) Superman," and throughout the album's songs Ray Davies turned his ironic gaze upon himself as a loser who could not follow social trends and who could not significantly affect the world around him.

The 1980's and Beyond. *One for the Road* (1980), the band's second live album, featured some of the songs from *Low Budget* as well as newly arranged versions of older songs that other artists, such as the Pretenders and David Bowie, had covered ("Stop Your Sobbing," "Where Have All the Good Times Gone," and "Till the End of the Day"). Also present was the previously unreleased "Prince of the Punks," an acidic comment on the punk movement and its hypocrisies. If there was

For the Record

In 1970 the Kinks' song about transvestism, "Lola," hit a snag in Great Britain when the BBC would not allow it to be played on the radio. The problem was not with the song's gender-bending lyrics, but rather with its explicit mention of Coca-Cola—which violated a rigid BBC rule against mentioning commercial product names. To get the song much-needed airtime, Ray Davies changed the lyrics for a radio version, substituting "cherry cola" for the brand name.

any doubt about their viability as a rock band, *One for the Road* put the question to rest. *Give the People What They Want* (1981) found Ray Davies back in top form with rock tunes "Around the Dial," "Better Things," and "Destroyer" (a 1980's reworking of "All Day and All of the Night"). *State of Confusion* (1983) was another solid effort featuring the beautiful "Come Dancing" and the biting commentaries of "State of Confusion" and "Young Conservatives."

Dave Davies released three solo albums in the 1980's, *AFL1-3603* (1980), *Glamour* (1981), and *Chosen People* (1983), each of which features some superb writing and deft musicianship. Mick Avory, a mainstay of the band, left before *Word of Mouth* (1984), a less successful album than the previous two, was released. It was followed by *Think Visual* (1986), a collection that reprises themes that Davies had better addressed elsewhere. A third live album, *Live: The Road*, appeared in 1987, and *U.K. Jive* was released in 1989; four years later came *Phobia* (1993) and a disappointing U.S. tour. Both Ray and Dave Davies then published memoirs, Ray's *X-Ray: The Unauthorized Autobiography* (1995) and Dave's *Kink: An Autobiography* (1996). In 1995 Ray Davies embarked on a critically successful solo tour, and just when the band's epitaph appeared to be written, they released *To the Bone* (1996), an acoustic collection of older songs and the title track, which suggested there was still life in one of the most enduring bands of the 1960's.

—David W. Madden

SELECT DISCOGRAPHY

■ SINGLES

"You Really Got Me," 1964
"All Day and All of the Night," 1965
"Tired of Waiting for You," 1965
"A Well Respected Man," 1966
"Sunny Afternoon," 1966
"Lola," 1970
"Come Dancing," 1983

■ ALBUMS

You Really Got Me, 1964
The Kinks Kontroversy, 1966
Face to Face, 1967
Something Else, 1967
Arthur: Or, the Decline and Fall of the British Empire, 1969
Lola Versus Powerman and the Moneygoround, 1970
Muswell Hillbillies, 1971
Schoolboys in Disgrace, 1975
Sleepwalker, 1977
Misfits, 1978
Low Budget, 1979
One for the Road, 1980
Give the People What They Want, 1981
State of Confusion, 1983
Word of Mouth, 1984
Think Visual, 1986
U.K. Jive, 1989
Phobia, 1993
To the Bone, 1996

SELECT AWARDS

Rock and Roll Hall of Fame, inducted 1990

SEE ALSO: Beatles, The; Bowie, David; Pretenders, The; Rolling Stones, The.

Rahsaan Roland Kirk

BORN: Columbus, Ohio; August 7, 1936
DIED: Bloomington, Indiana; December 5, 1977
FIRST ALBUM RELEASE: *Triple Threat*, 1956
MUSICAL STYLES: Jazz, swing, rhythm and blues

Blind at the age of two, Rahsaan Roland Kirk, tenor saxophonist and multi-instrumentalist, was reared in Columbus, Ohio. Having started with the bugle, he played trumpet at age ten, clarinet in his junior high school band, and C-melody saxophone at age twelve or thirteen. At the Ohio State School for the Blind in Columbus, he was exposed to classical recordings, and at home he heard recordings of such jazz artists as John Kirby and Buster Bailey. In the early 1970's, as the result of a dream, Kirk began using the name Rahsaan.

By age fifteen, Kirk had become a professional musician, performing in rhythm-and-blues groups in Columbus and with band leader Boyd Moore. Kirk journeyed to Los Angeles, where he sat in with Wardell Gray, and in Texas he played in a rhythm-and-blues band. In St. Louis, Kirk was encouraged by Charlie "Bird" Parker, who had heard him play a plastic flute. After Kirk's return to Columbus, he formed his own group, performed in other Ohio cities, traveled to Louisville, Kentucky, and moved to Chicago in 1960, where he made his second recording as a result of a referral to Argo Records by pianist Ramsey Lewis.

Recordings and Performances. Kirk, who performed in jazz clubs and at festivals in the United States and abroad, recorded in his own name many albums for various labels. In Europe, he made a number of live recordings between 1963 and 1975. His initial recording, flavored with blues, *Triple Threat* (1956), featured his work on stritch and manzello, two rare types of saxophone. After his move to Chicago, he recorded *Introducing Roland Kirk* (1960), a bop-inspired work that featured trumpeter-saxophonist Ira Sullivan and displayed Kirk's triple-saxophone technique. Following a European tour in 1961, Kirk played with Charles Mingus at the Five Spot in New York, recorded with Mingus on Mingus's *Oh Yeah!* (1961), and secured a contract with Mercury Records. From this point, Kirk, who employed such sidemen as Brother Jack McDuff, Art Taylor, Joe Benjamin, and Jaki Byard, performed primarily with his own group known as the Vibration Society. In 1962, the year he played the Newport Jazz Festival, he won the miscellaneous-instrument category of the *Down Beat* Critics Poll and, the next year, the *Down Beat* Readers Poll miscellaneous–instrument award. Throughout his career, he was recognized in a number of *Down Beat* polls.

Rahsaan Roland Kirk (left) about 1960 (Archive Photos/Frank Driggs Collection)

One of his well-received recordings of the 1960's that showed his stylistic variety, *Rip, Rig, and Panic* (1965), for EmArcy, teamed Kirk with Jaki Byard, Richard Davis, and Elvin Jones. *The Inflated Tear* (1968), recorded for Atlantic, featured Kirk's title composition; *Volunteered Slavery* (1969), another Atlantic release, included the 1968 Newport Jazz Festival performance. *Rahsaan/Rahsaan* (1970) was noted for Kirk's simultaneous playing of two melodies as part of a medley, and *Natural Black Inventions: Root Strata* (1971) further demonstrated Kirk's multiple instrument abilities, black consciousness, and unique approach to an audience.

In 1971, Kirk played on *The Ed Sullivan Show* and two years later recorded *Bright Moments*, inspired by Kirk's positive meditations on society. Recorded live at San Francisco's Keystone Korner, *Bright Moments* featured Kirk's witty commentaries. Another worthy recording, *Prepare Thyself to Deal with a Miracle* (1973) was noted for a twenty-one minute rendition of "Saxophone Concerto." In 1974, Kirk again recorded with Charles Mingus, *Mingus at Carnegie Hall*, and two years later Kirk's first Warner Bros. release appeared, *The Return of the 5000 Lb. Man* (1976), which featured "Theme for the Eulipions." *Kirkatron* (1976), also for Warner Bros., was followed by *Paris 1976*, with pianist Hilton Ruiz and trombonist Steve Turré, recorded in France for Royal Jazz. Despite the aftereffects of a paralyzing stroke in 1975, Kirk recorded *Boogie Woogie String Along for Real* in 1977, his final album, which did not include simultaneous saxophone performances.

For the Record

In an August 15, 1974, article in *Down Beat*, Rahsaan Roland Kirk said, "I feel a responsibility placed upon me when I pick up a saxophone. People like Ben Webster and Coleman Hawkins and John Coltrane left music here to be *played*. And I feel it's part of my calling to keep this music alive."

Multi-instrumental Approaches. Kirk, who identified his style as "black classical music," played a wide range of forms: New Orleans jazz, swing, bop, rhythm and blues, hard bop, and avant-garde or free jazz. His diversified musical style was also influenced by European classical music and East Indian music. He is especially known for the playing of three saxophones at once, tenor, manzello, and stritch, the latter two associated with Spanish marching bands of the late nineteenth century. An award-winning clarinetist and flutist, Kirk developed his own fingering techniques and became a master of circular breathing, which allowed him to play without stopping. He could produce a drone on the manzello while playing a melody on the tenor; the sound of the drone and melody were reminiscent of East Indian music. Having played some forty instruments, Kirk was proficient at the nose flute, claviette, harmonica, and piccolo. He also invented the trumpophone, a trumpet played with a saxophone mouthpiece; the slidesophone, a saxophone with a slide assembly; the black puzzle and black mystery pipes; and, used at points in his solos, the siren whistle, a metal hunting horn. Kirk, sometimes accused of gimmickry, defended his multi-instrument technique with the example of African musicians who played two instruments simultaneously.

Audience Relationship. Often commenting on the state of jazz in the United States and the predicament of black musicians, Kirk was known for being witty and establishing audience contact, similar to Dizzy Gillespie. Kirk, who believed that an audience should experience joy and intellectual satisfaction, claimed a musical affinity with John Coltrane and objected to certain transitions in jazz styles of the mid-1970's, decrying simplification by jazz legends. He often mocked electronic instrumentation, which he thought should not supplant the acoustic sound. Furthermore, Kirk observed that the treatment of jazz musicians in Europe in the mid-1970's had deteriorated because of commercial interests, and he ultimately preferred the U.S. scene because of the common language facilitating audience communication.

In the 1970's, Kirk organized the Jazz and People's Movement to encourage performance opportunities for jazz musicians. He was involved in protest demonstrations for equal time for "black classical music" directed at the television shows of Merv Griffin, Johnny Carson, and Dick Cavett. Kirk's interest in black issues is also reflected in the titling of such albums as *Blacknuss* (1971). In 1977, for the benefit of saxophone players, Kirk established the Vibration School of Music. Vocalist Jon Hendricks considered Kirk to be part of the legacy of saxophone players that included Coleman Hawkins, Charlie Parker, and John Coltrane.

—*Joseph McLaren*

SELECT DISCOGRAPHY

■ ALBUMS

Triple Threat, 1956 (rereleased as *Early Roots*, 1977)
Introducing Roland Kirk, 1960
Kirk's Work, 1961
Domino, 1962
Roland Kirk Meets the Benny Golson Orchestra, 1963
Kirk in Copenhagen, 1963
Rip, Rig and Panic, 1965
Here Comes the Whistleman, 1966
Volunteered Slavery, 1969
Rahsaan/Rahsaan, 1970
Natural Black Inventions: Root Strata, 1971
Prepare Thyself to Deal with a Miracle, 1973
Boogie Woogie String Along for Real, 1977

SELECT AWARDS

Down Beat Readers Poll, named Best Miscellaneous Instrument Player, 1963-1977
Down Beat Critics Poll, named Best Miscellaneous Instrument Player, 1962, 1964-1967, 1971-1976

SEE ALSO: Coltrane, John; Mingus, Charles; Parker, Charlie.

Kiss

ORIGINAL MEMBERS: Peter Criss (b. Peter Crisscoula, 1947), Ace Frehley (b. Paul Frehley, 1951), Gene Simmons (b. Gene Klein, 1949), Paul Stanley (b. Stanley Eisen, 1952)

OTHER MEMBERS: Eric Carr (1950-1991), Mark St. John (b. 1956), Bruce Kulick (b. 1953), Eric Singer (b. 1958), Vinnie Vincent (b. Vincent Cusano, 1952)

FIRST ALBUM RELEASE: *Kiss*, 1974

MUSICAL STYLES: Rock and roll

Kiss came on the rock and roll scene in the early 1970's and immediately gained notoriety for wearing distinctive makeup and playing concerts that included smoke bombs, extravagant pyrotechnics, fire breathing, and blood spitting. Kiss's live performances, coupled with their hard-driving rock music, set the standard for arena acts throughout the 1970's and early 1980's.

The Beginnings. A mutual friend introduced guitarist Paul Stanley to bass player Gene Simmons in 1973, and a concept was born. The pair found drummer Peter Criss and guitarist Ace Frehley through advertisements they placed in *Rolling Stone* and *The Village Voice*, and together the four musicians became Kiss. Inspired by Alice Cooper and the New York Dolls, the new group wanted to emphasize the theatrical side of rock and roll.

Both the lineup and the concept clicked, and within one year Kiss had a recording contract with Casablanca Records and a self-titled debut album in the record stores. That album, *Kiss* (1974), and the two studio efforts that followed sold well but did not come close to capturing the thrill of the band's live performances. The live album *Alive* (1975) finally managed to capture the band's in-concert energy and featured the hit single "Rock and Roll All Nite." Inspired by the success of *Alive*, Kiss followed it up with what many critics considered their best studio effort, *Destroyer* (1976), which became the band's first platinum album. Produced by Bob Ezrin (who had previously worked with Alice Cooper), it also featured their first Top-10 single, "Beth," a power ballad written and sung by drummer Criss.

Throughout the mid-1970's, Kiss released albums at the remarkable rate of two per year. The stores were filled with Kiss merchandise, Marvel Comics released two Kiss comic books, and the band even starred in a television special, *Kiss Meets the Phantom of the Park* (1978). In 1978, when

Kiss (Archive Photos)

things were already at the saturation point, they did something even more remarkable: Each of the four band members released a solo album. The simultaneous release of the four albums elicited both applause and negative responses from the critics and fueled rumors of an impending breakup.

The Makeup Comes Off. One of the band's many gimmicks was that they were never photographed without their makeup. At the height of their popularity, this provided the members with some semblance of anonymity. It also provided a shield as the lineup began to shift in the early 1980's. Criss left in 1981 and was replaced by Eric Carr. Frehley departed in 1982 and was replaced by Vinnie Vincent. Despite the changes, Kiss continued to produce albums, each less successful than its predecessor.

In 1983, the makeup provided yet another gimmick when band members removed it for the release of *Lick It Up*, a stunt that returned the band to platinum status. Vincent left in 1984 and was replaced by Mark St. John, who, because of health problems, stayed with the band for only a short time. Bruce Kulick became the new lead guitarist in 1984. Carr died of cancer in 1991 and was replaced by Eric Singer in 1992. In 1996, the original lineup of Criss, Frehley, Simmons, and Stanley marked their twenty-five year anniversary with an MTV Unplugged special and an album of the same name. They also reunited for one of the year's most successful tours, complete with makeup and pyrotechnics. —*Peggy Ramsey*

For the Record

In addition to cofounding Kiss, Gene Simmons made an important contribution to the next generation of rock and roll when he financed the first demo recording by a fledgling California band called Van Halen.

SELECT DISCOGRAPHY

■ ALBUMS

Kiss, 1974
Alive, 1975
Destroyer, 1976
Rock and Roll Over, 1976
Love Gun, 1977
Dynasty, 1979

Lick It Up, 1983
Crazy Nights, 1987
Revenge, 1992
Unplugged, 1996

SEE ALSO: Cooper, Alice; Van Halen.

Gladys Knight and the Pips

ORIGINAL MEMBERS: Gladys Knight (b. 1944), Merald "Bubba" Knight (b. 1942), Brenda Knight, Elenor Guest, William Guest (b. 1941)
OTHER MEMBERS: Edward Patten (b. 1939), Langston George
FIRST SINGLE RELEASE: "Whistle My Love," 1957
MUSICAL STYLES: Soul, rock and roll

Gladys Knight's childhood singing career and her early familiarity with both blues and gospel music paved the way for a successful adulthood. With a backup group composed of family members, she recorded a string of Top-40 hits in the 1960's and 1970's. Her raw but powerful voice and her expressive singing style rank her as one of the great female soul singers.

The Beginnings. Gladys Knight began singing in public when she was still a toddler. Her first public performance was at the Mount Moriah Baptist Church in her hometown of Atlanta, Georgia, at the age of four. This and other local performances led to her winning the two thousand dollar first prize on the *Ted Mack Original Amateur Hour* in 1952 at the age of eight. Aside from earning a small fortune at that time, she surprised many because she was the youngest contestant and an African American. Shortly after, she formed a group with her brother, sister, and two cousins. The backup group was named after their first manager, cousin James "Pip" Woods.

The group, still children, was hired to sing at the Royal Peacock, one of Atlanta's most prominent clubs. This led to additional performances throughout the Southeast on what was known as the "chitlin' circuit." As they became popular the group played larger auditoriums throughout the eastern United States. In 1961 they had their first hit single, "Every Beat of My Heart." Curiously, this single was recorded and released by two different record companies, Vee Jay and Fury. The two recordings were in competition with each other, with the Vee Jay version climbing to number 1 on the rhythm-and-blues charts and the other reaching only number 15. "Letter Full of Tears" was another hit in 1962.

The Soul Years. In the following years the Pips slipped from their former popularity, as Knight took time off to marry and have several children. The group resumed touring in the mid-1960's and signed with the Motown subsidiary label Soul in 1967. They had a major hit that year with "I Heard It Through the Grapevine," written by Marvin Gaye. They had a string of hits in the years following, including "If I Were Your Woman" (1970) and "Neither One of Us (Wants to Be the First to Say Goodbye)" (1973), both of which went to number 1 on the rhythm-and-blues charts.

The recordings from these years show the group at its best, despite the fact that they did not have the polished sound typical of other Motown artists in the 1960's. As Knight has written, "Even as a child, I was a belter, not a vocalist. I guess you could compare my style of singing to that of Aretha Franklin or Janis Joplin among women contemporaries, or James Ingram, Michael Bolton, and maybe Rod Stewart among the men." Her singing has a raw power and emotion that contrast sharply with the smooth, tight harmonies of the Pips. The result is a sound with the intensity of hard gospel in the framework of controlled accompaniment.

For the Record

Three years after beginning her singing career in a Baptist choir at age four, Gladys Knight made her television debut on Ted Mack's *Original Amateur Hour.* Perhaps appropriately, the seven-year old Knight won the $2,000 first prize for singing the Nat "King" Cole song "Too Young."

Buddah Records. During the six years with Soul Records, despite a number of major hits, the group drifted away from their hard-edged sound to more of a middle-of-the-road sound. In 1973 they moved to Buddah Records, where they recaptured the raw intensity of their earlier recordings. They were rewarded with a rapid succession of huge hits: "Midnight Train to Georgia" (1973) went to number 1 on both the pop and rhythm-and-blues charts, "I've Got to Use My Imagination" (1973) went to number 4 on the pop chart and number 1 on the rhythm-and-blues chart, "You're the Best Thing That Ever Happened to Me" (1974) peaked at number 3 on the pop chart while topping the rhythm-and-blues chart, and "I Feel a Song (in My Heart)" (1974) went to number 21 on the pop chart and number 1 on the rhythm-and-blues chart. The group garnered two Grammy Awards in 1974 as one of the most popular groups in the United States.

Pain and Glory. The successes of 1973 and 1974 were not matched in the years ahead. The Pips continued to release albums and singles, but none had the popularity of their first releases with Buddah. Knight made her debut as an actress in *Pipe Dreams* (1976), a film costarring her husband Barry Hankerson and financed with her own money. The film was a disaster that cost Knight millions of dollars. To make matters worse, the singing group fell into a legal dispute with Buddah over royalties, with the result that Knight was barred from recording with the Pips in the late 1970's. An out-of-court settlement in 1980 allowed the group to reunite in recordings for Columbia. Two initial albums were unsuccessful, but in 1983 their album *Visions* went gold. The album contained their first hit single in nearly a decade, "Save the Overtime for Me." In 1986, Knight sang with Dionne Warwick, Stevie Wonder, and Elton John on the Grammy Award-winning single

Gladys Knight and the Pips (Fotos Internationsal/Archive Photos)

"That's What Friends Are For." She and the Pips had another hit single in "Love Overboard" (1988) before Knight turned to a solo career in 1989.

In 1995, Gladys Knight and the Pips were inducted into the Rock and Roll Hall of Fame, a fitting tribute for more than forty years in show business. The year 1996 saw the release of an album of recently discovered recordings from their glory years, *The Lost Live Album.* The year 1997 was a big one for Knight, with the release of two albums, *The Ultimate Collection* (a Pips greatest hits compilation) and *I Feel a Song* (a solo album).

The year 1997 also saw the publication of Knight's autobiography, *Between Each Line of Pain and Glory.* In this book she offered recollections from every stage of her career, from a detailed account of the Ted Mack competition to an intimate discussion of the failure of her third marriage. She also dealt frankly with such troubling issues as racism in the 1950's, her addiction to gambling, and her sometimes frosty relations with other singers (of Aretha Franklin she wrote, "She could sing it and spell it, but she wasn't interested in giving *any* respect to me"). The title of the book is taken from the chorus of the 1973 hit single, "You're the Best Thing That Ever Happened to Me," whose opening lines summarize the remarkable career of this talented singer: "I've had my share of life's ups and downs/ But fate's been kind, the downs have been few/ I guess you could say that I've been lucky." —*E. Douglas Bomberger*

SELECT DISCOGRAPHY

■ SINGLES

"Every Beat of My Heart," 1961
"I Heard It Through the Grapevine," 1967
"If I Were Your Woman," 1970
"Neither One of Us (Wants to Be the First to Say Goodbye)," 1973
"Midnight Train to Georgia," 1973
"I've Got to Use My Imagination," 1973

■ ALBUMS

Letter Full of Tears, 1961
Gladys Knight and the Pips, 1964
Everybody Needs Love, 1967
Silk 'n' Soul, 1968
Nitty Gritty, 1969
If I Were Your Woman, 1971
Neither One of Us, 1972
Imagination, 1973
Claudine, 1974
I Feel a Song, 1974
Bless This House, 1976
Still Together, 1977
About Love, 1980
Touch, 1981
Visions, 1983
Life, 1985
All Our Love, 1987
The Lost Live Album, 1996

SELECT AWARDS

Grammy Awards for Best Pop Vocal Performance by a Duo, Group or Chorus for "Neither One of Us (Wants to Be the First to Say Goodbye)" and Best R&B Vocal Performance by a Duo, Group or Chorus for "Midnight Train to Georgia," 1973
Grammy Award for Best Pop Performance by a Duo or Group with Vocal for "That's What Friends Are For," 1986 (Gladys Knight solo with Elton John, Dionne Warwick, and Stevie Wonder)
Grammy Award for Best R&B Vocal Performance by a Duo or Group with Vocal for "Love Overboard," 1988
Rock and Roll Hall of Fame, inducted 1996

SEE ALSO: Bolton, Michael; Franklin, Aretha; Gaye, Marvin; Ingram, James; John, Elton; Joplin, Janis; Stewart, Rod; Warwick, Dionne; Wonder, Stevie.

Mark Knopfler. *See* Dire Straits / Mark Knopfler

Kool and the Gang

ORIGINAL MEMBERS: Robert "Kool" Bell (b. 1950), Khalis Bayyan (b. Ronald Bell, 1951), Dennis "Dee Tee" Thomas (b. 1951), Claydes Smith (b. 1948), Robert "Spike" Mickens (b. Jersey

City), Rickey Westfield (b. Jersey City), George "Funky Brown" (b. 1949)
OTHER MEMBERS: Clifford Adams (b. 1952), James "J. T." Taylor (b. 1953), Curtis Williams (b. 1962), Michael Ray (b. 1962), Skip Martin, Odeon Mays, Gary Brown
FIRST ALBUM RELEASE: *Live at the Sex Machine*, 1971
MUSICAL STYLES: Pop, funk

For the Record

Kool and the Gang's 1981 number 1 hit "Celebration" quickly became a victory anthem. It was the theme song of the 1981 Super Bowl football game; it was sung to American hostages when they returned home from Iran that same year; and it was sung at the 1984 Democratic Party's national convention when Walter Mondale was nominated for president in 1984.

Beginning as jazz musicians in the mid-1960's, the original Kool and the Gang were at various times called the Jazziacs, the Soultown Revue, and the New Dimensions. When they emerged as their final incarnation in 1969, they also shifted toward a more popularly accessible pop-funk style. Their horn-driven rhythm-and-blues sound earned them four platinum and four gold albums between 1974 and 1986.

Beginnings. While all of the original band members except Claydes Smith were attending Lincoln High School in Jersey City, New Jersey, they fell under the influence of eminent jazz musicians Thelonious Monk, Miles Davis, John Coltrane, Pharoah Sanders, and Leon Thomas. When the Jazziacs became part of the Soultown Revue in 1968, however, they had to learn contemporary soul tunes in order to back up the troupe's singers. The 1970's pop-dance sound, which featured staccato horn blasts and party chants, was in many ways a technique for musical survival. According to Thomas, "We had to make sure our jazz roots didn't overpower the funk. This way it is more acceptable to the kids . . . who buy most of our records." In the next several years they enjoyed modest success on the rhythm-and-blues charts with dance tunes.

Kool and the Gang landed squarely on the pop charts with their fifth album, *Wild and Peaceful* (1973), which spawned three hit singles: "Jungle Boogie" (number 4), "Funky Stuff" (number 29), and "Hollywood Swinging" (number 6). This mainstream success was short-lived, however, and for the next five years they settled for a string of Top-10 rhythm-and-blues hits while searching for new direction.

Making the Pop Charts. Kool and the Gang began their move back into the musical mainstream with the 1978 additions of balladeer J. T. Taylor and producer Eumir Deodato. With Taylor handling lead vocals and providing more variety, *Ladies Night* (1979) went platinum, peaking at number 13 on the pop charts and including two Top-10 hits, "Ladies Night" (number 8) and "Too Hot" (number 5). A string of twenty-one Top-20 hits in the United States and the United Kingdom between 1974 and 1988 (the year of Taylor's departure) made Kool and the Gang one of the foremost pop bands of the 1970's and 1980's. *Celebrate!* (1980), *Something Special* (1981), and *Emergency* (1984) all went platinum.

Ironically, as the group's hits became more mellow, their audiences became more white. After Taylor's departure, Kool and the Gang continued to play into the 1990's, registering a number of rhythm-and-blues hits, but never recapturing the pop market. Their last chart action was "Raindrop" (1989), which peaked at number 27 on the rhythm-and-blues charts. *—John Powell*

SELECT DISCOGRAPHY

■ ALBUMS

Live at the Sex Machine, 1971
Music Is the Message, 1971
Live at P. J.'s, 1972
Wild and Peaceful, 1973
Kool Jazz, 1973
Kool and the Gang Greatest Hits, 1975 (compilation)
Love and Understanding, 1976

Ladies Night, 1979
Celebrate!, 1980
Emergency, 1984
Sweat, 1989
The Best of Kool & the Gang, 1969-1976, 1993 (compilation)

SELECT AWARDS
Grammy Award for Album of the Year for *Saturday Night Fever*, 1978 (with others)

SEE ALSO: Commodores, The.

Kool Moe Dee

(Mohandas DeWese)

BORN: New York, New York; August 8, 1963
FIRST ALBUM RELEASE: *Kool Moe Dee*, 1986
MUSICAL STYLE: Rap

Kool Moe Dee was in the vanguard of the rap music wave as it flooded the New York scene in the late 1970's. He was part of Harlem, New York's Treacherous Three in the early 1980's when they were spotted by veteran producer Bobby Robinson. The Treacherous Three landed a deal with Robinson's Enjoy Records, producing "The New Rap Language" in 1980 and following with other singles before their contract was sold to the pioneering Sugarhill Record label. After recording several undistinguished singles, the band broke up, and Dee enrolled in college, earning a communications degree from the State University of New York.

Old School. Kool Moe Dee's big break came when he hooked up with an untested, seventeen-year-old producer, Teddy Riley, who would later become immensely popular for his work with Keith Sweat, Bobby Brown, and Michael Jackson. Together they delivered "Go See the Doctor" (1987, number 89), a cautionary safe-sex tale which became an underground classic. Dee's simple but direct debut album, *Kool Moe Dee* (1986), became a classic of old-school rap.

It was the follow-up, however, that made him a star. *How Ya Like Me Now* (1987) went to number 35 on the pop charts and went platinum at the cash register. His "Wild, Wild West" from the album was his first single to break into the rhythm-and-blues Top 10. The title track (number 22, rhythm and blues) inaugurated a long running feud with rapper L. L. Cool J, whom Kool Moe Dee accused of cheap imitation. The "rap war," carried out in various songs across more than two years, can be traced from Dee's perspective in his *Greatest Hits* package of 1993.

Social Conscience. From the late 1980's, Dee's work has been informed by a social conscience, opposing drugs and teaching an African philosophy of life. At the same time his work was becoming more clearly sexist, full of sexual posturing. At his creative peak, Dee released *Knowledge Is King* (1989), which went to number 25 on the pop charts and earned him an invitation to become the first rapper to perform at the Grammy Award ceremonies. In 1989 he also participated in Quincy Jones's *Back on the Block* album, which brought hip-hop stars together with their early influences; he recorded the single "Self–Destruction" in conjunction with KRS-One's "Stop the Violence" movement that fought violence among African Americans.

Subsequent albums were less commercially successful. *Funke Funke Wisdom* (1991) was a critical disappointment but did feature two notable singles. "Rise 'n Shine" brought Dee together with KRS-One and Chuck D from Public Enemy, while "How Kool Can One Blackman Be?" rose to number 49 on the rhythm-and-blues charts. Un-

For the Record

Kool Moe Dee learned to love rhyming by listening to Dr. Seuss's *How the Grinch Stole Christmas* (1957) and to the arrogance of heavyweight boxing champion Muhammad Ali.

§

"How Ya Like Me Now" opens with a sample of James Brown's "All Aboard the Night Train!"

der attack from the Internal Revenue Service for $180,000 in back taxes, Kool Moe Dee released a second *Greatest Hits* package, in 1993, and in the following year reunited the Treacherous Three to take advantage of the public interest in early rap influences. Together they released *Old School Flava* in 1994.

—John Powell

SELECT DISCOGRAPHY

■ ALBUMS

Kool Moe Dee, 1986
How Ya Like Me Now, 1987
The Best, 1987 (compilation)
Knowledge Is King, 1989
Greatest Hits, 1989 (compilation)
Funke Funke Wisdom, 1991
Greatest Hits, 1993 (compilation)
Interlude, 1994

SELECT AWARDS

Grammy Award for Best Rap Performance by a Duo or Group for "Back on the Block," 1990 (with others)

SEE ALSO: L. L. Cool J.

Alison Krauss

BORN: Decauter, Illinois; July 23, 1971
FIRST ALBUM RELEASE: *Too Late to Cry*, 1987
MUSICAL STYLE: Bluegrass

Alison Krauss, who won the Illinois state fiddling championship at age eleven, achieved a high level of popularity as a bluegrass artist. Krauss recorded for a small, independent record label, Rounder Records, but that did not stop her from becoming a two-time Grammy winner and a member of country music's Grand Ole Opry by the age of twenty-two. In addition to her dazzling fiddle playing, Krauss boasts one of the purest, sweetest voices in bluegrass music. Krauss's singing is often compared to the voice of Suzanne Cox of the Louisiana-based Cox Family, the group Krauss worked with on her 1994 album *I Know Who Holds Tomorrow*. Krauss has also been noted for her ability to uncover great contemporary bluegrass songs and arrange bluegrass versions of songs from other genres such as rock and gospel.

Child Prodigy. Krauss's story is one of amazing ability displayed at an early age. The daughter of a real estate agent, Krauss began playing fiddle at the age of five in her hometown of Champaign, Illinois. She was competing in bluegrass instrumental contests by age eight and started singing at ten. Initially trained as a classical violinist instead of a fiddler, Krauss fell in love with bluegrass after hearing it at local music festivals. When she joined a bluegrass band called Silver Rail, she was given a cassette of material to learn that contained music by instrumentalists such as banjoist J. D. Crowe, guitarist Tony Rice, and Ricky Skaggs. After hearing the tape, Krauss became hooked on bluegrass, which she describes as the equivalent of "acoustic rock and roll."

At age fourteen, Krauss joined Union Station, a local bluegrass quartet. That same year, word of

Alison Krauss in 1995 (AP/Wide World Photos)

an amazing performance at the Newport Folk Festival by Krauss and her new group reached Rounder Records. Krauss, not yet fifteen, was signed to a recording contract.

True to Her Roots. Once in the studio, Krauss demonstrated musical skill that went beyond her voice and fiddle playing. On her second album, *Two Highways* (1989), Krauss acted as Union Station's bandleader. Her next effort, *I've Got That Old Feeling* (1990), netted Krauss her first Grammy by age nineteen.

As success came, Krauss faced increasing pressure from Nashville music executives to water down her sound and become a commercial country artist. Krauss refused, citing her love for the traditional bluegrass sound, particularly the banjo, an instrument rarely heard on country music radio. Still, she remained in demand as a session musician and guest vocalist, having worked with stars such as Dolly Parton and Linda Ronstadt.

Krauss also went out of her way to promote little-known bluegrass artists such as the Cox Family, led by former oil worker Willard Cox and his three singing daughters. Krauss, who met the group at a Texas music festival, got the act signed to her record label after she sent a tape to a Rounder Records executive.

Bluegrass Royalty. Krauss became the seventy-first member of the Grand Ole Opry, an elite circle of country musicians, in 1993. Garth Brooks did the induction honors, pointing out that Krauss, then only twenty-one years old, was the first inductee from the bluegrass world since Jim and Jesse joined in 1964. "This woman wasn't even thought of in 1964," Brooks said. —*Lou Carlozo*

SELECT DISCOGRAPHY

■ ALBUMS

Too Late to Cry, 1987
Two Highways, 1989
I've Got That Old Feeling, 1990
Every Time You Say Goodbye, 1992
I Know Who Holds Tomorrow, 1994 (with the Cox Family)
Now That I've Found You: A Collection, 1995 (previously released material)
So Long So Wrong, 1997

For the Record

When Alison Krauss lived outside of Nashville, tour buses full of music fans would drive by her house. In a 1997 interview with *Chicago Tribune* country music writer Jack Hurst, Krauss insisted that the tourists must have been on their way to someone else's home. "Nobody would get on that tour bus to go see my house," Krauss said. "Driving by, it looked like crap, a big mudhole with dogs running around and trash in the yard. I could just hear [the tourists] going home saying, 'I tell you what! That Alison Krauss, she lives like a pig! And you should have seen her wearing that towel and that awful robe! Smoking that cig!'"

SELECT AWARDS

Grammy Award for Best Bluegrass Recording for *I've Got That Old Feeling*, 1990
Grammy Award for Best Bluegrass Album for *Every Time You Say Goodbye*, 1992 (with Union Station)
Grand Ole Opry, inducted 1993
Grammy Award for Best Southern Gospel, Country Gospel or Bluegrass Gospel Album for *I Know Who Holds Tomorrow*, 1994 (with the Cox Family)
Grammy Awards for Best Female Country Vocal Performance for "Baby, Now That I've Found You" and for Best Country Collaboration with Vocals for "Somewhere in the Vicinity of the Heart" (with Shenandoah) 1995
Grammy Award for Best Country Collaboration with Vocals for "High Lonesome Sound," 1996 (with Vince Gill and Union Station)
Grammy Awards for Best Country Performance by a Duo or Group with Vocals for "Looking in the Eyes of Love," for Best Country Instrumental Performance for "Little Liza Jane," and for Best Bluegrass Album for *So Long So Wrong*, 1997 (with Union Station)

SEE ALSO: Gill, Vince; Mattea, Kathy; Monroe, Bill, and the Blue Grass Boys; Parton, Dolly.

Kris Kristofferson

BORN: Brownsville, Texas; June 22, 1936
FIRST ALBUM RELEASE: *Kristofferson*, 1970
MUSICAL STYLE: Country

Multitalented Kris Kristofferson has made a name for himself as a hit songwriter, singer, movie star, and recording artist. He is also known for his support of antiwar, antipoverty, and other social causes.

Starting Out. Although he became an antiwar activist during the Vietnam era, Kris Kristofferson grew up in a military environment. His maternal grandfather served in the Swedish army, and his father was a major-general in the U.S. Air Force who served in World War II and the Korean War. Kris was a well-educated Rhodes Scholar who studied at Oxford University and started his career in Europe. He performed under the name Kris Carson for impresario Larry Parnes while still at Oxford, and later sang and played at army bases for five years while he was a helicopter pilot stationed in Germany. Kris left the army as Captain Kristofferson in 1965 to concentrate on songwriting.

Kristofferson moved to Nashville and worked as a cleaner at the CBS studios until Jerry Lee Lewis became the first to record one of his songs, "Once More with Feeling." Johnny Cash was interested in Kristofferson's work and persuaded Roger Miller to record "Me and Bobby McGee" (cowritten with Fred Foster) in 1969. The bluesy song was a country hit and became a rock standard after Janis Joplin's melodramatic cover in 1971. Another classic among Kristofferson's early songs was "Sunday Morning Coming Down," which Cash recorded. In 1970, Kristofferson's passionate "Help Me Make It Through the Night" reached the charts, a song that later crossed over to the pop and rhythm-and-blues audiences with Gladys Knight's version. Knight was also among the numerous artists who recorded the tender "For the Good Times," which later became a huge country hit for Ray Price. Kristofferson's own hits began with "Loving Her Was Easier (Than Anything I'll Ever Do Again)" and "Why Me," a ballad that Elvis Presley frequently performed in concert.

Since 1972, when Kristofferson did his first concert benefiting César Chávez and the United Farm Workers, all of his shows have included politically progressive songs and commentary. His many benefit concerts have helped the causes of Native Americans, human rights, environmental preservation, and world peace. He has appeared frequently at county fairs as well as in chic nightclubs, and his fans constitute a wide cross section of the public.

Movies and Marriage. Kristofferson married singer Rita Coolidge in 1973 and recorded three albums with her before their divorce six years later. As his singing career declined, he made his film debut in *Cisco Pike* (1972) and also appeared with Bob Dylan in *Pat Garrett and Billy the Kid* (1973). He achieved star status when he appeared opposite Barbra Streisand in a 1976 remake of the 1937 film *A Star Is Born.* For the next few years he concentrated on his film career until the unsuccessful *Heaven's Gate* in 1980.

Kristofferson returned to country music in 1983 with the album *The Winning Hand,* which featured duets with Brenda Lee, Dolly Parton, and Willie Nelson. Another collaboration, *Highwayman,* with Nelson, Cash, and Waylon Jennings, headed the country chart in 1985. The group subsequently toured as the Highwaymen and issued a second collaborative album, *Highwayman 2,* in 1990. The four musicians were known as "the bad boys," self-described outlaws who in-

For the Record

Kris Kristofferson volunteered for service in Vietnam in 1965, but he was turned down because he was slated for a teaching position at the United States Military Academy at West Point. Instead, he left the military and headed for Nashville.

troduced a bold frankness to country songwriting and declared their independence from country music formulas. New traditionalists such as Dwight Yoakam and even renegades such as Hank Williams, Jr., celebrated for his rock-and-roll sound, owe a great deal to Kristofferson, Cash, Nelson, and Jennings, who defined the country-pop style of the 1970's known as progressive-country music.

Still, Kristofferson was not ready to abandon his acting career. He was offered the script for the television miniseries *Amerika*, a fantasy about a Soviet invasion of the United States in which Kristofferson would play the anticommunist leader of the U.S. resistance. Although he turned down the script twice, the director, Don Rye, persisted, and Kristofferson starred in the miniseries in 1986. Although he effected many changes in the script, which appeared to promote a right-wing agenda, Kristofferson received heavy criticism from both liberal and conservative audiences. Later, he called the decision to accept the role the toughest career choice he had ever made; yet the role helped him clarify his political ideas about U.S. policy in Central America.

Music and Message. Optimistic from the success of *Highwayman*, Kristofferson released *Third World Warrior* in 1990, his personal statement regarding the United States' involvement in Central America. The album received mostly bad reviews, despite its good intentions. In songs such as "The Eagle and the Bear" and "Sandinista," the message was considered heavy-handed and the music minimal and instantly forgettable. Images that recur in the album, such as soldiers killing babies, were considered trite and overused. Even PolyGram, which released the album, seemed cool toward it. The company printed a mimimum number of copies and then dropped Kristofferson from the label. Within a year, the album was no longer available.

Perhaps hoping to recapture the golden period of the 1970's when he revolutionized Nashville with his romantic ballads, Kristofferson struck out in a new direction. In 1995, he celebrated signing on with Randall Jamail's Houston-based Justice Records label with the release of *A Moment of Forever*. Don Was, who had given Willie Nelson's career a needed boost with *Across the Borderline* in 1993 and had produced *Highwayman*,

Kris Kristofferson in 1977 (AP/Wide World Photos)

worked on the album, which featured the first new material by Kristofferson since *Third World Warrior.* The release of *A Moment of Forever* was accompanied by heavy press coverage and a full-length BBC television special centered on Kristofferson. Yet the reviews were negative, criticizing what one reviewer called "substandard material."

Kris Kristofferson is a versatile artist who made his biggest impact in the entertainment world as a songwriter. Although his career as a singer was hindered by a gruff, monotonous style and limited range, his autobiographical road songs, combining elements of folk, country, rock, and simple ballads display an aphoristic gift and often contain gritty, realistic details of the itinerant life.

—Sheila Golburgh Johnson

SELECT DISCOGRAPHY

■ ALBUMS

Kristofferson, 1970
Me and Bobby McGee, 1971
Full Moon, 1973 (with Rita Coolidge)
Breakaway, 1974 (with Rita Coolidge)
A Star Is Born, 1976 (film sound track)
Natural Act, 1979 (with Rita Coolidge)
The Winning Hand, 1983 (with Willie Nelson, Dolly Parton, and Brenda Lee)
Highwayman, 1985 (with Willie Nelson, Johnny Cash, and Waylon Jennings)
Third World Warrior, 1990
A Moment of Forever, 1995

SELECT AWARDS

Country Music Association Song of the Year (Songwriter's Award) for "Sunday Morning Coming Down," 1970
Grammy Award for Best Country Song for "Help Me Make It Through the Night," 1971
Grammy Award for Best Country Vocal Performance by a Duo or Group for "From the Bottle to the Bottom," 1973 (with Rita Coolidge)
Grammy Award for Best Country Vocal Performance by a Duo or Group for "Lover Please," 1975 (with Rita Coolidge)

SEE ALSO: Cash, Johnny; Jennings, Waylon; Nelson, Willie; Parton, Dolly.

L

L. L. Cool J

(James Todd Smith)

BORN: Queens, New York; August 16, 1968
FIRST ALBUM RELEASE: *Radio*, 1985
MUSICAL STYLES: Rap, hip-hop

L. L. Cool J released his first single when he was still in high school and went on to become one of the most popular hip-hop artists of the 1980's and 1990's. By treading a fine line between streetwise rap and pop music, L. L. Cool J was able to attract a large and diverse audience and maintain his popularity, even in the face of periodic widespread criticism.

L. L. Kool J (Paul Natkin)

Early Releases. James Todd Smith was born in Queens, New York, in 1968 and began rapping at the age of nine. When he was eleven, his grandfather bought him disc-jockey equipment, and Smith began recording demo tapes, which he sent out to various record companies in New York City. His music eventually caught the attention of Russell Simmons and Rick Rubin, two students at New York University who had recently formed Def Jam Records. In 1984, Smith released his and Def Jam's first single, "I Need a Beat," under the name L. L. Cool J (an acronym for Ladies Love Cool James). After the song sold over 100,000 copies, L. L. Cool J dropped out of high school to record *Radio* (1985), which was lauded by critics who were impressed by the young rapper's ability to instill rap music with a pop sensibility. The album achieved platinum sales the following year.

Stardom. L. L. Cool J continued his success in 1987 with the release of his second album, *Bigger and Deffer*, which eventually went double platinum on the strength of the romantic ballad "I Need Love." The song established L. L. Cool J as a pop and rap superstar. In 1988, he contributed the song "Going Back to Cali" to the sound track of the motion picture *Less Than Zero*, then released his third album, *Walking with a Panther*, the following year. Despite the fact that the album rose to number 6 on the album charts, many hip-hop fans complained that L. L. Cool J had strayed too far from his roots in the streets of New York City. He was loudly booed at a performance at Harlem, New York's Apollo Theatre in support of the album. L. L. Cool J answered accusations that he had sold out with *Mama Said Knock You Out* (1991), a hard-edged rap album that not only silenced most critics but also earned a Grammy Award for the Best Rap Solo Performance of 1991 for the single "Mama Said Knock You Out." In 1993, he performed at President Bill Clinton's inauguration.

L. L. Cool J seemed to lose direction again with 1993's *14 Shots to the Dome*, a confused and insincere

For the Record

In addition to his career as a musician, L. L. Cool J also found success as an actor. He appeared in several motion pictures, including *The Hard Way* (1991) and *Toys* (1992), and he landed a starring role on the television sitcom *In the House.*

attempt to profit from the popularity of "gangsta" rap. The follow-up album, *Mr. Smith* (1995), returned L. L. Cool J to the top and was eventually certified double platinum. The album included the single "Hey Lover," a duet with Boyz II Men. The following year saw the release of *All World: Greatest Hits.* In 1997, L. L. Cool J released the album *Phenomenon,* which he stated was a follow-up of sorts to his 1997 autobiographical book *I Make My Own Rules.* The album included the singles "Phenomenon," "4,3,2,1," and "Father."

—*Douglas Long*

SELECT DISCOGRAPHY

■ ALBUMS

Radio, 1985
Bigger and Deffer, 1987
Walking with a Panther, 1989
Mama Said Knock You Out, 1991
14 Shots to the Dome, 1993
Mr. Smith, 1995
All World: Greatest Hits, 1996 (compilation)
Phenomenon, 1997

SELECT AWARDS

Grammy Award for Best Rap Solo Performance for "Mama Said Knock You Out," 1991

SEE ALSO: Boyz II Men.

Patti LaBelle

(Patricia Louise Holt)

BORN: Philadelphia, Pennsylvania; October 4, 1944

FIRST ALBUM RELEASE: *Dreamer,* 1967 (as Patti LaBelle and the Blue Belles)

MUSICAL STYLES: Rhythm and blues, pop, soul, disco

In 1959 Patti LaBelle and Cindy Birdsong (b. 1939) formed a Philadelphia high school group, the Ordettes. Around 1960, promoter Bernard Montague took Sarah Dash (b. 1942) and Nona Hendryx (b. 1945) from another local group, the Del Capris, and created the Blue Belles with LaBelle and Birdsong. Throughout the 1960's, they enjoyed a number of minor hits, including "I Sold My Heart to the Junkman" (number 15, 1962), "Danny Boy" (number 76, 1964), and "You'll Never Walk Alone" (number 34, 1964). The group was mismanaged, however, and became best known as the group which gave Cindy Birdsong to the Supremes in 1967.

Labelle. The group was revitalized in 1970 when English manager Vicki Wickham shortened their name to Labelle, revamped their image, and sent them on the road with the Who. Though Patti LaBelle was at first reluctant, the makeover changed the whole image of 1960's girl groups. In the early 1970's Labelle helped introduce the glitter-rock trend, debuting the lamé space-cadet suits that would become their trademark and performing feverish stage routines which made them a top concert draw. Their music also was revitalized after signing with Epic Records in 1974. *Nightbirds* (1975) went to number 7 on the charts, largely on the strength of the number 1 single "Lady Marmalade," the group's only million–selling hit. After an unsuccessful album (*Phoenix,* 1975), Labelle broke up in 1976, mainly because of musical differences between Hendryx and LaBelle.

Solo Career. For almost a decade Patti LaBelle failed to put a solo album in the Top 40, continuing with a mix of funk and ballads. Though she produced no hits, she was highly respected in the music industry and was known for her duets with prominent performers such as Hendryx, Gladys Knight, Michael Bolton, and Bobby Womack. She also began an acting career, costarring with Al Green in the 1982 Broadway revival of *Your Arm's*

Patti LaBelle (MCA/Albert Sanchez)

Too Short to Box with God. In addition to various stage productions, LaBelle appeared on television in the Emmy Award-winning *Motown Salutes the Apollo* and *Sisters in the Name of Love* and a number of sitcoms.

LaBelle regained the national spotlight in the mid-1980's. *I'm in Love Again* (1983) rose to number 40 on the album charts. The following year her duet with Grover Washington, Jr., "New Attitude" (from the 1984 film *Beverly Hills Cop*) peaked at number 17. In 1986 she had her biggest album success when *The Winner in You* went to the top of the pop charts. It featured the number 1 duet with Michael McDonald, "On My Own." Though subsequent albums failed to make the Top 40, LaBelle won a Grammy Award in 1991 for for Best R&B Female Vocal Performance with *Burnin'*, which featured Hendryx, LaBelle, and Dash working together for the first time in almost fifteen years.

After leaving LaBelle, Hendryx established a reputation as a versatile funk rocker, with several rhythm-and-blues hits to her credit. At various times she collaborated with the Talking Heads, Valerie Simpson, Keith Richards, Peter Gabriel, George Clinton, Bobby Brown, Prince, and Yoko Ono. Her 1985 album *The Heat,* produced by Bernard Edwards (formerly of Chic) and Arthur Baker, featured the Grammy-nominated "Rock This House." —*John Powell*

SELECT DISCOGRAPHY

■ ALBUMS

Labelle

Labelle, 1971
Gonna Take a Miracle, 1971 (with Laura Nyro)
Pressure Cookin', 1973
Chameleon, 1976

■ ALBUMS

solo

Patti LaBelle, 1977
It's Alright with Me, 1979
Best of Patti LaBelle, 1982 (compilation)
The Winner in You, 1986
Burnin', 1991
Gems, 1994

SELECT AWARDS

Grammy Award for Best R&B Vocal Performance, Female, for *Burnin',* 1991

SEE ALSO: Doobie Brothers, The / Michael McDonald; Supremes, The.

For the Record

Patti LaBelle and Michael McDonald did not meet until their number 1 hit single "On My Own" was already on the charts. They met for the first time at NBC studios, where they performed the song on *The Tonight Show.*

k. d. lang

BORN: Consort, Alberta, Canada; November 2, 1961

FIRST ALBUM RELEASE: *A Truly Western Experience*, 1984

MUSICAL STYLES: Country, country rock, pop, blues

Singer k. d. lang has one of the most critically acclaimed pop voices of the twentieth century. She is also one of the most dynamic performers on tour. Her stage presence is infectious and her concerts command high praise from critics across the United States. She has been honored with numerous awards including several Grammy Awards and Juno Awards (Canada's equivalent of the Grammy).

To attribute the music of lang to any given style is difficult. Since the beginning of her recording career, her music has explored diverse territory. Lang has experienced success in many genres from her folk/country-and-western beginnings to time spent on the top of the pop music charts. She has an array of powerful torch songs to her credit as well. Lang has recorded solo, with her band the reclines, and in duets with many artists. The most famous and significant duet of her career has been the recording of "Crying" with the late Roy Orbison in 1987 (available on his *King of Hearts* album). In addition to her success as a musician, lang has wide personal popularity for holding to her convictions and refusing to conform to conventional standards in the music industry as well as in society.

Biography. Kathryn Dawn Lang grew up in Consort, Alberta, Canada which is a small town with a population of approximately seven hundred people in the western Canadian plains. She was the youngest of four children. Kathryn began taking piano lessons at a very early age and began playing the guitar at age ten. By her early teens she was writing and performing her own music. Her talent for the stage apparent from the beginning, she began her career as a performance artist. Lang would be a staunch animal rights advocate and vegetarian.

Lang's androgynous good looks have been sought out by many famous photographers. She has done fashion layouts for *Elle* and *Vogue*, made the cover of *Vanity Fair*, and been the subject of numerous interviews and photographs in many widely circulated publications including *Rolling Stone* and *Interview*. Since the early 1990's lang has been open about her homosexuality, a fact that has not seemed to hinder her career. Lang has done many invited musical performances for shows including the Grammy Awards. She also starred in Percy Adlon's 1993 film, *Salmonberries*.

The Country-and-Western Years. Lang with her nonconventional looks and musical style took the country-and-western music industry by storm in the mid-1980's. Her first album, *A Truly Western Experience*, was independently released in 1984. This album was done with the band she formed, the reclines. Lang signed a contract with Sire Records shortly after the release of this album. In 1985, she met Ben Mink, a fellow Canadian musician with whom she began a collaboration that

k. d. lang (Paul Natkin)

would produce many successful albums.

The first release from Sire Records was *Angel with a Lariat* (1987). Lang's career really took hold, however, after her next release, *Shadowland* (1988), which eventually went gold. This record was produced by Owen Bradley of country-and-western fame. A compilation of classic country-and-western songs, the album showcased the power and magnificence of lang's voice. *Shadowland* stayed on the *Billboard's* country album chart for 121 weeks. Her next recording, *Absolute Torch and Twang* (1989), recorded with the reclines and in collaboration with Ben Mink, also was well received. It stayed on the *Billboard's* country album chart for 104 weeks. In addition, shows on the "Absolute Torch and Twang" tour were performed to sellout crowds. Audiences were enthralled with the show. Although *Absolute Torch and Twang* and *Shadowland* were well-received, lang still had a difficult time getting radio airplay on country-and-western music stations.

For the Record

K. d. lang made the boldest move of her career by being the first successful pop musician to announce her homosexuality publicly. Lang came out as a lesbian in *The Advocate,* a popular national gay and lesbian newsmagazine, on June 16, 1992. To the surprise of her recording company and others in the music industry, her coming out may have actually helped record sales for her newly released album *Ingénue.* Record sales increased after the interview was published. *Ingénue* went platinum after lang won a Grammy Award for "Constant Craving" in 1992.

Pop and Beyond. In 1991, lang made a tremendous shift in her musical career. After seven years, she felt she had accomplished what she set out to do in country-and-western and believed it was time for a change. Ten months of collaborative work with Ben Mink resulted in the release of *Ingénue* (1992). *Ingénue* was lang's most significant recording since *Shadowland.* Exploring the craving for love, it is the album that brought her work to a larger audience. *Ingénue* was an incredible success which resulted in the hit single "Constant Craving." The album was lang's first to go platinum and received significant radio airplay with "Constant Craving." After a highly successful tour for *Ingénue,* lang embarked on a new project, doing the motion picture sound track for *Even Cowgirls Get the Blues* (1993). Lang's next solo albums were *all you can eat* (1995) and *drag* (1997). *All you can eat* once again brought lang and Ben Mink together, continuing their collaboration that has lasted for more than a decade.

Lang's recording *drag* is a collection of songs that explores the addiction and craving for love through the metaphor of smoking. The inspiration for *drag* came from lang's admiration for the Peggy Lee classic, "Don't Smoke in Bed," a song lang had wanted to record for several years. Songs with smoking themes were not new to her. She previously recorded two others, "I'm down to My Last Cigarette" (*Shadowland*) and "Three Cigarettes in an Ashtray" (*Angel with a Lariat*), which are consistently popular with audiences. The realization of this pattern gave her the creative energy to explore the theme further in an album devoted to the topic. *Drag* was well received and the positive response prompted an unplanned tour.

Where lang's music will take her next would be impossible to predict. She is an artist whose creative energy is ever shifting. One thing is clear, however: With a voice that is suited to perform music of any style, k. d. lang will continue to take her audiences into new listening realms.

—*Stephanie Brzuzy*

SELECT DISCOGRAPHY

■ ALBUMS

A Truly Western Experience, 1984 (with the reclines)

Angel with a Lariat, 1987 (with the reclines)

Shadowland, 1988

Absolute Torch and Twang, 1989 (with the reclines)

Ingénue, 1992
Even Cowgirls Get the Blues, 1993 (sound track)
all you can eat, 1995
drag, 1997

SELECT AWARDS

Juno Award for Most Promising Artist of the Year, 1985

Juno Award for Best Female Country Vocalist and Female Vocalist of the Year for "Crying" (with Roy Orbison), 1988

Grammy Award for Best Country Vocal Collaboration for "Crying," 1989 (with Roy Orbison)

Grammy Award for Best Country Vocal Performance, Female, for *Absolute Torch and Twang*, 1989

Canadian Academy of Recording Arts and Sciences Female Artist of the Decade Award, 1990

Grammy Award for Best Pop Vocal Performance, Female, for "Constant Craving," 1992

American Music Award for Best New Female Artist, Adult Contemporary, 1993

SEE ALSO: Cline, Patsy; Orbison, Roy.

Cyndi Lauper

BORN: Brooklyn, New York; June 22, 1953
FIRST SOLO ALBUM RELEASE: *She's So Unusual*, 1983
MUSICAL STYLE: Pop

Capitalizing on her plaintive, multioctave voice and her offbeat public persona, Cyndi Lauper was one of the most critically acclaimed female singers of the 1980's and 1990's. Born Cynthia Ann Stephanie Lauper to Fred and Catrine Dominique Lauper, Cyndi grew up in an unorthodox family. Her sister, Ellen, joined the Socialist Workers' Party and ran for the office of mayor of Phoenix, Arizona. Lauper's mother later appeared in several of her daughter's videos.

At the age of twelve, Lauper began singing and writing songs, and by the mid-1970's she was performing in various New York City cover bands. Singing rock standards by the Jefferson Airplane, Led Zeppelin, and Bad Company for local groups such as Doc West and Flyer, in 1977 she reportedly recorded her first single, "You Make Loving Fun." Later that year, she severely injured her vocal cords.

After one year of therapy with voice coach Katie Agestra, Lauper's voice returned and she formed Blue Angel with multi-instrumentalist John Turi. This band released its self-titled debut album in 1980, which included Lauper's version of Gene Pitney's "I'm Gonna Be Strong," a single Lauper coproduced. The backup band included Paul Shaffer on keyboards and Anton Figg on drums, later the core members of television host David Letterman's studio band. While not released in the United States until 1994, the record initially was a minor hit in Holland, reaching number 37 on the Amsterdam charts.

Solo Success. In the spring of 1983, Lauper signed with Epic Records and by year's end released her solo debut, *She's So Unusual*. The album sold more than five million copies in the United States and was the first debut rock album in history by a female artist to feature four Top-5 singles, including "All Through the Night" and Robert Hazard's "Girls Just Want to Have Fun," which became Lauper's signature song. Lauper cowrote "Time After Time" and "She Bop," which quickly became staples on the newly flourishing MTV video network.

For the Record

Many people thought that Cyndi Lauper would be a one-hit wonder, but she proved them wrong. Not only did her second single, "Time After Time," hit number 1, her next single, "She Bop," reached number 3—making her the first female singer ever to have her first three chart entries reach the top three positions. Moreover, her next single, "All Through the Night," reached number 5, making her the *only* rock artist ever to have four songs from a debut album reach the Top 10 as singles.

Lauper was an immediate media star, recognized as much for her multicolored hair, new-wave fashions, and quirky personality as for her soft-pop hits. She was frequently compared to fellow newcomers Madonna and Annie Lennox of the Eurythmics, with whom Lauper would have friendly competitions at award shows. In 1984, Lauper worked 350 days and played almost 300 concerts. She performed or promoted her records in 150 cities and designed her own T-shirts for concert sales. In 1985, Lauper received special attention, including a cover story in *People* magazine, for her contributions to the various artists' collection, *The Goonies O.S.T.* Her songs "What a Thrill" and the hit "The Goonies 'R' Good Enough" publicized her off-the-wall public image as did her sponsorship of professional wrestlers. Still, she continued receiving numerous Grammy and MTV Video Award nominations, including those for her role in U.S.A. for Africa's benefit single, "We Are the World."

Cyndi Lauper (Paul Natkin)

In 1986, she released *True Colors,* an album she coproduced that demonstrated a maturation in her professional growth with more adventurous musical styles and a stretching of her singing capabilities. One highlight was the Caribbean-flavored remake of Marvin Gaye's "What's Going On." *True Colors* featured guest appearances by Billy Joel, Nile Rodgers, Rick Derringer, Aimee Mann, and the Bangles. In turn, she sang backup for Joel on "Code of Silence" on his 1986 album, *The Bridge.*

With growing respect in the music community, Lauper's image shifted from girlish extravagance to sexy chanteuse, appearing on television's *Late Night with David Letterman* and onstage in short skirts and high heels. In October, 1988, Lauper traveled to the Soviet Union as one of a group of U.S. songwriters collaborating with Soviet counterparts. An outgrowth of this project was the collaborative album *Music Speaks Louder Than Words,* for which Lauper contributed "Cold Sky."

In 1989, Lauper received a Grammy Award nomination for the song "I Drove All Night" from her thematically unified album, *A Night to Remember.* She continued to augment her solo work with collaborations such as her 1990 appearance on former Pink Floyd guitarist Roger Waters's *The Wall Live in Berlin* singing "Another Brick in the Wall Part II" and "The Tide Is Turning." She was a member of Sean Lennon's 1991 Peace Choir, which remade John Lennon's "Give Peace a Chance" to protest the war in Iraq. Lauper also performed "Santa Claus Is Coming to Town" for 1992's *A Very Special Christmas 2* and appeared on the Hooters' 1993 album *Out of Body.*

Changes. On November 24, 1991, Lauper married actor David Thornton at the Friends Meeting House in New York. Singer Little Richard conducted the nontraditional ceremony, and soul singer Patti Labelle sang the wedding theme, "Come What May." For her fourth album, *Hat Full of Stars* (1993), Lauper coproduced, cowrote, and directed three videos of her new material. The introspective "Sally's Pigeons" from the album remains among Lauper's best lyrical efforts.

In 1994, Lauper remade her first hit into "Hey Now, Girls Just Want to Have Fun" with a Caribbean, reggae-driven background. Also in that year, *Sisters of Avalon* was issued in Japan, with worldwide release in 1996. For the first time, Lauper cowrote all songs on the album with her collaborator and keyboardist, Jan Pulsford, including the hit "Come Home." While pregnant, Lauper toured as a special guest with Tina Turner for three months before her daughter, Declyn Wallace Thornton, was born on November 19, 1997.

In addition to her numerous nominations for music and video awards, including her 1984 Best New Artist Grammy, in 1995 Lauper won an Emmy Award for Outstanding Guest Actress in a Comedy Series for her second appearance on *Mad About You.* In 1998, she performed a live concert for the VH1 cable network. —*Wesley Britton*

SELECT DISCOGRAPHY

■ ALBUMS

The Goonies O.S.T., 1985 (with others)
True Colors, 1986
A Night to Remember, 1989
Tycoon, 1992 (with others)
Hat Full of Stars, 1993
Twelve Deadly Cyns . . . And Then Some, 1994 (compilation)
Sisters of Avalon, 1996
Largo, 1998 (with others)

SELECT AWARDS

Rolling Stone, named Best New Artist and Best Female Video Artist, 1983
MTV Video Music Award for Best Female Video Artist, 1983
American Music Awards for Favorite Female Vocalist, Pop/Rock, and Favorite Female Vocalist, Video, Pop/Rock, 1984
Grammy Award for Best New Artist, 1984
MTV Video Music Award for Best Female Video of the Year, 1984

SEE ALSO: Madonna.

Leadbelly

(Huddie Ledbetter)

BORN: Mooringsport, Louisiana; January, 1888
DIED: New York, New York; December 6, 1949
FIRST SINGLE RELEASE: "Honey Take a Whiff on Me," 1933
MUSICAL STYLES: Folk, blues

Huddie Ledbetter, or Leadbelly, made his first appearance before a New York audience in 1935, less than one year after his release from the Angola State Prison in Louisiana. He brought a broad range of folk, blues, and religious songs to the music scene, many of which reflected his rural and prison background. Over the next fifteen years he was to profoundly influence an entire generation of folksingers.

The Beginnings. In January, 1888, Huddie Ledbetter was born to a middle-aged couple, Wes and Sallie Ledbetter, in Mooringsport, Louisiana. Ledbetter demonstrated his musical talent at an early age, singing and playing the accordion and the mandolin before he was six years old. By 1903, he was playing a windjammer accordion, as well as a newly acquired guitar, on a regular basis at local dances, or "sukey" jumps. His repertoire included

Leadbelly (Archive Photos)

the folk and country blues songs of the Louisiana region as well as the hymns that he sang and played in his backcountry church.

Ledbetter left school at the age of fourteen, working during the week on his father's farm and performing at country dances on the weekends. When he was sixteen, he fathered a daughter, Arthur Mae. After refusing to marry the baby's mother, Ledbetter moved to Shreveport, Louisiana, where he performed in many of the clubs on Fannin Street, the center of Shreveport's nightlife. During the next few years, Ledbetter wandered through north central Texas and parts of Louisiana, learning a wide variety of songs. He briefly attended Bishop College, but left school in 1908, when he married Aletta Henderson of Marshall, Texas. By 1910, the couple was in Dallas, Texas, where Ledbetter became the protégé of another talented country-blues singer, Blind Lemon Jefferson. While he was living near Dallas, Ledbetter acquired his first twelve-string guitar, the instrument which was to become his favorite.

In 1915, Ledbetter and his wife moved back to the vicinity of Marshall, Texas, where Ledbetter was to have his first serious brush with the law. He was accused of attacking a woman in Marshall, but he was actually convicted of carrying a weapon and was sentenced to thirty days on the county road gang. Only three days into his sentence, he managed to escape, taking refuge with relatives in Bowie County, Texas. He changed his name to Walter Boyd and began work as a sharecropper near the town of De Kalb, Texas. On December 17, 1917, Ledbetter's neighbor, Will Stafford, was killed. Ledbetter, alias Walter Boyd, was arrested, tried, and found guilty of murder. Ledbetter faced a seven- to thirty-year sentence which began in the Texas penal system at Shaw Prison and ended at Sugarland Prison. In January, 1924, Texas Governor Pat Neff made a tour of various prison camps. Ledbetter, who had already established himself as an entertainer within the prison system, was asked to sing for the governor. His song was an eloquent plea for freedom. Governor Neff responded to this plea by signing a full pardon for Ledbetter on January 16, 1925.

From 1925 to 1930, Ledbetter spent most of his time between Houston and Shreveport, supporting himself as a driver and maintenance worker while building a reputation as a musician. On January 15, 1930, Ledbetter was involved in an altercation in Mooringsport, Louisiana. He was charged with assault upon a well-known local white man, Dick Ellet. Ledbetter was brought to trial and sentenced to six to ten years in prison. He was sent to the notorious prison in Angola, Louisiana, to serve his time. Since Ledbetter was a model prisoner at Angola, he hoped for early release in 1934. He was informed, however, that he would probably not be released until 1936.

At this juncture, Ledbetter met John Lomax and his son, Alan, who were visiting prisons throughout the South, collecting and recording folksongs for the Library of Congress. Ledbetter asked Lomax to take a letter to the governor of Louisiana, O.K. Allen. Through the possible intervention of Lomax, Ledbetter was released on August 1, 1934. Ledbetter returned to Shreveport and took up residence with his second wife, Martha Promise. Shortly thereafter, Lomax hired Ledbetter as a chauffeur and assistant, and the two traveled across the South recording songs at various prisons. Lomax then took Ledbetter to New York, where he was introduced to the public as Leadbelly, a name he most likely acquired in prison. Lomax became Leadbelly's manager for the next year, arranging recording sessions with various record companies and appearances in a number of universities. Unfortunately, the friendly relationship between Leadbelly and Lomax was not to last, and the two men parted company.

The Comeback. In 1936, Mary Elizabeth Barnicle, a professor at New York University, became Leadbelly's manager. In 1938, she began making extensive recordings of more than fifty of his new songs. Through Barnicle and other activists, Leadbelly forged tenuous links with the left-wing labor movement, but he never developed political beliefs that led to a permanent alliance with any group. The only political issue he felt strongly about was civil rights, but his willingness to perform for radical left-wing organizations caused the FBI to start a file on him in the 1940's.

In 1937, while in Washington D.C., for a recording session with Alan Lomax at the Library of Congress, Leadbelly wrote a song which indicted Washington as a racist city, "The Bourgeois Blues." Upon his return to New York, Leadbelly sang on behalf of the "Scottsboro Boys," nine black Alabama men who were arrested for the alleged rape of two white women in 1931, recording "The Scottsboro Boys Shall Not Die." He warned inhabitants of Harlem, New York: "Don't you ever go to Alabama," implying that black men there were often arrested on false charges. On March 5, 1939, Leadbelly was arrested in New York for assault. The details of this incident remain unclear as Leadbelly may have been acting in self-defense. His friends and supporters, looking for ways to finance his legal defense, made a record deal with a new company called Musicraft. As a result, Leadbelly recorded thirteen songs, including old favorites such as "Frankie and Albert" and "De Kalb Blues." Despite the efforts of friends and legal counsel, he was sentenced to serve eight months at New York's Rikers Island prison.

In 1940, Leadbelly recorded a number of songs for the nation's largest record company, RCA Victor. The songs, which were issued in an album entitled *The Midnight Special and Other Prison Songs*, became a landmark in African American folk music. Throughout 1941, Leadbelly made a series of radio appearances and audition programs at local and national levels. Next to "Irene" (known as "Goodnight Irene" after a cover version by the Weavers in 1950), the most requested song of this era was his "Good Mornin' Blues."

In 1945, Leadbelly spent a year in California, recording for Capitol Records and playing engagements in a number of cities. He was also recorded in 1945 for Pete Seeger's documentary film that was released in 1975, *Three Songs by Leadbelly.* After he returned to the East, he wrote songs such as "Jim Crow Blues" and "Equality for Negroes," which focused on the need for civil rights. In May, 1949, while in Paris for a series of concerts, he was diagnosed with amyotrophic lateral sclerosis, Lou Gehrig's disease. His health declined rapidly, and he died in Bellevue Hospital in New York on December 5, 1949.

Legacy. In addition to preserving turn-of-the-century folk music, Leadbelly served as a teacher and role model for a younger generation of folksingers which included Pete Seeger, Sonny Terry, Woody Guthrie, and Burl Ives. He has been called "America's Greatest Folksinger," with a repertoire of more than five hundred songs.

—*Yvonne Johnson*

SELECT DISCOGRAPHY

■ SINGLES

"Honey Take a Whiff on Me," 1933
"Frankie and Albert," 1933
"Irene," 1934
"Midnight Special," 1934
"C. C. Rider," 1933
"Good Mornin' Blues," 1940

SELECT AWARDS

Oklahoma Folklore Society Award of Merit, 1949
Rock and Roll Hall of Fame, inducted 1988

SEE ALSO: Guthrie, Woody; Seeger, Pete.

Led Zeppelin

MEMBERS: Jimmy Page (b. 1944), Robert Plant (b. 1948), John Paul Jones (b. 1946), John Bonham (1948-1990)

FIRST ALBUM RELEASE: *Led Zeppelin*, 1969
MUSICAL STYLES: Rock and roll, hard rock

Guitarist Jimmy Page formed Led Zeppelin in England in 1968. One of the most popular bands of the 1970's, Led Zeppelin perfected a style of dynamic hard rock which had its roots in American blues. Led Zeppelin was one of the most influential bands in rock history, spawning countless imitators and inspiring groups such as Pearl Jam and Stone Temple Pilots with its emphasis on energetic live performances and high-quality studio recording.

Origins. Page, who took up guitar after listening to Elvis Presley records, had become one of the leading studio musicians in England by the mid-1960's, playing on hits such as the Who's "I Can't Explain" and the Kinks' "You Really Got Me." Bored with session work, Page joined the Yardbirds in 1966, first as a bassist, then playing joint lead guitar with Jeff Beck. After Beck quit later that year, Page became the sole lead guitarist. When the Yardbirds disbanded in 1968, Page set about finding members for a new band that would reflect the changes that had taken place in rock music.

By the late 1960's, Eric Clapton and Jimi Hendrix had redefined rock and roll. Strongly influenced by American blues, these guitarists fronted groups that relied heavily upon energy and volume as they performed extended improvisations of their songs in concert. Page possessed both the musical skills and the ambition necessary to front a hard-rock supergroup, and word that he was seeking bandmates spread through the British rock community. John Paul Jones, a highly regarded studio musician in London, soon contacted Page. In addition to playing bass and keyboards, Jones had arranged music for such groups as the Rolling Stones, Herman's Hermits, and the Yardbirds. Jones impressed Page, and he soon became the second member of the new band.

The two music professionals turned to relative unknowns for their vocalist and drummer. Terry Reid, a vocalist already committed to another band, suggested that Page contact Robert Plant, a young singer who had worked in several unsuc-

Led Zeppelin (Archive Photos)

cessful groups. The first time that Page heard Plant perform, he was amazed that the teenage singer had not yet been discovered, and he feared that Plant must have a terrible personality that drove people away. Although Plant admired bands such as Buffalo Springfield and Moby Grape, groups which Page did not like, both men were blues enthusiasts and they got along well. Plant recommended that Page audition his friend and former bandmate John Bonham on drums. Page enjoyed Bonham's powerful and aggressive drumming and invited him to a rehearsal session. Meeting in a hot and cramped studio in London, the four men played the Yardbirds' "Train Kept a-Rollin'" and several blues standards. The rehearsal was a success, and Page had his new band.

Touring and Recording. After a short tour in Scandinavia as the New Yardbirds, the group, which would soon take the name Led Zeppelin, entered the recording studio. Completed in just thirty hours, the album *Led Zeppelin* (1969) showcased the band's talents and hinted at the future directions the band might take. Page produced the album and relied upon his extensive studio experience to use techniques such as backward echo on the guitar solo in "You Shook Me." Studio wizardry would later become an integral part of the Led Zeppelin sound. Bonham's explosive drumming and Jones's steady bass lines provided a solid foundation for Page's often sloppy yet inspired guitar solos and Plant's impassioned vocals. Covers of Willie Dixon's "I Can't Quit You

Baby" and "You Shook Me" revealed the band's interest in the blues, while "Communication Breakdown" and "Good Times Bad Times" showed that Led Zeppelin could rock hard. Two numbers, the traditional "Babe I'm Gonna Leave You" and Page's instrumental "Black Mountain Side," featured acoustic guitar and revealed yet another side of the band.

Recognizing Led Zeppelin's potential as a supergroup, Atlantic Records signed the band with a $200,000 advance without even hearing the tapes of the recording session. Band manager Peter Grant mapped out a strategy for success which relied upon extensive touring to build a fan base, and Led Zeppelin began its first tour in the United States during the last week of 1968, starting in Denver and visiting cities including San Francisco, Detroit, Chicago, and Boston before returning to England in February, 1969. The audiences loved the band, and fans rushed to purchase *Led Zeppelin* when it was released in January. The album stayed on the charts for more than a year, peaking at number 10 in May, 1969.

The band's commercial success did not result in critical praise. Most reviewers resented the hype surrounding the band and regarded Led Zeppelin as a cynical attempt on the part of Page and the record company to create a supergroup for profit. Some of the worst reviews appeared in *Rolling Stone*, the most influential rock magazine of the time. Music critic John Mendelsohn called Led Zeppelin a formula band and complained about their "willingness to waste their considerable talent on unworthy material." Mendelsohn argued that Page was "a very limited producer and a writer of weak, unimaginative songs" and denigrated "prissy Robert Plant's howled vocals" on "Babe I'm Gonna Leave You." The band hated the negative reviews and thereafter never trusted the press. In the coming years Led Zeppelin's members rarely gave interviews, a decision which angered many journalists but made the band all the more mysterious and interesting to their fans.

Rising to the Top. Led Zeppelin continued its relentless pace of touring and recording, starting their second U.S. tour in May, 1969. The concerts drew large crowds, and the band's performances grew longer and longer. Other bands dreaded appearing on the same bill with Led Zeppelin, rightfully fearing that they could not compete with the raw power which Led Zeppelin exhibited on stage. During the hectic concert schedule, the band recorded their second album, *Led Zeppelin II*, which was released in October, 1969. The album included a blues cover, "Bring It on Home," the semi-acoustic "What Is and What Should Never Be," and "Whole Lotta Love," which would soon become a rock anthem. *Led Zeppelin II* went gold the day it was released and reached the number 1 spot on the charts two months later. Although the band was adamantly opposed, Atlantic released an edited version of "Whole Lotta Love" as a single in the United States. The single sold nearly one million copies and reached number 4 on the charts. ("Whole Lotta Love" was a very close reworking of "You Need Love," a song written by American bluesman Willie Dixon and recorded by Muddy Waters. Dixon eventually sued Led Zeppelin and, in a 1986 out-of-court settlement, finally collect some royalties from Led Zeppelin's version of the song.) Manager Grant's strategy of relentless touring worked. During Led Zeppelin's U.S. tour in early 1970, which consisted of twenty-nine concerts in less than five weeks, the band performed without an opening act and earned more than one million dollars. Led Zeppelin was now one of the most popular bands in the world. Band members earned notoriety for their offstage antics, destroying hotel rooms, abusing alcohol, and, increasingly, using drugs. Although they basked in the attention which they received, band members began to long for a break. In 1970, Page and Plant retired to a rustic cottage called Bron-Y-Aur in rural South Wales for rest and the opportunity to write new songs. The material written at Bron-Y-Aur provided the foundation for the third album, *Led Zeppelin III*, which they recorded in a country manor outside London called Headley Grange. Released in October, 1970, *Led Zeppelin III* surprised many fans. It contained the usual rock songs, including the "Immigrant Song" and "Out on the Tiles," and a blistering blues number, "Since I've Been Loving You." However, several songs, including "That's the Way" and "Tangerine," were gentle acoustic pieces. Page had also expanded the group's sound, including banjo, mandolin, and pedal steel guitar in some songs. Fans responded favorably to the new direction the band had taken, and *Led Zeppelin III* reached number 1 on the charts two weeks after it was released. Critical response, however, remained tepid.

"Stairway to Heaven." Led Zeppelin ignored the rock media and forged ahead, returning to Headley Grange to record songs for their next album. Its release was first delayed by Page, who demanded perfection in the recording and mixing of the album, and then by Atlantic Records, which vehemently protested the band's decision to release the album without a title or any identification on the album cover. The band won out, though fans usually called it Led Zeppelin IV or Zoso, after the unusual rune that Page placed on the album's inner sleeve. Despite Atlantic's concerns, the record sold well, though it stalled at number 2 on the charts. By the late 1990's, the untitled fourth album had sold more than fifteen million copies, making it one of the best-selling rock recordings of all time. Moreover, the album included the song "Stairway to Heaven," which quickly became one of the most popular songs in rock history. Building from a quiet acoustic guitar complemented by soft recorders, "Stairway to Heaven" developed into a full-fledged rock masterpiece, complete with a furious guitar solo from Page. Critics complained that the song's lyrics, which Plant had composed while sitting in front of the fireplace at Headley Grange, were obscure or meaningless, but the fans loved its atmosphere of medieval mysteriousness. It quickly became the most well-known Led Zeppelin song. Twenty years after its release listeners in Los Angeles, Cincinnati, Portland and several other cities voted "Stairway to Heaven" the best song of all time. The members of Led Zeppelin also regarded it as a high point which assured their standing as creative artists.

During the years following the release of the untitled album, Led Zeppelin was the most popular rock band in the world. Their next album, *Houses of the Holy*, reached number 1 in May, 1973. The album contained acoustic elements such as "Over the Hills and Far Away ," roaring rock songs such as "The Song Remains the Same," and the mysterious "No Quarter," which again reflected Plant's interest in medieval fantasy. Concerts sold out immediately, and the band made attendance and profit records wherever they performed. In 1975 Led Zeppelin released *Physical Graffiti*, a double album which contained the exotic "Kashmir," the frantic "Trampled Underfoot," and the quiet acoustic instrumental "Bron-Y-Aur." It reached the number 1 spot two weeks after its release. A complex work which reflected Page's expertise in the studio, *Physical Graffiti* came to be regarded as Led Zeppelin's masterpiece by many of their fans. Although Page broke the tip of a finger on his left hand, the 1975 world tour was a triumph—the band sold 120,000 tickets in New York City and performed for eighty-five thousand fans over five nights in London. Led Zeppelin seemed to be on top of the world.

Bad Times. However, commercial success masked problems within the group. Touring had grown monotonous, and band members continued to abuse alcohol and drugs. Jimmy Page turned to heroin. The very future of the band was in doubt when they learned that Robert Plant had

For the Record

When Led Zeppelin visited Denmark in 1970, Eva von Zeppelin, a descendant of the count who had developed the zeppelin, threatened to sue if the band used her family name. Seeking to avoid a lawsuit, the band performed as the Nobs at their concert in Copenhagen.

§

As of 1991 more than one million copies of the sheet music to "Stairway to Heaven" had been sold, making it the biggest-selling sheet music for a rock song in history.

been severely injured in a car accident while on vacation in Greece in August, 1975. More than a year passed before Plant recovered enough to record *Presence* (1976), the band's seventh album, which was completed in less than three weeks. Page recorded all of the guitar solos in less than one day. The album contained no acoustic or keyboard numbers, concentrating exclusively on an electric rock sound. *Presence* reached number 1 on the charts in April, 1976. Later that year the band released the concert film *The Song Remains the Same* and a companion live double album with the same title. The film was popular with fans, but the band was disappointed with the results. Peter Grant belittled it as an "expensive home film." The 1977 tour again broke records, but John Bonham was arrested in San Francisco on assault charges. The tour was winding down with only seven dates remaining when Plant learned that his five-year old son Karac Plant had died in England of a respiratory infection.

His son's death sent Plant into a period of seclusion, but he returned to Led Zeppelin in mid-1978. Later that year the band traveled to Stockholm, Sweden, to record their ninth album. Page was distracted by personal problems, so John Paul Jones guided the production of *In Through the Out Door*, which was released in 1979. The album marked another departure for Led Zeppelin, with the gentle "All My Love," the country parody "Hot Dog," and an emphasis on keyboards on several songs. A brief European tour followed by a successful appearance at a festival in England marked the band's return to the stage, and in September they announced plans for an extensive European and North American tour. However, on September 24, 1980, John Bonham choked to death on his own vomit after consuming a large quantity of alcohol. In December Led Zeppelin announced that it "could not continue as (they) were," and the era when Led Zeppelin ruled as the biggest band in the world came to a quiet close.

After the Breakup. Though Led Zeppelin had formally disbanded, fans remained interested in the band and its members. Page released a collection of studio tracks entitled *Coda* in 1982. He also released two albums with the Firm during the 1980's, but that band never came near the success of Led Zeppelin. Plant worked on his solo career, releasing several successful albums, while Jones returned to studio work. The band reunited in 1985 for the Live Aid concert, and in 1988 they performed at the Atlantic Records fortieth anniversary celebration with John Bonham's son Jason on drums. Tour manager Richard Cole published his memoir, *Stairway to Heaven: Led Zeppelin Uncensored*, in 1992, and Ritchie Yorke, one of the few journalists whom the band trusted, released *Led Zeppelin: The Definitive Biography*, in 1993. In 1995 Page and Plant performed on MTV's *Unplugged*, released an album entitled *No Quarter*, and toured together, but Jones did not participate.

—*Thomas Clarkin*

SELECT DISCOGRAPHY

■ ALBUMS

Led Zeppelin, 1969
Led Zeppelin II, 1969
Led Zeppelin III, 1970
Untitled (also known as *Led Zeppelin IV* or *Zoso*), 1971
Houses of the Holy, 1973
Physical Graffiti, 1975
Presence, 1976
The Song Remains the Same, 1976
In Through the Out Door, 1979
Coda, 1982

SELECT AWARDS

Rock and Roll Hall of Fame, inducted 1995

SEE ALSO: Clapton, Eric; Dixon, Willie; Yardbirds, The.

John Lennon

BORN: Liverpool, England; October 9, 1940
DIED: New York, New York; December 8, 1980
FIRST SINGLE RELEASE: "Give Peace a Chance," 1969
MUSICAL STYLES: Rock and roll, pop

Born in 1940 in Liverpool, England, to Alfred and Julia Stanley Lennon, John Winston Lennon be-

John Lennon in 1972 (Bernard Gotfryd/Archive Photos)

came interested in music as a teenager, playing in various groups with friends from the same town, including future Beatles Paul McCartney and George Harrison. He also showed a talent for art and enrolled in the Liverpool Art College. There he met Cynthia Powell, who later became his first wife.

Success with the Beatles. By 1960 Lennon and his friends were playing in clubs in Hamburg, Germany, as the Beatles. John and Cynthia Lennon were married in 1962, and their son John Julian Lennon was born the year after. The Beatles had developed a following in their hometown of Liverpool. After recording their first hit single, "Love Me Do," in 1962, they quickly became internationally popular, and their lives were never the same. In 1964, soon after the Beatles' American debut on the Ed Sullivan television show (before an estimated 73 million viewers), Lennon's first book, *In His Own Write*, was published. This was followed by a second book, *A Spaniard in the Works*, in 1965 (the title is a pun on a British expression, "a spanner [wrench] in the works"). In that same year, Lennon and his fellow Beatles were awarded M.B.E.'s (naming them Members of Order of the British Empire) by Buckingham Palace.

Popularity was problematic for Lennon, who was very outspoken. In 1966 many conservatives in the United States were offended by his casual remark that the Beatles had become more popular than Jesus Christ. Lennon was also a part of the 1960's counterculture movement, which included experimentation with hallucinogenic drugs, rejection of nationalism and the polarities of the Cold War, self-exploration, and mysticism.

Although some of the same values and interests were shared by his bandmates, Lennon went through considerable personal change during this period, and he carried his interests to greater extremes than the others. From the beginning of their careers, he had coauthored most of the Beatles' songs with his somewhat more conservative partner Paul McCartney, but their lyrics began to change. Earlier songs typically had simple love lyrics such as "Love, love me do/ You know I love you." Later Lennon Beatles lyrics such as "Lucy in the Sky with Diamonds" and "I Am the Walrus" featured surreal, even obscure, lyrics.

John and Yoko. Lennon had retained his interest in the visual arts, and he met artist Yoko Ono, who was to become his second wife, at a London art gallery in late 1966. (When she met him, she had no idea that he was a member of the most famous band in the world.) She fostered his interest in avant-garde art, and in 1967 they became close. In 1968 John and Cynthia Lennon were divorced. John grew even closer to Ono, who was pregnant with his child but miscarried. Later that year he was prosecuted and fined for cannabis (marijuana) possession. Lennon continued to record with the Beatles but also began to work on projects with Ono. Their first album, *Unfinished*

Music No. 1: Two Virgins, was released the same year. Because its cover featured a nude photograph of them, there were controversies over its distribution. It was shipped in a brown wrapper.

In March, 1969, soon after Ono was granted a divorce from her husband, John Lennon and Yoko Ono were married. During this time the Vietnam War was raging, and many American and British musicians had been raising their voices in protest. In a style reminiscent of New York art "happenings," the Lennons staged a "bed-in for peace" at a hotel in Amsterdam while on their honeymoon. They later held another bed-in in Montreal. The event was heavily publicized, and as part of the proceedings they recorded "Give Peace a Chance," which was released as a single. This antiwar protest song contrasted a monotone string of rhythmic words with a simple, chantlike refrain. In the following years the refrain was widely sung by large crowds during antiwar marches and demonstrations. The couple became increasingly involved in political causes and social issues. As celebrities, they were often interviewed, and they used their status as public figures to call attention to their social concerns.

Lennon continued to work both with the Beatles and on other musical ventures until the Beatles' final recordings for the *Abbey Road* album. Lennon and Ono, with a group they named the Plastic Ono Band, performed in Toronto (at this time Lennon had been barred from entry to the United States because of drug convictions). The show was released on the album *Live Peace in Toronto*. In 1969 the Plastic Ono Band released "Cold Turkey," and in 1970 Lennon released "Instant Karma! (We All Shine On)." Produced by Phil Spector, it went to number 3.

For the Record

In 1969 Lennon returned his prestigious M.B.E. award, which had been awarded to each of the Beatles four years before, to Queen Elizabeth. He did this partly to protest Britain's alignment with the United States in the Vietnam War and partly to reject English class divisions. Yet Lennon could not resist making a joke: His letter also complained about the poor sales of his song "Cold Turkey."

After the Beatles. By the time the Beatles officially disbanded in April of 1970 with McCartney's public resignation, Lennon had already moved away from his professional and personal identification with his former songwriting partner. On Lennon's 1970 *Plastic Ono Band* album was the intensely personal song "Mother," which reflected his and Ono's involvement in Dr. Arthur Janov's "primal scream" therapy. Later that year Lennon released his solo album *Imagine*, which went to number 1.

The Lennons moved to New York City in 1971. Political conservatives made efforts to deport them, pointing to John's 1968 drug conviction, and a long legal struggle against the U.S. Immigrationa and Nationalization Service ensued. They remained in the United States, performing and recording, both together and with other musicians such as Eric Clapton. While his wife remained committed to experimental music in the spirit of modernist musicians such as John Cage, and her manner of singing was not in the popular style, Lennon continued to play in a more mainstream style. In 1974 he recorded a number 1 hit single, "Whatever Gets You Thru the Night," with Elton John.

After a year of separation in 1974, John and Yoko were reunited, and their child Sean was born in 1975. Lennon's immigration was approved in 1976, and Lennon retired from music for several years, spending time with his family. He and Ono quietly contributed to charitable causes, and without compromising their ideals, they began to express themselves in a less hard-edged, less shocking way. As a result, they were viewed more positively by the general public. In 1980, Lennon began composing again, and the couple recorded a new album, *Double Fantasy*, which was received with great excitement. Plans were made for more recordings, and there was even talk of possible live performances, but they would never take place.

On December 8, only two months after his fortieth birthday, Lennon was murdered in New York by a deranged fan named Mark David Chapman. Ono was with Lennon when he was killed; they were in front of their apartment building, the Dakota. Millions around the world participated in both spontaneous and organized vigils to mourn Lennon's shocking death.

Lennon's musical and social influence continued. In 1988 a film documentary was released, bearing the title of one of his most well-remembered songs, "Imagine," in which he gently sings of his dreams for a better world:

> You may say I'm a dreamer
> but I'm not the only one:
> I'll hope some day you will join us
> and the world will live as one.

—*Alice Myers*

SELECT DISCOGRAPHY

■ ALBUMS

Unfinished Music No. 1: Two Virgins, 1968 (with Ono)
Unfinished Music No. 2: Life with the Lions, 1969 (with Ono)
Wedding Album, 1969 (with Ono)
Live Peace in Toronto, 1969 (with Ono)
John Lennon/Plastic Ono Band, 1970
Imagine, 1971
Sometime in New York City, 1972 (with Ono)
Mind Games, 1973
Walls and Bridges, 1974
Rock 'n' Roll, 1975
Shaved Fish, 1975
Double Fantasy, 1980 (with Ono)
The John Lennon Collection, 1982
Milk and Honey, 1984 (with Ono)
John Lennon Live in New York City, 1986
Menlove Ave., 1986
Imagine: John Lennon, 1988 (music from the motion picture)
Lennon, 1990 (4-CD boxed set, compilation)
Anthology, 1998 (4-CD compilation)

SELECT AWARDS

Member of the Order of the British Empire, 1965
Grammy Award for Album of the Year for *Double Fantasy*, 1981 (with Yoko Ono)
Hollywood Walk of Fame, star awarded posthumously, 1988
Rock and Roll Hall of Fame, inducted 1994 (Lennon solo; Beatles inducted 1988)

SEE ALSO: Beatles, The; Clapton, Eric; John, Elton; McCartney, Paul.

Annie Lennox. *See* The Eurythmics / Annie Lennox

Huey Lewis and the News

ORIGINAL MEMBERS: Huey Lewis (b. Hugh Cregg III, 1950), Mario Cipollina (b. 1954), Johnny Colla (b. 1952), Bill Gibson (b. 1951), Chris Hayes (b. 1957), Sean Hopper (b. 1953)
OTHER MEMBERS: Marvin McFadden, John Pierce, Ron Stallings, Rob Sudduth
FIRST ALBUM RELEASE: *Huey Lewis and the News*, 1980
MUSICAL STYLES: Pop, rock and roll, rhythm and blues

Formed in San Francisco in 1979, Huey Lewis and the News was one of the first rock bands to be recognized as much for their music videos as for their music. At the peak of their success in the mid-1980's, Lewis and the News released two consecutive multiplatinum albums and put eight singles in the Top 10. While often perceived as a formulaic pop band and criticized for a lack of spontaneity, Huey Lewis and the News' experimentation with a variety of musical styles and commitment to high-energy but gimmick-free live concerts won them a broad spectrum of loyal fans.

Huey Lewis. Huey Lewis was born Hugh Anthony Cregg III, the son of an artist mother and a radiologist and jazz drummer father. The teenage Cregg was slated to study engineering at Cornell University when his father insisted that he first spend a year traveling. Cregg hitchhiked his way around Europe, whiling away the hours roadside by teaching himself to play the harmonica.

He attended college briefly, then returned to the San Francisco area and in 1971 joined a struggling country-rock band called Clover. He adopted the name Huey Lewis (a girlfriend's father had been calling him "Huey Louie") and held down a variety of jobs while Clover struggled to find a commercial niche. Clover released two albums, then in 1976 signed on with a British record label and toured England, but its efforts there were eclipsed by the meteoric rise of mid-1970's punk rock.

Lewis found inspiration in British punk musicians, who played what they liked instead of trying to please audiences or record companies. After Clover broke up, Lewis returned once again to California, now resolved to get his favorite musicians together and play just for fun. He began running a weekly jam session, dubbed Monday Night Live, at Uncle Charlie's, a San Francisco club.

The News. Bill Gibson, Mario Cippolina, and Johnny Colla, once members of Clover's rival band Soundhole, all joined in the Monday Night Live sessions, as did fellow Clover alumnus Sean Hopper, and possibly Chris Hayes (Hayes, a successful jazz guitarist, has spoken of auditioning for the News and learning to play rock and roll after joining the band). Offered studio time to record a demo tape, the band, at the time called Huey Lewis and the American Express, recorded a parody of the theme from *Exodus* called "Exodisco," in keeping with Lewis's determination to have fun instead of struggling to make hit records. Nonetheless, the demo caught the attention of manager Bob Brown and the band soon had a recording contract.

Their first album, *Huey Lewis and the News*, was released in 1980. Recorded using a minimum of takes in an effort to achieve a live sound, the album merely sounded amateurish and was a commercial failure. Lewis was beginning to recognize the difference between creating a sound in the studio and playing live: "If you want a live sound, you have to fake a live sound."

For the Record

Huey Lewis made a cameo appearance in the 1985 film *Back to the Future* as a high school teacher who auditions Marty McFly's rock band for a school dance and rejects them: "Hold it, fellas. I'm afraid you're just too darn loud."

The second album, *Picture This* (1982), gave the band an opportunity to hone its recording skills and a second chance to prove its commercial potential. The band made what Lewis would often call their "deal with the devil," recording "Do You Believe in Love" because Lewis believed it sounded commercial enough to receive radio airplay. Bolstered by the accompanying music video promoting the band as apple-cheeked, clean-cut regular guys, the song became their first Top-40 hit and the first of two hit singles from *Picture This.*

Huey Lewis and the News' popularity continued to rise, aided by frequent exposure on MTV. In 1981 MTV had begun airing the characteristically low-budget videos made to accompany the band's first album; their relationship with MTV grew with the release of music videos from *Picture This* and with the network's airing of a videotaped live performance showcasing the band's strengths as a live act. The concert performance introduced viewers to the News' visual and musical trademarks: Lewis, Hayes, and Colla jumping from the drum platform during "Workin' for a Livin'"; a cappella versions of classic 1960's tunes such as Curtis Mayfield's "It's Alright" and the Shirelles' "Mama Said"; and Lewis's jubilant shout, "You've just heard the News!"

With the News' third album, *Sports* (1983), the fan base built by MTV appearances melded with the band's acquired commercial sense and studio savvy, allowing the band to fashion an album incorporating both eclectic musical styles and potential hits. Released in 1983, *Sports* spent seventy-one weeks on *Billboard*'s album charts and generated three Top-10 singles, two of which, "The Heart of Rock 'n' Roll" and "I Want a New Drug," became the band's signature tunes. Riding the wave of major success, the band played sold-out shows worldwide and were invited to participate in the star-studded USA for Africa benefit project, "We Are the World" (Lewis's line on the single was originally written for Prince). They also had their first number 1 hit with "The Power of Love," from the 1985 film *Back to the Future.*

Success became burdensome as Lewis and the band struggled to write songs for a fourth album in the wake of the multiplatinum *Sports.* However, *Fore!*, released in 1986, while less musically diverse than *Sports*, matched its popularity and record sales, quickly becoming a number 1 album and reaffirming the band's earlier success.

Having proved themselves to be more than a commercial fluke, the band felt more able to experiment musically. Their next album, *Small World* (1988), offered their take on international rhythms, reggae, and zydeco, in addition to straight-ahead pop tunes. However, sales for *Small World* were disappointing, and the News again felt pressured to create a more commercially viable sound. Lewis and the News changed record labels and took three years off from touring and recording.

The 1990's. Their 1991 comeback album, *Hard at Play*, yielded only one hit single, "Couple Days Off." Lewis, however, seemed content with a lower profile than he had enjoyed in the mid-1980's. After another hiatus, the band regrouped to play vintage rock and roll and, according to Lewis, "fell in love all over again." The result was 1994's moderately successful *Four Chords and Several Years Ago*, an album of cover tunes showcasing the band's early influences.

In 1996 the band released a greatest hits album, *Time Flies. . . . The Best of Huey Lewis and the News.* Bassist Mario Cippolina had left the band and been replaced with Los Angeles-based session musician John Pierce on four new songs (originally intended for a long-delayed Huey Lewis solo project). Following the promotional appearances for this album, Lewis and the News maintained a limited touring schedule and delayed the release of new material while individual members became increasingly involved in outside projects.

—*Maureen J. Puffer*

SELECT DISCOGRAPHY

■ ALBUMS

Huey Lewis and the News, 1980
Picture This, 1982
Sports, 1983
Fore!, 1986
Small World, 1988
Hard at Play, 1991
Four Chords and Several Years Ago, 1994
Time Flies. . . . The Best of Huey Lewis & the News, 1996 (compilation)

SELECT AWARDS

Grammy Award for Best Music Video, Long Form, for *Huey Lewis and the News: The Heart of Rock 'n' Roll*, 1985

SEE ALSO: Geils, J., Band; Springsteen, Bruce.

Jerry Lee Lewis

BORN: Ferriday, Louisiana; September 29, 1935
FIRST SINGLE RELEASE: "Crazy Arms," 1956
MUSICAL STYLES: Rockabilly, rock and roll, country

Of all the early rock-and-roll stars, Jerry Lee Lewis was one of the most flamboyant and colorful. His frenetic performance style, which included kicking piano stools out of his way and literally beating on the instrument, appealed to audiences of teenagers intent on rebelling against all authority. Although his career, and in particular the less savory aspects of his personal life, have been widely publicized, Lewis survived every crisis and would continue to perform on a regular basis despite poor health.

Early Career. Jerry Lee Lewis's earliest experiences with music centered around the radio, most notably the popular country stations. His first performances took place in church and in the roadhouses and nightclubs around Ferriday. He was also influenced by the gospel music that was a large part of his early years. His family included cousins who were to become prominent in their own areas: television evangelist Jimmy Swaggart and country music singer Mickey Gilley.

He made his first contact with Sam Phillips and Sun Records in 1956 while visiting yet another cousin, bass player Jay Brown (who was also his future father-in-law). Phillips already had produced successful recordings by Carl Perkins, Johnny Cash, Roy Orbison, and Elvis Presley; Lewis became yet another of the white, semicountry artists to be added to this roster. He recorded "Crazy Arms" and several other country songs for the Sun label; these pieces achieved only moderate success. Despite pressure to continue in a rockabilly style, Lewis moved toward what he considered more mainstream rock with such hits as "Whole Lotta Shakin' Going On" (a cover of an earlier Commodores release) and "Great Balls of Fire" (both 1957). Both recordings hit number 1 on the country charts while making it to number 3 and number 2 respectively on the pop charts and placing high on the rhythm-and-blues charts.

Jerry Lee Lewis (Archive Photos)

Because of his increasing popularity between 1956 and 1957, Lewis undertook a British tour in late 1958. Against the advice of his promoters, he took along his new wife, Myra, who also happened to be thirteen years old and his third cousin. When the British press revealed her identity, the ensuing uproar surprised Lewis, who saw no problem with her age or her blood relationship to him. Lewis found the public to be particularly unforgiving, and concerts that were not canceled were marred by heckling. Upon returning to the United States he found U.S. audiences to be no more tolerant. It was also clear that many former supporters, including Sam Phillips, would no longer promote his records. He made a living by touring and playing county fairs and similar venues for a fraction of the fee he had once commanded. After a decade of this lifestyle it became obvious that his rock-and-roll career was over. The demand for his type of music and his outrageous performances was gone. He returned to his country roots, establishing himself in that genre and recording a number of hit songs while remaining on the tour circuit.

During the 1980's and 1990's, Lewis was plagued by health problems that resulted from his hard-driving lifestyle during his early career. In 1981 and 1985 he suffered from bleeding ulcers that almost claimed his life. In 1996 he suffered a mild heart attack, but he went back to performing and recording on a limited basis.

Style. Jerry Lee Lewis established a unique style within that substyle of rock and roll commonly known as rockabilly. While under contract to Sun Records (1956-1963), he recorded more than 160 songs, the majority of which had a distinctly country flavor (his later move to a strictly country style was an outgrowth of this influence). He promoted himself as a wild man on stage, eventually earning himself the nickname "Killer," and enjoyed the notoriety he gained through these performances.

As with many of the early rockabilly stars, Lewis did not write many of his own songs; he felt composition would take something away from his performing style. He concentrated, instead, on his stage personality and selected pieces from the country, rhythm-and-blues, gospel, and rock repertoires that he then covered in his own personal style.

The most notable element of his performances was the pounding piano part incorporated into each of his songs. The instrumentation most commonly used by artists recording on the Sun Records label included lead acoustic guitar, acoustic bass, and the beat played on the cymbals. The addition of the piano to this mix, often accompanied only by the acoustic bass and drums, produced a sound that was squarely between the country roots of Memphis-style rock and the blues-inspired rock of early personalities such as Little Richard. Lewis, like Little Richard, cultivated a piano style that was very similar to boogie woogie, supporting bombastic, virtuosic figures (glissandos, trills, repeated notes, and the right hand in the upper registers of the instrument) with the "walking bass" typical of the earlier genre ("Great Balls of Fire"). He added to these his flamboyant stage personality to create a wild, exciting rock style to which young people wanted to dance.

His lyrics were not the representations of typical teen life in the 1950's; instead they were suggestive and slightly sexual, much in the style of Little Richard's early pieces and definitely in the old blues tradition ("Great Balls of Fire," "Whole Lotta Shakin' Going On"). His love of women, a trait he admitted was one of the most dominant features of his personality, clearly influenced his choice of lyrics, challenging the conservatives who were already appalled by rock and roll. His bold lyrics, as well as his personal life, were later used against him by those determined to show the detrimental effects of rock music on young people.

Lewis's place in the history of rock and roll is assured, even though he made personal decisions that ultimately affected his popularity and his music, resulting in numerous interruptions in his career. He accomplished two objectives by returning to country music: It allowed him to pay tribute to a medium that was very influential on his early music, and it allowed him to keep performing in a genre where forgiveness was more easily obtained. On his 1995 album, *Young Blood,* Lewis once again shows us his rocking piano style and the self-confidence typical of his earliest work.

—Karen M. Bryan

For the Record

"When they look back on me I want 'em to remember me not for all my vices, although I've had a few, and certainly not for any mansions of high livin' money I made and spent. I want 'em to remember me simply for my music."

§

"If I am going to hell, I'm going there playing the piano."

—*Jerry Lee Lewis,* to Denny Ray Miller, 1996

SELECT DISCOGRAPHY

■ SINGLES

"Crazy Arms," 1956
"Whole Lotta Shakin' Going On," 1957
"Great Balls of Fire," 1957
"Breathless," 1958
"Another Place, Another Time," 1968
"What's Made Milwaukee Famous," 1968
"Chantilly Lace," 1972
"Middle-Age Crazy," 1977

■ ALBUMS

Together, 1969 (with Linda Gail Lewis)
The Session, 1973
Southern Roots, 1973
Jerry Lee Lewis Keeps Rockin', 1978
Jerry Lee Lewis, 1979

Killer Country, 1980
Young Blood, 1995

SELECT AWARDS

Academy of Country Music Best Piano Player Award, 1975

Grammy Award for Best Spoken Word or Nonmusical Recording for *Interviews from "the Class of '55" Recording Sessions*, 1986 (with others)

Rock and Roll Hall of Fame, inducted 1986

SEE ALSO: Little Richard.

Gordon Lightfoot

BORN: Orillia, Ontario, Canada; November 17, 1938
FIRST ALBUM RELEASE: *Lightfoot*, 1966
MUSICAL STYLES: Folk, country, folk rock

Gordon Lightfoot emerged from the clubs and coffeehouses of Toronto in the mid-1960's to become a prolific songwriter whose works were recorded by artists in styles ranging from country to rock. As a performer, he moved from folk music with a country flavor to a more upbeat rock sound that allowed him to rise to the top of U.S. rock charts in the 1970's. Later in his career, his traditional folk style did not produce chart-topping hits but kept his large number of loyal fans satisfied.

Early Life and Career. Gordon Meredith Lightfoot was born in Orillia, Ontario, north of Toronto. He loved to sing even as a small child. Before he was a teenager, he performed regularly at school, church, and local civic events. While in high school, he sang in several barbershop quartets.

Beginning in 1958, Lightfoot studied at a California music school for fourteen months. He later credited this formal training as crucial to his development as a songwriter and musician. Back in Canada in 1959, he settled in Toronto and took any part-time job he could get in the city's lively music business. He wrote commercial jingles, played drums in a band, and sang in a folk music duo called the Two Tones. Eventually, he landed a steady job dancing and singing on the Canadian Broadcasting Corporation television show *Country Hoedown*. This exposure led to other television work, including hosting a limited-run country music show in England in 1963.

In 1964 Lightfoot was back in Toronto playing in nightclubs for very little money. He became part of a new folk music movement sweeping through North America at that time. Inspired by Bob Dylan, who was Lightfoot's musical hero, and others, many young singers began performing traditional folk ballads and their own compositions in folk clubs and coffeehouses. Two of Lightfoot's fellow Toronto folksingers were a married couple, Ian Tyson and Sylvia Fricker, who performed as Ian and Sylvia. Tyson worked with Lightfoot to improve the latter's guitar playing and arranged for his manager to produce a Lightfoot album. While the project was in development, Lightfoot's new producer procured performing dates throughout Canada and released some of his album material as singles.

Consequently, 1965 became Lightfoot's breakthrough year. His first single, "I'm Not Sayin'," was a hit in Canada. Ian and Sylvia had a hit that year with Lightfoot's "Early Morning Rain," and folk icons Peter, Paul, and Mary did the same with "For Lovin' Me." Meanwhile, Nashville superstar Marty Robbins took a Lightfoot composition, "Ribbon of Darkness," to the top of the country charts. *RPM* magazine named Lightfoot Canada's 1965 Folksinger of the Year. In January, 1966, United Artists issued the album *Lightfoot* to critical and commercial acclaim in Canada.

During the next three years, Lightfoot produced four more albums for United Artists. While he was making money and receiving critical acclaim, Lightfoot was disappointed that his albums were not selling well in the United States. Thus, in 1969 he switched labels, to the Reprise subsidiary of Warner Bros., believing that it would better promote his music to an album-buying audience.

The Successful 1970's. Reprise issued its first Lightfoot album, *Sit down Young Stranger*, in May of 1970. The record's sales were disappointing until a Seattle radio station began playing one of its songs. Listeners began calling in, requesting

For the Record

Gordon Lightfoot's "If You Could Read My Mind" has been recorded by more than one hundred artists.

the soft ballad "If You Could Read My Mind." Warner Bros. recalled all copies of the album, and reissued them under the name of that particular song. This strategy allowed the album to reach sales that qualified it for gold-record status while the single rose to number 5 on the rock charts.

Lightfoot's success in the U.S. rock market soon seemed, however, to have been a fluke. None of his next three albums sold well nor yielded a hit single, although a few of his songs reached the lower levels of the charts and his ballad "Cotton Jenny" became a country hit for fellow Canadian Anne Murray. Thus Lightfoot decided to give his music more of a rock sound by adding new instruments and sophisticated orchestration.

The resulting album, *Sundown*, was released in 1974. Both the album and the single of the same name soared to the number 1 positions on the charts and attained platinum-record status. Lightfoot's 1976 album, *Summertime Dream*, eventually sold enough units to attain double-platinum status. It contained a single that went to the number 2 position on the rock charts, the enigmatic ballad "The Wreck of the Edmund Fitzgerald." A greatest hits compilation, *Gord's Gold*, released in 1975, also eventually achieved double-platinum sales.

Later Career and Assessments. In 1978 Lightfoot released another album, *Endless Wire*, which became a gold record. Over the next decade and a half, he produced five more albums; none, however, sold particularly well. His 1986 effort, *East of Midnight*, was a departure for him. The album had a smoother, more pop sound than Lightfoot's previous work. Reviewers liked it but sales were disappointing. Lightfoot reportedly was disgusted with the lackluster sales of his records in the 1980's and vowed never to record again. He did not do so for seven years, but then issued *Waiting for You* in 1993; it contained the familiar, classic Lightfoot sound. His aging but intensely loyal fans loved it, indicating that a market—though not large enough to produce big hits—nevertheless existed for his music. His spirit renewed by the album's reception, Lightfoot continued to book concerts throughout the United States and Canada and promised more albums to come in his later years.

Lightfoot seldom recorded songs written by others. Thus, his career epitomizes that of the traditional singer-songwriter who tells his own stories to his audience. While love themes and relationships form the basis of much of his work, Lightfoot has been inspired by other subjects. A magazine article about the sinking of an ore freighter led him to write "The Wreck of the Edmund Fitzgerald." Canada's environment figures prominently in several of his songs. "Carefree Highway" (another Top-10 single) was inspired by a road sign he observed in Arizona.

Nearly all folk aficionados love Lightfoot's poetic songs. Ballad singers continually turn to his compositions when searching for songs to record. Some critics have alleged that Lightfoot's music all sounds the same. Yet while his singularly soft, warm, and intimate delivery is apparent on all of his records, Lightfoot's carefully crafted lyrics give each of his songs a distinctiveness that captivates his many admiring listeners.

—Roger D. Hardaway

SELECT DISCOGRAPHY

■ ALBUMS

Lightfoot, 1966
The Way I Feel, 1967
Did She Mention My Name, 1968
Back Here on Earth, 1969
Sunday Concert, 1969
Sit down Young Stranger (also known as *If You Could Read My Mind*), 1970
Summer Side of Life, 1971
Don Quixote, 1972
Old Dan's Records, 1972
Sundown, 1974
Cold on the Shoulder, 1975

Gord's Gold, 1975 (compilation, rerecorded material)
Summertime Dream, 1976
Endless Wire, 1978
Dream Street Rose, 1980
Shadows, 1982
Salute, 1983
East of Midnight, 1986
Gord's Gold, Volume II, 1988 (compilation, rerecorded material)
Waiting for You, 1993

SELECT AWARDS

Juno Hall of Fame, inducted 1986

SEE ALSO: Dylan, Bob; Murray, Anne; Peter, Paul, and Mary; Robbins, Marty.

Little Feat

ORIGINAL MEMBERS: Lowell George (1945-1979), Bill Payne (b. 1949), Richie Hayward, Roy Estrada

OTHER MEMBERS: Kenny Gradney, Paul Barrere (b. 1948), Sam Clayton, Craig Fuller, Shaun Murphy

FIRST ALBUM RELEASE: *Little Feat*, 1971

MUSICAL STYLES: Southern rock, rhythm and blues, funk, country rock

Little Feat, a down-home, funky, rock-and-roll band with musical roots in Southern California and Louisiana, was formed in 1969 by guitarist-songwriter Lowell George and bassist Roy Estrada. The band quickly developed a devoted following of live-concert fans and a widespread reputation for outstanding musicianship. During the 1970's they produced a string of high-quality, modest-selling albums and toured extensively. George, a creative force whose clever, jesting lyrics graced much of the band's best material, died in 1979. The remaining members disbanded for most of the next decade, but reorganized in 1988. The comeback album, *Let It Roll* (1988), went gold and the group enjoyed a renaissance in the 1990's, continuing to tour and record regularly.

California Beginnings. The formation of Little Feat resulted from the breakup of the late 1960's edition of Frank Zappa's Mothers of Invention. Two of Zappa's alumni, Lowell George (guitar) and Roy Estrada (bass), set about forming a new band with an eclectic but earthy and aggressive style. The original quartet was completed with the hiring of Bill Payne on keyboards and Richie Hayward on drums. Based in Los Angeles, the band first performed under the name Country Zeke and the Freaks, but concern over typecasting as a country band led to the choice of Little Feat, a playful reference to George's shoe size.

George was the leader and primary creative mind behind the new band. A graduate of Hollywood High School, he began his career playing wind instruments for recording sessions. In 1965 he started a short-lived folk-rock group called the Factory, the personnel of which included Hayward. In 1969 George emerged from his stint as Zappa's rhythm guitarist to dominate the sound of Little Feat with his bluesy singing and excellent solo work on the slide guitar. He also became the chief songwriter, establishing the band's trademarks of humorous lyrics and a punchy rhythmic feel. His writing gained attention from other artists, such as the Byrds, who recorded two of his songs, "Truck Stop Girl" and "Willin'."

For the Record

Bill Payne on Little Feat's 1988 reorganization: "We tried it about four years ago [1984] but there were too many people on the set. . . . I thought at that time, if and when we ever do it again, let's just do it with the five of us.

§

"When we finally got together, the spark was still there—I felt like we had what was needed to say something. . . . We don't have any rules about what we play, or subject matter. It's all music, and that in itself is unusual." (*Mix* magazine, March, 1988)

Little Feat signed a recording contract with Warner/Reprise, but the company failed to promote either of its first two albums, and sales were disappointing, despite a wealth of material later considered vintage Little Feat. Highlights included George's "Hamburger Moonlight" and "Snakes on Everything" from *Little Feat* (1971) and "Tripe Face Boogie" from the decidedly funkier *Sailin' Shoes* (1972). Both albums displayed distinctive cover art by Neon Park, a feature that became a trademark of all the band's subsequent recordings. Despite good reviews, the lack of sales contributed to discord within the group, and the fall of 1972 saw a suspension of activity and the eventual departure of Estrada to join Captain Beefheart.

A Dash of Louisiana Spice. Little Feat reorganized as a sextet for its third album, *Dixie Chicken* (1973). The new personnel included Paul Barrere, a guitarist from Burbank, California, and two rhythm players from New Orleans—Sam Clayton (congas) and Kenny Gradney (bass). The result was a dynamic infusion of southern rhythm and blues to the overall sound. The album contained a number of songs destined to become concert anthems, including "Dixie Chicken," "Fat Man in the Bathtub," and "On Your Way Down," the latter penned by Allen Toussaint, patriarch of the classic New Orleans rhythm-and-blues sound.

In 1974 the band released *Feats Don't Fail Me Now*, a solid hit and the first Little Feat album to reach gold-record status. This effort marked the emergence of Barrere and Payne as songwriters, as they began to eclipse George as the creative force. A spectacular reception in Europe as a headliner on the 1975 "Warner Bros. Music Show" strengthened Little Feat's reputation as a live attraction. Its audience-oriented shows invited comparisons to the Grateful Dead, and the band developed a similar, if smaller, cadre of fans who tagged along on concert tours.

Hiatus. George's role in both the music and the decision-making process diminished over the next few years. Barrere and Payne moved Little Feat toward jazz rock, and George began to divide time between the band and various solo projects. Following the band's excellent live album, *Waiting for Columbus* (1978), he released his own album, *Thanks I'll Eat It Here* (1979), and toured with a new group. In the middle of the tour he suffered an apparent heart attack and died. Little Feat finished *Down on the Farm* (1979) and disbanded. The 1981 compilation *Hoy-Hoy!* included live tracks and alternate studio takes.

During the 1980's the members of Little Feat pursued separate careers. Barrere recorded a solo album, *On My Own Two Feet*, in 1983. Payne played keyboards in numerous recording sessions and made occasional tours, notably one with James Taylor. Hayward worked as a sideman with both Joan Armatrading and Robert Plant. A Little Feat greatest hits album appeared in 1986 under the title *As Time Goes By*.

Reincarnation. In 1988 Payne spearheaded a reunion of the mid-1970's Little Feat personnel. George's place was taken by two new guitarists, Craig Fuller (formerly of Pure Prairie League) and Fred Tackett (an L.A. session musician and old friend who had recorded with Little Feat before). The concert debut, an energized appearance with Randy Newman at the New Orleans Jazz Festival, recalled the best of the band's legendary live shows, and the ensuing comeback album, *Let It Roll* (1988), quickly outsold any of the recordings from the earlier era.

Little Feat served notice that it intended to stay together by releasing two more albums and touring regularly in the early 1990's. After the departure of Fuller in 1994, the group enhanced its sound with the soulful vocals of Shaun Murphy. Her sassy debut on *Ain't Had Enough Fun* (1995) helped shift Little Feat's self-proclaimed "battle to rock the planet" into a new gear. Firmly reestablished as a vital force in the industry, Little Feat completed its 1996 tour still dedicated to the fun of music and the art of the live concert.

—*Charles Kinzer*

SELECT DISCOGRAPHY

■ ALBUMS

Little Feat, 1971
Sailin' Shoes, 1972
Dixie Chicken, 1973

Feats Don't Fail Me Now, 1974
Waiting for Columbus, 1978
Down on the Farm, 1979
Hoy-Hoy!, 1981
Let It Roll, 1988
Representing the Mambo, 1990
Ain't Had Enough Fun, 1995
Live from Neon Park, 1996

SEE ALSO: Byrds, The; Zappa, Frank / The Mothers of Invention.

Little Richard

(Richard Wayne Penniman)

BORN: Macon, Georgia; December 5, 1932
FIRST SINGLE RELEASE: "Tutti Frutti," 1955
MUSICAL STYLES: Rock and roll, gospel

Richard Wayne Penniman was born in Macon, Georgia. There has been some dispute about both the year and the actual day of his birth, but his mother, in one interview, stated that Richard was born on December 5, 1932. He was one of twelve children. His mother, the guiding inspiration behind the family, was active in the Seventh Day Adventist Church; his father was a construction worker who was also involved in local bootlegging activities. This juxtaposition of lifestyles was one that would have a profound effect on Little Richard throughout his life, leading to a constant battle between Richard's devotion to the church and to a rather raucous lifestyle that accompanied his rock and roll career.

After having traveled with his family as the Penniman Family Gospel Troupe, Richard left home at the age of fourteen to work in various traveling shows and rhythm-and-blues bands, gaining valuable experience in both styles. After his father's death in a local brawl, Richard felt it was his duty to return home and help support his family. He got a job as a dishwasher at the local bus station and continued to perform, playing gigs with his band the Upsetters. Richard was proud of the band's reputation for being eccentric. Sporting outrageous hairstyles, makeup, and earrings, they earned fifteen dollars per night for their performances.

Little Richard (Freddie Patterson Collection/ Archive Photos)

Early Career. Richard recorded eight songs for Camden Records in 1951, all of which featured his signature boogie-woogie piano playing and a musical style that was typical of urban blues. His first break came in 1955 when he sent a demo tape to Specialty Records in Los Angeles. Producer Robert "Bumps" Blackwell decided to offer Richard a contract and supervised Richard's first recording session for the company. The initial recording session took place in New Orleans in late 1955, and the majority of songs recorded were safe, uninspiring blues pieces. During a break, Richard began to play a boogie-woogie piano version of "Tutti Frutti," a piece that had been a standard selection of his band back in Georgia. Once the lyrics were revised to make them more acceptable for airplay, the band recorded the song that same afternoon. It quickly became a hit,

For the Record

In his book *The Life and Times of Little Richard: The Quasar of Rock* (1985), Charles White quoted Little Richard as saying, "Rock music may be just a bunch of noise to some people, but to me it was the music of love. My music brought togetherness, happiness. My music broke barriers that had seemed unbreakable. It drove tunnels through walls that no one had been able to get through. My music did that. It was called 'race music' 'till I came on the scene. I'm grateful for that."

§

When Little Richard learned that the famous London wax museum, Madame Toussaud's, was planning to display a wax statue of him, he expressed a simple wish: "I just hope they don't make me look like James Brown."

selling almost 200,000 copies in ten days.

"Tutti Frutti" was typical of many of Richard's hits in his early years. A modified twelve-bar blues pattern was the basis for the verse, and the chorus was built on a deviation of the verse structure. The piano was a prominent instrument in the band, with Richard playing it in his typically frenetic boogie-woogie fashion. He incorporated the "walking bass" as well as the pounding, upper-register chords and frills that were typical of the boogie-woogie piano style. Richard played on most of these early recordings, although entries in session logs indicate that studio musicians occasionally filled in. The instrumentation for these early sessions included guitar, bass, tenor saxophone, baritone saxophone, and drums. The backup band comprised some of the finest session musicians available in New Orleans, including a number of musicians who regularly played behind Fats Domino. The style of these songs was incredibly energetic and appealed to many of the teenagers, both black and white, who made up the targeted listening audience. These teenagers were ready for a new sound; Muddy Waters and B. B. King were considered "too old" for this younger generation, and Richard's radical departure from tradition, including his pompadour hairstyle and his frenzied stage manner, to say nothing of the energetic musical style, appealed to their desire for something new and different.

In 1956 and 1957, Richard also appeared in the films *Don't Knock the Rock* (1956), *The Girl Can't Help It* (1956), and *Mister Rock 'n' Roll* (1957), which helped define a new genre of motion pictures known as "rock and roll movies." These feature films were popular with the teenage generation and increased the popularity of Richard's records and the demand for personal appearances.

Conflict. Richard's career after 1957 was illustrative of the two most influential factors from his childhood—the conflict between the entertainment lifestyle and the strong sense of loyalty and dedication to the church and its ideals. In 1957 he retired from the concert stage and decided to become a minister, literally leaving a concert tour in the middle of a performance when he received a "sign from God." He enrolled in Bible college, although it quickly became apparent that he was not suited to the more structured lifestyle demanded by the religious school. He also married a secretary from Washington, D.C., but the marriage was of even shorter duration than his stay at the Bible college. For the next few years he concentrated on preaching and recording gospel records.

Richard gradually turned back to show business, returning completely in 1962 with a tour of England. While on tour he met the Beatles and the Rolling Stones, and both groups paid tribute to a performer who had been a strong influence on their respective musical styles. His tour of England was a success, although a later series of concerts on the European continent were less so. In the meantime, his popularity in the United States did not match that of his British tours, and he resorted to a style that was a caricature of his early performances. He recorded a number of songs for a variety of labels, including Specialty,

Vee Jay and Okey Records, but most of these recordings barely made the Hot 100 charts. His performances increasingly turned to parody: He wore outrageous costumes and exaggerated such things as his hairstyle and makeup. He relied on the old-style rock and roll, music that had been his main repertory in the late 1950's, and he always felt he was on the verge of a comeback. His progress was slowed, however, by his involvement with drugs and alcohol.

Having failed in his efforts to achieve a notable comeback, Richard once more turned to religion in the early 1970's and began to alternate between periods of relative obscurity and periods of newly found popularity as younger audiences became more interested in the early years of the rock and roll era.

Influence. Richard influenced many of the performers of the late 1950's and early 1960's. The shrieks and nonsense syllables used by numerous later groups, including both the Beatles and the Rolling Stones, and the flamboyant performance style associated with the music of the Rolling Stones, were both attributable to Richard. His boogie-woogie piano style, considered wild and unique in his time, was adopted by a number of performers and was very similar to that used by Jerry Lee Lewis. Richard's legacy is evident in the number of cover recordings that were made by other artists, notably white artists of the same generation.

Many of Richard's lyrics and stage mannerisms were objectionable to the older generation of the American public, who felt that his performances were too decadent and should be censored. This was particularly true among white America, where racial prejudices combined with rigid morality to work against acceptance of Richard and his music. Recordings of Richard's songs made by white mainstream artists were more acceptable for a number of reasons. The lyrics were often sanitized and objectionable elements were removed, and the outrageous stage mannerisms were no longer in evidence (although there were still objections to the recordings by Elvis Presley for many of the same reasons). Bill Haley and the Comets recorded several of his songs, but the most notable cover versions were made by Pat Boone, who had a clean reputation and was widely popular with older and more conservative listeners. He released versions of "Long Tall Sally" and "Tutti Frutti" in which the lyrics were no longer objectionable and the frenzied style of Richard's recordings were toned down. Both recordings placed high on the popular charts.

Richard was still active in the 1990's, performing primarily in gala situations and for special events such as the closing ceremonies of the 1996 Summer Olympics in Atlanta, Georgia, less than one hundred miles from his hometown.

—*Karen M. Bryan*

SELECT DISCOGRAPHY

■ SINGLES

"Tutti Frutti," 1955
"Long Tall Sally," 1956
"Rip It Up," 1956
"Lucille," 1957
"Keep a Knockin'," 1957
"Good Golly Miss Molly," 1958

SEE ALSO: Berry, Chuck; Haley, Bill; Lewis, Jerry Lee; Presley, Elvis.

Loggins and Messina / Kenny Loggins

Loggins and Messina

ORIGINAL MEMBERS: Kenny Loggins (b. 1948), Jim Messina (b. 1947)

OTHER MEMBERS: Merle Bregante, Jon Clarke, Al Garth, Larry Simms

FIRST ALBUM RELEASE: *Kenny Loggins with Jim Messina Sittin' In,* 1971

Kenny Loggins

BORN: Everett, Washington; January 7, 1948

FIRST ALBUM RELEASE: *Celebrate Me Home,* 1977

MUSICAL STYLES: Soft rock, country rock, rhythm and blues, pop

Formed in 1972, this group featured Kenny Loggins and Jim Messina, both talented singer-songwriters and guitarists. It lasted until late 1976, when both Loggins and Messina launched solo careers. Loggins became a successful solo artist and composer, especially of film sound tracks. Messina had three moderately successful solo albums before he rejoined Poco for their *Legacy* album in 1989.

The Beginnings. As a child, Kenny Loggins had moved from Washington to Detroit, Michigan, and eventually to California with his family. Playing guitar from the age of twelve, he majored in music at Pasadena City College, where he was a member of a folk group. During the late 1960's he turned to rock and roll and joined Gator Creek, who recorded with Mercury Records, and later Second Helping, who recorded with Viva. He also toured with the Electric Prunes. In 1969 Loggins took a job as a songwriter for one hundred dollars per week with Wingate Music, a division of ABC Records. His first break came in 1970, when the Nitty Gritty Dirt Band used four of his songs on the album *Uncle Charlie and His Dog Teddy*. One of these, "House at Pooh Corner," was a minor hit. The following year CBS/Columbia Records signed him as a solo artist; his first album was to be produced by Jim Messina.

Born in California, Messina had grown up in Texas, playing guitar from the age of five. When he was twelve, his parents moved back to California. In high school he formed a surf instrumental group, Jim Messina and the Jesters (who recorded one album), and then the hot-rod inspired Dragsters. In 1967, after studio work as a guitarist, engineer, and producer, he joined Buffalo Springfield on bass and produced the band's final album, *Last Time Around* (1968). Later that year, with former Buffalo Springfield member Richie Furay, Messina formed the country-rock group Poco. Wishing to return to album production, Messina left Poco in 1970 and joined CBS/Columbia Records as a staff producer.

Messina's first assignment was to produce Loggins's debut album. However, the two men soon realized that their styles complemented one another, and they collaborated on the project. The resulting album, *Kenny Loggins with Jim Messina Sittin' In* (1972), which included "Danny's Song" (a Top-10 hit for Canadian singer Anne Murray in 1973) and the Caribbean-pop tune "Vahevala," began a partnership that was to last for five years.

Recording Classics. Although their first album was billed as a solo effort by Loggins with Messina "sittin' in," and their live debut at the Troubadour club in Los Angeles featured the Kenny Loggins Band with Jim Messina, the duo soon became known as Loggins and Messina. Their next album, *Loggins and Messina* (1973), which included the hit "Your Mama Don't Dance," was very successful, as was *Full Sail* in 1974. *Mother Lode* (1974) was a moderate success, but *So Fine*, a nostalgic album of 1950's rhythm-and-blues hits, such as Clyde McPhatter's "A Lover's Question," was a commercial and musical disappointment. In 1976, after recording *Native Sons*, the duo split to pursue solo careers. Two more albums were issued, however—the compilation album *The Best of Friends* (1976) and *Finale* (1977).

Kenny Loggins. As a solo artist, Loggins has been more successful than Messina. His first two solo efforts, *Celebrate Me Home* (1977) and *Nightwatch* (1978), were immediately successful. From the latter, "Whenever I Call You Friend," cowritten with Melissa Manchester and performed with Fleetwood Mac's Stevie Nicks, was a Top-5 hit. With Michael McDonald of the Doobie Brothers,

For the Record

In 1976 Kenny Loggins is said to have turned down the offer to costar with Barbra Streisand in *A Star Is Born*. The role went to Kris Kristofferson.

§

During their tenure with Columbia Records, Loggins and Messina were never under contract as a duo, but had individual contracts. Apparently they and the record company viewed their five-year collaboration as an informal one that could end at any time.

Loggins wrote "What a Fool Believes," which became a number 1 hit for the Doobie Brothers in 1979 and won a Grammy Award for Song of the Year in 1980. The following year, Loggins took another Grammy, for Best Pop Vocal Performance, for "This Is It," from the album *Keep the Fire* (1979).

During the 1980's Loggins began to compose for film sound tracks. "I'm Alright," the theme song from *Caddyshack* (1980), reached number 7 on the charts, and the title song from *Footloose* (1984) was nominated for an Academy Award in 1985. He also cowrote several of the songs for *Top Gun* (1986) and recorded the film's theme song, "Danger Zone," which reached number 2 on the charts. Other sound tracks include *Over the Top* (1987); *Caddyshack II* (1988), which featured the hit single "Nobody's Fool"; and *One Fine Day* (1996), whose "For the First Time" was nominated for an Academy Award.

On other albums, Loggins drew inspiration from his personal life. His painful divorce, as well as his interest in environmental issues, are addressed in *Leap of Faith* (1991). "Conviction of the Heart" from this album was declared by Vice President Al Gore the unofficial anthem of the environmental movement. *Return to Pooh Corner* (1994) contains songs and lullabies that he sang to his children. The album *The Unimaginable Life* (1997) shares its title with a book Loggins cowrote with his second wife, Julia, in which they chronicle their love through letters and poetry.

Legacy. Although sometimes dismissed by critics for their mellow soft-rock sound, Loggins and Messina were a popular and successful duo during the 1970's. Blending rock, country, and rhythm and blues with hints of Caribbean and other Latin styles, the pair toured regularly in North America. Most of their albums are certified gold or platinum. As a solo artist, Loggins is noteworthy for his warm, intimate, yet enthusiastic vocal style and his inventive lyrics. Messina's solo career has been less successful, but he has continued to perform and produce. In 1996 he created the Songwriters' Performance Workshop, which holds clinics that focus on all aspects of the songwriter's art.

—Mary A. Wischusen

SELECT DISCOGRAPHY

■ ALBUMS

Loggins and Messina

Kenny Loggins with Jim Messina Sittin' In, 1971
Loggins and Messina, 1972
Full Sail, 1973
On Stage, 1974
Mother Lode, 1974
So Fine, 1975,
Native Sons, 1976
The Best of Friends, 1976
Finale, 1977

Kenny Loggins

Celebrate Me Home, 1977
Nightwatch, 1978
Keep the Fire, 1979
Vox Humana, 1985
Back to Avalon, 1988
Leap of Faith, 1991
Outside from the Redwoods—An Acoustic Afternoon, 1993
Return to Pooh Corner, 1994
The Unimaginable Life, 1997

SELECT AWARDS

Grammy Award for Song of the Year for "What a Fool Believes," 1979 (with Michael McDonald)
Grammy Award for Best Pop Performance, Male, for "This Is It," 1980

SEE ALSO: Buffalo Springfield; Doobie Brothers, The / Michael McDonald; Fleetwood Mac; Murray, Anne.

Los Lobos

ORIGINAL MEMBERS: David Hidalgo (b. 1954), Cesar Rosas (b. 1954), Luis "Louie" Perez (b. 1953), Conrad Lozano (b. 1952)
OTHER MEMBERS: Steve Berlin (b. 1957)
FIRST ALBUM RELEASE: *Los Lobos del Este Los Angeles: Just Another Band from East L.A.*, 1978
MUSICAL STYLES: Rock and roll, Mexican folk, pop, folk rock, country rock, rhythm and blues

The four original members of Los Lobos grew up in East Los Angeles, where they formed their band

Los Lobos (Ken Settle)

in 1973. The band's name is a humorous play on the name of a band from Mexico, Los Lobos del Norte (the Wolves of the North). In the early days, the band members would refer to themselves as Los Lobos del Este Los Angeles (the Wolves of East Los Angeles).

Beginnings. Although originally a Top-40 rock band, Los Lobos soon dug deep into their Mexican roots and mastered intricate Mexican folk music played on acoustic instruments. Outfitted in Mexican wedding shirts, long hair, and beards, the early Los Lobos played local clubs, backyard parties, weddings, and Latino cultural events. In 1978, they self-produced their first album, a beautiful acoustic collection of authentic Mexican folk classics such as "Sabor a Mi" and the Latino standard "Guantanamera." Four songs from this out-of-print album appear on the 1993 album *Just Another Band from East L.A.: A Collection.*

There are two lead singers in Los Lobos. David Hidalgo uses his sweet high-pitched voice on most of the group's folk and country-rock ballads, while Cesar Rosas belts out blues-based rock numbers in a lower and louder voice. The majority of songs are written by Hidalgo and percussionist Louie Perez. Bass player Conrad Lozano also plays the guitarron (or big guitar) popularized by Mexican mariachi bands. In addition to guitars, Rosas plays the bajo sexto (a Mexican folk guitar) and mandolin, and Hidalgo plays the accordion, violin, and steel guitar.

Crossing Over. Los Lobos rediscovered electric instruments and their American rock roots in the late 1970's. They played supercharged versions of Mexican classics such as "Volver Volver" and original blends of Mexican roots music mixed with rock, rockabilly, rhythm and blues, and country to the delight of punk-rock audiences in Hollywood. In 1981, the Blasters, another L.A. roots rock group, asked Los Lobos to open for them at the Whisky-a-Go-Go in Los Angeles. From this opportunity, Los Lobos gained the admiration of rock critics and cross-ethnic audiences. They also gained a saxophone player in Steve Berlin, who left the Blasters to join Los Lobos in 1983. Berlin and T-Bone Burnett produced the group's 1983 Slash label debut, *. . . And a Time to Dance*, an extended-play single of ranchera rock-dance numbers that included "Anselma," an accordion-driven norteño two-step for which Los Lobos received a Grammy Award.

The Ups and Downs of Fame. With regard to Los Lobos' next album in 1984, Berlin noted that "In some ways, *A Time to Dance* was a postcard, but *How Will the Wolf Survive?* is more like a letter." Indeed, this album received rave reviews from music critics, and *Rolling Stone* magazine proclaimed it the Album of the Year and voted Los Lobos the Band of the Year. The album masterfully showcased the band's versatile command of multiple styles of popular American and Mexican music including blues-based rock ("Don't Worry Baby"), delicate acoustic string band ("Lil' King of Everything"), upbeat ranchera rock ("Serenata Norteña"), and country rock ("Just a Matter of Time," a sad song about the hopes and dreams of a migrant worker about to leave his family). The album's centerpiece, "Will the Wolf Survive?" became the group's signature song for its subtle portrayal of the struggle of Mexicans in America disguised as the story of a wolf battling the elements to save its family.

In 1986, Paul Simon asked Los Lobos to back him on a song from his smash album *Graceland*, but 1987 proved to be an odd year for Los Lobos. With expectations riding high, they released *By the Light of the Moon*, an album that disappointed Los Lobos despite some very good songs about life in the barrio (the bouncy country rock number "One Time One Night" and the lovely ballad "Tears of God"). Next, they contributed eight songs to the enormously successful sound track to the 1987 film *La Bamba* , the biography of Ritchie Valens. Although Los Lobos consider these songs to be their least interesting work, it was the *La Bamba* sound track that earned them international stardom with both the album and the single "La Bamba" reaching number 1 on the charts. Said Berlin, "To have all this adulation for something that was not really much a part of us was discomforting. It's not that I'm whining about selling all these records. It's just mildly surreal that it was about a favor to Ritchie's family more than anything else, and it didn't necessarily reflect the breadth and depth of the work we had come up with at that point and since." Indeed, Los Lobos grew so tired of requests to play "La Bamba" that they began referring to the song as the "B word."

Back to the Future. In an effort to preserve their musical integrity following the La Bamba craze, Los Lobos produced their second album of acoustic Mexican folk music in 1988, *La Pistola y El Corazón*. The group also resumed touring with the advertised warning to La Bamba fanatics: "An evening of acoustic folkloric music with Los Lobos." In 1990, the reenergized band released *The Neighborhood* as a confident return to rock and roll, Los Lobos style. However, it was their 1992 album *Kiko* that was hailed by critics as a rock-and-roll masterpiece. Most of the album's sixteen songs are dreamy and mysterious. In the studio, the band experimented with unusual old instruments and devices, avoided modern digital processing, and recorded songs in two or three fresh takes. The hypnotic dragging tempo of "When the Circus Comes" is reminiscent of the Beatles' "Fool on the Hill," while "Kiko and the Lavender Moon" is a haunting swing/samba style suggestive of Duke Ellington, which captures a child's dreamy imagination. In a rare lead vocal, Louie Perez entranced listeners with "Saint Behind the Glass," a Mexican string-band song with surreal words and images of a saint statue interacting with the singer's family. True to form, Cesar Rosas brought listeners back to rock-and-roll basics with "That Train Don't Stop Here Anymore."

The magic of *Kiko* was still alive in 1994 when Hidalgo and Perez produced *The Latin Playboys*, an excellent experimental album of studio sounds and fun. This playful record laid the foundation for *Colossal Head* released by Los Lobos in 1996, a solid album on which this band continued to display its immense talent for blending Mexican and American forms of popular music.

While rock critics and musicians consider Los Lobos one of the greatest bands in the United States, they may yet go down in history as the greatest band nobody has ever heard. Airplay of their music has been minimal, and they have never graced the cover of *Rolling Stone.* Whether this problem is due to poor marketing or the uncompromising originality of their sound, Los Lobos' music will need to speak for itself.

—*Kurt C. Organista*

SELECT DISCOGRAPHY

■ ALBUMS

How Will the Wolf Survive? 1984

La Bamba, 1987 (sound track)

Kiko, 1992

Just Another Band from East L.A.: A Collection, 1993 (compilation)

SELECT AWARDS

Grammy Award for Best Mexican/American Performance for "Anselma," 1983

Rolling Stone, named Best Band of the Year, 1984

Grammy Award for Best Mexican/American Performance for *La Pistola y El Corazón,* 1989

SEE ALSO: Valens, Ritchie.

Lyle Lovett

BORN: Klein, Texas; November 1, 1957

FIRST ALBUM RELEASE: *Lyle Lovett,* 1986

MUSICAL STYLES: Country, country rock, pop, blues, folk

Lyle Lovett has been an admired and respected songwriter and performer. Despite never completely breaking into the mainstream, he has built a devoted following with his sense of humor, his witty lyrics, and his fun stage persona. While many would know him more for his small parts in films and his short marriage to actress Julia Roberts in the early 1990's, his unique songs have made him an American original who has defied labels or categorization.

Texas Son. Lyle Pearace Lovett was born in Klein, Texas, near Houston, Texas. Klein was a community of German immigrants founded by Lovett's great-great-grandfather, Adam Klein. Young Lovett graduated one semester early from high school and attended the prestigious Texas A&M University, where he studied journalism and German.

The year he enrolled in college he was eighteen and already playing at local coffeehouses, bars, and restaurants. He spent 1979 studying abroad in Rothenburg, Germany, where he made friends with some musicians. It was there he recorded his first four-song demo tape. After graduating from college with his dual degree, he traveled to Nashville and sang backup vocals on Nanci Griffith's third album, *Once in a Very Blue Moon* (1985). On that album Griffith sang Lovett's "If I Were the Woman You Wanted." He also sang on her *Last of the True Believers* (1986). That exposure, in addition to country artist's Guy Clark's recommendation, earned Lovett a recording contract with MCA/Curb Records.

The Uncountry Star. His self-titled debut album was a solid effort that gained him an immediate, if small, following. Though recorded in Nashville, the album contained pop-influenced songs that marked it as something other than the usual country album. In the song "Cowboy Man," he sings, "I ain't never been no cowboy/ heaven knows I've tried." "Cowboy Man," along with "God Will," included clever lyrics and warm melodies that caught the ears of younger country listeners, although the established patriarchs of country did not know what to think of the album (it actually sold better in Europe than in the United States). Despite limited airplay on traditional country stations, his constant touring made his debut a respectable commercial success.

Pontiac (1987) was a more polished effort and included engaging storytelling in the style of country artists such as Guy Clark and Townes Van Zandt, whom Lovett considered mentors. Songs

Lyle Lovett in 1990 (Paul Natkin)

such as "If I Had a Boat" and "She's Hot to Go" showed more folk influences than country. Well liked in the music community, the album featured many guest stars, including Emmylou Harris.

The next release was *Lyle Lovett and His Large Band* in 1989. On this hit album, he departed further from his country roots and dabbled in jazz and blues. For this, he enlisted an eighteen-piece band that was heavy on brass. The album opened with "Here I Am," a powerful slow-tempo rhythm-and-blues song spiced with bits of comic monologue. He furthered showed his sense of humor by covering Tammy Wynette's "Stand by Your Man."

The tour that supported this album was extremely successful and often sold out. Artists such as Shawn Colvin, who sang on some of his songs (and he on hers), opened for him. He would always join her onstage for a song, then she would sing on one of his, making both songs concert highlights.

Detours. It would be three years before the release of his next album, but Lovett was not idle. He continued writing songs for others, worked on the Grateful Dead tribute album *Deadicated,* and produced albums for other up-and-coming artists such as Walter Hyatt.

During this time, famed director Robert Altman, creator of films such as *Nashville, M*A*S*H,* and many others, saw Lovett in concert in Los Angeles and approached him about being in one of his films. Lovett reluctantly agreed and appeared in 1992's *The Player,* one of Altman's most successful films. In it he had a small but amusing role as a detective trying desperately to be part of the elite Hollywood crowd. He followed this up with larger parts in two other Altman films: *Short Cuts* (1993), in which he portrayed a humorous baker with weak social skills, and the less successful *Ready to Wear* (1994), in which he played a Texan millionaire. Other directors were taking note of his ability to play quirky comic characters, and he later appeared in 1998's *The Opposite of Sex.*

Film star Julia Roberts also appeared in *The Player,* but the two never shared a scene and actually met after having done the film. Roberts was a self-proclaimed fan of Lovett's original, offbeat music, and upon his discovery of that fact, he let her know he would like to meet her. The two soon began a very public courtship that was often featured on the covers of tabloid and entertainment magazines. The tall, beautiful Roberts and the gawky, odd-looking Lovett made an unusual couple. The media hounded them and, soon after their marriage, immediately started predicting their demise. The marriage did not, in fact, last. They were married in 1993 and were divorced by 1995.

More Recordings. In 1992 Lovett recorded *Joshua Judges Ruth* (titled after three books in the Bible). It included few country-influenced songs, veering more toward gospel and pop, and as usual, it was a critical success. He was increasingly compared to Tom Waits and Randy Newman: an artist who could not be labeled and whose intelligent songwriting would never be commercial enough to reach mainstream radio listeners. The track "You Never Been So Good up to Now," received some airplay, but again it was his cult following that made his album a modest commercial success. That year, he also went on a world tour, opening for the popular band Dire Straits. This proved fortunate, as it increased his international following.

Lovett released *I Love Everybody* in 1994. The title track was a country waltz, and there were other tracks with a country feel, but there were also songs, such as "Ain't It Somethin'" and "Record Lady," that had a rhythm-and-blues and gospel feel and featured extensive background vocals. The album was dedicated to his then wife, Julia Roberts.

In the summer of 1996, Lovett released *Road to Ensenada,* which sold well, with sales most likely boosted in part by people searching for songs about his breakup with Roberts. It proved to be a typical well-crafted album, with songs such as "Her First Mistake" and "Don't Touch My Hat" containing his well-known sense of humor. There were darker moments on the album as well, such as in the touching, sad "It Ought to Be Easier." The catchy song "Long Tall Texan," which Randy Newman sang backup on, received the most airplay of any song on the album. With this album, the country establishment finally seemed comfortable embracing him, and Lovett was no doubt surprised when the album broke into the *Billboard* Top 10 on the country charts. —*Kevin M. Mitchell*

For the Record

Making fun of his own uncountry persona, Lyle Lovett usually walks onstage holding a huge ten-gallon cowboy hat that he then sets down and never wears.

SELECT DISCOGRAPHY

■ ALBUMS

Lyle Lovett, 1986
Pontiac, 1987
Lyle Lovett and His Large Band, 1989
Joshua Judges Ruth, 1992
I Love Everybody, 1994
Road to Ensenada, 1996
Step Inside This House, 1998

SELECT AWARDS

Grammy Award for Best Country Vocal Performance, Male, for *Lyle Lovett and His Large Band,* 1989

Grammy Awards for Best Country Performance by a Duo or Group with Vocal for "Blues for Dixie" (with Asleep at the Wheel) and Best Pop Vocal Collaboration for "Funny How Time Slips Away" (with Al Green), 1994

Grammy Award for Best Country Album for *The Road to Ensenada,* 1996

SEE ALSO: Colvin, Shawn; Griffith, Nanci; Harris, Emmylou; Newman, Randy; Waits, Tom.

The Lovin' Spoonful

ORIGINAL MEMBERS: John Sebastian (b. 1944), Zalman (Zal) Yanovsky (b. 1944), Steve Boone (b. 1943), Joe Butler (b.1943)
OTHER MEMBERS: Jerry Yester, others
FIRST ALBUM RELEASE: *Do You Believe in Magic,* 1965
MUSICAL STYLES: Rock and roll, folk, rhythm and blues, country

Led by uniquely talented singer-songwriter John Sebastian, the Lovin' Spoonful was one of the first commercially successful folk-rock acts of the mid-1960's. Although lasting only two years, the group charted an amazing seven songs in the Top 10 during a time when the Beatles and Motown nearly had a monopoly on popular tastes. After the band's split, Sebastian continued performing as a solo act, eventually scoring the hit single "Welcome Back" from the television program *Welcome Back Kotter* in 1976.

The Beginnings. The origins of the 1960's folk-rock scene are sometimes thought to be located solely on the West Coast, in Los Angeles and San Francisco. The music found its first home in New York, however, amidst a thriving coffeehouse folk circuit. (It nurtured the budding genius of Bob Dylan before he "went electric" at the Newport Folk Festival in 1965.) Among the throng of hopefuls left in Dylan's wake were New York native John Sebastian and Canadian-born Zalman (Zal) Yanovsky. They met, jammed together, and decided to pool their talents. Before forming the Lovin' Spoonful in 1965, Sebastian and Yanovsky had been members of the Mugwumps, a little-known New York group that featured future Mamas and Papas members Cass Elliot and Denny Doherty. After the Mugwumps' demise, Yanovsky stayed active in New York's thriving underground scene while Sebastian made a pilgrimage to the South in search of hard-to-find folk music. While in the South, Sebastian spent considerable time with blues legend Sam "Lightnin'" Hopkins and met another bluesman who would prove to be an influential figure for Sebastian and the Lovin' Spoonful, Mississippi John Hurt.

Eager to start a new group, Sebastian reconnected with Yanovsky upon his return to New York. They recruited fellow New Yorker Joe Butler and North Carolina native Steve Boone to form the Lovin' Spoonful. Sebastian sang and played guitar, autoharp, piano, and harmonica. He was known as an exceptional harmonica player, having learned from his father—a classical player who was also responsible for introducing his son to Lightnin' Hopkins—before honing his skills on the streets of Greenwich Village near New York University. Yanovsky handled lead guitar, Butler played drums, and Boone played bass, guitar, and piano.

First appearing in New York-area clubs, the band gained a large following for their happy mixture of blues, folk, country, and rock and roll. As chief songwriter, Sebastian had many influences but his own unique voice. Combined with Sebastian's witty lyrics and buoyant melodies, the band's energy and down-home sense of fun proved irresistible. Young audiences were flocking to their shows, which quickly gained the attention of record labels.

A Fast Start. Signed by the Kama Sutra label in 1965, the Spoonful was on the fast track to stardom. They immediately recorded and released their debut album, *Do You Believe in Magic.* They issued the title song as a single, and the tune reached number 9 on the Billboard charts in August of 1965, remaining there for an incredible thirteen weeks. Epitomizing the band's musical style, upbeat sensibility, and their meteoric rise up the charts, "Do You Believe in Magic" could not have been a more fitting first hit.

Although the song has been called a "celebration of rock and roll," the lyrics "Do you believe in magic?/ don't bother to choose/ whether it's jug band music or rhythm and blues" indicates the

For the Record

The band took their name from the line "I love my baby by the lovin' spoonful" from Mississippi John Hurt's "Coffee Blues."

Spoonful's genre-bending tastes for any kind of music that had the right feeling. The band referred to their sound as "good time music." By the end of 1965, their first album had settled in at number 32 on the charts.

A string of hit singles followed throughout 1966. Their next two hits, "You Didn't Have to Be So Nice" (number 10) and "Daydream" (number 2) continued in the same breezy feel-good style, as did the lilting "Rain on the Roof," which charted at number 10 later in the year. Another side of the band was heard on "Did You Ever Have to Make Up Your Mind" (number 2), a whimsical ditty written by Sebastian in a taxi en route to the studio session at which they would record it. "Nashville Cats" (number 8), a clever tribute to country-music session musicians, displayed Sebastian's lyrical sense of play and the band's versatility.

Their biggest hit, the number 1 "Summer in the City," was somewhat uncharacteristic of their newly established sound. The lyrics "Hot town, summer in the city/ back of my neck gettin' dark and gritty/ been down, isn't it a pity/ doesn't seem to be a shadow in the city" immediately create an oppressive mood. Recent race riots in many U.S. cities probably contributed to the song's foreboding feeling, as did its stark chord progressions onto which recorded sounds of the city, with all its noise, traffic jams and bustling crowds, were superimposed. Yet before the song gets too depressing, the chorus switches melodic gears and offers a blast of cool, fresh air to relieve the day's heat and glare. The lyrics return to familiar Spoonful territory—"at night it's a different world" where all one needs to do is "go out and find a girl . . . dance all night" and "it'll be alright."

Good-Time Music Gone Bad. Through 1967 the Spoonful made three excellent and commercially successful albums. Their walk down easy street took a sudden detour, however, and the band broke up following a marijuana bust in which Yanovsky incriminated others, apparently including the rest of the band, in exchange for immunity. Details of the event remain obscure, but its effects clearly resulted in the Spoonful's demise. Yanovsky quit immediately, and after a lackluster year with his replacement, Jerry Yester, Sebastian departed in August of 1968.

Legacy. Their music remained on the charts through 1969, and Sebastian, foreshadowing what would be a solid solo career, left an indelible mark with his tie-dyed solo performance at the Woodstock festival that same year. Though the subsequent seven years were lean for Sebastian, he was once more on top of the charts with his number 1 hit "Welcome Back" from the television series *Welcome Back Kotter* in 1976. The accompanying album reached number 79. The original Lovin' Spoonful lineup reunited briefly in 1980 for a cameo in Paul Simon's film, *One Trick Pony*, and in the early 1990's the group began touring, minus Sebastian. Sebastian remained active in a variety of musical projects, including composing for television and films. —*Dave Junker*

SELECT DISCOGRAPHY

Lovin' Spoonful

■ SINGLES

"Do You Believe in Magic," 1965

"You Didn't Have to Be So Nice," 1965

"Daydream," 1966

"Did You Ever Have to Make Up Your Mind?" 1966

"Summer in the City," 1966

"Rain on the Roof," 1966

"Nashville Cats," 1966

"Darling Be Home Soon," 1967

■ ALBUMS

Do You Believe in Magic, 1965

Daydream, 1966

Hums of the Lovin' Spoonful, 1966

What's Up Tiger Lily? 1966

The Best of the Lovin' Spoonful, 1967 (compilation)

Everything Playing, 1968

John Sebastian

■ ALBUMS

John B. Sebastian, 1970

Cheapo Cheapo Productions Presents the Real Live John Sebastian, 1971

The Four of Us, 1971

The Tarzana Kid, 1974

Welcome Back, 1976

Tar Beach, 1993
I Want My Roots, 1996

SEE ALSO: Mamas and the Papas, The.

Loretta Lynn

BORN: Butcher Hollow, Kentucky; April 14, 1935
FIRST SINGLE RELEASE: "I'm a Honky Tonk Girl," 1960
MUSICAL STYLE: Country

Born Loretta Webb in 1935, the woman who was to become the country legend Loretta Lynn met and married Mooney Lynn when she was thirteen years old. A few months after their marriage, Mooney and Loretta's brother Junior hitchhiked to Washington to find work, leaving the pregnant Loretta behind. As soon as there was enough money, Mooney sent his wife a train ticket and she too moved to the West Coast. By the time she was seventeen Loretta had four children. (She became a grandmother at the age of thirty-one.) On her eighteenth birthday Mooney bought his wife a guitar which she taught herself to play. Encouraged by her husband, Lynn began playing with a band on Saturday nights. She also began competing in talent contests; as a prize from one of these contests, she won a watch and the opportunity to appear on a Tacoma, Washington, country music radio program hosted by Buck Owens.

A manager at Zero Records, a small Vancouver recording company, heard her on the Buck Owens program and gave her a record contract. In 1960 Lynn recorded "Honky Tonk Girl" for Zero Records. Zero, however, did not have enough money to promote the record. Lynn and her husband, therefore, mailed copies of the record to radio stations around the country. They then set out driving from Washington to Nashville, stopping at radio stations along the way to promote the record. By the time they reached Nashville, "Honky Tonk Girl" had become a hit on the *Billboard* country charts.

Success. On October 15, 1960, Lynn was introduced on the Grand Ole Opry by Ernest Tubb.

Loretta Lynn in 1974 (Max B. Miller/Fotos International/Archive Photos)

In 1962 Lynn became an official member of the Opry. From 1961 through 1968 Lynn also sang with the Wilburn Brothers, appearing on their syndicated television program.

From 1963 to 1969, twenty albums of Lynn's recordings were released. Two of Lynn's albums from the 1960's, *Don't Come Home a' Drinkin'* (1967) and *Loretta Lynn's Greatest Hits* (1968), were certified gold. Many of the songs in these albums were written by Lynn herself. They are songs about country life, love, and the relationships between men and women. As Lynn has explained it, she looked at life and saw what it was:

"Women staying at home while the guy's going out for a card game. Game didn't last all night, but the men did. Men going out with the boys, but they're not out with the boys. It was something nobody else was writing or singing about. It really got to me. I thought, 'This is a great thing,' so I started writing songs."

Lynn's observations about the relationships between men and women yielded such songs as "You Ain't Woman Enough (to Take My Man)" (1966) and "Don't Come Home a' Drinkin' (with Lovin' on Your Mind)" (1967). When writing, performing, and recording her songs, Lynn uses the colorful language, diction, and phrasing which are part of her Appalachian heritage. Thus, Lynn has been seen as a traditional country singer, retaining the original roots of country. (Lynn herself expressed this idea in her 1971 hit "You're Lookin' at Country.") However, Lynn's presentation of a particularly feminine point of view—in fact, a feminist point of view—was new for country music. Thus, in the 1960's and 1970's, when feminism had become a part of the political scene in the United States as well as a factor in male-female relationships, Lynn incorporated particularly feminist viewpoints in her traditional country songs. Lynn's approach made her particularly popular with female country fans during these two decades. By the mid-1960's Lynn was recognized as America's most popular female country singer.

During the 1970's Lynn teamed up with another country performer, Conway Twitty, to record a series of duets. From 1971 to 1988 Lynn and Twitty released eleven albums; four of these (*Only Make Believe*, 1971; *Lead Me On*, 1972; *Louisiana Woman, Mississippi Man*, 1973; and *The Very Best of Loretta and Conway*, 1979, were certified gold. On her own Loretta Lynn released twenty albums from January, 1970, through February, 1980. Some of these had provocative titles such as *When the Tingle Becomes a Chill* (1976), *You're Looking at Country* (1971), and *Out of My Head and Back in My Bed* (1978). Two of Lynn's albums from the 1970's went gold. They were *Coal Miner's Daughter* (1970) and *Loretta Lynn's Greatest Hits Volume 2* (1974). In the 1970's Lynn also courted controversy with such songs as "The Pill" (1973) and "Rated X" (1973).

Throughout her career Lynn has appeared on albums with other singers besides Conway Twitty. In 1966 she appeared on *The Wilburn Brothers Show* album. She has recorded four albums with Ernest Tubb. In 1979 she appeared on the sound track of *The Fish That Saved Pittsburgh* and in 1993 she recorded *Honky Tonk Angels* with Dolly Parton and Tammy Wynette. This album was also certified gold. In 1977 Lynn offered a tribute album to Patsy Cline, *I Remember Patsy*.

In 1976 Lynn coauthored, with George Vecsey, her autobiography *Coal Miner's Daughter*; this account of Lynn's life became a best-seller and, in 1980, served as the basis for the motion picture of the same name, which was nominated for an Academy Award as Best Picture of 1980. Music from Lynn's 1970 gold album *Coal Miner's Daughter* served as the sound track for the film.

Legacy. Lynn has been very successful as both a writer and a performer of country music. In both her writing and her performances she has been recognized as a traditional country performer. She has written and sung about topics which have always been the stuff of country music (family, religion, male-female relationships.) Her use of language (vocabulary, diction, accent, phrasing) has adhered very much to the language of Appalachia where traditional country music originated.

Nevertheless, Lynn gave her own twist to country music, which made her unique as a country music writer and performer. In her music Lynn emphasized the life of everyday women in America, and she gave a feminist slant to her rendition of these lives. When Lynn sang such songs as "Don't Come Home a' Drinkin' (with Lovin' on Your Mind)" or "Your Squaw's on the Warpath," she offered the perspective of a strong woman who takes care of her own affairs, which was new to country music. Lynn's strength and her popularity made it possible for female country writers and performers after her to bring a feminist perspective to their work.

Lynn, through her own life, has served as a role model for women everywhere. She has combined the life of wife and mother with a highly successful writing and performing career. She has also been a very successful businesswoman, establishing a dude ranch, worked by members of her family, in Hurricane Mills, Tennessee; running her own music publishing company; and establishing a chain of western clothing. In doing these things she has served as a strong role model for women trying to determine whether they can work outside the home and still manage a marriage and family.

—Annita Marie Ward

SELECT DISCOGRAPHY

■ ALBUMS

Don't Come Home a' Drinkin' (with Lovin' on Your Mind), 1967
Loretta Lynn's Greatest Hits, 1968
Coal Miner's Daughter, 1970
Only Make Believe, 1971 (with Conway Twitty)
Lead Me On, 1972 (with Conway Twitty)
One's on the Way, 1972
Louisiana Woman, Mississippi Man, 1973 (with Conway Twitty)
Loretta Lynn's Greatest Hits Volume 2, 1974
I Remember Patsy, 1977
The Very Best of Loretta and Conway, 1979 (with Conway Twitty)
Just a Woman, 1985
Honky Tonk Angels, 1993 (with Dolly Parton and Tammy Wynette)

For the Record

Loretta Lynn, the daughter of a poor Kentucky coal miner, grew up in a house that did not have running water, but eventually the phrase "coal miner's daughter" made her wealthy. Her 1970 album *Coal Miner's Daughter* was certified gold. Her 1976 autobiography *Coal Miner's Daughter* was a best-seller, and the 1980 motion picture *Coal Miner's Daughter*, based on Lynn's autobiography, was nominated for an Academy Award for Best Picture of 1980.

SELECT AWARDS

Country Music Association Female Vocalist of the Year Award, 1967
Grammy Award for Best Country Vocal Performance by a Group for "After the Fire Is Gone," 1971 (with Conway Twitty)
Country Music Association Entertainer of the Year, Female Vocalist of the Year, and Vocal Duo of the Year (with Conway Twitty) Awards, 1972
Country Music Association Vocal Duo of the Year Award, 1973, 1974, 1975 (with Conway Twitty)
Academy of Country Music Artist of the Decade Award, 1979
Nashville Songwriters Hall of Fame, inducted 1983
Country Music Hall of Fame, inducted 1988

SEE ALSO: Cline, Patsy; Gayle, Crystal; Twitty, Conway; Wynette, Tammy.

Jeff Lynne. *See* Electric Light Orchestra

Lynyrd Skynyrd

ORIGINAL MEMBERS: Ronnie Van Zant (1948-1977), Gary Rossington (b. 1951), Allen Collins (1952-1990), Billy Powell (b. 1952), Leon Wilkeson (b. 1952), Bob Burns (b. c. 1952), Larry Jungstrom (b. c. 1950)

OTHER MEMBERS: Artimus Pyle (b. 1948), Ed King (b. c. 1951)

FIRST SINGLE RELEASE: "Need All My Friends," 1968 (as Lynard Skynard)

MUSICAL STYLES: Rock and roll, southern rock, country rock

Lynyrd Skynyrd emerged in the early 1970's as both a best-selling group and a creator of hard-edged southern-rock music. Although the group's personnel fluctuated, it consistently produced high-powered, rhythm-driven records which covered an array of often politically incorrect topics.

Although an airplane crash in 1977 killed four members of the band and their entourage, their reputation has survived, and their legacy has become more powerful with the passing years.

The Beginnings. Gary Rossington, Larry Jungstrom, Bob Burns, and Ronnie Van Zant (all high school students in Jacksonville, Florida) formed a group in 1964. Later adding guitarist Allen Collins, the group underwent various transformations in style, membership, and name (at various times the group was known as the Noble Five, the Wildcats, Sons of Satan, One Percent, and My Backyard). The group's first single, "Need All My Friends," was released on a small local label in late 1968, and for the rest of the decade the band continued its experimentation and played wherever a willing audience could be found. In 1970, the band adopted the distinctive name it was to be best known as and began recording demos at a small studio in Sheffield, Alabama. One of these demos, titled "I've Been Your Fool," became the band's second released single.

In 1972, Lynyrd Skynyrd was playing at Funocchio's, a tavern in Atlanta, Georgia, when musician and producer Al Kooper happened to drop in and observe the band's performance. Kooper, a former member of Blood, Sweat, and Tears and a well-respected member of the music industry, was searching for young regional talent for a new recording company, Sounds of the South, a subsidiary of MCA. Kooper appeared to be primarily attracted by the band's thorough and sincere embracing of southern culture and the driving power chords fueled by their unique three-lead-guitar

Lynyrd Skynyrd (MCA)

setup. MCA signed the band to a contract worth nine thousand dollars and then promoted them heavily through 1973. Lynyrd Skynyrd also profited that year by going on their first national tour, opening for the veteran British band the Who. Their first album, titled *Pronounced Leh-Nerd Skin Nerd,* was released in November of that year and climbed the charts to number 27, eventually earning gold status. By the end of 1973, the band with the bad attitude and indecipherable name had secured the success it had tried so hard to win.

Recording Classics. The debut album featured a song destined to be a rock anthem and a radio mainstay for decades, "Free Bird." This recording was unlike most other Lynyrd Skynyrd offerings in that it was both a ballad and a tribute. The band had long been both fans and friends of another southern-rock group, the Allman Brothers Band. The latter group's leader and guitar virtuoso, Duane Allman, was liked and admired by Lynyrd Skynyrd's guitarists, and when Allman was killed in a 1971 motorcycle accident, Lynyrd Skynyrd chose to honor him with the song.

In 1974, the band's second album (aptly named *Second Helping*) produced their first song to hit the charts, eventually reaching the eighth position. This was a guitar-driven masterpiece that addressed several topical issues while reaffirming the group's southern roots. The very title, "Sweet Home Alabama," demonstrated the group's regional allegiance, but it was far more than a chauvinistic tribute. The song defended both scandal-plagued President Richard Nixon and segregationist Alabama Governor George Wallace while also bemoaning the group's arduous efforts to find success. The most controversial aspect of the song, however, was a very direct attack on singer-songwriter Neil Young. Young had criticized the southern "redneck" mentality in his 1971 song "Southern Man." Lynyrd Skynyrd had clearly felt insulted, and they retaliated with lyrics such as "Well I hope Neil Young will remember/ Southern man don't need him around anyhow." This action was consistent with the band's attitude and image of uncompromising confrontation.

In 1975 and 1976, the group continued their chart success. The albums *Nuthin' Fancy* (1975), *Gimme Back My Bullets* (1976), and *One More from the Road* (1976) all reached the Top 20. The singles "Saturday Night Special" and "Double Trouble" were also well received, and the band toured nonstop in both Europe and the United States to sold-out audiences. Sadly, Lynyrd Skynyrd's long run of good fortune was about to come to a disastrous end.

For the Record

The group used many different names before deciding to use Lynyrd Skynyrd. The two words in the title were not nonsensical rhyming gibberish, as many believed. Most of the founding members had attended high school together, where they shared a love of music and hatred for physical education teacher Leonard Skinner, who was notoriously hard on long-haired males. The group's name was a derisive poke at the despised educator.

Tragedy. In late 1975, the group had undergone additional personnel revision, adding another lead guitarist, Steve Gaines, and a trio of female backup singers, one of whom was Gaines's younger sister Cassie. The group had reached such a high level of popularity and was so strongly associated with the South that the band members, all baseball fans, were honored by a ceremony before the Atlanta Braves home opening game in 1977. On October 20, 1977, the band was traveling from Greenville, South Carolina, to Baton Rouge, Louisiana, when their plane crashed in Gillsburg, Mississippi. Although there was much speculation about the crash, later investigations would indicate low fuel as the main cause. Everyone on board suffered injuries, and four were killed: lead singer Van Zant, Steve and Cassie Gaines, and manager Dean Kilpatrick. Ironically, an album titled *Street Survivors* had just been released that had pictured the group standing amid flames; MCA withdrew and repackaged the album after the crash. The original version of the album had also contained a facetious order form for a Lynyrd Skynyrd survival kit. Even more chilling was the release of the popular single "That Smell," a song written by the late Van Zant about one of his favorite topics, death.

Legacy. Not surprisingly, *Street Survivors* sold even better after the crash. Another single, "What's Your Name," climbed as high as number 13 in March, 1978, and the group's final charting single was "You Got That Right," which peaked at number 69 the following month. A greatest-hits album released in 1980 did well, but subsequent material released by MCA would be of lesser quality.

In October, 1979, most of the surviving band members formed a group called the Rossington-Collins band, featuring lead vocalist Donnie Van Zant, Ronnie's brother. To this day, several bands consisting of various Lynyrd Skynyrd members continue to tour, but none have approached the appeal and success of the original group.

As a musical influence, Lynyrd Skynyrd is legendary. The band single-handedly originated the three-lead-guitar concept often associated with heavy-metal music of the 1980's and 1990's. They were a curious and unlikely hybrid of hedonism, belligerence, and social commentary, a mixture guaranteed to appeal to all erstwhile rebels.

—Thomas W. Buchanan

SELECT DISCOGRAPHY

■ ALBUMS

Pronounced Leh-Nerd Skin-Nerd, 1973
Gimme Back My Bullets, 1976
One More from the Road, 1976
Gold and Platinum, 1979

SEE ALSO: Allman Brothers Band, The; Frampton, Peter; Who, The; Young, Neil.

M

Paul McCartney

BORN: Liverpool, England; June 18, 1942
FIRST SOLO ALBUM RELEASE: *McCartney*, 1970
MUSICAL STYLES: Rock and roll, pop, classical

After the breakup of the Beatles, Paul McCartney established himself as a hugely popular—although uneven—recording artist. He was blessed with superior melodic skills, and the challenge always for McCartney as a solo artist was to motivate himself to go beyond simple musical solutions. As a man who cherished his family, McCartney made his music fit into his world of marriage and parenting. While critics often found fault in the music that came out of this domestic tranquillity, McCartney kept true to his priorities and produced a body of work worthy of respect.

The Beginnings. Born James Paul McCartney, he became interested in music as a child. Encouraged by his father—who was a part-time jazz musician—McCartney first learned how to play the trumpet. In 1956, his mother died of breast cancer. Saddened by the loss, McCartney found refuge in learning to play the guitar. On July 6, 1957, he met John Lennon. A bond between the two was established, and before long the two of them became the principal songwriters for the band that evolved into the Beatles. Revolutionizing popular music during the 1960's, the Beatles finally broke up in 1970. On March 12, 1969, McCartney married American photographer Linda Eastman in London. While personal and professional differences were pushing the Beatles apart, McCartney took sanctuary within his marriage and began recording songs in his living room on a four-track machine he had borrowed. Writing all the songs and playing all the instruments himself, McCartney created an album that was very casual and had a homemade feel to it. He was asked by Beatles' management to postpone the release of *McCartney* until after the release of the Beatles' album *Let It Be.* Instead, McCartney released his solo album in April, 1970, which was weeks before *Let It Be* would hit the stores. During an interview to promote his solo album, he announced that he was leaving the Beatles.

Including one classic song, "Maybe I'm Amazed," and a number of pleasant—if somewhat "throwaway"—songs such as "Every Night" and "That Would Be Something," *McCartney* climbed to number 1 on the U.S. pop charts and number 2 on the British pop charts. While the album sold more than three million copies, it was not well received critically. It was generally considered self-indulgent of McCartney to record such a low-key solo album while the Beatles crumbled around him. Lennon even called *McCartney* "rubbish." Surprised and hurt, McCartney clung even more tightly to the life he and his wife had created for themselves. From his perspective, it was now Paul and Linda against the world. In April, 1971, the first solo single, "Another Day," was released. The single was credited to both Paul and Linda McCartney. It was a hit, but it was not included on his second solo album, *Ram* (1971). For *Ram,* McCartney brought in Denny Seiwell to play drums and Dave Spinoza and Hugh McCracken to play guitars. McCartney considered the album a collaboration between himself and his wife. For this reason, *Ram* was credited to Paul and Linda McCartney. While more polished than his first album, *Ram* still had that carefree feel, and critics found it a flawed effort. The album went to number 1 on the British pop charts and to number 2 on the U.S. pop charts. The Beatlesque single from *Ram* "Uncle Albert/Admiral Halsey" reached number 1 in America. In addition to "Uncle Albert/Admiral Halsey," the album included some other strong songs like "Too Many People" and "Dear Boy." His former close friend and songwriting partner, John Lennon, took issue with both of these songs. He believed that McCartney was attacking him personally, and so Lennon

Paul McCartney on tour in 1989 (AP/Wide World Photos)

struck back on his *Imagine* album (1971) with his song "How Do You Sleep?" During the first half of the 1970's, McCartney and Lennon carried on a petty public feud.

Growing Wings. After the release of *Ram,* McCartney decided to put together a new band. Settling on the name Wings, the group included McCartney (bass, guitar, keyboards, lead vocals), his wife (keyboards and backing vocals), Seiwell (drums), and former Moody Blues guitarist Denny Laine (guitar and vocals). Wings went into the studio and hastily recorded an album. In December, 1971, Wings' first album, *Wild Life,* was released. While it reached number 10 on the U.S. pop charts, *Wild Life* was a very weak album. In 1972, McCartney asked guitarist Henry McCullough to join Wings. After playing at some British universities, the band released the single "Give Ireland Back to the Irish." McCartney had written this song in response to British soldiers killing Irish civilians in Londonderry, Northern Ireland, on January 30, 1972. This tragic incident became known as "Bloody Sunday." The song was banned by the British Broadcasting Corporation (BBC). So as not to upset the BBC again, the next single was a version of the nursery rhyme "Mary Had a Little Lamb."

In 1973, the album *Red Rose Speedway* was released. It included the hit ballad "My Love" and went to number 1 on the U.S. pop charts. McCartney also wrote the song "Live and Let Die" for the James Bond film of the same name. While the single "My Love" went to number 1 in the United States, "Live and Let Die" stalled at number 2. For Wings' next album, McCartney decided to record in Lagos, Nigeria. Before the band was to leave for Lagos, Seiwell and McCullough quit. The McCartneys and Laine forged ahead anyway, determined to make the best of a shaky situation. During their stay in Lagos, McCartney passed out from bronchial spasms, the McCartneys were mugged, the recording studio they used was under construction, some African musicians were afraid that Wings was going to steal their music, and it was the monsoon season. Out of the turmoil, the album that resulted was a grand success. *Band on the Run* was released at the end of 1973 and quickly shot up the charts. The album was both a critical and commercial success. It topped the U.S. pop charts and included the stellar McCartney compositions "Band on the Run" and "Jet." While selling more than six million copies worldwide, *Band on the Run* more importantly proved that McCartney could still make music worthy of a former Beatle. By 1975, Jimmy McCulloch (guitar) and Joe English (drums) had been added to the group. The next album, *Venus and Mars* (1975), was a solid effort and also topped the U.S. pop charts. Employing Tom Scott on saxophone, the single from the album, "Listen to What the Man Said," became a number 1 hit in America.

On September 9, 1975, Wings began its first and only world tour. The tour took the group to ten countries and lasted for thirteen months. For the next album, *Wings at the Speed of Sound* (1976), each band member was allowed to sing lead on at least one song. This democratic approach dramatically weakened the album. On the strength of two of McCartney's contributions—"Silly Love Songs" and "Let 'Em In"—*Wings at the Speed of Sound* went to number 1 in the United States. The world tour was extremely successful and broke a number of attendance records. *Wings over America*, a live album from the tour, was released on December 10, 1976. It became the biggest selling triple album in recording history. The live version off the album of "Maybe I'm Amazed" became a hit single. While some recording was done for the next Wings album during the early part of 1977, the most significant recording of the year came toward the end of 1977 with the Scottish song McCartney and Laine did together titled "Mull of Kintyre." The song was a tribute to the McCartneys' Scottish retreat. Released in November, 1977, "Mull of Kintyre" remarkably sold more than 2.5 million copies in the United Kingdom alone. During the year, both English and McCulloch left Wings. The album *London Town* (1978) was uneven but did include the hit single "With a Little Luck." McCartney recruited guitarist Laurence Juber and drummer Steve Holly to join Wings. Wings recorded one more album, *Back to the Egg* (1979), before officially disbanding in 1981.

For the Record

Paul McCartney on songwriting: "Sometimes you've only got an airline sickbag to write on, hotel notepaper, backs of envelopes, toilet paper. It's been done on everything, you know. So it's just an adventure every time I do it. On these promotion things I do, they ask, 'Paul, why do you do it? It can't be the money, it can't be the fame.' And it's just that each time you do it there's some kind of mystery to it as to whether you're going to pull it off."

New Challenges. In 1979, McCartney was honored by *The Guinness Book of World Records* for being the most successful popular songwriter of all time. While entering Japan on January 16, 1980, in order to begin a Japanese tour, McCartney was arrested for possession of marijuana. He remained in custody for ten days before being released without charges. Returning to England, Wings began a British tour during the spring of 1980. After the tour, McCartney went home to do the solo album *McCartney II* (1980). On December 8, 1980, John Lennon was shot and killed near his home in New York City. Shocked by the senseless death of Lennon, McCartney withdrew from the public eye. Receiving death threats on his own life, security guards surrounded him twenty-four hours per day. While Juber and Holly had left Wings after McCartney's arrest in Japan, Laine left in 1981 because McCartney refused to tour.

In 1982, McCartney returned with his strongest album in years. *Tug of War* was both a critical and commercial success. It included a touching tribute to Lennon in "Here Today" and a duet with Stevie Wonder, "Ebony and Ivory." For his 1983 album, *Pipes of Peace*, McCartney collaborated with Michael Jackson on "Say Say Say." While there were isolated recording gems during the 1980's, for the most part McCartney's musical experiments were not succeeding. During the late 1980's, he began collaborating with Elvis Costello. This collaboration helped spark the generally outstanding album *Flowers in the Dirt* (1989).

Although McCartney cannot read music, he boldly attempted to write classical pieces during the 1990's, including the *Liverpool Oratorio* (1991) and *Standing Stone* (1997). While critics of classical music were leery of McCartney's efforts, the public was appreciative and flocked to the performances of his classical works. Inspired by his work on the Beatles' anthologies during the late 1990's, McCartney released one of his best albums in years with *Flaming Pie* (1997). Over the years, the McCartneys had been involved in promoting vegetarian foods and supporting animal rights. It was Linda McCartney who was the force behind these positions. Sadly, she died of breast cancer on April 17, 1998, in Arizona. McCartney and the children were with her when she died.

—*Jeffry Jensen*

SELECT DISCOGRAPHY

■ ALBUMS

Wings

Wild Life, 1971
Red Rose Speedway, 1973
Band on the Run, 1973
Venus and Mars, 1975
Wings at the Speed of Sound, 1976
Wings over America, 1976 (live)
London Town, 1978
Back to the Egg, 1979

McCartney solo

McCartney, 1970
Ram, 1971 (with Linda McCartney)
McCartney II, 1980
Tug of War, 1982
Pipes of Peace, 1983
Flowers in the Dirt, 1989
Unplugged: The Official Bootleg, 1991
Off the Ground, 1993
Flaming Pie, 1997

SELECT AWARDS

Grammy Award for Best Arrangement Accompanying Vocalist for the song "Uncle Albert/ Admiral Halsey," 1971
Grammy Award for Best Pop Vocal Performance by a Duo, Group, or Chorus for the single "Band on the Run," 1974
Grammy Lifetime Achievement Award, 1990
Knighthood granted by Queen Elizabeth II of England, 1997
Rock and Roll Hall of Fame, inducted 1999

SEE ALSO: Beatles, The; Costello, Elvis; Everly Brothers, The; Holly, Buddy / The Crickets; Joel, Billy; John, Elton; Lennon, John; Moody Blues, The; Squeeze; XTC.

Michael McDonald. *See* The Doobie Brothers / Michael McDonald